Sources of Chinese Economic Growth, 1978–1996

Studies on Contemporary China

The Contemporary China Institute at the School of Oriental and African Studies (University of London) has, since its establishment in 1968, been an international centre for research and publications on twentieth-century China. *Studies on Contemporary China*, which is edited at the Institute, seeks to maintain and extend that tradition by making available the best work of scholars and China specialists throughout the world. It embraces a wide variety of subjects relating to Nationalist and Communist China, including social, political, and economic change, intellectual and cultural developments, foreign relations, and national security.

Sources of Chinese Economic Growth, 1978–1996

CHRIS BRAMALL

OXFORD
UNIVERSITY PRESS

OXFORD
UNIVERSITY PRESS

Great Clarendon Street, Oxford OX2 6DP
Oxford University Press is a department of the University of Oxford.
It furthers the University's objective of excellence in research, scholarship,
and education by publishing worldwide in

Oxford New York

Athens Auckland Bangkok Bogotá Buenos Aires Calcutta
Cape Town Chennai Dar es Salaam Delhi Florence Hong Kong Istanbul
Karachi Kuala Lumpur Madrid Melbourne Mexico City Mumbai
Nairobi Paris São Paulo Shanghai Singapore Taipei Tokyo Toronto Warsaw

and associated companies in Berlin Ibadan

Oxford is a registered trade mark of Oxford University Press
in the UK and certain other countries

Published in the United States
by Oxford University Press Inc., New York

First published 2000

British Library Cataloguing in Publication Data
Data available

Library of Congress Cataloging in Publication Data
Bramall, Chris.
Sources of Chinese economic growth, 1978–1996 / Chris Bramall.
p. cm. — (Studies on contemporary China)
Includes bibliographical references and index.
1. China—Economic conditions—1976– 2. China—Economic policy—1976–
3. China—Politics and government—1976– I. Title. II. Series.
HC427.92.B736 2000 338.951—dc21 00–032700

ISBN 0–19–829697–5

1 3 5 7 9 10 8 6 4 2

Typeset by Graphicraft Limited, Hong Kong
Printed in Great Britain
on acid-free paper by
Biddles Ltd., Guildford & King's Lynn

Preface

During the course of writing this rather long book, I have been greatly cheered and encouraged by a number of colleagues and friends. It is therefore with no little pleasure that I should like to acknowledge the assistance of Bob Ash, Terry Byres, Stuart Corbridge, and W. J. Macpherson in formulating the arguments which underlie my analysis. I am grateful to Steve Purdom for his enthusiastic research assistance. Michael Pollitt, my fellow Director of Studies, willingly shouldered more than his share of the burden of undergraduate teaching and in doing so gave me that invaluable margin of time in which to research and to think about the Chinese economy. I have also benefited enormously from discussions with Marion Jones and Liu Minquan, both of whom have been instrumental in encouraging me to reject the siren call of the conventional wisdom. However, my principal intellectual debt is to Mushtaq Khan, who rightly persuaded me that any explanation of Chinese growth couched simply in terms of industrial policy was far too glib unless proper weight was given to the political dimension of transition. I hope he feels that the end product is at least an improvement on my earlier ideas. I should also like to pay tribute to my former colleagues at Sidney Sussex College, Cambridge University. I have crossed swords with many of them over the years, but I have long been grateful for their fellowship and for the research environment offered by that wonderful institution.

In addition, I am grateful to Oxford University Press and to the Contemporary China Institute for the efficient manner in which my manuscript has been turned into a finished product. Two anonymous referees did much to strengthen and improve my argument in a number of places, and I am grateful to Frank Dikötter, Andrew Schuller, Jason Pearce, and John Callow for expediting the production process.

My greatest debt is a personal one, but the contribution of Beate Müller to the writing of this book is not to be measured in mere words.

Chris Bramall

Cambridge
February 2000

Contents

Glossary

1. General

This book covers the period between the 11th Plenum of 1978, and Deng's death in early 1997. Growth rates therefore generally refer to the period between 1978, the last year of the 'Maoist' system, and 1996, the last full year of Deng's rule. All growth rates are per cent per annum and calculated by ordinary least squares unless otherwise stated.

2. Abbreviations

BR	*Beijing Review*.
CD	*China Daily*.
CT	*China Today* (formerly *China Reconstructs*).
FDI	foreign direct investment.
FEER	*Far Eastern Economic Review*.
GVAO	gross value of agricultural output.
GVIO	gross value of industrial output.
JPRS	Joint Publications Research Service.
NDMP	net domestic material product.
neg.	negligible.
NVAO	net value of agricultural output.
NVIO	net value of industrial output.
SCMP	*South China Morning Post*.
SOEs	enterprises owned by central government, including those enterprises owned by county governments.
SWB	*Summary of World Broadcasts*.
TFP	total factor productivity.
TVCE	township and village collective enterprises. 'Collective' is strictly a misnomer here; these are enterprises owned by township and village governments and are more accurately described as local, state-owned, enterprises. The TVCE sector is thus a sub-set of the TVE sector.
TVE	township and village enterprises. This category includes township (*xiang*), village (*cun*), team (*dui*), cooperative (*lianying*), and individual (*geti*).

Part I

Chinese Economic Growth in Outline

1

Introduction: The Dengist Restoration

Few events in the post-war era have matched in either scale or scope the economic transformation of the countries of East Asia.[1] In 1952, Japanese per capita GDP was barely half that of Europe. By 1994, it was almost 40 per cent higher (Maddison, 1998: 13); and the economies of South Korea and Taiwan seemed well advanced along the same process of catch-up. Yet this transformation has been accomplished within an economic framework very different from the capitalist system developed in the United States. These systems have been described in various ways—the 'governed market' and the 'developmental state'—but their hallmark has been a pervasive yet selective industrial policy which has gone far beyond the securing of property rights.

Yet according to the dominant tradition in economic theory, the developmental state in East Asia ought to have failed in its bid to promote growth because it is capitalism, not state-directed industrialization, which constitutes 'the end of history'. The only response for the conventional wisdom—the master discourse as it will be called[2]—is to deny that the East Asian model has been successful, and to pursue policies which destabilize the East Asian economies. Initially, and despite the evidence of widespread and successful state interventions extensively documented by writers such as Chalmers Johnson (1985), Alice Amsden (1989), and Robert Wade (1990; 1996), the economies of Japan, Taiwan, and South Korea were labelled capitalist or market-conforming by the master discourse (Kuznets, 1979; World Bank, 1993*a*). In other words, the role of the state was simply denied. In the mid-1990s, however, the master discourse began to argue that these economies had not really performed successfully at all because of their failure to generate rapid (total factor) productivity growth (Young, 1995; Krugman, 1996). And the crisis of 1997–8 allowed the orthodoxy to claim that the East Asian economies had always been financially fragile and that this was the reason for their inability to sustain even the accumulation-based growth achieved over the preceding decades.

The third strategy adopted by the propagators of the master discourse has been to destabilize the East Asian economies, and this was very evident in the crisis of 1997–8 (Wade and Veneroso, 1998; Cumings, 1998). It would be wrong to imply that this was the sole cause of East Asia's economic problems. Domestic mismanagement created Japan's property bubble, and a persistent failure to raise aggregate demand aggravated it. In South Korea, Kim Daejung's long-standing hostility towards the chaebols (because of their links with the repressive regimes presided over by Presidents Park, Chun, and Roh) undermined the tradition of cooperation between state and private sector. In addition, all the East Asian economies suffered a decline in competitiveness because of the massive depreciations that occurred in Thailand, Indonesia, and Malaysia. Nevertheless, the Washington-based institutions also played a crucial role in creating the East Asian crisis. First, they pressurized the East Asian economies into liberalizing their foreign trade and exchange rate regimes, thus making them vulnerable to speculative attack. Second, Japan was prevented from bailing-out the South Korean economy, thus allowing the IMF to make emergency loans conditional upon market-orientated restructuring; this conditionality destroyed a large part of South Korea's industrial capacity. In consequence, an essentially cyclical crisis was transformed into a full-blown crisis, thus providing grist to the theoretical mill of the master discourse.[3]

The master discourse has been faced with a similar problem in explaining away the growth of transition-era China. As is well known, economic growth in the People's Republic during the years of transition between the plenary session of the Chinese Communist Party in the autumn of 1978, and the death of Deng Xiaoping in 1997, was remarkably fast.[4] But as soon as the question 'why?' is posed, the master discourse is in trouble. The problem arises because this discourse—as in the case of the other East Asian economies—holds that capitalism is a necessary condition for rapid and sustained economic growth. From this perspective, there is an obvious contradiction between the 'fact' that China was not a capitalist economy even in the mid-1990s (still less the early 1980s), and the 'fact' that its economy grew extremely quickly. Moreover, and in contrast to the rest of East Asia, China's economic growth was not undermined by the crisis of 1997–8. It therefore continued to pose a serious threat to the hegemony of the master discourse.[5]

As a result, attempts to deny China's post-1978 achievements have become numerous in recent years (Sachs and Woo, 1994; Fan, *et al.*, 1996; Friedman, 1990; Kornai, 1989; World Bank, 1996; Woo, *et al.*, 1997). First, it is claimed that a large part of the growth, both agricultural and industrial, is a statistical artefact. Second, growth is regarded as having fallen below its potential because of the persistence of 'inefficient' resource allocation and incompetent enterprise management, especially in the state sector. An implicit counterfactual is thus presented: China grew at close to 10 per cent per annum, but could have grown at (say) 15 per cent 'if only' the economy had been capitalist. The third form of denial centres on sustainability. Whatever the achievements of the transition era, Chinese economic growth is not sustainable in the long run without innovation, and this can only be delivered by capitalist institutions. China grew so rapidly in the 1980s only because of high rates of factor accumulation and (to a lesser extent) favourable initial conditions, especially its abundance of surplus labour which could easily be redeployed in industry.[6] The final form of denial centres on the existence of interventions. For example, it is routinely claimed by the populist organs of the master discourse (such as *The Economist*) that *de jure* enterprises owned by local government are *de facto* private enterprises operating under a 'flag of convenience'. It is also claimed that FDI-driven foreign trade is the engine of growth precisely because trade accounts for as much as 30 per cent of GDP; there is little role for the state in this sort of story. To be sure, even the more sceptical have become more positive in their assessments following the acceleration of growth in the early 1990s and the successful stabilization policies of 1994–5. For instance, the World Bank was impressed by the way in which inflation was brought under control without a sharp reduction in growth (World Bank, 1996), and the outgoing head of the Bank's mission in China went out of his way to emphasize just how much the People's Republic had achieved since 1978 (SCMP, 16 June 1997). Even the World Bank's (1997) report *China 2020* stressed the strengths of the Chinese strategy—high savings, rapid structural change, and 'pragmatic reform'.[7]

Nevertheless, the master discourse is adamantine in its refusal to acknowledge the underlying dynamism of the Chinese 'model'. Admittedly some writers schooled in the discourse are more positive than the Washington institutions (McMillan and Naughton, 1992; Naughton, 1995*b*; Rawski, 1994; Wong, 1994; Lin, *et al.*, 1996). Not only, they argue, was Chinese growth rapid but also it was based upon significant growth in total factor productivity. That productivity growth occurred even in state-owned enterprises. Although privatization was minimal before the mid-1990s, the growth of competition from rural enterprises and foreign firms—as well as changes to the way in which state-owned enterprises were managed—forced SOEs to improve their performance. Although some work (for example Jefferson, *et al.*, 1996) has recognized that the official figures issued in the late 1980s and 1990s exaggerate the growth of rural industry and that widespread static inefficiencies remained in the late 1990s, rapid economic growth and improvements in material living standards are unchallenged. In essence, therefore, these writers argue that a gradual transition to capitalism has served China well. If, they argue, the kind of shock therapy advocated by the mainstream advocates of the master discourse had been implemented in the early 1980s (as was the case in Russia), it would have failed.

Yet these disagreements between the advocates of shock therapy on the one hand, and the advocates of gradualism on the other, are cracks in the façade of the master discourse rather than in its foundations. For all their emphasis on the achievements of transition-era China, gradualist writers such as Naughton and Jefferson are united with shock therapists like Sachs and Woo in believing that China's economic performance will be yet more successful once a fully-fledged market economy is created by the privatization of state enterprises. More fundamentally, even the gradualists did not believe that China's economic strategy in the late 1990s was sustainable. Industrial policy along the lines adopted in Japan and South Korea was dismissed as being 'unwise' and in any case in conflict with membership of the WTO. Without privatization, the deficits of the SOEs would mount, thus creating a fiscal crisis for the state. Without free trade, static inefficiencies would proliferate unchecked and the rate of technical progress would be suboptimal. According to Jefferson, *et al.* (1996: 171):

> Even the highest estimates of TFP growth in China's state industry cannot obscure the presence of massive potential for additional productivity gains. . . . the recent deceleration of productivity growth in Chinese industry may foreshadow a return to earlier patterns of extensive growth.

More generally, the gradualists argue that a series of contradictions between the marketized and state-controlled sectors of the economy had appeared by the mid-1990s, and intensified over time; this encouraged rent-seeking behaviour and prevented genuine competition (Lin, *et al.*, 1996: 272). The argument clearly parallels the type of criticism made by Kornai in his later writings on market socialism in Hungary. And the solution is the same. The only way to avoid crisis was to embrace the market while it was not too late, and thereby exploit China's comparative advantage in the same way that the other Asian economies were forced to do. In other words, the Dengist transitional strategy was fast approaching its limits by the end of the 1990s, whatever its early successes. Seen in historical perspective, the orthodox approach in effect likens the Dengist era to a restoration (*chongxin*): a period in which the old regime enjoys an Indian summer as a prelude to its final collapse. The orthodoxy thus views the post-1978 transitional era as a late flowering of Chinese Communism, rather than the creation of a durable new regime—in the same way that the Tongzhi Restoration (1862–74) delayed, but did not prevent, the final collapse of the Qing dynasty (Wright, 1957).[8]

These doubts about sustainability not only united the 'shock therapy' and 'gradualist' wings of the orthodoxy, but were shared—albeit for very different reasons—by many heterodox scholars at the time of Deng's death. Some of these were contemptuous of the entire Dengist project (Chossudovsky, 1986; Bettleheim, 1988; Weil, 1996). But most of these heterodox accounts centred on specific problems. For example, some pointed to the environmental implications of rapid growth; the falling water-table in northern China, the aerial and water pollution caused by growing rural enterprises and the perceived folly of the Three Gorges dam underpin this approach (e.g. Edmonds, 1994). Others were worried about the capacity of agriculture to meet the growing demands of the population in the face of the closure of the arable frontier, the competing demands for land from industry and infrastructural projects and the high level of yields already reached (Brown, 1995). Yet others saw the succession as the major problem. With Deng's death, China faced a crisis of legitimacy in which the rival claims of leaders like Jiang Zemin, Qiao Shi, and the military (Yang Shangkun and Zhang Wangnian) had to be resolved. Additionally, there are those whose primary concern was the impact of spiralling income inequality on social stability. Not only, it is argued, had regional disparities grown dramatically over the course of the 1980s but also class-based income inequalities had re-emerged. Finally, there were those who questioned not merely the instrumental value of the Dengist approach to economic growth but also its intrinsic merit. For these, it was unclear that a strategy based upon the suppression of basic human rights, the occupation of Tibet and Eastern Turkestan, the neglect of infant girls, and spiralling inequalities of income and wealth had anything to commend it. From this perspective, the instrumental value of the Tian'anmen massacre in promoting growth by suppressing dissent is irrelevant.

Some of these concerns about sustainability are well founded. The sustainability of the Chinese road to transition was in doubt in the summer of 1989, and so it was again in the aftermath of Deng's death. There will be continuing debates over China's trade policy in Washington and Beijing. And even though the 1996 grain harvest was a record, the underlying performance of agriculture rightly remains a worry; the moderate grain harvests of the late 1990s showed that it was no easy matter to achieve consistent year-on-year output gains even with favourable internal terms of trade. Yet the longer the 'transition' era lasts, the more apposite it becomes to describe the era as a *weixin* not a *chongxin*. Indeed there is a strong element of wishful thinking in criticisms of the sustainability of economic growth in the People's Republic. The 'final crisis' of Chinese transition always lurks around the next corner; it is never at hand. In Joan Robinson's phrase, 'we are always tending, never arriving'.

In any case, the focus of this book lies not in the long-run sustainability of the Chinese 'model' but rather with the reasons for the remarkable growth that was achieved in the period between the deaths of Mao and Deng. It is here, on what the orthodoxy deems to be its own ground, that it is most deficient—in its analysis, in its use of data, in its conclusions and in the causal factors which it deems important. Three issues will be discussed in the chapters which follow. First, what will be called the 'proximate' sources of growth: initial conditions, factor accumulation, and productivity growth. Secondly, the extent to which these proximate sources of growth can themselves by explained by the role of the state in the growth process will be considered. Finally, the origins of the growth-promoting state of the post-Mao era will be addressed.

Of these three, the proximate determinants of growth are the centrepiece of the conventional theoretical literature on the economics of growth, and feature prominently in analyses of China's trajectory. The bulk of this literature concludes that initial conditions played an extremely important role in determining the pace of post-1978 Chinese economic growth. To be more precise, it was the very extent of underdevelopment that led to explosive growth. Real per capita GDP was low; that in itself ensures abundant scope for rapid convergence on the stationary state within the confines of the standard Solowian model. China's isolation under Mao meant that it could grow rapidly simply by introducing Western technology, in the same manner as Japan in the Meiji era.[9] Additionally, the limited extent of structural change that had occurred by 1978—China's labour force was still to be found primarily in the rural sector—ensured that growth could be underwritten by the transfer of surplus agricultural labour to labour-intensive industries producing consumer goods. The Maoist development strategy, it is argued, did little to endow China with the necessary social capability for catch-up growth. As importantly as anything else, Maoist institutions provided little motivation for growth-promoting behaviour by private individuals. Private enterprise was banned. Income differentials provided scant incentive for high productivity. The overriding emphasis on grain production prevented the exploitation of regional comparative advantage in agricultural production. This negative perspective on the Maoist era is shared even by a majority of those who are heterodox in other respects. Thus even writers who, as we will see, assign a great deal of credit for China's rapid growth to the interventions of the Dengist state in the industrial sector are dismissive of the Maoist legacy. The irrigation network is castigated for poor workmanship and deficient design. The educational gains of pre-1965 are seen as fatally eroded by the Cultural Revolution and the sending down of the urban intelligentsia into the countryside. Maoist technical progress is derided.

The other distinctive feature of the orthodox analysis of the proximate sources of growth is that it emphasizes the role of factor accumulation rather than technical progress. To be sure, growth-accounting treatments of Chinese growth are in their infancy, and it is recognized that foreign technology has played a role in creating comparatively efficient industrial enterprises in some parts of the non-state sector. Nevertheless, as in the writings of Krugman (1996) and Young (1995) on the post-war growth of East Asia, Chinese economic growth in the Dengist era was supposedly built on perspiration rather than inspiration. For example, a World Bank (1996: 13–14) report attributed 6.6 per cent of China's GDP growth of 10.2 per cent between 1985 and 1994 to accumulation, and a further 1.4 per cent to sectoral reallocation from agriculture and the SOE sector, with only 2.2 percentage points explained by total factor-productivity growth.[10] This emphasis on factor accumulation as the motor of growth is particularly evident in analyses of state-owned industry. Although, it is generally acknowledged, total factor productivity rose after 1978 (in contrast to the stagnation and perhaps even retardation of late Maoism) it did so slowly. In this respect, the state-owned sector lagged well behind the private sector, township and village enterprises, and joint ventures alike. The productivity gains achieved in agriculture in the early 1980s are also seen as merely one-off.

The second key issue addressed in this book is the role played by the Chinese state in promoting growth after 1978. In this regard, the key role played by the state according to the orthodoxy was in the promotion of marketization and privatization.[11] By eliminating some of the growth-retarding features of late Maoism (egalitarianism and many obstacles to factor and product mobility), and by establishing in their stead both the rudiments of a market economy and more secure property rights, transaction costs were reduced and the growth rate increased. Additionally, incentive structures were improved and investment promoted by transferring the ownership of assets to the private sector.

The process, it is argued, began with the rapid transformation of agriculture. The collectives of the Maoist era were despatched with alacrity, their assets transferred to farm households to do with as they felt fit. Maoist insistence on regional grain self-sufficiency was abandoned, allowing the untrammelled exploitation of comparative advantage. Prices were first moved closer to marginal costs, and then left to be determined by the emerging rural markets for most commodities. These processes were still incomplete by the end of the 1990s. Local governments continued to control land use, cropping patterns, and rural infrastructure; and factor markets remained signally underdeveloped. Nevertheless, the People's Republic had moved far in the direction of creating a market economy in rural areas, and sustained agricultural growth was (so the argument goes) the reward. Within the industrial sector, the Chinese state set its face against privatization, and as a result many potential efficiency gains remained to be exploited. Nevertheless, the removal of restrictions on the creation and operation of industrial enterprises led to the re-emergence of a vigorous private sector, albeit one that often sheltered under the political umbrella offered by the title 'township and village enterprise'. As significantly, the streets of China's cities echoed to the sounds of an active service sector which had been all but eliminated in the late Maoist era. Perhaps most importantly of all, the Dengist regime embraced the open door. By doing so, China allowed in the bracing wind of external competition, which did much to ensure the vitality of the private sector by offering intense competition. The open door also allowed a rapid surge in foreign direct investment, especially from Hong Kong; this served to initiate a process of much-needed technological modernization of plant and equipment. To be sure, the door was at best only half open; in more prosaic language, China's integration into the world economy was shallow, rather than deep. Much of the direct investment was confined to the eastern seaboard, and China's trade regime ensured that the lifting of tariff barriers was no more than partial. Nevertheless, the draught proved invigorating and the door opened further during the 1990s. As a result, the foreign sector provided a powerful stimulus to growth.

The validity of this orthodox appraisal of the role of the Dengist state is considered in this book from a number of perspectives. It considers, *inter alia*, whether marketization and privatization were as instrumental to the process of rapid economic growth as the exponents of the orthodoxy allege. Did they perhaps do more harm than good? This book also considers whether the orthodoxy is guilty of sins of omission in assigning to the state little more than the roles set out above. For instance, was any part of China's rapid growth due to interventionist macroeconomic policy? Might not tariffs and industrial policy have played a positive role? Did local government do more than act as a veil for private enterprise and entrepreneurial endeavour? Did the state play any role in the surge of agricultural production in 1978–84, and again in 1994–96? In fact, as will be seen, the Chinese state did all of this and more in the transition era. In doing so, it went far beyond the role assigned to it in (for example) Nozick's vision of the 'night-watchman' state. It was not developmental, but it actively—and successfully—promoted economic growth.

The final question leads on from this conclusion, although it is more easily posed than answered. For perhaps the greatest puzzle for heterodox economists is to explain why the Dengist state (like those elsewhere in East Asia) was so much more effective than the states of sub-Saharan Africa and South-East Asia in its economic interventions. From the perspective of the master discourse, the question is not worth asking. The Chinese state did not play a growth-promoting role after 1978, except in progressively absenting itself from the economic arena; the origins of its effectiveness is a question that simply does not arise because the state was ineffectual—especially in the industrial sphere. Perhaps more surprisingly, those who adopt a heterodox perspective on Chinese transition—for example, Nolan (1995*a*) or Lo (1997)—rarely ask this question about the origins of the growth-promoting state. For them, the main point is that the Chinese state chose the 'right' economic strategy, a strategy combining industrial policy, strategic integration into the world economy, and marketization of those segments of the economy where instances of market failure were rare. They argue that the 'lesson' from China—as with other East Asian countries—is that the strategy works, and by implication that it can work in other poor countries as well. More generally, the aim of the heterodoxy is to explode the myth of East Asian uniqueness. Rapid economic growth was the product neither of luck nor culture, but of design.

When the heterodoxy does confront the issue of the origins of Chinese success, it attributes success to the (Myrdalian) 'hard' or 'autonomous' state, which overcomes the forces of vested interest and institutional inertia. As narratives go, this is unexceptionable; the East Asian states have not been captured by powerful interest groups pursuing narrow agendas. And, by extension, it is hard to disagree with the notion that the countries of sub-Saharan Africa would grow faster if they could but insulate their states from rent-seeking coalitions. But this explanation begs the question of the origin of the hard state. When one probes deeper, the hard state is usually explained as being the product of visionary statesmen who have exercised control via a benevolent dictatorial regime. Moreover, the willingness of a country to acquiesce in dictatorship is attributed to historical contingency, rather than anything more fundamental. Nolan (1995*a*: 5) for instance suggests that China was inspired by the example of East Asia, and that its turbulent past made the CCP reluctant to experiment with democracy. Nevertheless, this still does not get us very far. All would agree that dictatorship per se is not a recipe for success. Not all dictators have a growth-promoting vision, and many of those who do may nevertheless be constrained in their freedom of manœuvre. The key to explaining China's hard state therefore seems to be the relative absence of constraints on the implementation of the Dengist transition strategy after 1978. Indeed Nolan (1995*a*: 5, 309–10) hints at such an explanation by arguing that Gorbachev's freedom to follow a 'governed market' approach in the USSR was constrained by the continuing strategic realities of the Cold War. Perhaps one should go further and argue that *perestroika* was an attempt to follow the Chinese road, and that it failed in the USSR because of a series of binding economic and political constraints, not because of any intrinsic flaw in the strategy.

Nevertheless, despite this weakness, we should not be too critical of the heterodox analysis. The orthodoxy remains so well entrenched that the task of persuading its advocates (and victims) that there is an alternative to both capitalism and state socialism is demanding enough in itself without also having to explain the origins of the state. Indeed, despite the illuminating work of Johnson, Amsden, and Wade on East Asia, the orthodoxy continues to seek ways of undermining the notion of an alternative to Anglo-Saxon capitalism, as we have seen. That objective was massively enhanced by the crisis that has affected many East and South-East Asian economies in 1997–8. The immediate task was therefore to show that the crisis was no more than a temporary problem brought on by a (mistaken) attempt to implement the dictates of the master discourse[12]—rather than indicative of a structural weakness in the East Asian model itself.

However, the advocates of the governed market approach need to consider seriously whether the East Asian model really can be applied in other parts of the world. It is not at all obvious that the state can emulate the East Asian model in sub-Saharan Africa, South-East Asia, or even the OECD countries; Krugman (1993*b*) is surely right in being sceptical about the applicability of industrial policy (the centrepiece of the governed market approach) in the USA or many LDCs. Perhaps one can even argue that the renunciation of traditional socialist prescriptions by Britain's Labour government of 1997 reflected a recognition of the impossibility of implementing an alternative economic strategy—whatever its intrinsic merits—in the United Kingdom. The states in all these countries are arguably very soft, and it may well be that the orthodox prescription is likely to bring about better results than attempting to undertake the impossible and create a governed market. But before we can be sure of that, it is essential to isolate the economic and political preconditions under which selective intervention can succeed before advocating it as a universal solution to the problems of underdevelopment—or dismissing it as wholly irrelevant. This ought to be the essence of any 'new' political economy.

2

The Process of Economic Growth

Chinese economic transition began neither with the death of Mao Zedong in September 1976, nor the arrest of the 'Gang of Four' in October.[1] Mao's death simply ushered in a two-year interregnum, dominated by a struggle for ascendancy between two factions in which the only real area of agreement was on the need to repudiate the Gang. The 'Two Whatevers' faction, led by Hua Guofeng and so-called for its commitment to upholding whatever policies and whatever instructions had been issued by Mao, was initially ascendant.[2] However, it gradually lost power to the 'Practice' faction, a group centred around Deng Xiaoping and committed to two key slogans. 'Seeking truth from facts' and 'practice is the sole criterion of truth' amounted to a view that the ideas of Party leaders (and especially those of Mao) were not above evaluation in the light of current evidence.[3] Deng himself was reinstated as a member of the Standing Committee of the Political Bureau and as Vice-Chairman of the Central Military Commission in July 1977. However, Deng's faction did not emerge triumphant until the autumn of 1978, and even then its triumph was incomplete: the 'little gang of four' did not lose office until the 5th National People's Congress in February 1980, while Hua Guofeng remained as Chairman of the Central Military Commission and Chairman of the Central Committee until June 1981.

To all intents and purposes, however, the 3rd Plenum of the 11th Central Committee of the Chinese Communist Party held in Beijing between 18 December and 22 December 1978 marked the de facto assumption of power by Deng Xiaoping. With it came the beginning of a new phase of Chinese economic development as the Party committed itself to correcting what it called the 'structural imbalances' of the Chinese economy.[4] It therefore signalled the end of the Maoist era. This largely symbolic purpose apart—Chen Yun took the view that the actual process of 'readjustment' did not begin until after December 1980 (Sun, 1995: 55)—the Plenum was very important in that it ratified a number of economic experiments. Most significantly, it upheld the process of rural liberalization which had been launched in some of the provinces after the death of Mao. In the van was Sichuan, where Zhao Ziyang, the provincial Party Secretary, encouraged the growth of private-sector farm production as early as December 1976. A similar policy was encouraged in rural Anhui by Wan Li (appointed in June 1977) in the early autumn of 1978 in response to drought conditions. The pivotal role played by these two in the transition process was encapsulated in the famous slogan *yao chifan zhao Ziyang; yao chimi zhao Wan Li* ('if you want to eat grain, call Ziyang; if you want to eat rice, call Wan Li') (Zhonggong zhongyang xuanchuanbu xuanchuanju, 1988: 5).

Reform experiments had also begun in the industrial sphere in October 1978, when a number of state-owned factories were granted financial autonomy on an experimental basis (again notably in Sichuan).[5]

1. Gradual Transition and 'Learning from Japan'

Even after 1978, the pace of economic change was slow.[6] Indeed, in the early days, most Chinese economists saw the most pressing problem as being sectoral imbalance (which needed 'readjustment') rather than any inherent systemic flaw (which would require 'reform').[7] The key statement of intent here was the slogan 'readjusting, restructuring, consolidating, and improving the national economy' advanced by the Central Committee in April 1979. As Yu (1984: 39) pointed out, of these 'Readjustment, however, is most important: it is the key link.' Not only did it require the correction of imbalances between rates of growth of agriculture and industry, and between the various subsectors of industry (notably between machine-building and metallurgy on the one hand and consumer goods, energy, and transport on the other), but also it encompassed the need to reduce gestation periods and to raise material living standards. Perhaps most importantly of all, and the reason why Yu and other Chinese leaders viewed it as the 'key link', the readjustment programme involved drastic reductions in expenditure on defence industrialization, and in particular the 'Third Front' projects that had been built in western China after 1964.

Nevertheless, the early emphasis on readjustment also reflected the comparative political weakness of those within the CCP committed to more market-orientated transition. In retrospect, three different groups within the upper echelons of the Party can be identified. The first of these was the 'Whatever' faction already mentioned. Allied to it was the 'Petroleum' faction which was committed to defending the comparatively privileged position enjoyed in respect of investment allocation by the heavy industrial and defence sectors.[8] Occupying the centre ground was a group committed to readjustment, but opposed to both extensive marketization (reducing the role of the plan) and privatization. Its leader was Chen Yun, but other notables included Li Xiannian, Peng Zhen, Wang Zhen, Bo Yibo, Deng Liqun, Hu Qiaomu, and Yao Yilin. Its economic analysis was supported by the bulk of economists based at the State Planning Commission and the People's University in Beijing. These 'Readjusters' largely held sway until 1984. Thereafter, however, the reform faction dominated. Led by Hu Yaobang, Zhao Ziyang, Wan Li, and Hu Qili, this faction's economic analysis (market-based price determination and at least some degree of privatization) was based upon the ideas of Xue Muqiao and CASS-based economists including Dong Fureng, Yu Guangyuan, Sun Shangqing, Liu Guoguang, and Chen Yizi.[9]

Three phases of economic transition can be distinguished in subsequent years. After a furious debate on whether price reform should preceded privatization, it was decided to push ahead with the former. The idea of establishing joint-stock companies was rejected by the NPC in 1986, and dramatic price reforms were announced in 1988. However, the commodity speculation that this provoked and the association of many of the reformers with corruption undermined the position of Zhao Ziyang, de facto leader of the reform camp. The Tiananmen massacre led to his fall, and with it came a halt to transition until 1992. That year saw Deng Xiaoping himself take the lead in advocating transition. Following his spring tour (*nanxun*), price reform was completed and a gradual drift towards enterprise reform began anew.[10] This renewed emphasis on transition—rather than the consolidation of 1989–92—continued until Deng's death in 1997.

Just as economic transition in China did not begin with the death of Mao Zedong in September 1976, so it did not end with the death of Deng Xiaoping in February 1997. Nevertheless, it is clear that, by the mid-1990s, Chinese economic transition had transformed late Maoist structures in state-owned industry, farming, rural industry and foreign trade and investment. That said, and despite the slogans of the era exhorting Chinese citizens to enrich themselves as soon as possible, the hallmark of the transition process between 1978 and 1997 was experimentation and gradualism.[11] The aim was to 'cross the river by touching the stones' (*mo shitou guohe*).[12] The emphasis placed on gradualism and the need for an initial period of 'restructuring' was most apparent in the urban industrial sector, where privatization was deliberately eschewed in favour of a more gradual introduction of incentive systems, and the increased exposure of firms to competition from goods produced abroad and in the rural sector. Even in agriculture, where the reforms were most radical, the emphasis (certainly in the beginning) was on experimentation and evolutionary change. For example, agricultural reform began as early as 1977 yet the contracting of farm production to households had barely begun in early 1980. Furthermore, some provinces (such as Heilongjiang) did not move in this direction until ordered to do so in 1983. It is therefore difficult to agree with Sach's (1993*a*) view that 'the rural reform was quite radical and had "somewhat of a 'big bang' character"' (p. 140) and 'it is wrong to describe China's transition as gradual in this area' (p. 144). Naughton's (1995) notion of 'growing out of the plan' seems altogether more apposite.

The other main characteristic of Chinese economic transition, more obvious in retrospect than it was at the time, was the influence of Japan. Some of this was overt, notably the Japan–China Long-Term Trade Protocol of February 1978 (Ishikawa, 1987). This committed China to the importation of complete, state-of-the-art, heavy industrial plants, e.g. the Baoshan Iron and Steel Complex established on the outskirts of Shanghai. In order to finance these imports, the Protocol established that China would export coal and oil to Japan.[13] But even more important was the way in which China's transition strategy was modelled on that of Japan in the inter-war period, and after World War II. The Chinese government could not announce that its aim was to 'learn from Japan' because of its political implications. Yet the influence of the Japanese approach is apparent across the economic spectrum. For example, China's macroeconomic policy after 1978 was generally expansionary; this willingness to tolerate inflation rates of 5 per cent or more was also the norm in Japan, especially before World War II.[14] In the sphere of education, the Dengist leadership focused on the promotion of primary education and rather neglected the secondary sector (as will be seen below). Japan had done the same in the late Meiji period, and even in 1940 the average number of years spent by a Japanese in secondary education was well below the norm in Western Europe. As for industrial policy, transition-era China rapidly abandoned the Maoist commitment to universal state ownership. The role of the state sector was to complement the private sector, just as it had in Japan during the 1950s and 1960s (Yamamura, 1986). And although rural light industry flourished in China, there was no attempt to adopt a wholly 'textile-first' strategy; rather the inspiration seems to have been the blend of heavy and light industry which was the norm in Japan during the 1930s. Perhaps most interestingly of all, the approach to market structure was very similar; the Japanese *keiretsu* (successors to the pre-war zaibatsu) had their equivalent in the Chinese *jituangongsi* which were promoted in the early 1990s. The parallels are also evident in respect of foreign trade. When Japan regained tariff autonomy at the turn of the century, it put in place a regime of selective protection in which tariff rates on imported primary commodities and capital goods were kept low, whereas consumer products faced a high rate of protection. This helped to support infant industries, and at the same time facilitated the process of technology transfer. China's post-1978 approach was remarkably similar; autarky was abandoned and replaced with a policy of strategic integration.

China's willingness to learn from Japan made a great deal of sense. Both were 'large' economies and therefore had no need to rely exclusively on the world market to exploit economies of scale. Moreover, and as Minami (1994: 226–30) points out, it can at least be argued that China in 1978 was little more advanced in its development than Japan in the early twentieth century (except in the sphere of industry). It therefore made sense for China to look to pre-war Japan, as well as to the Japanese industrial strategy of the post-war era, in formulating its transition strategy. Perhaps more importantly, the Japanese approach to development had 'succeeded', and not only in Japan but also in South Korea and Taiwan.[15] It was to prove equally effective in the People's Republic of China.

2. Macroeconomic Outcomes

The pre-1978 data on China's economy are subject to considerable margins of error, especially for the period of the Second Five-Year Plan (1958–62) and the Cultural Revolution (1966–76). During these periods, the SSB practically ceased to function and many of its key personnel were dispersed across China. The data published since 1981 represent an attempt to reconstruct the national accounts of the People's Republic for the Maoist period, as well as charting economic performance during the transition era.

The reconstructed data on the Chinese economy show that it grew much more quickly in the 1980s than it had in the late Maoist era (1957–78). The basis for this claim are the official data published by China's State Statistical Bureau (SSB) on net domestic material product (Table 2.1).[16] They show that NDMP growth during 1978–93 was more than double that for 1957–78 when measured using 1990 prices (8.8 compared to 4.3 per cent); at 1952 prices, it was 'only' 75 per cent greater (10.3 compared to 5.9 per cent).[17] Clearly, then, a comparison of growth rates between the late Maoist and Dengist eras is not especially sensitive to the choice of relative prices. The use of 1990 prices may exaggerate the improvement in growth performance after 1978, but the contrast between late Maoist and post-1978 periods is clear even if 1952 prices are used.[18]

TABLE 2.1. *Growth of Chinese NDMP and Population, 1952–1993* (per cent per annum)

Period	NDMP		NDMP per capita		Population
	1952 prices	1990 prices	1952 prices	1990 prices	
1952–7	9.0	6.2	6.6	3.8	2.3
1957–78	5.9	4.3	3.6	2.1	2.1
1978–93	10.3	8.8	8.7	7.3	1.5

Note: Output values for each of the five main sectors of the Chinese economy (agriculture, industry, construction, commerce and transportation, and communications) have been rebased to 1952 and 1990 prices, and then aggregated. NDMP data have ceased to be published since 1993.

Sources: ZGTJNJ (1992: 32–3, 77); ZGTJNJ (1994: 33, 59).

The growth rate of GDP is similar to that in NDMP (Table 2.2).[19] Real GDP grew annually by 9.9 per cent, significantly higher than the 8.8 per cent growth rate recorded by NDMP (both at 1990 prices). But the GDP data include the growth of 1994, 1995, and 1996, whereas the NDMP series ends in 1993. As growth rates in 1992–6 were significantly higher than for the transition period as a whole, this partly explains why GDP growth is faster than NDMP growth. Again, however, the key feature of the post-1978 era is the marked acceleration of growth compared to the late Maoist period—even if the disastrous fall in output that occurred during 1957–65 is excluded from the Maoist data. Of course the slowdown in population growth after 1978 contributed to faster post-1978 per capita growth, but the key ingredient in the transformation was faster output growth.

In longer term historical perspective, the growth achieved since 1978 is also extremely fast. Although Chinese economists writing in the late 1970s and early 1980s tended to look back on the early 1950s as a 'golden age', the data in Table 2.2 show that post-1978 growth rates were even faster—and that despite starting from a much higher base. At least as significantly, the growth rates achieved during the post-Mao era were far in excess of those achieved during the Republican period (1912–49) when the Chinese economy was much more market-orientated. Even according to Rawski's (extremely optimistic) estimates, real Chinese GDP grew by only about 2 per cent per year between 1914/18 and 1931/6, and by a mere 1.2 per cent in per capita terms (Rawski, 1989: 330).[20]

In comparative international terms, the post-1978 growth of the Chinese economy is equally impressive. Although the growth of most other developing countries

TABLE 2.2. *Growth of Chinese GDP, 1914–1996*
(growth of GDP at 1990 prices, per cent per annum)

Period	GDP	GDP per capita	Population
1914–36	1.1	0.3	0.8
1952–7	9.2	6.8	2.4
1957–65	−0.7	−1.9	1.2
1965–78	4.9	2.6	2.3
1978–96	9.9	8.4	1.4

Notes: The growth rate for 1914 to 1936 is based on 1933 constant prices. The growth rates for the 1950s are for GNP at 1952 constant prices and Yeh's figure for population growth is used. Data for 1957–78 are for net domestic material product, which excludes 'unproductive' services; reliable GDP data are not available. Output growth rates for post-1978 are at 1990 constant prices; individual sub-sectors have been rebased to 1990 prices before aggregation The growth rates for post-1978 are much faster using the GDP series given in ZGTJNJ (1995 and 1996) than in previous editions. This is because of higher estimates for tertiary sector growth.

Sources: Yeh (1979: 104); LSTJ (1990); ZGTJNJ (1993: 31–2, 81); ZGTJNJ (1996: 42, 69); ZGTJNJ (1997: 42, 69); WDR (1990: 178, 180, 228); Yeh (1992: 502).

—especially in sub-Saharan Africa and much of Latin America—was comparatively slow during the 1980s because of depression in the principal OECD economies and by the debt crisis, China's partial integration into the world economy meant that she was practically immune to these fluctuations. Thus the Chinese growth rate comfortably exceeded those of comparably large developing countries such as Brazil and India, which managed 2.7 and 5.3 per cent rates of increase respectively. Furthermore, compared to the averages for the (heavily indebted) regions of sub-Saharan Africa (2.1 per cent) or Latin America and the Caribbean (1.6 per cent), the Chinese rate was miraculous. Perhaps most importantly of all, China's record is impressive even when compared with the Asian NICs; South Korea (which achieved a GDP growth of 8.6 per cent, 1960–90) and Taiwan (8.7 per cent, 1953–90) did no better than the People's Republic even during their halcyon days (Lau, 1996: 75).

In comparison with the transitional economies of Eastern Europe and the Soviet Union (many of which privatized state industry early on, and which have placed an inordinate emphasis on the creation of formal property rights[21]), China has been well served in terms of its short- and medium-term growth rate by its more gradual approach to transition. The consequence of 'shock therapy' has been a collapse of real wages and industrial production, and spiralling unemployment in the former Soviet Union, and the countries along its western border.[22] Between 1990 and 1994, real GDP fell on average by 3.7 per cent per annum in Rumania, 4.7 per cent in the Czech Republic, 5.9 per cent in Bulgaria, 10.6 per cent in Russia, 14.4 per cent in Ukraine, and 31.2 per cent in Georgia. Only in Poland did it rise, and then by a modest 1.6 per cent (WDR, 1996: 208–9). It may be that these losses will be made good in the long run, but it is evident that a great deal of ground has been lost; in this regard, the contrast with China is striking.

Furthermore, there is little evidence that the high growth rates achieved in the years of transition in China were merely recovery from a depressed late Maoist base. It is certainly true that agricultural growth was exceptionally fast before 1985, and that it slowed down thereafter. It is also true that the overall growth rate slowed down in the late 1980s. But there are two reasons for doubting the idea that Dengist growth was merely a one-off movement onto a production frontier. First, rural growth did not slow after 1984. That was because of the growth of rural industry, which more than compensated (at least in accounting terms) for faltering agricultural growth. As a result—and despite the recession of 1989–90—output growth between 1984 and 1991 was virtually identical in its pace to growth between 1978 and 1984 (Table 2.3). Secondly, the slowdown in the late 1980s was a direct consequence of macroeconomic policy (and, to a lesser extent, the impact of the Tiananmen massacre on inward investment) rather than a secular decline in the growth rate. The temporary nature of slow growth during 1989–90 is abundantly clear from the renewal of rapid growth in 1991.

TABLE 2.3. *Phases of economic growth since 1978*
(real annual percentage growth rates, 1990 prices)

Period	GDP	GDP per capita
1978–84	8.5	7.0
1984–91	8.3	6.7
(1988–91)	(5.5)	(4.0)
1991–6	12.1	10.9

Sources: As for Table 2.2.

In fact, as is clear from Table 2.3, the growth rate in the early 1990s was actually faster than it had been in the early 1980s. Now it may be that this growth rate is unsustainable; the macroeconomic contraction of 1994–6 to check rising inflation certainly points in that direction. But the fact that the CCP was able to bring down inflation and still maintain an output growth rate of around 10 per cent suggests that the underlying potential growth rate of the economy may well be close to that figure. In that sense, it is hard indeed to see the Dengist period as a mere transitory phase.

Nevertheless, and despite the many euphoric commentaries on the People's Republic that are to be found in the literature, it is wise to be cautious before proclaiming China's 'success'. The first problem relates to the data. More precisely, official Chinese growth rates suffer from a significant element of upward bias. This is because the prices used to value industrial output are significantly above probable marginal cost. It is not true of every sector; coal is a case in point. But for metallurgy and machine building in particular, it is more than arguable that even the 1990 prices used to value final output are unrealistically high in the light of the low quality of these goods. As these sectors have continued to grow quickly since

1978, overall GDP growth is exaggerated. In addition, the data on the service sector are unreliable. This is largely because few data were collected in the late 1970s and early 1980s when it was still common for service sector activity to be regarded as 'unproductive'; the corrections made following the first tertiary sector census in 1992 do not address this problem.

Furthermore, the implicit GDP deflator is probably too low, largely because of the tendency of industrial enterprises to report their output in current prices even though it is presented as constant price data. If industrial factory gate prices are used instead, the GDP growth rate is reduced significantly. Instead of a real GDP growth rate of 9.7 per cent between 1985 and 1993, Sachs and Woo (1997: 75) estimate a figure of 7.5 per cent per year for GDP at 1990 prices. Maddison's (1998*b*: 56) revisions have the same sort of effect; his estimate of real GDP growth for 1978–95 is 7.5 per cent compared to an official figure of 9.8 per cent. A more radical revision still is suggested by Ren (1997: 108). By deflating primary output by the farm and sideline purchase price index, secondary output by the industrial products producer price index and tertiary output by the overall residents' consumer price index, he obtains an annual growth rate (at 1985 prices) of only 6 per cent for 1985–94.

Finally, the 1995 Industrial Census found widespread over-reporting of production, especially in the rural industrial sector. The number of enterprises was exaggerated by 2.68 million and total output by as much as 40 per cent in some sectors (CD, 3 Apr. 1997),[23] problems serious enough to cause the introduction of a new law in 1996 making falsification of data an offence.[24] This 1995 Census has, of course, allowed industrial output data for 1991–5 to be corrected; the extent of the over-reporting of gross output value was about 5 per cent in 1991, rising to 10 per cent in 1995.[25] But it is still the case that industrial output data for the 1990s remain problematic outside the Census years of 1990 and 1995.

Yet for all these problems, it is not clear that the official data produce a *qualitative* distortion of China's growth record after 1978. A 10 per cent over-reporting of industrial output is neither here nor there in terms of its impact on a growth rate as high as China's. The use of misleading deflators is more serious, but it is not certain that the revised figures are much better. Factory gate prices offer in principle a reliable way of deflating current price output, but only if they are based upon a representative sample of enterprises and products. The reluctance of China's State Statistical Bureau to use them as deflators—even though it publishes the deflators on a regular basis, most obviously in the *Statistical Yearbooks*—suggests that the arguments in their favour are by no means clear cut. Taking all these arguments together, it is probable that China's growth rates are exaggerated but not by as much as is often claimed.[26]

The second problem with China's growth rates relates to their interpretation. In order to evaluate China's record, we should not compare it against either historical performance or the growth rates achieved in other countries—but rather against a counterfactual based upon the underlying potential of the economy. Once the issue is posed in this way, it is evident that, given the 'right' growth strategy and an adequate infrastructural capability (both social and physical), China ought to have grown very quickly indeed. To start with, it enjoyed all the 'advantages of backwardness' that accrue to any late industrializer: a low level of GDP per capita combined with a backlog of technology and an abundance of surplus labour.[27] In addition, China's 1978 output level was well below its potential because of cyclical factors. Output at the end of the Maoist period was unusually depressed because of a run of poor harvests (see below) and the disruption of the economy caused by the struggle for succession in 1975–6.

From this perspective, China's record appears much less impressive compared with other East Asian NICs. Taiwan, South Korea, and Japan began their modern economic growth with very low levels of (purchasing power parity) GDP per capita compared to the USA. China, however, stood at a lower base still in 1978. Yet despite this advantage, and as Table 2.4 shows, China's per capita growth rate of 4.1 per cent between 1978 and 1992 was significantly less than the rates achieved by Taiwan, South Korea, and Japan at a comparable stage of their industrialization.

TABLE 2.4. *The scope for catch-up: Late industrializers and the USA* (levels and growth rates of GDP per capita at PPP)

Country	Year	Real GDP per capita relative to USA (USA = 100)	Growth of GDP per capita (per cent p.a.)
China	1978	5.3	
	1992	8.3	4.1 (1978–92)
Taiwan	1953	11.1	6.1 (1953–90)
S. Korea	1960	9.1	7.1 (1960–91)
Japan	1950	16.3	7.2 (1950–80)

Note: Estimates of GDP per capita and per capita growth rates are at 1985 prices and at purchasing-power parity.

Source: *Penn World Tables*, version 5.6 (1995).

Even in 1992, and despite the rapid growth of the 1980s, per capita GDP in China was lower relative to the USA than for Taiwan (1953) and South Korea (1960) at the beginning of their modern economic growth. In other words, China's growth rate after 1978 was actually rather disappointing; it should in principle have done better than the East Asian NICs because it started from further behind.[28] Even though work on purchasing power parity estimates GDP for the People's Republic is in its infancy, China's growth record during its transition fell short of being 'miraculous' when placed in an international perspective.

A third problem with the euphoric assessments of Chinese progress is that sustainability is by no means guaranteed. As Sachs (1993*a*: 141) rightly observed:

> Despite the enormous economic progress under the reforms, and the intoxicating GDP growth rates of the past two years, it is much too early to proclaim victory for China's reforms. Political and economic liberties are not protected; property rights are not clearly established, regional disputes threaten national unity, and there are no settled arrangements linking the central and regional governments. The recent growth of output and living standards is heartening but hardly conclusive with regard to China's future.

Moreover, although output also grew extremely quickly during 1992–4, the inflationary pressures that resulted suggest that growth rates of around 10 per cent may not be sustainable. Perhaps even more importantly, Deng left no successor able to command the unquestioned loyalty of army and Party.

It should also be pointed out that the period after 1978 was not one of continuously rapid economic growth. For example, output growth was relatively slow during the period 1979–81 when the rate fell below 8 per cent. Nevertheless, this slowdown was deliberately engineered[29] following the decision of the 3rd Plenum in December 1978 to correct widely perceived structural imbalances in the economy. The degree of imbalance was even greater than it had been in the early 1970s largely as a result of what was contemptuously dismissed by the reformers as Hua Guofeng's 'foreign leap forward' (because of its reliance on the import of capital goods from overseas) launched during 1976.[30] The programme of 'readjustment' that followed was designed to reduce the share of heavy industry in national income, thereby raising the share of light industry (predominantly consumer goods). It proved extremely successful. The share of accumulation in NDMP was reduced from 36.5 per cent in 1978 to 28.3 per cent by 1981, with the total value of accumulation declining by 5 per cent in nominal terms during that year. At the same time, the share of heavy industry in gross industrial output value was reduced from 57 per cent to 49 per cent (ZGTJNJ, 1992: 40, 57).

The growth rate of the economy also fell during 1986, declining from almost 14 per cent in 1985 to a little under 8 per cent in 1986. This 'recession' was precipitated by inflationary pressures within the economy; the retail price index rose by about 9 per cent in 1985 (ZGTJNJ, 1992: 235). Given the continuing sensitivity of the Party leadership to inflationary pressures (the memory of the hyperinflation of the late 1940s remained sharp), it was perhaps unsurprising that deliberate policy measures were taken during the second half of 1985 to slow the rate of output growth. These measures certainly had the desired effect, with the rise in the retail price index falling back to about 6 per cent in 1986. The most severe recession was that of 1989–90, which occurred because of contractionary fiscal and monetary policies designed to check the inflation which emerged in the early autumn of 1988. These deflationary measures included the compulsory purchase of state bonds by urban workers and a cut of about 20 per cent in state fixed investment. As a result, the growth rate of NDMP fell from 10.1 per cent in 1988 to only 3.2 per cent in 1989 and 5 per cent in 1990.

The transition era also saw phases of very rapid economic growth. The boom of 1984–5, for example, was dramatic. It was based on the bumper harvest of 1984 and the removal of many controls on the formation of new rural industries. In addition, there was growing investment by state enterprises (the financing of which added directly to the fiscal deficit); the investment share in national income leapt from about 30 per cent in 1983 to about 35 per cent in 1985, the highest share attained in any year during the 1980s (ZGTJNJ, 1992: 40). In 1985 alone, nominal accumulation increased by 46 per cent. The other period of dramatic growth was that which followed Deng Xiaoping's spring tour to south-east China in 1992. In the four years which followed, GDP growth registered 14.3, 13.5, 12.7, and 10.5 per cent respectively.[31] These rates were well above the average rate of 9.9 per cent for the post-1978 era (Table 2.3).

Yet these macroeconomic cycles need to be put in perspective. Even in 1989–90, when growth was at its slowest, national income still increased by nearly 4 per cent whilst the supposed 'recession' year of 1986 saw output growth of almost 8 per cent. Compared to the collapse of output that occurred in several Latin American countries in the early 1980s,[32] these Chinese cycles were mild. To be more precise, the coefficient of variation for Chinese NDMP between 1978 and 1991 was 0.35 whereas the corresponding figures (for real GDP) were 0.5 for South Korea, 0.75 for India, and 1.33 for Brazil. Japan, with a coefficient of variation of 0.26, was one of the very few countries to do better than China in this regard (WT, 1992: 144–5, 320–1, 348–9, 360–1).

In summary, the Dengist growth record was flawed: the growth rate fluctuated, the official data probably contain an element of upward bias, the success of the transition programme is by no means assured and the growth rate achieved was not 'miraculous' given the level of output in 1978. Nevertheless, the success of the transition era in terms of growth is plain. Even if we accept some of the revisions suggested by Ren (1997)—which reduce the growth rate by more than 3 percentage points—China's growth rate in the transition era remains high. Whether one compares it with the late Maoist era, to the Chinese economy before 1957, or to the performance of most other developing countries, the growth record of the People's Republic during the transition era was impressive.

3. The Agricultural Revolution

The success of the transition package introduced after 1978 depended upon an acceleration in the growth rate of agriculture.[33] With extensive grain imports ruled out by the desire to avoid 'dependency' and a recognition that rising Chinese import demand would be partially self-defeating in that it would raise world grain prices, a level of production close to self-sufficiency was deemed as essential under Deng as it had been under Mao. However, few in the leadership believed that it would be easy to increase agricultural production at a rate much in advance of population growth. This was because the scope for extensive growth had disappeared decades earlier, and even low-yield, upland, areas had long since been brought under the plough in the most densely populated areas of the country. In fact, and as a result of the encroachment of buildings, factories, and roads on to farm land (as well as erosion in many mountainous areas), the official data show cultivated area falling from a peak of about 1.677bn. *mu* in 1957 to 1.491bn. *mu* by 1978 (LSTJ, 1990: 14). This trend continued in the 1980s, and by 1991 the figure had dwindled to 1.435bn. *mu* (ZGNYTJZL, 1992: 12–13). These official data undoubtedly under-report true cultivated area; satellite photography suggests an understatement by between 30 and 45 per cent in the 1990s (Crook, 1991, 1997). However, official sources have confirmed that this understatement is offset by the overstatement of yields (Crook, 1997: 129).[34] In other words, understatement of cultivated area does not imply understatement of total output.

As it transpired—at least according to the *official* data—even the most sanguine expectations of the Chinese leadership were exceeded. First, agricultural production diversified at a remarkable pace (Table 2.5). The farm subsector, growing at an annual rate of 4.1 per cent, fared well, but most other subsectors did even better, with fisheries registering an annual growth rate of almost 13 per cent. Within farming, too, diversification proceeded rapidly. The growth of grain output, at 2.4 per cent per year, was positively sluggish by late Maoist standards. It lagged well behind the rates achieved between 1965 and 1978 (3.4 per cent) and even further behind the rate of 4 per cent per year achieved between 1952 and 1957.[35] By contrast, the production of cotton and vegetable oils increased annually by 3.2 and 6.7 per cent respectively during the years after 1978. These differences in relative growth rates had much to do with the changing composition of sown area. At the time of Mao's death, grain accounted for about 80 per cent of all sown area. Thereafter, grain sown area decreased at a rate of about 0.5 per cent per year with the result that its share had fallen to about 73 per cent by 1994. Conversely, the area sown to other crops tended to rise. In the case of the very important cotton crop, the share rose only marginally from about 3 per cent in 1978 to about 4 per cent by 1980. The area planted with oil crops increased more quickly; an annual rate of increase of about 3.4 per cent meant that its share had risen to 8 per cent in 1994 compared to a modest 4 per cent in 1978 (ZGTJNJ, 1995: 344–6; Nongye bu, 1989: 140–3). All this was largely in accordance with the objectives of the reformers. The share of cash crops was pushed up to meet the growing demand for non-grain products but at the same time the bulk of arable land continued to be sown with grain crops to guarantee near self-sufficiency. That grain production continued to grow at about 2.4 per cent per year—well above the population growth rate of 1.4 per cent—is an indication that they were comparatively successful.

TABLE 2.5. *Agricultural diversification after 1978* (percentage growth rates, 1978–1996)

Subsectoral output value (1990 prices)		Crop output, 1978–96 (volume)	
Farming	4.1	Grain	2.4
Forestry	5.0	Vegetable oil	6.7
Animal husbandry	9.0	Cotton	3.2
Fisheries	12.9		

Note: Subsectoral growth rates are for net output value at 1990 constant prices (value-added ratios by subsector are unavailable before 1983; the 1983 ratios are used as an approximation for 1978–82). The category 'sidelines' was discontinued after 1993; sidelines are therefore included within farming in this table. Crop output growth rates are calculated from unprocessed volume data.

Sources: Nongye bu (1989: 108–9); ZGNYTJZL (1988: 22–3); ZGTJNJ (1992: 358–9); ZGTJNJ (1995: 332–3, 347–8); ZGTJNJ (1996: 356, 371–2); ZGTJNJ (1997: 369, 383); Nongye bu (1997: 292–5).

Yet significant though diversification was, it was less significant from a leadership perspective than the dramatic increase in the overall growth rate shown in Table 2.6. The productivity miracle in agriculture is even more apparent when one looks at the trend in labour productivity for specific crops (Table 2.7). Labour productivity in rice production rose by no less than 129 per cent between 1975 and 1984, and the increase in labour productivity in wheat farming was an even more remarkable 140 per cent. Even in cotton cultivation, the rise in labour productivity was 112 per cent. As a result of this massive advance, a huge labour surplus was created in the farm sector for potential release to rural industry.

TABLE 2.6. *Agricultural growth in historical perspective* (growth rates of agricultural output at 1990 prices, per cent per annum)

Period	NVAO	NVAO per capita	Labour productivity
1952–7	4.1	1.7	2.0
1957–78	2.8	0.6	−0.2
1978–96	5.6	4.2	4.6
(1978–84)	(7.7)	(6.3)	(5.9)
(1984–9)	(3.1)	(1.5)	(1.7)
(1989–96)	(6.0)	(4.7)	(6.5)

Notes: The population denominator used to calculate NVAO per capita is total population. The labour force is the total number employed in farming, forestry, animal husbandry, and fisheries in both urban and rural areas and is taken from Renkou yu jiuye tongjisi (1997: 10). NVAO growth is calculated post-1977 (before 1978, the standard ZGTJNJ NVAO data are used) by expressing the gross output value of each subsector at 1990 prices, factoring out input costs and then reaggregating.

Sources: ZGTJNJ (1993: 33–4, 81, 101); ZGTJNJ (1994: 328, 330); ZGTJNJ (1995: 330, 332); ZGTJNJ (1996: 69, 356); ZGTJNJ (1997: 42, 69, 369).

TABLE 2.7. *The rise in labour productivity in farming, 1975–1984* (kg. per labour day)

Year	Rice	Wheat	Cotton
1975	7.3	5.3	0.7
1976	6.6	5.0	0.6
1977	7.6	4.3	0.6
1978	7.3	5.1	0.6
1979	9.6	6.4	0.7
1980	9.5	6.4	0.8
1981	10.6	7.9	0.8
1982	14.0	9.9	1.0
1983	15.1	13.6	1.1
1984	16.7	12.7	1.5

Source: Han and Feng (1992: 506–12).

All this evidence appears to show that the post-1978 period was an era of almost unprecedented growth—and that nothing less than an agricultural 'miracle' occurred between 1978 and 1984. The remarkable character of growth in the early 1980s is particularly evident when placed in its historical and international contexts.

During 1952–57, net output value in China grew by 4.1 per cent per year and the rate fell to an average of 2.8 per cent between 1957 and 1978 (ZGTJNJ, 1992: 33). By comparison with the Republican period, when annual growth averaged no more than 0.8 per cent (Yeh, 1979: 126), growth during the 1980s was truly astonishing.[36] Indeed, the growth of the agricultural sector during the early 1980s was so rapid that its share in NDMP actually increased from 33 per cent in 1978 to peak at 41 per cent in 1983 (ZGTJNJ, 1992: 35). In comparative international perspective, too, Chinese agriculture performed impressively. Between 1980 and 1991, agricultural output in Brazil and India grew annually by 'only' 2.6 per cent and 3.2 per cent respectively. The average for low and middle income countries (excluding China and India) over the same period was 2.5 per cent, whilst that for sub-Saharan Africa was a mere 1.8 per cent (WDR, 1993: 240–1). Furthermore, Chinese growth was substantially faster than in Meiji Japan, often cited as an example of successful agricultural development. Chinese growth between 1978 and 1994 was more than twice as fast as even the most optimistic estimates of Japanese growth between 1878 and 1919, which put the rate at only 2.4 per cent per annum (Nakamura, 1965: 255).[37] Finally, it is worth noting that the arguments put forward in the late 1980s that Chinese agriculture was in crisis—not an entirely unreasonable analysis given the slowdown after 1984—seem exaggerated in retrospect. Although performance was not especially good between 1984 and 1989, growth rates rose substantially in the early and mid-1990s. The growth of labour productivity in particular was very impressive.

The problem with this kind of positive assessment of Chinese agricultural performance after 1978 is that it ignores four factors. First, there is substantial evidence that crop production was significantly under-reported at the end of the 1970s, and that under-reporting was greatly reduced by 1984. Therefore a part of the growth recorded in Table 2.6 is a statistical artefact. For example, many of the provinces under-reported output to central government, and at a local level various practices were used to understate grain yields in the late 1970s (Oi, 1989: 89, 117). Shue (1988: 139–41) makes a similar point on the basis of interviews with local officials, concluding that under-reporting typically varied between 5 and 15 per cent. The main incentive for under-reporting was the procurement system, by which the state extracted the lion's share of recorded 'surplus' production. Additionally, central government may have tacitly condoned under-reporting for provinces such as Anhui and Sichuan which had suffered severe famine during the Great Leap Forward, partly as a result of an excessive procurement burden.[38] Furthermore, it seems extremely unlikely that the official series reported in the *Chinese Agricultural* and *Statistical Yearbooks* employ consistent definitions. The crop reporting system broke down with the demise of the commune in 1982–3, and it seems likely that 1984 output was inflated because of the incorporation of private-sector production into the data for the first time. These doubts are reinforced by year-on-year trends in production. The reported real agricultural growth rates—9 per cent in 1983 and 13 per cent in 1984 (ZGTJNJ, 1994: 34)—are extraordinarily high even for an economy experiencing recovery from an output trough. The fact that growth drops dramatically after 1984 reinforces the view that the data for the early 1980s are suspect. Some idea of the impact of under-reporting on output can be obtained by looking at grain production, which officially rose by about 34 per cent between 1978 and 1984. If under-reporting was widespread and on the scale reported by Shue (perhaps 10 per cent of 1978 output), that alone reduces the growth rate between 1978 and 1984 to 21 per cent.

A second qualification is that much of the agricultural growth of the 1980s was due to a combination of recovery from the depression of the mid-1970s, and the continuing impact of long-run trend factors. In other words, agricultural growth in the transition period was only partly the product of post-1978 policy changes. Part of the rise in output was simply due to recovery from the output trough of the mid-1970s. The much-used comparison between 1978 and 1984 is especially misleading here because it compares a poor harvest year (1978) with an excellent harvest year (1984); according to Kueh's (1995: 299) series, the weather in 1978 was 54 per cent worse than the 1952–84 mean, whereas it was only 3 per cent worse in 1984. In other words, the 1978–84 comparison is clearly biased.[39] In fact, if grain output during 1975–8 had grown at the rate achieved during 1965–75 (3.7 per cent per annum), 1978 output would have been 317m. tonnes—over 10m. tonnes higher than actual output. More importantly, trend factors—irrigation, new seed varieties, and increased application of chemical fertilizer—were an even more powerful stimulus. In fact, if one assumes that the growth rate of grain production for 1965–75 had simply been maintained between 1975 and 1984, output in 1984 would have reached around 390m. tonnes—only a little below the figure of 407m. tonnes actually recorded and purportedly the product of decollectivization. In short, a continuation of late Maoist agricultural policies would have achieved almost the same level of grain production as the new transition policies.

To put this another way, Chinese agriculture was not in crisis at the end of the 1970s. Indeed, the continuity in agricultural performance between the early 1970s and late 1980s was rather greater than many of the reformers have cared to admit. Although output levels in the mid-1970s appear extremely low, these had much to do with the vagaries of the weather experienced during 1975–8. In any case, even these depressed levels of output were actually quite adequate. For example, per capita food consumption averaged 2,294 kcal per person per day during 1976–8, a level undoubtedly in excess of subsistence and probably marginally above the average for 1955–7 (Piazza, 1986: 77).[40] Of course, increases in grain production were needed if the Chinese diet was to become more varied; increased output of meat and dairy products could only be achieved by enhanced production of grain for use as animal feed. But that should not detract from the Maoist achievement in ensuring an adequate level of food consumption for a population that had increased in size by more than 380 million between 1952 and 1978 against a background of an unchanging arable area.[41] Furthermore, the path of the reformers was greatly eased by the diffusion of new agricultural technologies pioneered in the late 1960s and early 1970s and which centred on chemical fertilizer, plastics, and hybrid varieties (Stone, 1988*a*).

To be sure, this rather critical analysis is biased against the policies pursued in the transition era because it focuses exclusively on grain—one of the slowest growing subsectors within agriculture. If one looks at total agricultural output, the picture is somewhat different. In the late Maoist period, NVAO grew at only 2.5 per cent per year between 1965 and 1975, to reach 262bn. *yuan* (at 1990 prices) in 1975; this was significantly slower than the growth of grain production (3.7 per cent) over the same period. Projecting that growth rate forward to 1984 produces a level of NVAO in 1984 of 328bn. *yuan*. This is well below the 399bn. *yuan* figure actually achieved. In other words, the transition policies did produce a significant rise in *total* agricultural output over and above what would have been achieved if Maoist policies had been continued. Nevertheless, the rise in output is perhaps better seen as 'significant' rather than 'miraculous' when the under-reporting previously discussed is also incorporated. If one assuming under-reporting of NVAO by 10 per cent in 1975, and that the 1965–75 growth rate was sustained after 1975, that implies that true NVAO would have reached about 360bn. yuan in 1984 if Maoist policies had been maintained. Official NVAO rose by about 52 per cent between 1975 and 1984, but in the absence of any policy change, and allowing for under-reporting, it would have increased by about 25 per cent over the same period anyway. The difference between these two figures of 25 and 52 per cent—a growth rate of about 2.7 per cent per year—is therefore a measure of the boost to agricultural production provided by the policy changes introduced after 1978. If this constitutes a miracle, it was rather a modest kind of miracle.

A third reason for being wary of the claim that agricultural performance post-1978 was miraculous is that the vulnerability of production to poor weather persisted. In that sense, Chinese agriculture in the 1990s has much more in common with (say) the late 1960s than is often recognized. 1979, for example, was probably the best single year of the decade and this had much to do with the startling 10 per cent increase in grain yields that was recorded (Nongye bu, 1989: 148). By comparison, 1980 and 1981 were poor years, especially 1980, and this served to mask the underlying improvement in agricultural performance taking place at the time. It also served to exaggerate the degree of improvement that occurred during 1982–4 when three years of good weather culminated in a 1984 grain yield of 241 kg per *mu*, no less than 43 per cent higher than the 1978 yield and implying an annual rate of increase of close to 6 per cent. Such rates of improvement were manifestly unsustainable, and so it proved. With the good weather of the early 1980s being followed by a four-year period of poor weather, the grain yield stagnated at a little below the 240 kg mark (Nongye bu, 1989: 148; ZGNYTJZL, 1988: 56–7). The 1988 harvest was particularly bad because the area severely affected by 'natural disasters' (meaning a yield of more than 30 per cent below normal) was some 22 per cent higher than the average for the decade, and more than 50 per cent higher than in 1984 (ZGTJNJ, 1992: 385). 1991 was an even more difficult year. The total area severely affected by 'natural disasters' was some 16 per cent higher than in 1988 (ZGTJNJ, 1992: 385). Even this disguises the intensity of the problem at a provincial level. The area worst hit centred on Anhui and Jiangsu, where very extensive flooding occurred. Hefei, the capital of Anhui, was inundated and total provincial grain production was about 29 per cent lower than it had been in 1990 (ZGNYTJZL, 1991: 72–3). Even during the Great Leap Forward, there was no decline in production for a single year comparable to this.[42] Shanxi province was also badly hit in 1991; grain production there fell by 23 per cent as a result of a severe drought (ZGNYTJZL, 1991: 398).

Nevertheless, the Chinese agricultural sector was comparatively resilient even in the face of bad weather in the late 1980s and 1990s. One cannot, for example, argue that the poor weather of 1988 led to an agricultural crisis. The volume of imported grain (15.3m. tonnes) was below the level of 1982 and amounted to no more than 4 per cent of total production, and net output value was 2.2 per cent higher than in 1987 (ZGTJNJ, 1992: 34, 358, 638), largely because the growth of the non-farm sectors of agriculture continued unimpaired. The value of aquatic products increased in real terms by 11.6 per cent compared to 1987 whilst that of household sidelines rose by 12.6 per cent. Still more remarkably (and perhaps implausibly), the value of animal products also increased by 12.7 per cent—despite pressure on the availability of grain for use as animal feed (ZGNYTJZL, 1988: 18–19). Even the floods of 1991 had a limited national effect. The problems experienced in Anhui and Jiangsu notwithstanding, national net output value was 2.3 per cent higher than in 1990; and even national grain production fell by only a modest 2.1 per cent (ZGNYZL, 1991: 72–3). More generally, according to the index devised by Kueh (1995), the trend decline in the instability of agricultural output that occurred between 1952 and 1978 continued after 1984.[43] In short, Chinese agriculture was vulnerable to weather-induced fluctuations even in the 1990s, but this vulnerability was undoubtedly of an order of magnitude less than in Bangladesh or Sudan.

Fourth and finally, one should be sceptical of the notion of post-Mao agricultural 'miracle' because of the clear slowdown in agricultural growth after 1984. As Table 2.6 shows, NVAO grew at only 3.1 per cent between 1984 and 1989. Although this rose to 6 per cent during 1989–96, this was still below the rate achieved during the period up to 1984. Moreover, the growth of farm production itself was only 3.8 per cent per year even in 1989–96, compared to 7.3 per cent between 1978 and 1984. Of course that was hardly a disastrous outcome. The 1989–96 growth rate comfortably exceeded the average rate of agricultural growth attained in poor countries over the course of the 1978–91 era (2.5 per cent) and was far above the rate achieved in sub-Saharan Africa. Even so, the performance of Chinese agriculture in the late 1980s and early 1990s was rather disquieting given a population growth rate which remained obstinately high, and growing pressure to make more arable land available for industrial and residential development.[44] Moreover, the level of farm investment was manifestly inadequate even to maintain, let alone expand, the irrigation infrastructure. As the 1990s progressed, the search for a solution to what is increasingly seen as the agricultural 'problem' intensified.

None of this is to suggest that one could reasonably expect the growth of the early 1980s to be maintained. That growth was wholly exceptional, and the very fact that farm production could grow at no more than 3.8 per cent per year between

1989 and 1996—despite a marked improvement in the internal terms of trade, renewed attempts to promote grain self-sufficiency at the provincial level,[45] and impressive labour productivity—demonstrates the exceptional nature of the early 1980s. Yet the underlying problem is that Chinese agricultural output needs to grow at a rate close to that achieved in the early 1980s if growing demand is to be satisfied without large increases in imports. In other words, China's agriculture has done well since 1978—but probably not well enough.

At root, the agricultural problem in the People's Republic is a combination of growing grain demand, stagnant per capita grain production, and the difficulties inherent in trading on a significant scale on world markets. On the demand side, the very success of the transition in raising real incomes has led to growing consumer demand for meat and dairy products. As is well known, it is not especially efficient in terms of calorie production to feed grain to cattle. However, the drift towards a market economy (and hence the effective abandonment of consumer-goods rationing) as well as rising disposable incomes has ensured that there is no simple means of controlling demand for these grain-intensive products. Reliance on the price mechanism is tantamount to an acceptance of spiralling inflation. On the supply side, domestic production of grain increased throughout the 1980s, but per capita output reached a peak in 1984 and then fell back.[46] Only in 1996 was the 1984 per capita level reattained (Table 2.8). The alternative to domestic production is of course to import, and in principle, China could meet its grain needs in this way. But the difficulties here are substantial. China is a 'large' country in the sense that it is not a price taker in world markets. This means that its terms of trade would deteriorate significantly were the People's Republic to become a major grain importer. That in turn would require China to become a much more significant exporter of industrial commodities. The net result would be a China far more dependent on the world economy for both imports and exports—even supposing that the OECD countries would accept a greatly increased volume of imports from China. All this would leave the economy rather vulnerable to political pressures and to poor harvests in grain-exporting countries. Not entirely surprisingly, the Chinese leadership is wary of going down this path, and OECD countries will have to go far to provide adequate reassurance (Anderson, 1992).

4. Industrialization

The growth of Chinese industrial output after 1978 was also rather erratic. The 'readjustment' of the balance between light and heavy industry served to reduce the overall industrial growth rate to a mere 1.7 per cent in 1981 and to 5.7 per cent in 1982. Heavy industry in particular was hit hard. The growth rate of heavy industrial gross output value fell from 16 per cent in 1978 to 2 per cent in 1980; in 1981, gross output value fell by almost 5 per cent. Over the same period, the growth rate of the light industrial sector remained consistently in excess of 10 per cent (ZGTJNJ, 1992: 56). This 'readjustment' is equally apparent in the production of specific industrial commodities. For example, steel output fell by 4 per cent

TABLE 2.8. *Total and per capita grain production in China, 1978–1996*

Year	Grain output (m. tonnes)	Grain output per capita (kg.)
1978	304.8	317
1979	332.1	340
1980	320.6	325
1981	325.0	325
1982	354.5	349
1983	387.3	377
1984	407.3	390
1985	379.1	358
1986	391.5	364
1987	403.0	369
1988	394.1	355
1989	407.8	362
1990	446.2	390
1991	435.3	376
1992	442.7	378
1993	456.5	385
1994	445.1	371
1995	466.6	385
1996	504.5	412

Sources: ZGTJNJ (1992: 358–9); ZGTJNJ (1996: 69, 352); LSTJ (1990: 2); ZGTJNJ (1997: 69, 383).

in 1981, machine tools by 23 per cent and vehicles by 21 per cent; and despite widespread energy shortages, coal production was unchanged compared to 1980. This was in sharp contrast to the production of the light industrial sector where the output of cotton cloth and bicycles rose by 6 and 35 per cent respectively in 1981 (Yu, 1984). Industrial output, especially in the rural sector, also suffered a severe decline during 1988–90; two million private companies went out of business in the first half of 1989 alone (BR, 10 Dec. 1990).

The regional pattern of industrial growth was also uneven (Table 2.9). On the positive side, the dominant position of Shanghai and Liaoning—the centres of Chinese industry since the 1890s—was gradually eroded. In 1978, the two were 'over-industrialized' in the sense that their share in national industrial output was close to four times their share in national population. By 1996, the two were still over-industrialized but to a far lesser extent than at the beginning of transition. More generally, the extent of over-industrialization in the North-East and the North Coastal regions also declined after 1978.

However, the main gains were not registered by the under-industrialized Western and Central regions. North-West China saw a big increase in under-industrialization as mineral extraction and heavy industrial production became relatively less important; this was especially true for Gansu (which had done comparatively well in the Maoist period). By contrast, the Central and South-Western regions at least enjoyed increases in their relative shares. Nevertheless, these rises

TABLE 2.9. *Regional shares in industrial output and population, 1978–1996* (percentages)

Region	1978		1988		1996	
	Output share	Population share	Output share	Population share	Output share	Population share
North-East	11.6	7.5	8.6	7.3	5.8	7.2
Northern Coastal	29.8	18.1	26.4	18.1	23.7	17.9
Southern Coastal	24.4	19.1	29.7	19.1	36.2	19.2
Central	18.2	28.5	19.8	28.6	20.1	28.8
South-West	9.5	19.9	10.4	19.9	10.1	19.6
North-West	6.4	7.0	5.0	7.0	4.0	7.2
TOTAL	100.0	100.0	100.0	100.0	100.0	100.0
Of which:						
Old Centres	17.9	4.7	14.2	4.7	10.1	4.6
Southern Coastal (excl. Shanghai)	15.7	18.0	23.2	18.0	31.1	18.0

Notes: North-East = Heilongjiang, Jilin, and Nei Menggu; Northern Coastal = Beijing, Tianjin, Hebei, Shandong, and Liaoning; Southern Coastal = Shanghai, Jiangsu, Zhejiang, Fujian, and Guangdong; Central = Shanxi, Henan, Hubei, Hunan, Anhui, and Jiangxi; South-West = Sichuan, Guizhou, Yunnan, and Guangxi; North-West = Shaanxi, Ningxia, Gansu, Qinghai, and Xinjiang. Old Centres = Shanghai and Liaoning. 'Total' is the sum of these 28 province-level units (Tibet and Hainan are therefore excluded). 'Industry' here is the secondary sector (manufacturing plus construction). Output is measured on a GDP basis at 1990 prices.

Sources: LSTJ (1990); ZGTJNJ (1991–7). For Beijing and Jilin, GDP-based measures of output for industry and construction are not available for 1978 and 1988. These have been estimated from current price NDMP-based measures of industrial and construction output; the data were first converted to 1980 prices (using the LSTJ 1990 deflators for gross output value) and then to 1990 prices (by using the ratio of 1980 to current prices for industrial output in 1990—see ZGTJNJ, 1991: 397).

were small. In consequence, both remained substantially under-industrialized by 1996; in that year, the two regions accounted for almost 50 per cent of China's population but only about 30 per cent of industrial production. In addition, the redistribution of industrial production which had occurred in the 1980s did not continue into the 1990s. Most obviously, Shanghai's relative standing no longer deteriorated. This was because of the CCP's decision to allow the city to retain more of its tax revenue (so that it could begin the development of Pudong, the area to the east of the old city centre). It allowed Shanghai to grow extremely quickly in the mid-1990s.

The biggest relative gains—as is well known—were registered by the Southern Coastal region, which recorded an increase in its share of national industrial production from 24 to 36 per cent. Moreover, even these figures understate the true concentration of industrial production because they incorporate Shanghai, which suffered a declining industrial share until the 1990s. If Shanghai is excluded, the share of the four provinces along the south-eastern coast of China (Jiangsu, Zhejiang, Fujian, and Guangdong) almost doubled (from 15.7 to 31.1 per cent) of the national total. By 1996, these four were plainly over-industrialized; their share in national population was only 18 per cent.

The uneven pattern of industrial growth summarized above had the effect of increasing spatial income inequality, with all its intrinsic and instrumental implications. However, two things need to be said in defence of the post-1978 regional pattern of industrialization. First, the definition of 'over-industrialization' used here—a share in production in excess of population—is very crude.[47] Given the well-developed transport infrastructure and the favourable physical geography of the south-eastern provinces, one would expect this region to have a higher share in national industrial output than implied by its population. Conversely, one would not expect provinces like Sichuan, Qinghai, and Gansu to be centres of Chinese industrial production; economic geography is very much against them. Second, the rapid relative growth of industrial production was not so much an unintended consequence of economic policy but rather its very purpose. As the writings of Chinese economists and political leaders have made clear, it was hoped that the fruits of industrial growth in the south-east would gradually 'trickle-down' to the central and western provinces. For example, the 'grand international cycle' (*guoji da xunhuan*) theory—which was put forward by Wang Jian in the 1980s and which heavily influenced Zhao Ziyang—envisaged for China a pattern of export-led growth centred on the south-east.[48] By attracting migrant labour (who would remit part of their income to their home towns and villages) and by sub-contracting production, the south-east would ensure that central and western China obtained a share in the fruits of growth.

Nevertheless, and despite these regional and cyclical fluctuations, there is little doubt that the pace of industrial output growth during the Dengist period was impressive, especially compared to the pace of agricultural growth.[49] Over the period between 1978 and 1996, constant price industrial output (GDP definition) grew annually by 12.1 per cent (Table 2.10). This was significantly greater than both the 7.5 per cent rate achieved by the modern sector between 1914/18 and 1931/6, and the 8.7 per cent rate achieved between 1957 and 1978. Symbolically, the Dengist era culminated with China becoming the world's single largest steel producer as output exceeded 100 million tonnes in 1996. Nevertheless, the contrast between the post-1978 and the preceding periods is less sharp than is usually thought. This partly reflects the high base from which industrial growth in the 1980s began. After close to thirty years of Maoist industrialization, the 1978 (current price) share of industrial output in GNP stood at 45 per cent, compared to only about 17 per cent of GDP in 1952 and a paltry 12 per cent in the 1930s (ZGTJNJ, 1992: 31; Liu and Yeh, 1965: 66; Yeh, 1979: 107).[50] The size of China's industrial sector in 1978 was also far greater than in most other low and middle income countries. Even in 1990, the industry share of low income countries (excluding India and China) was only 34 per cent and that of middle income countries little better at 37 per cent (WDR, 1992: 222). Yet despite this high 1978 base, China's industrial growth rate during the 1980s comfortably exceeded the averages for low, lower-middle, and upper-middle income of 3.7, 2.8, and 2 per cent for 1980–90 (WDR, 1992: 220–1).

TABLE 2.10. *Chinese industrial growth rates, 1914–1996*
(per cent per annum; constant prices)

Period	Industrial output	Industrial output per capita
1914/18–1931/6	2.1	1.5
(Modern)	(7.9)	(7.3)
(Traditional)	(0.7)	(0.1)
1952–7	18.8	16.0
1957–78	8.7	6.4
1978–96	12.1	10.5
(Rural)*	(18.1)	

* 1978–94.

Notes: Pre-1949 growth rates calculated at 1933 constant prices. 'Modern' and 'Traditional' sectors include mining and utilities as well as manufacturing. 1952–94 growth rates are at 1990 constant prices and based on net domestic material product data; data on Chinese GDP and its components are not available for pre-1978. 1978 data and after use the GDP definition of industrial output. 'Rural' industry (TVE industry) is the sum of township (*xiang*), village (*cun*), team (*dui*), cooperative (*lianying*), and individual (*geti*); see ZGTJNJ (1992: 399) or Byrd and Lin (1990). The consistent series used here is obtained by splicing together the data given in Nongye bu (1989: 104) and ZGTJNJ (1995: 365) for 1984 and after; the ZGTJNJ series for pre-1984 covers industries owned only by townships and villages (the old commune and brigade—*shedui*—enterprises). Value-added ratios used for rural industry are for *xiang* industry only; they are calculated for 1979–83, 1985, and 1990 by interpolation. Constant price output data are deflated using the all-industry producer price deflator. As Field (1992) notes, the data on rural industry are not especially reliable; official figures tend to mix current and constant price data and often define the scope of rural industry in different ways from year to year. This widely shared perception was confirmed by the results of the 1995 Industrial Census; the data used in this table reflect the resulting revisions to total industrial output value (though not to rural industry).

Sources: Output data are from Yeh (1979: 107, 126), ZGTJNJ (1992: 327, 406), ZGTJNJ (1995: 32, 365), ZGTJNJ (1996: 42, 69), ZGTJNJ (1997: 42, 69) and Nongye bu (1989: 104). Value-added ratios are from Zhongguo tongjiju (1985*a*: 108), ZGTJNJ (1987: 263), ZGTJNJ (1988: 320), ZGTJNJ (1989: 292), ZGTJNJ (1990: 419), ZGTJNJ (1991: 399), and ZGTJNJ (1992: 411). Rural industry price deflator from ZGTJNJ (1995: 249).

The growth of Chinese rural industry (TVE), as is well known, was extremely fast.[51] The base level of output in 1978 was not insignificant because of the development of commune and brigade industry in the late Maoist period. Nevertheless, the growth of rural NVIO was an astonishing 18 per cent between 1978 and 1994, and that despite the closure of many rural industries during the recession of 1988–90. By 1994, 70 million Chinese worked in the township and village-level (TVCE) subsector of rural industry alone, compared to only 17 million in 1978 (ZGTJNJ, 1995: 364).[52] Furthermore, the growth of rural industry did not really get under way until 1984; output rose by 'only' 10.7 per cent between 1978 and 1983, compared to 15.2 per cent between 1983 and 1990, and a remarkable 34.5 per cent between 1990 and 1994. Probably the most dynamic industrial subsector in rural China—largely because it began from such a low base—was private industry.[53] Between 1985 and 1994, for example, total employment rose from 6.9 million to 25.6 million workers (ZGGYJJTJNJ, 1990: 407; ZGTJNJ, 1995: 407). This meteoric growth does in part reflect its extremely low base in the early 1980s, and the reclassification of former *xiangzhen* enterprises as private companies once late Maoist prohibitions on the private sector had been lifted. It is also important to point out that the data on rural industry are very unreliable. As noted earlier, the Third Industrial Census of 1995 found that the number of enterprises had been overstated by 2.68 million. Even so, none of this seriously brings into question the idea of extremely rapid rural industrialization during the transition era.

Yet industrial growth was not confined to the countryside during the transition era. Indeed, state-owned industry contributed much more in quantitative terms to industrial growth than its rural counterpart (Nolan, 1996; Lo, 1997). In part this was simply because of the sheer size of the state sector at the end of the 1970s; measured at 1990 constant prices, state industry accounted for no less than 77 per cent of net output value compared to a rural share of only 12 per cent (the remainder was produced by urban collective industry). As a result, the growth of the state sector was the key determinant of China's industrial growth in an accounting sense. As significantly, the performance of state industry was by no means poor in the 1980s. For one thing, its impressive real growth rate of more than 7 per cent per year was achieved from a relatively high base. In addition, and equally importantly, productivity increased significantly during the transition era.[54] As a result, the state sector continued to dominate the Chinese industrial landscape with an output share of 54 per cent even in 1991.[55]

Chinese industry also enjoyed significant export success (Zweig, 1991). Measured in US dollars, total exports increased 6.7 fold between 1980 and 1994 whereas manufactured exports increased 11.2 fold (ZGTJNJ, 1995: 538).[56] As a result, the share of primary products in export value fell from about 50 per cent in 1980 to 16 per cent by 1994 (ZGTJNJ 1995: 538). Rural industry contributed significantly to this process, accounting for some 15 per cent of all Chinese exports by US dollar value in 1988 (ZGNYTJZL, 1988: 244; ZGTJNJ, 1992: 627). Nevertheless, the production of rural industry was geared primarily towards the domestic market; less than 4 per cent of gross *xiangzhen* output value was exported in 1988 (ZGNYTJZL, 1988: 214, 244). In many respects, of course, these trends are unsurprising given the combined impact of the closed nature of the economy in the early 1970s, and the rapid pace of rural industrialization after 1978. Moreover, the growth of industrial exports reflected China's comparative advantage in labour-intensive export products and her comparative disadvantage (limited arable area per head) in farm products. Nevertheless, Chinese industry did more than simply exploit its comparative advantage (Lo, 1997). As will be seen in later chapters, the pace of productivity growth and technical progress was also impressive.

5. Regional Perspectives on Growth

One of the more remarkable features of Chinese growth in the transition era is that almost every part of the People's Republic participated in the process. To be sure, there was substantial variation; most obviously, eastern China grew more rapidly than the interior. But the very fact that rapid growth occurred even in areas which were handicapped by their economic geography is testimony to the underlying dynamism of the process of Chinese economic growth after 1978.

Shared Growth in the Provinces

The provincial data show that national output growth was reflected in rapid per capita growth in every one of China's provinces (Table 2.11). They all recorded a real per capita growth rate of over 5 per cent, an extraordinary achievement and an indication of just how widespread were the benefits of growth. In 1978, only four of the provinces had a per capita real income of more than 1,000 *yuan*; by 1996, all had surpassed that mark. Even more remarkably, four out of the five poorest provinces in 1978 achieved a growth rate which at least matched the national median. In other words, even poor provinces such as Guizhou and Henan benefited significantly from the dramatic growth of the 1980s and 1990s. By the standards of other poor countries which have enjoyed rapid overall growth in the past—Brazil in the 1960s and early 1970s comes to mind—the extent of participation by China's poor regions in the growth process is stunning. Perhaps only Taiwan has experienced a pattern of growth such as this—and Taiwan has a population barely half the size of an average Chinese province.

Growth Patterns in Four Prefectures

We need, however, to look at the pattern of growth at the prefectural, as well as the provincial, level to fully appreciate China's success after 1978.[57] Although an analysis of provincial trends offers considerable insight into the shared nature of economic growth (albeit with significant differences in the pace of industrialization), it is still unsatisfactory as a means of assessing the spatial impact of growth. This is because the typical Chinese province offers such a broad canvas for inspection that trends within provinces tend to be lost. It is entirely possible that a province could register a positive growth rate but that one or more of its prefectures might not. This possibility is hardly surprising; some of China's provinces are not only comparable in size to large European countries (France is Sichuan's closest European equivalent) but also contain far more diverse terrain. Even within the provinces of eastern China, the counties along the coast are almost a world apart from those of the mountainous interior.

One way of proceeding is to look at trends in county incomes in a given province. However, this approach is still not very satisfactory because, despite intraprovincial diversity, the range of conditions in any single province cannot do justice to the Chinese mainland. An analysis so confined is unlikely to properly identify the key elements in the growth process. The provinces of the interior are alike in lacking a window on the Pacific, and thereby proximity to the growth poles that have emerged in Japan, South Korea, and Taiwan since World War II. That matters little if one is analysing the growth process during the Maoist years because of China's isolation; although considerable trade was conducted via Hong Kong, the coastal

TABLE 2.11. *Per capita GDP in China's provinces, 1978–1996* (provinces ranked by 1978 per capita real GDP)

Province	GDP per capita, 1978 (1990 prices)	GDP per capita, 1996 (1990 prices)	Annual GDP per capita growth rate, 1978–96 (1990 prices)
Guizhou	350	1,215	7.1
Henan	426	1,939	8.2
Sichuan	450	1,866	7.9
Yunnan	462	1,723	7.8
Anhui	466	2,174	8.1
Gansu	487	1,697	7.7
Jiangxi	499	2,203	8.0
Shaanxi	515	1,913	7.6
Hunan	522	1,969	7.2
Guangxi	529	1,988	7.5
Ningxia	590	1,939	6.9
Fujian	606	4,041	10.5
Xinjiang	618	2,666	8.8
Nei Menggu	630	2,323	7.2
Shandong	646	3,611	9.8
Hubei	651	2,742	7.6
Hebei	681	2,804	8.0
Zhejiang	697	4,997	11.0
Shanxi	709	2,292	6.2
Jilin	731	2,851	7.7
Jiangsu	748	4,368	10.0
Guangdong	783	5,374	11.5
Qinghai	835	2,129	5.3
Heilongjiang	1,093	2,806	4.9
Liaoning	1,151	4,176	7.5
Tianjin	1,851	6,430	6.3
Beijing	2,298	7,163	6.6
Shanghai	2,944	10,991	7.2
Median	638	2,495	7.7
National Average	704	2,928	8.4

Notes: Growth rates are calculated by estimating the components of GDP at 1990 prices, and then reaggregating. Guangdong includes Hainan. The data for Tibet are incomplete.

Sources: LSTJ (1990); ZGTJNJ (1991–7).

provinces were largely unaffected—for good or ill—by the growth of the Pacific Rim. But one can hardly hope to offer a proper assessment of the growth of the Dengist era without considering these external factors. By the same token, the possibility that the harsh physical geography of the Chinese interior imposed a crippling handicap on growth in the north- and south-west needs a full discussion. To look simply at growth along the coast is to ignore this potentially crucial issue. For whatever the obstacles to industrialization in the interior of Guangdong, it seems—on the surface, at any rate—to pale into insignificance when set against the barriers to growth imposed by the soaring mountains of the interior. Of course, the answer to the question is in some senses extremely obvious. It is simply inconceivable, for example, that the extent of industrialization on the Tibetan plateau or across the Gobi desert will ever rival that achieved around Shanghai. But that does not necessary mean that the Himalayan plateau and its periphery—which, after all, is home to a very large population—is doomed to underdevelopment. Similarly the more fertile parts of Gansu, Ningxia, and Xinjiang provinces. And precisely because growth in these areas is not impossible, they cannot simply be ignored.

The best way to proceed is therefore to look at a number of areas drawn from very different parts of the People's Republic. This allows us more detail than provincial-level analysis, but still makes all-China generalizations more robust than (say) simply looking at a handful of counties in the same province. To that end, 4 distinctive Chinese prefectures have been selected for more detailed consideration in the chapters which follow: Suzhou, Wenjiang, Wenzhou, and Liangshan (Table 2.12).[58]

TABLE 2.12. *Four prefectures and their constituent counties*

Prefecture	Counties and cities
Suzhou (Jiangsu)	Suzhou and Wuxi cities. Jiangyin, Yixing, Xishan (formerly Wuxi county), Zhangjiagang (formerly Shazhou), Changshu, Taicang, Kunshan, Wuxian, and Wujiang counties.
Wenjiang (Sichuan)	Wenjiang, Pixian, Xindu, Guanghan, Shifang, Pengzhou (formerly Pengxian), Dujiangyan (formerly Guanxian), Chongzhou (formerly Chongqing county), Dayi, Qionglai, Pujiang, and Xinjin counties.
Wenzhou (Zhejiang)	Wenzhou city. Dongtou, Yueqing, Yongjia, Rui'an, Pingyang, Cangnan, Wencheng, and Taishun counties.
Liangshan (Sichuan)	Xichang city. Muli, Yanyuan, Dechang, Huili, Huidong, Ningnan, Puge, Butuo, Jinyang, Zhaojue, Xide, Mianning, Yuexi, Ganluo, Meigu, and Leibo counties.

Notes: Prefectural boundaries have changed at frequent intervals since 1949. The prefectures looked at here are essentially as defined in *Administrative Divisions of the People's Republic of China, 1980* (1981). Suzhou is the exception; the counties listed here under Suzhou are those given as falling under the jurisdiction of Wuxi and Suzhou cities in JSSXGK (1989). Changzhou city—which, with Suzhou and Wuxi, comprises the Suxichang region—is therefore excluded, but its inclusion would make very little difference to the conclusions drawn below. The term 'prefecture' is used throughout this book for simplicity in referring to all four areas, although Wenzhou and Wenjiang were both upgraded to municipality status in the 1980s. Wenjiang prefecture was broken up in the mid-1980s, with Guanghan and Shifang transferred to the new municipality of Deyang, and the rump making up the new Chengdu municipality. Ouhai county was incorporated into Wenzhou city in the early 1980s, which also saw part of Pingyang county renamed as the new county of Cangnan. Liangshan's Xichang city includes the old Xichang county.

The first prefecture, that of Suzhou, is located in the Sunan (or Jiangnan) region of eastern China and bounded by Lake Tai to the west and the great metropolis of Shanghai to the east. In the late 1970s, the region comprised the famous cities of Suzhou and Wuxi, and 9 other counties. This is one of the most prosperous parts of China, as the data for 1982 reveal. GDP per capita in these 9 counties and 2 cities averaged 1,546 *yuan* in 1982 (Table 2.13), well above the Chinese average of 867 *yuan* (LSTJ, 1990). Even if Suzhou and Wuxi cities are excluded, the average of the 9 counties was still 1,194 *yuan* (Population Census Office, 1987: 13).

The second group of (12) counties make up Wenjiang prefecture, located on the Chengdu plain in Sichuan. Although this area is immensely fertile, it is far from the coast. Moreover, though Chengdu is a major city, it does not compare as a market for agricultural and industrial products with the metropolitan centre of Shanghai. As a result, it is not surprising that per capita GDP in Wenjiang's counties (663 *yuan*) was considerably below the average in Suzhou. In fact, the Suzhou average was not exceeded by a single one of Wenjiang's counties even though the latter included Shifang, the most prosperous county in the entire province.

TABLE 2.13. *Regional differences in growth rates, 1980–1996*

Prefecture	Per capita GDP (1990 *yuan*)		Real growth rate (% p.a.)
	1982	1996	1980–96
Suzhou	1,546	10,022	13.5
Wenjiang	663	3,432	11.7 (1982–96)
Wenzhou	590	3,221 (1,995)	11.8 (1980–95)
Liangshan	453	1,263	7.9 (1982–96)

Notes: All data and growth rates are based on 1990 constant prices (the provincial price deflator is used where county deflators are unavailable). For Suzhou, growth rates are derived from GDP data for 1980, 1982, 1985, 1988, 1991, 1993, 1995, and 1996. For Wenjiang and Liangshan, the GDP data are for 1982, 1985, 1988, 1991–4, and 1996. For Wenzhou, the data points are 1980, 1982, 1987, 1988, and 1992–5. In all four cases, the prefectural growth rate is estimated by first aggregating the GDP of each county and city in the prefecture. The data are taken mainly from the relevant provincial statistical yearbooks. The exception is 1982. This is the first year for which it is possible to calculate GDP for every county-level unit in China. GDP is calculated for that year from county GVAIO (at 1980 prices) and data on the sectoral composition of county workforces as follows. First, GVAIO is disaggregated into GVIO and GVAO by using employment data and provincial GVIO per worker. GVAO and GVIO are then converted to NVAO and NVIO at 1990 prices by using provincial value-added ratios and price deflators. Tertiary output value is calculated as the tertiary workforce multiplied by average NVAIO per worker for each county. The sum of net tertiary output and NVAIO still understates GDP, largely because it excludes depreciation. It is therefore multiplied by the ratio of true provincial GDP to estimated provincial GDP (as calculated by the method just outlined). This methodology is of course crude, but it gives a far better estimate of GDP than the other alternatives which have been employed at other times in the literature. For example, NVAIO is too narrow (it excludes tertiary production), gross social output data are unavailable until the late 1980s (and then still need to be converted into value-added terms) and attempts to use the county data in the ZGFX series—see, for example, Knight and Song (1993)—are flawed because these data exclude industries located in the counties but owned by provincial and national government.

Sources: ZGRKTJNJ (1988); Jiangsu tongjiju (1989; 1992); JSTJNJ (1994; 1997); Suzhou tongjiju (1996); Wenzhou tongjiju (1985; 1989); ZJTJNJ (1988; 1989; 1990; 1991; 1992; 1993; 1994; 1995; 1996); Sichuan tongjiju (1986); SCTJNJ (1987; 1989; 1990; 1992; 1993; 1994; 1995; 1997).

The third prefecture consists of the city and 9 counties that make up Wenzhou prefecture in Zhejiang. Wenzhou was a Treaty Port before 1949, and it is therefore perhaps rather surprising that per capita GDP (590 *yuan*) was lower than in either Suzhou or Wenjiang at the start of the transition era. Part of the explanation is that Wenzhou is not especially close to any large metropolitan centre and, in addition, the topography of the area consists predominantly of rolling hills. Two of Wenzhou's counties (Wencheng and Taishun) were in fact classified as poor by the Office of the Leading Group in 1986 and allocated central government relief as a result.

The final group of counties to be analysed make up Liangshan prefecture in southwestern Sichuan, one of the poorest areas in China. This prefecture was (and still is) by far the poorest of the 4 with a 1982 per capita GDP of only 453 *yuan* and a population density of considerably less than 100 people per square kilometre (compared to over 500 on the Chengdu plain). This reflects Liangshan's weak transport links and its exceptionally mountainous terrain. This region is the poorest part of Sichuan and a high proportion of its population is made up of ethnic minorities (predominantly Yi). Even by national standards, the prefecture is poor. Of China's 45 poorest counties—where per capita peasant income averaged less than 500 *yuan* in 1996—5 were in Sichuan. Of these, 4 (Butuo, Leibo, Ganluo and Xide) were to be found in Liangshan (ZGNYNJ, 1997: 463).

In the light of these differences in physical and economic geography, and the widely varying levels of per capita output at the start of the 1980s, it is not surprising that the 4 prefectures grew at the different rates shown in Table 2.13. Suzhou, for example, grew more than three times faster than Liangshan. Yet all 4 prefectures, despite their very different economic geography and per capita income levels, achieved annual growth rates that were extremely impressive by the standards of the developing world in the 1980s and early 1990s.[59] This points to the shared nature of the growth process in China during the Dengist era.

Ascent from Poverty: Growth in China's Poorest Counties

Perhaps the most compelling regional feature of Chinese economic growth in the years after 1978 is that even the poorest counties in the People's Republic saw a significant rise in their real per capita incomes. This is evident from looking at 8 of the 10 poorest counties in China in 1982 (Table 2.14). These 8 are all located in Gansu (the remaining 2 were in neighbouring Ningxia), and their low income stemmed directly from the inhospitable desert topography. As a result, median GDP per head in the 8 was only 137 *yuan* in 1982 (compared to which even Liangshan appears prosperous). Yet despite this low base, the 8 counties as a whole achieved a (median) growth rate of almost 11 per cent. Even Dongxiang, the most sluggish county, achieved a rate of increase of 9 per cent—a phenomenal achievement by the standards of most contemporary developing countries.

This significant rise in output was not, however, simply a result of growth itself. World Bank loans, as well as national policy designed to relieve poverty in China's poorest counties overseen by the Leading Group on Economic Development in Poor Areas, played a large part. In fact, the gains made in Gansu may have been at the

TABLE 2.14. *Growth of GDP per capita in China's poorest counties, 1982–1996*

County	GDP per capita, 1982 (in 1990 *yuan*)	GDP per capita, 1996 (in 1990 *yuan*)	Annual growth rate (1982–96)
Dongxiang	105	353	9.0
Zhuanglang	129	642	12.1
Huining	132	493	9.9
Minxian	136	475	9.3
Zhangjiachuan	138	640	11.6
Tongwei	139	606	11.1
Jishishan	142	551	10.2
Guanghe	155	817	12.6
Median	137	579	10.8

Notes: GDP per capita in 1982 is calculated using the method outlined in Table 2.13. 1996 current price data have been converted to 1990 prices using the provincial price deflator. Growth rates are by natural logs using end-point data only.

Sources: ZGRKTJNJ (1988); GSNJ (1997: 332, 641–3).

expense of much slower progress in other parts of China, especially the south-west. One indication is that there were still 31 counties in Yunnan where per capita net peasant income averaged less than 500 *yuan*, compared to only 3 in Gansu by 1996 (ZGNYNJ, 1997: 453). Furthermore, the growth rates given in Table 2.14 may exaggerate the true growth rate because they are based on two data points only. In addition, there is considerable evidence that the bulk of China's success in poverty relief was achieved *before* 1989 (largely because of rapid agricultural growth), and that comparatively little progress has been made since. Finally, the spatial approach to poverty is rather misleading because it is known that many of China's poorest citizens live in counties which have average incomes in excess of the poverty line (Riskin, 1993). Even so, the Chinese record in respect of poverty relief at the provincial, prefectural, and county level between 1978 and 1996 was remarkable.

In explaining these divergent patterns of growth in the Chinese economy, we need a theory which is capable of two things. First, it needs to be able to explain why the overall pace of growth was rapid by Chinese historical standards and the standards of other developing countries. Second, the theory needs to be flexible enough to explain marked regional variations in growth rates across the People's Republic at every level of the administrative hierarchy. These twin tasks are taken up in the chapters that follow

6. Conclusion

It has often been said that the process of Chinese economic transition undertaken after 1978 was unplanned. In a sense, that is true: there was no carefully scripted programme of economic change, and hallmarks of the transition process were pragmatism and gradualism. However, this portrayal understates the coherence of the vision which underlay transition. This vision, at least initially, was nothing less than a return to the 'golden age' of the years before 1956 when a vigorous and dynamic private sector coexisted alongside state ownership of the commanding heights. To be sure, there were important differences between transition-era China and the People's Republic during the First Five-Year Plan (1953–7). Price controls were less widespread between 1978 and 1996 than they were in the 1950s. The Chinese economy was significantly more open, and its trading links extended well beyond the orbit of the former Soviet Union and its satellites that was the norm during early Maoism. The burden of military spending, very high in the early 1950s as a result of the Korean war, was much less. Furthermore, rural industrialization, largely ignored in the 1950s when the emphasis was on large-scale urban industry, was the leitmotiv of the Dengist era. These differences have tended to increase as the transition process has gathered momentum. Nevertheless, the core of the post-1978 programme is recognizable from the economic structures of the early 1950s. None of this is surprising given the conspicuous roles played by Deng Xiaoping and Chen Yun in both phases of economic growth.

The policies pursued during the Dengist era were also similar to those of the 1950s in being extremely successful at promoting economic growth. Transition-era growth, in absolute and per capita terms, was impressive in both historical and comparative international perspective. Structural change took place at an unprecedented rate; indeed the landscape of many parts of rural China has been utterly transformed by the emergence of modern industry. Inflationary pressures were, for the most part, kept under control, and economic growth brought in its train an improvement in material living standards evident even to the casual observer. Some failures were apparent at the time of Deng's death—in particular, regional divergence in growth rates and little progress on poverty reduction since the mid-1980s. And it is arguable that China could have grown even more quickly given its low level of output in 1978. Nevertheless, taken as a whole, it is scant wonder that so many have seen the era of transition as one of remarkable achievement.

3

The Sectoral Contributions of Industry and Agriculture

This chapter considers the sectoral contributions of industry and agriculture to output growth in the transition era. It begins by looking at the accounting contributions of the two sectors. The discussion is then widened to look at the more intangible contributions of agriculture and industry to the growth process.

1. A Sectoral Decomposition of Output Growth

The key sectors in Chinese economic growth since 1978 are readily identified in a narrow accounting sense by the size of their contribution to GDP growth. This contribution is a function of the size of the sector, and the sectoral growth rate. A small sector—even if it grows quickly—will therefore have only a small effect on the rate of growth of GDP. The contributions of each sector to GDP growth in China after 1978 are shown in Table 3.1.

TABLE 3.1. *Sources of post-1978 GDP growth by sector* (percentage share of change in real GDP)

Sector	1978–84	1984–96	1978–96
Agriculture	30	10	13
Secondary	37	62	58
Tertiary	33	28	29

Note: Shares are calculated with reference to constant 1990 price GDP. In the Chinese accounts, the primary sector is defined as agriculture. The secondary sector comprises industry and construction, and all other subsectors are classified as tertiary. Sectoral contributions are measured as the increase in output value for a given sector as a percentage of the total output increase over the same period.

Source: ZGTJNJ (1993: 31–2); ZGTJNJ (1995: 32); ZGTJNJ (1996: 42); ZGTJNJ (1997: 42).

One of the most marked features of these data is that the service-sector's contribution was approximately the same throughout the post-1978 era. This is not especially surprising. The service sector was so small in the late 1970s in relation to other sectors because of Maoist policies designed to minimize the scale of activities deemed to be unproductive. As a result of this neglect, services accounted in 1978 for 29 per cent of real Chinese GDP, compared to 1978 figures of 42 per cent in Brazil, 35 per cent in India, 45 per cent in Kenya, and 47 per cent in Pakistan

(WT, 1994). The average for all low income countries in 1992 was 40 per cent (WDR, 1994: 167). In other words, the contribution of services in late Maoist China was remarkably small by international standards. As a result, even though the service sector grew quickly in the early 1980s as Maoist restrictions were lifted, its overall contribution to output growth was limited precisely because it was so small to begin with. After 1984, by which time the service sector was much larger, its contribution to GDP growth actually declined.

Table 3.1 also shows that one cannot generalize about sectoral contributions across the entire transition era. In the first period before the agricultural 'high tide' of 1984, the sectoral contributions of the three sectors were very similar; all three contributed about a third of real GDP growth. After 1984, however, industry played the leading role in accounting terms. To be sure, the data for 1978–84 probably overstate the contribution of agriculture. As discussed in the previous chapter, there is some evidence that agricultural output was under-reported at the end of the Maoist era in some of China's poor provinces in order to minimize the procurement burden, especially for grain (Oi, 1989: 88–91, 116–17). This under-reporting declined in the early 1980s as comparatively rapid output growth obviated the need for such deceit. Furthermore, a run of good harvests in 1982, 1983, and 1984 also helped to inflate the growth rate; only after 1984 did China's weather revert to its more usual pattern and this brought in its train a marked slowdown in the agricultural growth rate. As a result, the estimation of agricultural growth between the trough of 1978 (albeit a more shallow trough than in 1975–6) and the peak of 1984 imparts an undoubted upward bias to the growth rate. Nevertheless, and even allowing for these biases, the data in Table 3.1 broadly support what is now the conventional wisdom on China: agricultural output growth played an important role in the early years of Dengist rule.

By contrast, the post-1984 period has been dominated by industrialization. During the period between 1984 and 1996, industry accounted for fully 62 per cent of output growth—and this despite a downward revision of industrial output following the Third Industry Census in 1995. By contrast, the agricultural sector contributed only 10 per cent of the increase, and services held their own with a contribution of about 30 per cent. Industry was thus very much the 'leading sector' in this narrow statistical sense after 1984, and this is true (albeit to a lesser extent) for the transition era as a whole. Although agricultural growth was important in the early years, its contribution to growth in the Dengist era as a whole was swamped by that of industry: for the entire period between 1978 and 1996, agriculture contributed only 13 per cent of output growth, less than a quarter of the contribution of industry. In other words, if this period in Chinese history was an era of miraculous growth, it was very much an industrial miracle.

2. The Role of Industry

One of the most famous propositions in growth theory is that industry, and especially manufacturing, is the 'engine of growth' in a capitalist economy:

It is the rate of growth of manufacturing production (together with the ancillary activities of public utilities and construction) which is likely to exert a dominating influence on the overall rate of economic growth: partly on account of its influence on the rate of growth of productivity in the industrial sector itself, and partly also because it will tend, indirectly, to raise the rate of productivity growth in other sectors. (Kaldor, 1966: 294)

Kaldor's conclusion was prompted by three interlocking ideas. The first of these was Verdoorn's Law: output growth causes productivity growth in manufacturing or, to put it another way, there are dynamic economies of scale in manufacturing. This idea was of course put forward originally by Adam Smith, and it reappeared in the writings of Allyn Young and Alfred Marshall (though Marshall treated economies of scale as external to firms). For all these writers, manufacturing was unique in that production was subject to increasing returns, whereas returns were diminishing in agriculture and services. The second Kaldorian idea was that manufacturing matters because of its linkage effects. Its growth absorbs labour from agriculture (an idea which featured prominently in the writings of W. A. Lewis). Manufactured goods also make possible higher productivity growth in both the service and agricultural sectors.[1] Thirdly, Kaldor argued, manufacturing is vital because its products are tradeable. Its success is therefore essential for the removal of the balance of payments constraint. For, and in sharp contrast to the bulk of the products of the service sector, manufactured products can substitute for imports and can be exported. One of the aims of this chapter is to look at whether Kaldor's analysis along these lines holds for Chinese industry after 1978.

But we need to consider the structure, as well as the overall rate, of industrial growth. Industrialization per se need not promote growth in other sectors; we need to ask whether the goods produced were of any use; did they satisfy consumer and export demand, or were they merely stockpiled? This issue is particularly relevant because the late Maoist industrial structure has often been derided as hopelessly unsuited to the task of promoting modern economic growth. Industrial growth in the 1980s might therefore signal nothing more than a duplication of the failures of the 1960s and 1970s. This is precisely the view offered by Naughton (1995*a*: 322) of a significant proportion of industrial output produced after 1978:

. . . this factory [CMB: a truck-assembly plant in Chengdu] will have no future in a fully reformed economy. Only larger, more efficient auto assembly plants will survive, and only those possessing some kind of integrated and partially automated assembly line. Moreover, the investments made to that time [CMB: 1988] will do virtually nothing to prepare this small factory to make the leap into production at a competitive scale. Yet all this investment —surely destined to be wasted ultimately—has been made since the beginning of China's second phase of reforms in 1984.

Finally, we need to consider whether post-1978 industrial growth was little more than an illusion. This would be the case if heavy industry was a slow-growing sector and the actual price used to value heavy industrial products was lower than its shadow price.[2] The low actual price would amount to assigning a low weight to a slow-growing sector; the overall industrial growth rate would not, therefore, be dragged down by slow-growing heavy industry.

2.1. Industry and the Literature on China

Most Chinese economists saw the major problem of China's industrial sector in the late 1970s as structural, and therefore structural reform as the appropriate remedy. However, many Western economists have doubted the degree of structural change actually achieved within Chinese industry over the course of the transition. According to Lardy (1989: 284):

> The interindustry allocation of investment also changed, but only for a brief period. . . . The traditional emphasis on heavy industry or producer goods was modified, at least in the short run, with its share of industrial investment falling from about 90 per cent during 1966–75 to about 80 per cent in 1981–2. But heavy industry's share began to rise after 1981, exceeding 82 per cent in 1982 and 88 per cent by 1984.

A similar viewpoint was expressed by the World Bank (1990: 157), according to which 'Ten years of reform have brought significant changes in certain areas but left largely unaltered the provincial dispersion of industry as well as the subsectoral distribution of product.' This conclusion reflects in part the view that structural change is virtually impossible without systemic change and this was China's problem in the mid/late 1980s. According to Prybyla (1991: 213):

> Policy errors are the standard communist explanation, in China and elsewhere, for much that goes awry in the system . . . There is some substance to this diagnosis, but it fails to account for the fullness and persistence of static and dynamic inefficiencies. If taken seriously by those who offer it, it can result in intrasystemic policy adjustments that do little to improve the situation, and often make things worse.

In essence, this type of critique is a general attack on economic planning; thus Prybyla (1991: 214), cites admiringly Hayek's view that the advocates of central planning suffer from a 'fatal conceit' in believing in the very possibility of planning. The solution to structural problems from this perspective is systemic reform, because 'market signals' expressed via the price mechanism will lead to an optimal allocation of resources. In other words, systemic reform renders unnecessary state-led industrial restructuring because 'reform' is in itself a sufficient condition for market-induced structural change.

However, this type of analysis is not very convincing. The total factor productivity estimates on which it is based are subject to large margins of error, and therefore the relative 'efficiency' of comparative economic systems is not easy to establish. Furthermore, most of those assessments which single out the inefficiencies of state socialist industrial sectors ignore the defence externalities generated by investment in heavy industry and the defence sector. More importantly from the viewpoint of this chapter, and notwithstanding the opinions expressed by Prybyla, Lardy, and others to the contrary, important changes have occurred in the structure of

Chinese industry during the course of transition despite the limited extent of systemic reform. As Field (1992) rightly observes:

> In the late 1970s, Chinese industry was on the verge of collapse [p. 577] . . . the reforms undertaken since 1978 had a considerable impact on the structure of growth . . . Every branch [of industry] in which output consists primarily of consumer goods grew faster than its historic rate, while most branches with a primary output of producer goods grew more slowly. Of the four exceptions, machinery has a large consumer-goods component, and building materials and timber have been in chronic short supply. [p. 592]

In other words, the structural reforms of the 1980s have been *remarkably successful* in addressing and correcting many late Maoist structural imbalances. Given Field's view that Chinese industry was on the verge of collapse in the late 1970s, the transition policies can hardly have been anything else because the industrial growth rate averaged well over 10 per cent after 1978. The same (heterodox) point is made by Lo (1997), whose book is very much in the Kaldorian tradition. For Lo, it was structural change within the industrial sector that played a key role in the explosive growth of the transition era. China did not merely follow a strategy which exploited its comparative advantage as asserted by Lin, *et al.*, (1996) but moved quickly into high technology, capital-intensive, types of production.

2.2. Sectoral Trends in Industrial Growth

The obvious way to demonstrate the extent of structural change in China's industrial sector after 1978 is to measure it. A first look at the extent of the post-1978 industrial transformation is provided by sectoral trends in industrial output value during between 1978 and 1990 (when industrial sectors were redefined) as compared with the decades of Maoist rule (Table 3.2). Perhaps the most striking feature of these data is the changing fortunes of light and heavy industry. During the Maoist period, heavy industry grew more quickly than did light industry (11.3 compared to 8.9 per cent per year). After 1978, however, the position was reversed; light industry grew at 12.5 per cent, compared to a heavy industry growth rate of only 9.2 per cent. Although heavy industry certainly did not grow slowly by international standards according to the data in this table, it did grow more slowly than light industry.[3]

Yet though the data in Table 3.2 do offer some insight, they are not very useful for an analysis of post-1978 Chinese growth. One problem is that the degree of disaggregation is very limited; it is not at all clear that a relatively unimportant sector such as paper production should be identified separately whereas the performance of key engineering sectors—such as the production of electrical and electronic equipment—is hidden. Secondly, it is impossible to identify the growth rate of the manufacturing sector from these data. This matters because central to the Kaldorian analysis is that it is the performance of manufacturing—rather than the performance of industry as a whole—that determines the overall rate of economic growth. We need instead a method of disaggregation which distinguishes between, for example, petroleum extraction (mining) and petroleum processing (manufacturing), and between ferrous-metal mining and ferrous-metal smelting (manufacturing).

TABLE 3.2. *Sectoral trends in industry, 1978–1990*

Sector	Output growth rates (per cent per annum)		Sectoral shares (per cent)	
	1952–78	1978–90	1978	1990
Metallurgy	10.3	9.0	8	7
Power	13.9	6.9	7	5
Coal	7.0	5.9	5	3
Oil	20.4	5.9	10	6
Chemicals	16.6	12.0	10	12
Machinery	13.8	13.7	24	30
Building materials	9.3	12.4	5	5
Timber	1.9	6.4	3	2
Food	4.6	9.4	10	9
Textiles	5.7	10.4	10	10
Paper	6.4	9.9	1	1
Other	8.9	12.1	9	11
Light	8.9	12.5	35	46
Heavy	11.3	9.2	65	54
TOTAL	9.1	10.7	100	100

Notes: The output series terminates in 1990 when China adopted the ISIC method of disaggregation. It is therefore not possible to use this method of disaggregation for the whole transition period. Data are for net industrial output value of township-level and above enterprises at 1980 constant prices—except for heavy and light industry, which include *cun* enterprises and below.

Sources: Calculated from Zhongguo tongjiju (1985*a*), ZGGYJJTJNJ (1991: 72–3) and Field (1992: 607) for 1980. 1978 value-added ratios are used for 1978 and before; for subsequent years, 1984 value-added ratios are used. From Zhongguo tongjiju (1985*a*: 108).

Fortunately, the Chinese have adopted a method of disaggregation that approximates the International Standard Industrial Code (ISIC) following the 1985 industrial census. Although this census does not provide us with full information on industrial output in the early years of the transition era, data were collected on production in 1980 and 1984. We can therefore analyse industrial performance over the course of the 1980s with some degree of certainty. Using this ISIC disaggregation, industrial growth rates were as set out in Table 3.3, and Table 3.4. In order to facilitate comparisons with the data in Table 3.2, growth rates are provided for 1980 to 1990 at 1980 prices in Table 3.3. Table 3.4 by comparison extends the series to 1992, and uses 1990 prices. As will be seen, this makes a substantial difference to the analysis.[4]

One obvious feature of these data is that the growth rate achieved by extractive industries was slow. It averaged only 3.3 per cent for the decade, barely one-third of the industry average and even further below the rate achieved by manufacturing (9.4 per cent). Furthermore, it contributed less than 4 per cent of total industrial output growth between 1980 and 1990. As a result, manufacturing was the leading industrial sector by some distance. Its growth was not spectacular by international standards; South Korean manufacturing output grew by 17 per cent per year between 1970 and 1980, and 12 per cent between 1980 and 1992 (WDR,

TABLE 3.3. *Industrial growth rates by ISIC disaggregation, 1980–1990* (percentages)

Industry	Growth rate, 1980–90	Contribution to total industrial output growth
Forage manufacture	40.4	0.5
Electronic equipment	18.7	7.0
Chemical fibres	18.5	3.1
Other	15.7	0.7
Pharmaceutical products	15.4	3.4
Other mineral mining	15.0	neg.
Arts and crafts	14.5	1.9
Electrical equipment	13.1	6.3
Plastic goods	13.0	2.6
Tobacco manufacture	12.3	5.9
Clothing	12.3	3.3
Beverage manufacture	10.8	2.1
Transport equipment	10.8	5.1
Metal products	10.6	3.6
Printing	10.3	1.3
Cultural and sporting	9.8	0.7
Machine building	9.7	11.8
Leather and fur	9.6	1.1
Food manufacture	9.4	3.9
Non-ferrous metal mining	9.3	0.6
Furniture manufacture	9.1	0.6
Paper-making	9.1	1.8
Building materials	9.0	4.8
Chemicals	8.9	7.5
Non-metal mineral mining	8.1	0.7
Instruments and meters	7.8	1.0
Timber processing	6.7	0.4
Textile manufacture	6.6	7.7
Non-ferrous metal smelting	6.6	1.1
Ferrous-metal mining	6.5	0.2
Coke and coal gas	6.2	0.1
Rubber goods	5.9	1.5
Ferrous-metal smelting	5.9	3.1
Water supply	5.2	0.2
Coal mining	3.5	1.2
Petroleum processing	2.9	0.8
Salt mining	2.5	neg.
Power generation	2.0	1.7
Petroleum extraction	1.4	0.9
Logging	1.2	neg.
Extractive industries	3.3	3.8
Manufacturing	9.4	96.2
TOTAL	8.7	100.0

Notes: Growth rates are for net output value at 1980 constant prices. Data are for *xiang*-level enterprises and above only.

Sources: Constant price data are not directly available for every year. They have therefore been calculated using figures on labour productivity in constant prices and employment taken from ZGGYJJTJNJ (1993). The exception is 1986, where output value comes from ZGTJNJ (1987: 259–60). Constant price GVIO data are converted into NVIO using the ratio of *current* price NVIO to GVIO given in ZGGYJJTJNJ (1993).

1994: 165). Nevertheless, the dynamism of Chinese manufacturing after 1978 supports Kaldor's view that a vibrant manufacturing sector is an essential condition for rapid GDP growth.

Secondly, the acceleration of growth in what might be styled the 'traditional' light-industrial sector (food, beverages, tobacco, and clothing) is striking. After languishing during the Maoist period, it grew at an average rate of 9.8 per cent, significantly in excess of the industrial average after 1978. Although the textiles subsector grew rather slowly, that was more than offset by the rapid rates of increase achieved by the clothing and tobacco subsectors; and even food processing grew more quickly than the industry average. Nevertheless, it is the growth of tobacco manufacturing that deserves to be emphasized because this subsector contributed no less than 5.9 per cent of total industrial output growth—well in excess of the contribution of the food sector. Thirdly, the growth of the furniture, building materials, and timber-processing sectors stands out. Together, these subsectors grew at average rate of 8.3 per cent. This grow was substantially faster than during the Maoist period, and reflected the housing boom—especially in rural areas—that began at the start of the 1980s.

A fourth aspect of these data—and it is one which supports those who argue that Chinese industrial structure changed little after 1978—is the slow growth of energy production. The output of the petroleum-processing subsector rose by less than 3 per cent per year, and power generation by only 2 per cent despite the desperate energy shortages that plagued the economy during the 1980s. Nevertheless, this slow growth may have been unavoidable. For example, massive investment in hydroelectricity production would have raised the growth rate of the power-supply subsector. However, this ignores the likely environmental consequences; the building of a dam in the Three Gorges of the Yangzi River between Sichuan and Hubei will doubtless relieve some of the pressure on power supplies in the long run, but it provoked protest in both China and the West because of the need to relocate some 3 million people and the likely impact on water supplies and ecology both upstream and in the Yangzi delta. An alternative would have been increased coal production, China's key energy input; a higher level of production would doubtless have allowed a somewhat faster rate of economic growth. But even setting aside the consequences for urban air pollution, the level of production in 1978 was already very high; by 1990 output had increased to almost 1.1bn tonnes, making China the largest producer of coal in the world (ZGTJNJ, 1992: 440, 854). To be sure, per capita production lagged well behind. However, it not easy to raise production dramatically because of the gestation periods involved in producing deep-mined coal. In modern retreat mining, long underground roadways need first to be driven and shored up before cutting can begin, and production often falters in the early months because of unexpected geological problems. If seams are thin and run diagonally between roadways, the problems of mechanization become even greater. Increased levels of production also require higher investment in cleaning and grading facilities on the surface. Moreover, a faster rate of extraction might even have been counter-productive because of the immense transport bottlenecks incurred in moving it from north-central China to the Sunan area and the south-east coast: as is well known,

TABLE 3.4. *Industrial growth rates by ISIC disaggregation, 1980–1992* (percentages)

Industry	Growth rate, 1980–92	Contribution to total industrial output growth
Coal mining	5.0	2.8
Petroleum extraction	2.3	2.2
Ferrous-metal mining	8.9	0.3
Non-ferrous metal mining	9.4	0.7
Non-metal mineral mining	9.9	0.7
Salt mining	1.5	0.1
Other mineral mining	12.8	neg.
Logging	1.5	0.3
Water supply	9.8	0.5
Food manufacture	9.8	3.5
Beverage manufacture	11.8	2.7
Tobacco manufacture	11.3	5.0
Forage manufacture	36.0	0.5
Textile manufacture	6.4	6.2
Clothing	13.3	2.4
Leather and fur	11.8	1.0
Timber processing	7.6	0.5
Furniture manufacture	8.7	0.4
Paper-making	9.1	1.6
Printing	11.2	1.1
Cultural and sporting	11.5	0.6
Arts and crafts	15.2	1.3
Power generation	3.5	3.7
Petroleum processing	3.0	1.3
Coke and coal gas	7.8	0.2
Chemicals	9.8	7.6
Pharmaceutical products	18.1	3.1
Chemical fibres	19.9	2.4
Rubber goods	8.8	1.8
Plastic goods	14.6	2.3
Building materials	10.0	6.8
Ferrous-metal smelting	6.2	5.5
Non-ferrous metal smelting	7.0	1.7
Metal products	10.7	2.7
Machine building	10.0	10.2
Transport equipment	13.1	5.8
Electrical equipment	13.2	4.8
Electronic equipment	17.6	4.5
Instruments and meters	9.0	0.9
Other	15.9	0.5
Extractive industries	4.2	7.6
Manufacturing	9.5	92.4
TOTAL	8.8	100

Notes: As for Table 3.3 except that growth rates are for net output value at 1990 constant prices.

Sources: As for Table 3.3.

China's energy problem in the late 1980s and early 1990s was as much a problem of transport as it was of production.[5]

Yet the most remarkable feature of Table 3.3—and one which suggests that the critics of post-1978 Chinese industrial growth have overstated their case—is the impressive growth rate achieved by 'new' industries.[6] The production of the chemical fibre and pharmaceutical subsectors grew at a rate in excess of 15 per cent, almost double the industry average. Moreover, because the two did not start from an especially low base, they contributed about 6.5 per cent of total output growth. Equally significant was the startling rate of growth achieved by electrical and electronic engineering. These two sectors together contributed no less than 13 per cent of total output growth, with electronic equipment production second only to the (insignificant) forage subsector in its rate of growth.

Consider next the sectoral growth rates for 1980 to 1992, this time at 1990 prices (Table 3.4). The results here are broadly similar to those given in Table 3.3. However, extending the period for two years to 1992, and using 1990 prices has two effects. First, the early 1990s saw a revival of the growth rate of extractive industries, largely because of government worries over (in particular) the constraint on growth imposed by inadequate energy supply. For example, output growth in the key coal sector rose from 3.5 per cent in 1980–90, to 5 per cent for 1980–92. By contrast, the growth rates of the 'new' industries like electronics fell back somewhat, partly because production had reached a comparatively high base level by 1990. The second effect of using 1990, rather 1980, prices is that they raise the contribution of extractive industries to the growth rate. This reflects the increases in relative energy and mineral prices from the very low levels that prevailed at the beginning of the transition era, and which arguably moved these prices closer to (private) marginal costs. It has the effect of changing the weights implicitly assigned by prices to the various subsectors of industry. As a result, the contribution to output growth made by the new industries falls when 1990 prices are used for the 1980 to 1992 period; for example, the combined contribution of electronic and electrical equipment goes down from over 13 per cent to 9.3 per cent.

Nevertheless, the key conclusion is the same, whether one uses 1980 or 1990 prices. Chinese industrial growth in the Dengist era was extremely rapid, and it is hard to argue from these data that Chinese industrial growth merely duplicated Maoist industrial development. The surge in growth achieved by the industries of the present and future shows that Chinese industry not only grew but became far more 'modern' in its structure after 1978. For although traditional industries grew more quickly than under the Maoist regime, it is the growth of the new industries which really stands out. By the early 1990s, the most obvious feature of Chinese industrial production was its diversity.

2.3. Industrial Output in the Prefectures

Even poor and relatively inaccessible parts of China such as Liangshan shared in post-1978 industrial growth. As Table 3.5 shows, industrial output in this isolated

TABLE 3.5. *Industrial output growth in Liangshan, 1980–1996* (at 1990 prices, counties in ascending order by industrial growth rates)

County	Annual growth rate (%)
Butuo	−0.4
Leibo	3.6
Zhaojue	5.8
Mianning	6.3
Huili	6.5
Puge	7.1
Yuexi	7.7
Yanyuan	9.8
Meigu	10.3
Ningnan	10.4
Muli	11.2
Dechang	11.2
Jinyang	11.2
Huidong	11.3
Xide	15.5
Xichang	18.8
Ganluo	19.9
OVERALL	11.3

Notes: Industry includes construction and is measured here on a GDP basis. To obtain these data for 1980–8 (the figures for other years are readily available), GVIO at 1980 prices is first converted to a GDP basis using the value-added ratios for independent accounting industrial enterprises by county. The provincial ratio of (industry + construction) to industry is used to calculate secondary output; and the provincial price deflator is used to convert from 1980 to 1990 prices. The basic GVIO data given in SCZL (1990) exclude SOEs owned by central and provincial government, but there were so few of these in Liangshan that the growth rates calculated above are unlikely to be significantly affected.
Sources: SCTJNJ (1993; 1994; 1995; 1997); SCZL (1990).

part of south-western Sichuan grew at 11.3 per cent per year, a very respectable growth rate by any standard. Furthermore, industrial output increased even in the least accessible parts of Liangshan. In Leibo county, linked to the rest of the prefecture only via difficult mountain roads, industrial production grew at over 3 per cent per year after 1980. Although coal production declined during the 1980s, this was offset by increased production of processed timber (*renzaoban*), cement, and electricity. In Zhaojue, where the topography is even more difficult than in Leibo, industrial output nevertheless grew at 6 per cent per annum. As with Leibo, electricity generation and cement production were major growth areas (SCZL, 1990: 604, 610). Liangshan's other counties did even better. Mianning county, although on the Chengdu–Kunming railway and therefore more accessible than other parts of Liangshan, suffered from the decline of its mining sector in the late 1980s. In particular, the production of talcum—Mianning is the only county in Sichuan where there are significant reserves (Dangdai Sichuan congshu bianjibu, 1991: 85)—fell

TABLE 3.6. *Industrial output growth in Suzhou prefecture, 1980–1996* (industrial value-added at 1990 prices, counties in ascending order of growth)

County	Annual output growth (%)
Suzhou city	11.0
Wuxi city	11.1
Changshu	18.6
Jiangyin	21.0
Wuxian	21.5
Yixing	22.6
Xishan	23.5
Wujiang	23.8
Taicang	24.2
Zhangjiagang	25.2
Kunshan	26.6
OVERALL	18.4

Notes: Gross output data are for 1980, 1985, 1988, 1991, 1993, 1995, and 1996. Industrial output includes construction; in other words, it measures total output of the secondary sector. Secondary sector value-added is estimated from GVIO for 1980–8 using the ratio of provincial secondary output value to GVIO in 1991. The provincial price deflator was used to estimate output at 1990 prices.

Sources: Jiangsu tongjiju (1989; 1992); JSTJNJ (1994; 1997); Suzhou tongjiju (1996).

sharply from 13,556 tonnes at peak in 1985 to only 1516 tonnes in 1988 (SCZL, 1990: 606). Nevertheless, real output growth still exceeded 6 per cent per year. Butuo is the one exception; there, industrial output rose until 1992, and then fell back—resulting in a negative growth rate for 1980–96 period. In statistical terms, this was largely due to big falls in output in 1993 and 1994 in light industry in particular; the growth rate for 1978–91 was almost 8 per cent. The main reason appears to have been the decline of coal and sugar-cane production.

In sum, and despite the comparatively slow growth of industrial production in some of Liangshan's counties, it is clear from this prefecture's experience that the growth process in China after 1978 was confined neither to coastal regions nor to those areas close to the great metropolitan centres. Almost every county—even those heavily disadvantaged in terms of their physical geography—saw tangible output increases.

Nevertheless, the rates of industrialization achieved in less isolated regions exceeded those achieved in western China. Nowhere was this rapid growth more apparent than in Sunan (Table 3.6). Modern industrialization had commenced there in the late nineteenth century and continued during the Maoist era. As a result, the levels of industrial output reached in Suzhou and Wuxi cities by the late 1970s was comparatively high, and this is reflected in slower growth there in the 1980s.[7] In Sunan's other counties, however, the growth rates achieved were much higher than those achieved in other parts of China. Whilst Liangshan's Zhaojue and Mianning counties were achieving industrial growth of 6 per cent per annum, the rate achieved in Kunshan was an amazing 27 per cent. More startling still, only the two fastest-growing counties in Liangshan (Xichang and Ganluo) were able to match the rate achieved by the slowest growing county in Suzhou (Changshu at 18.6 per cent).

Of course, these figures should not be taken too literally; there is no doubt, as discussed in the last chapter, that the value of industrial output in the *xiangzhen* sector has been consistently overestimated and the necessary adjustments have not yet been incorporated into the historical statistics. The price deflators are also suspect. If the provincial data for Jiangsu are to be believed, nominal GVIO grew by 51.8 per cent and real GVIO by 42 per cent in 1993 alone (JSTJNJ, 1994: 20–1). The difference—about 10 per cent—is obviously the implied inflation rate for industrial products. However, the same source records an increase of 18.5 per cent in factory-gate prices for industrial products (JSTJNJ, 1994: 96), and it is certain that the rate of inflation in Suzhou was well above the provincial average because of the explosive nature of the growth in that area. Nevertheless, these biases have little effect on the overall conclusion; the gap in growth rates between Liangshan and Suzhou is simply too large (and the statistical biases in Suzhou were also to be found in Liangshan).[8] There can therefore be no doubting the substantial spatial disparities in the pace of industrialization across China during the transition era.

It was seen earlier that there was a strong relationship between industrial and overall output growth at a provincial level. This same finding is largely true of the four prefectures of Suzhou, Wenzhou, Wenjiang, and Liangshan, although not perhaps to the same degree (Table 3.7).

TABLE 3.7. *Regional trends in GDP and industrial growth* (1990 prices, prefectures ranked by GDP growth)

Prefecture	Growth of GDP, 1982–96 (% p.a.)	Growth of industrial output, 1980–96 (% p.a.)
Suzhou	14.3 (1980–96)	18.4
Wenzhou	13.2 (1980–95)	21.4
Wenjiang	12.8	16.3
Liangshan	9.2	11.3

Notes: Industrial output for Wenjiang was calculated in the same way as for Liangshan. For Wenzhou, 1984 output is the sum of construction and industrial output (NDMP measure) multiplied by the ratio of provincial secondary output to the provincial sum of the NDMP measures of industry and construction. For 1991 and 1992, GVIO was converted to secondary output using the 1993 ratios of GVIO to secondary output for each county. For other years, secondary sector output is available directly. Provincial price deflator are used to obtain 1990 prices.

Sources: as for Tables 2.11, 3.5 and 3.6.

In the case of each prefecture, the growth of industrial output exceeded the growth of overall output by a comfortable margin. In other words, agriculture and tertiary production were growing much slower than industrial production—a rather unsurprising result, but a clear demonstration that industry was the leading sector right across the People's Republic.

TABLE 3.8. *Sectoral growth rates in Suzhou, 1980–1996*
(annual growth rates, counties ranked by industrial growth)

County	Industrial output (1990 prices)	Agricultural output (1990 prices)	Grain output (volume)
Kunshan	26.6	4.3	0.0
Zhangjiagang	25.2	4.3	0.0
Taicang	24.2	5.2	0.4
Wujiang	23.8	5.2	−0.7
Xishan	23.5	3.8	−1.7
Yixing	22.6	6.2	−0.1
Wuxian	21.5	12.6	−0.8
Jiangyin	21.0	5.4	−0.6
Changshu	18.6	3.0	−0.1
Wuxi	11.1	8.3	−1.4
Suzhou	11.0	14.2	+8.7
OVERALL	18.4	5.6	−0.3

Notes: Agricultural and industrial output are measures of value-added on a GDP basis. Agricultural output for 1980–8 is calculated from GVAO using the ratio of GVAO to primary output by county in 1991. They are converted to 1990 prices using the provincial price deflator. Boundary changes in the mid-1990s have inflated agricultural and grain production in Wuxi and Suzhou cities. Between 1993 and 1996, non-agricultural population in Wuxi rose by 57,000 whereas total population rose by 129,000 (compare JSTJNJ (1994: 276) with JSTJNJ (1997: 352). For Suzhou the comparable figures were 67,000 and 192,000).

Sources: As for Table 3.7.

This is reinforced by a closer examination of the growth process in relatively successful areas such as Suzhou, Wenzhou, and Wenjiang. Suzhou is a boundlessly fertile area, and historically much of the region's growth was centred on the growth of agriculture. Since the late 1970s, however, the performance of agriculture has been very poor. As Philip Huang (1990) has pointed out, grain yields largely stagnated in the Yangzi delta region during the 1980s. For instance, in Songjiang county—part of the Shanghai conurbation—rice and wheat yields largely stagnated around their 1978/79 levels (Huang, 1990: 224). Moreover, if one looks at trends for the transition period as a whole, the evidence is that grain production fell in most of Suzhou's counties (Table 3.8).

More generally, these data show that the overall rate of industrial growth in Suzhou was about three times faster than the rate of agricultural growth. For some counties, the differential was even higher; for example, industrial growth was almost six times faster than in agriculture in Changshu. If one compares the growth rate of industrial output with that of grain production, the contrast is even more marked. Whereas industrial output was growing at 18 per cent per year, grain output fell (or increased at an insignificant rate) in every county. But perhaps most significantly of all, those parts of Suzhou where industrial growth was slowest

—the cities of Suzhou and Wuxi—agricultural growth was well above the average. All this shows that industrialization was the key to rapid economic growth in the transition era.

In sum, the experience of the Suzhou area provides a stark illustration of the limited contribution of agriculture in the most dynamic Chinese regions after 1978. This is not to say that the performance of agriculture in Suzhou was necessarily bad. As Table 3.8 shows, real net output was growing at over 5 per cent per annum during the transition era: by any international standard, Suzhou's agriculture was performing rather well. To be sure, the performance of the grain sector was poor; but that was hardly surprising given the extremely high yields that were being recorded in the late 1970s. Nevertheless, the overwhelming characteristic of the Suzhou experience is the dominance of the industrial sector. As Huang rightly says, the modernization of the 1980s was altogether different from the involution of the Maoist era and before.

There is only one conclusion to be drawn from this analysis of industrial growth by sector, and at the level of the prefecture. That conclusion is firmly Kaldorian: industry was the leading sector in the growth process during the transition era. Where industrialization was rapid, an area thrived even if its agricultural performance was not outstanding. Suzhou, with its especially poor record on grain production, is the classic demonstration. Moreover, the process of industrialization that swept across the People's Republic after 1978 did not merely repeat the Maoist pattern of industrialization. Rather, the structure of industrial production increasingly reflected changing patterns of technical progress and demand; in other words, a clear process of modernization was taking place.

3. The Role of Agriculture

One of the main themes in development economics is that agricultural success is crucial for sustained economic growth. According to Johnston and Mellor (1961) there are five distinct contributions made by agriculture to growth process: (a) the supply of food; (b) market size; (c) the supply of savings; (d) the release of labour; and (e) the earning of foreign exchange. Of these, savings and investment, and their contribution to growth, are discussed in Chapters 6, 8, and 9, along with human capital. Labour release, and its impact on productivity, is assessed in Chapter 7. The part played by aggregate demand is one of the central themes of Chapter 13, and foreign trade is discussed in Chapter 15.

The discussion of agriculture in this chapter therefore concentrates on two issues. First, the extent to which agriculture contributed directly to the growth process in accounting terms. The national picture has been sketched in broad outline already, but we need to look in more detail at agriculture's contribution in the different provinces. Secondly, we must consider whether rapid agricultural growth was a necessary condition for economic growth as a whole in terms of the *linkage effects* between agriculture and the wider economy.

3.1. The Accounting Contribution of Agriculture: Provincial Evidence

The role played by agriculture in leading industrialization is a controversial issue. The idea, for example, that agriculture was the leading sector in early modern British and Japanese growth depends upon the dating of the beginning of 'modern' economic growth, and on the interpretation of the (scanty) data on agricultural growth. In the British case, 'take-off' has often been dated from the Restoration of 1660 which—it is argued—marked the transition from feudalism to capitalism. Furthermore, much work suggests that the English 'agricultural revolution' occurred between 1660 and the middle of the eighteenth century—with the clear implication that 'take-off' ought properly to be dated well before 1800, and that the agricultural revolution might have been a necessary precondition for later industrialization. For example, Kerridge's (1967) work suggested that the agricultural revolution occurred in the two centuries prior to 1700, a view recently restated by Gregory Clark (1993). Furthermore, work by Allen (1992) has distinguished explicitly between what he has called the 'Yeomen's Revolution' of pre-1750 and the 'Landlords' Revolution' that followed it. In the first of these, corn yields doubled and GDP rose in consequence. In the second, however, agricultural output remained largely unchanged; the period was revolutionary in terms of its effect upon employment rather than its impact on output (Allen, 1992: 21). The issues are similar in the case of pre-Meiji Japan. If one accepts the 'revisionist' view (Smith, 1959; Hall, 1962; Hanley and Yamamura, 1977) that modern economic growth began in the late Tokugawa period, and even more so if one accepts Nakamura's (1965; 1966) upward revision of agricultural output growth for the period before 1868, agriculture can be viewed as Japan's 'leading sector'.

However, this notion that agriculture led the growth process in the 'classical' British and Japanese cases is open to a number of serious objections. In the instance of Britain, for example, Crafts' estimates show agriculture growing at 0.8 per cent per year between 1780 and 1801, and at 1.2 per cent between 1801 and 1831. In both time periods, however, agriculture was comfortably outperformed by industry, which grew annually by 2.0 and 2.8 in the respective periods (Crafts and Harley, 1992: 715; Crafts, 1994: 47). Much the same is true of Meiji Japan. Between 1885 (the first year for which we have reasonable estimates of GDP) and 1919, agricultural output grew by 1.7 per cent in real terms, well below the 6.4 per cent recorded by the industrial sector (Ohkawa, Takamatsu, and Yamamoto, 1974: 225, 227).

Moreover, although Allen (1992; 1994) has stressed the importance of institutional rather than output changes in the second half of the eighteenth century, his estimate of output growth between 1750 and 1850 (a total increase of 129 per cent) is far in excess of Clark's (39–85 per cent);[9] indeed Allen's 1994 paper draws back from his 1992 emphasis on the Yeoman's Revolution of pre-1750. Allen's caution is reinforced by the work of Overton (1996), which shows that Clark's estimates are extremely implausible. He concludes that:

> . . . the arguments for an 'agricultural revolution' commencing in the sixteenth century fail to carry conviction [p. 197] . . . it was not until the century after 1750 that the dramatic and unprecedented improvements in output, land productivity and labour productivity, associated with equally dramatic and unprecedented changes in husbandry, were under way on a broad front. (Overton, 1996: 198)

In Japan's case, few specialists have fully accepted the revisionist conclusions.[10] To be sure, it is widely agreed that technical progress did occur in agriculture in the late Tokugawa period, and there is little doubt that Nakamura was right in arguing that agricultural output was underestimated at the beginning of the Meiji period. But Nakamura's adjustment is too great (Minami, 1986; Francks, 1992) and it is generally agreed that the key transformation in Japanese agriculture occurred during the Meiji era—even though many of the crop varieties were pioneered in the previous century. In other words, the conventional wisdom on both Japan and Britain by the end of the twentieth century was that industrial and agricultural revolutions occurred simultaneously, and that, in accounting terms, industry made the main contribution to GDP growth.

In the Chinese case, the evidence at first glance also suggests that agriculture was not the leading sector. In fact, provincial data seem rather to demonstrate the overwhelming importance of industrial growth (Table 3.9). If we define a leading sector as one which raises its share in total output over time, these data demonstrate that industry played that role. It is, for example, particularly revealing that the growth rate of GDP exceeded that of industry in only 5 of the 26 provinces and municipalities on which we have data. Moreover, of the top 6 provinces in terms of industrial growth, 5 were also in the top 6 for GDP growth; Zhejiang, Guangdong, and Fujian in particular achieved phenomenally rapid rates of industrialization after 1978, and it is hardly surprising that this is reflected in rapid growth of GDP. The only province which experienced rapid GDP growth despite comparatively slow industrial growth was Xinjiang. Xinjiang achieved this rather unlikely outcome by virtue of an agricultural growth rate (based upon animal husbandry) of over 9 per cent per annum—the fastest rate achieved by any Chinese province.

Of course, rapid industrial growth did not guarantee a rapid overall growth rate. Hubei, Jiangxi, and Anhui all achieved industrial growth rates substantially above the national median, yet their overall growth rates were comparatively disappointing. Nevertheless, and despite these exceptions, there is a much stronger relationship between industrial and total output growth than between (say) agricultural and total output growth. If GDP growth is regressed on industrial growth, the adjusted R^2 is 0.71 and the industry coefficient is highly significant. In the case of agricultural output growth, the adjusted R^2 is only 0.01 and the agricultural coefficient is not significant.

Yet before dismissing agriculture, we need to look at its contribution more closely. In particular, it is worthwhile investigating the possibility that agriculture was cast in the leading role in the growth of China's *poor* provinces. The logic behind this idea is that the contribution of a sector to growth depends upon both its growth and its initial size. Even if agriculture had not grown especially quickly, it might

TABLE 3.9. *Provincial rates of growth of GDP and industrial output, 1978–1996* (provinces ranked by industrial growth rate)

Province	Real GDP growth (% p.a., 1990 prices)	Real industrial growth (% p.a., 1990 prices)
Guangdong	13.6	17.9
Zhejiang	12.0	17.6
Fujian	12.4	17.5
Anhui	9.7	15.4
Jiangsu	11.3	14.6
Shandong	11.2	14.6
Guangxi	9.0	13.9
Jiangxi	9.6	13.1
Sichuan	8.9	12.5
Henan	9.8	12.2
Hubei	9.1	12.2
Yunnan	9.5	12.0
Shaanxi	9.2	11.3
Hunan	8.6	11.0
Hebei	9.6	10.9
Guizhou	8.8	10.5
Ningxia	9.2	9.7
Xinjiang	10.7	9.6
Shanxi	7.8	9.3
Nei Menggu	8.7	9.2
Liaoning	8.7	8.4
Shanghai	8.7	8.4
Gansu	9.4	8.2
Tianjin	8.0	8.0
Qinghai	7.2	7.5
Heilongjiang	5.9	5.7
Median	9.2	11.2

Notes: 'Industry' here comprises industry and construction. There are no data available on real sectoral output trends in LSTJ (1990) on Beijing, Hainan, Jilin, or Tibet; these provinces are therefore omitted.
Sources: LSTJ (1990); ZGTJNJ (1991–7).

still have been the key sector in poor provinces like Guizhou because it was so large relative to other sectors in 1978. Table 3.10, however, suggests that was not the case for the transition era. In all 10 of China's poorest provinces, the contribution of the primary sector to growth was much less than industry's; in not one of these 10 did the contribution of the primary sector come even close to matching that of the secondary sector. The best that can be said of agriculture was that it made more of a contribution in poor provinces than it did in richer ones. In the 5 poorest provinces, it contributed 20 per cent of growth. In the 5 richest, agriculture contributed only 11 per cent. Perhaps more significantly, agriculture played only a minor role in those provinces which achieved very rapid growth. In Jiangsu, industry contributed five times more to growth than the primary sector and in Guangdong the

TABLE 3.10. *Sectoral contributions to real GDP growth, 1978–1996* (percentages, provinces ranked in ascending order of real GDP per capita in 1978)

Province	GDP per capita, 1978 (*yuan*)	Growth of GDP per capita, 1978–96	Primary contribution	Secondary contribution
Guizhou	350	7.1	24	45
Henan	426	8.2	20	52
Sichuan	450	7.9	18	54
Yunnan	462	7.8	22	53
Anhui	466	8.1	15	67
Gansu	487	7.7	21	41
Jiangxi	499	8.0	22	50
Shaanxi	515	7.6	18	55
Hunan	522	7.2	16	54
Guangxi	529	7.5	26	53
Ningxia	590	6.9	23	42
Fujian	606	10.5	16	58
Xinjiang	618	8.8	28	37
Nei Menggu	630	7.2	36	41
Shandong	646	9.8	16	61
Hubei	651	7.6	17	58
Hebei	681	8.0	12	59
Zhejiang	697	11.0	8	71
Shanxi	709	6.2	12	61
Jiangsu	748	10.0	12	64
Guangdong	783	11.5	10	59
Qinghai	835	5.3	15	44
Heilongjiang	1,093	4.9	20	54
Liaoning	1,151	7.5	13	56
Tianjin	1,851	6.3	7	61
Shanghai	2,944	7.2	1	64

Notes: All data are at 1990 constant prices. There is inadequate information for a sectoral decomposition in the cases of Beijing, Hainan, Jilin, and Tibet.
Sources: As for Table 3.9.

contribution was six times larger. In Zhejiang, the ratio was a massive nine to one.[11] For the 5 fastest growing provinces, indeed, agriculture contributed only 12 per cent of GDP growth. More generally, the contribution of agriculture fell short of that of industry for every single provincial-level unit in China between 1978 and 1996. More than anything else, this finding illustrates the overwhelming dominance of industry in the Chinese growth process.

Nevertheless, this sort of analysis is very misleading because it ignores the key contribution of agriculture during 1978 to 1984, the crucial early years of growth (Table 3.11). For although the dominance of industry was overwhelming in the late 1980s and throughout the 1990s, rapid agricultural growth was important early on. As these data show, the contribution of agriculture exceeded that of industry in 14 of China's provinces between 1978 and 1984. Moreover, agriculture was crucial for

TABLE 3.11. *Sectoral contributions to real GDP growth, 1978–1984* (percentages, provinces ranked in ascending order of real GDP per capita in 1978)

Province	GDP per capita, 1978 (*yuan*)	Growth of GDP per capita, 1978–96	Primary contribution	Secondary contribution
Guizhou	350	7.1	43	36
Henan	426	8.2	41	32
Sichuan	450	7.9	41	25
Yunnan	462	7.8	43	37
Anhui	466	8.1	42	35
Gansu	487	7.7	39	26
Jiangxi	499	8.0	43	31
Shaanxi	515	7.6	29	33
Hunan	522	7.2	33	39
Guangxi	529	7.5	40	30
Ningxia	590	6.9	43	27
Fujian	606	10.5	33	31
Xinjiang	618	8.8	40	29
Nei Menggu	630	7.2	40	33
Shandong	646	9.8	48	30
Hubei	651	7.6	33	39
Hebei	681	8.0	42	35
Zhejiang	697	11.0	25	43
Shanxi	709	6.2	31	42
Jiangsu	748	10.0	40	47
Guangdong	783	11.5	33	37
Qinghai	835	5.3	23	30
Heilongjiang	1,093	4.9	27	42
Liaoning	1,151	7.5	23	51
Tianjin	1,851	6.3	6	57
Shanghai	2,944	7.2	7	56
National	704	8.4	30	37

Notes: All data are at 1990 constant prices. There is inadequate information for a sectoral decomposition in the cases of Beijing, Hainan, Jilin, and Tibet.

Sources: As for Table 3.9.

many poor provinces in these early years. As Table 3.11 shows, agriculture's contribution exceeded that of industry in every one of the poorest 7 provinces during 1978–84, and in many of these 7 it was by a substantial margin. In the provinces of Sichuan, Gansu, and Ningxia, in fact, we can almost say that agriculture was overwhelmingly dominant. Moreover, of the poorest 15 provinces in 1978, the contribution of industry exceeded that of agriculture in only the cases of Hunan and Shaanxi.

Only in the richer and more industrialized provinces as a rule did industry's contribution outweigh that of agriculture. It is of course not surprising that industry was so dominant in the large cities of Shanghai and Tianjin, nor that it was crucial in the industrialized province of Liaoning, the heartland of so much industry in 1978. But it is a telling commentary on the growth process that industry was the decisive factor even in the early years for the fast-growing provinces of Zhejiang, Guangdong, and Jiangsu. That said, it is important in retrospect to remember that agriculture contributed so much early on even in these areas. Particularly remarkable here is the case of Guangdong. It is often thought that Guangdong's growth in the 1980s and 1990s was driven primarily by investment in industry—particularly clothing and consumer electronics carried out by Hong Kong-based companies, and therefore that the province was very different from the rest of China. Yet these data show that agriculture was almost as important as industry in the early days, with the share of the primary sector falling only 4 percentage points below that of the secondary. And in Fujian and Shandong—two of China's other rapidly growing provinces along the eastern seaboard—agriculture was actually more important than industry before 1984, and in the case of the latter by a very significant margin.

The importance of agriculture in the early years of Dengist rule is reinforced by looking at trends in the *share of agriculture in output*. If agriculture truly played a leading role in the growth process, one would expect to see its share in output rising; that is, one would expect agricultural output to rise more quickly than industrial output. The evidence here is summarized in Table 3.12. In many ways it confirms that presented in Tables 3.10 and 3.11. If one considers the national share of agriculture in NDMP measured at 1990 constant prices, the trend for the entire 1978–92 period is of a steady decline.[12] In 1978, the share was 46 per cent. By 1984, it was down to 44 per cent, and it had fallen to 26 per cent by 1992. The decline was not continuous; there were year-on-year rises in 1982 and 1990. Nevertheless, at no time did the share of agriculture regain its 1978 level in the transition era. At the provincial level, every single provincial-equivalent registered a decline in the share of agriculture in NDMP between 1978 and 1992.[13] Of course, the magnitude of the decline varied substantially. In Ningxia the fall was only 1 percentage point and 7 areas in all registered declines of less than 10 percentage points. In Jiangsu, however, there was a decline of 26 percentage points and a colossal 36 points in Zhejiang.

However, as seen in Table 3.11, the importance of agriculture was far greater during 1978–84 than it was during the transition period as a whole. One of the most interesting features of Chinese growth is that the agricultural share exceeded its 1978 level in most parts of mainland China at some point in the early 1980s.[14] As Table 3.12 shows, it was extremely common for the agricultural share to rise in the early 1980s. For example, in Sichuan and Shandong, two of China's biggest producers of agricultural commodities, the agricultural share peaked in 1982 and 1983–4 respectively. Moreover, the rise in the agricultural share was in some cases very large indeed. For example, the 1983 share in Jilin was 5 percentage points higher than in 1978, and in Ningxia, there was a colossal 9 percentage point difference between the share of agriculture in 1981 and in 1978. More generally, in only 7 of China's provinces and municipalities (Shanghai, Zhejiang, Fujian, Henan, Hunan, Guangdong, and Yunnan) did the agricultural share never exceed its 1978 level at some point during the Dengist era.

TABLE 3.12. *Share of agriculture in NDMP in China's provinces*
(share of NVAO in NDMP at constant 1990 prices)

Province	1978	1984	1991	1992	Peak year post-1978 (share in parenthesis)
Beijing	11	12	11	10	1982–4, 1987–90 (12)
Tianjin	11	9	12	10	1991 (12)
Hebei	41	44	30	27	1983 (45)
Shanxi	36	35	22	22	1982 (38)
Nei Menggu	48	48	44	42	1981 (50)
Liaoning	26	27	21	20	1983 (30)
Jilin	42	44	36	33	1983 (47)
Heilongjiang	30	32	27	27	1983–4 (32)
Shanghai*	10	10	5	4	1978 (10)
Jiangsu	50	45	27	24	1979 (52)
Zhejiang*	60	45	28	24	1978 (60)
Anhui	63	60	38	39	1981 (66)
Fujian*	53	46	37	33	1978 (53)
Jiangxi	61	58	48	45	1982 (63)
Shandong	50	53	37	32	1983–4 (53)
Henan*	56	54	39	35	1978 (56)
Hubei	58	50	40	39	1979 (59)
Hunan*	60	56	46	43	1978 (60)
Guangdong*	47	44	30	26	1978 (47)
Guangxi	60	56	51	49	1979, 1982 (61)
Sichuan	55	53	41	38	1982 (57)
Guizhou	60	57	48	45	1982 (63)
Yunnan*	62	58	44	42	1978 (62)
Shaanxi	47	43	34	32	1979 (50)
Gansu	35	38	29	28	1983 (39)
Ningxia	36	43	35	31	1981 (45)
Xinjiang	45	48	45	42	1984, 1986 (48)

* Indicates a province or municipality where the share of agricultural output in material product did not exceed its 1978 level at any point after 1978.

Notes: No data are available for Hainan, Qinghai or Tibet. Shares calculated at 1990 constant prices.

Sources: LSTJ (1990, *passim*); ZGTJNJ (1991: 38); ZGTJNJ (1992: 32–3, 37–8); ZGTJNJ (1993: 41).

Of course, some care is needed when interpreting Tables 3.10, 3.11, and 3.12. There is no apparent correlation between income levels and changes in the agricultural share of output. In other words, increases in the agricultural share occurred after 1978 in rich provinces such as Jiangsu and Liaoning as well as in poor provinces like Gansu and Guizhou. Furthermore, one of the reasons why the agricultural share was comparatively high in the early 1980s in some parts of China was that the weather—especially during 1982–4—was much better than it had been in 1978. For that reason, 1978 is not an especially good base year to use in assessments of Chinese agricultural growth in the 1980s; it tends to impart a significant upward bias to growth rates. It also needs to be emphasized that an almost continuous decline in the share of agriculture occurred in some provinces. Zhejiang is the best example. In 1978, provincial production was still dominated by farming; with a share of agriculture in NDMP of 60 per cent, Zhejiang was much closer to the very poor province of Guizhou than Jiangsu, its neighbour. But after 1978, the transformation of the structure of Zhejiang's economy was exceedingly swift. By 1984, the share of agriculture was down to 45 per cent, and by 1991 it had fallen even further to a mere 28 per cent. In Zhejiang, therefore, the dominant role played by industry in the growth of the 1980s is exceptionally clear. Nevertheless, the fact remains that agricultural output was growing quickly in the early 1980s in most parts of China for reasons entirely unconnected with good weather, and that Zhejiang's experience was very much the exception rather than the rule. This was reflected in many instances in a rise in the agricultural share in NDMP. In other words, agriculture was indeed the leading sector in much of China in the early 1980s. Furthermore, as was apparent in Table 3.11, the main beneficiaries were China's poorest provinces.

The Accounting Contribution of Agriculture: Local Evidence

The issues raised in the previous section can be pursued further at a local level, and the evidence here confirms that agriculture was the leading sector in many impoverished areas in the early part of the transition era.

A case in point is Zhejiang province's Wenzhou municipality. Although Zhejiang as a whole was comparatively prosperous by Chinese standards in 1978, Wenzhou was not. However, Wenzhou's agricultural geography was favourable; there was no insuperable a priori obstacle in the way of prosperity. Some of the data on the post-1978 role of agriculture are presented in Table 3.13.[15] Perhaps the most striking feature of these data is the important accounting contribution made by agriculture to growth in the early years of transition. For the whole prefecture, agriculture provided about 42 per cent of output growth. For 3 of the counties (Pingyang, Wencheng, and Taishun) the contribution exceeded 50 per cent, clear evidence of the vital role played by the sector. Nevertheless, agriculture was less important in Wenzhou than in other parts of China in this period. Indeed, in parts of Wenzhou, agriculture was of extremely limited accounting significance even in the early 1980s. In Wenzhou city and Yueqing, for example, agriculture accounted for only 14 per cent of output growth, far below the median. In the case of Wenzhou city, this is not surprising given the dominance of industrial production in that urban centre. In Yueqing's case, it reflects very poor agricultural performance. Between 1980 and 1984, farm production actually declined there in real terms; so did grain output.

The stagnation of Yueqing's farm sector reflects in part the rapid growth of household industry that was the most salient feature of the Wenzhou experience in the transition period. The dominance of industry is more apparent after 1984. With the exceptions of Dongtou, Wencheng, and Taishun—and even there agriculture contributed much less than 50 per cent of output growth after 1984—the contribution made by agriculture to output growth in the second half of the transition period

TABLE 3.13. *The contribution of agriculture to NVAIO growth in Wenzhou municipality, 1978–1993* (counties ranked by NDMP per capita in 1980)

County	Percentage contribution of agriculture to NVAIO growth (1980 prices)		NDMP per capita (current *yuan*)
	1978–84	1984–93	1980
Wenzhou city	14	1	503
Rui'an	43	0	269
Yueqing	14	9	265
Pingyang	57	−2	188
Yongjia	36	−1	177
Dongtou	41	35	174
Taishun	86	22	172
Wencheng	58	29	165
Median	42	5	183

Notes: These calculations are based on NVAO and NVIO in 1978, 1984, and 1993. In every case, *cun*-level industry is included in NVIO to ensure a consistent series. This is achieved for 1984 by disaggregating the pre-1985 Chinese measure of GVAO and adding the value of *cun* industrial output to GVIO. This disaggregation is not possible for 1978, but *cun* industrial output value was too small in that year to significantly affect the results. No disaggregation is needed for 1993 because *cun* industry was included in industry in official Chinese data after 1984. Value-added for industry is calculated using the ratio of NVIO to GVIO in 1980 for 1978, 1984, and 1993. This is slightly misleading because 1980 data exclude *cun* industry from both GVIO and NVIO. However, value-added in *cun* industry was not so different from value-added in other industrial sectors to affect the result. Value-added in agriculture is calculated using the ratio of NVAO to GVAO in 1988 for both 1978 and 1984; 1993 value-added in agriculture is based on the ratio of provincial GVAO to NVAO. Wenzhou city incorporates Ouhai *xian*, and Pingyang incorporates Cangnan *xian*. Separate data are not available on these administrative units for 1978.

Sources: Wenzhou tongjiju (1985; 1989); ZJTJNJ (1994: 20, 24, 165, 414, 416); Zhejiang sheng jingji yanjiu zhongxin (1986).

was slight. In 5 of the 8 *xian*-level units, agriculture contributed less than 10 per cent of the growth of NVAIO, and in two cases it made a negative contribution. In statistical terms, growth in Wenzhou was thus driven by industry.

Even so, and as the cases of Wencheng and Taishun illustrate, agriculture was the key to the acceleration of growth that occurred in poor counties throughout the Chinese mainland after 1978. By Wenzhou standards, the two were underdeveloped in 1978. Per capita NDMP was below the municipality average in both and, in Taishun especially, industrialization had barely begun; the share of industry in NDMP there was only 10.5 per cent in 1980 (Wenzhou tongjiju, 1985: 343). It is therefore especially interesting that agriculture contributed well over 50 per cent of growth in the two before 1984. Indeed, with no less than 86 per cent of output growth generated by agriculture in the first six years, one may reasonable state that economic growth in Taishun was led by its agricultural sector.

This evidence on Wenzhou is reinforced by considering the role of agriculture in one of the poorest parts of Hunan, itself a relatively—but not extraordinarily

—poor Chinese province. The data in Table 3.14 show the contribution of agriculture to economic growth in Xiangxi prefecture. This mountainous prefecture, which borders on Sichuan, was the poorest in Hunan in the early 1980s. An indication of Xiangxi's poverty comes from *xian* levels of per capita NDMP in 1986, which were well below mean income levels in both Hunan and Zhejiang.

TABLE 3.14. *The contribution of agriculture to the growth of NVAIO in Hunan's Xiangxi prefecture, 1978–1986*

	Percentage contribution of agriculture to NVAIO growth (1980 prices) 1978–86	NDMP per capita (current *yuan*) 1986
Jishou city	26	592
Dayong city	74	588
Luxi	52	356
Fenghuang	51	442
Huayuan	61	307
Baojing	60	315
Guzhang	75	344
Yongshun	84	370
Sangzhi	77	333
Longshan	48	407
Median	61	363
Hunan	n/a	609
Zhejiang	n/a	1,042
China	n/a	743

Notes: Agricultural value-added is derived from *xian* GVAO and NVAO in 1985. Industrial value-added is the provincial average for 1978 and 1986.

Sources: Hunan tongjiju (1987: 393, 423); ZGFX (1989: 341–3); LSTJ (1990: 588–91).

As these figures show, the contribution of agriculture was decisive in the early years of transition. Except in Jishou city, where the industrial base was comparatively well-established in 1978, and Longshan *xian*, agriculture provided more than 50 per cent of the change in output in the remaining 8 *xian*. Moreover, in 4 of the *xian*, the agricultural contribution exceeded 70 per cent. All this made for a median contribution of 61 per cent—far in excess of the Wenzhou median of 42 per cent recorded in Table 3.13. This finding is doubly significant because the period used for Xiangxi is 1978 to 1986. With industry beginning to grow rapidly after 1984 in most parts of China, the use of 1986 as the terminal year ought to understate the contribution of agriculture compared to 1978–84 (the Wenzhou reference period). Part of the reason for the surge in agricultural production was a reaction to the overemphasis placed on industrialization during the 1960s.[16]

Perhaps even stronger evidence for the centrality of agriculture to the growth process in the early 1980s comes from the ethnic minority counties of Gansu province in north-west China (Table 3.15). The share of industrial production in total output was very small in these *xian* in the late 1970s. The median share was only 7 per cent, and 13 of the nineteen counties had NVIO shares of single figures. Only in Linxia city and the counties of Jone and Zhugqu was the extent of industrial production at all significant. One therefore might have expected industry, beginning from such a lowly basis, to have been crucial in impelling growth momentum after 1978. In practice, however, industrial production actually *declined* in many of these *xian* in the early 1980s. In fact, a decline was recorded in 9 of the 19 *xian* in the province, and the fact that industrial output increased in the sample as a whole reflects the dominant contribution of a mere 2 *xian* (Tianzhu and Zhugqu) which together accounted for 81 per cent of the increase between 1978 and 1984.

In consequence, agriculture was the mainstay of output growth in Gansu's ethnic minority areas. In the 9 *xian* in which industrial output fell, agriculture necessarily accounted for more than 100 per cent of total output growth. In a further 6 of the 19, the contribution of agriculture exceeded 50 per cent of total output growth. Only in Zhangjiachuan and Aksay (where agricultural production declined) and in Zhugqu (where agriculture accounted for only 32 per cent of growth) can one argue that agriculture did not play the role of leading sector. This suggests that these areas of Gansu and Hunan, in common with other parts of China, were 'over-industrialized' in the late Maoist period. With the shift away from the Third Front that occurred in the 1980s, it was largely inevitable that the importance of agriculture in the growth process would increase, and that of industry diminish. Moreover, although it might seem odd to talk of 'over-industrialization' in counties where agriculture accounted for over 90 per cent of output value in 1978, it is a remarkable fact that 7 of the *xian* where the share of agriculture exceeded 90 per cent of output in 1978 increased that share even further by 1984. There is thus a strong similarity between the poor *xian* of Zhejiang and poor *xian* in other provinces of China such as Hunan and Gansu in terms of the decisive impact of agriculture in the early stages of transition.

In sum, although the contribution of industry dominated that of agriculture for the Dengist period as a whole, the importance of agriculture in the early years of transition was crucial. Only in the municipalities and a handful of prosperous rural regions was agriculture largely insignificant in the period 1978 to 1984. In the poorest parts of China, the role of agriculture in initiating and sustaining broadly based economic growth was crucial in the early 1980s.

3.2. Agricultural Linkage Effects

The accounting analysis pursued in the previous section is a narrow way of assessing the impact of agriculture. We need to look not only at its direct statistical contribution but also at the linkages between agriculture on the one hand and industry on the other. Was it the initial growth of agriculture that caused the rapid industrial growth in the early 1980s? Did agriculture make possible the continued economic growth of the second half of the decade, or was industrial growth after 1984 self-sustaining and largely independent of agriculture?

TABLE 3.15. *The role of agriculture in the growth process in ethnic minority counties of Gansu province, 1978–1984*

County	Contribution of agriculture to growth, 1978–84 (%)	Growth of GVIO, 1978–84 (% p.a.)	Share of NVIO in NVAIO, 1978
Linxia city	158	−1.3	42
Linxia	96	5.0	2
Yongjing	103	−2.2	9
Hezheng	111	−1.3	8
Guanghe	87	16.9	4
Kangle	99	1.2	4
Dongxiang	102	−9.0	4
Xiahe	102	−1.0	7
Lintan	103	3.8	7
Jone	242	−8.4	37
Zhugqu	32	3.7	50
Tewo	69	21.2	13
Luqu	102	−5.8	4
Maqu	102	−9.2	2
Subei	135	−0.9	7
Sunan	94	2.7	8
Tianzhu	55	20.3	17
Zhangjiachuan	107	5.4	6
Aksay	−251	17.0	14
Median	102	1.2	7

Note: All the estimates are based on data valued in 1980 constant prices. Industrial value-added is the provincial average. Agricultural value-added is calculated for each *xian* from 1985 data on NVAO and GVAO at current prices. The 1984 data probably exclude *cun* industry (the figures given in the Gansu source for 1985 are not explicitly identified, but they are the same as those given in ZGFX, which expressly exclude *cun* industry. Moreover, if the 1984 data did include *cun* industry, there ought to be inconsistencies when they are compared with the 1985 figures; in fact, there are no obvious inconsistencies in the Gansu series; GVAO increased by 9 per cent in 1985, and GVIO by 3.6 per cent). The Zhangjiachuan sign is positive because both NVAO and NVAIO declined. The sign for Aksay is negative because agricultural output declined, whereas total output increased.

Sources: *Gansu sheng shaominzu diqu jiben tongji ziliao* (1988: 25, 30–64); ZGFX (1989).

It has long been argued that there are important linkages between agricultural and industrial sectors in developing countries which make it impossible for a government bent upon regulating economic growth to treat either sector as independent (Owen, 1966; Ishikawa, 1967; Mellor, 1973). Construction and many industrial subsectors—notably textiles and food processing—are dependent upon agriculture as a source of input supply, and therefore a degree of sectoral balance is essential if growth is not to grind to a halt in the face of strong inflationary pressures. As Lewis (1954: 173) argued:

> . . . if the capitalist sector produces no food, its expansion increases the demand for food, raises the price of food in terms of capitalist products and so reduces profits. This is one of

the senses in which industrialisation is dependent upon agricultural improvement. . . . This is also why industrial and agrarian revolutions always go together, and why economies in which agriculture is stagnant do not show industrial development.

Lewis was writing here of a closed economy (although he later generalized it to include foreign trade). Where opportunities for foreign trade exist, a dynamic domestic agriculture is less important. British industrialization, for example, was made possible by raw cotton imports fashioned by the great mills of south-east Lancashire into the cotton textiles which, in turn, earned the foreign currency required to buy the raw cotton in the first place. However, reliance upon external sources of supply produces difficulties of its own. A source of export earnings is needed in the first place to finance raw material imports; the primary sector must needs perform that role initially (in the absence of a foreign loan). That in turn necessitates a dynamic primary sector, as well as a willingness to accept the risks involved in primary commodity export; the evidence for a long-run decline in the terms of trade of primary producers may be equivocal but there is no doubting the instability of primary commodity prices (Prebisch, 1949; Singer, 1950; Spraos, 1983). Reliance on domestic agriculture is therefore a safer option than integration into the world economy.

For most countries, therefore, the fortunes of industry are inextricably linked to those of agriculture. The precise nature of the link in China during the early 1980s can be seen from input–output data on agricultural subsectors (Table 3.16).[17]

TABLE 3.16. *Use of agricultural output by non-agriculture in 1981* (per cent of current price agricultural output)

	Agricultural subsector of origin				
	Farming	Forestry	Livestock	Sidelines	Aquatic
Agriculture	18	9	11	17	3
Heavy industry	1	33	1	5	neg.
Light industry	31	31	43	27	5
Construction	neg.	neg.	neg.	44	neg.
Transport	neg.	neg.	neg.	neg.	neg.
Commerce	neg.	neg.	1	neg.	7
Intermediate	50	73	55	93	15
Depreciation	neg.	neg.	neg.	neg.	neg.
Consumption	51	3	38	5	79
Accumulation	3	21	3	1	1
Net exports	–5	3	1	neg.	4
Other	neg.	neg.	2	neg.	neg.

Notes: These figures are percentages of gross current price output in each agricultural sub-sector. Sidelines exclude *cun* and below-*cun* level rural industry. 'All intermediate' is the sum of the first six rows; it shows the proportion of output used as inputs by other economic sectors.

Source: Calculated from data in CEF (1987: Table 12).

The forward linkages shown vary considerably in degree between subsectors. Almost all aquatic production, for example, was destined for final consumption; rapid output growth in this subsector would do little to promote industrialization. By contrast, the link between farming and Chinese industrialization was far stronger. Of the output of the farm sector, some 50 per cent was used as intermediate inputs, especially for the food-processing industry. Not less than 20 per cent of farm output was used by this industrial subsector, and a further 6 per cent was used by the textile industry. This input–output relationship demonstrates that increased farm output had an importance for Chinese industrialization in the 1980s that was much greater than is implied by its share in GDP. Accordingly, although Bhalla (1992) is right to say that farming had fewer linkages with industry than many other sectors and subsectors, the linkage effects which did exist suggest that the development of light industry would have been virtually impossible without rising farm production.

Even more significant were the linkages between forestry, sidelines, and the rest of the Chinese economy. Some 73 per cent of the products of the forestry subsector were intermediate inputs, with heavy and light industry being the key recipients. A staggering 93 per cent of all sideline output served as inputs for other sectors, with only 5 per cent going to final consumption. The links between sidelines and the construction sector were particularly strong; no less than 44 per cent of sideline output was used by China's construction sector in 1981. All this suggests that a pattern of agriculture growth in which sideline and forestry subsectors feature disproportionately would be of greatest advantage for the industrialization process.

This conclusion is to some extent supported by provincial-level data (Table 3.17).

TABLE 3.17. *The composition of agricultural output growth, 1978–1992* (annual growth rates of output value at 1990 prices)

Province	Farming	Forestry	Livestock	Sidelines	GVAO	NDMP
Zhejiang	2.0	4.9	4.9	23.9	4.6	10.9
Guangdong	4.6	7.3	9.2	13.3	7.2	11.3
Jiangsu	3.1	2.5	7.9	48.1	5.7	10.3
Anhui	4.2	7.2	7.5	14.9	5.6	8.5
Henan	3.9	6.2	9.5	23.5	5.8	9.0
Guizhou	3.9	6.1	9.4	13.3	6.2	8.2
Sichuan	3.3	5.9	10.1	13.1	5.7	8.0
Hunan	3.0	2.6	7.6	14.7	4.9	7.0
China	4.4	7.3	9.2	13.3	7.2	8.7

Note: Growth rates are for gross output value because data on subsectoral value-added are either unreliable or unavailable for the late 1970s and early 1980s. The data do not go beyond 1992 because sidelines are included in farming from 1993 onwards.

Sources: LSTJ (1990); ZGTJNJ (1991: 318–21); ZGNYTJZL (1992: 24–5); ZGNYTJZL (1993: 22–3); SCTJNJ (1993: 222).

The most obvious feature of this table is the incredible growth of the sideline sector throughout China. Ranging from 13 to almost 50 per cent per year, this far exceeded the rate of growth of both agricultural and total output. Of course, the relationship between NDMP and sideline growth was not precise. For example, NDMP grew at similar rates in Henan and Anhui, yet sideline production increased much more quickly in the former than the latter. Furthermore, although Guangdong achieved the fastest NDMP growth of any Chinese province, the rate of sideline increase was below the national average. Nevertheless, and despite this imprecision, it is apparent from these data that there was a link between the growth of the sideline subsector and the overall rate of economic growth. In essence, this was because many sideline products (e.g. timber, furniture, and tools) were inputs for the construction sector. Thus, for two of the provinces where NDMP grew much more quickly than the national average (Zhejiang and Jiangsu), the growth of sideline production was also far in excess of the national average. Even though the overall rate of agricultural growth was below the national average, the dynamism of the sideline sector was far more important there than big rises in crop production. By contrast, sideline growth was much slower in Sichuan, Guizhou, and Hunan (perhaps because the construction sector grew comparatively slowly)—and in all three cases the overall rate of NDMP growth was correspondingly slower.

Yet, and notwithstanding this evidence of correlation, the precise causal link between sidelines and the wider economy is difficult to determine. One can argue that sideline growth caused industrial growth. Or one can assert that sideline production responded passively to prior industrial growth. All that is really clear is that the growth of the two went hand-in-hand. The importance of rapid growth in the forestry subsector seems even less clear-cut. In Jiangsu, forestry output grew slowly—hardly a surprise in view of the lack of forest cover—and yet NDMP growth was rapid. In Guizhou, forestry output grew quickly, but there was no apparent benefit in terms of overall output growth. Nevertheless, it is possible that Hunan's growth was constrained by its forestry subsector; as the table shows, Hunan came bottom in terms of both NDMP and forestry output growth.

More generally, the contribution of agriculture as a supplier of inputs to the growing industrial sector can be evaluated by considering whether the agricultural sector was able to meet industrial demand without recourse to imports. The degree of import penetration thus serves as a measure of the extent of excess home demand for particular agricultural commodities. For example, growing imports of agricultural commodities by Britain in the half century after 1750 has often been taken as signifying agricultural failure (O'Brien, 1977; Thomas, 1985; Beckett, 1990).

The degree to which agriculture in the People's Republic was successful in this regard is apparent from Table 3.18. Grain production was probably the biggest success story. Despite soaring demand (driven by the direct consumption needs of a growing population and the rising input needs of the food-processing industry), China was able to restrict grain imports to 5 per cent of domestic production in every year between 1976 and 1996. This success reflected the predominant share of grain crops in sown area and the marked increase in yields achieved, especially in the early 1980s.

Together, these ensured that production increased by about a third over the course of the first decade of transition.

TABLE 3.18. *Agricultural production and imports, 1978–1996*
(imports as a percentage of domestic production)

Year	Grain	Cotton	Wool
1976	1	9	6
1977	3	9	7
1978	3	24	8
1979	4	25	11
1980	4	33	21
1981	5	26	19
1982	5	13	35
1983	4	5	37
1984	3	1	31
1985	2	neg.	59
1986	2	neg.	83
1987	4	neg.	72
1988	4	1	84
1989	4	1	44
1990	3	1	24
1991	3	1	66
1992	3	6	87
1993	2	neg.	99
1994	2	12	125
1995	4	16	102
1996	2	15	76

Note: The import series is not consistent. Data for pre-1987 were collected by the Ministry of Trade, others by Chinese Customs.

Sources: Output—Nongye bu (1989: 190, 241); ZGNYTJZL (1987: 68, 121; 1988: 71, 126; 1989: 46, 54, 148; 1991: 50, 53, 140; 1994: 345–6, 353; 1995: 347–8, 355), ZGTJNJ (1996: 371–2, 379); ZGNYNJ (1997: 301, 311, 343). Imports—Nongye bu (1989: 535, 537); ZGTJNJ (1987: 600; 1989: 642; 1991: 365, 376, 626; 1993: 644; 1994: 518; 1995: 549; 1996: 593; 1997: 600).

Some regions, of course, did less well. In parts of eastern China, grain output per capita grew hardly at all during the 1980s. Total production in Shanghai, for example, was on average lower in 1983–5 than it had been in 1978–80 (LSTJ, 1990: 320). In Zhejiang, per capita grain production declined annually by 0.5 per cent between 1978 and 1991; in Guangdong, the rate of decline was 0.7 per cent.[18] Nevertheless, it is hard to characterize any of this as 'failure'. For one thing, actual production—as opposed to per capita production—continued to grow by 0.5 per cent in Zhejiang and 1.1 per cent in Guangdong. In other words, the decline in per capita production was more due to population growth than to falling production. Furthermore, in so far as per capita production fell, it reflected a deliberate reaction against the Maoist drive for grain self-sufficiency; this reaction took the form of a reduction in grain sown area and an increase in the area sown to cash crops and vegetables. In Guangdong, for instance, grain sown area in 1988 was more than 25 per cent lower than it had been in 1978 (LSTJ, 1990: 627). So the slight rise in the national ratio of grain imports to production reflected (at least in the early years of transition) a deliberate policy decision to raise grain imports rather than any incapacity on the part of the grain subsector to meet rising demand. Given the high income elasticity of demand for cash crops and vegetables in eastern China, it was in many respects less costly to meet the needs of the urban population by imports than from domestic production given the transport costs involved. As a result, wheat accounted for more than 90 per cent of imported grain in the mid-1980s (Nongye bu, 1989: 535).

The capacity of the cotton subsector to meet the demands placed on it by the growth of the textile industry was rather less impressive. Cotton production increased by about 30 per cent between the mid-1970s and 1980 but that was wholly inadequate to satisfy rising demand, which had to be met by resorting to foreign supply. As a result, cotton imports rose from 188,000 tonnes in 1976 to almost 900,000 in 1980—amounting to more than 33 per cent of domestic production. Nevertheless, this failure was transitional rather than deep-rooted. The pronounced shift in the structure of industrial production from producer to consumer goods at the end of the 1970s not unnaturally led to bottlenecks which could only be resolved in time by increases in cotton yields. By the early 1980s this process was in full swing, with the yield rising from about 29 to 61 kg. per sown *mu* between the late 1970s and 1984. By 1984, indeed, cotton production reached 6.3m. tonnes or about three times higher than its level in 1976. In consequence, the ratio of imports to production fell from its 1980 peak of 33 per cent to a mere 0.5 per cent by 1984. From that point on, and despite the decline in cotton production to around 4 million tonnes per year, the problem of ensuring adequate supplies of raw cotton to the cotton industry was temporarily resolved by the late 1980s. After 1991, however, reliance on cotton imports began to rise, and by 1995 imports accounted for 16 per cent of production. Nevertheless, China's dependence on the foreign sector for cotton was clearly rather limited at the time of Deng's death.

The picture in the case of wool production was very different. Although production increased by 85 per cent between 1978 and 1994 (ZGTJNJ, 1995: 355), this was well below the rate needed to satisfy demand. The problem faced by the industries of eastern China in securing adequate supplies of wool were exacerbated by transport bottlenecks, local protection in the main wool-producing regions of western China, and heavy provincial investment in the (highly profitable) wool-processing industry; ultimately, it precipitated a 'war' over wool supplies (Watson and Findlay, 1992; Watson, *et al.*, 1989). This excess demand could only be met by imports, which rose from less than 10 per cent of production in the late 1970s to over 80 per cent between 1986 and 1988. Moreover, although the import ratio fell back substantially in 1989 and 1990, it rose again thereafter; by 1994, wool imports exceeded domestic production by a factor of 25 per cent. The position improved very substantially in 1995 and 1996, but nevertheless China remained very dependent on the world economy for supplies of this product.

Wool production aside, however, the supply contribution of agriculture to the process of 1980s industrialization in China was impressive; a mere accounting treatment does little to bring out the true significance of agriculture to the national economy during the 1980s and early 1990s. There were important forward linkages running from agricultural subsectors like sidelines and forestry to industry; as a result, and especially in those regions where these subsectors proved especially dynamic, agricultural growth spurred industrialization. Even for commodities like grain and cotton, both of which were vital to the Chinese economy and yet scarce before 1978, there is scant evidence that the growing demand was running up against insoluble production bottlenecks. Furthermore, whilst wool imports were very substantial by the mid-1990s, domestic production still met about 50 per cent of total demand, no small achievement given China's limited grazing land.

4. Conclusion

This chapter suggests that China's industrial sector played the leading role in post-1978 growth. In purely accounting terms, industry's contribution was greater than that of agriculture in *both* the sub-period 1978–84 and the sub-period 1984–96. In the post-1984 era in particular, it is plain that industry was overwhelmingly dominant; its contribution was six times that of agriculture in the decade after 1984. Furthermore, the role of industry in China's growth was even more significant than its accounting contribution suggests. It provided inputs to both services and to agriculture. Moreover, it experienced a process of profound structural change which, by the late 1980s, made it far more responsive to the needs of other sectors than it had been at the time of Mao's death. Perhaps most importantly of all, Chinese industry became increasingly 'modern' over the course of the 1980s. Traditional consumer-orientated industries such as tobacco thrived in the market atmosphere but so too did undeniably modern products like pharmaceuticals, plastics, electrical equipment, and electronics. The pace of industrial growth and this changing pattern of industrial output together ensured that industrial growth was the key element in Chinese growth during the Dengist era.

Yet this conclusion that industry was the leading sector is not to imply that agriculture acted as a constraint on growth. On the contrary. Agriculture played the key role in the growth process between 1978 and 1984 in most parts of China, and in poor regions, agriculture was of critical importance throughout the post-1978 era. Take the poor provinces of Yunnan and Gansu. The two entered the transition era with similar levels of per capita GDP (462 and 487 *yuan* respectively) and achieved very similar rates of growth (7.8 compared to 7.7 per cent). Yet by 1996, there were still 8.4 million people living in counties throughout Yunnan where average net peasant income fell below 500 *yuan* per year. In Gansu, however, only 1.18 million were still in poverty by this measure (ZGNYNJ, 1997: 453). This comparison is somewhat misleading because of harvest fluctuations, the substantial volume of aid received by Gansu, and the fact that Yunnan's population was nearly twice as big. Yet it is hard to believe that Gansu's more successful record on poverty reduction was entirely unrelated to its having achieved an agricultural growth rate of 7.8 per cent between 1978 and 1996, whereas Yunnan managed 'only' 5.6 per cent.

But when all is said and done, it is the rapid pace of industrialization that is the most salient characteristic of the exceptionally fast growth achieved by the People's Republic during the transition era. Not a single province experienced industrial growth of less than 5 per cent after 1978. No less than 16 provinces achieved rates of more than 10 per cent and, as has been seen, rates of more than 20 per cent were commonplace in areas like Suzhou. By the time of Deng's death, China had gone far towards establishing a modern industrial sector.

4

Theories of Growth

The dominant feature of the transition era in China was the sheer acceleration in the pace of growth in agriculture, industry, and in total GDP. The most 'miraculous' aspect of the Dengist growth experience is therefore the way in which the relatively slow growth of late Maoism gave way to the explosive growth presided over by his successor. To what extent can this transformation be explained by theories of economic growth?

Growth theory comes in many guises. It was pioneered by Adam Smith, and by David Ricardo. It was elaborated upon by Marx. And in the period immediately before and after World War II, it was given a Keynesian slant by the work of Roy Harrod (1939); at the same time, many of Marx's ideas were formalized in the Soviet Union by G. A. Feldman. However, perhaps the best-known approach is the neoclassical one. This dates from the work of Robert Solow (1956; 1957) on one-sector models, and Solow's work gave rise to a large-scale research programme in the 1960s which was in turn given empirical substance by the pioneering work on growth-accounting by E. F. Denison. Yet by the early 1980s, even neoclassical economists had lost interest in this research programme. According to Frank Hahn (1986: 379):

> The theory of growth is now definitely somewhat in eclipse and I am not sure that this fate is not deserved. The major part of this theory was concerned with steady states and it was never clear why, even given the commitment to equilibrium analysis, this particular equilibrium should be of central interest. Moreover the models invariably failed to show concern for the real engines of growth: innovations and perhaps population growth. Indeed most of them are simply mechanical toys sans history and sans human ingenuity.

This sort of criticism, coming as it did from a leading neoclassical practitioner (Hahn had co-authored both a well-known survey of neoclassical growth theory and one of the key texts on general equilibrium)[1] gives an indication of the extent to which growth theory languished in the early 1980s. Growth theory has since, however, undergone a dramatic revival. In part this reflects the need for economists to explain the central event of the post-war era, the rise of East Asia. Perhaps more importantly, the revival of interest in growth theory has occurred because of the work of Paul Romer (1986; 1990; 1991; 1993; 1994; 1995) who has sought to address head-on (within a well-defined theoretical framework) the central features of neoclassical theory—the prediction of diminishing returns to capital, and the absence of a theory of technical progress.

Not surprisingly, the emergence of endogenous growth theory has spawned a flood of papers, a new journal dedicated to growth issues and extensive critical debate.[2] The neoclassical response has taken various forms. Some have denied that endogenous growth theory is of any use in explaining the event most in need of explanation—the rise of East Asia (Young, 1995; Krugman, 1996). Others, such as Greg Mankiw (Mankiw, *et al.*, 1992; Mankiw, 1995), have argued that the insights offered by Lucas (1988) and Romer are easily incorporated into a Solowian model by broadening the meaning of the term capital to include human capital. And economic historians have argued that perhaps the most important episode of all—Britain's Industrial Revolution—cannot be explained using an endogenous theory of technical progress (Crafts, 1995).

These debates are important because, although there is considerable agreement on the proximate determinants of growth (initial conditions, capital accumulation broadly defined, and technical progress), there is extensive disagreement about which is most important. The question has important policy implications. For example, if growth can be sustained for long periods of time by capital and labour accumulation, one can reasonably question whether the governments of LDCs should pay much attention to spending on research and development. If growth depends primarily upon the growth of human capital, there is a strong case for high government spending on education. By contrast, if investment in plant and equipment generates significant externalities (De Long and Summers, 1992; 1993), equipment subsidies are indispensable. And if the closing of what Romer (1993) calls the 'ideas gap' is most important, that strengthens the case for free trade and the encouragement of multinational investment. Moreover, if the creation of new blueprints will only occur when firms can be tempted by the inducement of large supernormal profits (quasi-rents) along neo-Schumpeterian lines, there are clear implications for patent and competition policy.

Nevertheless, much of this new growth theory remains superficial. In essence, it offers little more than a description of growth. We need to go deeper and look at the institutional structures which underlie the growth process.[3] How do economies make the transition from stagnation or extensive growth to a growth path along which per capita income rises (intensive growth)? How can they move from a low growth to a high growth path? Is it inevitable that growth-promoting institutions will emerge via endogenous processes? This perspective on the growth process leads immediately to heavily disputed terrain: the respective roles of the private and the public in promoting growth. In one sense, of course, the debate here is merely trivial; very few would disagree with the view that effective private and state institutions are both important. However, intrinsic to the master discourse is a much stronger proposition: that the state has only a small role to play in promoting economic growth and, more especially, as a direct producer of goods and services. That proposition was taken to be a self-evident truth by many governments in the West during the 1990s, not surprisingly as it is they who have played a key role in the very construction of the master discourse. But it needs to be properly evaluated, especially in the light of the experience of East Asia and continental Europe.

To begin, however, we need to outline the central issues and conclusions spawned by growth theory. Broadly speaking, four factors promoting per capita growth have been identified. First, favourable initial conditions. A country able to adopt new technologies pioneered abroad will be more successful if it has a highly developed level of human and physical capital. Alternatively, a country's labour force may be deployed in low-productivity sectors, or its institutions may discourage risk-taking and hard work; such a country may be able to achieve big output rises by eliminating this static inefficiency and moving on to its production frontier. In addition, a country may grow rapidly if it is away from its (higher) steady state. Second, an economy can grow by building up its stock of physical capital via an increase in its savings rate. Third, the country can instead invest heavily in human capital, thereby raising the quality of its labour force. Finally, growth can be based around technical progress. A country can, for example, grow quickly by importing ideas from abroad or by simply diffusing technologies developed indigenously; this is the notion of technological diffusion, or 'catch-up' growth. Alternatively, a country can spend heavily on research and development, thereby generating a high rate of indigenous invention and innovation. Let us consider these arguments in turn.

1. The Role of Initial Conditions

Favourable initial conditions can promote growth via four mechanisms. First, they may make it easier to adopt new technology from abroad (dynamic gains). Second, a country may be able to grow swiftly by redeploying factors of production from low- to high-productivity sectors. Third, a country can raise output by eliminating the incentive failures associated with growth-retarding institutions. Fourth, rapid growth will occur during the period in which an economy, starting from a (low-level) disequilibrium, moves towards its steady state.[4]

Let us begin with the first case. Consider a country (A) with a high (equilibrium) capital–labour ratio and operating on its production function. Suppose A suddenly gains access to a new technology pioneered in some other country—by, for example, opening its economy up to foreign trade and foreign direct investment. Then A will enjoy a big increase in per capita output as its production function is shifted dramatically outwards at the point where the capital–labour ratio is high. This is because its high level of human capital allows the foreign technology to be absorbed and diffused more quickly. By contrast, country B (operating on the same initial production function but with a lower capital–labour ratio) will not gain as much in terms of output from the same technology because of its lower capital–labour ratio; the shift in the production function will be less at the lower than the higher capital–labour ratio. This reflects country B's inability to absorb the new techniques. Its workforce is simply not skilled enough to benefit from the technological opportunities presented to it.

In other words, the extent to which the production function shifts out as foreign technology becomes available is a function of the capital–labour ratio. The rise in output will be large at high capital–labour ratios, and less at low capital–labour ratios. Countries like A therefore have much more scope for growth based on 'catch-up'—or what Amsden (1989) calls 'industrialization by learning'—than countries like B.

In effect, we are assuming here that there are increasing returns to human capital or what Abramovitz has called social capability.

Let us now turn to the second case of static inefficiency caused by sectoral misallocation of factors of production. Here country A might have a high capital–labour ratio but this is not being translated into a high level of per capita output because its capital and labour are being deployed in the wrong (i.e. low-productivity) sectors. For example, the bulk of investment might be going into the military sector; the value of the capital stock of the country is therefore high, but the capital is relatively unproductive. Alternatively, the country's problem might be that the bulk of its labour is working at low levels of productivity in agriculture. This is of course the sort of model outlined by W. A. Lewis. In both cases, the solution is the same. By redeploying labour and capital to more productive sectors, per capita output will rise. Accordingly, country A has the ability to grow much faster than a country (B) which has already deployed its factors of production to the optimal sector.

The third set of initial conditions that might allow a country to grow quickly also relate to the elimination of static inefficiency. Again suppose that country A is off its production function. But suppose this time that the inefficiency arises not because factors have been allocated to the 'wrong' sectors, but rather that the intra-sectoral productivity of these factors is less than their potential because of growth-retarding institutions. For example, the tax system may discourage risk-taking, or collective farming discourages a high level of labour productivity because it goes unrewarded. Or suppose that the level of demand is inadequate to ensure full employment of factors of production. Then country A can in principle grow quickly by eliminating these institutional inefficiencies, and in the process move on to its production function.

Let us consider these three possibilities in more detail.

1.1. Diffusion and Social Capability

The importance of social capability has been written about extensively by Moses Abramovitz (1986; 1989; 1994). He argues that what matters for growth is not access to ideas per se but the capacity to absorb them—that is, social capability. Although poor countries may in principle be able to catch up with rich countries, the scope for such catching up is constrained by their low levels of human capital formation. Thus the post-war recovery of Japan and Germany occurred because their stocks of human capital (a skilled and educated workforce) were largely intact. Abramovitz is however careful to note that social capability is a slippery concept. He measures it as a combination of years of education and quality of institutions, but acknowledges the problems involved.[5] For example, educational systems may be good at diffusing ideas but less good at producing a workforce which is flexible and capable of adapting to technological change. Moreover, social capability is recognized in some sense to be endogenous; it will tend to change in response to technological opportunities. Additionally, social capability may have less to do with formal education and institutions than with attitudes and the extent of vested interest. Finally, Abramovitz points out that social capability and a technology gap do no more than define the potential growth rate of an LDC. To achieve that potential, the pace of the diffusion of knowledge, capital accumulation, and demand growth all need to be rapid. These conditions came together in post-war Europe, but they have not always done so (Abramovitz, 1986: 395). Nevertheless, the central conclusion from Abramovitz's analysis is that it identifies weaknesses in the initial level of human capital as an obstacle to diffusion-based economic growth:

> Countries that are technologically backward have a potentiality for generating growth more rapid than that of more advanced countries, provided their social capabilities are sufficiently developed to permit successful exploitation of technologies already employed by the technological leaders. (Abramovitz, 1986: 390)

> By comparison with America and Britain, many, though not all, of the 'followers' were also latecomers in respect to social capability. In the decades following 1870, they lacked experience with large-scale production and commerce, and in one degree or another they needed to advance in levels of general and technical education. (Ibid. 397)

The influence of Abramovitz's work can be seen in the writings of Paul Romer (1993). Romer argues that the main problem faced by LDCs is an idea—rather than the object—gap. In other words, and in contrast to augmented Solowian models in which technology is seen as a public good, LDCs are constrained by their limited access to Western technology. This is precisely because 'blueprints' are non-rival but partially excludable goods. Their instantaneous diffusion from advanced to poor countries is restricted by transaction costs (limited information), by patent protection, and by deliberate, government-established, barriers to the spread of foreign ideas. LDCs should therefore, Romer argues, pay more attention to closing the ideas gap than to investing heavily in physical and human capital formation.

A third perspective is offered by Gomulka (1986) as the basis for his 'hat-shaped' theory of technological diffusion in Eastern European economies. His argument is that these economies were unable to absorb the available Western technologies because of their inadequate initial levels of human capital. But once this latter was remedied by the wholesale expansion of education after their revolutions, the Eastern European economies experienced a period of one-off catch-up growth based upon technological diffusion. However, growth then slowed down as the scope for further diffusion was exhausted. Gomulka (1986: 52–3) summarized his argument thus:

> For any particular country, the innovation rate tends to be highest at medium levels of development, when the country in question still has much to learn from the outside world and, at the same time, has already developed the means—a high level of education, an R&D sector, an investment goods sector, an export capability—of transferring directly or being otherwise capable of absorbing outside knowledge. . . . the Soviet method of compensating for allocative inefficiency and innovation resistance with larger conventional and innovation inputs would cease to be feasible as a way of sustaining a high innovation rate once the initial reserves of these inputs have been exhausted. (pp. 52–3)

To be sure, the evidence from Britain on the role played by its level of human capital is equivocal. If there is a conventional wisdom on the subject, it is the view expressed by Bowman and Anderson (1963) that a literacy rate of more than 30 per cent is necessary for modern economic growth. As English literacy rates by the late eighteenth century averaged around 60 per cent for grooms and 40 per cent for brides (as measured by their ability to sign the marriage register—Schofield, 1973), England clearly satisfied the Bowman–Anderson criterion. However, it is hard to argue that England was the 'first industrial nation' merely because her literacy rates were high. In fact, English literacy rates were fairly close to the Western European average (Mitch, 1993: 269–70, 305). Perhaps the key feature of English industrialization was instead the way in which the inventions and even the innovations of continental Europe were modified and diffused across the economy; the steam engine provides the classic example.[6] In other words, even though its literacy rate was not especially impressive, Britain seems to have had a high level of social capability.[7]

Japan's experience during the late nineteenth century offers an even more interesting test of the hypothesis because, after it was opened up to foreign trade (following the imposition of the 'Unequal Treaties' in the 1850s), the country was in a position to grow by exploiting the technologies already developed in Europe and the USA. Indeed, as Abramovitz notes (1986: 387 n.), the term 'social capability' was first used by Ohkawa and Rosovsky as one way of explaining why Japanese industrialization was comparatively successful in the second half of the nineteenth century and many scholars have interpreted the growth of Meiji Japan in this light. The argument put forward by a group of writers usually called 'revisionists' (Smith 1959; Hall 1962; Nakamura, 1966; Hanley and Yamamura, 1977; Hanley and Wolf, 1985) was that the pace of Japanese development in the Tokugawa period (1603–1867) was far faster than suggested by the largely Marxist conventional wisdom exemplified by the writings of E. H. Norman (1940). According to the revisionists, agriculture was growing quite quickly, internal trade was flourishing, fertility was being deliberately held in check by late marriage and infanticide, and literacy rates were rising.[8] This latter was particularly important according to Minami (1994: 16–17) because it provided Meiji Japan with a high quality labour force which was willing to accept new types of technology:

> Meiji Japan's greatest inheritance from the Tokugawa period was an abundance of eligible labour . . . The quality of the labour force . . . was excellent. It was able to adapt easily to the new social and economic order, and meet the needs of modern industries when they began to expand rapidly. The extent of education is, we believe, the major reason for the quality of the labour force. . . . It was probably because of their education that labourers from agricultural areas were able to absorb the necessary training and become skilled at their new jobs.

This same argument is repeated in Minami, *et al.* (1995: 17–19), and made clearly by T. C. Smith (1988: 44) in respect of the Japanese textile industry:

> My argument is that the growth of the modern textile industry was made possible by the specific skills, attitudes, roles, capital accumulations, and commercial practices brought into being mainly during the period of 'premodern growth'. . . . The preindustrial values incorporated in the emergent factory system were not immemorial. Insofar as they included willingness to work for long periods off the farm for wages and were associated with industrially

useful skills, they were mainly the product of the Tokugawa period, and of its last century especially. Modern Japanese industry took over these new preindustrial values, changing them in the process, although—as many observers have noticed—less than one would think.

More generally, one might argue that Japan's high social capability was instrumental in allowing it to exploit Western technology. There is no question that imported (largely British) innovations were extremely important in the late nineteenth century;[9] most of the equipment used in the cotton textile industry came from Platt Brothers of Oldham (Saxonhouse, 1985; Francks, 1992; Minami, *et al.*, 1995; Morris-Suzuki, 1995). But without its high level of social capability, Japan would have been unable to exploit this scope for catch-up to the full.

Yet the paradox in the social capability argument is that it is supported by the Japanese evidence, but *not* in the way that these economists imply. Rather, it is more plausible to portray Japanese growth in the late nineteenth century as comparatively slow because social capability was limited. The evidence on this is rather strong. First, the Japanese growth rate was not very impressive when compared with countries at a similar level of development in the same era. At 2.6 per cent per annum between 1885 and 1919, Japanese growth was below the rates achieved in Germany (2.8 per cent) and the USA (3.9 per cent) between 1870 and 1913 (Ohkawa, *et al.*, 1974: 225; Maddison, 1991: 49–50). It also fell short of the growth rates achieved by Taiwan and Korea as Japanese colonies in the 1930s (Myers and Peattie, 1984). Secondly, the Tokugawa record on education was not—pace Dore—especially distinguished. The obvious comparison is with Britain on the eve of her Industrial Revolution. There, male literacy rates stood at 56 per cent in 1775 rising to 65 per cent by 1800 (Sanderson, 1991; Crafts, 1995: 754). Even more significantly, analysis of convict data suggests that female literacy rates exceeded 80 per cent by about 1800 (Nicholas and Oxley, 1993: 740). From this perspective, Japanese social capability was poor. Third, there is little to suggest that the Japanese workforce was well-suited to the factories of the late nineteenth and early twentieth centuries. The reality of late nineteenth-century Japanese modernization was therefore that the Tokugawa legacy played at best only a modest role. Rather, Meiji Japan created its own social capability. Even then, its creation was rather belated. As late as 1890, more than two decades after the restoration, only 49 per cent of 6–9-year olds were enrolled in primary education. Only thereafter did the pace of advance increase, such that the figure reached 99 per cent by 1920 (Inada, *et al.*, 1992: 236). Not surprisingly, the rate of economic growth accelerated as a result; during the 1930s, driven by rising government spending and the impact of devaluation, growth exceeded 5 per cent per year (Ohkawa, *et al.*, 1974: 225).[10]

This is not to argue that human capital played no role in propelling the growth of the Meiji economy. As Kiyokawa (1984; 1987) has pointed out, the growth of cotton textiles, Japan's leading sector in the second half of the Meiji period, would surely not have been as impressive but for the skills of its 'factory girls'. Furthermore, some accounts of working conditions in Japan's cotton mills are exaggerated. As Mosk (1996: 94–6) has recently shown, females recruited by the cotton mills were on average more undernourished than the female population as a whole, but there is little evidence that having to work in the cotton sector was the cause of that under-nutrition. Even so, the very fact that the dominant technology in the cotton sector was ring-, rather than mule-spinning, was a partial reflection of the low quality of the Japanese labour force (Francks, 1992; Howe, 1996). In sum, therefore, we may fairly conclude that Japan's social capability was more limited in the late nineteenth century than has sometimes been alleged.

By contrast, rapid diffusion of European technology to the USA during the nineteenth century (and later its capacity to generate innovation) can be explained by the higher social capability of the USA (North, 1994; Abramovitz and David, 1996). Traditional class structures, a greater emphasis on class distinctions and 'the persistence of pre-industrial social values' (Abramovitz and David, 1996: 55) all operated to Europe's disadvantage. As Abramovitz and David (ibid. 59) say:

> America's third advantage lay in the sphere of social capability. Its egalitarian and secular outlook made wealth and economic attainment the basis of social distinction, made business a respected occupation, and directed education and science to material ends. In Europe, by contrast, the social outlook was still colored by an aristocratic residue.

Of course, social capability was not the only factor determining American technological leadership. As Abramovitz and David point out, it also enjoyed the benefits of abundant natural resources and a large market. It also benefited from an influx of skilled migrants from Europe itself. Further, Abramovitz and David perhaps exaggerate America's superior social capability; there was nothing egalitarian about prevailing attitudes towards women or the indigenous population. Moreover, it is not clear that the spread of capitalist 'attitudes' from the USA would have helped Britain very much. For example, a number of Marxist writers have suggested that Britain's 'failure' after 1870 occurred because its transition to capitalism was too thorough. By eradicating some of the pre-capitalist institutions—such as a strong and interventionist state—Britain's capacity to modernize its economy was reduced (Wood, 1991). For all that, however, there is still more than an element of truth in the Abramovitz–David analysis.

Finally, a word about the way levels of human capital facilitated technological diffusion in post-war LDCs. The evidence for a number of Asian countries is summarized in Table 4.1. It reveals what is already well known: the successful East Asian NICs (Hong Kong, Singapore, Taiwan, and South Korea) all began their period of rapid growth with adult literacy rates that were well over the 30 to 40 per cent level typically regarded as a requirement for rapid growth. In the cases of Hong Kong and South Korea in particular, literary rates were exceptionally high by LDC standards. It is hard to believe that these literacy rates were unimportant in facilitating the diffusion of new industrial technologies from the West and from Japan. As Amsden (1989) rightly observes, South Korean growth—and late industrialization more generally—was based firmly upon a process of industrialization by learning.

TABLE 4.1. *Initial literacy rates and the pace of growth in Asia, 1960–1980*

Country	1960 adult literacy rate (per cent)	Growth of real per capita GNP (per cent per annum)
Hong Kong	70	6.8
South Korea	71	7.0
Singapore	50	7.5
Taiwan	54	7.2
Sri Lanka	75	2.4
India	28	1.4

Sources: WDR (1982: 110–11, 154–5); James, *et al.* (1989: 194–5); *Taiwan Statistical Databook* (1990: 1).

And according to Rodrik (1996: 20):

by the late 1950s the East Asian economies had for the most part a much better educated labor force than would have been expected on the basis of their income levels . . . This may have made it much easier to establish a competent bureaucracy (as well as enhancing the productivity of interventions aimed at boosting private investment.

The data in Table 4.1 also provide a clear reason for India's failure to generate rapid industrial growth despite the abundant scope for catch-up in the post-war era. With a literacy rate of only 28 per cent in 1960, India's level of human capital formation was well below the norm in the successful Asian economies. According to Drèze and Sen (1995: 13):[11]

The remarkable neglect of elementary education in India is all the more striking given the widespread recognition, in the contemporary world, of the importance of basic education for economic development. Somehow the educational aspects of economic development have continued to be out of the main focus, and this relative neglect has persisted despite the recent radical changes in economic policy.

Much the same seems true for sub-Saharan Africa, where literacy averaged less than 30 per cent in 1970 (WDR, 1990) and for Pakistan and Bangladesh, where literacy rates had reached only 36 per cent even by 1992 (Drèze and Sen, 1995: 215). Moreover, amongst rapidly growing developing countries after 1960, only Nigeria combined a low initial level of literacy (15 per cent) with fast growth and this undoubtedly reflected her development of oil production, which required little by way of a large, literate workforce. But note that Table 4.1 also illustrates the dangers inherent in seeing human capital levels as the sole determinant of growth. Sri Lankan GDP per capita, despite its 75 per cent literacy rate in 1960, grew at only 2.4 per cent between 1960 and 1980, largely because of greater emphasis on meeting basic needs and redistribution (as well as a high per capita income level in 1960) instead of growth at all costs.

1.2. Sectoral redeployment of factors of production

Initial conditions may also favour a country if it 'finds itself' (perhaps after a revolution of some sort) with its factors of production deployed in low-productivity sectors. One obvious example of a low-productivity sector is defence. However, the more usual approach emphasizes the role of surplus labour. The classic analysis of this phenomenon is the two-sector model outlined by Lewis (1954).[12] The meaning of surplus labour is as follows:

> an unlimited supply of labour may be said to exist in those countries where population is so large relatively to capital and natural resources, that there are large sectors of the economy where the marginal productivity of labour is negligible, zero, or even negative. . . . Whether marginal productivity is zero or negligible is not, however, of fundamental importance to our analysis. (Lewis, 1954: 141–2)

Lewis (1954: 141–45) identifies at least five sources of surplus labour: agriculture, traditional services (employers and employees), retainers, women in the household, and population growth. This model is, however, essentially one which focuses on the demand-side. In it, capital accumulation is the engine of growth; it is this which shifts outwards the demand for labour in the modern sector (Lewis, 1954: 151–2). The role of surplus labour is to ensure that the labour supply curve is horizontal; it thus prevents the real wage from rising (which could choke off accumulation).

The process whereby surplus labour is absorbed by industry implies that labour is redeployed from a low-productivity sector (typically agriculture) to a high-productivity sector (industry). Total output therefore rises as static inefficiency is eliminated. It follows that, because LDCs are typically characterized by an abundance of surplus labour, they can grow explosively in the early stages of development. It is in this sense that surplus labour constitutes a favourable initial condition for growth.[13]

The Lewis model in effect assumes that surplus labour exists because of market failure. The real wage rate in the modern sector is higher than in the traditional sector, and this causes a deadweight loss. In addition, unless the capital market functions perfectly, the (financial) surplus will also be misallocated. As Williamson (1991) points out, this latter is likely to involve a much more serious economic cost (at least if one makes plausible assumptions about the propensities to invest out of profit and rent respectively). But both problems stem from the failure of the labour market to clear. If that market was efficient, labour would migrate from the low- to the high-wage sector, thus equalizing real wage rates. This type of market failure is particularly acute, it is usually argued, in state socialist economies. There, institutional barriers to labour mobility, e.g. the need for internal passports, will interact with limited information and transaction costs to severely restrict labour mobility. The solution to the problem is therefore apparent. LDCs, especially state socialist ones, need to create an efficient labour market. By so doing, they will be able to grow extremely quickly.

However, the Lewis model is vulnerable to a number of very serious objections. For example, it is by no means obvious that labour can be released from agriculture except during the seasonal slack period; many LDCs are characterized by full employment in rural areas during the harvest peak. Nor is it obvious that traditional sector labour is paid a (subsistence) wage higher than its marginal product (Jorgenson, 1966). A further problem is that there may be obstacles to migration which are not easily removed because they are not due to a readily identifiable institution. In Industrial Revolution Britain, for example, most surplus agricultural labour was to be found in the south midlands and south-east of England (Allen, 1992), whereas modern industry was centred in Lancashire and Yorkshire. Even though there were few institutional constraints on mobility, much of the labour 'released' by agriculture simply remained underemployed in its region of origin (Williamson, 1991). In other words, its contribution to industrialization was negligible. As Allen (1992: 262) concluded:

During the eighteenth century agriculture in the south midlands was modernized, so that labour on the farm would be used efficiently. This reorganization did not accelerate the rate of economic growth, however. All it did was to turn the midlands into an even more perfect example of an underdeveloped country. The problem was not overcome, the surplus labour not sopped up, until the end of the nineteenth century. The basic problem was that the agricultural revolution came too soon. Instead of contributing to the growth of manufacturing, the premature release of labour from agriculture caused nothing but poverty.

Another criticism of the Lewis model is that labour may not be absorbed by the modern sector because of labour-saving technical progress; migrants are still attracted because migration decisions are based on expected rather than actual income (Todaro, 1969). In addition, as Krugman (1995) points out, the conditions necessary for the very existence of a modern sector are stringent.[14] Given that the modern sector has to attract workers from the traditional sector by paying a wage premium, it can only do so if its productivity is also relatively higher. Furthermore, it may only be able to generate such low unit-labour costs (via economies of scale) if product demand is high. In other words, a 'Big Push' (Rosenstein-Rodan, 1943) may be needed to establish a viable modern sector in the first place. It is also often argued that the Lewis approach is no more than a justification for 'urban bias' because, in common with Third World *praxis* in countries as diverse as Kenya and the USSR, the model ignores the need to increase agricultural production (Lipton, 1977; Bates, 1981; Varshney, 1993). This view is also to be found in the writings of other economists, such as Hans Singer (1992: 73):

The Arthur Lewis model was also indicative of another weakness in the type of development prevalent during the Golden Years, namely a comparative neglect of agriculture. In this model and much related thinking, the main function of agriculture was to provide rural surplus labour as the cannon fodder of industrialization. . . .

Moreover, even if industry is constrained by labour shortages, the problem is often solved in developing countries by population growth in *urban* areas instead of migration. In fact, much of Britain's urban population was born in the cities themselves, a process brought about by a fall in the age of marriage for women (Wrigley and Schofield, 1981). To be sure, massive spatial and occupational labour transfers took place during the First Industrial Revolution.[15] Crafts (1985: 62–3) estimates that the share of the male labour force in agriculture fell from 61 per cent in 1700 to 29 per cent by 1840, and Williamson (1991: 44) shows the rate of rural out-migration rising from 0.6 in 1811–16 to a peak of over 1.5 per cent per year in the 1840s and 1850s. As a consequence, immigration accounted for 60 per cent of urban population growth between 1776 and 1811. But the experience of Britain in the *early* years of industrialization was very unusual. At the height of the Industrial Revolution (1811–46), rural–urban migration in Britain accounted for only 46 per cent of urban population growth. In developing countries during the 1960s and 1970s, it accounted for only 40 per cent of city growth (Williamson, 1990: 28). Moreover, the absolute size of the rural population often remains constant or even rises during the industrialization process; that was the experience of Britain, just as it was the experience of Japan until the 1930s. Only in a relative sense was there a release of labour. In other words, the 'normal' experience during the development process is for the bulk of the increase in urban population to come from natural growth within the cities themselves. There was therefore in principle no reason why China could not have gone down the same route during its transition.

In addition to these criticisms, there are three further very serious objections to the Lewis model. First, labour-transfer models typically ignore potential demand-side problems. It is, for instance, not difficult to develop a theory in which—by assuming mark-up pricing, spare capacity, and a differential savings function along standard Kaleckian lines—a rise in the mark-up (or conversely a fall in the real wage rate) will reduce investment (Dutt, 1984). This is because aggregate demand falls as income is redistributed from workers to capitalists. In other words, falling real wages in the urban sector caused by in-migration may cause a realization crisis which could bring the growth process to a halt. Lewis argued that a *rise* in the real wage rate might be fatal for economic growth based on unlimited supplies of labour but the possibility of a realization crisis makes the impact of a *fall* in the real wage equally devastating.

Second, labour surplus models ignore the point that labour is different from other factors of production in that it is not a mere commodity. If agricultural labour is transplanted from rural areas, and put to work in a factory environment, alienation is almost inevitable. This is precisely what happened in the 'dark satanic mills' of Lancashire and Yorkshire in the early nineteenth century, and in the textile factories of Japan in the late Meiji period. Indeed, as Tsurumi (1990) shows, the 'factory girls' were so alienated by their conditions of work that turnover rates were extremely high (compared in particular to textile mills in British India). Factory owners responded by trying to keep their workforce *in situ* by housing it in dormitories sealed off by barbed-wire fences and patrolling guards. Nor was their motivation helped by their limited education. In Osaka, the capital of the textile industry, 42 per cent of women employees had received no education at all and only 8 per cent had received the compulsory four years of elementary education (Taira, 1978: 198). According to Francks (1992: 204):

> It would be hard, however, to present the experience of the early Japanese textile industries in creating their factory labour force as a model of the transformation of surplus labour resources into productive industrial workers. Neither does it suggest that the attitudes and approaches of early Japanese industrial workers and employers embodied traditional values which. . . . eased the transition into factory work.

The labour force employed in proto-industry in rural Japan was similarly alienated, at least to judge by the wave of strikes that occurred in the early Meiji period.

Alienation has serious implications for labour-surplus models. The Lewis result depends upon marginal labour productivity remaining more or less constant (at a given wage rate) in the industrial sector as labour migrates. But if the migrating workforce is alienated, that will certainly not be the case. In fact, marginal productivity will fall sharply—and may fall so much that there is no net output gain at all from labour transfers.[16] In other words, the entire model is exploded in the presence of alienation. There is no point in transferring labour to industry because the migrants become so disaffected that labour productivity is depressed to the level prevailing in agriculture. And although this result is likely to be an extreme case (and is an unlikely long-run result), it is simply invalid to assume—as most surplus-labour models do—that marginal labour productivity can be assumed unchanged during the analysis.

Finally, the transfer of surplus labour may not promote growth because of its implications for capital accumulation. It may even retard growth. Precisely because the effect of migration is to hold down the industrial real wage, firms may be discouraged from undertaking both investment and labour-saving innovation.[17] Why invest in new machinery when labour is available in abundance? Arguably this is what happened in Britain during the Industrial Revolution when the investment share was only about 10 per cent of GDP (Crafts, 1985), far less than has been the norm in labour-scarce Asian economies like Singapore and Hong Kong.

To be sure, some of these criticisms of the Lewis model have been overstated. An activist government can regulate aggregate demand and thereby ensure that the realization problem mentioned by Krugman and Dutt is avoided. In addition, a careful reading of both evidence and literature suggests that agriculture has rarely been 'dismissed' as being unimportant; in that sense, the 'urban bias' school is criticizing a straw man. Stalinist theory certainly saw rapid growth as dependent upon investment in heavy industry, which in turn required the extraction of resources from the agricultural sector. Nevertheless, even Stalin recognized the need to raise agricultural output. The only way to attain that end was by means of institutional change designed to redistribute inputs in favour of the most productive class in the countryside—the peasantry. Land reform was the first step along that road, but it was to be followed by collective farming and mechanization. Now one can of course argue that this dual strategy of investment in heavy industry and institutional reform in agriculture was misconceived; but it can hardly be alleged that there was no attempt to develop agriculture even in the Soviet Union.

Moreover, Lewis himself was at pains to point out that agriculture could not be neglected if development was to be successful:

Now if the capitalist sector produces no food, its expansion increases the demand for food, raises the price of food in terms of capitalist products, and so reduces profits. This is one of the senses in which industrialisation is dependent upon agricultural improvement; it is not profitable to produce a growing volume of manufactures unless agricultural production is growing simultaneously. This is also why industrial and agrarian revolutions always go together, and why economies in which agriculture is stagnant do not show industrial development. (Lewis, 1954: 173)

The importance of agriculture was also underlined in the writings of Michal Kalecki (1963: 51) who saw the principal financial constraint on economic development as the slow growth of farm production:

In other words the rate of increase of supply of necessities . . . as fixed by institutional barriers to the development of agriculture, determines the rate of growth of national income. . . . This seems to me the gist of the problem of financing economic development in a mixed economy. . . . the main 'financial' problem of development is that of inadequate agricultural production. The key to 'financing' a more rapid growth is the removal of obstacles to the expansion of agriculture, such as feudal land-ownership and domination of peasants by money-lenders and merchants.

At the end of the day, however, it is the criticisms of the Lewis model that carry most conviction. In the British case, there is little evidence that the misallocation of labour cost the economy a great deal. According to Williamson, the deadweight loss due to wage gaps was only 0.6 per cent of GNP in 1831. Even if one makes capital quasi-mobile—i.e. recognize that some of the profits made in agriculture would have migrated to industry if the wage gap between the two sectors had been eliminated, thus raising industrial investment—the cost of labour-market failure is still only 3.3 per cent (Williamson, 1991: 71–3). Given that real GDP was growing by that order of magnitude per year, it is hard to see labour-market failure as a significant break on industrialization.

Furthermore, the attempt by Kaldor (1966) to use a labour surplus model of the Lewis type to explain slow growth (relative to other countries) in post-war Britain proved ultimately unconvincing even for Kaldor himself. Central to Kaldor's original model was the idea that growth depended upon a large manufacturing sector because there was much more scope for productivity growth there than in other sectors of the economy. The required labour could not be extracted from agriculture because Britain's agricultural sector was already far smaller in employment terms than most other OECD economies and because its labour productivity was quite high relative to both its industrial sector and the agricultural sectors of other European economies. According to Kaldor (1966: 303):

Britain, having started the process of industrialization earlier than any other country, has reached 'maturity' much earlier—in the sense that it has attained a distribution of the labour force between the primary, secondary and tertiary sectors at which industry can no longer attract the labour it needs by drawing on the labour reserves of other sectors . . . manpower shortage is the main handicap from which we are suffering, and once our thinking becomes adjusted to this, we shall, I hope, tend to concentrate our efforts on a more rational use of manpower in all fields, and to limit the absorption of labour into those sectors in which . . . the marginal social product is likely to be appreciably below the marginal private product.

The only option open to the Labour government of the 1960s was therefore to extract labour from the service sector; and this it tried to do using selective employment tax. A similar sort of idea underpinned the model put forward by Bacon and Eltis (1976) that the non-market sector was 'crowding out' market-sector investment.

But the argument was not very convincing. Rowthorn (1975) was rather dismissive, and Kaldor (1975) admitted that he had by then changed his mind about his 1966 approach: the British problem was one of inadequate demand growth caused by a balance of payments of constraint, not labour shortages.[18] Furthermore, there is very little empirical evidence to support the Bacon and Eltis view (McCombie and Thirlwall, 1994: 103–19). None of this is especially surprising; it is hard indeed to argue that Britain was suffering from labour shortages following the re-emergence of mass unemployment after 1973.

There is of course ample evidence that agriculture released labour in most countries during their early industrialization. For the Soviet Union, recent estimates by Barber and Davies suggest a fall in the agricultural workforce from 61.6 million in 1926 to 48.2 million by 1939; over the same period, industrial employment rose from 6.3 to 23.6 million (Davies, *et al.*, 1994: 91, 277). Ellman (1979: 94, 98) makes the point more forcefully: 'The increase in the labour force came mainly from agriculture and was fed on food obtained from agriculture.' But it is hard to argue that this process promoted output growth; the release of labour from agriculture during 1928–32 was of course associated with a massive famine. Consider also Taiwan. There, the share of agriculture in total employment fell from 55 per cent in 1953–6 to 14 per cent by 1988 (Thorbecke, 1992: 16). According to Fields (1980; 1991), this is a classic example of what he calls 'modern sector enlargement growth'—that is, the Lewis model—driven by the relatively labour-intensive nature of Taiwanese industrialization. As Fields (1980: 230–2) says: 'Taiwan's ability to create sufficient industrial jobs for the workers released from agriculture contrast with the experience in most LDCs of growing underemployment in low-level jobs, especially in the cities, in areas like commerce and services.' However, the abundance of cheap labour in the 1950s and early 1960s may actually have delayed the development of capital-intensive modern industrial products; certainly Taiwan's growth performance during the 1950s was unimpressive.

In short, and even though the labour surplus model has been a central part of the explanation for growth usually offered by the master discourse, it is very unconvincing. Surplus labour may offer a potential advantage to developing countries, but the pitfalls are arguably much greater than the opportunities. This suggests on *a priori* grounds that it probably will not help very much in explaining growth in transition-era China, but a full discussion is deferred to Chapter 7.

1.3. Growth-Retarding Institutions

The third way in which initial conditions may facilitate growth is the most general in that we can think of all manner of institutional obstacles which prevent an economy with a high capital–labour ratio from operating on its production function even though labour and capital have been deployed in (notionally) high-productivity sectors. Typical obstacles which have been singled out in the literature include collective farming, high marginal rates of taxation, state ownership of industrial enterprises, and insecure property rights. This sort of analysis has been applied to Eastern Europe in 1989. These countries had created an extensive capital stock by then (especially their stock of human capital), but were unable to exploit its potential because of their state socialist economic systems. But once capitalist institutions were properly introduced, these economies grew quickly. Arguably this has happened in Eastern Germany, Poland, and the Czech Republic in the early 1990s.

However, this takes us into the vexed question of the role of the state in the economy, which not only influences institutional frameworks but every other aspect of the growth process. It takes us away from what have been called above the 'proximate' determinants of growth, and towards the deeper forces at work. A discussion of the role of the state is therefore deferred to the end of the chapter. But what does need to be said at this stage is that it is hard in practice to translate the high capital–labour ratio into a high level of per capita output. It is one thing to say that all a country has to do to grow quickly is to replace socialist institutions with capitalist ones, but quite another to do it (even supposing that the capitalist institutions are more efficient). As Russia (in particular) has discovered, the creation of well-defined and enforceable property rights is a long and painful process.

2. The Accumulation of Physical Capital

Although Adam Smith wrote extensively on the subject of economic growth, the first systematic account was offered by David Ricardo (Pasinetti, 1974; Pasinetti, 1977; Hènin, 1986). At the heart of Ricardo's theory of growth was investment by industrial capitalists. Whereas landlords were unproductive 'wastrels', industrial entrepreneurs consumed little and instead allocated their profits to capital accumulation, thus raising the level of output and employment. Nevertheless, Ricardo's theory was imbued with Malthusian pessimism. Pasinetti (1974: 6) summarizes Ricardo's view thus:

> The process of transforming profits into capital, however, cannot go on indefinitely. Owing to diminishing returns of new capital (and labour) applied to the same quantity of land, or to less fertile lands, rent increases over time . . . and consequently the profit-rate continuously falls. When the rate of profit has fallen to zero, capitalists are prevented from accumulating any more; the growth process stops and the system reaches a *stationary state*.

Ricardo did not doubt that technical progress would occur. However, it would be resisted by landowners and its labour-saving bias would make it unsustainable because of the unemployment consequences. As a result, technical progress could only delay and not prevent the advent of the stationary state. The same was true of free trade. By making wage goods available at a low price, free trade would help to hold down money wage demands and hence increase profits; Ricardo's campaign for the abolition of the Corn Laws followed directly from this analysis. But once again, these profits would not sustain accumulation indefinitely because of diminishing returns to capital. From a modern perspective, it is evident that Ricardo was too pessimistic. Long-run technical progress has not gone hand-in-hand with spiralling unemployment and the stationary state has not been reached. Nevertheless, the emphasis placed on capital accumulation as a motor of economic growth is hard to gainsay, and in this sense Ricardo's contribution to explaining economic growth was extremely important.

Accumulation was also of course at the heart of Marx's theory of capitalist economic growth. The reason for this was neither animal spirits (Keynes), nor religion (Weber), but the impact of competition:

> . . . the development of capitalist production makes it constantly necessary to keep increasing the amount of capital laid out in a given industrial undertaking, and competition makes the immanent laws of capitalist production to be felt by each individual capitalist, as external coercive laws. It compels him to keep constantly extending his capital, in order to preserve it, but extend it he cannot, except by means of progressive accumulation. . . . Accumulate, Accumulate! That is Moses and the prophets!. (Marx, 1867: 555, 558)

Although Marx seems to have argued that accumulation enabled the capitalist to benefit from increasing returns and the embodiment of new technology, these assumptions are not needed to produce the Marxian result. Provided there is at least one capitalist prone to reinvest and that investment is financed out of profits (i.e. investment is self-financing), competition will force other capitalists to follow suit unless they wish to see their share in the stock of capital becoming progressively smaller (Marglin, 1984: 54–5).[19]

The emphasis in Marx's writings on the role of capital accumulation in the growth process provided the starting point for the development of the celebrated theory of G. A. Feldman (1928). Feldman seized upon the distinction made by Marx (1885: 399) between Department I (that sector of the economy producing means of production) and Department II (producing articles of consumption). Feldman showed that the rate of growth would be faster if the proportion of the capital stock (and therefore investment) allocated to Department I was higher. This result is admittedly very sensitive to its assumptions. Unless one assumes identical gestation periods and capital–output ratios in the two sectors, a very long time horizon, and a closed economy, the Feldman result does not hold (Ellman, 1979: 126). Nevertheless, the Feldman model provided the foundation for economic policy in the Soviet Union and in Maoist China, and a variant of it formed the basis of the policy advocated by Mahalanobis for post-independence India.[20]

Many of the ideas of the classical economists are also to be found in the celebrated work of Lewis (1954). As we have seen, Lewis' central message was that economic development requires the mobilization of surplus labour in agriculture and its reallocation to the industrial sector. But Lewis also argued that it was investment by capitalists in the modern sector that drove the growth process. Indeed capital accumulation was indispensable for economic growth:

> The central problem in the theory of economic development is to understand the process by which a community which was previously saving and investing 4 or 5 per cent of its national income converts itself into an economy where voluntary saving is running at about 12 to 15 per cent of national income or more. This is the central problem because the central fact of economic development is rapid capital accumulation (including knowledge and skills with capital). (Lewis, 1954: 155)

Keynes' work too led to an emphasis on the role of investment in the growth process. Although *The General Theory* was confined to analysing the short period, his key idea—that investment determines output and hence savings—led naturally to the proposition that the rate of growth of output was also a function of the rate of growth of the capital stock. This notion was formalized by Harrod (1939), who offered what was in essence a model of multiplier–accelerator interaction (Samuelson, 1939). With investment determining output via the multiplier, and output in turn determining investment via the accelerator, here was a clear model of the growth process in a capitalist economy.[21] To be sure, the model was not especially convincing. One of Harrod's conclusions was that the natural and warranted growth rates could only be equal by a fluke—thereby suggesting that economies would be condemned either to secular inflation or stagnation. The result rested on his rather improbable assumption that the four variables in question (growth of the labour force, the pace of technical progress, the savings propensity, and the marginal capital–output ratio) were all exogenously determined, as Solow (1956) pointed out. We can perhaps agree that the four are unlikely to change rapidly in the short term even if they are endogenous (as is true of the capital–labour ratio in neoclassical models); in that sense, the spirit of the Harrod model is correct. However, his conclusion seemed strongly at odds with the 'golden age' growth experienced in the OECD countries between 1950 and 1973—as did his second result that divergence between actual and warranted rates was likely to produce explosive results. Nevertheless, the importance of capital in the growth process is as clear in the Harrodian approach as it was in the earlier models of Ricardo and Marx.

Two more appealing theories of growth were those developed by Michal Kalecki and Joan Robinson. Kalecki's *Theory of Growth in a Socialist Economy* (1963, iv. 16) has the growth rate of output (r) determined by the investment share (I/Y), the capital–output ratio (m), depreciation (a) and the degree of capacity utilization (u) via the equation:

$$r = (1/m) \cdot (I/Y) - a + u.$$

The task for the planners is therefore to vary the investment share so as to bring the actual growth of output into line with potential output growth (as determined by technical progress and the growth of the labour force). However, and contrary to the views of many of the planners, Kalecki did not regard investment increases as an instant panacea (Kalecki, 1963, iv. 28–9). Indeed, a feature of his work is the recognition of a government decision curve whereby the state must decide whether the gains from a higher investment share in terms of higher long-run consumption outweigh the costs in terms of lower short-run consumption (Kalecki, 1963, iv. 32–7, 274–6). Kalecki, however, offered little in this theory on the determinants of technical progress, which is assumed exogenous. His focus was rather on the need to embody knowledge and novel ideas in new capital.

By contrast, Joan Robinson's *Accumulation of Capital* (1956) and *Essays on the Theory of Economic Growth* (1962) stressed the two-way relationship between profits and investment, an idea first developed by Kalecki as a way of explaining the business cycle. On the one hand, investment created profits by raising the level of aggregate demand. On the other hand, the level of (expected) profit determined the desired rate of accumulation (Asimakopulos, 1977; 1991; Marglin, 1984). According to Robinson (1962: 47):

> The central mechanism of our model is the desire of firms to accumulate, and we have assumed that it is influenced by the expected rate of profit. . . . Valuing the existing stock of capital on the basis of the same rate of profit . . . the double-sided relationship between the rate of profit and the rate of accumulation now appears.

There is no presumption in this model that the rate of profit falls as accumulation increases; the relationship between the two is linear in Robinson's diagram. And technical progress is not ignored; Robinson's notion of a 'golden age' is an equilibrium between the desired growth rate (determined by animal spirits and the savings propensity) and the natural growth rate (determined by population growth and technical progress). Nevertheless, accumulation is to the fore throughout the model and indeed technical progress is at least in part determined by animal spirits (largely ignored by Kalecki) via investment.

The best-known model of growth is that of Robert Solow (1956).[22] In the long run, the growth of output is determined exogenously by the rates of growth of technical progress and the labour force; per capita growth therefore depends solely on technical progress. In this long run, investment plays no role in determining growth. Increases in capital per worker raise output per worker—but at a dwindling rate because of diminishing returns—until finally the marginal productivity of capital becomes zero.[23] In other words, the economy simply moves along its production function. Nevertheless, Solow (1970: pp. xxii–xxiv) later accepted that this type of model rather downplayed the role of investment because it took no account of its importance in embodying technical progress. That is, investment does not *cause* technical progress, but increases in knowledge are of no avail unless embodied in new investment:

> The formal model omitted one mechanism whose absence would clearly bias the predictions against investment. That is what I called 'embodiment', the fact that much technological progress, maybe most of it, could find its way into actual production only with the use of new and different capital equipment. . . . A policy to increase investment would thus lead not only to higher capital intensity, which might not matter much, but also to a faster

transfer of new technology into actual production, which would (p. xxiii). . . . if we suppose that all . . . these countries had access to roughly the same pool of technological innovations, then it appears that the ones that invested fastest were best able to take advantage of the available knowledge. (Solow, 1970: p. xxiv)

In the short and medium term—up to 100 years in a neoclassical model according to Sato (1966)—investment is likely to be much more important. This is because an increase in savings (which is assumed to translate one-for-one into investment in the Solow model) will change the steady state capital–labour ratio. In the process of transition from one steady state to another, the growth rate of per capita income will rise.

As already mentioned, two rather different processes need to be distinguished. In the first, the economy is moving from a disequilibrium towards its already existing superior steady state. In the second, the economy starts in equilibrium, and then experiences a increase in its savings rate which creates a new superior steady state. In the first case, the economy starts from a position of disequilibrium in which per capita output and the capital–labour ratio are low (it is assumed to be on its production function). In this scenario, the savings rate has increased in a previous time period, making possible the attainment of a superior long-run steady state. Growth occurs because the supply of savings is greater than investment demand. In effect, this economy is still in the process of converting its higher savings rate into a higher capital–labour ratio. It will take time for it to converge on its steady state, and during that transitional period growth will be rapid.

In the second case, achieving growth is more difficult. By contrast, the problem is that the increase in the savings rate already achieved in the first case has still to be accomplished. In other words, policies and institutions need to be devised to raise the savings rate. Without such a shift in the savings function, no growth will occur (ceteris paribus) because the economy is already in a low level equilibrium. Once, however, an increase in the savings rate can be achieved, growth will occur in exactly the same way as in the first case.

The Solow model does not imply that technical progress has no role in the short term; it will still raise growth by shifting the production function outwards. But in the transition to the steady state, it must share the limelight with capital accumulation. In other words, movements along and shifts in the production function together drive short-run growth. The *relative* importance of technical progress and investment in the short run thus remains an open question in the Solow model. It can only be resolved by country-specific empirical evidence. Some countries may be better at (or prefer to rely on) capital accumulation. Others may wish to remain in the steady state and grow simply by shifting their production function outward at a given capital–labour ratio. And, as will be discussed at the end of this chapter, the respective roles of state and market in the economy may be critical in determining the relative importance of technical progress and capital accumulation.

An interesting attempt to quantify the roles of accumulation and technical progress is the recent work of Young (1992; 1995). His growth-accounting exercise applied to Hong Kong, South Korea, Singapore, and Taiwan found that total factor productivity growth[24] had played only a small role in their post-1945 economic miracles—whereas investment was crucial; the view was supported by Krugman (1996). Young's results are summarized in Table 4.2.

TABLE 4.2. *The contribution of total factor productivity to economic growth in East Asia, 1966–1991*

Country	Total factor productivity growth (per cent per annum)		
	Period	Economy-wide	Manufacturing
Hong Kong	1966–91	2.3 (3.4)	n/a
Singapore	1966–90	0.2 (1.3)	–1.0
South Korea	1966–90	1.7 (2.2)	3.0
Taiwan	1966–90	2.1 (2.1)	1.7

Note: Data in parentheses are World Bank estimates for 1960–85 (World Bank, 1993*a*: 52–3).
Source: Young (1995: 672).

Young (1995: 674–5) concluded that the emphasis on factor accumulation in neoclassical theory allowed it to readily explain the East Asian experience:

If the remarkable postwar rise in East Asian living standards is primarily the result of one-shot increases in output brought about by the rise in participation rates, investment to GDP ratios, and educational standards and the intersectoral transfer of labour from agriculture to other sectors with higher value-added per worker, then economic theory is admirably well suited to explain the East Asian experience. Neoclassical growth theory . . . can explain most of the differences between the performance of the NICs and that of other postwar economies.

Perhaps the most important implication of these results is that the long-run future for the Asian economies (especially Singapore) is bleak. Precisely because their growth has been based almost entirely upon unsustainable factor accumulation, there is every reason to expect their growth to slow markedly in the near future. It is therefore an easy step to argue that the 1997–8 crisis heralded the onset of this period of slower growth. If these Asian economies wish to achieve sustained growth, they must raise their productivity growth rates by means of technical progress. As Young says (1992: 50) 'it is clear that Singapore will only be able to sustain further growth by reorienting its policies from factor accumulation toward the considerably more subtle issue of technological change' (Young, 1992: 50). It is partly for this reason that Krugman (1996) argues that there are clear similarities in the growth process in Singapore and the former Soviet Union.

The results obtained by Young and others are controversial, as we will see. But their conclusion that investment in physical capital played an important role in East Asian growth is not. There is hardly an economist in the world who would disagree with that proposition. Many would go further, and argue that capital accumulation is usually one engine of growth for developing countries. In large measure, this is because the evidence that capital 'matters' for countries at the early stage of development is very strong. In Japan, modern industrialization coincided with an increase in the investment share in current price GNP from 12 per cent in 1885 (when reliable data start to be available) to 25 per cent on the eve of war with China in 1937 (Ohkawa, *et al.*, 1974: 178). Although some Japan specialists have argued that growth was export-led (Blumenthal 1972; Shinohara 1962), the overwhelming consensus is that investment was much more important (Minami 1986). And it has continued to be important even after 1945. In Kenya, GDP per capita grew at 3.9 per cent per annum between 1965 and 1973 under the presidency of Jomo Kenyatta; over the same period, gross domestic investment (GDI) grew by 16 per cent per annum. Between 1978 and 1992 (under Daniel Arap Moi), however, GDI fell by 0.3 per cent per year and GDP per head grew by only 0.3 per cent per annum (WT, 1992; 1994). In other words, there is a strong correlation between the trend in investment and the trend in GDP per head. Finally, the experience of the Soviet Union in the 1930s is worth a mention. There the share of net investment in NNP rose from 10 per cent in 1928 to 23 per cent in 1937. Over the same period, real GDP at purchasing power parity rose at 5.4 per cent per year (Davies, *et al.*, 1994: 270–2). Not surprisingly, perhaps, Harrison (1994: 48) concluded: 'The Soviet economic transformation of 1928–40 was driven largely by investment.'

The main area of disagreement amongst theorists centres on the long-run neoclassical conclusion that per capita growth ultimately depends solely on technical progress, and therefore that capital accumulation does not matter. There are three reasons for this. First, growth accounting studies have found that capital accumulation still contributes significantly to growth in the mature economies of North America and Europe. Second, studies using different methodologies have reached a similar conclusion. Third, a number of theories have been put forward to explain why investment in physical capital will always be important.

First, the growth accounting studies. In the case of the USA, Jorgenson and Griliches (1967) demonstrated that growth in the long run could be explained almost entirely in terms of factor accumulation, reducing the residual to a mere 0.1 per cent (Hènin, 1986: 207–8). Although Jorgenson later retreated from this rather extreme view and increased the contribution to 0.3 per cent (Hènin, 1986: 208; Fagerberg, 1994: 1150), Jorgenson (cited in Srinivasan, 1995: 55) put the contribution of TFP at only 22 per cent, well below that of capital (44 per cent).[25] A more recent general study of international economies is that of Kim and Lau (Lau, 1996). Kim and Lau made a number of important non-neoclassical assumptions: increasing returns to scale, non-neutral fully embodied technical progress, and profit maximization. These assumptions lead to TFP being reduced almost to zero across a wide range of countries (Tables 4.3 and 4.4).

These tables show two important results. First, they confirm Young's conclusion that capital accumulation was crucial in Asian growth. Irrespective of whether embodied technical progress is attributed to capital or to technical progress in the growth-accounting, the result is the same: technical progress explains none of the

TABLE 4.3. *Kim and Lau's growth-accounting results*

Country	Sources of growth since World War II (per cent)			
	Physical capital	Labour	Human capital	Total factor productivity
Hong Kong	63	20	17	0
Singapore	63	19	18	0
South Korea	61	20	19	0
Taiwan	70	14	16	0
France	86	−1	8	6
Japan	88	6	4	2
UK	57	4	9	29
USA	53	31	7	9
W. Germany	92	−7	9	6

Note: The precise years involved in this study are not specified. Here embodied technical progress is attributed to capital; see Table 4.4.

Source: Lau (1996: 80).

growth achieved in East Asia since World War II. Second, capital accumulation played a critical role even in the mature North American and European economies. Take the USA. Even if embodied technical progress is not attributed to capital, Kim and Lau still find that 64 per cent of post-war growth had nothing to do with technical progress. And if embodied technical progress is attributed to capital, then a massive 53 per cent (Table 4.3) of post-war US growth was due solely to investment in physical capital. For West Germany, the figure is an almost incredible 92 per cent. Lau (1996) summarizes these findings thus:

> Embodiment also reaffirms the central role of new gross fixed investment in economic growth—without new gross fixed investment, the benefits of technical progress cannot be realized. Thus, because of embodiment, physical capital turns out to be the most important source of economic growth not only for the developing countries in the postwar period, but also for the developed countries as well. (p. 89)
>
> . . . while the hypothesis of no technical progress can be decisively rejected for the developed countries, it cannot be rejected for the East Asian developing countries. Consequently, while technical progress, or the 'residual', is the most important source of economic growth for the developed countries, it plays no role in the economic growth of the developing countries, which can be attributed in large part to capital accumulation. (p. 88)

A second reason for believing that capital accumulation matters even in mature economies is the work done outside growth-accounting frameworks. In particular, many economists have sought to explain slow post-war British (and US) growth—both classic examples of mature economies—in terms of low rates of investment. The Cambridge approach of the 1970s and early 1980s (Kaldor, 1957; 1961; Singh, 1977; Eatwell, 1982) argued that the UK economy was balance of payments constrained. This constraint restricted the growth of aggregate demand, which in

TABLE 4.4. *The contribution of technical progress to growth*

Country	Percentage of output growth explained by technical progress, when:	
	Embodied technical progress attributed to technical progress	Embodied technical progress attributed to physical capital
Hong Kong	0	0
Singapore	0	0
South Korea	0	0
Taiwan	0	0
France	58	6
Japan	45	2
UK	49	29
USA	36	9
W. Germany	61	6

Source: Lau (1996: 80).

turn constrained profits and therefore investment. As investment was critical in embodying new technology (dynamic economies of scale), low rates of investment were doubly damaging. Many British economists continue to take this view (Glyn, 1992; McCombie and Thirlwall, 1994; Rowthorn, 1995; Godley, 1996). According to Kitson and Michie (1996: 200–1):

> the growth of the UK's manufacturing gross capital stock has been inferior to that of the other major industrial nations [CMB: the G5 countries]. This is most evident during the 1979–89 period, when although there was a worldwide slowdown in the growth of manufacturing investment, the United Kingdom was the only country of the five not to experience any growth in the manufacturing capital stock. . . . The dismal investment record of UK manufacturing since the 1960s has been a major cause of Britain's indifferent growth performance, constraining technological progress and the expansion of demand.

Will Hutton's *The State We're In* (1995: 98) made the same point to a wider audience: 'any explanation of British performance that does not incorporate poor investment is plainly inadequate.'

The relatively poor investment record of the UK emerges clearly from the comparative international data on manufacturing (Table 4.5). In each of the three periods, British investment in equipment grew significantly less fast than the G5 mean. Moreover, in every case but one (the USA during 1964–73) Britain lagged behind its principal competitors. Even when due weight is given to the relative maturity of Britain's manufacturing sector and the decline in manufacturing output that has occurred in the post-war era, Britain's poor investment performance is hard to deny. For an economy that has to produce and export manufactures if it wishes to balance the balance of payments at full employment and socially acceptable rates of inflation and inequality, this is a dismal record.

TABLE 4.5. *Growth of the gross value of equipment in G5 manufacturing sectors, 1964–1989* (per cent per annum)

	1964–73	1973–9	1979–89
UK	4.6	2.6	0.2
USA	4.2	5.0	2.4
W. Germany	7.6	2.9	1.7
France	7.8	3.5	1.7
Japan	14.0	5.5	5.0
Mean	7.6	3.9	2.2

Source: Kitson and Michie (1996: 41).

None of this evidence on Britain is decisive. Yet even those who are critical of the notion of a balance of payments constraint direct their criticism at the role of the balance of payments rather than at the assumption that profits matter for investment. Eltis (1996: 191–2), for example, argued that low UK investment in manufacturing was largely a consequence of low profitability, itself deriving in large measure from weaknesses in labour skills and management. And the Thatcherite project of the 1980s started off from the premiss that it was necessary to rebuild British profitability in order to promote investment in (*inter alia*) new equipment in order to raise labour productivity (Brenner, 1998). The route chosen—a full-scale attack on organized labour—may have been different from the Cambridge approach, but the underlying objective was much the same.

A third reason to believe that capital accumulation matters even in the long run for growth is the development of new theoretical perspectives on its role, and how its contribution should be measured. The ideas are not especially new. The essential point was made by Kaldor as early as the beginning of the 1960s:

> the rate of shift of the production function due to the changing state of 'knowledge' cannot be treated as an independent function of (chronological) time, but depends on the rate of accumulation of capital itself. Since improved knowledge is, largely, if not entirely, infused into the economy through the introduction of new equipment, the rate of shift of the curve will itself depend on the *speed of movement* along the curve, which makes any attempt to isolate the one from the other the more nonsensical. (Kaldor, 1961: 263)

However, more recent work has helped to clarify this point, and has added a number of new perspectives. Perhaps the most important recent theoretical attempt to focus the attention of economists on the role of investment is that of Maurice Scott (1989). In essence Scott argues that all technical progress is due to investment, and therefore that it is impossible to distinguish between shifts in, and movements along, a production function. Conventional growth accounting finds that TFP is significant only because it incorrectly measures the capital stock. That is, it fails to properly account for the relative price effects that stem from improvements in the quality of physical assets. McCombie and Thirlwall (1994: 129) summarize Scott's view thus:

> Scott contends that the treatment of technical progress in growth theory as an exogenous factor distinct from the rate of investment is meaningless. He argues that the residual found in the growth accounting approach must be attributable to measurement error, and in particular, is the result of the way that the capital stock is conventionally measured. Once this error is corrected, Scott finds that the residual disappears. . . . Scott's central thesis is that, as a matter of definition, all technical change should be attributed to investment if the latter is broadly defined to include all expenditures incurred to increase future consumption at the cost of forgoing some present consumption.

The importance of capital accumulation also features in other new growth theories. This is especially true of the work of De Long and Summers (1992; 1993). They agree that the rapid growth of East Asia (Hong Kong apart) largely reflects their success vis-à-vis factor accumulation:

> In our regressions, growth in East Asia has not been extraordinarily high, in the sense of diverging from the general pattern given the macroeconomic fundamentals. Growth has been rapid, yes: but we would have expected growth to be rapid because fundamentals—especially rates of equipment accumulation—have been very favorable. Hong Kong is the sole outstanding positive outlier. (De Long and Summers, 1993: 413)

The significance of this model is that it assumes that investment in equipment generates externalities; it is thus a model of endogenous growth In other words, the Solowian assumption of diminishing returns to capital is overturned and, by implication, long-run growth can be sustained by capital accumulation. Moreover, they found that the social rates of return to equipment investment were high (about 20 per cent per annum) and about half of it is in the form of higher TFP (De Long and Summers, 1992: 159). Equally importantly, they found strong evidence that even poor countries with limited human capital could benefit from higher equipment investment:

> One might think that . . . poorer developing countries lack the human infrastructure to support machine technology and are unable to benefit from high rates of accumulation. We believe this fear is overdrawn. Relatively poor economies appear to benefit as much as do richer economies from an investment effort concentrated on machinery and equipment. Rapid growth is found where equipment investment is high, and slow growth where equipment investment is low. (De Long and Summers, 1993: 396)

These theories stressing the long-run importance of investment in physical capital have not been without their critics. For example, Oulton and Young (1996) found little evidence of externalities to investment in capital equipment. Crafts (1996: 174) cites a number of sources suggesting that the post-war decline of the UK is due more to lack of spending on R&D and skills than to lack of equipment investment (which generates few positive externalities). D. N. McCloskey (1981; 1990) has long been sceptical of those who claimed that late Victorian Britain could have grown much more quickly if only overseas investment had been repatriated. Rather ironically in the light of his recent writings, Crafts was one of those criticized. McCloskey's view was simply that this investment would have had little effect because of diminishing returns:

> . . . Crafts apparently knows better than his grand-parents. They could have had a quarter more consumption in 1911 simply by passing a law in 1871 banning all investment abroad. What a marvel of ingenuity is such economics! . . . By keeping savings at home the British people could have had two Forth Bridges, two Bakerloo Lines, two London Housing stocks, two Port Sunlights. The common sense of this piece of political economy is, of course, that the rate of return would be driven down to nil. So deep is his fascination with arithmetic of growth, however, that Crafts does not notice this problem. (McCloskey, 1981: 133)

Furthermore, Romer (1993: 545) also sees the De Long and Summers perspective as dangerous in the sense that it implies that LDCs must sacrifice consumption in order to raise investment:

> Recent work emphasizing object gaps has therefore lent a pessimistic, almost Calvinistic tone to policy advice. 'These countries are poor because they consumed too much in the past and did not accumulate like we did. To achieve a better standard of living, they must tighten their belts, reduce their current standard of living, accumulate more capital and pay for a better system of public education.'

If instead, as Romer argues, the main problem in LDCs is an 'ideas' rather than an 'object' gap (limited access to ideas rather that any shortage of capital equipment), the problem can be solved by encouraging faster rates of technology transfer without requiring any restriction on consumption.

Nevertheless, despite these important qualifications, the three findings of plausible theoretical reasons for the continuing importance of capital,[26] growth-accounting results which attribute much of the growth of mature economies to investment, and non-accounting studies of the UK and USA which reach the same conclusion together present a compelling case. There is therefore every reason to suppose that Chinese growth after 1978 also owed much to the accumulation of physical capital.

3. Human-Capital Formation

In contrast to those who emphasize capital accumulation as the motor of economic growth, other economists have stressed the role of the labour force. This approach in turn can be divided into two theories: those which stress increases in the size of the labour force, and those emphasizing labour force quality.

Those writers who stress the size of the labour force as a source of growth accept that population growth will tend to reduce both the capital–labour ratio (Coale and Hoover, 1958) and the land–labour ratio (Malthus). In that sense, population increases are an obstacle to economic growth. However, it has often been alleged that population increases will still have a positive impact by promoting technical progress (Boserup, 1981; Simon, 1977; Kremer, 1993). The precise arguments vary. Boserup (1981) sees a rising population density as desirable because it makes possible the construction of irrigation and other infrastructure. But she also suggests that population growth spurs innovation by initially reducing per capita income ('necessity is the mother of invention'). For Kuznets and for Simon (1977, 1981), a larger absolute population means more inventive talent. This idea has been infused with new life by endogenous growth theory because knowledge is regarded there as a non-rival good. By linking this with the views of Kuznets and Simon, Kremer (1993) argues that technical progress will be a function of absolute population size.

All these theories are problematic. The empirical evidence is against them: the vast populations of China, India, and Bangladesh did not make them the home of the first industrial revolution. The Boserup 'necessity' argument seems to imply that low per capita income should be associated with technical progress—which again receives little support from the evidence. And an obvious objection to the Kuznets–Simon–Kremer view is surely that, if ability is randomly distributed amongst the population, for every genius there is also born a destroyer of civilizations. Even if there is a correlation between technical progress and the absolute size of world population, the more plausible causal hypothesis is from technical progress to population, rather than the converse.

More recent theories have stressed the importance of improving the quality of the labour force rather than merely increasing its size (Mankiw, *et al.*, 1992; Barro and Lee, 1993; Mankiw, 1995). Recent developments in neoclassical growth theory —responding to the challenge offered by endogenous growth theory—stress the importance of *raising* the level of human capital; that is, it posits a causal link running from rates of growth of human capital to rates of growth of per capita income.

This sort of approach is again not especially novel: development economists have long been aware of the importance of human capital. However, it is only recently that attempts have been made to incorporate human capital in an explicit fashion into the Solowian model (these theories are usually called augmented neoclassical models)—and then more by way of a response to endogenous growth theory than anything else. This augmented neoclassical approach has been formalized by Mankiw, *et al.* (1992) and Mankiw (1995). The basic equation is:

$$Y_j = K_j^{1/3} H_j^{1/3} A L_j^{1/3}.$$

Here Y is output, K capital, and L labour. A refers to knowledge, which is assumed to be the same in all countries. The subscript j indicates that this is a production function for firm j. The novelty lies in the introduction of H (human capital), which varies across countries. It functions in the same way as physical capital in that it too is subject to diminishing returns; the justification for this is essentially the work of Psacharopoulos (1985).[27] In this type of augmented neoclassical model, growth rates differ between countries because of differences in human capital. It is not that countries do not have access to knowledge. Rather, the problem is that they are unable to use it fully. Mankiw (1995) summarizes this view clearly:

> Knowledge refers to society's understanding about how the world works. Human capital refers to the resources expended transmitting this understanding to the labour force. Put crudely, knowledge is the quality of society's textbooks; human capital is the amount of time that has been spent reading them. (p. 298)

Even though knowledge is undeniably important for economic growth, theories of the creation of knowledge may be of little help in explaining international differences in growth rates. Knowledge, as opposed to capital, travels around the world fairly quickly. State-of-the-art textbooks are available in the poorest countries. . . . For understanding international experience, the best assumption may be that all countries have access to the same pool of knowledge, but differ by the degree to which they take advantage of this knowledge by investing in physical and human capital. (p. 301)

To be sure, this theory has done a rather better job of making sense of the empirical evidence than the original Solow model; introducing human capital does substantially raise the R^2 in cross-country regressions. Nevertheless, it has not found favour with endogenous growth theorists. It is easy to see why. For one thing, a model of this type implies a massive real wage differential in favour of poor countries where skill shortages are acute. That in turn suggests that we ought to see a large-scale migration of skilled workers from rich to poor countries. But neither migration nor wage differentials are anything like as large as predicted by the model (Romer, 1995: 317). The second objection is even more compelling, namely that there is widespread evidence of barriers to knowledge transfer *within* countries, let alone across countries. Patents, licensing agreements, the role of government (e.g. restricted access to libraries) or simply lack of interest in new ideas all serve to limit the international diffusion of knowledge. As Romer (1993) puts it, countries and firms alike suffer from an ideas gap.

Nevertheless, there is probably something in the view that growth is slow in many LDCs because of inadequate investment in human capital. Human capital may not rescue the Solow model, but it is entirely plausible that skill shortages can constrain growth. This sort of idea has been frequently discussed by development economists since World War II. Theodore Schultz (1960; 1961) was of course the pioneer in this field, arguing that 'While land per se is not the critical factor in being poor, the human agent is: investment in improving population quality can significantly enhance the prospects and welfare of poor people' (1990: 282–3). To be more precise, education can be viewed as promoting economic development in the following ways. First, by enhancing human capital, education increases (potential) labour productivity and real wages. The private rate of return to primary education in this respect is particularly high. Secondly, female education in particular is powerfully but inversely correlated with fertility, and its promotion thus serves to reduce the rate of population growth. Thirdly, education has been seen to play a powerful role in reducing undernourishment, as well as making possible the introduction of simple but extremely effective forms of preventive medicine (Drèze and Sen, 1990: 262).

Perhaps even more importantly, some new growth theorists have argued that human capital formation drives growth not just directly but also by producing externalities (Lucas, 1988; 1993). According to him, there are significant positive social rates of return to investment in human capital (externalities). A well-educated workforce tends to be more responsive to new ideas and new technology, and in this way the diffusion of knowledge is much faster. Moreover, a country well-endowed with human capital will be better able to attract and keep 'footloose' capital in the form of multinational enterprises. Respect for the law and a demand for democracy are also likely to be enhanced by universal education. Thus according to Lucas (1993: 270):

> The main engine of growth is the accumulation of human capital—of knowledge—and the main source of differences in living standards among nations is differences in human capital. Physical capital accumulation plays an essential but decidedly subsidiary role.

This quotation makes it clear that Lucas has in mind a slightly different notion of human capital than the standard Mankiw, *et al.* formulation. The idea can be expressed more formally as (Lucas, 1988):

$$Y_j = A(H)F(K_jH_j).$$

In this set-up, technical progress (A) is tied to human capital, rather than simply being exogenous.

Nevertheless, and even though both endogenous and neoclassical theorists see human capital as important, the idea is not without its critics, largely because high levels of expenditure on education in developing countries are thought to cause serious opportunity costs (Little, 1982: 189–93). At one level, as Little points out, it is not obvious how much education adds to human capital; qualifications are highly regarded by employers because they serve as a screening device rather than because qualifications carry with them firm-specific skills. Developing countries have invested heavily in education also have to contend with the emigration of skilled labour; in some countries, the emigration rate amongst graduates is 20 per cent (UNDP, 1994: 65). Given that it is virtually impossible to prevent emigration by professionals, it may be that countries would do better to invest less in higher education, and more in guaranteeing universal primary education. Furthermore, the payment of high real earnings to those possessing formal qualifications is not in itself a proof that education raises productivity or, indeed, of excess demand for skilled labour. Some LDCs are in fact typically characterized by an over-supply of educated workers, and the offer of high wages is a convenient device whereby a firm can signal its recruiting preferences rather than a manifestation of labour shortages. Moreover, for standard efficiency wage reasons (Akerlof and Yellen, 1986), firms typically pay a wage well above the market-clearing rate to discourage on-the-job shirking. An additional problem, at least from a policy viewpoint, is that the social returns to education are invariably below the private returns—which makes the case for state expenditure on education extremely problematic, at least on efficiency grounds. As Little (1982: 192) says, 'Private returns are almost without exception higher than social returns, government subsidies outweighing any tax recouped.'

In addition, education systems in LDCs have often to serve to promote anti-developmental values as much as skills. The Meiji government in Japan certainly used compulsory primary education as a means to enhance the skill level of the workforce. However, education also fulfilled a socializing function by inculcating habits of obedience, and deference to hierarchy. According to Crawcour (1988: 403): 'Its aim, like that of conscription, was to create loyal subjects and docile workers, and it was effective in producing Japanese who not only did what they were told but even believed and felt what they were told to believe and feel.' Of course, this subservience arguably helps to promote economic growth; the growth of both South Korea and (especially) Lee Kuan Yew's Singapore can, and has, been interpreted in this way. Nevertheless, the dangers of the approach are apparent from the Japanese experience. It is, for example, hard to believe that Japanese imperialism in the 1930s and 1940s would have occurred if its population had been educated in the liberal tradition, and if its institutions of government had been thoroughly democratic. Sen (1989) argues that famine avoidance may often depend upon a free press and a democratic opposition. The same may also be true of imperialism (and is arguably supported by the response of citizens to US involvement in Vietnam).

The evidence also suggests a positive link between the growth of human capital and that of per capita output. To be sure, the 'classical' British case suggests that industrialization can take place against a background of *declining* literacy. For example, Sanderson's (1991: 14–17) summary of the evidence shows clear evidence of declining literacy in Lancashire between *c*.1750 and 1820. More recent work by Nicholas and Nicholas (1992) shows that literacy rate of convicts transported to Australia as rising up to 1807 in urban areas, before declining to the levels of the 1790s by 1835 (Mitch, 1993: 276). For transported English females, the evidence suggests a virtually unbroken increase in illiteracy between 1795 and 1825 (Nicholas and Oxley, 1993: 740). Mitch (1993: 303–4) therefore concludes:[28]

> In sum, there is little evidence to suggest that education played a central role in England's Industrial Revolution, suggesting in turn that it has been possible for economies to compensate for poorly educated work forces with other offsetting advantages. This is not to say that education made no contribution whatever. . . . But there is little support for the view that the contribution of education was central. Perhaps the most telling point is the minimal extent of the shift of the labor force towards occupations likely to make use of formal education.

The broader international evidence points, however, to a different conclusion (Table 4.6). These data are, of course, far from easy to interpret. Few would claim that improved education is the only important factor in determining the pace of economic growth and accordingly there are a multitude of alternative explanations that can be suggested for the growth patterns observed in the table. Many, for example, believe that a programme of selective protection and subsidization of the nascent export sector lies at the heart of the East Asian economic 'miracle' (White, 1988; Wade, 1990; Amsden, 1989). Yet there is support in the table for the view that fast economic growth requires a rapid improvement in the educational level of the workforce, as well as a high initial level. This is most clear in the Taiwanese case, where fast economic growth has been associated with tremendous improvements in both secondary enrolment rates and literacy. Sri Lanka provides a negative example of the same phenomenon. Largely as a result of declining educational expenditure after 1960 (spending on education fell from 4.7 per cent of GNP

TABLE 4.6. *Education and economic growth*
(growth rates during 1960–1980; per cent per annum)

Country	Literacy	SECENR	GNP per capita
Sri Lanka	0.7	3.6	2.4
India	1.5	1.6	1.4
Brazil	1.3	5.8	5.1
Hong Kong	1.5	6.2	6.8
South Korea	1.6	5.6	7.0
Singapore	3.1	3.2	7.5
Taiwan	3.1	4.7	7.2

Note: SECENR = secondary school enrolment rates as percentage of age group. Literacy rates are for the population aged 15 and over.

Sources: WDR (1982: 110–11, 154–5); James, *et al.* (1989: 194–5); *Taiwan Statistical Databook* (1990: 1).

in 1960/1 to 2.9 per cent by 1980—Bhalla, 1988: 92), literacy and secondary enrolment rates show relatively modest rates of improvement over the period. According to Sen (1988), and not unreasonably, this suggests a positive relation between growth and educational improvement. Of course, the relationship is far from tight. Brazil provides the obvious exception. There, GNP per head grew by over 5 per cent even though the improvement in literacy was only modest, with primary school enrolment rates actually declining (unlike every other country in the sample). It is true that secondary enrolment rates did increase sharply but that had more to do with Brazil's extremely low base than an especially meritorious performance. Standing at only 11 per cent in 1960, Brazil's secondary enrolment rate was barely half that of India and, accordingly, a fast rate of improvement was a relatively simple matter.

More generally, most development economists agree that human capital growth is an important part of the growth process (World Bank, 1993*a*: 48–54). This conventional wisdom has been strongly reinforced by more detailed examination of the rise of East Asia. One such examination, in seeking to determine the percentage contribution of factor accumulation to East Asian growth, produce the results shown in Table 4.7. Although investment in physical capital was important, these data show the critical role played by investment in primary education. This result is confirmed by estimates of the private and social rates of return on different types of education. For primary education, the private rate of return is more than 25 per cent compared to about 17 per cent for secondary education. Primary education also yields a higher social rate of return, 18 compared to 11 per cent (World Bank, 1993*a*: 198).[29] Only Japan of the economies in Table 4.7 shows a very large return on secondary education. This doubtless reflects both her early transition to universal primary education and her comparatively high per capita income level by 1965.

TABLE 4.7. *Sources of per capita GDP growth in Asia, 1960–1985* (percentage contribution to GDP per capita growth by source)

Country	Primary enrolment rate	Secondary enrolment rate	Percentage share of investment in GDP
Hong Kong	86	23	46
Indonesia	79	7	49
Japan	58	41	38
South Korea	67	19	38
Malaysia	73	14	47
Taiwan	69	19	36
Singapore	75	22	43
Thailand	87	13	35

Note: As is the norm in growth-accounting exercises, the sum of the causal factors can be either significantly under or over 100.

Source: World Bank (1993*a*: 52–3).

The implications from all this for China seem clear. The international evidence (with a small number of exceptions) points to a positive role for human-capital formation in the growth process. This is very much in line with the predictions of both augmented Solowian and Lucasian models.

4. Technical Progress

Technical progress is an elusive notion, but broadly involves three different concepts: invention (the development of an idea), innovation (the translation of the idea into a workable piece of machinery), and diffusion (the widespread use of the new machinery in the economy). Most theories of technical progress have focused on invention and innovation, and to these we will come in due course. But countries can grow simply by diffusing an existing technology across their economies. Our discussion begins, therefore, with the process of diffusion.

4.1. Diffusion of New Technology

The role played by the diffusion of technology, and in particular the way it interacts with initial social capability, was discussed in the first part of this chapter. There is no need to repeat that discussion here. However, there is little agreement on whether diffusion always plays a key role in the growth process. That is obviously true for the world leader which by definition cannot base its growth upon the diffusion of technology developed elsewhere.[30] But there are other countries too which may have grown without diffusion playing a major role. In particular, the notion that technological diffusion has played a key role has been largely rejected by the master discourse as an explanation for East Asian growth. Its response to diffusion arguments is not to deny that technological diffusion has occurred in many countries, especially in East Asia. Nor does it deny that high levels of human-capital formation contribute to the absorption of diffused technology. Instead, the master discourse contends that diffusion contributed very little to growth: that must be the case because growth accounting for East Asia has found that TFP contributed only insignificantly. The logic here is that the East Asian economies were over-regulated. As a result, much of the technology transferred was inappropriate and, secondly, the technology that was transferred was misused. In other words, the development of sophisticated, heavy industrial plants in (say) South Korea did very little to raise output growth. This is the clear implication of Lau's (1996) results summarized in Table 4.4. Even if one classifies embodied technical progress as measured by TFP rather than by capital accumulation, the underlying result remains the same: embodied technical progress made a zero contribution to growth.

Ultimately the role played by diffusion in growth can only be addressed by considering the evidence. Before doing that, however, it is convenient to look at theories of invention and innovation.

4.2. The Role of Invention and Innovation

The literature on invention and innovation is far more extensive than that on diffusion. Marx viewed capital accumulation as the mainspring of economic growth in the nineteenth century; that much is clear from the title of his most famous book. Nevertheless, in so far as technical progress is discussed, Marx offers what amounts to an endogenous theory of innovation. For example, he argues that the development of the steam engine by James Watt was a response to the invention of machines rather an independent causal factor in UK industrialization (Marx, 1867: 355). Furthermore, the invention of a wide range of machinery in Britain during the eighteenth century—which heralded the dawn of Modern Industry, or machinofacture—was only possible because of the age of manufacture, by which Marx means handicraft industry. Manufacture was important because it created a skilled workforce which could later be used in the modern industrial sector (Marx, 1867: 361). In a sense, therefore, Marx argued that capital accumulation preceded the inventions of the Industrial Revolution.

Most modern theories of economic growth have seen technical progress as one of the key elements in the process, especially in the long run. In essence, these theories can be divided into four categories.[31] First, there is the traditional neoclassical view exemplified by the work of Solow (1956) in which innovations are an exogenous public good. The second type of theory, this time an endogenous approach to innovation, is the AK model. This takes the approach pioneered by Alfred Marshall, and John von Neumann (1937). That is, the mobilization of inputs, whether capital or human capital, creates spillovers or externalities in the form of new ideas and techniques. Here innovation occurs via the endogenous process of 'learning by doing'. More recently, AK models have been developed by Romer (1986) and Lucas (1988). The third class of models are usually called neo-Schumpeterian. They derive from Joseph Schumpeter's view that innovation depends upon the activities of entrepreneurs and that a degree of monopoly power is conducive to innovation because it allows firms to earn quasi-rents. Many of these ideas were taken up by Nelson and Winter (1982), Rosenberg (1994), and other institutional economists. More formal endogenous growth models in which innovation is no longer relegated to the status of a mere externality have of course been developed by Romer (1990), Grossman and Helpman (1989), and many other economists during the 1990s. The fourth and final approach to technical progress is that offered by Nicholas Kaldor (1966; McCombie and Thirlwall, 1994). Here technical progress is caused by demand growth, a relationship often known as Verdoorn's Law.

The basic Solowian model is based on a production function of the form:[32]

$$Y = F(K, AL).$$

Here Y is net output, A the level of technology, K is capital stock and L the labour supply.[33] The key point is that the growth of factor inputs has no effect on per capita output in the long run; technical progress alone determines the growth of per capita output. Moreover, technical progress (A) is fully exogenous and is a public good; in the words of Joan Robinson, technology is 'like the gentle dew that floats down from heaven'. In the more prosaic language of Solow:

> . . . the permanent rate of growth of output per unit of labor input is independent of the saving (investment) rate and depends entirely on the rate of technological progress in the broadest sense. (Solow, 1970: p. xii)

In fairness, we have seen earlier that Solow was not entirely happy with this approach because it ignored the role of capital in embodying technical progress; Solow wrote a number of papers which stressed that point. Nevertheless, the important point for our purposes is not the details of his approach, but the fact that here for the first time was a well-developed growth model that put technical progress in the forefront of a theory of long-run economic growth.

Formalization of the second approach to technical progress did not begin until the 1980s. However, the work of Arrow (1962) and Kaldor (1957) led the way by developing models of 'learning by doing' in which the act of investment resulted in learning by entrepreneurs—in other words, endogenous technical progress. Kaldor put the matter thus:

> The advance in scientific knowledge in physics or in the science of engineering in the laboratory cannot by itself secure the innumerable design improvements that result from the repeated application of particular engineering principles. The optimum design for the steam engine or for the diesel engine or the sewing machine has only been achieved after many years or decades of experience . . . The gain in design through experience is even more important in the making of plant and equipment. (Kaldor, 1972: 381)

This notion of technical progress could only be modelled by assuming that none of the gains accrued to the firm. Without that assumption, the axiom of convexity (perfect competition) would have to be abandoned. Not that this worried Kaldor overmuch; the title of the 1972 lecture from which the quotation is drawn was 'The

Irrelevance of Equilibrium Economics'. But the need to treat endogenous technical progress as an externality if neoclassical models were to be retained discouraged research on the subject. Moreover, when Paul Romer and Robert Lucas did succeed in reviving interest in the 1980s, the early models they put forward were little more than formalizations of the Kaldor–Arrow approach. The similarity of the approaches is clear from the following equations:

$$Y_j = A(K)F(K_j L_j). \qquad \text{(Arrow, 1962)}$$

$$Y_j = A(R)F(R_j K_j L_j). \qquad \text{(Romer, 1986)}$$

The notation is as before, except that R here is expenditure on research and development. In each case, there are spillover effects resulting from physical capital accumulation (Arrow)[34] and spending on research and development (Romer).[35] Crucially, these externalities offset diminishing returns at the level of the firm and allow growth to continue in the long run.

As these models were simple linear models which retained the assumption of perfect competition and gave firms no apparent incentive to engage in R&D spending—an implication plainly falsified by the evidence—they were not especially satisfactory even to their proponents. Romer (1994: 20) states explicitly that he was glad to be able to reject his own early model of endogenous growth. By doing so he was able to address the observed fact that firms conduct R&D in order to benefit from the quasi-rents that such expenditure generates (Romer, 1991: 104). Even so, he took the view that both neoclassical and linear endogenous models have contributed much to our understanding of growth:

> The neoclassical model made the fundamental contribution of showing that a nonrival good—knowledge or technology—has to be taken seriously within models of growth. Models with spillovers that focus on the effects of increasing returns at the level of society as a whole demonstrate effects that will still be present if the equilibrium is one with monopolistic competition instead of price taking with spillovers. (Romer, 1991: 107–8)

These insights are nevertheless eclipsed by those offered by neo-Schumpeterian models in which endogenous technical progress and oligopoly co-exist. The original insight was Schumpeter's, who characterized capitalism as an evolutionary process of creative destruction rather than a stationary mechanism for efficient resource allocation at a moment in time (Schumpeter, 1943: 82–3). That evolution was not driven by shocks, population, capital, or 'the vagaries of monetary systems'. Instead, the prime mover was innovation, broadly defined to comprise new methods of production, new methods of transportation, new forms of organization, new markets, and new goods for the consumer. His early writings (*The Theory of Economic Development*, first published in German in 1911) tended to glorify the entrepreneur himself as the source of innovative ideas,[36] and in the process neglected the role of industrial research (Nelson and Winter, 1982: 277–8). Catephores (1994: 28) summarizes this Schumpeterian attitude towards the entrepreneur thus:

> [Schumpeter] firmly believed that strong, brilliant and original individuals were the only ones who created wealth, material affluence, progress for themselves and for everybody else. He

believed in leaders. They were the only ones to merit serious consideration on the part of the social scientist. To them he gave his heart.

This whole approach is very Weberian.[37] Instead of Weber's 'charismatic leader' overcoming the trammels of bureaucracy, we have the heroic entrepreneur overcoming the timidity of his contemporaries (Schumpeter, 1943: 132). It is clear that Schumpeter rather cast himself in this role late in life; he yearned to be 'the best lover in Vienna, the best horseman in Europe, and the greatest economist in the world' (Catephores, 1994: 8). More generally, this analysis of the source of innovation was decidedly problematic in ignoring Marx's insight that the entrepreneur has no choice but to innovate if her firm is to survive and flourish. Marx (1867, ch. 14, section 5 n.) in fact emphatically denied a decisive role for the heroic individual:

The simple belief in the inventive genius exercised a priori by the individual capitalist in division of labour, exists nowadays only among German professors. . . . The more or less extensive application of division of labour depends on length of purse not on greatness of genius.

By the time he came to write *Capitalism, Socialism, and Democracy* (1943), Schumpeter too had come to see the sources of industrial innovation in a less romantic light.[38] For charismatic entrepreneurship, he substituted the hard graft of teams of industrial researchers. Innovation was increasingly being 'reduced to routine' that was carried out by teams of 'trained specialists', bureaux, and committees (Schumpeter, 1943: 96, 132–3).

Schumpeter's other critical insight was to see monopoly as a factor which promoted rather than retarded technical progress. To be sure, it was an obstacle to static resource allocation; if that were the only goal of an economic system, one could not but agree with the merits of perfect competition as extolled by orthodox economic theory. But if the aim was to promote economic growth, an element of monopoly power had much to recommend it. Pricing behaviour was one obvious case in point. Under monopoly, prices diverge from marginal cost in the short run. But in the long run, monopoly power brings benefits to the consumer because the technical progress which it allows makes possible the introduction of new products, which have the effect of reducing costs 'per unit of service' (Schumpeter, 1943: 92). Moreover, perfect competition is incompatible with technical progress because it eliminates the supernormal profits/quasi-rents needed to motivate the entrepreneur in the first place:

Perfect competition implies free entry into each industry. . . . But perfectly free entry into a new field may make it impossible to enter it at all. The introduction of new methods of production and new commodities is hardly conceivable with perfect—and perfectly prompt—competition from the start. And this means that the bulk of what we call economic progress is incompatible with it. As a matter of fact, perfect competition is and always has been temporarily suspended whenever anything new is being introduced. (Schumpeter, 1943: 104–5)

These sorts of ideas became the staple of the second wave of endogenous growth theories that appeared in the late 1980s and 1990s (Romer, 1990; Krugman, 1990, ch. 11; Aghion and Howitt, 1992; Grossman and Helpman, 1991; 1994; Young, 1993). The assumption of perfect competition was abandoned, and instead the interaction of monopolistic profits and innovation (especially the production of new products) was emphasized. The result was a formal theory of economic growth in which the creation of quasi-rents served as both motivation and reward for innovation. The policy implication was clear:

> . . . a subsidy to physical capital accumulation may be a very poor substitute for direct subsidies that increase the incentive to undertake research. In the absence of feasible policies that can remove the divergence between the social and private returns to research, a second-best policy would be to subsidize the accumulation of total human capital. (Romer, 1990: S99).

A final approach to technical progress is offered by Nicholas Kaldor (1957, 1961). Kaldor emphasizes the role of capital accumulation in embodying technical progress. In that sense, his model is one of endogenous technical progress. His starting point was the 'stylised fact' about economic growth that 'over longer periods, income and capital tend to grow at the same rate' (Kaldor, 1961: 230–1). In other words, there was no reason to accept the neoclassical assumption of diminishing returns to investment.[39] This was because technical progress was a function of investment:

> whether the increase in output will be more or less than proportionate to the increase in capital will depend, not on the state of knowledge or the rate of progress in knowledge, but on the *speed* with which capital is accumulated, relatively to the capacity to innovate and infuse innovations into the economic system (p. 264). . . . There is therefore no *unique* rate of technical progress—no unique rate at which alone a constant rate of growth can be maintained. There is a whole series of such rates, depending on the rate of accumulation of capital being relatively small or large . . . [this] explains why there is no long-run tendency to a falling rate of profit, or for a continued increase in capital in relation to output. (Kaldor, 1961: 264–5)

The key determinant of the investment that embodied technical progress was demand growth. Demand was important for three reasons. First, by raising profits, it allowed a faster rate of investment because the bulk of investment is financed out of profits. Secondly, higher profits provided the resources to finance a higher level of spending on research and development. Thirdly, higher demand increased the degree of capacity utilization. As firms typically maintain excess capacity as a way of deterring entry into the market, the increase in demand would prompt higher investment over and above any effect it had on the rate of corporate profitability. This analysis was the basis of Kaldor's version of Verdoorn's Law—that there is a direct causal link between the rate of growth of demand and the rate of (labour) productivity growth via the intermediation of technical progress in the manufacturing sector. According to Kaldor (1966: 288):

[there is an] empirical relationship between the growth of productivity and the growth of production which has recently come to be known as the 'Verdoorn Law'. . . . It is dynamic rather than a static relationship—between the rates of change of productivity and of output, rather than between the level of productivity and the scale of output—primarily because technological progress enters into it, and is not just a reflection of the economies of large-scale production.

Kaldor presented two alternative specifications of Verdoorn's Law:[40]

$$e = a + bq$$

where e is employment growth and q is the rate of growth of output. The law is supported if b is significantly less than 1 because this implies that employment is growing much less quickly than output, i.e. labour productivity is rising. Alternatively:

$$p = c + dq$$

where p is the growth of labour productivity. This time Verdoorn's law is supported if d is significant. To allow for the impact of investment—as the law stands, labour productivity growth might simply reflect higher investment—the law can be estimated using the equation:

$$p = a + bq + c(I/Q)$$

where I/Q is the share of investment in output (McCombie and Thirlwall, 1994: 177). In this approach, Kaldor in effect brings together the various Keynesian and post-Keynesian insights. Demand is central (Keynes) and operates via profits (Robinson, Kalecki) on the degree of technical progress (Kaldor) to produce productivity growth. The whole formulation is quintessentially non-neoclassical, not least in the sense that the dependent variable is labour productivity rather than total factor productivity.

4.3. The Evidence on the Role of Technical Progress

So much, then, for the various theories of technical progress and its importance in the growth process. We now need to consider whether there is any evidence to support this view that technical progress matters.

Perhaps the first thing to say is that the rejection of diffusion as an explanation for Asian growth by the master discourse does *not* imply a rejection of the role of technological diffusion as an explanation of growth in *all* circumstances. In some situations,[41] argues the master discourse, diffusion is indeed a mainspring of growth. This argument has been applied in particular to the period between 1950 and 1973, when output growth in Europe reached historically unprecedented rates. According to Crafts and Toniolo (1996), this growth was made possible by the diffusion of technologies developed during the 1930s and World War II, but not diffused until after 1950 because of the impact of the war and world depression during the 1930s. Once this scope for catch-up growth was exhausted (the early 1970s), European growth rates fell back to their secular trend. The 'golden age' was therefore a one-off event; the diffusion that made it possible was a once-and-for-all phenomenon. But the diffusion argument need not apply just to mature economies. Young's growth-accounting study on Asia discussed earlier made an important distinction between Hong Kong and Singapore. Whereas total factor productivity in Singapore grew by only 0.2 per cent per year, it rose by a very impressive 2.3 per cent per annum in Hong Kong between 1966 and 1991. In other words, one ingredient in Hong Kong' success was its ability to successfully apply imported technology (Table 4.2).

Second, many industrial case studies seem to suggest a key role for technical progress across a range of economies. This body of evidence suggests that, although scientific ideas are important, commercial exploitation of the ideas requires vast expenditure by industrial companies (Grossman and Helpman, 1994: 26–7). Rosenberg (1992: 116–19), for example, views American technological dynamism as a result of the key role played by the capital goods industry. Resource endowments 'pushed it in the direction of mechanization' but it was the growth of machinofacture itself that led to more invention and innovation. More generally, Rosenberg gives a whole series of industries—energy-efficient technologies, telecommunications, chemical processing, forest products, and scientific instrumentation—where technical progress was both endogenous and crucial to the industry's success. He cites the example of lasers, rejected initially as having nothing to do with telecommunications, now revolutionizing the whole industry (Rosenberg, 1992: 3). The Sony Walkman is another example of technological change that was revolutionary in its impact but simple in terms of the underlying technology involved. In short, there is a wealth of examples that shows how the evolution of capitalism since 1800 has been overwhelmingly associated with innovation. To regard it merely as the product of capital accumulation is manifestly wrong; in that sense, attempts to push the TFP residual down to zero in growth accounting are deeply ahistorical. It can be done, but it does not tell us much about the process of economic growth.[42]

An alternative approach to analysing the contribution of technical progress is to look at historical evidence. Once again, the British Industrial Revolution offers much insight. It is particularly interesting that many recent accounts of the British experience have downplayed the role played by innovation. For example, the pioneering work of Crafts on the growth accounting of the Industrial Revolution shows that the bulk (70 per cent) of the acceleration in output growth between 1701–60 and 1801–30 can be explained in terms of increased factor inputs (Crafts, 1985: 82; Crafts and Harley, 1992). Moreover, Crafts' (1994: 51) more recent estimates for the 1801–31 period show that TFP growth accounted for only 18 per cent of growth, whereas capital accumulation contributed 45 per cent and labour 37 per cent. Even the railway was not especially revolutionary in its impact (Hawke, 1970). Secondly, it is well known that the rate of diffusion of some of the best-known inventions—in coke smelting and the steam engine, for instance—was very slow (Hyde, 1977; von Tunzelmann, 1978).

Nevertheless, these criticisms of the pace of British innovation are probably overstated. The view that the Industrial Revolution should be seen as a 'wave of gadgets' (the phrase made famous by T. S. Ashton) is not a new one, and many of the writers of the last two decades have continued to see technology as the key mover in British industrialization. That is not surprising given that the most dynamic industry was cotton, where many of the innovations occurred. One of those who continue to emphasize the role of technical progress is David Landes. (1969; 1993). According to him:

When the British began to move ahead of their neighbors and inaugurated a new, more productive mode of production, they did so because, building on earlier gains, they found technological solutions to the stresses and opportunities of widening and deepening markets. . . . [Unlike French innovations] British innovations had wider economic consequences because the demand for these products was potentially larger and the supply more elastic (compare cotton and silk for cheapness) and because they had wider ramifications within the larger economy (thus multiple uses of iron and the general applicability of advances in power technology). They were the stuff of an industrial revolution. Pace Nick Crafts (1977), the French changes were not. (Landes, 1993: 162)

Mokyr (1993: 33) offers a similarly positive view of the role played by innovation. For him, the Industrial Revolution was not so much a wave of gadgets but a cluster of macroinventions (some of which undoubtedly come from France) which led to an acceleration in the rate of microinvention in which Britain had a comparative advantage. In addition, new work by Crafts (1995) increasingly reinstates the role of technical progress in early British industrialization. Even when capital is defined broadly in the fashion of Mankiw, *et al.* (1992) to include human capital, it is difficult to drive residual TFP down to zero. However, Crafts argues, it is hard to explain technical progress purely in terms of an endogenous growth model. Instead, what is needed is an approach which combines endogenous and exogenous elements, but nevertheless focuses firmly on technical progress: 'It seems probable that retaining the notion that exogenous macroinventions are part of the picture and that these give rise to bounded learning by doing, will be central features of any realistic model of growth in the period' (Crafts, 1995: 767–8).

Even more interesting is the debate on the contribution of technical progress to the post-war growth of Japan, Taiwan, and South Korea. We have already seen that Young (1995) and Krugman (1996) see the bulk of East Asian growth as reflecting factor inputs.[43] This is echoed by the work of Kim and Lau who 'cannot reject the hypothesis that there has been no technical progress in the NICs' (Srinivasan, 1995: 56). Easterly (1995: 281, 284) makes the same point; for him, rapid East Asian growth is 'consistent with the old prosaic fundamentals'. But all these estimates depend upon their neoclassical growth-accounting methodology and the underlying quality of the data. The problem here is that estimates of TFP growth are extremely sensitive both to their assumptions and the way in which factor inputs are measured. One example of this is the gulf between Young's estimate of economy-wide TFP in Singapore (0.2 per cent per annum between 1966 and 1990—Table 4.2, above) and the figure of 1.8 per cent for 1961 to 1991 calculated by van Elkan (1995: 9). Although van Elkan (1995: 10) accepts the importance of capital accumulation, she argues that 'the role of TFP over the past three decades should not be minimized'. Sarel's findings are also much more positive about the extent of TFP growth. According to him, it grew at 3.1 per cent in South Korea between 1975 and 1990 compared to Young's estimate of 1.7 per cent. And the Singaporean figure rises to 1.9 per cent, very similar to the estimate of van Elkan (IMF, 1998: 5).

Stronger evidence still for the unreliability of TFP estimates comes from data on TFP in South Korean manufacturing (Table 4.8). Two features of this table stand out. First, the World Bank estimate of TFP growth (8.8 per cent) is far higher than those of Park and Kwon (–1.6%, their preferred estimate, or 2 per cent if a neoclassical production function is used). Secondly, there is no correlation at all between the sectoral estimates. This discrepancy is at its most extreme in the case of chemicals; Park and Kwon report slightly negative TFP whereas the World Bank estimate is of no less than 13.1 per cent.

Given these varied and conflicting estimates, the only way to proceed is to look at industries on a case-by-case basis to see whether there was any technical progress. The evidence here is plain. Take South Korea, for example. In 1953 the economy was primarily agriculture; pre-war industry was located mainly in the north. By the end of the 1980s, however, South Korea had established a name for itself in world markets for steel, shipbuilding, chemicals, and cars, a clear indication of the underlying quality of its products (Amsden, 1989; Westphal, 1990; Chang, 1993*a*). As Amsden (1989: 269) says: 'Hyundai Heavy Industries (HHI), a subsidiary of the Hyundai Group, began building its first ship, a very large crude carrier, in March 1973. Less than a decade later, HHI had become the world's largest shipbuilder . . .' Moreover, POSCO, the Korean steel producer founded in 1968, was exporting technology to the USA by the mid-1980s (Amsden, 1989: 291). The same type of story of technical success could equally well be told for Taiwan; in the area of computer hardware in particular, Taiwan was remarkably successful (Wade, 1990, ch. 4). Singapore may be an exception to this story of East Asian success; the estimates of East Asian TFP are remarkably consistent in putting Singapore at the bottom. Nevertheless, the notion of negligible technical progress seems very implausible. As Lee Kuan Yew put it, if one interprets Krugman literally, Singapore Airlines would be indistinguishable from Aeroflot.

But the best example of successful innovation is Japan. Some of this dates from before World War II. Yawata Steel (founded in 1897 and productive from 1901 onwards) grew rapidly in the pre-war years. At the turn of the century, Japan imported 94 per cent of her steel, but by 1936—following the merger of Yawata with a number of small steel companies to form Nippon Steel—the figure was down to 9 per cent (Yamazawa, 1990: 92–3). More generally, the extent of Japanese technical progress by 1941 is evident from the quality of her weaponry—which reflected *innovation*, and not simply diffusion. Her *Yamato*-class battleships were the largest in the world, and Japanese 24-inch torpedoes were far more effective than the 21-inch models deployed by the Allies. Even the best US carrier-based

TABLE 4.8. *Estimates of total factor productivity growth rates in South Korean manufacturing, 1966–1990* (per cent per annum)

Estimates by:	Period	All manufacturing
World Bank	1968–88	8.8
Young	1966–90	3.0
Park–Kwon	1967–89	−1.6
Sector	Sectoral TFP	
	Park–Kwon 1967–89	World Bank 1968–88
Iron and steel	4.9	3.7
Non-ferrous metal	4.5	7.6
Non-metallic minerals	6.4	2.8
Chemicals	−0.4	13.1
Transport equipment	2.7	11.2
Machinery	3.8	8.0
Electrical and electronic	4.8	10.7
Heavy industry	0.5	
Food	−7.8	9.5
Textiles	4.4	10.7
Wood	13.9	10.8
Paper	−2.0	9.5
Other manufacturing	2.4	7.5
Light industry	−0.5	

Sources: Young (1995: 672); Kwon (1994: 637); World Bank (1993*a*: 307).

fighter of World War II (the Hellcat) was based upon the design of a Japanese Zero which crash-landed intact on American territory.

After World War II, there is no disguising growing Japanese technological prowess (Okimoto, 1989; Morris-Suzuki, 1994). By the early 1990s, Japan was the world leader in many areas of manufacturing; labour productivity on average had increased from 18 per cent of US levels in 1950 to 80 per cent by 1989 (Maddison, 1994: 54). Furthermore, Japan was moving into such high technology areas as nuclear power and space exploration. Of course much of the technology was imported; and, even though it was successfully applied in areas such as semiconductors and TV design, some economists are reluctant to award too much credit to the role of MITI in the process (Yamamura, 1986).[44] But whatever the size of the growth-accounting residual, and whatever the role of MITI, Japanese technological success is indisputable and it has played a key part in the country's economic growth.

In all these cases, it has been successful innovation and internal diffusion that has been the key to rapid economic growth. Many of the innovations in the British cotton textile industry were based upon inventions that originated in France.

The United States was able to catch up with, and ultimately surpass, Britain by building upon existing British technologies. The growth of Meiji Japan was facilitated by the acquisition from other countries of technologies which were deemed appropriate for Japanese circumstances; for example, ring-spinning—the dominant US technique in cotton spinning—was seen as much better suited to Japanese factor endowments than mule-spinning—the dominant British technique (see Saxonhouse, 1985; Francks, 1992; Howe, 1996).

It may even be the case that Soviet growth owed much more to technical progress than is usually admitted. Although the data remain problematic,[45] there is clear evidence of a trend decline in the growth rate of net material product (NMP) over time. In the 1950s, NMP grew at 9.3 per cent per year. By the late 1960s, however, that rate was down to 4.1 per cent and in the first half of the 1980s it fell to only 0.6 per cent (Shmelev and Popov, 1990). Dwindling technical progress could have been the source of this decline and there are in turn (at least) two ways to explain it. One possibility is that technical progress was quite rapid, but largely confined to the defence sector. As there was undoubtedly substantial innovation in the USSR's defence and space sectors, and as we know that defence may have pre-empted as much as 25 per cent of GDP by the 1980s (Aslund, 1995: 43), this explanation is entirely plausible. The second possibility is that, because the USSR was in large measure a closed and heavily planned economy, it suffered from an increasingly wide ideas gap.[46] The USSR was able to exploit catch-up opportunities in the early days precisely because the technological gap was so large (which is broadly the Gomulka argument mentioned earlier). But the pace of innovation later slowed down as the country became more closed, and the absence of competition became ever more apparent. Aslund (1995: 55) makes the point thus:

> . . . rapid innovation does appear incompatible with perfect competition. But Schumpeterian theory must not be stretched so far as to miss the vital point that in a competitive economy the incentive for a firm to innovate is, above all, survival, rather than the gain of windfall profit. . . . that force would be declining as competition declines; it would be small under monopoly and virtually absent under socialism. It follows that to secure a maximum rate of innovation, the degree of competition must be intermediate, neither high nor low.

However, the evidence on overall rates of Soviet technical progress as measured by TFP is hard to interpret (Table 4.9). Depending on whether one assumes a Cobb–Douglas or a CES production function, the rate of growth of TFP shows either a trend decline or virtually no change. The latter possibility is not implausible. Given the decline in Soviet growth, and assuming unchanged technical progress, it is a simple matter to reconcile the two by assuming a slower rate of factor accumulation. We know that the Soviet workforce was fully mobilized by the 1980s; around 97 per cent of women aged between 40 and 45 were working by 1985. There may also have been a slowdown in the pace of capital accumulation. The capital–labour ratio increased by only 4 per cent between 1980 and 1987, compared to 7.4 per cent between 1950 and 1959 (Gros and Steinherr, 1995: 65–6). Ultimately, however, we can only say that we do not know whether falling Soviet growth rates were caused

TABLE 4.9. *Estimates of TFP growth in the USSR, 1950–1987* (per cent per annum)

Period	Industrial-sector TFP		Economy-wide TFP	
	Cobb–Douglas	CES	Cobb–Douglas	CES
1950–60	6.1	0.4	1.3	−0.2
1960–70	1.9	0.4	−0.1	−0.2
1970–80	2.4	0.4	−0.8	−0.2
1980–7	−0.1	0.4	−1.2	−0.3

Note: CES is a constant elasticity of substitution function. These data are based on Western estimates of both GNP and industrial output.
Source: Gros and Steinherr (1995: 68).

by a declining pace of factor accumulation or a slowdown in the rate of technical progress. Perhaps the commonsense conclusion is that both occurred simultaneously.

Finally, let us consider the post-war OECD evidence on the Kaldor–Verdoorn relationship between demand growth and labour productivity growth. Much of the cross-sectional evidence for comparatively short time periods is rather equivocal (McCombie and Thirlwall, 1994: 171–2). However, the evidence for longer periods is much stronger. This is apparent if one looks at the rates of growth of labour productivity and GDP (a proxy for the strength of aggregate demand) in 1950–73 and 1973–89 (Table 4.10). This table shows the extent of the decline in demand growth after 1973; GDP growth between 1973 and 1989 was less than half the rate achieved during the halcyon days of Bretton Woods. This decline went hand-in-hand with a fall in the rate of labour productivity growth. In fact, these data show that both demand and productivity growth fell after 1973 in every one of the G5 countries. This is a striking demonstration of the underlying validity of the Kaldor–Verdoorn hypothesis.

TABLE 4.10. *Growth of real GDP and labour productivity in the G5 countries, 1950–1987* (per cent per annum)

Country	1950–73		1973–87	
	GDP	GDP per hour	GDP	GDP per hour
France	5.0	5.0	2.3	3.2
W. Germany	5.9	5.9	2.1	2.6
Japan	9.3	7.6	3.9	3.5
UK	3.0	3.2	2.0	2.3
USA	3.6	2.5	2.7	1.0
G5 Mean	5.4	4.8	2.6	2.5

Source: Maddison (1991: 50–1).

In summary, this discussion of a range of evidence suggests that technical progress is invariably an important source of growth. The view taken by the master discourse that it was unimportant in much of East Asia is not convincing because the conclusion rests on the methodologically flawed growth-accounting framework. In any case, even if the master discourse is right about East Asia, the Asian experience does not appear to have been typical. A wide range of economies—Industrial Revolution Britain, post-war OECD economies, Japan, and even perhaps the USSR—have grown at least in part by successful technical progress. Accordingly, there is no reason to rule out technical progress as a source of Chinese growth on a priori grounds.

6. Conclusion

This very brief survey of the field is more than enough to illustrate the immense variety of growth theories. It also demonstrates how far we are from a settled theory. This is not surprising; what is most apparent is the extent to which the supposedly 'independent' variables of labour-force growth, human-capital formation, the accumulation of physical capital, technical progress, and initial conditions interact. Despite the valiant efforts of the growth accountants, it is clear that we cannot differentiate between the relative contributions of these components to the growth process in any precise way. Kaldor and Abramovitz recognized many years ago that there is no easy way to distinguish between a shift in the production function and a movement along it. As Abramovitz (1993) has recently said in restating his view, the problem is that technical progress determines the pace of accumulation, and the pace of accumulation determines that of technical progress. And, as he points out: 'surely there can be few economists who do not sense that there are two-way connections between technological progress, economies of scale, tangible capital accumulation, and human and other intangible capital accumulation' (Abramovitz, 1993: 221).

That growth is over-determined is also clear when the evidence is considered. The most salient feature of the fastest-growing economies of the post-1945 era is that their growth has been powered by all of the factors identified in growth theory. In the case of post-war Japan, for example, initial conditions (a skilled labour force and some inherited physical infrastructure) were favourable, investment in physical and human capital was high, there was extensive scope for the diffusion of technologies developed in the West, and innovation was widespread. The same is true of other East Asian economies, and (necessarily crude) growth accounting does nothing to identify the interaction of these factors. In fact, its spurious precision serves only to obscure the underlying processes.

It follows as a matter of logic that the Chinese experience after 1978 can probably be explained using these same sorts of arguments. We have already seen that its growth rate was extremely rapid during its transition, and therefore (as with Japan) perhaps each and every one of the proximate determinants of growth identified in this chapter was of great importance. Certainly there is little case for offering a monocasual explanation of growth. It makes no sense to decry the importance of any of the factors that have been the centrepieces of the great theories of the past, precisely because the growth process is so complex. There is little purpose to be served by some facile a priori simplification in which (say) physical capital accumulation is the key ingredient. We need to recognize the complexity of the growth process, and to explore the *range* of proximate factors which together determined why growth was fast before going on to look at the deeper reasons for China's success. This is the approach adopted in the chapters that follow.

Part II

The Role of Initial Conditions

5

The Maoist Legacy and the Literature

As we have seen in the previous chapter, many theories emphasize initial economic conditions as a key determinant of the growth rate. Four sets of favourable preconditions have been identified: a high level of social and physical capability (which facilitates technological diffusion); scope for the redeployment of labour from low- to high-productivity sectors; the combination of a high savings rate and a modest capital–labour ratio; and scope for institutional improvement (which raises intra-sectoral productivity).

This part of the book looks at the first three of these preconditions. Did China have a high degree of physical and social capability at the commencement of the transition era (Chapter 6)? Did the transfer of labour from low- to high-productivity sectors contribute to growth (Chapter 7)? Was a high investment/savings rate a characteristic of the economy in 1978? (Chapter 8).[1] The central issue addressed in these chapters is whether the rapid pace of growth achieved in the People's Republic during the Dengist era reflected the legacies of the late Qing (1800–1911), the Republican (1911–49), and Maoist (1949–78) periods. The analysis begins in this chapter with the literature on the role of initial conditions.

1. The View of the Master Discourse

There is a tendency in some accounts of post-1978 growth to look no further than the changes undertaken after the death of Mao to explain the acceleration in China's growth rate. The conventional wisdom, in other words, is that the Maoist legacy was largely negative in the sense that China inherited a low level of social and physical capability which was reflected in its low capital–labour ratio. Accordingly, there was little scope for (productivity) growth based upon the diffusion of technology pioneered overseas. For example, Sachs and Woo (1994: 116–17) argue that after 1978:

> Coastal regions boomed, traditional areas of heavy industry grew more slowly than the national average, and agricultural regions lay in the middle. We offer a 'Russification' hypothesis: preceding industrialization (along Soviet lines) was a hindrance, not a help, to economic growth in the 1980s. . . . The small role played by import-substituting industrialization is consistent with the experience of East Asia more broadly. Throughout East Asia, rapid growth was spurred by labour-intensive export-oriented manufactures, developed independently of the heavy industry that had been fostered by import-substitution policies.

This same conventional wisdom claims that China was nevertheless advantaged in three of the ways discussed in Chapter 4: it had an abundance of surplus labour in its backward agricultural sector, its institutions were so inimical to growth that relatively simple reforms (e.g. decollectivization) would lead to big, one-off, output gains, and it had a high rate of savings and investment.[2] We focus here on the role of surplus labour, which occupies centre stage in the master discourse on China.

This Sachs–Woo analysis of the role played by surplus labour is little more than an application of a standard intersectoral labour-transfer model to the Chinese economy. In 1978, so the argument goes, China's labour market was in disequilibrium. As a result of market imperfections—to be precise, barriers to labour mobility erected by government—the real wage in agriculture was below its market-clearing level, whereas the real wage in industry was above market clearing. Hand in hand with this went high marginal productivity of labour in rural areas and low marginal urban labour productivity. Labour was therefore surplus in rural areas, and scarce in China's cities. The task then was to remove the barriers to labour-mobility, and thereby restore labour-market equilibrium. This would necessarily involve large flows of labour from agriculture to industry, and would have the effect of producing a large increase in total output.

These types of arguments are summarized in the following quotations:

> It was neither gradualism nor experimentation, but rather China's economic structure, that proved so felicitous to reform . . . China began reform as a peasant agricultural society, EEFSU [CMB: Eastern Europe and the former Soviet Union] as urban and overindustrialized. China faced the classic problem of normal economic development, the transfer of workers from low-productivity agriculture to higher-productivity industry. In EEFSU, the problem is structural adjustment: cutting employment in inefficient and subsidized industry to allow new jobs in efficient industry and services. . . . Crucially, China's agricultural workers had nothing to lose, indeed much to gain, from the dismantling of socialism, while much of the industrial and even agricultural work force in EEFSU has plausible fears that dismantling the old system could leave them worse off, at least in the short run. (Sachs and Woo, 1994: 102–4)

> The different fates of gradualism in different countries at various times were actually predetermined by their initial economic structures . . . Gradualism is more possible in an underdeveloped (under-industrialized) economy with a huge surplus rural labour force like China than in an 'over-industrialized' and 'over-state-sector-dominated' country like Poland. (Fan, 1994: 105)

> . . . it can be concluded that China's outstanding economic performance may be largely attributed to fortuitous initial conditions. (Raiser, 1995: 150)

In essence, so the argument goes, China was less advanced along the road to development in 1978 than EEFSU in the late 1980s. As a result, it still had a large agricultural sector in which labour productivity was lower than in industry. This distinction between China and EEFSU is supported by the fact that the share of agriculture in total output and employment was substantially higher in the former. Measured at factor cost in 1987 prices, industrial output in Poland in 1989 was 4.3 times greater than that of agriculture; in Russia, the ratio in the same year was 4.1.[3] By contrast, Chinese agriculture was 40 per cent larger in output terms than industry (WT, 1994).

Chinese agricultural productivity was, however, very low—even though absolute output (relative to industrial output) was high. In fact, it is argued, labour productivity in Chinese agriculture was not only low but close to zero as a result of the operation of collective farming. Moreover (and partly as a result), China's rural workforce was strongly predisposed to move out of agriculture. Per capita incomes were much higher in urban areas, and the welfare system there was far more developed than the primitive system of health care and old age support that existed in the communes. Indeed, the only reason labour migration did not occur on a vast scale in the Maoist era was because of the operation of a highly restrictive system of residence permits in conjunction with the virtual non-existence of private markets for food in urban areas (which meant that illegal migrants had no means of subsisting). Considerable surplus labour could be found in the state-owned factories of EEFSU, but many of these workers had little incentive to move to the private sector because of an elaborate factory-based system of welfare. In effect, the real (social) wage in the state sector was well above the marginal productivity of labour. Labour reallocation would reduce the deadweight loss but there was little incentive for the labour to move. The dismantling of the welfare state in EEFSU, it is therefore argued, was a necessary precondition for the creation of a more efficient allocation of labour.

It follows from this sort of analysis that the release of surplus labour after 1978 made an important contribution to the pace of economic growth in China. According to a World Bank (1996: 14, 67–9) study, labour reallocation out of agriculture contributed 1 percentage point towards China's GDP growth of 10.2 per cent between 1985 and 1994; the reallocation of labour out of other low productivity sectors contributed a further 0.4 percentage points. The same type of finding is offered by Sachs and Woo (1997: 76–8); for them, labour reallocation contributed 1.1 percentage points per year towards the annual GDP growth rate of 9.3 per cent between 1979 and 1993. This significant contribution reflected the extent of surplus labour in the countryside:

> The large labor allocation effect in China reflects the existence of a large amount of labor employed in low-productivity agriculture and the success of the post-1978 Chinese reforms in creating higher-productivity jobs in the industry and service sectors. (Sachs and Woo, 1997: 78)

The broader significance of these results is that they allow the master discourse to argue that China's growth performance after 1978 was much less miraculous than previously thought.[4] Early growth accounting exercises suggested that there was little alternative but to see the growth as a miracle precisely because TFP growth was so rapid. Indeed the Sachs–Woo estimates show that factor accumulation accounts for only 6.2 percentage points of the 8.4 per cent growth rate between 1979 and 1993. That implies, if TFP is conventionally measured, a productivity contribution of 2.2 percentage points—an impressive record for a country supposedly riddled with all manner of state-inflicted 'distortions', and perhaps even enough to cast doubt on the standard proposition that the market-based economies outperform those characterized by substantial intervention. The master discourse cannot be easily rescued by adding human capital to the production function because, if anything, its contribution declined as a result of reduced spending on secondary education (as will be discussed in Chapter 9). But disaggregating TFP provides an answer. By showing that a large component of conventionally measured TFP is no more than a one-off labour reallocation effect, any notion of an economic miracle in China can be discounted. The true import of this approach becomes very clear in a recent study by Woo (1998: 34). First, he adopts the methodology already discussed. Second, Woo assumes (not implausibly) that labour reallocation has been much greater than the official data suggests because of illegal migration by rural workers to TVEs located in the coastal provinces; he assumes that the non-agricultural labour force is in fact 100 million greater than officially reported. Third, he re-estimates industrial output value by deflating using the index of factory-gate prices. This produces a revised estimate of 'true' TFP growth of 0.7 per cent per annum for 1979–93 (Woo, 1998: 34). Even more strikingly, the estimate for true TFP growth for 1985–93 is −0.6 per cent—and therefore the whole notion of an economic miracle in China is exploded.

2. Other Western Assessments of the Maoist Legacy

Other scholars have elaborated on, and to some extent criticized, these arguments. According to many, China's irrigation network was of low quality. Moreover, because yields were already at a high level by 1978, they could only be raised by massive new investment. In other words, it is wrong to see Chinese agricultural growth in the 1980s as being based upon the inherited capital stock (Nolan, 1995*a*: 142–3). In the sphere of industry, Maoist defence industrialization—epitomized by the programme of 'Third Front' construction—was not best suited to the promotion of growth in the civilian sector. Much of the industry, located in the deep interior of western China, was incomplete, expensive, and extremely inaccessible (Naughton, 1987; Nolan and Ash, 1995: 993). Chinese economists themselves talked of the 'sheep shit' arrangement of this industry, whereby plants producing components for the same final product were widely dispersed across mountainous regions (Gu, 1985). Furthermore, precisely because the volume of resources allocated to the 'Third Front' was so vast, funds were not available for the modernization of light industry in the coastal region (Gan and Yang, 1984). Finally, the quality of the Chinese workforce, and especially that of China's scientific and technical personnel, was low. Many skilled personnel had been persecuted during the Cultural Revolution, or had deskilled thanks to the policy of sending intellectuals into the countryside (*shangshan xiaxiang*). Trained statisticians and economists were both in short supply because of the closure of key research institutes (Nolan and Ash, 1995: 990; Nolan, 1995*a*: 116–17).

Nevertheless, there is a considerable body of literature that takes a more positive view of Maoist legacies. For example, even though China's capital stock was less well developed than apologists for Maoism have claimed, Nolan's point is not that it was negligible. Rather, despite the investment failures of the Maoist regime, the Dengist leadership still inherited an economy with enormous underutilized stocks of physical and human capital. In other words (and thinking about the issue in neoclassical terms), China in 1978 had quite a high capital–labour ratio but was operating far below its production possibility frontier. Nolan's interpretation is therefore not so much that the Dengist leadership inherited little scope for rapid growth, but rather that China's position in this respect was no better than that of the USSR in the late 1980s. For example, Nolan points out that China had a high level of education by LDC standards, and that the Third Front programme left behind it a legacy of technical skills (Nolan, 1995*a*: 116; Nolan and Ash, 1995: 1990). If anything, Russia was advantaged relative to China because it had a much higher level of social capability as well as all the other advantages of backwardness. It was therefore better placed than China to take advantage of the diffusion of Western technology.[5] Nolan (1995: 159) summarizes his argument thus:

Both systems had relatively large amounts of technical skill and capital stock locked up in the military sector. In each case, the economic system was massively underperforming compared to the productive potential achievable with existing physical and human capital. In each case, relatively simple system changes were capable of generating an initial large improvement in system performance which could serve as a springboard to further more fundamental change and improvement. In other words, despite important differences, both the former Soviet Union and China possessed huge catch-up possibilities, as did most of the former Stalinist countries.

Others have gone further, arguing that China's capital–labour ratio was actually comparatively high by LDC standards at the time of Mao's death. Andrew Watson (1989*b*: 87), for example, is very positive about the potential of the irrigation system inherited in 1978:

. . . the main achievement of the reforms was to realize the full potential of the investments in land, water and technology that had been made under the commune system. The inefficiencies in commune management, the lack of incentives for peasant labour and the low prices paid by the state had hindered the proper exploitation of those communal investments. Once the reforms removed the constraints, the potential was realized. In this view, therefore, the rapid development of 1978 to 1984 was 'one-off', based as it was on the exploitation of the hitherto under-utilized infrastructure, capital and technology.

There are other favourable evaluations. Rawski (1995: 1171) has written positively of the role played by the famous 'barefoot doctors' in raising life expectancy, and Lardy (1995) notes that the Dengist leadership enjoyed the enormous advantage of inheriting an insignificant volume of international debt. In this respect, of course, China was in a very much better position than most of Eastern Europe (and especially Hungary). Additionally, Drèze and Sen (1995: 65, 67, 73–4) argue that China was well ahead of India in terms of basic education by the early 1980s, and that most of this advantage was due to the inherited educational system.

Finally, I have argued elsewhere that the experience of Sichuan in the Maoist era shows the available potential for future growth (Bramall, 1993, ch. 3). I emphasize there the regional benefits of the Third Front, the positive irrigation legacy, and the dramatic expansion of the transport system that was completed between 1949 and 1978. This particular Marxist approach goes beyond the Western view that there was simply unexploited potential in the Chinese economy of the late 1970s. It doubts whether it really makes sense to argue that the Maoist economy was 'underperforming' in the sense of promoting China's development before 1978. On the supply side, the development of the forces of production was hindered by the need for high levels of military spending to counter the threats posed by both the United States and by the Soviet Union after 1960. As a result, resources that might otherwise have been used to develop the capital stock in agriculture and in industry were diverted into 'unproductive' areas. On the demand side, even the infrastructure that was created via the mass mobilization of the labour force had to remain underutilized given the need to squeeze consumer demand to finance military spending. Only after consumer spending was restored by the shift in the terms of trade towards agriculture (which resulted in a substantial fiscal deficit in the late 1970s and early 1980s) could the infrastructure previously created be brought into full use. In short, the Maoist economy was underperforming in terms of growth, but not in terms of its promotion of China's social and economic development. After 1978, it was able to exploit this social capability and raise its growth rate.

3. Chinese Perspectives: The Maoist Legacy in Retrospect

As for post-1978 Chinese perspectives on these issues, most theorists and members of the Party were united in giving to the Maoist development strategy much of the credit for what was achieved, despite its deficiencies.[6] Inheriting an infrastructure that was either non-existent or badly damaged by war, the Maoist regime not only restored existing systems but created an array of new irrigation schemes and schools at both primary and secondary level. By mobilizing factors of production —especially unskilled rural labour—on an unprecedented scale, the necessary infrastructure for modern economic growth was created. For example, the illiteracy rate of the population was much reduced, thus increasing the stock of human capital. In addition to this, the Maoist years saw a massive investment in physical infrastructure: irrigation networks, plant and machinery, factories, and transport networks. Taken together, these policies shifted the Chinese production frontier far beyond that of 1949. Furthermore, for all the failings of Maoism, the majority view was that there had been no alternative to Maoism in the context of the 1950s. For theorists such as Hu Sheng, Chen Junsheng, He Xin, and Hu Qiaomu—and for Deng Xiaoping himself—capitalism had been tried before in China and found wanting. Much of this was because of Western imperialism, which had reduced China to semi-colonial status (Sun, 1995: 225–8); Hu Sheng, for example, followed the route taken by *dependencia* writers on Latin America in arguing that the 'golden age of the bourgeoisie' (Bergère, 1989) was during 1914 to 1918 when the Western powers were occupied in fighting themselves.

But despite the recognition of these achievements, the official approach adopted by the Party since 1978 argues that the late Maoist economy (that is, the post-1957 Chinese economy) signally failed to develop the forces of production because it placed too much emphasis on politics ('politics in command') and neglected the incentive systems needed to effectively develop and utilize the forces of production. In agriculture, for example, it is usually argued that the range of workpoints earned for a day's work was extremely narrow, and the system invariably operated in such a way that women received less than men, irrespective of their actual contribution. The policy of 'cutting off the tails of capitalism', at its height during the Cultural Revolution (1966–76), all but eliminated private sector production, thereby hampering entrepreneurship, experimentation, and hard work. Moreover, the position worsened after 1964 following the beginning of the 'In agriculture, study Dazhai' campaign (*nongye xue Dazhai*). The Dazhai approach involved time rather than piece-rate methods of payment, the allocation of a substantial proportion of workpoints on the basis of political rather than economic criteria, the elimination of private plots, and the brigade as the level of accounting—in other words, a system far removed from small-scale private farming.[7]

From a theoretical perspective, a renewed emphasis on incentives in the primary stage of economic development was justified by recourse to Marx's *Critique of the Gotha Programme* in which it is argued that 'the narrow horizon of bourgeois right' (distribution according to work done) could only be crossed once the forces of production had been sufficiently developed.[8] The idea, indeed, was given a theoretical basis as early as 1979 by Su Shaozhi and Feng Lanrui (Misra, 1998: 92). It was reaffirmed in Su's work throughout the 1980s (e.g. Su and Zhang, 1989) which argued that China would only end the 'primary stage of socialism' by the middle of the twenty-first century. The attraction of this notion that China had not progressed beyond the primary stage by 1978 was that it allowed the CCP to argue that Mao's policies were not so much incorrect as applied at the wrong moment in history (Misra, 1998: 91–2). Ultimately, such a doctrine would allow the CCP to embark upon on a full-scale restoration of capitalism.

The influence of the doctrine of the 'primary stage of socialism' is evident from the pronouncements of the leadership during the 1980s. Deng Xiaoping put the point thus in his 'Build Socialism with Chinese Characteristics' of 1984:

> Speaking of our shortcomings since the founding of the People's Republic, one was negligence in developing the productive forces. Socialism means eliminating poverty. Pauperism is not socialism, still less communism. The superiority of the socialist system lies above all in its ability to increasingly develop the productive forces and to improve the people's material and cultural life. (Central Committee, 1991: 2)

And Zhao Ziyang argued along these lines even as late as 1987 (Central Committee, 1991: 641):

> . . . China's socialist society is still in its primary stage. We must proceed from this reality and not jump over this stage . . . to believe that it is possible to jump over the primary stage of socialism, in which the productive forces are to be highly developed, is to take a utopian position on this question, and that is the major cognitive root of 'Left' mistakes [p. 641] . . . precisely because our socialism has emerged from the womb of a semi-colonial, semi-feudal society, with the productive forces lagging far behind those of the developed capitalist countries, we are destined to go through a very long primary stage [p. 642] . . . It will be at least

100 years from the 1950s, when the socialist transformation of private ownership of the means of production was basically completed, to the time when socialist modernization will have been in the main accomplished, and all these years belong to the primary stage of socialism [p. 644] . . . The practice of allowing everyone to 'eat from the same big pot,' egalitarianism and jealousy of other people's incomes still constitute the main tendency in income distribution at present. We must continue to tackle these problems both from an ideological perspective and in our practical work. Where possible, we should introduce piece-rate wages and wages based on work quotas, maintaining strict control over product quality and work quotas [p. 668].

From this type of perspective, the triumphal economic progress of the 1980s stemmed from the restoration of incentive systems (systemic reform). Once in place, these incentive structures had the effect of propelling the Chinese economy closer to its production frontier, and in developing the productive potential of the economy via accumulation and productivity growth. In agriculture in particular, the restoration of private farming raised sharply the labour productivity of the workforce because farm income were now much more closely related to production than they had been hitherto. There was no longer an incentive for shirking because such behaviour would be directly reflected in a smaller yield at harvest time. Furthermore, precisely because there was so much unexploited slack in the late Maoist economy—well-developed irrigation, electricity transmission, and transport networks existed in profusion but were being used to a degree well below their potential—the process of catch-up in agriculture was explosive, with annual growth rates—12 per cent in 1982 and 13 per cent in 1984 (ZGTJNJ, 1992: 34)—far in excess of any conceivable long-run trend.

In fairness, not all Chinese economists shared this view. However, the disagreement within Party ranks centres largely on the *reasons* for the economy's ability to move on to, and beyond, its Maoist production frontier during the 1980s. Instead of emphasizing the roles played by decollectivization, privatization, and the creation of formal (and individual) property rights, some Chinese stress the galvanizing effect of the shift in the terms of trade in favour of agriculture in 1979. By creating a surplus in the rural sector which could be invested in both agriculture and, more importantly, modern industry, the shift in the internal terms of trade set in train a process of cumulative causation that continued unchecked until the recession of 1989–90. To put the argument another way, the shift in the terms of trade raise the level of effective demand. The most obvious sign of this was the fiscal deficit that emerged in the late 1970s and early 1980s. This fiscal stimulus resulted in a sustained increased in output, and in the growth rate. These issues are discussed in Chapter 13.

6

Social Capability and the Capital Stock at the End of the Maoist Era

Our discussion of the role of initial conditions now turns to the part played in post-1978 growth by the inherited levels of physical and human capital. As we have seen, these arguments feature extensively in the literature, both on growth and on China in the transition era. The central question is: was growth so fast because of extensive investment in both physical and human capital in the Maoist era (and before)? Can we think of the China of 1978 as having inherited a well-developed stock of physical and human capital from the Maoist period such that it was in an excellent position to absorb technologies developed? The main issues surround the quality of the physical capital created between 1952 and 1978, and whether Maoist policies on education helped or hindered the development of human capital.

1. Capital Accumulation in Agriculture: The Development of Irrigation

The importance of irrigation as a means of raising crop production has been recognized in China for centuries. It serves to ensure stable yields in years of flood or drought by regulating the supply of water. It makes possible multiple cropping by allowing paddy fields to be drained once the rice harvest is collected so that crops of wheat and barley can be sown; a guaranteed water supply also helps to raise the yield of these dryland crops. In the absence of irrigation, paddy fields remain flooded throughout the year to ensure adequate water supplies for the new rice crop. And when combined with the 'Green Revolution' package of chemical fertilizer and modern varieties (MVs), irrigation can have a dramatic effect upon yields. According to Barker and Herdt (1985: 102): 'the yield of modern varieties under ideal irrigation is five times greater than the yield of traditional varieties under rain-fed conditions.' Moreover, although the impact of the Green Revolution technology is maximized when it is introduced as a package, it is arguably irrigation that is the most important complementary input in raising yields. For example, the new seed varieties have tended to be adopted almost exclusively in areas where water control is good (Barker and Herdt, 1985: 62–3). David and Otsuka's (1994: 413) study of the impact of the introduction of new technology on rice production concluded that:[1]

> In summary, the country studies consistently found that environmental factors—especially the degree of water control—rather than socioeconomic factors such as farm size and tenure, are the decisive factors affecting modern variety adoption.

The importance of irrigation is also clear from the experience of a wide range of countries. For example, the growth of Japanese agriculture in the first four decades after the Meiji restoration of 1868 was based on the development of an extensive irrigation system during the preceding Tokugawa period (Smith, 1959; Hayami and Yamada, 1991). Similarly, the impressive rice yields attained in the Punjab after 1947 owed much to the irrigation systems developed there by the British during the Raj. Conversely, a key reason for the slowdown in Japanese agricultural output growth after 1900 was the failure by the Japanese state to expand the irrigated area further. Irrigation is equally important for the successful application of the modern (Green Revolution) package of technology. It is by no means accidental that the package proved far more effective in the Punjab after its introduction in the 1960s; there, the irrigation part of the package was so much more complete than in other regions.

Given these demonstrations of the importance of irrigation, it is natural to ask whether the exceptional Chinese agricultural growth of the 1980s owed much—if anything—to the legacy bequeathed by the Maoist era.

1.1. Irrigation in China before 1949

One of the earliest, and perhaps the most famous, irrigation network in China was constructed on Sichuan's Chengdu plain radiating from Guanxian by Li Bing (255–206 BC) and his son, Er Lang. This damming of the river Du (hence the name Dujiangyan for the system) created one of the most fertile areas in China, and the system was faithfully maintained throughout the centuries that followed.[2] For example, silt was removed annually from the river beds during the low-water season (December–January) as advised in Li Bing's famous axiom *shen tao tan di zuo yan* ('Dig the channels deep and keep the banks low') and a ceremony was held every April to mark the reopening of the Inner River (Hutson, 1915). As a result, counties like Wenjiang were able to sow over 95 per cent of cultivated area with rice during the summer and plant the same land with a mix of wheat, barley, and rapeseed during the winter (Department of Agricultural Economics, 1941: 134). However, irrigation only became extensive during the medieval agricultural revolution that occurred under the Song dynasty (960–1275). During this era, agricultural was revolutionized: 'By the thirteenth century China thus had what was probably the most sophisticated agriculture in the world' (Elvin, 1973: 129). The network continued to expand during the centuries that followed. In the largely uninhabited area around Hunan's Dongting lake, water-conservancy work (principally dyke construction) only really began during the early years of the Ming dynasty. After a virtual collapse during the Ming–Qing transition, large scale construction of dykes was initiated by the Qing Emperors. According to Perdue (1987: 197): 'The building of waterworks was critical to the transformation of Hunan from a sparsely settled, frontier area to a densely populated, highly productive rice-exporting province.'

For all that, China's irrigation and water-conservancy systems were incomplete and, in many respects, increasingly ineffective in the first half of the twentieth century. This reflected the growing paralysis of the Qing and Republican governments at local and national levels. As irrigation systems are for the most part public goods, a mechanism for coordinating labour and capital at a supra-household level is essential if large-scale projects are to be completed. The state is an obvious coordinator, but its ability to function in this capacity is predicated upon an ability to raise enough money to finance such projects. By 1900, and continuing thereafter, the capability of the Chinese state was heavily circumscribed. Moreover, at least as importantly, few in the Republican regime were interested in improving the functioning of the rural economy.

Examples of failure in the sphere of irrigation and water conservancy in the late Qing and Republican periods abound, and there is some evidence that the incidence of failure was increasing over time. North China was particularly vulnerable because of the tendency of the Yellow River to flood. In 1855, it broke its banks near Kaifeng to create a new channel which emptied into the sea north of the Shandong peninsula; the flooding caused may have played a role in the Nian rebellion. In 1938, the dykes were destroyed at Chiang Kaishek's behest to halt the advancing Japanese. More than 4,000 villages were submerged and the river was diverted south of the Shandong peninsula, but the armies of Imperial Japan marched on. After 1947, and the reconstruction of the Yellow River's dykes, the river reverted to its pre-1938 course.

If anything, however, drought produced greater loss of life than flooding before 1949. In the great drought of 1876–9, which affected Shanxi, Shaanxi, Hebei, Henan, and Shandong, between 9 and 13 million Chinese are estimated to have died. Its impact also extended to the north-west; in Gansu's Ningxian, for example, 'very many deaths' occurred (*Ningxian zhi*, 1988: 141). The drought of 1892–4 was less severe but still led to perhaps one million deaths. That of 1920–1 was less severe still because the extension of the railway network allowed famine relief. Even so, the scale of suffering was still enormous; in Ningxian, an estimated 4,000 famine deaths occurred out of a population of perhaps 200,000 (*Ningxian zhi*, 1988: 142, 154). The total number of famine deaths throughout China was put at half a million. Additionally, between two and three millions died during the drought of 1928–31 in Shaanxi (Vermeer, 1988: 28–46). In Shajing village in north-east Hebei, there were four serious floods and one serious drought between 1911 and 1939; in the last three of the floods (1929, 1938, and 1939), more than 50 per cent of the crop was destroyed on each occasion (Huang, 1985: 213). In Wudian village in the central part of the province, there were three serious floods and two serious droughts between 1925 and 1941. The droughts destroyed more than 50 per cent of the crop on each occasion and the floods destroyed between 25 and 50 per cent of the harvest (Huang, 1985: 213). In Anhui province, there were droughts on average during three to five of every ten years, and flooding five to seven times per decade, during the 500 years before 1949. The severest flooding during the Republican period was caused by the Yangzi River in 1931 and the worst drought was in 1934 (*Anhui nongye dili*, 1980: 16).

For the most part, south China was less affected by flooding than the north. According to Huang (1990: 159–60): 'the [Yangzi] delta, though not without ecological problems, was much less unstable than North China: a mere twenty major floods in the 500 years between 1401 and 1900 . . . compared with almost annual flooding of the Yellow River on the North China plain.' In the great Yangzi flood of 1870, the high-water level reached 137.7 metres at Wushan county in Sichuan. This was the highest level attained at any time during the 1870 to 1986 period, and was some 24 per cent higher than the average high-water mark during 1951–86 (*Wushan xian zhi*, 1991: 77, 81). Flooding also occurred in 1896, 1905, 1920, and 1930, when the high-water levels were 125.7, 124.6, and 123.6 metres respectively; in 1931, about one-fifth of cultivated area was waterlogged and 24 people died (*Wushan xian zhi*, 1991: 77, 113). This latter was the occasion of perhaps the best documented Yangzi flood between 1900 and 1949: it created some 14 million refugees. In Kunshan county alone (located in Suzhou prefecture close to Shanghai and Lake Tai), about 330,000 *mu* were flooded, or about one-third of total cultivated area (*Kunshan xian zhi*, 1990: 26, 193). Even so, the damage done by flooding in this county was less than in 1921, when 450,000 *mu* were without crops due to flooding; and 410,000 *mu* were waterlogged in 1949 (*Kunshan xian zhi*, 1990: 127). Other parts of southern China were also subject to periodic flooding and droughts. In Zhejiang, more than 60 counties were affected by flooding in 1922 (Shang, 1989: 243; *Tonglu xian zhi*, 1991: 62). Far more severe in its impact, however, was the drought of 1934. More than 70 counties, and more than 50 per cent of the province's cultivated area was affected, with 'innumerable deaths' occurring (Shang, 1989: 243). In Jiangshan city, the drought lasted 130 days and 'almost half' of the city's 50,000 households went hungry (*Jiangshan xian zhi*, 1990: 12, 68). In Tonglu county in the same year, about 188,000 *mu* were drought-stricken (89 per cent of cultivated area) and the harvest was some 80 per cent below normal (*Tonglu xian zhi*, 1991: 66, 128). In Linhai county (also in Zhejiang), there was a severe drought in 1900 and a further drought due to 80 days without rain in 1929 (*Linhai xian zhi*, 1989: 154–5). Similar problems affected other parts of southern China. In Hunan, extensive flooding in the Dongting lake area in 1934 caused 30,000 deaths by drowning, especially in and around Lixian (Liu, 1990: 336). There were droughts of 50 and 56 days in 1937 and 1930 respectively in Sichuan's Wushan county, whilst that of 1944 went on for 72 days, affecting up to 90 per cent of the population; in 1942, again due to drought, the harvest was only about 60 per cent of normal (*Wushan xian zhi*, 1991: 75–6). In Sichuan's Qianwei county, flooding caused by the Min River led to 200 deaths in 1917 and 188 deaths in 1931. In 1937, a severe drought was caused by 150 days without rain, and that of 1943 was even worse; the paddy fields were parched and only about 10 per cent of arable area was sown to crops (*Qianwei xian zhi*, 1991: 105–6).

These numerous instances of drought and flooding had much to do with the parlous state of the late Qing and Republican irrigation systems. According to official Chinese data covering 26 provincial-level units, 200.5m. *mu* were irrigated in 1952 amounting to only about 13 per cent of cultivated area (see Table 6.1). This meant that vast areas of China were unirrigated in the 1940s, especially in the north-east. In Liaoning province, for example, there was a marshy area of about 25,000 square kilometres on the lower reaches of the Yalu River. According to the compilers of the 1959 *Agricultural Geography of the North-East* 'The plain is one of the greatest swamps in China' (Sun, 1959: 41). But even in areas of southern China close to major irrigation systems, water conservancy was signally underdeveloped. Sichuan's Dujiangyan covered only about 130,000 hectares before 1949 (it had increased to 570,000 hectares by the late 1970s) such that, in a county like Huayang, (adjacent to Chengdu city) irrigated area amounted to only about 50 per cent of the total (Buck and Chen, 1944). The major difficulty lay in pumping water to irrigate terraces on the hillsides in the south-eastern part of the county. In Dongguan county located in Guangdong province's prosperous Pearl River delta, there was a vast area of marshland alongside the Hanxi River that had yet to be irrigated despite its obvious potential (Potter and Potter, 1990: 76). Moreover, irrigation did make a vast difference to yields. In Huayang county, for instance, rice yields averaged 528 *jin* per *mu* on irrigated land compared to 304 *jin* per *mu* on terraced land; comparative wheat yields were 270 and 120 *jin* respectively (Buck and Chen, 1944: 35).

1.2. Maoist Irrigation

Many would accept that one of the major achievement of the Maoist regime in rural areas was to transform the inadequately developed irrigation network that it inherited. Provincial-level trends are summarized in Tables 6.1 and 6.2. Irrigated area in the provinces covered by these data grew at an annual rate of 8 per cent between 1952 and 1957, and continued to grow annually by 3.5 per cent in the 21 years that followed; the slowdown was inevitable given the relatively high base that had been reached by 1957. As a result, the area of land irrigated by 1978—614m. *mu*—was more than three times greater than it had been in 1952. Moreover, because arable area declined over the same period, the percentage of irrigated land climbed steadily from 20 per cent in 1952 to reach more than 50 per cent by 1978.

This investment in irrigation was financed from four sources: central government, the retained profits of collective farms, labour accumulation (labour mobilization during the winter for infrastructure construction), and bank/credit cooperative lending. The first was by no means inconsiderable. During the First Five-Year Plan, water-conservancy investment (*shuili jiben*) totalled 2,431m. *yuan*, a figure which rose to 7,014m. during 1966–70 and to 15,723m. *yuan* during the Fifth Five-Year Plan (1976–80) (ZGNCTJNJ, 1990: 265). Nevertheless, it was probably less important than labour accumulation. Some data for Xuhuai prefecture in Jiangsu, for example, show that the central government contributed 24 per cent of the total during 1976–80 whereas 'labour services by the masses' (*dazhong laowu*) contributed 51 per cent (Wakashiro, 1990: 492). The key institution in this process was the commune because it allowed an unprecedented mobilization of 'surplus' labour during the winter slack period. In Hunan, for example, several million people were mobilized annually during 1969–73, during which time 95 large and medium-sized projects were completed along with 3,200 small reservoirs; this extended irrigated area by 5.9m. *mu*, or by about 18 per cent of its 1965 level (Liu, 1990: 165). Some

TABLE 6.1. *Trends in Irrigated Area, 1952–1978* (area irrigated in million *mu*)

Province	1952	1957	1965	1978
Beijing	0.37	0.58	3.69	5.13
Tianjin	1.11	2.15	3.30	5.20
Hebei	14.40	23.66	26.29	54.87
Shanxi	3.81	8.72	10.53	16.36
Liaoning	1.51	5.43	4.57	12.78
Jilin	1.75	5.53	3.06	8.99
Heilongjiang	2.04	4.28	5.67	10.02
Shanghai	5.81	5.74	5.52	5.40
Jiangsu	3.33	17.13	29.09	49.08
Zhejiang	16.35	18.10	21.37	22.58
Anhui	15.44	18.74	24.37	35.93
Fujian	9.64	11.54	16.00	12.94
Jiangxi	14.80	19.91	30.01	24.62
Shandong	5.10	11.53	22.68	66.22
Henan	11.82	19.56	17.95	55.83
Hubei	12.47	21.09	33.84	35.33
Hunan	23.07	26.64	32.44	40.31
Guangdong	10.27	16.83	31.90	29.51
Guangxi	8.03	13.09	14.65	22.05
Sichuan	9.97	15.99	23.93	43.02
Guizhou	2.74	4.17	6.14	7.46
Yunnan	4.04	6.64	12.82	13.52
Shaanxi	4.49	7.58	9.42	18.21
Gansu	4.91	6.45	8.00	12.72
Qinghai	0.97	1.72	2.12	2.47
Ningxia	2.23	3.24	3.13	3.64
TOTAL	200.5	296.0	402.5	614.2

Notes: Data are for effectively irrigated area. The Heilongjiang figure for 1965 is by linear interpolation. Only incomplete time-series data exist for Inner Mongolia, Tibet, Xinjiang, and Hainan; they are therefore excluded from this table. Their inclusion would have added 67.31m. *mu* to the total in 1991.

Sources: LSTJ (1990); ZGTJNJ (1992: 344); ZGNYTJZL (1992: 14); Sichuan (1952)—ZSSWY (1984: 191); Guizhou (1952)—Guizhou sheng qing bianji weiyuanhui (1986: 177); Guizhou (1965)—Guizhou tongjiju (1984: 154).

12 billion labour days were expended between 1949 and 1987 (Liu, 1990: 294) which, on the basis of the 1965 rural labour force of 13.4 million (LSTJ, 1990: 598), implies 24 days per worker per year. As much of this 'labour accumulation' occurred under the commune (1958–82), the true intensity at the height of the late Maoist period was much greater. The corresponding figure for Zhejiang was 12 days per worker per year between 1949 and 1985 (LSTJ, 1990: 386; Shang, 1989: 246) but then that province's need was somewhat less: 53 per cent of arable area was irrigated in Zhejiang by 1952 compared to 42 per cent in Hunan where the threat of flooding offered by the Yangzi River via Dongting lake was in any case much more severe. Similar examples of labour accumulation can be compiled for virtually every Chinese province.

TABLE 6.2. *Growth of Irrigated Area, 1952–1978* (annual average growth rates, per cent)

Province	1952–7	1957–78
Beijing	9.3	10.9
Tianjin	14.2	4.3
Hebei	10.4	4.1
Shanxi	18.0	3.0
Liaoning	29.2	4.2
Jilin	25.9	2.3
Heilongjiang	15.9	4.1
Shanghai	−0.2	−0.3
Jiangsu	5.1	5.1
Zhejiang	2.0	1.1
Anhui	3.9	3.1
Fujian	3.7	0.5
Jiangxi	6.1	1.0
Shandong	17.7	8.7
Henan	10.6	5.1
Hubei	11.1	2.5
Hunan	2.9	2.0
Guangdong	10.4	2.7
Guangxi	10.3	2.5
Sichuan	9.9	4.8
Guizhou	8.7	2.8
Yunnan	10.4	3.4
Shaanxi	11.0	4.3
Gansu	5.6	3.3
Qinghai	12.2	1.7
Ningxia	7.7	0.6
Average	8.1	3.5

Sources: As for Table 6.1.

Provincial variation in the rate of growth of irrigated area was of course considerable. Growth rates were high in northern provinces such as Shanxi and Shandong, and exceptionally high in the Manchurian provinces in the 1950s, principally because so little land was irrigated before 1952 despite the omnipresent threat of drought. In the south, those provinces which began the 1950s with irrigation ratios far above the national average—Fujian, Zhejiang, and Hunan—showed little growth in their irrigated area; growth rates were much faster in those that started from a lower base. For the 21 years that followed 1957, provincial variation was much less marked, with irrigated area in the northern and north-eastern provinces growing little more quickly than it did in the south. Nevertheless, even after 1957, provincial variation existed. For 1952–78 as a whole, the greatest success story was in Shandong which had achieved an irrigation percentage well above the national average despite being well below it in 1952. By comparison, those provinces that lagged behind the national average by 1978 did so in general for obvious reasons. Endemic water shortages constrained irrigation expansion in the north-western provinces; in north-central China, the falling water-table hampered irrigation projects in Anhui, Hebei, and Shanxi. In the south-west, the topography made it difficult to extend irrigation to peripheral prefectures in Sichuan, Yunnan, and Guizhou. And in Manchuria, the primary focus was on land reclamation rather than irrigation until the 1980s. Perhaps most remarkably of all, only Shanghai registered a decline in irrigated land and that was because of the growing encroachment of industry and urban settlement on arable land; all of her cultivated area was irrigated in the 1950s and it remained so during the 1970s.

1.3. Maoist Irrigation Failures

These bare figures suggest that the Maoist achievement in raising the degree of irrigation was truly remarkable. The important issue, however, is whether these gains were chimerical. Did the apparent extension of irrigation networks lead to significant increases in yields and greater yield stability in the face of natural disaster?

One must immediately recognize that the official Chinese data on irrigation are misleading (Nickum, 1990; Vermeer, 1977). The term 'effectively irrigated area' means only that land can be irrigated in normal conditions (ZGTJNJ, 1992: 399). That is, there is no need for the old *dongshuitian* system in which paddy fields are kept flooded during the winter in order to ensure enough water during the spring. The term 'effective irrigation' does not mean that a supply of water is guaranteed in times of drought, although the standard laid down in the Twelve-Year Plan of 1956 required that irrigated land could sustain crops in the event of 30 to 50 days without rain (Vermeer, 1977: 183). Even in 1991, only about 60 per cent of irrigated area was irrigated by means of electrical pumps (ZGTJNJ, 1992: 344). Furthermore, although generally acknowledged that the irrigation programme was highly effective during the 1950s, it is equally commonplace to find accounts suggesting that much of the expansion undertaken after 1958 was misconceived. This was especially true for north China, where water shortages and siltation posed enormous problems. According to Vermeer (1988: 213), writing about Shaanxi province:

> After 1975, although the number of pump wells kept increasing in many areas . . . , ground water levels started sinking and the actual irrigated area could not be expanded much further. Rapid siltation of irrigation reservoirs severely limited their effective lifespan. By 1977, 47 per cent of the total capacity of Shaanxi's 120 medium and large-scale reservoirs . . . had been lost and 40 reservoirs were no longer in use. Many reservoirs had become dilapidated and dangerous. Yet reservoir building continued . . .

In Xiyang county in Shanxi (the home of Dazhai), construction work began in 1975 on the West–East Water Transfer (*Xishuidongdiao*) project, an 18.5 km tunnel to divert water from the Su River through the mountains to Xiyang and thus solve its chronic water shortages. In 1980, however, the project was halted, and it was criticized in *Renmin Ribao* (5 June 1980) in an article under the heading 'The Folly of Water Diversion Projects Like This Should Never Be Repeated'. The charges against it were inordinate expense, engineering incompetence and the downstream damage caused by diverting the water out of the Su River (Qin, 1995, chs. 33 and 38). A report by *Xinhua* (7 July 1980) added to the tide of criticism of the entire *nongye xue Dazhai* approach to water conservancy by claiming that Xiyang county had exaggerated its grain production figures during the five-year period 1973–7 by 26 per cent.[3] *Shanxi Ribao* (17 October 1980) went even further in its article 'Dazhai's Departure from the Spirit of Dazhai' (Qin, 1995: 540).[4] These criticisms continue into the 1990s; a book by Chen, *et al.* (1993) outlining rural development in China between 1949 and 1989 devoted more than 100 out of 650 pages to denouncing the Dazhai model as implemented in Xiyang.[5] Similar problems allegedly affected other Chinese provinces, even those south of the Yangzi River where water resources are much more plentiful. In Hunan province, for example, the problem of silting was particularly acute in the Dongting lake area. Water storage capacity in the lake was some 40 per cent lower than it had been in 1949, with the result that about half of the length of the flood prevention dykes was inadequate to cope with a really severe flood (Geography Department, 1981: 101, 130). Some 20 per cent of wetland area was affected annually by drought, whilst about 8 per cent was vulnerable to flooding. As a result 'there is a major drought every three years and one major flood every five years causing a seven to eight per cent reduction in total grain output' (Geography Department, 1981: 100). The worst drought occurred in 1960, when 29.8 million *mu* were affected, about four times the annual average for 1949 to 1979 (Geography Department, 1981: 100). It is no accident, according to some, that the worst flooding and/or drought conditions occurred throughout China during the Great Leap Forward, the period when the irrigated area was expanded most rapidly.

The number of apparent irrigation failures during the Maoist years is indeed considerable. Drought and flooding both contributed to the famine that followed the Great Leap Forward. In Sichuan, for example, drought in 1961 reduced output by more than 30 per cent on almost 46m. *mu* of farmland, about 40 per cent of provincial arable area. This drought-affected area was three times greater than in any other year in the entire 1961–91 period. Furthermore, the drought continued into 1962 when 21m. *mu* were severely affected, a figure that was surpassed only by the 24m. *mu* recorded in 1990 (SCTJNJ, 1990: 147; SCTJNJ, 1992: 135). In Qianwei county in southern Sichuan, the 1962–3 drought was caused by rainfall of only about 50 per cent of normal, which reduced 200,000 *mu* (about two-thirds of sown area) to parched fields (*Qianwei xian zhi*, 1991: 105). Conditions were comparable in Shandong, where there was no rain for seven months between the autumn of 1960 and the spring of 1961; 90m. *mu* were affected, almost 75 per cent of the provincial total. In three regions in the north there was no rain for nine months and it proved impossible to plant any crops on 3m. *mu* of arable land. But worse was to follow. When the weather finally broke during the summer, the rainfall was so heavy that flooding affected about half of grain land. As a result, the autumn harvest was 56 per cent lower than it had been in 1960 (ZSDSWY, 1989: 71–2). If these data are accurate—there must be doubts about any and all figures collected during the Leap—they strongly suggest that the Sichuan and Shandong famines, at any rate, did have a significant natural element to them (see also Bramall, 1993).

Furthermore, natural disasters had not been eliminated by the end of the 1970s. According to Vermeer (1988), the problems in Shaanxi had if anything intensified by the 1970s:

> . . . in Yan'an Prefecture alone 1.3 million ha of grasslands were destroyed between 1958 and 1978. Between 1971 and 1980, almost every year 700,000 ha or more of Shaanxi's farmland were struck by drought, in 1980 even 2.1 million ha; during the 1950s, both floods and droughts had been far less serious [p. 14]. . . . The harmful consequences of the on-going deforestation of hills and mountains, mainly due to reclamation and the felling of trees for fuel and timber, became most evident in the terrible floods in west Guanzhong and south Shaanxi in 1981 [p. 13].

This claim of a trend increase in the incidence of natural disaster has also been made about south-west China. In Sichuan, it is alleged, major droughts occurred four times between 1801 and 1900. Between 1901 and 1950, however, the incidence increased to a rate of once every 10 years and between 1951 and 1979, droughts were occurring every third year. In Guizhou, severe droughts occurred during one year in every three between 1957 and 1975, but at a rate of one year in two between 1972 and 1981. Still more dramatically, the incidence of flooding even in the well-developed Sichuan basin rose sharply. In the 1950s, floods occurred four times. In the 1960s, however, there were seven severe floods, and in the 1970s there were eight (Tang, 1986: 196).

Furthermore, there is no question that many parts of China were severely affected by drought and flooding in the late 1970s. In Anhui, a severe drought began in the winter of 1977 and continued through to the autumn of 1978. Serious flooding occurred in 1980, affecting 9m. *mu* of arable land, some 13 per cent of the total (*Anhui nongye dili*, 1980: 16; Wang, 1989: 2–4, 61). In Gansu, the drought of 1973 was exceptionally severe, affecting 17m. *mu*, or about 30 per cent of the total (Zhonggong Gansu sheng wei yanjiushi, 1988: i. 146). In Gansu's Ningxian, the drought lasted 80 days and the grain yield was a mere 82 kg per *mu*—barely 50 per cent of the average for 1971 and 1972, and only 38 per cent of that achieved in 1974 (*Ningxian zhi*, 1988: 239). In Henan, the collapse of dams at Zhumadian in 1975 following heavy rain led to 26,000 deaths (Zhang and Hou, 1990: i. 308–9). More generally, the agricultural sector was especially affected by poor weather during 1980 and 1981. In 1980, for example, there was serious flooding in Hubei, Hunan, and Jiangsu (SWB, 1980*a*). In the same year, much of northern China was affected by drought. Some 140m. *mu* of arable land was affected because rainfall was barely half its normal level (SWB, 1980*c*). In 1980 also, Sichuan suffered its worst flood since 1934 along the Minjiang River (SWB, 1980*a*). The situation in the province was little better in 1981 when flooding affected 49 million people and damaged 1.6 million homes (SWB, 1981*b*). Even on the Chengdu plain, the Dujiangyan system could not prevent flooding in mid-July. In the three counties worst hit—Jintang, Xindu, and Guanghan—200 people died and 210,000 were made homeless (SWB,

1981*a*). The level of the Yangzi River at Wushan reached 122 metres, a record for the 1951–86 period and well above the 111 metre average (*Wushan xian zhi*, 1991: 77–81). At Neijiang, the Tuojiang River emulated its bigger sister by also setting a post-1949 record, this time of 314 metres compared to its 1951–81 average of 305 metres (*Neijiang shi zhi*, 1987: 69). Even in 1982, flooding continued to pose problems. Although only a small part of Sichuan was affected, the 22 counties that were the principals involved suffered severely. The streets of Shizhu's county town (in south-eastern Sichuan) were flooded on three separate occasions, on the last to a depth of a metre and a half (JPRS, 1983: 87).

1.4. Maoist Irrigation: The Achievement

Nevertheless, the argument that Maoist investment in water-conservancy projects was misconceived is not convincing. To be sure, the record was sullied by failure, and the woes that afflicted rural China had certainly not been eradicated by the time of Mao's death. But for all that, the progress that had been made between 1949 and 1979 was remarkable. Much of this progress was obscured by the natural calamities of the 1970s.[6] It should not be, because much of the evidence is tendentious and misleading. Official Chinese data on natural disasters are unreliable. More generally, information on many provinces is simply missing, especially for the 1950s when it probably was not collected. For example, in the Sichuan case, there is no detail on the area severely hit by natural disaster prior to 1961 (SCTJNJ, 1990: 147; SCTJNJ, 1992: 135). Even were the data to be available, it is unlikely that the figures would be fully comparable with those for the 1970s. Reporting completeness is one problem; the trend increases in the incidence of natural disasters noted above unquestionably reflects much fuller reporting, a pattern that was encouraged by the availability of central government funds for disaster relief. Potentially more serious, however, is the definition of a 'severe natural disaster'. Chinese sources glibly, and routinely, assert that it means a situation in which output is 30 per cent or more below normal. But without a definition of 'natural', any substantial output fluctuation—whether natural or man-made—could in principle come into that category.[7] The allocation of an output loss between man-made and natural causes must necessarily be arbitrary, and that must have been true even more so during the Leap. We know that many historical Chinese data have been reconstructed during the 1980s, and it is hard to believe that the construction has not been influenced by political imperatives. In the case of the Leap, the political imperative is to show that a part of the output loss was due to bad weather but that the remainder was attributable to the pace of communalization. The data on natural disaster show precisely that. In 1961, when output reached its nadir, 28.8m. hectares suffered an output loss of 30 per cent or more. Assuming the actual output loss was 50 per cent, that would imply a fall in output due to natural disaster of about 7 bn. *yuan*. Actual output in 1961 was more than 13bn *yuan* lower than it had been in 1957. At best, then, 50 per cent of the output loss is attributable to natural disaster—which fits in very neatly with the official interpretation.

This official interpretation could, of course, be correct. But it is rather convenient. Given the slim data base from which natural disaster data are derived, and the ease with which the data can be manipulated, one ought to be very cautious before claiming, as Vermeer does (see above), that fluctuations in crop yields due to poor weather in Shaanxi were more frequent in the 1970s than they had been in the 1950s. That after all fits nicely alongside the official 'vision' of the 1950s as a golden age offered by the 'reformist' leadership of the CCP. In any case, in longer historical perspective, the 'disasters' of the late 1970s seem very tame. For all Vermeer's talk of the 'terrible' floods of 1981, there was no repetition of the famine of the early 1930s. In fact, the 1981 grain yield was a respectable 123 kg per sown *mu*, a mere 1 kg below the average yield for 1975–80 (Nongye bu, 1989: 186). Much the same is true of the other 'disasters' quoted. The high-water level of 122 metres in Wushan in 1981 was a post-revolution peak but it was still below the levels of 124 and 125 metres reached in 1920 and 1905 respectively, and well short of the record 138 metres registered in 1870 (*Wushan xian zhi*, 1991: 77–81). Moreover, the Neijiang level of 314 metres was still a metre below its level in 1898 (*Neijiang shi zhi*, 1987: 69). Far more importantly, the impact on output in the early 1980s was far from significant. Neijiang's grain yield was lower than in 1979 but that was because of an (unexplained) 27 per cent fall in potato yields; the yield of the crucial rice crop was 3 per cent higher (*Neijiang shi zhi*, 1987: 304). As for Wushan, the slight fall in the potato yield was more than offset by big yield increases for other grain crops; the rice yield, for instance, was 28 per cent higher whilst that of corn—quantitatively the most important grain crop—was 26 per cent higher (*Wushan xian zhi*, 1991: 124). In both cases, it appears, the vast improvement in water-conservancy facilities accomplished during the Maoist years was sufficient to ensure that the climatic variation which had caused devastation during the Republican and Qing era made little impact by the late 1970s.

This interpretation is reinforced by the microlevel evidence on the impact of irrigation on yields. As has been noted earlier, some writers have suggested that the rapid and uncontrolled expansion of the irrigation network that took place during the Leap aggravated the problems of drought and flooding during those years. Yet there is evidence of remarkably successful projects carried out during those years. A good example comes from Guangdong's Dongguan county (Potter and Potter, 1990: 76–81). Of Chashan commune's 30,000 *mu* of rice land, 18,000 were regularly flooded before 1949 such that the grain yield was only about 50 *jin* per *mu*. In 1959, however, it was decided to launch a massive water-control project. By dint of herculean efforts, the flow of the river Hanxi was redirected into a single central channel by the creation of embankments. The marshes on each side of the embankments were then drained, irrigated, and divided up into relatively large-scale fields that were readily accessible. Once the area had been planted with rice, the yields were extremely high. This, plus the enormous expansion in sown area, led to an increase in output from 5,000 tonnes in 1957 to 10,250 tonnes in 1962. As Potter and Potter note (1990: 80):

The four years from 1962 to 1966 are remembered by Zengbu [CMB: a production brigade in Dongguan's Chashan commune] peasants and cadres as a 'golden period'. . . . The material reasons were the legacy of the Great Leap Forward. The amount of arable land in the commune had been increased by 18,000 *mu*. There was an effective irrigation system, and flooding was prevented by the new flood control system. These material improvements improved the ratio of land to population, made the land able to be cultivated more effectively, and protected it from the flooding which had been a major reason for agricultural losses. Rice production shot up, both per capita and per *mu*.

There is far from universal agreement on these issues. The work of Friedman, *et al.* (1991: 221) on Raoyang county in Hebei offers a case in point. According to them:

Labor corvees of unprecedented scale tried to reduce Hebei's water problems. In subsequent decades central Hebei relied on the reservoirs and canals built in 1958–59 with the labor of millions using picks, shovels, and hand-carts . . . The hectic efforts at times backfired, misusing the water-table, increasing salinization and alkalinity of the soil, and bringing waste and great loss. As a horrendous flood in 1963 soon showed, the claims of great success for the labor corvee work were much exaggerated.

But this analysis is not convincing.[8] Nobody would deny that some problems did occur during the Leap but the fact remains that increases in irrigated area went hand in hand with increases in yields. Friedman, *et al.* (1991: 167) are dismissive: 'By 1954 Wugong [CMB: a village in Raoyang] had ninety-nine wells and 1,050 *mu* of irrigated land, only 300 *mu* more than before drilling began. In spite of enormous efforts, the irrigated area would increase only 450 *mu* during the next decade.' But their own figures show that these increases tripled irrigated area between 1953 and 1958, and that the average grain yield rose from 306 *jin* per *mu* on average during 1953–5 to 392 *jin* during 1959–61 (Friedman, *et al.*, 1991: 292). Certainly the Hebei flood of 1963 was a huge setback; grain output was lower than it had been in any year between 1950 and 1962 (LSTJ, 1990: 133). But it was only a temporary setback; output by 1966 was almost double its 1963 level. In other words, Friedman, *et al.* conflate levels and trends. It is undeniable that the natural disaster problem had not been definitively resolved by 1963; the same was equally true of 1988. But that should not be used as an excuse to ignore the progress that had been made. If the irrigation networks engineered between 1957 and 1965 were so misconceived, why is that they were not simply dismantled (the Hebei data show that the percentage of land irrigated rose from 21 to 25 per cent between 1957 and 1965)? The facts of the matter are that irrigated area increased virtually everywhere in China between 1957 and 1965; Table 6.1 shows an increase of 36 per cent. It did so for the very simple reason that the Chinese peasantry were only too well aware of the impact of irrigation on crop yields. Grain yields of course dipped during the debacle of the Great Leap Forward but thereafter grew strongly, much in line with (although a little more slowly than) the trend increase in irrigated area.

Perhaps more fundamentally, the record of irrigation projects commenced after the Leap—and the bulk of difficult, large-scale, water-conservancy projects were carried out in the late 1960s and throughout the 1970s—was generally rather good, especially in northern China. An example of success comes from Shulu county in Hebei (Blecher and Shue, 1996: 171). According to them:

> The state in Shulu, most notably the local state in the form of the county government, undertook sizeable infrastructure projects in the Mao years. In particular, in the last winter of that wintry era, it initiated and supervised the building of a massive water conservancy project that resolved very serious long-standing soil salinity problems in the southern third of Shulu, resulting in sharply increased crop yields.

This example is particularly interesting because Blecher and Shue's positive conclusion conflicts directly with the bleak assessment of Friedman, *et al.* about Raoyang, also in Hebei.

To be fair, when it comes to famous projects such as the Dazhai-inspired West–East Water Transfer project or the Red Flag Canal,[9] the propaganda war surrounding them between supporters and denigrators of the Maoist approach to water conservancy makes it almost impossible to assess their impact. It is probable that the scale of these ventures was excessive. Projects like the Red Flag Canal probably contributed to the famine which followed the Great Leap Forward by diverting labour from direct farm production. However, it is worth observing that grain yields in Linxian in 1980 were 35 and 12 per cent higher than in the neighbouring counties of Anyang and Qixian respectively (ZGFX, 1980–7). Moreover, Red Flag Canal was being promoted in the mid-1990s as a tourist attraction (and funded accordingly), a sign that—in some quarters of the CCP at least—it was not regarded as a white elephant (BR, 28 July 1997). As for Xiyang, the West–East Water Transfer project was probably too expensive. However, Xiyang faced an intensifying water shortage in the 1990s; the underlying problem which the water diversion project was designed to solve still exists.[10] Moreover, it was not the height of wisdom to stop the project in 1980, when much of it was close to completion. In fact, the decision to halt had far more to do with the project's association with Hua Guofeng and Chen Yonggui—both under vigorous attack in 1980 for their identification with Maoism—than with any assessment of the project's merit.

More generally, the data on Xiyang county reported in Chen, *et al.* (1993: 460–1) show GVAO rising by 5.7 per cent, and gross farm output value by 6.4 per cent, per year between 1957 and 1976 (at 1970 constant prices). Chen, *et al.* argue that this was mainly due to the massive mobilization of the workforce, and their data show the value of total labour inputs rising by 7.3 per cent per year between 1957 and 1976. However, this interpretation is by no means convincing. For one thing, their data on labour inputs are hard to take seriously; the massive flooding of 1963 led to a monumental mobilization of the labour force, yet the Chen, *et al.* data show a big *fall* in labour inputs in that year. The same applies to the drought year of 1973. Secondly, if one accepts their input data, the series for labour inputs into farming grew less quickly (5.4 per cent compared to 6.4 per cent) than the farm output series. In other words, labour productivity in farming was rising. Thirdly, Chen, *et al.* seem to ignore the point that Maoist China had very little choice but to mobilize labour in order to raise production. The external threat consumed the bulk of China's 'surplus' in the Third Front programme; all that was left was the labour force. In these circumstances, their claim that Chinese labour productivity lags far behind that of the USA is simply not very relevant.

2. The Accumulation of Industrial Capital

It is often said of Maoist industrialization (and there is much truth in the view) that it was geared overwhelmingly towards preparation for war; this gave rise to the slogan adopted at the start of the Third Front programme. The view is supported by the pattern of industrial growth (Table 6.3). Heavy industry in particular —metallurgy, chemicals, and machine-building—grew substantially more quickly than light industries such as textiles and food processing.[11] Curiously, the growth differential was especially marked during the 1950s, even though it is this period that Chinese economists typically characterize as being an era of balanced growth. By 1957, the share of light industry had fallen from 58 to 47 per cent.[12]

TABLE 6.3. *Growth of industrial output by sector, 1952–1978* (annual percentage growth of net output value, 1980 prices)

Sector	1952–7	1965–78	1952–78
Metallurgy	29.0	7.9	10.3
Power	20.1	10.9	13.9
Coal	17.4	8.6	7.0
Oil	34.3	15.9	20.5
Chemicals	29.6	13.1	16.6
Machine building	28.5	14.9	13.8
Building materials	18.8	11.6	9.3
Timber	12.0	4.9	1.9
Food processing	12.5	7.1	4.6
Textiles	8.2	6.9	5.7
Paper	18.1	6.5	6.5
Other	18.0	8.7	9.4
Light	13.4	8.0	8.9
Heavy	24.5	12.6	11.3
TOTAL	15.8	10.4	9.1

Notes: These figures are for *xiang*-level enterprises and above, except for the categories 'light' and 'heavy', which include all industry. The sector marked 'Other' includes the sectors designated cultural products, clothing, leather, and 'other.' Data on these individual sectors are not available except for a handful of years before 1978, and therefore 'Other' is calculated as a residual. Data on the structure of industrial output at 1990 prices do not exist. This is because of the adoption of the ISIC method of disaggregation after 1985 which—although it conforms much more closely to international practice (Field, 1992)—has led to the old series (on which the above table is based) being discontinued.

Sources: Zhongguo tongjiju (1985*a*); ZGGYJJTJNJ (1990); ZGTJNJ (1993: 57–8).

These figures also show substantial differences in growth rates *within* heavy industry. Although most of the subsectors grew annually by more than 10 per cent between 1952 and 1978, building materials and especially coal lagged behind. Even so, the value of coal production still increased much faster than the output of food products and textiles. Interestingly, it is also evident that some of the preconceptions of Chinese economists about growth patterns are not borne out by the evidence. According to Dong Fureng (1988: 235), for example: 'within heavy industry [CMB: in socialist economies], the machine-building subsector (as in the Soviet Union) or the iron and steel subsector (as in China) was selected as the center of economic development.' This is misleading. Iron and steel output did increase significantly in China after 1952, but its growth rate was below that of machine building, and it grew more slowly than heavy industry as a whole. Only during the Great Leap Forward did metallurgy temporarily assume the position of leading sector. These sectoral trends in output value are reflected in the patterns of labour force growth. The median growth rate of employment in state industry (data are not available for collective industry by sector) was 8.5 per cent per year between 1952 and 1978, and every sector of heavy industry equalled or exceeded this rate with the exception of the building materials sector. By contrast, employment in textiles and food processing grew by 3.6 and 4.7 per cent per year respectively over the same period (Zhongguo tongjiju, 1985*a*: 74).

The importance of heavy industry during the Maoist years is also borne out by the growth rates of selected industrial products (Table 6.4).

TABLE 6.4. *Growth rates of selected industrial products, 1952–1978* (annual percentage growth rates)

Heavy industry		Light industry	
Coal	7.2	Cotton cloth	3.6
Steel	10.1	Wool	9.8
Cement	11.4	Cigarettes	5.1
		Sugar	5.6

Source: ZGTJNJ (1992: 338–41).

The difference between the growth rates of light- and heavy-industrial products in the 1952–78 is clear from these data. For most heavy-industrial products, the growth rate was about twice that for light-industrial products. Even though the growth of wool output was an extremely impressive 9.8 per cent per year, it was exceeded by the growth rates of steel and cement production, both key elements in the Third Front construction programme.[13]

However, perhaps the clearest indication of the dominant position assigned to heavy industry in the Maoist development strategy is provided by the changing structure of industrial output (Table 6.5). Maoist industrial development led ultimately to a heavy-industry share in net industrial output value of 65 per cent by 1978, well up on the 42 per cent share registered in 1952. The extent of heavy-industry orientation is particularly apparent from the combined shares of metallurgy, chemicals, and machinery. In 1952, the three contributed 13 per cent of industrial output. By 1965, however, this had risen to 33 per cent, and in 1978 it stood at a massive 42 per cent. By contrast, the combined share of food processing and textiles—51 per cent in 1952—had fallen to 30 per cent by 1965, and was down to 20 per cent by 1978. This is testimony to the massive transformation of China's industrial sector that had taken place during the Maoist era. However, for a country bent upon a less defence-oriented development strategy in the 1980s, such a degree of mismatch between light and heavy industry appears extreme. In this respect, it is remarkable how different late Maoist China was to Britain towards the end of its first industrial revolution in 1841 (Horrell, *et al.*, 1994). Whereas textiles and food processing remained supreme in Britain, these two sectors together accounted for only 20 per cent of Chinese industrial output in 1978.

TABLE 6.5. *Shares in industrial output by sector, 1952–1978* (percentage shares in NVIO, 1980 prices)

Sector	1952	1965	1978
Metallurgy	5	10	8
Power	3	6	7
Coal	6	6	5
Oil	1	5	10
Chemicals	2	6	10
Machinery	7	16	24
Building materials	4	4	5
Timber	12	5	3
Food processing	27	16	10
Textiles	24	14	10
Paper	2	2	1
Other	9	9	9

Note: *Xiang* enterprises and above only.

Sources: Zhongguo tongjiju (1985*a*); ZGGYJJTJNJ (1990).

A final indication of the dominance of heavy industry comes from the scale of the programme of 'Third Front' construction. A particularly good example is provided by the growth of the Panzhihua conurbation in south-western Sichuan.[14] In 1945, the city—then called Dukou—barely existed and contained within its boundaries (and those of the adjacent counties of Miyi and Yanbian) a mere 13 industrial enterprises (SCZL, 1990: 342). Industrial output in 1952 was only 1.45m. *yuan*, barely a third of one per cent of that of Chongqing, Sichuan's largest city. Between 1952 and 1965, output grew more quickly than the provincial average (15.1 per cent per year compared to 11.6 per cent), but this was due primarily to logging and the development of a sugar-processing industry. Total industrial output value in 1965 was still barely 0.4 per cent of Chongqing's. The Third Front programme, which got under way in the mid-1960s, changed all that. Authority was given in February 1965 for the construction of a 'nationally unique river valley city built on both banks of the Jinsha river' (Cui, *et al.*, 1985: 143). In order to integrate the city into the national economy, approval was given for the construction of a railway linking Kunming and Chengdu via Panzhihua. As a result of a massive investment in steel and coal production in the years that followed, Panzhihua's industrial output grew by no less than 44 per cent per year between 1965 and 1978 compared to a provincial average of 10.4 per cent. Iron and steel production was non-existent in 1965; by 1978, the Panzhihua complex was producing over 1.6m. tonnes of steel and 1.4m. tonnes of iron. In the early 1980s Dukou was renamed Panzhihua to honour the name of the city's most important industry. Over the same period, coal production in Panzhihua rose from 9,400 tonnes to 3.5m. tonnes and about 80 per cent of output value was accounted for by the three steel, iron ore, and electricity bureaux (*ju*) alone (Cui, *et al.*, 1985: 147). By the late 1970s, Panzhihua's gross industrial output value amounted to 19 per cent of Chongqing's, a phenomenal achievement given the disparity in populations and the unremittingly hostile physical conditions in the Panzhihua area. In the sense that the Third Front Programme created an industrial sector capable of producing large quantities of output, it was a conspicuous success. But it is also testimony to the heavy-industrial bias of Maoist industrialization. In 1952, light industry accounted for 90 per cent of gross industrial output value in Panzhihua, and 53 per cent even by 1965. By 1978, however, the light-industrial sector accounted for barely 5 per cent of the total (SCZL, 1990: 342–3). Such was the transformation that had occurred on the banks of the Jinsha River in the late Maoist era to meet the threat posed by American involvement in Vietnam and Cambodia.

Yet for all the emphasis placed on heavy industry and defence by the Maoist industrialization strategy, it is quite wrong to see the industrial structure as petrified. The data on the pattern of investment show in fact a process of continually changing sectoral priorities. Some indication of this comes from Table 6.6, which shows the volume of new capacity created nationally in a number of selected industries over time. If the Maoist industrial structure was ossified, one would expect to see a similar amount of capacity being added to sectors over time. In fact, the volume of new capacity varied significantly across five year plan periods, depending on the priorities of the central government. In the sphere of energy, for example, one sees a decline in the volume of new coal-producing capacity from 81m. tonnes during 1971–5 to 65m. tonnes in 1976–80. This was offset by the development of the oil industry. During 1966–70, only 28m. tonnes of capacity were added. However, the figure rose to 41m. tonnes during 1971–5 and remained at 40m. tonnes during 1976–80; this of course reflected the coming on stream of new oilfields such as Daqing (with an installed capacity of 52m. tonnes) and Shengli (20m. tonnes).[15] In the case of cement, new capacity increased most quickly during 1966–70, when over 15m. tonnes of new capacity was installed. This reflected the commencement of the programme of Third Front construction. During the 1970s, however, the urgency

TABLE 6.6. *New production capacity installed in selected industries by five year plan periods, 1966–1980*

Industry	Units	1966–70	1971–5	1976–80
Steel	m. tonnes	6.5	6.0	5.9
Cement	m. tonnes	15.3	11.3	11.2
Coal	m. tonnes	68.1	81.2	64.9
Oil	m. tonnes	27.8	41.0	39.8
Chemical fertilizer	m. tonnes	2.0	3.7	4.7
Bicycles	million	0.7	0.7	2.4
Sewing machines	million	0.4	0.4	2.6
Synthetic fibres	000 tonnes	12.3	124.0	262.6
Cotton	m. bolts	3.2	0.9	1.9

Source: ZGTJNJ (1983: 348–59); ZGTJNJ (1985: 446–7).

gradually went out of the programme. As a result, only 11m. tonnes of new capacity was installed in each of the five year plan periods 1971–5 and 1976–80.

In other words, the Chinese planning system was well able to adjust to changing needs, and this conclusion is reinforced by looking at those sectors which expanded more quickly in the 1970s. One example is chemical fertilizer production. Installed capacity in the industry increased by only 2m. tonnes in 1966–70. But the figure leapt to 3.7m. tonnes during 1971–5 and climbed further to reach 4.7m. tonnes in 1976–80 as new plants purchased from Europe, Japan, and the USA were installed and came on stream. All this reflected a growing attention to the problems of the agricultural sector. Consumer-goods production was also allowed to expand in the late 1970s. Installed capacity in the bicycle industry increased by only 700,000 units in both the 1966–70 and 1971–5 plan periods. During 1976–80, however, the figure increased by a dramatic 2.4m. units. Much the same was true of another important consumer good, sewing machines. In this case, new capacity installation during 1976–80 (2.6m. units) was more than six times greater than in the previous plan period. Moreover, installed capacity in the synthetic fibres sector in 1976–80 was about 20 times greater than it had been during 1966–70.

In other words, the late Maoist industrial sector was gradually responding to the perceived need to provide more goods for consumers. None of this is to imply that the planners were always able to anticipate future demand. For example, new capacity installed in the cotton industry during 1976–80 was only about 60 per cent of that installed during 1966–70 (although that at least was something of an improvement over the rather dismal performance recorded during 1971–5). But the Maoist system of investment allocation was by no means as inflexible as is often suggested. Much of the capacity installed during the 1970s was increasingly well suited to the changing pattern of greater priority for consumption goods and inputs for use in agriculture. Accordingly, the industrial inheritance of the Dengist era was much more valuable for transition than is often recognized.

3. Investment in Transport Infrastructure

China's pre-1949 transport infrastructure was primitive. To be sure, the railway network inherited in 1949 was by no means negligible, comprising about 20,000 km of track in 1936. Furthermore, the network grew between 1915 and 1936 at a rate of about 3.3 per cent per year (Rawski, 1989: 209). Nevertheless, the network was woefully inadequate. In terms of its total size, the Republican railway system was smaller than those of Japan (24,036 km in 1930) and Brazil (33,106 km in 1943) (Minami, 1986: 120; Baer, 1995: 20); it was dwarfed by the 72,000 km network of British India. The Chinese railway system was also deficient in terms of its regional coverage and its quality. There were, for example, no railway bridges across the Yangzi River before 1949; trains were ferried across in sections. Additionally, most of the country's tracks were to be found in eastern China and Manchuria. Of the national total of 22,000 km in 1949,[16] very little was to be found in the south-west region; only 800 km existed in Guangxi, 656 km in Yunnan, 140 km in Guizhou and—given the size of the province—a paltry 67 km in Sichuan (Tang, 1986: 146). Furthermore, because of the differences in gauges, only the Guangxi network properly qualified as part of the national network; the Sichuan tracks, for instance, were no more than short, freight-carrying (mainly coal) lines around Chongqing city (*Chongqing shi jingji dili* 1987: 168–72). Much the same was true for the north-west, with the Longhai line—China's principal east–west trunk railway—extending only as far as Tianshui, 46 km into Gansu province, by 1949. Work had begun on extending the line from Tianshui to Lanzhou, the provincial capital, but this had made hardly any progress by 1949 (ZGSWY, 1988: i. 234). This slow pace of construction was typical; it had taken ten years to complete the 155 km stretch between Baoji and Tianshui.

The same pattern of underdevelopment is evident in the case of roads. Before 1949, the motor-road network did increased rapidly, growing annually by 15.8 per cent between 1927 and 1936 (Rawski, 1989: 214). But this growth began from an exceptionally low base. The pace of Republican construction still left far too many parts of China isolated. Wushan county—in the Yangzi Gorges—did not even begin its first motor road until 1956 (*Wushan xian zhi*, 1991: 210). Moreover, even comparatively affluent provinces like Zhejiang developed a comprehensive road network only extremely slowly. In Wenzhou prefecture, for instance, there were only about 100 km of motor road in 1949 (Wenzhou tongjiju, 1985: 175). As for China's ethnic minority counties, barely a handful had motor roads at the end of the Republican period.

Much of the transport infrastructure bequeathed in 1978 was therefore constructed during the Maoist era. The deficiencies of the Republican era began to be made good in the early 1950s, when a sustained effort was made to establish an extensive railway network in both the north- and south-west regions. As it transpired, no less than 75 per cent of all new track constructed during the Maoist period was in western China. Many of these were exceptionally impressive engineering achievements given the nature of the terrain; that was particularly true of the 1,892 km line linking Lanzhou with Urumqi built across the Gobi desert (completed in 1965) and the spectacular 1,100 km mountain line linking Chengdu and Kunming (completed in 1970).[17] In terms of the rate of construction, between 1952 and 1978, the national network expanded at an annual rate of 3.1 per cent; in the south-western provinces of Yunnan, Guizhou, and Sichuan, however, the rate averaged 3.7, 8.9, and 15.1 per cent per year respectively (ZYSWZY, 1986: 640; Tang, 1986: 146; Guizhou tongjiju, 1984: 242; SCTJNJ, 1990: 236). As was the case with railways, the Communist victory in 1949 ushered in a period of rapid expansion of the road system. Between 1952 and 1978, the metalled road network increased at an annual rate of 8 per cent (ZGTJNJ, 1992: 508) and very few counties were inaccessible by road at the end of the 1970s. For example, even Tibet possessed 15,912 km of roads by 1978, 75 per cent of which could be used by motor vehicles (Tang, 1986: 293), and only one of her counties (Medog) could not be reached by car. Furthermore, in Guizhou, China's poorest province, the road network density was 15.8 km of road per 100 square km, significantly higher than the national average of 9.4 km (Zhongguo Xinan minzu yanjiu xuehui, 1986: 217, 225).

For all these achievements, China's transport infrastructure was still underdeveloped in 1978. The annual growth rate of the railway network between 1952 and 1978 (3.1 per cent)[18] was lower than had been achieved during the war-torn 1915–36 period (3.3 per cent). Furthermore, the size of the 1978 network (48,600 km) was still inferior to those of India (62,000 km) and the USA (253,000 km).[19] In addition, a number of strategically important areas of China remained unconnected to the national network, most obviously Tibet. Finally, none of the new lines constructed in western China were double-tracked, and very few were electrified. The road network also remained backward. China was far from entering the motorway age; indeed the long-distance routes worked by her buses were often in a poor enough state of repair to be called diabolical. The road density—at 94 km per 1,000 square km of area—was substantially less than achieved in other large countries such as Brazil (164 km), India (539 km), and the USA (668 km) by the mid-1980s (World Bank, 1990*b*: 215). Furthermore, for all the much-vaunted Chinese 'achievements' in Tibet, about 40 per cent of her *xiang* (townships) were still inaccessible by motor vehicles at the end of the 1970s.

Nevertheless, one could hardly expect the Maoist regime to make good the neglect of a century within less than three decades. Maoist growth rates were a much more considerable achievement than those achieved prior to 1949 precisely because growth began from a significantly higher base, and one can argue about whether (for example) the massive cost of extending the railway network to link Golmud in Qinghai with Lhasa in Tibet was justified given Tibet's small population. Moreover, that so many of the incredibly isolated areas of south-west China were accessible by road in the late 1970s is a tribute to how much had been achieved in the Maoist period. Most importantly of all, and as will be seen in Chapter 8, it was the transport infrastructure created before 1978 that provided the foundation for the economic growth of the era of transition. Without that infrastructure, rapid growth would have been impossible.

4. The Development of Social Capability

4.1. Education in Late Imperial and Republican China

Late Imperial China was characterized by a reasonable level of male literacy. According to Rawski (1979: 23), male literacy rates hovered between 30 and 45 per cent of the total in the late Qing. By the Bowman–Anderson criterion, this may have been enough for China to begin modern industrial growth. However, female literacy rates were far lower; Rawski estimates them to have been in the range of 2 to 10 per cent. In other words, China's overall literacy rate seems to have fallen short of the 30 per cent threshold. This record, poor though it was, may even have deteriorated after the collapse of the Qing dynasty: the research carried out in the 1930s by J. L. Buck (1937: 375–7) and associates estimated rural literacy rates at perhaps 30 per cent for males aged 7 and over and barely 1 per cent for females. Given that Buck's sample was biased in favour of the more prosperous and accessible parts of the rural hinterland (Stross, 1986), these figures may even overstate literacy. Nevertheless, Buck's results are not markedly different from the most reliable data on this question, the age composition figures on illiteracy collected during the 1982 Population Census (Table 6.7).

Table 6.7. *Combined male and female illiteracy by age in 1982* (percentage of cohort)

Year of birth	Jiangsu	Zhejiang	Sichuan	Yunnan	Jilin
1963–7	8	7	n/a	27	4
1958–62	16	15	14	34	6
1953–7	28	23	22	42	11
1948–52	30	24	28	45	13
1943–7	31	27	30	49	16
1938–42	44	40	41	61	25
1933–7	58	52	53	69	43
1928–32	65	60	61	76	57
1923–7	69	64	69	81	65
1922 and earlier	80	77	80	89	80

Sources: Du (1987: 341); Wang (1988: 352); Liu (1988: 381); Zou and Miao (1989: 493); Cao (1988: 387).

The most obvious characteristic of these data is the exceptionally high rate of illiteracy amongst the older age groups. For those born before 1922, illiteracy rates averaged over 80 per cent. Even for the cohort born during 1923 and 1927—who would have been educated during the Nanjing decade—illiteracy rates were close to 80 per cent. Although there is considerable spatial variation in literacy rates amongst those born in the 1940s and later (with literacy rates in Jilin, for example, far ahead of those recorded in Yunnan), the pattern for those born in the pre-1937 period is remarkably consistent.

Four other points are worth making about the extent of illiteracy in the Republican period. First, the figures in Table 6.7 understate true pre-1949 illiteracy because they take no account of the positive effects of adult literacy programmes introduced after the Revolution (Lavely, *et al.*, 1990). In other words, many of those who missed primary education in the 1930s had another chance in the 1950s. Secondly, rural illiteracy rates were even lower than these averages suggest. In rural China, illiteracy rates for those aged 60 and over in 1982 as a percentage of the age cohort were 82 per cent for males and 97 per cent for females (Zhonghua quanguo funu lianhehui funu yanjiusuo, 1991: 64). Thirdly, the female literacy rates in the Republican period were incredibly low (Table 6.8); the gender bias within the traditional Chinese household is plain. Finally, illiteracy rates amongst ethnic minorities were even higher. Compare, for example, the illiteracy rates of Han Chinese resident in Sichuan with those of Tibetans resident in the western part of the same province. For males aged between 60 and 64 in 1990, the illiteracy rates for Han Chinese was 40 per cent whereas for Tibetans it was 76 per cent. For females in the same age range, the illiteracy rate for Han Chinese was 84 per cent but for Tibetans it was 98 per cent. For Tibetan woman born before 1925, the illiteracy rate was almost 100 per cent, compared to 92 per cent for Han females (Xizang zizhiqu renkou pucha bangongshi, 1992: 411). Evidently the extent of educational failure in ethnic minority areas was even greater than in Han China.

TABLE 6.8. *Female illiteracy rates in Republican China*
(female illiterates as percentage of female population)

Year of birth	Jiangsu	Zhejiang	Sichuan	Yunnan	Jilin
1928–32	88	83	86	93	79
1923–7	91	86	90	95	87
1922 and before	95	94	96	98	95

Sources: As for Table 6.7.

In sum, these systematic data from the 1982 Census bear testimony to the failure of the educational programmes of the Qing and Republican periods. Illiteracy rates in the China of the 1930s were uniformly high for males, and exceptionally high for females. As a result, Republican China fell well short of the literacy rates achieved by most of Western Europe on the eve of industrialization. The idea that China's growth rate after 1978 owed anything to a large population of pensioners who received their education before 1949 is an illusion.

4.2. Maoist Education

There is much criticism of the Maoist approach to education in the literature. That is especially true for the Cultural Revolution when educated urban youth and intellectuals were sent into the countryside in the *shangshan xiaxiang* programme and the university system closed down. Both policies have been roundly condemned (Bernstein, 1977; Liu and Wu, 1986: 422; Schneider, 1989).[20] Writing of the 'sending down' programme, Banister (1987: 342) concluded:

> This attempt to 'ruralize' the population was so counter to the needs and preferences of the affected people that it finally failed . . . The great majority of the sent-down youth were disaffected if not bitter, their parents struggled to get them back home, and peasants in areas where the youth were sent complained about the burden of supporting them.

Similar evidence of mutual disaffection emerges in the writings of Unger, *et al.* (1984); and Bernstein, writing in the late 1970s before it was fully apparent that the programme had been tacitly abandoned by the CCP, was also relatively pessimistic about its effectiveness. Although the programme did serve to mitigate urban unemployment and although the rural economy gained from the presence of urban youth, the costs were high: 'one of these costs is to the advanced sector, and it comes in the form of wasted talent, in that some of those who ought to be given high-level training do not receive it because they have been sent to the countryside' (Bernstein, 1977: 295).

Chinese accounts of the impact of the Cultural Revolution on the educational system are typically even more dismissive of Maoist policy:

> In the ten years of internal strife [1966–76], our intellectuals were widely discriminated against and suppressed and many scientists and professors were branded 'reactionary academic authorities' and denounced and insulted as such. The development of science and technology in our country suffered serious setbacks and were badly undermined. In many fields approaching the world's advanced level after gruelling work since the birth of New China, there was again a widened gap between us and the world's most advanced level.
>
> Education was the hardest-hit field during the 10 years of catastrophe. All schools were closed to 'make revolution' and the campus of some institutes of higher learning for a while became the arena of infighting between different factions of rebels. (Liu and Wu, 1986: 422)

Many 'autobiographical' accounts also testify to the degree of abhorrence felt by most educated Chinese towards the policies pursued during the late Maoist era (Cheng, 1986; Chang, 1991; Zhang, 1991; Mosher, 1994).[21]

What of the evidence? From the start it must be admitted that Maoist policy did fail in a number of areas. During the 1950s, for instance, the Soviet influence was overwhelming and brought in its train the dubious benefits of Lysenkoist genetics (Schneider, 1989). Perhaps more seriously, the emphasis on high-quality provision that was an integral part of the Soviet tradition led to the relative neglect of primary education in rural areas (Pepper, 1987*a*). The Yan'an-inspired goal of a *minban* school in every village was dropped and neither the total number of primary school children nor the number of primary schools showed much of an increase between 1952 and 1957 (ZGTJNJ, 1993: 699, 703); secondary schooling in rural areas was largely ignored. In fact, these systemic failings during the supposedly 'golden age' of the 1950s led to radical change during the Cultural Revolution. According to Pepper (1990):

> . . . the basic tasks that should be performed at the secondary level are to provide education that will be terminal for most and college preparatory for some. . . . During the early 1960s, the formula for achieving these tasks . . . was an increasingly stratified one with the urban-based, quality-oriented keypoint schools emerging clearly as the college-preparatory system. Other less regular work-study and vocational options were used to meet the inevitable demands for some kind of mass secondary schooling that grew out of the rapidly developing elementary school system. . . . The 'Maoist' solution as it finally crystallized during the 1966–76 decade, after the Red Guard phase had run its course, was to break up the whole bifurcated system. Despite all the rhetoric, the net effect was not just to politicize education but also to popularize and vocationalize it. (Pepper, 1990: 94–5)

The damaging effects of the Cultural Revolution on the educational system are well known. Most universities were shut from the mid-1960s until the early 1970s as teacher and student alike participated in the activities of the Red Guards. When most reopened (in 1972 and 1973), a mere 48,000 students was still listed on the enrolment registers compared to 674,000 in 1965 (ZGTJNJ, 1992: 702). Moreover, university admission depended far more upon experience and background than intellectual merit. This emphasis on egalitarianism in higher education was successful in its own terms, but it had damaging consequences for economic growth in the 1980s, which was constrained by shortages of skilled personnel. As for the *shangshan xiaxiang* campaign, few in either the West or China have had a good word for it. The majority of the 17 million or so urban youth sent to the countryside between 1966 and 1978 resented their exile every bit as much as Chinese peasants resented having to feed these unproductive mouths. By most criteria, the tangible benefits that accrued to rural China were small. According to Bernstein (1977: 238–9) 'When it is possible to appraise the program against some kind of external standard, however crude, it turns out that the urban youth contribution is relatively modest.' As he points out, only a very small fraction were employed as doctors, teachers, or scientists and, if the rationale for the programme was merely to provide additional unskilled labour (50 per cent seemingly did nothing else—Bernstein, 1977: 239), it hardly made sense to employ expensively educated urban youth in that role. That the exodus was reversed so quickly and so completely in the late 1970s and early 1980s give some indication of the degree of feeling on both sides of the rural–urban divide. The impact of the Cultural Revolution on primary school completion (*gugong*) rates was also significant. In Sichuan, completion rates were running at about 90 per cent in 1965. However, they averaged only about 40 per cent during 1966–73 (Liu, 1988: 385). In Yunnan, the completion rate dwindled from 35 per cent in 1966 to 28 per cent during the Cultural Revolution (Zou and Miao, 1989: 498).

Nevertheless, the educational record of the Maoist era is not so easily dismissed. Perhaps the most obvious indicator of success was the upward trend in the literacy rate. By 1982, the position was radically different from that of 1949 (Table 6.9). By then, illiteracy had been reduced to an overall rate of 32 per cent (ZGRKNJ, 1986: 617) and, if one looks at the population aged 15 and over,[22] adult illiteracy was 23 per cent (National Population Census Office, 1991: 30). Over 50 per cent of the female population aged 12 and over was literate (in very sharp contrast to the position in the 1930s), whilst male literacy was up to 80 per cent. Furthermore, the rise in literacy was spread across China's provinces; even in the very poor north-western and south-western regions, female literacy rates were close to 50 per cent by the early 1980s.

TABLE 6.9. *Illiteracy by Chinese region, 1982* (per cent)

	Male	Female
Regional illiteracy rates, 1982:		
North-East	16.5	32.8
Northern Coastal	16.9	40.9
Southern Coastal	15.1	43.9
Central	20.1	47.5
South-West	24.8	53.1
North-West	26.7	50.6
National illiteracy rates:		
1930s		
Rural	64	97
Urban	40	85
1982		
Overall	19	45
Ethnic	30	56

Notes: N-E—provinces of Heilongjiang, Jilin, and Nei Menggu. Northern Coastal—Beijing, Hebei, Tianjin, Shandong, and Liaoning. Southern Coastal—Shanghai, Jiangsu, Zhejiang, Fujian, and Guangdong (including Hainan). Central—Shanxi, Henan, Hubei, Hunan, Anhui, and Jiangxi. South-West—Sichuan, Guizhou, Yunnan, Tibet, and Guangxi). North-West—Gansu, Ningxia, Shaanxi, Qinghai, and Xinjiang. Illiteracy rates are illiterates aged 12 and over as a share of total male or female population. Regional rates are based on provincial means weighted by 1978 population. Data for the 1930s are based on illiteracy rates amongst those aged 60 and over at the time of the 1982 Census.

Sources: ZGRKTJNJ (1988: 470–1); Zhonghua quanguo funu lianhehui funu yanjiusuo (1991: 64); ZGRKNJ (1986: 630).

This extremely rapid reduction in the degree of illiteracy was due mainly to the expansion of primary and secondary education during the Maoist era. Although the number of children in primary education increased rather slowly in the 1950s, the number enrolled by 1957 nevertheless accounted for 62 per cent of the cohort —well in excess of the 1952 rate of 49 per cent. More importantly, primary education became virtually universal after the dramatic change in policy that occurred in the early 1960s. By 1965, the enrolment rate has reached 85 per cent and approached 97 per cent by 1975 (ZGTJNJ, 1992: 717). Moreover, primary school completion rates rose over time (although, as we have seen, they declined temporarily during the early stages of the Cultural Revolution). In Jilin, for example, the completion rate rose from 37 per cent in 1964, to 83 per cent in 1978 (Cao, 1988: 392). In Yunnan, the rate rose from 29 per cent in 1957 to 35 per cent by 1966 and to 52 per cent in 1978 (Zou and Miao, 1989: 498).

Almost as importantly, rural secondary education expanded enormously in the late Maoist period (Table 6.10).

TABLE 6.10. *Secondary school enrolment rates, 1965–1978* (per cent)

Year	Lower middle school	Upper middle school
1965	44.9	26.4
1966	30.3	13.0
1967	22.0	7.5
1968	45.4	12.1
1969	68.7	28.8
1970	71.1	38.6
1971	89.8	38.4
1972	88.1	46.2
1973	84.4	40.0
1974	88.4	51.0
1975	90.6	60.4
1976	94.1	71.4
1977	92.0	63.7
1978	87.6	40.9

Notes: Enrolment rates calculated as the number entering lower or upper middle school as a percentage of those graduating from primary and lower middle school respectively in the same year.
Source: ZGJYNJ, 1949–81 (1984: 1,001, 1,021).

The programme of mass secondary education only really began in 1955, but by 1958 the numbers enrolled in secondary school had increased threefold (ZGTJNJ, 1992: 702). However, the proportion of those going on from primary to secondary school was still only about 45 per cent by 1965 (ZGTJNJ, 1991: 688, 690). These numbers fell further during the first years of the Cultural Revolution.

Thereafter, secondary education increased very rapidly. This expansion was a result of the rejection after 1966 of the views of educational professionals that had prevailed during the 1950s—according to which secondary education was unnecessary for the rural population. When this elitist model of the early 1960s—which focused on channelling a small number of predominantly urban children into 'key-point' middle schools—was jettisoned, the 'staying-on' rate rose to reach over 94 per cent by 1976 (ZGTJNJ, 1991: 688, 690; Pepper, 1990).[23] In part, this expansion of the secondary sector was financed by the state. However, the bulk of resources were raised by the communes themselves, either from the collective accumulation fund or by charging tuition fees; these amounted to around 4 *yuan* per annum in relatively prosperous areas like the Chengdu plain (Endicott, 1988: 239). By the 1970s, then, near-universal secondary education existed in rural areas for the first time, and—not surprisingly—the closure campaign of 1977–82 (see Chapter 16) met with considerable resistance. This was because mass secondary education in rural areas not only raised literacy rates but also contributed enormously to the rapid rural industrialization of the 1980s; indeed many communes were reluctant to close their secondary schools during 1977–82 precisely because of an awareness of the importance of a skilled labour force for rural industrial enterprises (Pepper, 1996: 504). Indeed, without the massive expansion of secondary education in the post-1966 period, it would have been impossible to have started rural enterprises on the scale undertaken in the early 1980s.

The Maoist years also saw a concerted attempt, apparently successful, to provide a technical rather than a liberal arts education at the tertiary level. According to Richman (1969: 168):

> The most spectacular growth in Chinese education has been in engineering fields. From 1928 to 1947—a period of about twenty years—China produced only 31,700 engineering graduates; from 1948 to 1963—a period of fifteen years—the country produced 387,840 graduates, or almost thirteen times more than it did during the earlier period . . . In recent years one third or more of all higher education graduates have been in engineering fields.

Even though China lagged well behind most developed countries in terms of scientists per 100,000 people, she had clearly made enormous progress compared to pre-1949 and there can be no doubt that this helped make possible the massive expansion of industry that occurred during the Maoist years.

5. Chinese Culture and Economic Growth

One of the least appealing aspects of economic theorizing to those working outside the profession is its tendency to ignore cultural factors. Economists tend either to take a deterministic view (the economic base determines the superstructure, including culture) or simply assume that culture is given (as in standard neoclassical theorizing, in which preferences and cultural factors are taken as exogenous) without really considering whether this culture promotes or retards economic growth.[24]

Economic determinism continues to have its advocates. Fredric Jameson, for example, has long seen economic forces as critical in determining cultural outcomes; in his early work, capitalism led to individualism and thus to the differentiation of ideas and texts.[25] In his more recent work, late capitalism (postmodernism) is seen as obliterating these distinctions (Veeser, 1989: 13 n.). It is thus the changing nature of capitalism (the economic base) which has brought about changes in the cultural realm (the superstructure). However, it has long been argued by others that cultural factors will have an independent impact on the economy. The most celebrated argument along these lines is that of Max Weber. Weber believed that the development of capitalism could be partly explained by religion (the emergence of the Protestant work ethic in the wake of the Reformation), and regarded this conclusion as a direct critique of Marx's historical materialism (Giddens, 1995: 65–6). Nevertheless, Weber's aim was not simply to replace one form of determinism (economic) with another (cultural); rather, it was to recognize the interaction of economic and cultural factors:

On the other hand, however, we have no intention whatever of maintaining such a foolish and doctrinaire thesis as that the spirit of capitalism . . . could only have arisen as the result of certain effects of the Reformation, or even that capitalism as an economic system is a creation of the Reformation. In itself, the fact that certain important forms of capitalistic business organization are known to be considerably older than the Reformation is a sufficient refutation of such a claim. On the contrary, we only wish to ascertain whether and to what extent religious forces have taken part in the qualitative formation and the quantitative expansion of that spirit over the world. (Weber, cited in Käsler, 1988: 81)

Weber's analysis is not without its problems. As Tawney (1937) noted, the genesis of capitalism arguably lay in the Catholic city states of the fifteenth century and not in Protestant England and Holland; moreover, one can always restate the materialist position by arguing that the Reformation, far from being exogenous, was itself a product of economic factors. Nevertheless, in both its rejection of determinism and in arguing that 'culture matters', the Weberian approach has obvious appeal and has been influential in much of the theorizing of the twentieth century. Writers of the Frankfurt school such as Adorno and Marcuse emphasized the role of culture in influencing class consciousness and therefore class action; similarly E. P. Thompson's (1968) study of the English working class. Much of Althusser's work had as its objective the criticism of all forms of Marxist determinism (economism and humanism), and a restatement of the importance of the superstructure. This provided the foundation for Althusser's own interpretation of Marxian theory, in which neither economic nor superstructural factors are any more fundamental than each other. Rather, outcomes are overdetermined:

. . . Marx has at least given us the 'two ends of the chain', and has told us to find out what goes on between them: on the one hand, determination in the last instance by the (economic) mode of production; on the other, the relative autonomy of the superstructures and their specific effectivity [p. 111]. . . . the economic dialectic is never active in the pure state; in History, these instances, the superstructures, etc.—are never seen to step respectfully aside when their work is done or, when the Time comes, as his pure phenomena, to scatter before His Majesty the Economy as he strides along the royal road of the Dialectic. From the first moment to the last, the lonely hour of the 'last instance' never comes [p. 113]. (Althusser, 1990)

More generally, the intense debates on the Left since the 1960s and the emergence of postmodernism have led to several widely-held conclusion. One is that there is no good reason to assign a privileged position to economic forces as an explanation of oppression. Subordination, it is argued, can reflect (inter alia) gender, crime, ideology, and race as well as economic factors.[26] This in turn has led to growing emphasis on the role of cultural and ideological factors in influencing economic development. For example, Chomsky has emphasized the role of media in 'manufacturing consent', and Fukuyama (1995) the role of trust in reducing transaction costs and thus promoting growth. Scott (1976) has stressed the way in which the 'moral economy' of the peasant has led to resistance to market forces, and Lal (1995: 1,475) argued that economic reform in India (and China) was bound to fail because of cultural resistance, and especially 'continuing atavistic attitudes toward trade and commerce'. None of these accounts are entirely convincing: Chomsky probably overrates the impact of the media, and the empirical basis of Fukuyama's identification of high- and low-trust societies is problematic (successful economies are identified as exhibiting high trust, and vice versa, irrespective of actual conditions); Scott neglects the willingness of peasantries to respond to suitable economic incentives, and Lal makes the same mistake (as well as suggesting that culture is immutable). But despite these problems, one clear conclusion from all this work is that culture does matter in terms of its independent impact on the economy.

A second clear conclusion is that culture does not change quickly. Lal is surely wrong in seeing contemporary Indian culture as immutable, but there is little doubting the glacial pace of cultural change. According to Bailey (1966: 296–7), writing of India:

> Any plan for modernization which is based on the assumption that peasants will feel an immediate moral commitment to modernity as such, and will persist voluntarily in the face of failure and frustrations because they are so committed, must be ineffective. . . . Cognitive maps do change; but for the most part they do so slowly as the result of experience. As the flow of water can change the course of a river, so experience can erode received ideas and allow others to settle in their place. With this, most modernizers must be content.

Over any short time period, one can therefore assume that culture is given. It follows that Chinese culture during the 1980s must have been wholly or substantially as it was in the late 1970s.

The central question as far as China is concerned is of course whether the culture of the late 1970s, itself a product of the Maoist, Republican, and Imperial eras, was conducive to economic growth. On this, the conventional wisdom for many years was that Chinese culture was inimical to development, a view primarily based upon the poor economic performance of the economy over the *longue durée* from 1700 to the end of the 1970s. For Marx, for instance, China was 'Asiatic', a country 'without history'. Wright (1957) argued that the Tongzhi Restoration (1862–74) failed because, in the last instance, modernization was rejected because it was seen as conflicting with the Confucian order. More recently, Morishima ascribed the difference in the development paths of China and Japan to the nature of Confucianism in the latter—which promoted loyalty to the state rather than to family or lineage group; and Fukuyama (1995) makes a similar point, stylising China as a 'low-trust' society. Moreover, against a background of growing nepotism and corruption in the late 1980s, some intellectuals in the People's Republic despaired of Chinese culture; the series 'River Elegy' is the best example.

However, these notions of cultural conservatism are not very convincing. One problem is that pre-1949 Chinese culture was not an obstacle to growth when other institutional factors were broadly growth-promoting. There was, for example, extraordinary technical progress in China during the Tang and Song periods, and even the Ming dynasty was not characterized by technological stasis (Needham, 1970). The work of Rowe (1984; 1989), and Chuan and Kraus (1975), has shown that long-distance commerce was not unusual under the late Ming/early Qing, and the sophistication of a number of China's water-conservancy projects along the Yellow River, in northern Hunan, and in Sichuan is well known (Perdue, 1987). It is therefore more logical to look for an explanation of the late Qing slowdown in terms of institutional, economic, and ecological structures rather than culture. As Elvin (1983: 380) puts it:

> The explanation in terms of economic and ecological factors [CMB: the Elvin high-level equilibrium trap] . . . does not deny the general importance of cultural factors—on the contrary!—but suggests that late traditional Chinese values and ideas were in most respects already suitable for modern economic growth, and that the key inhibiting constraints were not cultural.

This type of view is reinforced by the rapidity of economic growth in those parts of China most influenced by the impact of Western imperialism after 1840. Most obviously, it is hard to explain the growth of the textile industry in Shanghai and Sunan after 1900 without acknowledging the receptive nature of Chinese culture to capitalism and innovation. Moreover, the extent of growth in the Republican era was considerable; as Bergère (1989) has shown, the period between the beginning of World War I and the end of the 1920s was indeed 'the golden age of the Chinese bourgeoisie'. In fact, the pace of growth of modern industry was so fast during the Nanjing decade (1928–37) that China on the eve of the Japanese invasion is portrayed as being on the verge of economic take-off (Rawski, 1989); between 1914/18 and 1931/6, the modern industrial sector grew at almost 8 per cent per year in 1933 prices (Yeh, 1979). It is more than questionable whether take-off was likely given the institutional obstacles to agricultural growth, the limited development of infrastructure, and the corruption of the Kuomintang regime, but it is transparent that Chinese culture was in itself no obstacle to the growth of modern industry. This proposition is fully affirmed by the dramatic growth rates achieved in Taiwan and Hong Kong after 1950.

Some Maoist institutional structures and policies probably had the unintended effect of increasing sympathy within China for some 'Western values'. There is little doubt that collective farming, though popular in some areas, was widely hated (Kelliher, 1992; Zhou, 1996). Paradoxically, therefore, almost any alternative was perceived as attractive, and for that reason decollectivization proceeded quickly in many regions in the early 1980s; for the majority of the Chinese peasantry, decollectivization was a second land reform (Kueh, 1985) or a second revolution (Garnault, *et al.*, 1996). Another positive factor (albeit paradoxically) was China's involvement in the Korean war. Chinese cemeteries and the new local gazetteers alike pay testimony to the number of Chinese soldiers who died fighting on the North Korean side, but those who came through that experience relatively unscathed were marked by it for ever. On returning to their villages, they brought with them an understanding of modernity (massive American firepower) that helped to weaken traditional Chinese village culture. The same applied to the sending down of urban citizens to the countryside during the Cultural Revolution (Bernstein, 1977). Although mutual incomprehension invariably marked these encounters, the programme did bring a flow of new ideas and educated men and women to many previously closed village communities.

Maoist campaigns also took their toll of Chinese cultural traditions. The successful prohibition of footbinding, the introduction of a divorce law, and the availability of contraception when family planning policies began to be implemented in the late 1960s, helped to emancipate women. The introduction of modern health-care technologies (especially vaccination) weakened the position of traditional Chinese doctors. Electricity, roads, and mobile cinemas facilitated communication. Collectivization was probably most important of all. By undermining the traditional village hierarchy (already severely weakened by the persecution of landlords during the land-reform campaigns of 1947–53) and by facilitating the introduction of new agricultural technologies, many village traditions were irreparably damaged. Hated the collective may have been, but there was no easy way back to the past. Even the Great Leap Forward promoted modernity by introducing the Chinese peasantry to iron and steel-making technology; that period was also one of female emancipation (communal dining; child-care facilities; sewing circles).

Not all the changes that were wrought to village life in the Maoist era promoted the cause of modernity. Some of the dubious technologies propagated by the collective helped to discredit modernizing ideas. The emancipation of women during the Leap provoked a male backlash. The obstacles to internal migration tended to make rural China more, rather than less, cellular. Limited contact with the outside world made China much more insular than before 1949, with the result that those Chinese travelling abroad in the early 1980s were amazed by the extent of material progress that had occurred in Japan, South Korea, Taiwan, and Hong Kong. Jiang Qing's revolutionary operas and the writings of the Chinese literary establishment provoked derision rather than any affection for modernity.[27] Furthermore, some Maoist campaigns which ostensibly focused on changing Chinese culture served only to mask a more malevolent intent; for example, the movement to 'Criticize Lin Biao and Confucius' of the early 1970s was directed not against the latter but against Zhou Enlai. Nevertheless, Chinese culture on the eve of transition was arguably much less hidebound and traditional than in many other countries precisely because of the impact of pre-1949 Western imperialism and, above all, the effects of the Maoist pursuit of modernity. It is hard to believe that this culture did nothing to serve the cause of economic growth in the years that followed Mao's death.

6. Summary: The Capital Stock and Social Capability in 1978

The picture that emerges from this discussion is that China entered the transition era with reasonably well-developed levels of physical and human capital. The economy therefore had a significant level of social and physical capability which it could use to generate growth. The extent of this capability should not be exaggerated; as we have seen, there were many deficiencies in the stock of both human and physical capital. Not all Maoist educational policies were a success. Some of the irrigation projects undertaken in the 1960s and 1970s were misconceived. The transport network remained deficient despite heavy investment. And China's cultural transformation was incomplete. Nevertheless, China's capability was well enough developed to allow it to utilize effectively the technology pioneered abroad that became available after China opened its frontiers to foreign trade and FDI in the 1970s. This process of technological diffusion played a key role in the rapid growth of the transition era, but it was the development of social and physical capability—especially in the Maoist period—which made it possible.

7

The Role of Surplus Labour

The analysis of surplus labour offered by the master discourse is based upon the famous labour-surplus models developed by Lewis (1954) and others; these were discussed in Chapter 4. They have been used by a number of writers to explain China's rapid growth since 1978. One of the key conclusions from this literature is that China grew more quickly than the countries of Eastern Europe and the former Soviet Union (EEFSU) because of its relative abundance of surplus labour (Sachs and Woo, 1994; 1997; Woo, 1998). Its relative under-industrialization, it has been argued, worked to China's advantage after 1978.

1. Productivity Fantasies

Right from the start, it is important to recognize the limitations of the well-known analysis developed by Sachs and Woo. One of the problems with their approach to accounting for Chinese growth is that the methodology adopted in estimating TFP is flawed. A key difficulty is that the results are very sensitive to the valuation of output. The whole TFP approach works only if the prices used to value output and factor inputs are equal to long-run social marginal cost, i.e. if they are equilibrium prices. However, equilibrium prices do not (for a number of well-known reasons) exist and therefore are not observable. The only way to make the approach operational is to look for a year in which the prevailing prices can be deemed 'close' to the equilibrium price vector. But this can never be more than guesswork, especially when economies are characterized by extensive government intervention because then a view has to be taken about whether observed prices are closer to social marginal cost (because intervention by government corrects for externalities) or whether they are even more distorted. And precisely because of these sorts of problems, widely differing estimates of East Asian TFP have proliferated in the literature over the last decade.

Perhaps the most useful aspect of the work of Sachs and Woo is that it helps to lay bare the wholly tendentious nature of TFP estimates for China. Woo is happy to aggregate wildly varying qualities of labour to produce an estimate of aggregate labour input, and to use a Cobb–Douglas production function (which rules out economies of scale). Even assuming this approach to be a reasonable approximation, his estimate of TFP growth for 1979–93 varies from 0.2 to 2.3 per cent depending on the deflation procedure and the assumed share of labour in income. And this before any attempt is even made to ask whether observed prices in China bear any relation to long-run social marginal costs. Woo is hardly alone in offering a wide

TFP range; Borensztein and Ostry (1996) suggest TFP growth of −1.0 to 3.8 per cent for 1979 to 1990. But if this is the likely order of error even before fundamental questions are asked about how inputs and outputs ought to be priced, we can fairly conclude that growth accounting offers no useful insights into the growth process in China. It follows that attempts to measure the impact of labour reallocation in this sort of way are wholly spurious.

We therefore need to abandon empty formalism and rely instead on a more qualitative analysis of the contribution of surplus labour to China's growth. The place to begin is to ask whether surplus labour existed at all in the People's Republic in the mid-1970s.

2. The Existence of Surplus Labour in the 1970s

It is by no means fanciful to argue that there was actually very little surplus labour in Chinese agriculture in the mid-1970s. A labour surplus certainly did not exist during the peak periods of sowing and harvesting; attempts at the removal of labour from farming during the Great Leap Forward (1958–62)—when farm labour was used to produce iron and steel, and therefore unavailable during the harvest period—led directly to the disastrous famine of the early 1960s (Walker, 1984; Kueh, 1995). But even during the winter slack season, the abundant surplus labour identified by Buck and others in pre-war Chinese agriculture had largely disappeared. This was because, as observed in Chapter 6, a substantial part of the workforce was absorbed by the large-scale labour accumulation projects which were begun in the late 1960s and early 1970s. Yet, and paradoxically, on-farm labour productivity in Chinese agriculture was much lower than in other Asian countries and compared with Chinese industry, implying very large underemployment.

The key to understanding this paradox is to recognize the nature of the question being asked. If the question is: 'Was sectoral labour allocation in late Maoist China first-best?' the answer is clearly 'No'. But if the question is: 'Was labour optimally allocated given the prevailing incentive structures?' the answer would be 'Yes'. Although labour productivity was higher in industry than in agriculture, releasing labour from agriculture would not have raised total output under late Maoism. For one thing, the process of labour release would have reduced farm output because labour productivity in agriculture was non-negative. This in itself need not have been a disaster. The first-best solution would have been to employ the released labour in export-orientated light industry, and use the export revenue to pay for food imports. But the military orientation of the Maoist development strategy ruled this approach out on two counts. First, there was little demand for industrial labour because industry was geared towards military ends and therefore capital intensive. Any labour released in these circumstances would have been underemployed in urban instead of rural China and, for being more easily organized, would have posed a greater threat to regime stability. Second, the approach would have implied dependence on food imports, a very dangerous policy given China's strategic isolation and the (perceived) threat posed to the Maoist regime by both the USA and the Soviet

Union. In other words, *given* China's perception of the external threat, the development of light industry using agricultural labour was not an option.

In addition, incentives within farming were such that labour productivity was very low. In part, this was because of the way collective farms operated. The primary aims of the collective were to satisfy basic needs, to hold in check income inequalities in the countryside, to extract the financial surplus from the rural sector and transfer it to industry, and to provide an institutional framework within which labour could be mobilized for military defence if required. No other institutional framework could easily satisfy these goals in the Chinese context. However, there was little scope within this overall plan for powerful incentive systems. Precisely because material incentives would divide the rural population into opposing camps, it would threaten the very solidarity that was deemed both intrinsically important and instrumentally significant for national defence.

The result was an on-farm incentive system that did little to encourage high levels of productivity. By the late 1960s, time-rate systems proliferated and there were immense difficulties in adequately supervising the rural workforce. In Liu's (1991*a*) phrase, the amount of time spent ('time allocation') on farm work was high but the intensity of effort per hour ('effort allocation') was very low. The problem was compounded by the way in which the internal terms of trade were biased against agriculture. In order to finance Third Front construction, it was necessary to depress rural consumption and extract the surplus (in the form of high profits in those industries selling to collective farms) via high input prices and low farm-procurement prices. The negative substitution effects this process of extraction set up served to weaken farm incentives even further. With productivity per labour day low and declining (as mobilizational campaigns lost their effectiveness through repetition), there was evidently a need to raise farm output in some other way. Unfortunately there were few substitution possibilities. Capital was far too scarce to be reallocated to agriculture; it was needed for the Third Front. And, although HYVs were on the way, they were still not available in the early 1970s. The only way, therefore, to maintain output growth was by continuing involution (Huang, 1990): the application of ever larger volumes of labour to farm production to offset the adverse incentive effects on productivity.

Little surplus labour existed in other sectors of the economy. Again the Third Front was the culprit in the 1960s and early 1970s because, at the margin, it used significant amounts of labour to construct new factories in inaccessible parts of the hinterland, and to build transport infrastructure. The Chengdu–Kunming railway, the centrepiece of the infrastructural programme, was especially demanding because of the terrain across which it was built. And within industry itself, it was hard to free up labour because of constraints on labour-saving technological imports from the West.

Until the early 1970s, therefore, it was not easy to see how China could achieve rapid increases in per capita output *given* its military orientation. The late Maoist development strategy had gone far towards ensuring military security, raising the educational level of the labour force and creating an extensive physical infrastructure even in western China. And the continuing high rate of saving (discussed in the next chapter) meant that the capital–labour ratio would continue to rise—and with it per capita output—over the forseeable future. But the incentive structures necessitated by this pattern of development meant that there was extensive slack within the economy.

3. Surplus Labour in Transition-Era China

In fact, of course, the way out of the impasse of moderate growth was already clear by the mid-1970s. China's developing rapprochement with the USA, and the growth of its nuclear arsenal, signalled the end for the Third Front programme. Once that programme was brought to an end, the main obstacle to the development of labour-absorbing light industry were removed. Furthermore, it was then possible to shift the internal terms of trade in favour of agriculture, with likely favourable effects on farm production. As importantly, the need for collective farming would be much reduced once military objectives were less important. The other solution to the impasse was the development of high-yielding varieties. By bringing about a dramatic increase in output per worker, HYVs made possible a simultaneous increase in total agricultural output and the release of labour. HYVs were labour-using in the sense that more labour was needed per unit of land but, because they raised yields, it was possible to reduce sown area and still increase output levels.

These twin solutions were adopted at the beginning of the transition era. It was therefore the transition strategy itself—the end of the Third Front (and with it the end of collective farming and biased internal terms of trade) and the wholesale adoption of HYVs—which created surplus labour in the Chinese countryside in the late 1970s and early 1980s. As incentive structures improved, labour productivity rose and became apparent that a large proportion of the labour force was no longer needed for agricultural production; these improved incentives are reflected in the much-reduced labour norms of 1984 compared to those of 1978. The labour made available could be reallocated to the urban industrial sector and, even more importantly, to rural industry.

The extent of the labour surplus created by the new transition strategy is not easily established. Conceptually, it is simple enough to define surplus labour as actual employment minus 'necessary' employment for a given level of production and a given structure of incentives. But there are two problems. The first centres on the estimation of the optimal labour requirements or labour norms for each agricultural activity (which must then be aggregated to obtain a measure of total 'necessary' labour). Many of the approaches adopted in the Chinese literature for defining necessary labour appear relatively ad hoc, partly because assumptions need to be made about how much labour time had to be devoted to indirect tasks such as housework and transportation.[1] As these estimates tend to be based upon survey evidence, the results vary quite considerably across localities. In Jiangsu, for instance, it is typically assumed that a worker can manage between 6 and 7 *mu* of cultivated land (Ho, 1994: 87). But in Sichuan, it was assumed in the late 1980s that a labourer could operate only 4.6 *mu* of land and that a fifth of labour time had to be spent on housework (*jiawu laodong*). On this basis, the labour requirement in Sichuan for farming was estimated as 25.36 million workers for 1987. Assuming a farm workforce of 32.81 million, this implied a surplus of 7.45 million workers or 23 per cent of the labour force (Sichuan shehui kexueyuan, 1988: 144).

The second problem concerns the estimation of the size of the actual labour force. Many children aged under 16 are usually employed in the Chinese countryside; so, too, men aged over 60 and women aged over 55. A substantial portion of the labour force worked on private plots in the 1970s, but might have participated in the formal economy if more jobs had been available. These categories are often excluded from the usual definition of the workforce but the measurement of surplus labour is very sensitive to their treatment. As seen above, the labour surplus in Sichuan based upon the official definition of the labour force was 7.45 million workers in 1987. But if the 'other' categories are included in the actual labour force—which they should be—the surplus rises to about 15 million, or 40 per cent of the rural workforce (Sichuan shehui kexueyuan, 1988: 144). This is one of the reasons why estimates of surplus labour for China vary so greatly.

Nevertheless, we can estimate the extent of the labour surplus by using national estimates of labour norms in different years and by using official estimates of the size of the actual labour force. This is the procedure adopted in Table 7.1. It shows the volume of necessary labour in 1978 and 1984 *given* the labour norms and the structure of output in the two years. In other words, the questions being answered are: (a) how much labour was needed to produce 1978 output given the (incentive-dependent) labour norms of 1978; and (b) how much labour was needed to produce 1984 output given the (incentive-dependent) labour norms of 1984? The table shows that labour norms were much lower in 1984, largely because of the improved incentive system. As a result, necessary labour is much lower in that year than in 1978. By comparing total necessary labour in 1978 and 1984 with actual employment in those years (estimating the length of the labour year as a very conservative 250 days), it is possible to calculate the extent of surplus labour in agriculture.

These calculations show a labour *deficit* in 1978 of 10.9 billion workdays or almost 44 million workers, about 15 per cent of the workforce. This deficit was presumably made good by working more labour days per year, or by mobilizing more of the rural population (no less than 790 million in 1978) at peak times. By 1984, however, such expedients were no longer necessary. As a result of the improved array of incentives, the volume of necessary agricultural labour had fallen from 82 to 55 billion labour days. As a result, 22.2 billion labour days (almost 89 million workers) were now surplus. In percentage terms, this amounted to about 29 per cent of the labour force, a massive transformation compared to 1978. This figure is towards the bottom end of the range of estimates made by Chinese economists: these typically range between 30 and 40 per cent (Taylor, 1988: 750).

Of course we need to be rather wary before automatically assuming that some 90 million workers could be transferred out of agriculture in 1984. Although direct labour requirements during the winter slack period were comparatively slight, this

TABLE 7.1. *Surplus labour in Chinese agriculture, 1978 and 1984*

	1978			1984		
	Area	*Necessary labour*		Area	*Necessary labour*	
	(m. *mu*)	Per *mu* (days)	Total (m. days)	(m. *mu*)	Per *mu* (days)	Total (m. days)
Rice	516.3	28.1	14,508	497.7	21.2	10,551
Wheat	437.7	30.7	13,439	443.6	14.8	6,566
Maize	299.4	31.1	9,312	278.0	16.7	4,643
Other grain	271.2	31.1	8,436	229.8	16.7	3,837
Soya beans	107.2	22.2	2,379	109.3	10.1	1,104
Tubers	176.9	31.1	5,503	134.8	16.7	2,252
Cotton	73.0	60.5	4,416	103.8	40.9	4,247
Groundnuts	26.5	35.7	947	36.3	25.6	930
Rapeseed	39.0	30.4	1,185	51.2	21.4	1,096
Fibres	11.3	54.3	612	7.3	40.5	295
Sugar cane	8.2	65.2	537	10.9	49.8	544
Sugar beet	5.0	11.3	56	7.5	25.4	191
Tobacco	11.8	83.9	987	13.5	54.9	739
Other cash crops	41.9	83.9	3,513	58.7	54.9	3,225
Vegetables	50.0	83.9	4,192	64.8	54.9	3,558
Tea	15.7	57.4	902	16.2	48.4	782
Fruit	24.9	115.6	2,873	33.3	84.5	2,814
Pigs (m. head)	301.3	24.9	7,502	306.8	17.4	5,338
Fisheries			435	48.9	45.6	2,230
Total necessary labour (m. days)			81,734			54,941
Actual employment (m. days)			70,795			77,170
Surplus (m. days)			−10,939			+22,229

Note: The figure given in the World Bank source for the rice labour norm in 1978 (38.1 workdays per *mu*) should read 28.1 workdays per *mu*. Actual employment in labour days is calculated by multiplying the total primary workforce by 250 days per worker, which is the assumed length of the labour year.

Sources: ZGNCTJNJ (1985: 154–68); World Bank (1992: 71); Renkou yu jiuye tongjisi (1997: 9).

was the period when extensive irrigation and water-conservancy work was carried out. Without this 'labour accumulation'—and as became clear during the late 1980s—agricultural production would suffer either through flooding or drought. The figures in Table 7.1 take no account of this indirect labour requirement. In addition, labour demand was also extremely high during the harvest period, when surplus labour virtually disappeared. The best indication comes from the 1982 Population Census. This revealed a total rural working population of 407.2 million, well above the standard labour force survey estimate of 333 million. The differences reflects the seasonal demand for labour. The 1982 Census was taken in the middle of the summer, and even those who were working for only a short period of time were included as members of the workforce. By contrast, the survey data only include workers employed for the whole year (Li, 1992: 65). Nevertheless, even allowing for this additional demand for labour, it is hard to believe that the labour surplus could have been much less than 20 per cent at all times of the year except during the peak harvesting and sowing periods. In many of the more prosperous parts of China, the limits to what could be accomplished by labour accumulation had been reached by the late 1980s. Labour was still needed to maintain water-conservancy facilities, but the scope for large increases in irrigated area based on mass mobilization had passed. Furthermore, although the rural workforce was close to being fully employed during the peak sowing and harvest periods, that did not preclude the use of that labour in rural industry during the remainder of the year.

An alternative approach to the measurement of surplus labour is to look at differences in average sectoral labour productivity. In general, one would expect to see higher levels of labour productivity in industry than in agriculture. It is, for example, much harder to mechanize agricultural production—especially rice—because of the ecology (Bray, 1986). The lower relative labour productivity of agriculture is reflected in sectoral differences in productivity in OECD economies in the 1980s. In France, Germany, Japan, Holland, UK, and the USA, economy-wide productivity was about 40 per cent higher on average than labour productivity in agriculture (Maddison, 1991: 151). In China's case, the productivity differential was very much higher (Table 7.2). These data clearly imply substantial surplus labour in China. Moreover, the extent of the productivity gap between the secondary and the primary sector widened inexorably during the transition period.[2] The progressive mechanization and modernization of industry during the course of the 1980s, a period during which agricultural mechanization has barely advanced at all, has served only to widen the differential—despite the growth of employment in the off-farm rural sector.

To be sure, these figures are difficult to interpret. As has been argued already, the 1978 surplus was much more notional than real. In a first-best world, labour could have been transferred from agriculture to industry, but that was not possible given China's development strategy and the poor incentive structures it implied. Only after the implementation of the transition strategy in the early 1980s was this labour surplus effective rather than merely notional. In addition, it is not entirely fair to compare Chinese sectoral productivity differentials with those found in modern OECD economies. The OECD economies are much more orientated towards wheat production, which is easier to mechanize than rice; one might, for example, interpret the sectoral productivity ratio in Japan in 1987 of 3.7 : 1 (Maddison, 1991: 151)—little different from the ratio in China—as implying that it was not a simple matter for the People's Republic to reduce the productivity gap given its dependence on rice production. But on the other hand, most studies of contemporary Japanese agriculture have concluded that an abundance of surplus labour exists there too. The same logic implies an extensive labour surplus in China as well.[3]

In sum, we can be relatively confident that, despite some serious measurement problems, the transition strategy had given rise to an abundance of surplus labour in agriculture by the mid-1980s. In principle, therefore, the agricultural sector could

TABLE 7.2. *Sectoral differences in labour productivity in China, 1978–1996* (productivity levels in 1990 *yuan* per worker)

Year	Labour productivity			Productivity ratios	
	Primary	Secondary	Tertiary	Secondary : Primary	Tertiary : Primary
1978	929	3,653	3,284	3.9	3.5
1979	975	3,796	3,343	3.9	3.4
1980	945	4,054	3,318	4.3	3.5
1981	989	3,978	3,300	4.0	3.3
1982	1,064	4,025	3,565	3.8	3.4
1983	1,141	4,280	3,702	3.8	3.2
1984	1,301	4,430	4,069	3.4	3.1
1985	1,313	4,856	4,455	3.7	3.4
1986	1,351	4,965	4,738	3.7	3.5
1987	1,397	5,405	5,083	3.9	3.6
1988	1,406	5,961	5,443	4.2	3.9
1989	1,406	6,250	5,624	4.4	4.0
1990	1,306	5,652	4,914	4.3	3.8
1991	1,327	6,337	5,179	4.8	3.9
1992	1,402	7,483	5,498	5.3	3.9
1993	1,504	8,582	5,606	5.7	3.7
1994	1,605	9,901	5,592	6.2	3.5
1995	1,733	11,004	5,559	6.3	3.2
1996	1,858	11,915	5,641	6.4	3.0

Note: Labour productivity is expressed in terms of real GDP (at 1990 constant prices) per employed worker. The term 'primary sector' here refers exclusively to agriculture, i.e. it does not include employment in the mining sector; compare the series for agriculture (ZGTJNJ 1995: 86) with the series for primary industry (ZGTJNJ 1995: 83).

Sources: LSTJ (1990); ZGTJNJ (1996: 42, 69); ZGTJNJ (1997: 42, 69); Renkou yu jiuye tongjisi (1997: 5).

have played a key role in promoting growth by releasing this labour for use in industry. But this is very different from the Sachs and Woo argument that transition-era China inherited abundant surplus labour. On the contrary; it was the adoption of China's transition strategy which *created* the surplus.

4. Surplus Labour in the Military Sector

An additional argument that has been used to explain the contrasting paths of China and the USSR during transition is that the military sector was much larger in the latter, and that it was therefore impossible to mobilize this labour for productive civilian purposes. This line of reasoning assumes that Eastern Europe had no alternative but to maintain its defence capability in the face of the NATO threat. It follows that there was only a negligible 'surplus' of labour available for redeployment to the dynamic subsectors of the civilian economy. These problems acted as a powerful constraint on the *perestroika* programme launched by Gorbachev. The

USSR's problem was compounded by its isolation. The Warsaw Pact was still seen as a threat to the West in the late 1980s, and accordingly NATO was extremely unwilling to allow trade with, and capital flows to, Eastern Europe. In consequence, a large proportion of Soviet 'surplus' was pre-empted by the military sector and, additionally, the surplus itself was reduced because of a lack of foreign investment. Limited trade had the same effect because it prevented technology transfer and therefore depressed productivity growth. In China, by contrast, defence industrialization had proceeded much less far, and the American threat had dwindled to almost nothing by the late 1970s. The proportion of the labour surplus needed to maintain China's military capability was small and the remainder could be readily diverted to civilian production. Furthermore, trade between China and the West increased rapidly in the 1970s and in its wake came direct foreign investment. As a result, the surplus available for reinvestment in the China of the late 1970s was much greater than in Gorbachev's Soviet Union. This chain of reasoning is summarized by Harding (1994: 105):

> The willingness of the West in general, and the United States in particular, to accommodate China's engagement with the international economy stands in sharp contrast to the more skeptical attitude towards the Soviet Union in the 1980s. . . . the main rationale was strategic: the desire (in the case of the United States) to solidify China's place in an anti-Soviet coalition, or the hope (in the case of Japan and many Asian nations) to ensure that China would play a more responsible role in the region as its economic interdependencies increased. This explains why the United States granted China most-favored-nation status early while refusing to do so for the Soviet Union.

However, this argument of low productivity labour locked into Eastern Europe's military sector in abundance compared to China is not as compelling as it seems. For one thing, the military sector in the People's Republic was by no means small; the scale of China's post-1965 Third Front programme of defence industrialization was in fact immense (Naughton, 1988; Bramall, 1993) and may have been comparable in relation to GDP to Soviet defence expenditure. The scale of 'defence conversion' required at the end of the 1970s was therefore enormous. To be sure, there is evidence of successful conversion. Many of the Third Front industries now produce civilian outputs as varied as motorcycles, cars, TVs, and religious bronzes (Folta, 1992; Brömmelhörster and Frankenstein, 1997). But, isolated examples apart, retooling was not a viable proposition for many of the more geographically isolated factories in the western provinces, and much of this capital stock had to be written off.

A second problem in the USSR-China comparison is that, even if the USSR did have more labour in its military sector, it is at least arguable that it could have followed China in abandoning defence industrialization. The Soviet nuclear arsenal was more than adequate to deter US aggression by 1980; moreover, it is hard to construe the stationing of SS-20 missiles in Europe and the creation of a 'blue-water' fleet as purely defensive moves. Furthermore, the invasion of Afghanistan was hardly calculated to convince the West of the peaceful intentions of the Soviet Union.

In principle, therefore, the USSR could have done more towards establishing better relations with the West before Gorbachev took over, and made disarmament a reality. Finally, the problems of the Russian economy in the early 1990s cannot be attributed to the need to maintained a bloated defence establishment. Partial nuclear disarmament, and the abandonment of Eastern Europe, meant that there was considerable scope for wide-reaching defence cuts in Russia—and therefore for the release of surplus labour.

Nevertheless, it is probably fair to conclude that China was relatively advantaged in the early 1980s compared to the period in the USSR when Gorbachev was attempting to carry out a process of gradual transition. Nixon had made considerable efforts to assuage Chinese fears in the early and mid-1970s, and that continued during the 1980s. In the Soviet case, the election of Reagan in 1980 led to an intensification of anti-Soviet rhetoric and, most threateningly of all, the launch of the Star Wars programme. This escalation of the cold war was one of the factors which in the end proved the undoing of the USSR: it was simply unable to match these increases in US defence spending. Moreover, the Soviet Union had long committed itself to achieving at least strategic parity with the USA and therefore it was politically extremely difficult to cut back on defence spending; the General Secretary risked being toppled. In China, where military spending had never been anything other than geared to the defence of the People's Republic, the political repercussions were likely to be far less. Moreover, as will be seen in Chapter 17, the absence of powerful political opposition in China made Deng's task far easier than that of Soviet Party Secretaries.

As a result, we may conclude that both Russia and China had substantial reserves of surplus labour in their military sectors at the beginning of their respective transitions. Nevertheless, there was more ample scope for a scaling down of Chinese military expenditure, and a corresponding transfer of resources to the civilian sector. But once again, it was the transition strategy that created the surplus labour. It was the decision to abandon the Third Front that created the labour surplus in the military sector.

5. Incentives for Occupational Mobility in China

We have seen in the two preceding sections that a vast pool of surplus labour appears to been created by the radical reorientation of the Chinese development strategy at the end of the 1980s. Yet it is one thing to show that surplus labour existed in China, and quite another to show that this labour could readily have been mobilized. A crucial issue here is whether there was any incentive for labour to move out of agriculture and into the industrial sector. For if such incentives did exist, then labour would release itself; it did not need to be made redundant first as was the case in much of EEFSU.

In some respects, material incentives to find a job outside farming in the late 1970s were not especially powerful. First, many rural industries struggled to make profits and that tended to depress wages (Potter and Potter, 1990: 140–2; Chan, *et al.*, 1984:

244–6). Secondly, many brigade and team leaders sought to maximize industrial profits by keeping wages as low as possible. Unmarried women in particular were easily 'exploited'; their employment in low-wage drudgery such as servicing brick kilns was commonplace (Potter and Potter, 1990: 116–17). Thirdly, the very egalitarianism that characterized the late Maoist era itself had the effect of preventing officials from paying high wages to any sub-group of rural workers. Nevertheless, the positive incentives to take industrial work outweighed the negative. More often than not, only a modest premium was needed to attract workers from farming because of the relatively unpleasant nature of so much farm work.[4] In consequence, as the value of the labour day in farming stagnated or even declined in the 1970s,[5] there were increasingly compelling incentives for farmers to leave the land.

By the early 1980s, even the small-wage differential between farm and industrial employment in the countryside began to widen. The reasons are well known. Egalitarianism had been effectively abandoned. Higher peasant incomes allowed higher prices to be charged for industrial products, which in turn allowed the payment of higher wages. As a result, a clear gap emerged between incomes received in farming and incomes from industrial employment. According to a 1984 survey of 37,000 households across China, the income per labour day spent in crop farming was only 4.9 *yuan*, compared to 8.4 *yuan* in food processing and 15 *yuan* in transportation and manufacturing (AS, 1988: 29). Another way to look at incentives for the abandonment of farming is to compare the difference in income between rural and urban areas; those parts of China where industry was extensively developed were of course urban. Some indication of these differentials is offered by the per capita output data assembled in Table 7.3. This table make two types of urban–rural comparisons. The first contrasts the incomes of China's big metropolitan centres with those of the adjacent provinces. This is not a true urban–rural comparison because cities like Shanghai and Beijing included a number of rural counties within their jurisdiction. Conversely, parts of Hebei (such as Shijiazhuang, the provincial capital) and Jiangsu (Nanjing) are manifestly urban. Nevertheless, the comparison is not too heavily distorted by these factors. The second type of comparison contrasts per capita GNP (and other income measures) in provincial capitals with adjacent counties. This is perhaps a better way of assessing the urban–rural gap (although output data in the counties adjacent to urban centres are not a true indicator of income because of commuting). As the data show, the gap ranges from 3.2 : 1, to 5.8 : 1 if one compares Shanghai with its hinterland. These figures are well above official Chinese data on the expenditure (*xiaofei*) gap between rural and urban populations which, in 1978, was put at 2.9 : 1 (ZGTJNJ, 1993: 280). They are in line with those estimates made by Western specialists using those fragmentary data on subsidies and welfare payments that are available, and range from 3 : 1 to 6 : 1. They indicate a clear material inducement to abandon farming in favour of industrial employment. In short, Chinese farmers had very little to lose, and indeed everything to gain, from the growth of off-farm employment. Accordingly, it seems extremely likely a priori that agriculture must have been the principal source of surplus labour.

TABLE 7.3. *Urban–rural income differentials in China, 1978–1982*

Urban income (*yuan* per capita)		Rural income (*yuan* per capita)		Ratio	Year	Measure, per capita
Beijing	1,290	Hebei	364	3.5 : 1	1978	GDP
Tianjin	1,160	Hebei	364	3.2 : 1	1978	GDP
Shanghai	2,498	Jiangsu	430	5.8 : 1	1978	GDP
Nanjing	1,519	Jiangning	312	4.9 : 1	1978	GNP
Wenzhou	800	Yongjia	205	3.9 : 1	1980	NDMP
Lanzhou	3,082	Yongdeng	744	4.1 : 1	1982	GVAIO
Guiyang	1,417	Longli	316	4.5 : 1	1982	GVAIO
Chengdu	2,297	Xindu	685	3.4 : 1	1982	GVAIO

Note: GDP, GNP and NDMP are at current prices and GVAIO at constant 1980 prices.

Sources: LSTJ (1990: 64, 92, 124, 311, 343); Jiangsu tongjiju (1989: 381, 385); Zhejiang tongjiju (1984: 86–103); ZGRKTJNJ (1988: 650, 656, 661, 662, 684).

6. Surplus Labour in Eastern Europe

Yet all this having been said, surplus labour at the beginning of transition was not a uniquely Chinese phenomenon. Surplus labour also existed in abundance in Eastern Europe, especially in the industrial sector, within which there were wide intersectoral differentials in profitability and productivity. In other words, the Eastern Europe countries could have raised their output by redeploying labour and capital from industries with low rates of profit into industries with higher rates of profit. The extent of these intersectoral differentials is shown in Table 7.4 in the case of the Soviet Union.

These profit differentials should not be interpreted as measures of efficiency; profitability in the Soviet Union of Brezhnev and the China of Mao was very much dependent upon the product prices set by the state. With market price determination, it is likely that the profitability of railways, farming, and energy would have been far higher. Nevertheless, if one accepts the price used by the Soviet state as the appropriate shadow price, it is clear that even the logic of Soviet planning dictated a shift in capital and labour away from metallurgy and chemicals towards light industry. By exploiting that profit differential, there is no reason in principle why Soviet output could not have been increased. As it was, the proportion of investment going to the production of means of production was about eight times greater than investment going into the production of consumer goods in the early 1980s (Dyker, 1992: 173).[6]

The situation in China was similar to that in Eastern Europe in that there were large profit differentials between industries, as well as between industry and agriculture. To be sure, the bulk of China's labour was concentrated in agriculture, and therefore that was the logical source of surplus labour. But it is not clear why this process was qualitatively different from the redeployment of labour and capital

TABLE 7.4. *Profit Rates in Soviet Industry, 1986* (per cent)

Sector	Profit rates
Light industry	24
Communications	18
Construction	16
Food processing	14
Machinery	14
Metallurgy	12
Chemicals	11
Fuel and power	10
Collective farms	7
Railways	5

Source: Shmelev and Popov (1990: 310).

between industries in Eastern Europe. In *both* China and Eastern Europe, it is arguable—depending on which prices are used to make the calculation—that the productivity of factors of production in certain sectors was very low. And in both cases this opportunity cost was small. The argument made by the advocates of the 'Polish road'—that very little surplus labour existed; it had to be created by industrial restructuring—would make sense only if intersectoral productivity differentials within Eastern Europe industry were negligible. However, as pervasive shortages of consumer durables indicate, that plainly was not the case. In other words, there does seem to have been scope for intersectoral reallocation of labour and capital in both China and Eastern Europe.

However, the critics of Sachs and Woo (notably Nolan and Ash, 1995) tend to neglect two critical points in emphasizing the similarities of China and Eastern Europe. First, although there certainly was surplus labour in Eastern Europe in the late 1980s, its extent was small compared to China. There were differences in labour productivity within Eastern Europe's industrial sector, and between agriculture and industry, but these differentials were comparatively small because of the extent of modernization that had occurred throughout the Eastern European economy by the late 1980s. Almost every economic activity—including agriculture—used significant quantities of machinery and the labour-intensive traditional sector had largely disappeared. By contrast, an enormous productivity gulf existed between traditional and modern sectors in China; this was exemplified by the labour-intensive collection of night-soil on a daily basis throughout her cities on the one hand and the comparatively advanced technology deployed in her steel mills and oilfields on the other.

Secondly, Nolan and Ash underestimate the obstacles to reallocating labour between sectors and subsectors in Eastern Europe: the obstacles to the *mobilization* of the labour surplus were less in China than in Eastern Europe. As we have seen, there was certainly considerable scope for such a reallocation in Eastern Europe. But powerful considerations militated against worker migration to the private sector. A migrant would, for example, lose her entitlement to free housing. Her pension would be much reduced. She would also lose her right to a whole range of other job-related subsidies such as childcare, health, and meals. And all this sacrifice in exchange for the dubious prospect of a high wage in the private sector. By contrast, and as we have seen, the Chinese peasant stood to gain a great deal. The rural economy of the early 1980s offered scant provision by way of housing, childcare, or other welfare benefits. The drudgery of work in all kinds of weather was an inescapable part of farm life. Although the return from farm production did increase markedly in the golden years between 1982 and 1984, the terms of trade swung against the farm sector as the 1980s wore on; by the mid-1980s, the relative rates of return per day were far higher outside the farm sector. In other words, the Chinese peasant faced a choice between a stagnant income and negligible welfare benefits on the one hand, and at least the prospect of a well-paid job on the other. It goes without saying that many still opted for relative security (peasants were still guaranteed a substantial market for their grain by the state in the late 1980s). However, many of them were easily enticed to work in the new township and village enterprises even in provinces like Zhejiang and Jiangsu where a reasonable living was to be made from farming. These powerful incentives to occupational mobility in China gave it an undoubted advantage at the beginning of the transition process.

7. The Release of Surplus Labour

It has been shown in the previous sections that abundant surplus labour existed in the Chinese military and agricultural sectors by the early 1980s, and that this labour had a strong material incentive to move out of agriculture and into the non-farm sector. To what extent, however, did this process of labour release actually occur, and did it contribute to rapid growth? Did farm labour simply become surplus to the needs of the non-farm sector, and in the process contribute little to industrial growth? Or did labour shortages serve as a powerful break on the expansion of rural industry?

It certainly seems true that agriculture released labour at a significant pace after 1978 (Table 7.5). Up to 1989, the absolute numbers employed in agriculture increased by about 50 million.[7] However, the share of agricultural in total employment declined by some 10 percentage points. In other words, there was a *relative* release of labour by agriculture. The speed of labour release was even more marked within the rural sector itself. In 1982, some 91 per cent of rural employees were employed in agriculture but, by 1988, this had fallen to 79 per cent (Nongye bu, 1989: 16–17; ZGNYTJZL, 1987: 12; ZGNYTJZL, 1988: 6). This process was of course made possible by the sharp yield increases achieved throughout most of China in the early 1980s. The grain yield, for instance, averaged 179 kg per *mu* during 1978–80 but rose to an average of 236 kg by 1984–6 (Nongye bu, 1989: 148). This allowed agricultural output to rise with a much less than proportionate increase in agricultural

TABLE 7.5. *Share of agricultural employment in total employment, 1978–1996*

Year	Employment in agriculture (m.)	Total employment (m.)	Share of agricultural employment (%)
1978	283.18	401.53	70.5
1979	286.34	410.25	69.8
1980	291.22	423.61	68.7
1981	297.77	437.25	68.1
1982	308.59	452.95	68.1
1983	311.51	464.36	67.1
1984	308.68	481.97	64.0
1985	311.3	498.73	62.4
1986	312.54	512.81	60.9
1987	316.63	527.84	60.0
1988	322.49	543.34	59.4
1989	332.25	553.3	60.0
1990	341.17	639.1	53.4
1991	349.56	647.99	53.9
1992	347.95	655.54	53.1
1993	339.66	663.73	51.2
1994	333.86	671.99	49.7
1995	330.18	679.47	48.6
1996	329.09	688.5	47.8

Notes: These are year-end data; agriculture comprises farming, forestry. Fisheries, sidelines, and animal husbandry. The series breaks in 1990; before then, no distinction was made between primary-sector and agricultural employment.

Source: Renkou yu jiuye tongjisi (1997: 9, 10).

employment; the 'surplus' labour thus created was available for use by industry. As a result, the rate of local labour release in the early 1980s was particularly impressive. One indication is the rate of growth of labour productivity in agriculture. Nationally, labour productivity in agriculture grew by 3.8 per cent per year between 1978 and 1985 (LSTJ, 1990). In the second half of the 1980s, however, productivity growth was less fast; the national average growth rate for labour productivity in agriculture fell to 3 per cent per year. But such a fall in the growth rate was hardly calamitous; one might reasonably suppose that the initial growth of the early 1980s was unsustainable based as it was on an inherited Maoist infrastructure less than fully exploited. Accordingly, on the basis of national data such as these, it is hard to conclude that there was much by way of failure on the part of agriculture to release labour in the late 1980s. After 1991, the process of labour release changed in character. From then on, the *level* of total agricultural employment declined; by 1996, it was about 20 million workers less than it had been at its 1991 peak. In other words, the release of labour after 1991 was both relative and *absolute*.[8]

The most important issue, however, is not whether labour was released by agriculture but whether the pace of agricultural labour-productivity growth, and hence the rate of labour release, was fast enough to avoid industrial labour shortages. From the perspective of the mid-1990s, of course, this was no longer the right question to ask. As the restructuring and privatization of SOEs gathered momentum, the labour problem was increasingly that of unemployment—rather than labour shortages—in urban China. Even the official data, for example, reported that there were 9.7 million surplus urban workers by 1996, 6.59 million of them in state-owned enterprises (Renkou yu jiuye tongjisi, 1997: 405). But was it also true that few labour shortages existed in the first decade and more of transition? One indication that labour shortages were uncommon is the extent of population migration to labour-scarce cities and regions. The central Chinese government could have done much to improve the operation of the labour market by providing subsidies to would-be migrants, and to those areas that acted as magnets to the migrants. However, despite some officially sanctioned resettlement programmes, Chinese central government did little to expedite labour flows between regions (World Bank, 1992: 59–60; Banister, 1992).

Nevertheless, and despite the limited role played by government, data collected in the census of 1987 (which surveyed 1 per cent of the population) show substantial migration. Between 1982 and 1987, 30.6 million people migrated (some 2.9 per cent of the population) and there was a trend increase over the period; about 3.64 million migrations occurred in 1983 and 6.9 millions in 1986 (Li, 1992: 226). The 1990 Population Census found that 2.63 per cent of the population were permanent migrants, or 30.4 million people (ZGTJNJ, 1992: 88). According to Banister (1992: 20), the 10 per cent sample from the Census found that there were 33.8 million permanent migrants (3 per cent) between 1985 and 1990. In addition to these official migrants, there was a much larger number of temporary migrants in China's big cities and more prosperous delta regions. Estimating the size of this floating population (*liudong renkou*) is of course difficult. However, the first proper rural labour-force survey carried out in China found that 21,397 of the labourers in the survey were temporary migrants, or about 11.3 per cent of the sample (Yu, 1989: 15, 17). The survey also identified an additional 3 per cent of the labour force who were permanent migrants, a figure very similar to that estimated from the 1987 1 per cent censuses. Applying these rates to the national labour force (ZGTJNJ, 1992: 98) implies a migrant population of 73 millions in 1986, of which 58 millions were temporary migrants. This figure accords well with most ad hoc Chinese estimates, which have put the size of the floating population at between 50 and 70 millions for the late 1980s (Banister, 1992: 20).

Substantial though these figures are, and although migration was far more extensive by the late 1980s that it had been at the beginning of the decade, China fell far short of having a properly functioning national labour market. Some obstacles were official, notably the reluctance of the city authorities to grant urban-residency status to in-migrants from rural areas (Delman, *et al.*, 1990). These barriers had been set up during the Maoist period and continued to exist even if they were somewhat less effective (largely because the existence of private markets made it easy for unofficial migrants to purchase food and other necessities). Other barriers to labour migration were rooted in cultural factors. Prominent amongst these was prejudice against those arriving from other regions of the country. Native place hierarchy was a well-defined feature of China before 1949, and it remained extremely powerful in the 1980s. As Emily Honig (1990; 1992) has shown, the obstacles placed in the way of those migrating from Subei (northern Jiangsu) into Shanghai and its suburbs were formidable. These barriers both slowed down the rate of migration and led to the emergence of well-defined labour-market segmentation, with in-migrants confined largely to the secondary labour market. Much the same is true in other parts of China, where opposition by the population of county towns to in-migrants has encouraged town officials to erect barriers to entry (Siu, 1990). Some of this behaviour reflected ethnic prejudice directed against the rural population in Subei, and in Guangdong's neighbouring provinces, which was perceived to be bucolic in its habits and outlook. However, opposition probably owed much to a desire on the part of 'insiders' to preserve their pay and conditions in the face of the threat posed by the cheap labour offered by 'outsiders'.

Nevertheless, the picture was complex at the provincial level. It is by no means true that the peasant population of poor provinces found it more difficult to migrate than the population of richer provinces. To be sure, Ningxia's 1986 migration rate (5.8 per cent) was well below the national average of 14.3 per cent but Guangxi and Qinghai—hardly rich provinces—achieved migration rates of 12.9 and 18.6 per cent respectively (Yu, 1989: 234, 237, 257, 260, 280, 283). Nevertheless, the rates of labour release in poor provinces were generally slow. In Guizhou, for example, the rate of release was so slow that the 1988 share of agricultural employment was only about 3 percentage points lower than in 1978, far down on the national pattern (12 percentage points lower). In general, it seems that the capacity of poor provinces to release labour from agriculture—and still maintain a high and growing level of agricultural output—was limited. In Hunan, productivity growth was somewhat less fast than the national average between 1978 and 1985; for 1985–8, however, the growth rate was only 1.9 per cent, well below the national figure of 3 per cent. In Guizhou, agricultural productivity growth was marginally above the national trend before 1985. But after that year, output per worker fell by 2 per cent per year until 1988, whereas the all-China level was rising by 3 per cent per year (LSTJ, 1990). The disappointing performance of poor provinces was undoubtedly a consequence of the torpid pace of farm-sector modernization. To be sure, the application of chemical fertilizers and other modern inputs did rise after 1978 but it did not do so at a rate sufficient to sustain rapid labour-productivity growth in the poorest parts of China. As a result, their capacity to release labour was limited.

By contrast, China's most prosperous provinces stand acquitted of any charge of a failure to release labour from agriculture. In Fujian, for example, the annual rate of increase of labour productivity was 5.4 per cent between 1978 and 1985, well above the national average. At 3.4 per cent between 1985 and 1988, it again exceeded the national trend. In Zhejiang, the pace of labour release was even faster, with the agricultural share in employment almost 30 percentage points down on 1978. As a result, although Zhejiang and Guizhou started from about the same base, there was a marked difference in the share—50 per cent compared to 78 per cent—reached by 1988. This of course reflected the extremely fast pace of industrialization (which raised the demand for labour). The Sunan area was particularly remarkable in this respect; in some parts of the region, the agricultural labour force had dwindled to a very low level by the end of the 1980s. In Wuxi county, for instance, the share of the non-agricultural labour force rose from 20 per cent in 1978 to 80 per cent by 1988 (WXGY, 1990: 435). Indeed, 61 per cent of the entire labour force was employed in *xiangzhen* industry alone in 1988 (Jiangsu tongjiju, 1989: 212). Not that the area was able to avoid labour shortages entirely; by the mid-1980s, Wuxi county was recruiting labour from outside the province (WXGY, 1991: 61–2; Xin, 1990: 318–19). But there is little evidence that these local shortages proved a binding constraint on industrialization. As Ho (1994) points out, the number of labour days worked per year in his sample of Jiangsu villages rarely exceeded 300, and seasonal underemployment remained commonplace even in the southern part of the province. Furthermore, the relative ease of access to the Anhui labour market (a traditional source of workers for Sunan) meant that even counties like Wuxi—which was very untypical of China—faced no crippling labour shortage even in the medium term.

It is also worth adding that there is little real evidence that the release of labour led to the collapse of agricultural production even in Sunan where the demand of the non-farm sector for labour was so high. To be sure, the trajectory of the grain yield after 1984 does, on the face of it, suggest a degree of agricultural failure. In Zhejiang, for example, the grain yield declined at an average rate of 1.7 per cent between 1984 and 1988; in Jiangsu, the rate of decline was 0.2 per cent. By contrast, the national yield rose by 0.1 per cent annually whilst poor provinces like Gansu and Hunan managed annual rates of increase of 2 and 0.2 per cent respectively. However, the decline in grain yields observed in Zhejiang and Jiangsu after 1984 in essence reflected the virtual impossibility of pushing yields much beyond the mark of 300–20 kg per sown *mu* in combination with the high yield already reached by the late 1970s. In that period, average grain yields in Zhejiang were about 40 kg higher than those achieved in Jiangsu and about 100 kg (some 50 per cent) higher than those reached in Guangdong (Nongye bu, 1989: 174–89). Even by 1988, when the average grain yield in Zhejiang was 323 kg, the national average was only 239 kg (ZGNYTJZl, 1989: 56). In other words, Zhejiang's grain sector was achieving yields close to the potential maximum yield given the existing state of technology. It was therefore extremely difficult to raise yields further and this largely explains yield stagnation. By contrast, China's poor provinces enjoyed enormous potential for catch-up growth in the grain sector even in the late 1980s and so were still able to push yields up after 1985. More generally, and directly contradicting the charge of agricultural failure, the rate of growth of agricultural labour productivity in Sunan was extremely impressive throughout the 1980s. In Zhejiang, productivity growth averaged 5.2 per cent between 1978 and 1985, compared to 3.8 per cent nationally. Furthermore, and perhaps more significantly, productivity continued to grow at 5 per cent per year even after 1985, a period when the national rate fell back to 3 per cent. In short, and due in no small measure to the phenomenal rate of growth achieved by her sideline subsector, Zhejiang's agriculture comprehensively outperformed the other provinces.

In sum, the Chinese agricultural sector was successful in releasing some labour for industrial use during the 1980s. The share of agricultural employment in total employment declined steadily in most provinces as rising labour productivity in agriculture allowed output to be maintained (and even increased) using a smaller workforce. Moreover, and despite numerous obstacles to labour migration, some 100 million Chinese peasants had, by the end of the decade, found permanent or temporary employment outside the township in which they originally resided. Most had *litu bu lixiang* ('left the soil but not the countryside'); in other words, they remained resident in rural areas even though no longer working in agriculture for the bulk of the year. A relatively small proportion did, however, find their way into China's great metropolitan centres. Nevertheless, and especially in poor provinces, there is some evidence that the pace of agricultural modernization was relatively slow. As a result, rural industrialization may have been held back by an inadequate rate of labour release (though slow demand growth was probably the primary obstacle).

Not so in rich provinces. Despite an astonishing pace of rural industrialization throughout the course of the 1980s, the agriculture economy in Sunan (in particular) was able to raise its labour productivity at a rate fast enough to maintain agricultural output and at the same time meet much of the industrial demand for labour. It was Sunan, in other words, that conformed to the path of the 'classical' agricultural revolution as exemplified by Great Britain in the eighteenth century. Without the transformation of agricultural productivity that occurred, and which was the truly revolutionary aspect of the Sunan experience, the massive intersectoral labour transfers that occurred would have been impossible.

8. The Contribution of Surplus Labour to Industrialization

It is at this point, however, that the surplus labour argument breaks down. We have already seen that China did not inherit an abundance of surplus labour. Rather, surplus labour was created by the transition strategy itself. Moreover, although we have shown that labour was released by the agricultural sector without any massive decline in farm production, and that this labour was absorbed by Chinese industry, we have not yet considered the effect on industrial productivity. It is this which is the crux of the issue: if labour release led to no more than an offsetting decline in industrial productivity, there is no reason to see surplus labour as contributing to China's growth in the transition era.

We know, of course, that labour productivity growth accelerated after 1978.[9] Labour productivity in the industrial sector grew at an annual rate of 6.5 per cent (in 1990 prices) between 1978 and 1996, a significant rate of increase (Table 7.2). But that in itself does not show that the impact of labour release on the industrial sector was benign. That is because of the range of other factors at work in influencing productivity. As we will see in Chapter 10, China increased its level of spending on research and development, and employed more personnel to carry out scientific research. State-owned industrial enterprises were subjected to the discipline of the market, which might have been expected to reduce organizational inefficiencies. The wage system was restructured such that a part of the income of workers was related to their productivity. And the economy was opened up to foreign trade and FDI which embodied many new ideas and technologies. Given that China was almost a war economy in 1978—largely closed, spending heavily on defence and with an industrial structure dominated by state-owned firms—one would have expected the transition policies to have led to marked increases in labour productivity.

In fact, given all these positive 'shocks', China's labour productivity record looks rather poor, which suggests that the impact of labour transfers out of agriculture may even have been to offset these otherwise favourable influences. That seems still more likely if the 1978–96 period is subdivided. For the years between 1991 and 1996, annual labour-productivity growth rose by an impressive 13.6 per cent (Table 7.2). But between 1978 and 1991, the rate of increase was a much more modest 4.6 per cent per year (and becomes smaller still if the official estimate of GDP on which it is based is accepted to be an exaggeration). This evidence seems to imply that only when FDI-based technological diffusion from abroad became significant (after 1992) did productivity growth really begin to accelerate in the face of the adverse effects of labour transfers.

The notion that labour transfers might have depressed productivity levels in the industrial sector is lent support by some of the microeconomic evidence. One problem was the social impact of migrant labour on China's established urban centres. Many of the migrants to the Pearl River Delta in particular found it difficult to fit in because of linguistic differences. Even though many of these migrants found work, Chinese cities were forced to spend substantial sums on infrastructure, and the presence of migrants was often resented by the local population. As a result, migrant incomes were lower because they were systematically discriminated against as 'outsiders' in terms of access to housing and education, as well as marriage prospects (Solinger, 1995). In the Pearl River Delta, for example, young migrant woman were referred to as *dagong mei* (working girls) or *wailai mei* (outside girls) (G. Lin, 1997: 97). More recently, city authorities have tried to limit the incomes of migrants by restricting the range of jobs in which they can be employed. In Beijing, for example, a list of 198 types of permitted work was published in February 1998 which sought to push migrants into unpopular and low-paid jobs such as abattoir work, burning corpses, and mining (SCMP, 17 April 1998). The Deputy Party Secretary of Liaoning openly encouraged unemployed workers to 'grab back' the jobs held by migrants (SCMP, 15 Oct. 1997). Even 'academic' accounts have stressed the way in which migrants necessitate high infrastructural spending, cause overcrowding and crime, and drain funds out of urban areas and back to the villages (Li, 1996*a*; 1996*b*; Ba dachengshi, 1990: 224, 246; Wang, 1998: 72). All this diverted attention (as well as funds) away from the more pressing task of raising the labour productivity of the new industrial workforce.

The other problem is that most of the migrants ended up working in factories where labour productivity was below the norm in China's most modern plants so that their contribution to industrial output was far below the average labour productivity of the industrial sector. The principal reason was that many of China's modern enterprises used highly capital-intensive technologies and, if anything, shed labour during the transition period. The Baoshan Iron and Steel plant is the classic example (Otsuka, *et al.*, 1998: 116–19). As a result, the labour released by the Chinese agricultural sector ended up working in enterprises which were typically small, rural, and controlled by local government. Such enterprises had much inferior productivity levels compared to factories which were large, urban-based, and run by central government. For example, many firms set up in areas like Wenzhou (Nolan and Dong, 1990*a*) and Nanhai (G. Lin, 1997) were far too small to take advantage of economies of scale. Similarly, rural enterprises were much less efficient than urban enterprises. A study of the textile industry in 1986 estimated labour productivity in urban plants at 20.7 thousand *yuan*, compared to 13.1 thousand *yuan* in rural plants (Wu, 1996: 133). At a macrolevel, rural industrial enterprises averaged 1,336 *yuan* in 1978 compared to 3,006 *yuan* in urban industrial enterprises (Wu and Wu, 1994: 151). Enterprises owned by central government also had a productivity advantage over those owned by local government (which were much more likely to employ released labour). For the iron and steel industry, for example, Wu (1996: 111) put the differential at 11.5 to 7.3 thousand *yuan* in 1988–9. And the productivity comparison between collectively owned and state-owned industrial enterprises was even more striking; in 1978 (1980 prices) labour productivity in the collective sector was just 934 *yuan*, compared to 3,837 *yuan* in the state sector (Wu and Wu, 1994: 158). Given that the overwhelming majority of migrants were employed by collective industry, this is an especially significant finding. Worse still, the very availability of cheap labour probably served as a disincentive to the adoption of more efficient, capital-intensive, techniques.

If these two pieces of evidence—that migrants tended to have a depressing effect on labour-productivity levels, and that they were disproportionately employed in industrial enterprises where labour productivity was comparatively low to start with—are put together, it is entirely possible that the impact of labour release on industrial output may have been much less than implied by the labour-surplus models typically used by the master discourse.

Finally, there is some evidence that labour migration caused a realization problem. One of the characteristics of migrant labour is that much of it is temporary. That is particularly true of young women, whose aim was invariably to work in a factory for a few years before ultimately returning to their home village. One consequence was that this group of migrants had a relatively low marginal propensity to consume, especially in the region to which they temporarily migrated. In addition, migrants typically remitted a large part of their wage to their home village. Their savings were therefore not available for reinvestment in the region in which they worked. In other words, there could well have been a substantial drain of funds away from areas like the Pearl River Delta.

This interpretation is lent support by the evidence. According to the World Bank (1997*c*: 57), out-migrants from Sichuan and Anhui typically remitted between 20 and 50 per cent of their income to their home village. Data on Guizhou suggest that each rural inhabitant received a per capita remittance of 18.56 *yuan* in 1995 (about 1 per cent of their gross annual income), implying a total inflow of remittance income of about 557 million *yuan* per year. If we assume that those making the remittances—there were 725,000 outside workers in 1995—each earned around 4,475 *yuan* (the average wage for industrial workers in Guizhou), that implies a remittance rate of about 9 per cent of migrant income (GZTJNJ 1997: 29, 35, 124). Clearly outflows of this order of magnitude implied a significant loss for those provinces (mainly in eastern China) where the migrants were working.

Industrialization in areas employing large numbers of migrants may therefore have been checked by slow demand growth. We can take the argument a step further by assuming in Kaldorian and neo-Schumpeterian fashion that the pace of innovation is positively related to the growth of aggregate demand via the reinvestment of quasi-rents. The realization problem caused by migration then implies that labour release may have served to slow down the rate of productivity growth by reducing the pace of innovation.

9. Conclusion

The argument advanced by Sachs and Woo that the release of labour from agriculture played a key role in raising productivity in China is not convincing. To be sure, there was surplus labour in China by the early 1980s, and in much larger amounts than in Eastern Europe and the former Soviet Union. The large income gap between the rural and urban sector gave agricultural labour a very strong incentive to migrate. And there is abundant evidence that this released labour was employed, and in large numbers, in the industrial sector.

But there remain huge gaps in the argument put forward by the master discourse. For one thing, it was the transition strategy itself that created surplus labour, not late Maoist development policies. Only when the Third Front was brought to an end, and agricultural productivity increased by the reforms of the late 1970s and early 1980s, was surplus labour created. More importantly, it is likely that the release of labour depressed industrial productivity. The migrant workers were alienated by their new surroundings, and succeeded (unknowingly) in alienating the existing urban population by their very presence. In addition, most of these migrants were not employed in state-of-the-art modern factories but in low-productivity enterprises, typically small in scale and located in rural areas. In so far as the employment of migrants boosted industrial output, it cannot have been by very much. Finally, migrant labour created a realization problem in the areas in which they worked by saving the bulk of their wages and remitting them to their home village. In short, the Lewis model does not appear especially helpful in explaining Chinese growth in the transition era. The release of surplus labour may have boosted output, but the increase was probably no more than slight.

8

The Rates of Saving and Investment

A central argument identified in the literature linking initial conditions to rapid growth can be easily stated in neoclassical terms. A country will be in a position to grow quickly if it enjoys the combination of a high savings rate and a low capital–labour ratio (relative to its steady state capital–labour ratio). If the savings rate per head exceeds the investment requirement per head, the capital–labour ratio will grow and with it per capita income. In other words, an economy starting off in disequilibrium will grow swiftly during the process of moving towards its steady-state equilibrium.

We saw in Chapter 6 that China's social and physical capability was relatively well-developed, but by no means exceptional, at the end of the Maoist period. Was this because China's savings rate was comparatively low, such that the economy had reached a (modest) equilibrium capital–labour ratio by 1978? Or did late Maoist China actually have a high savings rate, such that the modest capital–labour ratio in the late 1970s simply reflected the fact that the economy was still moving towards its steady state? In other words, was it just the case that China was still in the early stages of growth, and that much more time would have to elapse before the full benefits of the high savings rate fed through into the capital–labour ratio? If this second theory is right, and China did have a high savings rate at the end of the Maoist era in 1978 but was still in the process of making the transition to its (high-level) equilibrium, we have a very powerful explanation of growth after 1978: it was in no small measure merely a continuation of the process of capital accumulation that was already taking place. The Maoist regime had already accomplished the hard part; it had succeeded in raising the savings rate. The Dengist regime was therefore in the enviable position of being able to reap the benefits.[1]

1. The Rate of Savings and Investment in the Maoist Period

Precise data on Chinese savings rates for the period between 1949 and 1978 are unavailable. However, they can be proxied by trends in the investment share (Table 8.1). The Maoist period can be viewed as one in which the share of accumulation in material product was increased from just over 20 per cent in the early 1950s to just over 30 per cent by the mid-1970s.[2] By international standards, this latter was not an especially high figure, and although the rate was above 30 per cent in every year between 1970 and 1978, it needs to be emphasized that the median rate for the entire 1952–78 period was only 27.1 per cent. It is therefore extremely misleading to characterize the Maoist era as one of breakneck accumulation.

Nevertheless, the increase in the accumulation rate was still impressive by the standard of most developing countries.

TABLE 8.1. *The share of accumulation in net national material product* (per cent; current prices)

Year	Accumulation share	Year	Accumulation share
1952	21.4	1966	30.6
1953	23.1	1967	21.3
1954	25.5	1968	21.1
1955	22.9	1969	23.2
1956	24.4	1970	32.9
1957	24.9	1971	34.1
1958	33.9	1972	31.6
1959	43.8	1973	32.9
1960	39.6	1974	32.3
1961	19.2	1975	33.9
1962	10.4	1976	30.9
1963	17.5	1977	32.3
1964	22.2	1978	36.5
1965	27.1		

Source: ZGTJNJ (1991: 40).

There is little in the statistical record to suggest that the People's Republic was incapable of sustaining accumulation at this sort of pace. To be sure, the accumulation rate did drop in two periods: during 1961–5 in the aftermath of the Great Leap Forward, and again during 1967–9. But those declines were hardly surprising given the famine, and the disruptions to production in the early years of the Cultural Revolution. In 'normal' times, the rate was much higher: it exceeded 30 per cent in every year between 1970 and 1978, and was even rising in the late 1970s.[3] In short, the austerity drive of the Maoist era does seem to have made possible a large and sustained increase in the investment rate.

2. The Absence of Macroeconomic Crisis in the late 1970s

One of the key reasons why China was able to sustain a high rate of savings and investment in the twilight of the Maoist era was the absence of any severe macroeconomic crisis. This is something on which the general theoretical literature relating to the preconditions for economic growth has said little. Yet an argument often heard in the debate about transition is that success depends upon the extent of economic stability when the transition programme begins (Rodrik, 1996). An economy entering transition from a state of economic crisis is less likely to do as well as an economy enjoying macroeconomic stability. This is because instability (especially inflation) creates uncertainty, which in turn adversely affects domestic savings and investment, and the willingness of foreign companies and governments to invest. In the Chinese context, it is argued that initial macroeconomic conditions in the People's Republic were far more benign on the eve of reform than they were in either Latin America or Eastern Europe, where the reformers inherited full-blown macroeconomic crises. The Polish inflation rate in 1989, for example, was no less than 640 per cent (Balcerowicz, 1994*b*: 74). It is thus suggested that Poland had no option but to embrace shock therapy (Balcerowicz, 1994*a*: 44):

> The range of sensible options depends very much on the initial situation, and especially on macroeconomic conditions. If the macroeconomic situation is catastrophic (near hyperinflation and massive shortages, as in Poland in mid-1989) the 'cold turkey' approach to stabilization is the *safest* [original emphasis] one.

Other Eastern European countries also faced difficulties at the end of the 1980s as the USSR began to shift towards charging market prices for its oil and gas exports. As a consequence, Eastern Europe suffered a massive adverse terms of trade shock. According to Kenen (1991), the decline in the terms of trade varied between 23 per cent in Poland to 37 per cent in Hungary. As Krugman and Obstfeld (1994: 721) note, this was on average twice the size of the first oil-price shock in the OECD countries. To be sure, the Soviet Union undoubtedly enjoyed an improvement in her terms of trade as a result. However, much of this was offset by the continued decline in world oil prices, one of the USSR's key exports. Other countries attempting transition faced similar problems, especially in Latin America. The Chilean economy inherited by Pinochet in late 1973 was on the verge of collapse. Admittedly, that was largely the doing of Pinochet and his collaborators, but the same cannot be said for other parts of South America. In Brazil, the inflation rate climbed steadily during the 1980s to reach over 2,000 per cent by 1994. Populism in Peru under Garcia led to an inflation rate of 2,800 per cent by 1989 and 12,400 per cent in 1990. The Bolivian inflation rate on the eve of stabilization surpassed even that, reaching more than 23,000 per cent (Rodrik, 1996: 22, 26).

By contrast, it is alleged, China faced no such problems (Fan, 1994: 101). Following Mao's death, and the arrest of the 'Gang of Four' which signalled the end of the Cultural Revolution, the Chinese economy recovered relatively quickly and the authority of the CCP was maintained.[4] This ensured both that the CCP retained at least a degree of legitimacy, and that there was little momentum for a radical economic reform in the late 1970s. According to Fan (1994: 101):

> Gradualism was adopted at the end of 1978 not because there were no proposals for more radical reform programmes but because a majority of society and the leadership were not in favour of them. The fact was that the Chinese economic situation in the late 1970s was 'too good' for a radical reform package to be adopted. . . . The noticeable recovery of economic performance immediately after the end of the Cultural Revolution seemed to many people evidence of the virtues of the old system. It was hence natural for a majority of people not to choose an abrupt change of their life when their real income was not only growing but was also expected to continue to grow under the current regime.

Now there is unquestionably something in this characterization of the Chinese economy in the 1970s. Real GDP was growing quickly in 1977 and 1978, and life expectancy probably also continued to rise. Furthermore, very few of the Chinese reformers thought systemic reform necessary at the time: as was noted in Chapter 2, the prevailing view was that, by abandoning Maoist emphasis on class struggle and shifting the focus instead to economic construction, the planned economy could be made to work better. This was true even of some of the provinces that experienced very little per capita output growth in the late Maoist period. In Sichuan, the province hit hardest by the famine of the early 1960s, there was no attempt at agricultural privatization in the late 1970s despite the presence of Zhao Ziyang as First Party Secretary. Rather, the emphasis was on readjustment—removal of restrictions on private markets and lower procurement quotas—instead of systemic reform (Bramall, 1995*a*).

However, this view that the economy was in relatively good shape ignores the pervasive sense of crisis that one finds in the pronouncements of the Chinese leadership and the Chinese literature of the late 1970s. Deng Xiaoping and Chen Yun were united during the 1980s in their mistrust of any political or economic change that might lead to the re-emergence of the chaos (*daluan*) that had characterized the Cultural Revolution. Moreover, they both believed that Chinese agriculture was in crisis at the end of the 1970s. In their view, per capita agricultural output had been stagnant since the late 1950s, and this is supported by the (official) data. Measured at 1990 constant prices, per capita agricultural output averaged only 269 *yuan* in 1976–8 compared to 297 *yuan* in 1955–7.[5] In Sichuan, one of China's poorest provinces, per capita agricultural output fell by 18 per cent over the same period. Furthermore, extreme material poverty was commonplace in many parts of central and western China. It was this perception of crisis that encouraged the Chinese leadership to acquiesce in early decollectivization in parts of Anhui, Sichuan, and Gansu provinces. This acquiescence was reinforced by the drought that hit agricultural production in Anhui in 1977 and 1978. In fact, it is not hard to argue that the crisis was much more severe in parts of rural China than it was in Poland. Polish hyperinflation was, to be sure, a source of concern but it was hardly comparable to the outright starvation that was perceived to threaten some of the poorest parts of the Chinese countryside.

Of course one can argue that, in 'objective' terms, there was no real crisis even in rural China in the late 1970s. The state was able to transfer grain from surplus provinces to meet the needs of deficit provinces in the late 1970s. It could also purchase grain on the world market if necessary. These measures had been more than sufficient to avert starvation in Sichuan in 1976 (where the harvest was very poor) and there is no reason to suppose that they would not have been in effective in Anhui. In other words, the problems of rural China of the late 1970s related more to weather-induced temporary fluctuation rather than any long-run crisis. Furthermore, the relatively minor readjustment undertaken in Sichuan in the late 1970s were quite enough to raise per capita output above its 1957 level by 1979–80; there was no obvious need for reform.[6] Nevertheless, there is no denying the fact that there was *perceived* to be a crisis in rural China, and that these perceptions encouraged the Chinese leadership to act. If nothing else, the Dengist leadership saw two tasks as requiring urgent attention. First, the trained personnel who had languished in the countryside since the late 1960s had to be restored to office if the regime was to have the skilled cadres necessary for rapid economy growth. Secondly, Hua Guofeng's ambitious 'foreign leap forward'—and all it entailed in terms of higher investment and large increases in imports—had to be halted if consumption levels were to be raised.

In fact, there are clear parallels between China in the late 1970s and the USSR in the late 1980s. There was, for example, no real crisis in the Soviet economy: at the time of Gorbachev's accession (March 1985), the USSR was in much better shape than that of Eastern Europe in 1989–90. Some indication of growth rates is given in Table 8.2.

TABLE 8.2. *Soviet Growth Rates, 1970–1985* (real annual percentage growth rates)

	Net material product	Agricultural output	Agricultural output (per capita)
1970–5	5.9	1.4	1.5
1975–80	4.2	1.4	1.8
1980–5	3.6	2.0	2.0
1970–85	4.4	1.1	1.3

Note: Growth rates calculated at (unspecified) constant prices.
Source: Dyker (1992: 42, 104).

These figures may overstate the true growth rate (CIA estimates for GNP growth are somewhat lower). Nevertheless, the Soviet growth rate in the early 1980s was not disastrous, and the data on agriculture show that, if anything, the growth rate was increasing. Indeed, in respect of agriculture, the Soviet performance was much superior to that of China. As we have seen, there was no growth in per capita output in China, whereas the USSR achieved an increase of more than 1 per cent per year. In other respects, too, the Soviet Union inherited by Gorbachev in 1985 did not teeter on the brink of disaster. The budget deficit was only about 2 per cent of national income in 1985, and the current account was actually in surplus in 1985 (Dyker, 1992: 177, 183). This was despite the fall in the world oil price after 1983.

Nevertheless, as with China, the USSR was *perceived* to be facing a crisis in 1985. This perception reflected a number of factors. For one thing, the growth rate was declining over time, and it was generally held that this reflected a combination of dwindling scope for extensive growth and a failure to generate productivity increases. In addition, many (e.g. Shmelev and Popov, 1990) argued that the planning system was endemically inefficient in the static sense, with large subsidies being paid to agriculture and heavy industry. Finally, the decline in world prices was a harbinger of the problems the USSR would face if it attempted to modernize its industry by importing modern capital. All these factors together were instrumental in persuading Gorbachev to embark upon the path of *perestroika* at the 27th Congress in 1986.

In sum, the difference between China and the economies of Eastern Europe in terms of the situation they inherited is greatly exaggerated. The parallels—especially between late Maoist China and the Soviet Union of Chernenko—seem greater than the differences. Macroeconomic conditions were not ideal in either China or the USSR at the beginning of transition, but it is hard to argue that either economy was in crisis. That, of course, was not the perception at the time.

3. External Sources of Capital

China entered the transition era not only with a substantial physical and social capability but also with privileged access to the overseas savings needed to develop and expand that capital stock during the 1980s. Not only was the People's Republic free from external debt but it was able also to call upon the savings of Chinese living abroad, notably in Taiwan and Hong Kong. This meant that China entered the transition era not having to finance its investment solely on the basis of domestic savings.[7]

3.1. International Debt

China was remarkable amongst LDCs in beginning transition with no accumulated foreign debt. World Bank data show a total external debt in 1977 of zero, with China taking out her first significant loan (of US$623m.) in 1978. By 1990, this had risen to US$52,555m. or about half of that contracted by Brazil for the same year (WT, 1992: 186–7). China thus entered the 1980s free of the constraints faced by most other countries throughout the developing world. The comparison here between China, and both Eastern Europe and sub-Saharan Africa, is instructive (Table 8.3).

TABLE 8.3. *Ratio of total external debt to GNP*

Country (year)	Total external debt (US$bn.)	GNP (US$bn.)	Debt/GNP ratio (per cent)
Russia (1985)	28.31	535.31	5
Hungary (1989)	20.39	27.90	73
Poland (1989)	43.13	79.02	55
Bulgaria (1989)	10.12	21.10	48
Kenya (1985)	4.11	5.91	70
Nigeria (1986)	23.40	38.71	61
Tanzania (1986)	4.30	4.78	90

Notes: Russian GDP is extrapolated 1994 GDP and World Bank estimates of growth rates between 1985 and 1994 (WDR, 1996: 173, 211). In this calculation, the entire debt of the USSR is assigned to Russia. The dates reflect the end of Soviet domination for Hungary, Poland, and Bulgaria, the beginning of *perestroika* for Russia, and the onset of the debt 'crisis' in sub-Saharan Africa.

Source: World Bank (1993*c*).

The debts of the Soviet Union itself—for which Russian debt serves as a proxy—were not high at the beginning of *perestroika* in 1985; it is hard to believe that a debt burden of 5 per cent of GDP amounted to a significant obstacle in the way of transition in Russia. The same was true of some of the Soviet Union's former satellites such as Czechoslovakia. However, the situation was very different in other countries undergoing transition. In sub-Saharan Africa, debt–GNP ratios of well over 50 per cent were normal by the mid-1980s. Moreover, although the extent of debt in Bulgaria, Poland, and Hungary was less crippling (at around 50 per cent) in 1989, it was still significant enough to impose a balance of payments constraint on them. By contrast, China's freedom from debt allowed it to use its export earnings with impunity to purchase both capital and consumer goods on international markets.

The fate of Mexico and Brazil in the 1980s shows what might have happened to China but for its negligible debt burden. In Brazil, the ratio of debt to GNP stood at about 50 per cent in 1985 (World Bank, 1993*c*: 54). It is no coincidence that its economy grew at a meagre 2.7 per cent per year during the 1980s compared to 9 per cent during the preceding 15 years (WDR, 1992: 221). Much of this was because the share of gross investment in GNP fell from 29 per cent in 1979–81 to 22 per cent by 1988–90. A particularly severe recession occurred in 1983; with investment at only about two-thirds of its real value at the end of the 1970s, employment was 23 per cent down on 1980 (WT, 1992: 144–5). The longer term inflationary consequences were at least as damaging. With Brazilian firms denied access to foreign capital, investment levels could only be financed by increasing the mark-up (with the aim of boosting retained profits) or by domestic monetary expansion. In conjunction with the election of Sarney's government, which was weak because it was immediately faced by a host of competing claims for distributional justice, these factors made the hyperinflation of the late 1980s virtually inevitable (Baer, 1995). The Mexican experience was not dissimilar. There, the debt–GNP ratio climbed to 55 per cent in 1985 and to 83 per cent in 1986 (World Bank, 1993*c*: 298). Against this background, the investment share in GNP fell from an average of 35 per cent during 1979–81 to 23 per cent by 1988–90, and, between 1981 and 1987, the index of real earnings fell from 146 to 100. Most dramatically of all, GNP per capita fell from US$3,000 in 1981 to US$1,770 by 1988. Although this had much to do with the depreciation of the currency, GNP per capita in 1987 pesos was still about 10 per cent lower than it had been in 1981 (WT, 1992: 416–17). As for private sector spending, Brazilian consumption at its trough (1990) was more than 10 per cent down on its peak (1986) whilst Mexican consumption levels in 1987 were 18 per cent lower than in 1981. These two instances illustrate the good fortune of the Dengist government. China began its transition with an extensive infrastructure and was able to build upon it by allocating her export earnings to the purchase of capital good imports rather than to the servicing of a foreign debt.

The absence of accumulated external debt in China during the late 1970s reflected two factors. First, Mao had little choice in the matter of foreign borrowing (at least if one accepts Maoist ideology as a given); after the split with the Soviet Union in the early 1960s, all sources of foreign funds were denied her. Second, the People's

Republic had been scarred by her experience of borrowing from the Soviet Union in the 1950s and therefore the auguries were not good. China had, to be sure, benefited from those loans. Soviet 'aid' during the 1950s came in the form of credits to finance the bilateral trade balance, which was in deficit in every year between 1950 and 1955 (Eckstein, 1964). These loans totalled 5.294bn. *yuan* between 1950 and 1957; they averaged about 1 per cent of national income, although the ratio was probably as high as 2.5 per cent during 1950–1 (Eckstein, 1964: 149; ZGTJNJ, 1992: 32). This external funding not only helped finance China's involvement in the Korean War but also played a key role in the industrialization of the 1950s, much of which centred around the 156 key plants purchased from the USSR (Yu, 1984: 681). As a result of the installation of this capacity, China was able to restrict its imports of capital goods to about 8 per cent of its total imports between 1950 and 1960 (Yu, 1984: 679; Nongye bu, 1989: 532).

However, there was a price. In order to service the debt, China ran a trade surplus with the Soviet Union after 1956 (Eckstein, 1964: 153); by the mid-1960s —ahead of time, in fact—China's debts had been repaid in full (Yu, 1984: 683). However, most of China's exports were of textiles and agricultural products: 56 per cent of exports by value were agricultural commodities in 1953 and a further 27 per cent (rising to 42 per cent in 1958) was accounted for by light industrial products (Nongye bu, 1989: 516). This pattern of trade necessarily depressed consumption levels in the short run, and although the impact was comparatively slight before 1958, these exports were a significant drain during the Great Leap Forward (Walker, 1984). In fact, grain exports accounted for more than 2.5 per cent of production during 1959–60.[8] The regional impact was even more severe. The bulk of China's grain exports came from Sichuan, the province worst hit by the famine of the early 1960s. The province's grain exports (by volume) increased fifteenfold between 1957 and 1959; by 1959, indeed, grain exports accounted for about 6 per cent of production (Bramall, 1993). Of course, the famine in Sichuan, and elsewhere in China, was caused primarily by a fall in production, and the collapse of effective redistributive mechanisms. Nevertheless, given that only about 1500 kcals per capita per day of food were available in Sichuan during 1959 to 1961, it is clear that grain exports to the USSR contributed significantly to the high levels of excess mortality.[9] Against this background, the reticence of the Maoist leadership to have recourse to foreign borrowing after 1960 is understandable. It is by no means coincidental that China began to borrow significant sums only after the extremely rapid rise in agricultural output in the late 1970s and early 1980s.

3.2. Overseas Chinese Capital

A second argument often made about external capital is that the People's Republic enjoyed the advantage of capital inflows from overseas Chinese (e.g. Sachs and Woo, 1994). These transfers, it is said, played a crucial role in financing Chinese investment during the 1980s. By contrast, and partly because of the legacy of the debt crisis of the early 1980s, Western banks and governments were most reluctant to make financial transfers on this scale to Eastern Europe. According to Balcerowicz (1994*a*): 'the large influx of foreign capital into Southern China (predominantly of overseas Chinese origin) also seems to have been a largely specific factor, i.e. difficult to reproduce on such a large scale in most of the Central and East European countries.'

There is some truth in this analysis. For example, the bulk (61 per cent) of direct investment in China between 1983 and 1991 came from Hong Kong (Yabuki, 1995: 162). This undoubtedly contributed to economic growth in Fujian, Guangdong, and Hainan, as will be discussed in Chapter 11. To be sure, and as Nolan and Ash (1995) rightly point out, there was no a priori reason why Eastern Europe could not have attracted *some* direct foreign investment. The cheap and well-skilled labour force that existed certainly ought to have provided an incentive for European and Japanese firms to invest. To put the argument in another way, if relatively high-cost Britain was capable of attracting Japanese investment, why not Eastern Europe and the Soviet Union?

Nevertheless, though it was not impossible for them to attract capital, the disadvantages of investment in Eastern Europe from the perspective of an international company were plain. First, it involved non-negligible transport costs in supplying goods to the markets of the EU; as Krugman (1991) has pointed out, transport costs remain an important consideration in determining location. Secondly, the Eastern European countries stood outside the tariff barriers that surrounded the EU and their accession to the Treaty of Rome promised to be a slow process. Thirdly, the language barriers were, and are, formidable. In that respect in particular, the advantage to 'footloose' Japanese and European companies of investing in an English-speaking country are extremely strong. By contrast, China's advantages were plain. The common language and similar procedures adopted in formulating deals eased the path of the overseas Chinese investor. The potential size of the market was also an enormous attraction. To be sure, the calculus of profit and loss was still primary; if overseas Chinese had doubted the scope for profits in the People's Republic, they would not have invested. Nevertheless, China's links with this pool of overseas savings were still significant at the margin.

4. Conclusion to Part II

China was comparatively fortunate in its initial conditions for growth in the transition era. Indeed, there is little question that a part of post-1978 Chinese economic growth can be explained by initial conditions. By exploiting the infrastructural legacy painfully constructed during the Maoist era, the CCP was able to launch economic transition with a burst of rapid growth. This was especially true of the period up to 1984, when growth centred on the exploitation of previously completed irrigation systems in agriculture, and the extensive foundation of fixed capital in both industry and in transport. To be sure, agricultural growth depended upon the application of large quantities of chemical fertilizer and not just the use of existing fixed capital. However the bulk of this fertilizer itself came from plants completed during the mid- and late-1970s.

The People's Republic was also lucky in entering the transition era without external debt, with privileged access to sources of external capital, and with a high rate of savings. China benefited too from its comparatively well-developed level of human capital. Finally, Chinese culture was relatively receptive to modern economic technologies, structures, and ideas. It had never been entirely unreceptive, as indicated by the fact of rapid growth in the Treaty Ports before 1949. But there is no doubt that the Maoist period accelerated the process by its destruction of traditional peasant culture and customs.

The only argument which does not seem especially plausible in the Chinese context is that which relates to surplus labour. The standard Lewis-type surplus labour is unconvincing, both in general terms and in its application to China. China does not seem to have profited significantly by redeploying labour from (notionally) low productivity to (notionally) high productivity sectors.

Nevertheless, and despite the arguments put forward in Chapters 6, 7, and 8, it would be wrong to explain post-1978 growth *purely* in terms of the economic inheritance. First, there is no doubt—as will be seen in the next few chapters—that China owed some of its growth to a further increase in its savings rate, and to a rise in its rate of productivity growth. In other words, the economy did not grow simply by exploiting its potential. Secondly, the inheritance argument does not explain *why* China suddenly began to exploit its favourable preconditions after 1978. For example, the large, literate, labour force of the late 1970s had to be mobilized if it was to benefit the economy; its mere existence was certainly not a sufficient condition for rapid economic growth. In fact, as will be seen, it was to be the Chinese state which unlocked the economy's potential.

Part III

Other Proximate Sources of Growth

9

Capital Accumulation after 1978

Having discussed the role played by the Dengist economic inheritance in Part II, we now go on to look at other sources of growth. This chapter looks at the extent to which the pattern of investment changed after 1978. Did the investment rate increase above the very respectable level of the 1970s? Did the savings function shift to an even higher level after 1978, thus making possible the (long-run) attainment of an even higher steady-state level of per capita output? Merely a continuation of the pre-1978 investment and savings record would have generated growth after 1978. But an increase in the savings rate, if that is what happened, might have made possible yet faster growth. For example, as was seen in Chapter 6, the Dengist regime inherited an extensive social and physical capability. Nevertheless, the planners of the late 1970s were well aware of the deficiencies of this Maoist legacy: the capital–labour ratio, though high by the standards of many developing countries, was still well below the level found in both the rapidly growing East Asian economies and those of the OECD. Could it not be raised by a still higher savings rate?

The second issue relates to the pattern of investment. Is there any evidence that investment after 1978 went into sectors with a higher level of capital productivity than the sectors selected before 1978? This chapter addresses this by looking at the role of investment in agriculture, and considers three broad types of agricultural capital—machinery, irrigation, and fertilizer. This focus on agriculture is then shifted to physical capital formation in industry, and in transport infrastructure. The final section addresses the role played by human capital formation. In this respect, it will argued that the Chinese leadership during the transition era was much less successful in sustaining the achievements of the Maoist regime.

1. The Macroeconomics of Investment

The trend in investment after 1978 is shown in Table 9.1. In 1993, the investment share exceeded 43 per cent, a remarkable figure for a country still relatively poor. Some idea of just how extreme this is comes from looking at the comparable data on East Asia for 1991. The Japanese investment ratio of 32 per cent seems extremely modest by comparison, and even the 38 per cent recorded by South Korea seems unexceptional. Perhaps most significantly of all, the Chinese investment rate eclipsed even that of Singapore (40 per cent), a country long seen as having placed almost overwhelming—and, according to some, unnecessary—emphasis on capital accumulation. Compared with the early 1980s (when accumulation was not very different in its scale than in the Maoist period), the investment share rose from around

33 per cent of GDP to nearly 40 per cent of GDP in the mid-1990s. In other words, a further big leap in the investment rate occurred in China in the transition era—and that from a late 1970s rate that was already high.

TABLE 9.1. *The share of investment in GDP* (per cent; current prices)

Year	GDI/GDP	Year	GDI/GDP
1978	38.0	1988	36.8
1979	36.5	1989	36.0
1980	35.2	1990	34.7
1981	32.5	1991	34.8
1982	33.2	1992	36.2
1983	33.8	1993	43.3
1984	34.4	1994	41.2
1985	37.8	1995	40.8
1986	37.7	1996	39.2
1987	36.1	Mean	36.7

Note: Due to data revisions, the figures published in ZGTJNJ (1997) are different from those published earlier; these latest figures are used here.

Sources: ZGTJNJ (1996: 46); ZGTJNJ (1997: 46).

Furthermore, an examination of fluctuations in the share of investment in GDP after 1978 suggests an intimate relationship between investment and economic growth. Between 1978 and 1982/3, the investment share fell from around 38 per cent of GDP to about 32 per cent. During this sub-period, GDP growth was only 7.2 per cent—well below the 1978–94 average of 9.7 per cent. By contrast, the rise in the investment share from 33 per cent of GDP in 1983 to 37.5 per cent in 1988 was associated with a surge in the GDP growth rate to 11.7 per cent. The relationship continues for the remainder of the post-1978 period. Between 1988 and 1991, the investment share fell (36.8 per cent to 34.8 per cent, with a 1990 trough of 34.7 per cent), and so did the growth rate, to a modest 5.5 per cent per year. After 1991—when the investment share picked up from 34.8 to over 40 per cent—GDP growth accelerated to 13.2 per cent between 1991 and 1994. If anything—and rather ironically given that one of the main aims of the readjustment process in the early 1980s was to correct what was seen as the over-investment of the Maoist years and Hua Guofeng's interregnum—it was the transition era that saw an extreme emphasis on investment. The median share of accumulation in NDMP was 33 per cent during 1978–92, significantly higher than the Maoist average. In fact, the share was never below the Maoist median of 27 per cent (see Chapter 8), even in the readjustment period of 1981–3 or the depression of 1989–90. Moreover, as growth accelerated after 1991, so the accumulation share climbed to 38.7 per cent in 1993 (ZGTJNJ, 1994: 40).

1.1. Investment Hunger

Yet the increase in the investment rate after 1978 has been seen as involving costs. One problem from the viewpoint of the CCP was that it was hard to control 'investment hunger' because that required central government to discipline local interests. As Huang (1996) points out, the inflation caused by excessive investment is (at least in part) an externality for those regions which create it. Regions able to invest heavily in rural industry, and existing locally-controlled SOEs, benefit far more from the capacity created by the investment than they lose from its costs; they therefore have only a weak incentive to control investment levels. The calculus of costs and benefits is of course very different for central government, and this has brought it into collision with local government on many occasions.

To be sure, the centre has always been able to assert its will, but only at the cost of periodic re-centralization and pronounced growth slowdowns. There is in fact a very general view amongst Chinese economists (including Huang) that investment hunger was the prime cause of the inflationary pressures that erupted in China during 1985–6, 1988–9 and 1993–4. This analysis starts from the assumption that the bulk of investment is carried out by state enterprises. This fact created problems because of the weakening of controls on state enterprises as the 1980s progressed. Not only did the granting of greater autonomy weaken the direct ability of the state to intervene but also market forces were still too weak to act as an alternative disciplinary force; state enterprises in fact continued to face only soft budget constraints, and if they over-invested, there was only a remote possibility of either bankruptcy or takeover.[1] As a result, state enterprises were prone in periods of monetary expansion to expand their investment. As investment necessarily involves more or less lengthy gestation periods, this increased demand for investment goods is not matched in the short term by an increase in production. The macroeconomic consequence is inflation, and it can only be quelled by a period of intense monetary contraction.

This analysis gains considerable support from the evidence. The first inflationary episode in 1985 took place against the background of a rise in the investment share in GDP from 32 per cent in 1982 to 39 per cent in 1985. In the early 1990s, the investment share rose from 35 per cent in 1991 to 43 per cent in 1993 (Table 9.1). There is, however, much less of a link between investment and the inflation of 1988–9; the investment share changed very little in this period. That episode of inflation had more to do with price liberalization, both actual and announced (this latter produced intertemporal commodity speculation on an extensive scale in 1988).

More generally, Huang probably exaggerates what he sees as the conflict between the growth-promoting and inflation-inducing effects of decentralization. The Chinese transitional strategy has involved inflationary costs, but it is hard to argue convincingly that these costs have outweighed the benefits of rapid growth. In that sense, the CCP has been happy (rightly so) to accept a measure of inflation during the transition era, and has acted firmly only when the inflation rate has threatened to accelerate dramatically.

1.2. Unproductive Investment

A second criticism that can be directed against the investment record during the transition era is that much of it was 'unproductive' in that it went into the production of consumption goods rather than means of production. Using the official Chinese distinction between productive and unproductive accumulation, it is clear that unproductive accumulation surged in the early 1980s. In 1976, the share of unproductive accumulation was barely 21 per cent, and even in 1978 it was only 28 per cent (LSTJ, 1990: 7). But by 1980, the share had increased to reach 45 per cent and in 1982 it reached a post-1978 peak of 54 per cent. Although it fell back considerably after that, the figure still averaged 37 per cent during 1991–3 (ZGTJNJ, 1994: 7).

Table 9.2. *Investment in housing, 1978–1996*

Year	GDP per capita (1990 prices; *yuan*)	Rural floor space (m^2 per capita)	Urban floor space (m^2 per capita)	Share of private rural housing investment in GDI (per cent; current prices)
1978	704	8.1	3.6	n/a
1979	744	8.1	3.7	n/a
1980	781	9.4	3.9	n/a
1981	808	10.2	4.1	n/a
1982	867	10.7	4.4	n/a
1983	943	11.6	4.6	n/a
1984	1,094	13.6	4.9	n/a
1985	1,214	14.7	5.2	9.2
1986	1,299	15.3	6.0	10.1
1987	1,421	16.0	6.1	11.3
1988	1,548	16.6	6.3	10.5
1989	1,584	17.2	6.6	10.5
1990	1,622	17.8	6.7	10.1
1991	1,750	18.5	6.9	10.1
1992	1,976	18.9	7.1	7.0
1993	2,217	20.7	7.5	5.1
1994	2,470	20.2	7.8	5.2
1995	2,701	21.0	8.1	5.7
1996	2,928	21.7	8.5	6.6
Growth rates (%):				
1978–83	5.7	8.1	5.3	n/a
1983–96	9.9	4.3	4.4	n/a
1978–96	8.4	5.8	5.0	n/a

Sources: ZGTJNJ (1995: 32, 59, 290); ZGTJNJ (1993: 31–2, 81); LSTJ (1990: 21, 35); ZGTJNJ (1996: 42, 69, 279); ZGTJNJ (1997: 42, 46, 69, 197, 324).

However, the scale of unproductive investment was probably not high enough to adversely affect the economy in a significant way. Consider investment in housing. There are few comprehensive data, but an indication of the trends comes from the statistics presented in Table 9.2. Investment in housing certainly did increase extremely rapidly in the early 1980s. Over the period up to 1983, the rate of growth of floor space per capita (8.1 per cent in the countryside and 5.3 per cent in urban areas) was faster than the rate of growth of real per capita GDP. But this frenetic pace of housing construction did not last. Its intensity reflected the need to make good years of neglect in both urban and rural areas. By 1983, the more immediate demands had been satisfied, and the pace of growth slackened off. Similarly, by the late 1980s, private investment in housing in rural areas as a proportion of gross domestic investment was falling back, and by 1994 it was less than half its 1987 peak. Indeed, in the period after 1983, the growth of per capita floor space in both urban and rural areas was less than half the rate of GDP per capita growth—in marked contrast to the early years of transition. Moreover, for the transition period as a whole, per capita floor space grew less quickly than per capita GDP—hardly a sign that housing was taking a disproportionate share of resources. Furthermore, it is hard to argue that investment in housing 'crowded-out' productive spending even in the early 1980s. In the countryside in particular, the reality was that booms in house construction and agricultural production went hand in hand in the period up to 1984. After 1984, the rate of growth in both slowed appreciably.

We are left with two broad conclusions about investment. Firstly, the post-1978 period saw significant increase in the share of investment in GDP to a level not seen since the heady days of the Great Leap Forward. In other words, an increase in the investment rate to a level substantially higher than during the Maoist period does appear to have played a role in the acceleration of growth after 1978. Both Maoist and Dengist periods were characterized by investment rates which were high by the standards of most contemporary developing countries, but that was especially true of China after 1978. Secondly, although some of this post-1978 increase in investment went towards making good the deficiencies in the housing stock, the bulk appears to have gone into productive assets; there is little sign of a trade-off between the two.

2. Agriculture

2.1. Agricultural Mechanization

As far as fixed investment by the agricultural sector is concerned, the evidence is summarized in Table 9.3.[2] There are two distinct trends. First, one of the most marked characteristics of these data is the way in which the capital stock—as measured by horsepower—climbed in the late 1970s, growing by more than 10 per cent in every year between 1975 and 1980. After 1980 the growth rate slowed substantially.[3] Even so, the capital stock was vastly higher by 1996 than it had been in 1978. As a result, the 1996 level was much more than double the level in 1980. Measured by the value of the capital stock—a rather less reliable measure—the value of agricultural machinery increased from 34bn. *yuan* in 1980 to nearly 63bn. *yuan* in 1992 (ZGNCTJNJ, 1993: 272).[4] In other words, although observers have drawn attention to China's relatively poor investment record for agriculture in the late 1980s (Watson, 1989*a*; Watson, 1989*b*), the state of affairs was by no means disastrous.

Whether this capital stock growth did much to further the cause of yield increases is a moot point. In fact, the only reason that mechanization proceeded at the pace it did in the 1970s was because of the campaign to 'learn from Dazhai' that was such a feature of the decade. Although tractorization made sense in the predominantly wheat-growing regions of northern China—as is evident from the development of cooperation over ploughing between households even after decollectivization—(Sicular, 1991; Gold, 1988; OECD, 1997), it was misguided when applied to rice-growing paddy fields of southern China. Accordingly, as soon as the campaign to emulate Dazhai was abandoned, the growth in stock of large and medium-sized tractors slowed sharply (and finally came to a halt in 1987).

TABLE 9.3. *Capital formation in agriculture, 1975–1996*

Year	Agricultural machine power (m. kW)	Annual percentage change	Trucks (000s)	Annual percentage change
1975	74.79	26.1	39.6	29.5
1976	86.30	15.4	48.7	23.0
1977	102.62	18.9	59.9	23.0
1978	117.50	14.5	73.8	23.2
1979	133.79	13.9	97.1	31.6
1980	147.46	10.2	134.7	38.7
1981	156.80	6.3	175.1	30.0
1982	166.14	6.0	206.4	17.9
1983	180.29	8.5	274.8	33.1
1984	195.33	8.3	349.2	27.1
1985	209.13	7.1	429.7	23.1
1986	229.50	9.7	499.2	16.2
1987	248.36	8.2	550.2	10.2
1988	265.75	7.0	591.4	7.5
1989	280.67	5.6	625.1	5.7
1990	287.08	2.3	624.4	–0.1
1991	293.89	2.4	616.6	–1.2
1992	303.08	3.1	642.4	4.2
1993	318.17	5.0	690.5	7.5
1994	338.03	6.2	748.0	8.3
1995	358.37	6.0	778.0	4.0
1996	385.47	7.6	836.9	7.6

Sources: Pre-1986 data are from Nongye bu (1989: 310); other data come from ZGTJNJ (1995: 334), ZGNYNJ (1996: 397, 405) and ZGNYNJ (1997: 401, 409).

The second trend evident in Table 9.3 is the increased use of trucks. As the data show, the stock of trucks in rural areas rose at average rate of more than 20 per cent, and sustained that pace of growth over the entire decade after 1975. In this case, there is little doubt that the trend was a clear response to increased demand, not least because the demand for walking tractors—which were cheap and served as a substitute of sorts for trucks—rocketed at a time when the demand for other types of tractors was falling.

That demand increase in turn had its origins in a number of factors. First, the removal of many late Maoist restrictions on private commerce served as a spur to investment in trucks. Secondly, the dramatic increase in the purchasing price of agricultural commodities gave the rural population a windfall income gain that was available for reinvestment and for consumption. It is hardly a coincidence that the growth of the number of trucks in use actually accelerated from 23 per cent in the mid-1970s to over 30 per cent between 1979 and 1983. Again, however, it remains debatable whether this had much of an impact on agricultural yields. Trucks no doubt facilitated specialization, and made it easier for farmers to acquire fertilizer and other modern inputs. But it is unlikely that the effect was substantial in the early 1980s when the economy was far from being fully market-orientated (and therefore offering extensive scope for income increases via specialization).

2.2. Investment in Irrigation after 1978

As for the record on investment in irrigation after 1978, there is little doubt that it was rather poor, in marked contrast to the Maoist era. As Tables 9.4 and 9.5 show, irrigated area appears to have declined up to 1988, falling at an annual average rate of 0.1 per cent after 1978. This amounted to a cumulative decline of about 7m. *mu* or about 1 per cent of the total irrigated area of 1978. The south-west (Sichuan, Guizhou, and Yunnan) and north-east (Heilongjiang, Jilin, and Liaoning) regions both registered a modest increase. Elsewhere, however, decline was very much the norm as irrigated land came under pressure from industrial and housing development, with both Guangdong and Liaoning to the fore. Only eleven provinces recorded any sort of an increase in the decade after 1978.

This neglect of the water-conservancy facilities so painstakingly created during the Maoist era was one important factor in the slowdown of farm output growth after the *annus mirabilis* of 1984. The relatively poor harvest of 1985 led to the claim that decollectivization had resulted in *chi laoben* (living off old capital), i.e. the neglect of the irrigation infrastructure (Fewsmith, 1995: 159). This argument was heard with increasing regularity as the decade progressed:

> During a period of 30 some years after the liberation, with indomitable will-power, people built numerous large and small water reservoirs and dams on the great earth of Hunan. These water-conservancy facilities have played a foundation-laying role in the development of Hunan's agriculture. In the 10 years that followed, they were, however, ignored, neglected, and gradually slid to the delicate condition they are in today. . . . Some people call water-conservancy facilities the 'patron' of agriculture. But due to its deteriorating condition, this patron can no longer 'make its presence or power felt'. During the summer drought of 1988, many large and small reservoirs dried up, which not only caused a sharp

decline in the production of crops, but also threatened the drinking-water supply of humans and animals. (Mo, 1989: 36–7)

In large measure, the problem was caused by a sharp decline in state investment. Measured in real terms, investment in water conservancy by the state fell from just over 3bn. *yuan* in 1978 and 1979 to a mere 1.6bn. in 1988; even in nominal terms, state investment in 1988 (2.36bn.) was lower than it had been in the late 1970s (3.5bn. *yuan* in 1978–9) (ZGNCTJNJ, 1990: 265). By any standards, this was a sharp decline. The crisis—the term is hardly an exaggeration—occurred, however, because the fall in state investment coincided with a decline in collective investment and labour mobilization following decollectivization.

TABLE 9.4. *Trends in provincial irrigated area, 1978–1996* (area irrigated in million *mu*)

Province	1978	1988	1991	1994	1996
Beijing	5.13	5.07	4.86	4.64	4.85
Tianjin	5.20	5.14	5.21	5.23	5.27
Hebei	54.87	54.48	57.59	59.44	63.72
Shanxi	16.36	16.46	17.24	17.81	18.08
Liaoning	12.78	11.43	16.34	17.76	18.42
Jilin	8.99	11.62	13.85	13.65	14.04
Heilongjiang	10.02	11.93	16.77	15.23	20.03
Shanghai	5.40	4.91	4.76	4.37	4.28
Jiangsu	49.08	52.43	57.75	56.99	57.57
Zhejiang	22.58	22.27	22.14	21.42	21.19
Anhui	35.93	33.19	40.79	43.17	44.57
Fujian	12.94	13.87	14.10	14.06	14.03
Jiangxi	24.62	27.24	27.72	27.26	28.34
Shandong	66.22	64.86	68.29	69.63	70.39
Henan	55.83	50.40	55.51	58.97	62.87
Hubei	35.33	32.59	34.96	33.58	35.77
Hunan	40.31	39.92	39.19	40.19	40.01
Guangdong	29.51	25.24	25.24	21.98	22.34
Guangxi	22.05	20.04	22.53	22.33	22.06
Sichuan	43.02	41.39	42.40	43.11	43.88
Guizhou	7.46	8.07	7.68	9.10	9.28
Yunnan	13.52	14.84	16.23	17.71	19.25
Shaanxi	18.21	18.59	19.25	19.88	19.31
Gansu	12.72	12.56	13.01	13.71	14.09
Qinghai	2.47	2.45	2.63	2.65	2.64
Ningxia	3.64	3.83	3.98	4.15	4.22
Xinjiang	39.12	41.48	42.75	41.98	42.62
TOTAL	653.31	646.30	692.77	700.00	723.12

Notes: Data refer to effectively irrigated area. The data given in the ZGTJNJ series are slightly different from those to be found in the Agricultural Yearbooks.

Sources: Table 5.2; ZGTJNJ (1992: 344); ZGTJNJ (1995: 337); ZGTJNJ (1997: 373). For Xinjiang, in addition, LSTJ (1990: 930);

TABLE 9.5. *Growth of irrigated area, 1978–1996*
(annual percentage growth rates; provinces in ascending order of growth)

Province	1978–96	1978–88	1988–96
Guangdong	−1.5	−1.6	−1.5
Shanghai	−1.3	−0.9	−1.7
Zhejiang	−0.4	−0.1	−0.6
Beijing	−0.3	−0.1	−0.6
Hunan	0.0	−0.1	0.0
Guangxi	0.0	−1.0	1.2
Tianjin	0.1	−0.1	0.3
Hubei	0.1	−0.8	1.2
Sichuan	0.1	−0.4	0.7
Shandong	0.3	−0.2	1.0
Shaanxi	0.3	0.2	0.5
Qinghai	0.4	−0.1	0.9
Fujian	0.5	0.7	0.1
Xinjiang	0.5	0.6	0.3
Shaanxi	0.6	0.1	1.2
Gansu	0.6	−0.1	1.4
Henan	0.7	−1.0	2.8
Hebei	0.8	−0.1	2.0
Jiangxi	0.8	1.0	0.5
Ningxia	0.8	0.5	1.2
Jiangsu	0.9	0.7	1.2
Anhui	1.2	−0.8	3.8
Guizhou	1.2	0.8	1.8
Yunnan	2.0	0.9	3.3
Liaoning	2.1	−1.1	6.1
Jilin	2.5	2.6	2.4
Heilongjiang	3.9	1.8	6.7
TOTAL	0.6	−0.1	1.4

Note: Growth rates are between endpoints only.
Sources: as for Table 9.4.

To be sure, there was no *collapse* of local investment in irrigation. Local governments in many parts of China mobilized some of the soaring tax revenue contributed by the rapidly expanding non-farm sector for infrastructural purposes. For example, Renshou county (Sichuan) successfully completed in 1988 a large reservoir which had been begun in the early 1970s. In order to finance its completion, and to implement complementary projects that the reservoir made possible, the county was able to rely on collective and other industries to provide 13.1m. of the 20.1m. *yuan* required in 1989 (Odgaard, 1992: 137–8). More generally, investment by rural households (*nonghu jiben*) in agriculture as a whole rose sharply from 4.98bn. *yuan* in 1981 to 20.03bn. *yuan* in 1988 (Nongcun zijin ketizu, 1990: 22). The fact remains, however, that this investment was inadequate to fill the gap left by the declining state contribution. Most peasant investment was outside the agricultural sector in housing, industry, and commerce, and very little of the investment within the farm sector itself went into water conservancy. The reasons for this pattern are not difficult to explain. In essence, agriculture offered a much lower rate of return than industry and commerce, largely because of the relative price structure. Furthermore, and notwithstanding repeated government 'assurances', many households remained concerned about the uncertainty involved; agriculture had been collectivized once, and many were by no means convinced that it would not happen again. In addition, water-conservancy projects have a powerful public goods component; individual households, and even small groups of households, could not hope to bring large-scale projects to fruition.

The neglect that occurred during the early 1980s was underlined by the widespread flooding that occurred in Anhui and Jiangsu provinces in 1991 (Kueh, 1995).[5] The Yangzi flooding of 1998 points to a similar conclusion (although deforestation due to excess logging in western Sichuan was as much to blame as the inadequacies of the irrigation system). Accordingly, though some of the pessimism concerning Chinese irrigation voiced in the late 1980s was overdone, it is hard to argue that post-1978 investment in irrigation contributed very much to the acceleration in the pace of agricultural growth. It was the Maoist legacy which was crucial, and little was done to build upon it until the early 1990s.

2.3. Fertilizer Inputs

Fertilizer inputs are widely recognized as having an importance at least equal to irrigation systems in raising agricultural output. The relationship between the application of nitrogen and rice yields is quadratic: yields initially increase dramatically as more fertilizer is applied, before stagnating and eventually declining. A second general result is that modern varieties are more fertilizer-responsive than traditional types across a wide range of countries. As a result, and though yields using modern varieties are higher than using traditional varieties for a given application of fertilizer, the adoption of Green Revolution varieties has led to increased chemical fertilizer use (David and Otsuka, 1994: 16). Thirdly, chemical fertilizer applications are of major significance for rice yields; fertilizer alone is estimated to have accounted for about 25 per cent of the total increase in rice output in eight Asian countries between 1965 and 1980 (Barker and Herdt, 1985: 76, 79–80, 81, 84).

The importance of fertilizer was of course well known in Qing and Republican China; indeed the yield growth of the eighteenth, nineteenth, and early twentieth centuries was very much predicated upon a growing use of organic fertilizers such as manure and night-soil from urban centres (Perkins, 1967). By the late 1950s, however, the scope for increasing yields by the further application of these organic fertilizers had almost reached its limits (Ishikawa, 1971). In the view of most agricultural specialists, whether Western, Soviet, or Chinese, the only way to raise yields beyond existing levels was by the application of chemical fertilizer (Buck, 1947; Afans'yeskiy 1960, 1962; Sun, 1960). In the mid-1960s, however, the use of chemical fertilizer in China was still very limited. In 1964, only about 9 kg of chemical fertilizer (nutrient weight) was being used per hectare of sown land (Nongye bu, 1989: 340). In Zhejiang province, where agriculture was more developed than most, chemical fertilizer use was running at only 90 kg per hectare in 1965. Even in Shanghai, where 180 kg of chemical fertilizer were being applied per hectare in 1965 (LSTJ, 1990), application rates fell well below what was to be the norm in the most advanced parts of Asia by the early 1990s. For example, according to FAO statistics for 1992/93, average application rates of fertilizer per hectare were running at 439 kg in Japan, 507 kg in South Korea, and 928 kg in Malaysia (ZGTJNJ, 1995: 774).

From the mid-1960s onwards, however, the growing use of chemical fertilizer became increasingly the norm in Chinese agriculture. By 1980, application rates had reached 128 kg per hectare and rose to 375 kg by 1995. In the most advanced areas such as Guangdong and Fujian, the figure had risen to 840 and 870 kg per hectare respectively (ZGTJNJ, 1995: 331, 337). Even in poor areas like Henan and Guizhou, 480 and 330 kg of chemical fertilizer were being applied to every hectare of cultivated land in the respective provinces. More generally, and as the data in Table 9.6 show, chemical fertilizer use per hectare grew at 8.7 per cent per year between 1970 and 1975, before accelerating to a phenomenal 20.8 per cent per year between 1975 and 1980. The growth rate fell back thereafter, but still averaged 8 per cent per year in the first half of the 1980s, and over 6 per cent between 1985 and 1996.

TABLE 9.6. *Growth of farm output and chemical fertilizer use, 1970–1996* (annual percentage growth rates)

Period	Chemical fertilizer use	Farm output	Grain yields
1970–5	8.7	3.3	3.4
1975–80	20.8	3.4	3.9
1980–5	8.0	7.3	5.9
1985–90	6.9	1.6	2.0
1990–6	6.3	4.7	2.2

Notes: Farm output is at 1990 prices. It is gross output value before 1983 (no value-added data are available) and net thereafter; it refers only to crop production. Chemical fertilizer-use data are based on nutrient weights applied in kg per sown hectare. Yields are measured in kg of unprocessed grain (*yuanliang*) per sown hectare.

Sources: Nongye bu (1989: 106–9, 138–43, 146–8, 341); ZGTJNJ (1995: 332, 337, 344); ZGTJNJ (1996: 356, 361, 368, 374); ZGTJNJ (1997: 373, 380, 383).

However, it is not clear from the data in Table 9.6 that there was a strong link between fertilizer use and farm output. When output growth accelerated in the early 1990s, for example, there was little change in chemical fertilizer use. More important was probably the rise in procurement prices and the incentive effects it induced. The weak nature of the fertilizer–output relationship is probably best illustrated, however, by looking at the period between 1975 and 1985. In the second half of the 1970s, the growth of chemical fertilizer use accelerated from 8.7 per cent in 1970–5 to 20.8 per cent. But the growth of farm output measured at constant prices rose only marginally (from 3.3 to 3.4 per cent) and the impact of fertilizer is no more clear if one looks at grain yields (on the assumption that the new varieties of hybrid wheat and dwarf rice were more fertilizer-responsive than other crops). Grain-yield growth rates did accelerate, but only modestly; the rates were 3.4 per cent between 1970 and 1975, and 3.9 per cent between 1975 and 1980. Furthermore, when the analysis is extended to 1980 to 1985, the link between fertilizer use and farm output becomes even weaker. Over that period, farm-output growth accelerated dramatically to average 7.3 per cent; grain-yield growth also accelerated significantly, to an average of 5.9 per cent. Yet the growth rate of chemical fertilizer use actually fell, and fell sharply. As the data in Table 9.6 show, fertilizer use per unit area grew at only 8 per cent per year in the first half of the 1980s, compared to nearly 21 per cent in the previous five years. In other words, the evidence seems to suggest that fertilizer inputs played at best only a modest role in the agricultural miracle of the early 1980s.

This conclusion is, however, probably too pessimistic. For one thing, the comparison is loaded against the 1975–80 period because the end years involved imply a normal to trough comparison; in 1975, grain yields were at their 1965–85 trend whereas in 1980 yields were some 4 to 5 per cent below trend because of poor weather. By contrast, the 1980–5 period involves more of a trough to peak comparison; although 1985 was a poor year compared to the extremely good years of 1982–4, yields in that year were still slightly above trend. Additionally, the impact of increased fertilizer use was probably relatively modest in the late 1970s because this was very much a period of learning; the new fertilizer-responsive hybrid varieties of rice had only made their appearance in 1975 and there is no doubt that the collectives were unsure about the optimal way in which to employ them. As a result, a substantial proportion of the applied fertilizer was wasted. But perhaps most importantly of all, other aspects of economic policy were still far from conducive to high growth rates of farm production. To be sure, a programme of readjustment and partial decollectivization had been launched in several provinces, notably Anhui and Sichuan. But policy remained unconducive to rapid output growth in a number of respects. The 'readjustment' programme did not really get under way until 1977 even in Anhui and Sichuan, and a number of blatantly inappropriate late Maoist policies were still being pushed, notably double rice cropping (even in areas where the growing season was too short) and Dazhai-style mechanization in the rice-growing areas south of the Yangzi River. More significantly, the purchasing price of farm products was still far too low until the 22 per cent adjustment of 1979; as a result, there was little incentive for output maximization. Moreover, most economists would argue that until decollectivization—and the reassertion of a powerful link between effort and remuneration—collective incentive systems did little to spur efficient production. In other words, the application of fertilizer was wasteful and ineffectual precisely because there little motivation for farm workers to use it in any other way.

In short, increased use of fertilizer was by no means a sufficient condition to bring about a dramatic rise in yields. That much seems evident from the slow national growth rate of farm production in the late 1970s. Yet it is unlikely that the output gains of the early 1980s could have been achieved in its absence; the positive incentive effects that resulted from the 1979 increase in procurement prices and from decollectivization would almost certainly have faltered in the face of diminishing returns without increased application of chemical fertilizer. This hypothesis that fertilizer did indeed play a key role is strengthened by looking at the provincial data (Table 9.7).

These data reveal no precise fit between growth of chemical fertilizer use and growth of grain yields. But that is not surprising in view of the range of other factors that affected provincial output: weather, the yield level reached in the late 1970s, and availability of other complementary inputs. Indeed, many features of these data suggest that chemical fertilizer played a key in the explosive agricultural growth of the early 1980s. First, consider Anhui. It has frequently been suggested that the province's rapid growth after two decades of stagnation was inextricably linked to decollectivization. The data in this table suggest a more prosaic explanation: a rapid increase in chemical fertilizer usage. As fertilizer growth was extremely rapid *prior* to decollectivization—growing at 35 per cent between 1978 and 1980—it is difficult to argue that decollectivization caused the increased use of fertilizer. A second (more general) point is that, of the ten provinces in which fertilizer usage grew most quickly, seven experienced a rate of grain-yield growth above the national median, and the three which did not—Zhejiang, Henan, and Shaanxi—are readily explicable. In Zhejiang, grain yields were already very high in the late 1970s; only Shanghai was achieving a higher yield. In other words, one would not expect to see rapid growth in the 1980s from an already-high base. In the case of Shaanxi, the problem was almost certainly a lack of complementary inputs. Only 32 per cent of arable area was irrigated in 1978 compared to a national average of 45 per cent. Henan, therefore, is the only really anomalous province in the top ten, and its grain yield growth was only a fraction below the national median growth rate (5.0 compared to 5.1 per cent). This suggests a comparatively robust relationship between chemical fertilizer use and grain yields, and it is supported by the experience of those provinces where chemical fertilizer use increased modestly or not at all in the early 1980s. Of the bottom five provinces in terms of fertilizer use growth, only Ningxia enjoyed grain yield growth in excess of the median. However, given that Ningxia had a population of only about 5 million people in 1994, one would not wish to infer too much from its experience.

The bulk of the econometric studies of the sources of Chinese agricultural growth in the early 1980s also support the contention that increased use of chemical fertilizer played a pivotal role. According to Lin (1992), 32 per cent of Chinese crop output growth between 1978 and 1984 across China was attributable to fertilizer. Once the one-off gains from decollectivization had been enjoyed, the role of fertilizer became even more important, accounting for 54 per cent of crop output growth between 1984 and 1987. However, because state-procurement prices fell relative to input prices, fertilizer growth was much slower after 1984. A study by Fan (1991) also assigns a key role to fertilizer. According to this, chemical fertilizers accounted for 31 per cent of the output increase between 1965 and 1985. To be sure,

TABLE 9.7. *Trends in provincial grain yields and use of chemical fertilizer per hectare, 1978–1985* (average annual percentage growth rates)

Province	Chemical fertilizer per hectare	Grain yield per hectare
Anhui	19.3	6.9
Jilin	15.0	9.3
Xinjiang	12.7	7.7
Jiangxi	12.3	5.7
Henan	11.8	5.0
Shaanxi	10.0	4.7
Hebei	9.8	5.6
Zhejiang	9.8	2.4
Jiangsu	9.5	5.2
Hubei	9.0	5.4
Fujian	8.0	2.9
Yunnan	7.1	3.9
Sichuan	7.0	5.3
Guangxi	6.6	2.1
Guizhou	6.5	3.4
Liaoning	6.0	2.3
Guangdong	5.8	5.2
Hunan	5.7	5.7
Shandong	5.4	6.4
Heilongjiang	5.2	0.9
Shanxi	4.4	5.2
Ningxia	1.4	6.9
Gansu	0.7	2.7
Shanghai	0.2	0.8
Tianjin	−1.1	4.7
Beijing	−3.4	4.5
Median	6.8	5.1

Notes: 1978 and 1985 are chosen for the comparison because both were years of comparatively poor weather. The yield growth is based upon data for every year between 1978 and 1985; chemical fertilizer figures are for 1978, 1980, 1982, 1984, and 1985 only. Grain yields and fertilizer application are both per unit of sown area. Fertilizer application figures are in terms of nutrient weight. The provincial figures given in LSTJ (1990) are often inconsistent, usually because fertilizer-use rates are given in actual rather than nutrient weight. Where the series is obviously inconsistent given (a) provincial per capita income, and (b) chemical fertilizer-use rates for 1984 and 1994 (as given in ZGTJNJ, 1995: 331, 337 and ZGTJNJ, 1985: 283), it is assumed here that use has been given in actual rather than nutrient terms. These figures are then converted to nutrient weight using the 1980 national conversion factor of 4.62 (Nongye bu, 1989: 341). The provinces where adjustments have been made in this way are Hubei, Tianjin, Shandong, Henan, Shaanxi, and Guizhou. Data for Qinghai and Nei Menggu are unreliable and therefore these two provinces are excluded from the analysis. Data for Fujian and Guangxi are for 1980–5 only. The Jiangsu figure for 1978 is by calculation from Jiangsu tongjiju (1989: 127, 135) and JSTJNJ (1994: 137).

Sources: Nongye bu (1989: 174–88); LSTJ (1990); ZGTJNJ (1983: 199); ZGTJNJ (1985: 283).

McMillan, *et al.* (1989) and Kim (1990) put chemical fertilizer's contribution at 7 and −1 per cent respectively. But the Kim study is severely limited in its scope: the single township of Dahe between 1981 and 1984. Furthermore, there is some evidence that yields and fertilizer use were already very high in Dahe township in the early 1980s (Putterman, 1993: 95–6); accordingly, increased chemical fertilizer application may have faltered in the face of diminishing returns. The McMillan study is perhaps the least plausible of all because it looks at total agricultural production, rather than just farm output. It is therefore not surprising that there is little evidence that chemical fertilizer was a critically important input.

Nevertheless, it would be wrong to conclude that chemical fertilizer application by itself was other than a partial solution to the agricultural problems of the late 1970s. We have already seen from Table 9.7 that Ningxia and Henan are anomalous. The same table shows that the same is also true of Jiangsu, Shandong, and Hunan: the three all experienced grain-yield growth rates (6.5, 6.4, and 5.7 per cent respectively) significantly above the national median even though fertilizer application grew only slowly in each case. The reason for these and other anomalies is that agricultural technology is a package. Each input taken separately will raise yields, but when applied together the impact is much greater than the sum of the parts. And it was taken together that investment in chemical fertilizer and irrigation played a crucial role in China's agricultural success (Stone, 1988; Bramall, 1995*a*). Although the irrigation network expanded only slowly after 1978, the massive construction programmes of the late Maoist era together with a minimal programme of maintenance spending after decollectivization—as we have seen, the network did not collapse—was enough to guarantee a high level of water control. Substantial investment in chemical fertilizer use in the late 1970s and during the transition period served to exploit the full potential of this infrastructure.

3. Capital Formation in Industry

3.1. Investment in the State Sector

If investment played an important role in promoting agricultural growth, it was even more important in the industrial sector. However, the precise growth rate of the capital stock is a matter of heated debate. As Table 9.8 indicates, there are three basic series for fixed investment by state-owned enterprises.

The various series for the industrial capital stock given in Table 9.8 produce significant differences in growth rates. The Chen–Jefferson series in particular generates capital-stock growth which is much slower (7.3 per cent) than the ZGTJNJ series (9.6 per cent) for 1980–92. This is the main reason why some of the more recent estimates of total factor productivity (TFP) growth show a more definite increase in the 1980s than earlier studies of productivity growth.

Nevertheless, the most important point about the growth of state-sector industrial capital stock after 1978 is that it shows little change in the 1980s compared to 1965–78. As Chen, *et al.* (1988*a*: 266) show, the net capital stock—using the old

TABLE 9.8. *Real fixed capital stock of state-owned industrial enterprises, 1980–1995* (billion *yuan*; net value)

Year	LSTJ (1980 prices)	ZGTJNJ (1980 prices)	Chen–Jefferson (1990 prices)
1980	252.8	236.65	493.5
1981	270.9	251.83	503.45
1982	291.4	271.38	524.43
1983	316.1	296.06	548.50
1984	339.2	310.20	568.44
1985	392.4	339.70	615.39
1986	441.7	383.14	675.13
1987	498.3	425.77	724.6
1988	554.6	474.55	786.95
1989	613.6	523.92	858.15
1990	n/a	565.78	930.00
1991	n/a	626.91	1,016.04
1992	n/a	681.35	1,107.14
1993	n/a	748.25	n/a
1994	n/a	821.55	n/a
1995	n/a	1,068.02	n/a
Growth rates (%):			
1980–8	10.6	9.0	6.1
1980–92	n/a	9.6	7.3
1980–95	n/a	10.1	n/a

Notes: The net capital stock is calculated by assuming that the capital stock at the end of 1979 is in 1980 prices, i.e. that there was negligible inflation before the 1980s; this is the procedure adopted by Jefferson, *et al.* (1992*b*: 260). The net capital stock in the 1980s is then calculated by computing net investment in each year from the change in the capital stock, deflating investment and reaggregating. The first two are both based upon current-price series compiled by the State Statistical Bureau. They include all types of fixed investment, including investment in such items as housing and health care for workers employed by the SOEs. The LSTJ series is the older one. The newer ZGTJNJ series reflects the additional information collected in the 1985 Industrial Census as well as other improvements. Both series have been deflated using the industrial-product price indices given in ZGTJNJ (1996: 271). The third series compiled by Chen, *et al.* (1988*a*) and later modified by Jefferson, *et al.* (1992*b*) uses the original LSTJ data. However, Chen–Jefferson modify that series by trying to exclude investment in 'unproductive' items. In practice, because of the limitations of the data, the authors are only able to remove expenditure on housing for state-sector workers. Nevertheless, this is a large item of SOE spending, and its exclusion has the effect of significantly reducing the capital stock totals. In addition, Chen–Jefferson employ a number of methods to deflate non-residential construction and equipment investment. Their series is, however, more sensitive to the exclusion of housing than it is to the deflation procedure. It is perhaps debatable whether this procedure is much of an improvement. The Chen–Jefferson logic is clear, but there is a value judgement about what constitutes 'unproductive' investment here.)

Sources: ZGTJNJ (1995: 28, 249); ZGTJNJ (1996: 39, 271); ZGTJNJ (1997: 39, 283); LSTJ (1990: 19); Chen, *et al.* (1988*a*); Jefferson, *et al.* (1992*b*: 245); Jefferson, *et al.* (1996: 176).

LSTJ series—grew at about 7.1 per cent between 1965 and 1978 (at 1980 prices), a rate only a little higher than the 6.6 per cent recorded between 1980 and 1988. In other words, the rise in TFP growth in the 1980s is explained—in accounting terms—by a rise in output growth rather than any real decline in capital-stock growth. The net capital stock in the state industrial sector continued to grow at a comparatively steady rate over the entire period between 1965 and the late 1980s. In short, the Maoist investment effort in state industry continued largely unabated into the Dengist era. The acceleration in growth that occurred in the economy as a whole after 1978 does not appear to have been driven by any *increase* in the overall rate of growth of investment in state-owned industrial enterprises.

3.2. Investment in Rural Industry

In the case of rural industry, there are also many problems involved in accurately determining the rate of growth of the capital stock. For one thing, the data that exist are for all rural enterprises, not just industrial enterprises. Secondly, there is no unbroken series for the capital stock of rural enterprises. The data for 1984 and before are confined to enterprises managed at the level of *xiang* and *cun*; see, for example, Nongye bu (1989: 286–9). These figures therefore exclude cooperative, team, and private enterprises. Only after 1984 are all rural enterprises covered by the data. Thirdly, although figures are available for the net capital stock, doubts about the biases in measurement of the gross capital stock, as well as the reliability of depreciation procedures, abound. Finally, there are no proper deflators available.

For all that, even if one allows for more than a little imprecision in the data, there is no question that the capital stock grew exceptionally quickly during the transition era. Some estimates of the growth rates are given in Table 9.9.

Table 9.9. *Growth of the net capital stock in township and village enterprises (TVEs), 1978–1996* (per cent p.a.)

Period	All TVEs (1990 prices)	TVE industry (1980 prices)
1978–84	14.0	15.1
1984–8	25.8*	29.3
1988–91	11.0	14.4
1991–5	22.0	n/a

* 1985–8.

Notes: The capital stock estimates from which these rates are derived are net of depreciation. The industry series is at 1980 prices and estimated by Wu. The all-TVE series is only for *xiang* and *cun* non-farm enterprises before 1985, whereas the later data including all types of non-farm enterprises; in view of this break in the series, no attempt has been made to calculate a growth rate for the entire period. Annual changes in the net capital stock have been deflated by the GDP deflator and then reaggregated.

Sources: Wu and Wu (1994: 172); ZGTJNJ (1993: 397); ZGNMYTJZL (1986); ZGNYTJZL (1987, 1988, 1989, 1991, 1992, 1993, 1994); ZGNYNJ (1990); ZGNYNJ (1996: 366); ZGNYNJ (1997: 369).

The table shows that the non-farm capital stock did not grow consistently quickly across the post-1978 period. Between 1978 and 1984 the low profitability of farming heavily constrained investment, and fiscal/monetary contraction in the late 1989–90 had the same effect. Nevertheless, it is clear that one feature of the Dengist era was the explosive growth of investment in rural industry. This distinguished the 1980s from the Maoist era; for although the latter saw a considerable development of rural industries in provinces such as Jiangsu and Zhejiang where the agricultural sector was comparatively prosperous, this was not the norm in China. In most provinces, the surplus generated within agriculture was simply inadequate to finance more than a handful of rural enterprises. But with the resurgence of agricultural prosperity in the early 1980s, it was increasingly possible to develop industry even in areas which were relatively poor in the Maoist period.

4. Investment in Transport Infrastructure

The pace of construction of transport networks after 1978 appears disappointing, even allowing for the substantial base that had been created by the end of the Maoist period. Thus the size of the road network increased annually by only 1.5 per cent between 1978 and 1994, and that of the railway network by a mere 0.6 per cent (Table 9.10). This rate of increase was especially disappointing given the vastly increased demand for transport after 1978.

TABLE 9.10. *The extent of China's road and railway networks, 1978–1995* (thousand km)

Year	Railways			Roads	
	Total	Double-track	Electrified	Total	Paved
1978	49	8	1	890	651
1979	50			876	
1980	50			883	
1981	50			890	
1982	51			907	
1983	52	9		915	706
1984	52	10		927	725
1985	52	10	4	942	
1986	53			963	
1987	53			982	
1988	53			1,000	
1989	53			1,014	
1990	53	13	7	1,028	883
1991	53			1,041	
1992	54	14	8	1,057	
1993	54	14	9	1,084	960
1994	54	15	9	1,118	998
1995	55	17	10	1,157	1043
1996	56	18	10	1,186	1078
Growth rate (%)	0.6	4.6	13.4	1.7	3.0

Sources: ZGTJNJ (1995: 467, 473); ZGTJNJ (1985: 385, 389); ZGTJNJ (1996: 500, 501, 508); ZGTJNJ (1997: 512, 518).

In consequence, the enormous rise in the movement of passengers and freight in the 1980s and 1990s was only made possible by exploiting more fully the existing capacity of the system. In the case of the movement of goods by rail, the rate of utilization had risen from 2.5m. tonne-km per km of track in 1952 to 9.5m. tonne-km by 1978. Between 1978 and 1988 alone, however, it increased by a further 5.8m. tonne-km (ZGTJNJ, 1992: 508, 513). The resulting utilization rate of 15.3m. tonne-km was far above the 3.2m. figure recorded in India, and substantially higher even than the 8.9m. tonne-km attained in the USA (World Bank, 1990*b*: 218).[6] The growth of passenger traffic was even faster. China's utilization rate was 5.1m. passenger-km by 1988, up from only 1.9 in 1978 and a mere 0.8 in 1952. This implies an annual growth rate of 10 per cent per year between 1978 and 1988, compared to only 3.4 per cent in the Maoist period (ZGTJNJ, 1992: 508, 511). As a result, the intensity of passenger use of the railway system by 1988 was far above the figures of 1.8, 3.2, and 0.1m. passenger-km registered in the Soviet Union, India, and the USA respectively in the early 1980s. With a virtually identical pattern for road use—network size increased by 1.2 per cent per year, whereas freight traffic (in tonne-km) rose by only a fraction under 28 per cent per annum (ZGTJNJ, 1992: 508, 513)—it is clear that the rapid economic growth of the 1980s would have been quite impossible without the Maoist transport legacy. As it was, both road and railway networks were massively overcrowded by the late 1980s, and little changed in the early 1990s.

The deficiencies of the transport network were most apparent in western China (as will be seen in Chapter 8 in the case of Liangshan). Although the Third Front programme had provided a basic transport infrastructure of sorts, many of China's poorest areas lacked access to national markets. Tibet, the only province not connected to the national railway grid, was the most obvious example, but there were many villages in the mountainous Tibetan borderland (Qinghai, western Sichuan, and western Yunnan) that lacked even rudimentary road connections as late as the mid-1990s. These communities are of enormous interest to anthropologists as a result, but the signal underdevelopment of their infrastructure goes far towards explaining their low income levels.

5. Education in the Transition Era

The expansion of education in the years after 1978 could have helped to promote growth because of its high rate of return. The data available for China during the 1980s suggest that primary education yielded a particularly significant private rate of return. Some evidence for Sichuan province is presented in Table 9.11. These figures show a clear correlation between educational status and per capita income in every case. The implied private rate of return to primary education for the province is 23 per cent. The return to lower secondary education is by contrast only 9 per cent, and that to upper secondary education only 7 per cent. These rates of return are somewhat lower than in other countries; World Bank data suggest an average

TABLE 9.11. *Income differentials by level of education in Sichuan, 1983* (average per capita income in *yuan*)

Educational level	Pengshui	Jianyang	All Sichuan
Illiterate	623	225	198
Primary	805	245	243
Lower secondary	877	292	264
Upper secondary	1,970	355	282

Note: Data on Pengshui are for gross income; others are net. The all-Sichuan data are drawn from a survey of 2,760 households across 43 counties.

Source: Nongcun yanjiuzu (1986: 671, 720, 721).

rate of return to primary education for Asia of 32 per cent, and one of 29 per cent for all developing countries (World Bank, 1988: 355). Nevertheless, the order of magnitude is clearly plausible. Other Chinese data also suggest a rate of return to primary education that is both positive and significant. In rural Gansu, the rate of return in terms of non-farm income was found to be about 12 per cent for an extra year of schooling. For farm income, however, a lack of good quality arable land severely restricted the potential return to education (World Bank, 1988: 357).

In addition, the evidence on infant mortality testifies to the importance of education. Data, for example, on Shanxi province suggests that the infant mortality rate for children born to mothers who had completed primary education was 45 per thousand, compared to 73 per thousand for mothers without any education (World Bank, 1992: 84). Some more general all-China evidence is presented in Table 9.12.

TABLE 9.12. *The relationship between education and infant mortality*

Mother's education	Infant mortality rate (per 1000)
Illiterate	74
Semi-literate	68
Primary school	51
Lower secondary school	34
Upper secondary school	26
Higher education	15

Note: The infant mortality rate data are for males and females combined. Data were collected in a 1988 survey.

Source: Gu, *et al.* (1991: 29).

Again, the relationship is clear. Children born to mothers without any education were almost five times more likely to die in infancy than those born to mothers with higher education.

5.1. Chinese Education after 1978

On the face of things, faster economic growth in the transition era appears to have been correlated with improvements in education after 1978. Consider trends in the literacy rate between the 1982 and 1990 Population Censuses, and between the 1982 Census and the 1987 Population Survey (Table 9.13). These data show that the percentage of the population aged 15 or over and classified as illiterate or semi-literate declined to 15.9 per cent by 1990 compared to the 22.8 per cent illiteracy rate

Table 9.13. *Provincial illiteracy rates, 1982–1990*
(literates and semi-literates as percentage of total population)

Province	Men and women, aged 14+		Women, aged 11+	
	1982	1990	1982	1987
Beijing	12	9	22	20
Tianjin	14	9	26	23
Hebei	22	15	42	35
Shanxi	18	11	33	28
Nei Menggu	22	15	41	31
Liaoning	13	9	23	19
Jilin	16	11	29	23
Heilongjiang	16	11	30	25
Shanghai	14	11	26	23
Jiangsu	27	17	50	41
Zhejiang	24	18	44	35
Anhui	32	24	64	54
Fujian	25	16	57	49
Jiangxi	21	16	48	46
Shandong	28	17	52	42
Henan	26	16	51	43
Hubei	23	16	45	36
Hunan	18	12	35	30
Guangdong	16	11	37	32
Guangxi	17	11	39	35
Hainan	19	14	n/a	n/a
Sichuan	23	16	45	36
Guizhou	30	24	67	57
Yunnan	32	25	64	57
Tibet	46	44	84	n/a
Shaanxi	24	18	45	39
Gansu	32	28	65	59
Qinghai	29	28	63	67
Ningxia	27	22	58	47
Xinjiang	20	13	36	25
China	23	16	45	38

Sources: National Population Census Office (1991: 30); ZGRKNJ (1985: 617); Li (1990: 12).

registered in 1982 (National Population Census Office, 1991: 30). Furthermore, the illiteracy rate declined in every Chinese provincial-level administrative unit, including Tibet (though there the decline was very modest; illiteracy stood at 96 per cent of its 1982 level in 1990 compared to 70 per cent nationally). The data on changes in female literacy rates between 1982 and 1987 also show a good deal of progress. The extent of illiteracy declined in every province except Qinghai, and in some cases (Inner Mongolia, Guizhou, Anhui, and Ningxia) the decrease was spectacular. Policy measures do seem to have contributed to these improvements. For example, a number of initiatives were launched during the 1980s to improve the quality of education. The late 1970s saw the termination of the extremely unpopular programme of sending urban youth to the countryside and, by the early 1980s, most of these unwilling migrants had returned (Banister, 1987: 340–8). Unified and competitive university entrance examinations were restored in 1977 (Pepper, 1990: 140). Furthermore, in 1985 the Central Committee decreed that 9 years of compulsory education were necessary in rural areas and the decision became law at the Sixth National People's Congress on 12 April 1986 (Central Committee, 1991: 907). Note also that rising real incomes enabled parents to educate their children and themselves by purchasing books, radios, and televisions; it was not just formal education which expanded.

Yet these positive developments disguise a number of trends which point towards educational failure after 1978. In both Zhejiang and Jiangsu, two of the fastest-growing provinces during the 1980s, the illiteracy rate was above the national average in 1982. In 1990, that remained the position—despite their rapid growth. In other words, the 'fruits of growth' were not used in any systematic way to fund improvements in educational quality. In the short term that may not have mattered much because both were well above the literacy threshold needed to allow modern economic growth. But it hardly boded well for the long term. In order to follow the path taken by East Asian economies such as Japan, Taiwan, and South Korea, Jiangsu and Zhejiang will have to create a highly skilled and educated workforce. That can hardly be accomplished overnight, and the ground lost during the 1980s will be hard to regain. Not the least of the problem is that Zhejiang appears to have made much less progress than other Chinese provinces. In 1982, illiteracy in Zhejiang was about 5 per cent above the national average. By 1990, however, this had increased to 10 per cent (National Population Census Office, 1991: 30). In other words, Zhejiang's relatively rapid growth was achieved despite a decline in her relative literacy rate.

Zhejiang's poor record is symptomatic of a more general problem that afflicted Chinese education throughout the post-1978 period: low primary education completion rates. The problem at the beginning of the transition era was a decline in the enrolment rate. The return to an 'urban-biased quality-oriented system' led to a fall in the number of children enrolled in primary schools from 151 million in 1975 to 136 million by 1984 and 125 million by 1988 (Pepper, 1990: 78, 80). The proportion of the age group enrolling (the enrolment rate) also declined from a peak of almost 97 per cent in 1975, to 93 per cent by 1980. In the poorer provinces, the decline was even more abrupt. In Gansu, for example, the enrolment rate rose from 58 per cent in 1957 to reach 97 per cent in 1976. By 1979, however, it was down to only 87 per cent (ZGSWY, 1988, i. 417). To be fair, this problem had largely been overcome in Han areas by the end of the decade. By 1988, the rate was back up to 97 per cent (ZGTJNJ, 1992: 717) and according to the most recent Population Census, the rate was 97.8 per cent in 1990 (ZGRKTJNJ, 1993: 273). Even in Gansu, the rate was back up to 89 per cent by 1985.

Yet there was still serious cause for concern. In ethnic minority areas, for example, enrolment rates remained exceptionally low at the beginning of the 1990s. In Tibet, the 1990 enrolment rate averaged only about 55 per cent of the population aged between 7 and 11. This in itself disguises considerable spatial variation. In Lhasa itself, the enrolment rate was 62 per cent and in the eastern prefecture of Qamdo and Shannan, the rate was 68 per cent. But in the western prefectures of Nagqu and Ngari, the figures were only 27 and 19 per cent respectively. Furthermore, drop-out rates in ethnic minority areas seem to have risen. Amongst Gansu Tibetans attending school, for example, those born between 1966 and 1970 had received on average 3.4 years of education by the time of the 1990 Census. But for those born between 1971 and 1976, the figure had dropped to 3.2 years; and for those born between 1976 and 1980—who thus received their education after 1978—it had dropped to 2.9 years. There was also a considerable gender mismatch. Amongst females aged 10 to 14 in 1990, the average number of years of education completed was 2.2; amongst males, the figure was far higher at 3.6 years (Xizang zizhiqu renkou pucha bangongshi, 1992: 227, 527, 528).

Furthermore, although the enrolment problem in Han areas had been largely solved by the late 1980s, it had been replaced by a new problem: that of high drop-out rates (Pepper, 1990: 90–1; Rosen, 1990: 300–1). This phenomenon had everything to do with the transition policies themselves. Decollectivization of farming, and the sharp increase in the internal terms of trade, raised the rate of return per labour day in the agricultural sector. In consequence, the opportunity cost incurred by a family in sending its children to school was raised substantially and many responded by putting them to work in the fields instead. In this respect, the 'responsibility system' attracted almost universal criticism in the countryside (Pepper, 1990: 83). Evidence on this again comes from the 1982 Census in the guise of declining primary school completion rates (Table 9.14). In every case, the completion rate dropped during the late 1970s. Although it generally recovered in the early 1980s, only in Inner Mongolia was the 1982 rate higher than the peak completion rate in the mid- to late-1970s.

The problem if anything intensified in the mid-1980s with the removal of controls on the rural private non-farm sector. The relative profitability of transport, commerce, and industry was significantly higher than that of farming and this raised even further the opportunity costs of education. The scale of the problem is illustrated in Table 9.15.

In the poorest areas of China such as Gansu, Guizhou, and Yunnan, these results are not especially surprising. Part of the problem in the more remote areas was the

TABLE 9.14. *Primary school completion rates, 1978–1982*
(percentage of enrolled children completing primary education)

Year	Jilin	Yunnan	Anhui	Guangxi	Nei Menggu
1976	73	n/a	58	68	65
1977	76	n/a	58	66	n/a
1978	83	52	49	59	67
1979	70	n/a	43	55	n/a
1980	70	n/a	49	49	61
1981	70	n/a	52	56	62
1982	71	44	57	58	70

Sources: Cao (1988: 392); Zou and Miao (1989: 498–9); Gao and Zheng (1987: 367); Huang (1988: 379); Song (1987: 418).

TABLE 9.15. *School drop-out rates in 1990*
(percentage of population aged 6–14 not in school in 1990)

Province	Both sexes	Females
Jiangsu	9.8	12.0
Beijing	11.1	10.9
Shanghai	11.2	11.2
Hebei	11.7	12.6
Shanxi	11.9	12.9
Henan	13.1	15.7
Liaoning	13.3	13.7
Hubei	14.0	16.9
Tianjin	14.2	14.4
Shandong	14.8	17.6
Hunan	15.5	18.1
Shaanxi	15.9	14.6
Heilongjiang	16.3	17.4
Guangdong	17.9	20.6
Jilin	18.8	16.7
Sichuan	20.5	23.7
Nei Menggu	20.7	22.5
Hainan	21.8	25.8
Anhui	23.1	29.2
Fujian	23.7	29.5
Guangxi	23.6	27.3
Zhejiang	23.8	25.5
Xinjiang	24.0	24.2
Jiangxi	26.1	32.9
Ningxia	27.2	32.9
Gansu	28.9	35.6
Guizhou	34.0	43.5
Yunnan	35.4	41.8
Qinghai	39.3	45.1
China	19.1	22.3

Source: ZGRKTJNJ (1993: 274).

sheer distance involved in travelling to and from school; this did much to discourage attendance. In addition, educational provision requires expenditure by local government or by private agents, and neither are very likely in areas where the level of economic development is limited. Low personal incomes restrict the tax base and force local governments to charge school fees to raise additional revenue to provide education. But low personal incomes militate against a shift in consumption from necessities like food and clothing to luxuries like schooling, still less the payment of school fees. Thus children in poor provinces typically enrolled and received a few years of education before being removed from school to work on the family farm. Perhaps even more worryingly, there were few signs of improvement in the late 1980s. For example, the drop-out rate for 1990 in Ningxia for the 6–14-year cohort was identical to that recorded in a 1987 survey (Zhonghua quanguo funu lianhehui funu yanjiusuo, 1991: 206). In Yunnan, the non-attendance rate increased dramatically from 26 per cent to 35 per cent during this short period.

But perhaps the most revealing aspect of these data is again the mismatch implied between the rate of economic growth and participation in primary education in some of China's most advanced provinces. Guangdong's per capita growth rate after 1978 (11.5 per cent) was well above the national norm, and yet the drop-out rate was very close to the Chinese average. The contrast is (again) even more dramatic for Zhejiang. Although per capita income in this province grew faster than in any other in China, the Zhejiang drop-out rate stood at 23.8 per cent, substantially above the national average of 19 per cent. The contrast in ranking is even clearer. Ranked first in terms of per capita growth, Zhejiang ranked twenty-second in terms of its educational completion rate. Worst of all, the Zhejiang drop-out rate seems to have increased in the late 1980s. The 1987 survey, for example, discovered that the drop-out rate in that year was 17 per cent, well below the 24 per cent recorded three years later (Zhonghua quanguo funu lianhehui funu yanjiusuo, 1991: 206). By contrast, the rate seems to have fallen in seven of the nine provinces covered in 1987 (the other exception, Yunnan, has already been mentioned). One need look no further for an explanation of Zhejiang's relatively poor performance in reducing her illiteracy rate between 1982 and 1990. Much the same was true for Fujian, ranked fifth in terms of growth but only twentieth in terms of completion rates. The only exception to this rather dismal pattern was Jiangsu, ranked third in terms of growth and first in terms of educational completion rate. The reasons for this are not entirely clear, but it may reflect the preponderance of *xiangzhen qiye* as opposed to private enterprises in the rural sector. If one assumes that the *xiangzhen* enterprises were far more reluctant to employ child labour than private firms, the sharp contrast between Jiangsu and Zhejiang (where private industry is far more widespread) is explained. In Zhejiang's Wenzhou municipality, where the development of the private sector was extraordinarily fast in the 1980s, some 20 per cent of the workforce employed even in large firms were children by the middle of the decade (Chen, 1990: 141).

On the face of it, there is a contradiction between these data on drop-out rates, and the continuing fall in the illiteracy rate between 1982 and 1990. However, there is little comfort to be drawn from the decline in illiteracy, which largely reflects an age-composition effect. The data on the age structure of illiteracy collected nationwide in 1982 show that 60.8 million of the total illiterate population of 237.7 million were aged 60 or over (ZGRKNJ, 1985: 618). In age-specific terms, this amounted to an illiteracy rate for the population aged 60 and over of 79 per cent (and a staggering 95 per cent for women). By contrast, the illiteracy rate for those aged between 12 and 19 was less than 10 per cent—and this despite the disruption caused by the Cultural Revolution. The same pattern is evident in the data from the 1990 Population Census (Table 9.16).

TABLE 9.16. *Age specific illiteracy rates in 1990* (per cent)

Age range	Cities	Towns	Counties
15–19	1.3	1.1	6.6
20–4	1.6	1.7	7.8
25–9	1.8	2.2	9.3
55–9	33.6	32.3	61.1
60–4	43.3	42.9	68.6
65 and over	60.8	63.1	79.4

Source: Zhongguo 1990 nian renkou pucha ziliao (1993, ii. 282–93).

Precisely because mortality after 1982 was heavily concentrated amongst those aged over 60 (for obvious reasons), this meant that more illiterates tended to die every year than did literate persons. Consider Sichuan. The 1987 One Per Cent Survey found that 3,343 persons had died during 1986 in the 158,242 households (646,922 people) covered by the 1987 survey (Sichuan sheng renkou pucha bangongshi, 1988: 2–6, 684–5). Of the 3,343 who died, no less than 2,200 were illiterates, and 1,687 of these were aged 60 or over. This type of interaction between the age-structure of literacy and age-specific mortality rates therefore reduced the rate of illiteracy—even though drop-out rates were high and rising amongst children aged between 6 and 14. Furthermore, and paradoxically, those areas that were most successful in reducing mortality rates amongst the elderly were penalized in the sense that their rates of illiteracy remained high as a result.

Finally, the quality of Chinese secondary education also deteriorated in several respects. An attempt was made in the transition era to turn back the clock and restore the elitist system—keypoint schools and all—of the early 1960s, under which there was no pretence at providing a universal secondary education and only a handful of predominantly urban youth were provided with the quality of teaching to equip them to compete for scarce tertiary places. Despite widespread popular criticism, directed especially against keypoint schools (Pepper, 1990: 113), the new system was pushed through and caused a sharp decline in the number of secondary schools, and in secondary school numbers. Thus the number of secondary schools fell from 204,000 in 1977 to 105,000 by 1983, and the number of students enrolled dwindled from 68 million in 1977 to 46 million by 1983 before recovering to 52 million by 1988 (ZGTJNJ, 1992: 702; Pepper, 1990: 97).

6. Conclusion

It was argued in Chapter 6 that a substantial proportion of the physical capital stock which formed the basis of post-1978 economic growth was created in the Maoist period. In irrigation, despite the failures of the Great Leap Forward, a substantial and extremely effective network had been established. Of all the legacies of the commune, this was the most enduring. It provided the basis for the agricultural revolution of the early 1980s, which in term provided the basis for the development of rural industry. In the sphere of transport, the isolation of western China was brought to an end. In industry, the heavy industrial sectors provided a firm foundation for the more broadly based growth of the 1980s.

Even so, and precisely because post-1978 growth was driven in large measure by China's industrial sector, the Maoist legacy in terms of the capital stock was not the only factor at work. In fact, a key feature of the transition was a marked increase in investment, and this in turn had much to do with the phenomenal growth of the industrial capital stock. On the one hand, the high level of investment undertaken by state-owned industrial enterprises in the late Maoist period continued; given that this sector was by far the largest component of Chinese industry, it was critical in ensuring a high overall rate of investment. But secondly, and marking out the era of transition from that of late Maoism, there was an explosive growth of investment in rural industry. Whereas this had been largely confined to a few prosperous areas before 1978 (notably Sunan), it was increasingly general in rural China thereafter. Even in poor provinces like Guizhou and Yunnan, substantial increases in rural industrial investment were recorded.

Nevertheless, one would be hard put to conclude from this chapter that it was greater factor accumulation that was *primarily* responsible for the acceleration in the rate of output growth in China after 1978. For one thing, the rate of accumulation in the late 1970s was already high by the standards of other developing countries. For another, a number of key sectors were neglected: irrigation, transport, and energy. Moreover, some of the attempts to raise the investment rate yet higher in the late 1980s and 1990s triggered inflation. Perhaps even more importantly, the record on human capital accumulation after 1978 was unimpressive. It is, for example, difficult to argue that improved educational provision during the 1980s contributed to accelerating economic growth—precisely because Chinese education went backwards over the course of the decade. Rates of illiteracy did fall between 1982 and 1990 but this was because high (natural) mortality rates amongst elderly illiterates offset the adverse effects of falling enrolment rates in the early 1980s, and rising drop-out rates in the second half of the decade. Furthermore, the literacy rate increased least in Zhejiang, the very province where the pace of economic growth was fastest. As a result of all this, Chinese educational provision was on a par with that offered by Japan at around the time of World War I. According to Minami (1994: 50):

China's 97 per cent primary school enrolment rate is at the level Japan's was from 1905 to 1910 and its 39 per cent secondary school enrolment rate is where Japan's was between 1915 and 1920 . . . These figures suggest that primary and secondary education in China lags 60 to 80 years behind Japan.

In short, although the extent to which growth during the transition era was dependent upon the Maoist educational legacy is debatable, there is much to suggest that conclusion. The Maoist development strategy does appear to have raised the abysmally low Republican literacy rates up to a point where modern economic growth was possible. The system of education inherited from Mao may not have been ideal but it seems to have been effective enough to allow rapid economic growth despite the best efforts of the Dengist regime to promote its dissolution. More generally, factor accumulation was important after 1978, but it is hard to argue that it was a surge in accumulation which accelerated the growth rate.

10

The Growth of Productivity

Central to the master discourse is the proposition that East Asian economic growth was driven by the combination of a low initial level of per capita output and a high rate of factor accumulation. In other words, the East Asian economies moved from a low-level equilibrium capital–output ratio towards a higher equilibrium capital–labour ratio by raising their rates of saving and investment. By contrast, slow growth in sub-Saharan Africa and South Asia reflected the low rates of investment that were the norms in these countries.

It is an easy step to argue that transition-era China can be fitted comfortably into the (pre-1997) East Asian pattern. In so far as productivity did rise after 1978, the gains were simply one-off according to writers like Sachs and Woo. They reflected the redeployment of surplus labour from agriculture to industry and, secondly, the replacement of institutions (like collective farms) which retarded growth by institutions which were growth-promoting. This chapter assesses the truth of these claims. Were there no other types of productivity growth in the transition era?

1. Productivity Growth in the Industrial Sector

1.1. Industrial Productivity in the Maoist Era

The rate of technical progress in the industrial sector even during the Maoist era was much faster than is often alleged.[1] The area of most conspicuous success was defence. China exploded her first atomic bomb, a 20 kiloton device, on 16 October 1964. That represented the culmination of almost a decade of intensive effort during which an extraordinary range of technical hurdles were overcome. Some of this was accomplished with Soviet assistance, but much of it was not. For instance, the uranium ore which provided the material for the bomb was collected originally by farmers during the early years of the Great Leap Forward.[2] Another example was the use of nickel-plated copper pipe instead of the (unobtainable) Monel alloy used in the West and the USSR to produce uranium hexafluoride (Lewis and Xue, 1988: 88, 101). China was also ultimately successful in building submarine-launched ballistic missiles (Lewis and Xue, 1994) and, more generally, in developing satellite delivery systems.

Yet technical progress was not confined to the defence sector.[3] One of the more remarkable features of the Maoist era was the pace of technological diffusion. A case in point is the steel industry, where a whole series of new plants using best practice technology were constructed after the Revolution.[4] In Sichuan, only four small steel plants existed in 1949, two in Chongqing (founded in 1937 and 1941), one at Wanfu (1941), and the fourth at Weiyuan (also founded in 1941). After 1949, however, the industry grew swiftly. Of the 75 plants in operation by 1981, 14 began production in the 1950s, 11 in the 1960s and no less than 44 in the 1970s (ZSSWY, 1984: 387–93). In Henan province, steel production was virtually non-existent in 1949. By 1983, however, 12 major steel plants had been established. Of these, 2 began production in the 1950s, 3 in the 1960s, and 5 in the 1970s (Henan sheng renmin zhengfu diaocha yanjiu shi, 1987: 214–16). Much the same story is true of Anhui and Yunnan. In both a steel industry barely existed in the 1940s; by the late 1970s it was well established (Anhui sheng renmin zhengfu banggongting, 1987, iii. 31–47; ZYSWZY, 1986: 540–1).

Steel was by no means exceptional: across the range of industrial products, a vast number of new plants were constructed after 1949. The national picture by the early 1980s is recorded in the results of the 1985 industry census (Table 10.1).

TABLE 10.1. *China's large and medium-sized industrial enterprises in 1985 classified by year of beginning operation*

Years of beginning operation	No. of enterprises		Net output value (current prices)	
	Total	Per cent	Value (bn. *yuan*)	Per cent
Pre-1949	1,624	21	49.268	33
1950–2	664	8	12.607	8
1953–7	1,026	13	16.442	11
1958–62	1,513	19	29.996	20
1963–5	389	5	10.562	7
1966–70	1,216	15	14.293	9
1971–5	696	9	7.853	5
1976–80	380	5	6.659	4
1981–5	370	5	3.268	2
TOTAL	7,878	100	150.949	100

Source: Guowuyuan quanguo gongye pucha lingdao xiaozu bangongshi (1987, i. 536–7).

Of the 7,878 large and medium-sized industrial enterprises in existence in 1985, only 1,624 had been founded before 1949. Of the others, no less than 1,912 had been founded during the allegedly chaotic period of the Cultural Revolution (1966–76), and these accounted for about 15 per cent of net industrial output value in 1985. Perhaps even more remarkably in the light of the criticism habitually directed against the Great Leap Forward, large and medium enterprises set up at that time accounted for some 20 per cent of production in 1985.

But Maoist technical progress was about more than just the diffusion of technologies that were known about in China in 1949. The period also saw genuine innovation—that is, the introduction of new goods and new methods of production never previously seen in China's provinces. In Sichuan, for example, goods such as sewing machines, watches, televisions, chemical fertilizer, plate glass, railway locomotives, and even civilian airliners were all being produced by the end of the 1970s (ZSSWY, 1984: 263–8). Some of this new technology was pioneered within China. Every Chinese knows the story of how the bridge over the Yangzi River at Nanjing was built even though Soviet experts had declared it impossible, and Chinese biogas generators were regarded as so innovative that many of them were exported. However, the technology was for the most part from the Soviet Union in the 1950s, or came to China via Hong Kong during the 1960s.

The key development towards the end of the Maoist era was the gradual improvement of relations with the USA and the OECD economies in the early 1970s: this enabled the People's Republic to import openly the latest technologies. Improved relations were especially important for Chinese agriculture because they allowed China to import 13 pairs of synthetic ammonia plants from the USA, Britain, and Japan in January 1973 (Bramall, 1995*a*), and to employ new technologies such as drip-feed irrigation (Qin, 1995). It is in fact the early 1970s rather than the 1980s which mark a decisive change in China's reliance on technology imports, and which culminated in Hua Guofeng's 'foreign leap forward' in 1977–8 during which some 120 new, import-reliant, projects were scheduled. All this is very clear from the data on the value of imports. In 1973, the value of imports—which hovered at around US\$20m. per year between 1958 and 1972—soared to US\$52m. and rose further to \$76m. in 1974. As a result of Hua's Ten-Year Plan, import value soared again between 1977 and 1980, rising from US\$72m. to US\$200m. (State Statistical Bureau, 1994: 19).

However, despite all this undeniable technical progress, the evidence suggests little sign of rising industrial productivity in the late Maoist era. The clearest sign of this comes from estimates of the growth rate of total factor productivity in state-owned enterprises (Table 10.2).

TABLE 10.2. *Growth of total factor productivity in independent-accounting state-owned industrial enterprises, 1952–1980* (per cent per annum; at 1952 prices)

Period	Cobb–Douglas production function	Translog production function
1953–7	5.6	5.0
1965–78	0.9	0.9
1972–80	neg.	1.6

Notes: These are my estimates from the Chen, *et al.* data. The growth rates differ slightly from those estimated by Chen, *et al.* By excluding housing from the official Chinese data, the Chen, *et al.* approach produces a much better measure of the value of equipment and machinery used by the industrial sector. A second critical adjustment was to properly deflate the capital stock series, which merely uses current prices to value annual additions to the capital stock. In order to calculate total factor productivity, output elasticities are estimated using a Cobb–Douglas or translog production function; these are then used to calculate an aggregate input series for labour, capital, and (in the most recent studies) intermediate material inputs. This procedure is undoubtedly superior to those which proxy output elasticities by income shares (e.g. McGuckin, *et al.* (1992)) because this latter *de facto* assumes perfect competition (where marginal productivity can be proxied by factor returns).

Source: Chen, *et al.* (1988*b*: 583).

These data on industrial total factor productivity growth show that the record of Maoist industrial enterprises was poor. This was not so in the 1950s, when the rate of growth of TFP was a more than a respectable 5 per cent. But after the Great Leap Forward, the rate of growth was extremely slow. Moreover, there is not much evidence of any improvement towards the end of the period when one might have expected some of the gains from learning to begin to come through in the productivity data; the translog function does show an increase, but it is hardly very significant. Jefferson (1990: 346) has produced similarly pessimistic results for the late Maoist iron and steel industry. His estimates for TFP growth show a clear fall from the remarkable 9.7 per cent annual rate achieved between 1952 and 1957 to −1.6 per cent between 1957 and 1980. As with the Chen, *et al.* study, Jefferson excludes non-productive capital and labour from the input series used.

To be sure, these estimates are exceptionally problematic. As noted earlier, estimates of TFP growth are very sensitive to their underlying assumptions. In the case of the Chen, *et al.* study, one obvious weakness is that it makes no attempt to allow for improvements in the quality of the labour force. In other words, the role of human capital—so important in augmented neoclassical growth theory (Mankiw, *et al.*, 1992)—is ignored. Moreover, the Chinese data have their own weaknesses. Although Chen, *et al.* (1988*a*) have adjusted official estimates of the capital stock, this cannot disguise the poor quality of the underlying data; the collection of reliable statistics was not one of the aims of the Cultural Revolution. There is an even more critical problem. It is often alleged that much of the capital used by Chinese state-owned industry was effectively useless because of its very low quality. If that is true, then it surely follows that the official Chinese prices used to value the capital stock are far higher than is justified by the marginal productivity of that capital. That in turn would imply much higher pre-1978 industrial productivity than is shown by the Chen, *et al.* revised series. This is part of the general problem that affects any analysis of trends in an economy where prices bear little relation to marginal costs. Precisely because the relative price structure of output (including capital goods) is not related to relative marginal costs, the calculation of an aggregate like capital in an unbiased way is problematic. The weighting given to each industrial subsector in calculating the capital stock is the price of each type of output. Unless these prices reflect marginal costs (or all sectors grow at the same pace), the value of aggregate capital will be biased. There is also the problem posed by the rapid development of the defence sector, especially during the post-1965 'Third Front' construction period. Two questions arise. First, are the outputs of the military sector included in the official output series? The answer is almost certainly 'no', and in that sense pre-1978 capital productivity is underestimated. Secondly, there is the problem of valuation. The social benefits of military output undoubtedly exceeded their private benefits but the problems involved in valuing nuclear and conventional weapons are insuperable. Given, however, the size of the Chinese defence sector, these issues are of great significance.

These are serious problems and are not easily ignored. But it is hard to believe that one should reverse the basic Chen, *et al.* conclusion for three reasons. First, there is a virtual consensus in the literature—Chinese and Western alike—that the rate of productivity growth under the Maoist regime was unimpressive. The following is representative of the conventional wisdom amongst Chinese economists:

> China's present technical level is still fairly low and some people still lack a full understanding of the role of science and technology. . . . the blind pursuit of the high growth rate of the economy, and, therefore, the blind expansion of capital construction resulted in neglecting the upgrading of equipment and technology of existing enterprises. Moreover, shortcomings in planning led to a failure to recognize in good time the important role of equipment retooling and technology upgrading. (Ma, 1990: 235–6)

This assessment is all the more interesting because it follows (Ma, 1990: 234) a list of China's technological achievements up to the mid-1980s.

Secondly, one would not expect to see rapid productivity growth in the short run in an economy introducing new technology at a breakneck pace. It is one thing to produce civilian airliners, as Sichuan province did by the late 1970s. It is another matter entirely to translate that technological advance into high productivity levels given a basic unfamiliarity with the techniques and the product. Moreover, the very pace of technical progress compounded the problem. There was no chance to learn a new technique before an even newer technology or product was introduced. This is arguably the reason why post-war Singapore has registered such low TFP growth. Paradoxically, it is a sign of extremely fast rather than slow innovation.

Thirdly, there is a vast array of examples that demonstrate Maoist failures in introducing new technology. Take the case of biogas digesters (Smil, 1988: 54–63). These were seen in the late 1970s by many in the West as a great achievement and a direct result of the Maoist emphasis on the promotion of small-scale rural industry. They provided energy in a relatively environmentally friendly way for rural areas, as well as good quality fertilizer. In reality, however, many of the digesters were badly manufactured, and cracked in the second year of operation. Much the same story is true of the famous 'five small industries'.[5] Many of the chemical fertilizer plants were exceptionally inefficient and were subsidized by central government (Wong, 1991*a*). Small scale electricity plants were not only too small but also created widespread pollution (Wirtshafter and Shih 1990). More generally, '"easy money" [CMB: provided by the central government for rural industrialization] fed excessive growth in the program so that, by the mid-1970s, rural industries had expanded beyond optimal scales and local supply capabilities, creating enormous technical, supply, and financial problems . . .' (Wong, 1991*c*: 185). Chinese integrated circuit technology was allegedly almost on a par with the West by the mid-1960s, but thereafter progress ceased (Zita, 1991: 490). Moreover, the legacy of the Maoist period even within China is widely seen as one of obsolete and worn-out technology in many industries:

> According to a 1980 survey, about one-fourth of the fixed assets of the country's industrial and transport enterprises are overused and about 36 per cent of the equipment in light industry needs to be improved. In the metallurgical industry, two-thirds of the equipment dates from the 1930s–1950s. In the machine-building industry, with two-thirds of its machine tools

used less than 10 years, most of them were manufactured during the ten chaotic years, many being poor in performance and quality. (Ma, 1990: 235)

For all these reasons, it is difficult to disagree with the conclusion that the Maoist record on industrial productivity growth was poor.[6] According to Baark (1991: 533): 'The system failed to provide a significantly higher technological level in the majority of industrial enterprises. Apparently less than 10 per cent of the results of research and development activities were put into production in the 1970s, and the designs of the vast majority of equipment dated from the 1950s.' Moreover, it is also perhaps fair to say that rapid productivity growth was never really the aim of the Maoist regime. To be sure, the CCP was more than willing to harness the potential of new technology. But the quality of the final product was the main consideration, not the efficiency of input use. The Third Front is perhaps the classic example; the economics of locating factories in caves is more than problematic but the strategic logic is clear. In emulating both the relocation of Soviet industry to the Urals in 1941–2 and the relocation of Chinese industry in 1937–8 after the Japanese invasion, the CCP leadership was following an obvious strategy in preparing for a conventional war. That productivity was sacrificed in the process was entirely unsurprising.

1.2. Industrial Productivity Growth after 1978

The trajectory of total factor productivity in Chinese industry after 1978 is also uncertain. Many economists are relatively optimistic, at least in the sense of arguing that productivity growth was much faster after 1978 than before. Some of the estimates that have been made are summarized in Table 10.3.[7]

These studies share three common features.[8] First, TFP growth was substantially faster in state-owned industrial enterprises after 1978 than it had been in the late Maoist period. This is the key conclusion, and it has been supported in a wide range of studies, many of them fairly recent (Groves, *et al.*, 1994, 1997; Lo, 1997). Secondly, TFP growth in collective enterprises was faster than in state enterprises. Whether this means very much in terms of the impact of ownership on performance is a moot point. The capital-stock data are exceptionally unreliable but, even more importantly, the Third Industrial Census of 1995 found extensive evidence of over-reporting of physical output and the use of flawed price deflators; as Jefferson, *et al.* (1996: 155, 170) rightly record—having downgraded their estimates of TVCE TFP in any case—these figures are not robust. Furthermore, any attempt to conclude that differences in ownership explain the TFP gap between the two sectors is rendered treacherous by the need to normalize for differences in product (for example, the state sector includes a large number of extractive industries where one would not expect to see rapid TFP growth), location, and the much lower base-level of collective TFP. Moreover, as is well known, most of the collective enterprises were owned by local government in any case. In effect, the comparison is between centrally and locally owned state enterprises—rather than between collective and state ownership. The third general conclusion from the data is that the

TABLE 10.3. *Estimates of total factor productivity growth in state and collective industrial enterprises, 1980–1992* (per cent per annum)

State enterprises:	
Chen, *et al.* (1988)	1978–85—5.2
Jefferson (1990)	1980–5—2.5
McGuckin, *et al.* (1992)	1980–4—-1.1; 1984–5—1.2
Jefferson, *et al.* (1992)	1980–4—1.8; 1984–8—3.0; 1980–8—2.4
Jefferson and Rawski (1994)	1980–4—1.8; 1984–8—3.0; 1988–92—2.5
Wu and Wu (1994)	1978–83—1.9; 1984–8—2.8; 1989–91—2.2; 1978–91—1.8
Jefferson, *et al.* (1996)	1980–4—2.2; 1984–8—3.7; 1988–92—1.6; 1980–92—2.5
Otsuka, *et al.* (1998)	1978–84—2.2; 1984–8—6.8; 1988–93—2.2
Collective enterprises	
Jefferson, *et al.* (1992) (all)	1980–4—3.5; 1984–8—5.9; 1980–8—4.6
Jefferson and Rawski (1994)	1980–4—3.4[a], 7.3[b]; 1984–8—5.9[a], 6.6[b]; 1988–92—4.9[a], 6.9[b]
Wu and Wu (1994)[b]	1978–83—4.4; 1984–8—6.5; 1989–91—13.8; 1978–91—5.5
Jefferson, *et al.* (1996)	1980–4—2.8; 1984–8—4.5; 1988–92—3.0; 1980–92—3.4

Notes: The Chen, *et al.* study estimates TFP growth between endpoints only and uses NVIO as the measure of output. The results reported here are for a Cobb–Douglas production function, although they provide results for a translog production function as well (for which the fit is less good). The Jefferson study is for the iron and steel industry only and again uses NVIO as the output measure. The studies by Jefferson, *et al.*, and by Jefferson and Rawski, use GVIO as the output measure, and therefore measure intermediate material inputs as well as labour and capital inputs. The estimates by Wu and Wu use unrevised data on net capital stock and a GDP rather than an NVIO measure of output. The Otsuka estimate uses a methodology very similar to Chen, *et al.*

Sources: Chen, *et al.* (1988*b*: 585); Jefferson (1990: 346); Jefferson, *et al.* (1992*b*: 253); Jefferson and Rawski (1994: 56); Wu and Wu in Findlay, *et al.* (1994: 168); Jefferson, Rawski, and Zheng (1996: 155); Otsuka, *et al.* (1998: 14).

growth rate of state-sector TFP was not especially impressive in the first years of the reforms (i.e. up to about 1984/5), and that the growth rate may have slowed during 1988–92.[9]

This direct evidence of improved performance after 1978 is supported by additional evidence on convergence in both productivity levels and profit rates across industrial SOEs. As far as productivity is concerned, the cross-sectional analysis of Otsuka, *et al.* (1998: 68–70) found that the introduction of the profit retention system in the late 1970s, profit contracts in the mid-1980s and the shareholding system in the early 1990s all had positive effects on production efficiency in the iron and steel industry. The study also found that TFP in the garment industry was much higher in collective enterprises and joint ventures than in SOEs. More interestingly, they found that SOEs in the machine-tool sector which were more market-orientated and less vertically integrated (that is, those that were forced to purchase parts) had much higher TFP levels than those which were not (Otsuka, *et al.*, 1998: 142–3, 171–2). This study therefore suggests that the growing market-orientation of the economy (the growth of TVEs and reduced vertical integration) as well reforms to the management of SOEs (profit retention, profit contracts, and the shareholding system) served to raise productive efficiency.

Studies which have looked at the dispersion of profit rates have tended to reach a similar conclusion. Naughton (1992; 1995*a*: 237) estimates that the standard deviation of sectoral profit rates fell from 19.7 in 1980 to 7.4 in 1989; over the same period, the coefficient of variation fell from 0.78 to 0.44. This convergence occurred against a background of a decline in the average rate of profit from 25.2 per cent in 1980 to 16.8 per cent in 1989 (Naughton, 1995*a*: 238). The process, Naughton (1995*a*: 240) argues, largely reflects the erosion of supernormal profits (quasi-rents) by the forces of competition rather than any loss of technical efficiency:

> . . . all the available evidence is consistent with the hypothesis that increased entry and competition has been the primary cause of equalization of profit among China's industrial sectors.

Lo (1999) had reached the same conclusion. The hypothesis of convergence of factor returns is supported by evidence collected by Jefferson and Xu (1991: 61) from a sample of 20 firms in Wuhan city, and a larger sample of 352 enterprises drawn up by the State Statistical Bureau. These samples show convergence of returns to labour, intermediate inputs and capital between 1978 and 1987. Evaluation of a larger sample of 226 state-owned industrial enterprises produced a similar conclusion:

> . . . this article reports evidence that during 1980–89 returns to labor, capital and materials became more equal among large and medium-sized enterprises within China's state sector. We also find a significant convergence of technical efficiency. (Jefferson and Xu, 1994: 598)

Further evidence on the state and collectively owned industrial sectors *in toto* shows that the marginal revenue products of capital and labour converged between 1980 and 1988 (Jefferson, *et al.*, 1992*b*: 255). This reflected a relative increase in marginal labour productivity in collective industry, and a relative fall in marginal capital productivity in collective industries (which was higher than in the state sector in 1980).

The view that growth in the industrial sector after 1978 was driven at least in part by productivity growth is reinforced by what we know of the accelerating pace of technical progress in the 1980s.[10] The new emphasis on the importance of science and technology was signalled by the resurrection of the slogan 'the four modernizations'—one of which was the modernization of science and technology—after 1975. This gained concrete expression in the re-establishment of the State Science and Technology Commission (which had existed before 1966) in 1977 (Conroy, 1989). And Deng himself seems to have regarded science and technology as instrumental in the transition process:

> Science and technology is the foremost productive force. Economic development relies on science and technology. Without the help of science and technology, we would not have achieved such a high growth rate in the past ten years or so. (Deng in Yabuki, 1995: 292)

Scientific and technological modernization was pursued in two ways. First, considerable financial and material emphasis was placed on increasing China's own technological capability. This was clearly signalled in government policy. For example, the Sixth Five Year Plan (published in 1982) contained for the first time a science and technology plan. In addition, the State Council established a Science and Technology Leading Group (Conroy, 1989). More concretely, the level of expenditure on R&D expanded substantially (Table 10.4). As these data show, the proportion of investment allocated to improving the quality of the capital stock (as opposed to its quantity) increased from about a third in the late 1970s to an average of over 45 per cent in the early 1990s. It reached a peak of 62 per cent in 1988, the year in which the emphasis by Zhao Ziyang on technological modernization reached its apogee. The story for the number of scientific and technical personnel is yet more spectacular; their numbers increased from about 4.3 million in 1978 to over 18 million by the mid-1990s. It is true that much of this increase took the form of a greater number of teachers (the bulk of whom were employed in schools). Furthermore, the number of scientific researchers remained constant at around 3.3 million. Nevertheless, and especially significant as an indicator of China's ability to successfully assimilate new technology, the number of engineers rose from 1.6 million in 1978 to 5.5 million by 1994. Finally, and just as significantly, the increased emphasis on science and technology was reflected in the composition of the state budget. In the late 1970s, when the threat of war with the USSR still loomed large, state spending on technical progress accounted for only about a fifth of the defence budget. As 1980s progressed, and the threat of war receded, so the proportion allocated to technical progress increased. By the late 1980s, spending on technology was running at around 60 per cent of spending on defence—and in 1993 it (briefly) almost matched defence expenditure before falling back to about 70 per cent. These absolute ratios are of course misleading in that defence spending is understated by the official data used here. Nevertheless, the rising trend is undeniable, not least because it is well documented that military spending was cut back in the early 1980s.

The second means by which technical progress was advanced after 1978 was by encouraging technology transfer. Much of this is well known (though it should be pointed out that the pace of technology transfer was rather slow until 1992, after which FDI grew extremely quickly). Indeed a number of non-China specialists have argued that China's rapid growth after 1978 reflects its success in closing the 'ideas gap'. According to Paul Romer (1993: 562–3):

> The superficial view of reform in China . . . [of a] . . . movement to an undistorted market system. . . . no doubt helps explain much of the early success in agricultural reform, but it does not fit the recent, spectacularly successful development of manufacturing in the special economic zones of the coastal provinces . . . the notion of a purely domestic response to policy reform misses the enormous flow of direct foreign investment that China has received. . . . entrepreneurs and traders from Hong Kong have acted as intermediaries with investors from other countries. In both capacities, they have supplied crucial expertise in areas such as marketing, management, training and technology acquisition.

The transmission mechanisms for foreign technology have varied. Coastal economic zones, ranging from the original 4 SEZs[11] and the 14 coastal cities, to Hainan and

TABLE 10.4. *Technological transformation, 1976–1996*

Year	State enterprises		State spending on technology as percentage of defence spending
	Technology spending as percentage of investment in capital construction	Nos. of scientific and technical personnel (millions)	
1975	33.1	n/a	22.1
1976	39.2	n/a	n/a
1977	43.4	n/a	n/a
1978	33.5	4.345	37.7
1979	33.6	n/a	n/a
1980	33.5	5.276	41.5
1981	44.1	n/a	n/a
1982	45.1	6.264	n/a
1983	49.0	6.852	44.4
1984	41.6	7.466	61.8
1985	41.8	7.817	54.0
1986	52.6	8.253	64.7
1987	56.5	8.894	60.0
1988	62.3	9.661	69.3
1989	50.8	10.351	58.2
1990	48.7	10.809	53.0
1991	48.4	17.168	54.7
1992	48.5	17.597	59.2
1993	47.8	18.124	99.0
1994	45.3	18.659	75.4
1995	44.6	19.134	77.7
1996	42.1	19.856	72.6

Notes: The first column is investment in technical updates and transformation as a percentage of investment in capital construction by state-owned enterprises in current prices. The second column is the total number of scientific and technical personnel (including engineering, agricultural, health care, research, and teaching personnel) in state-owned enterprises. The third column is government expenditure on technical updates and transformation as a percentage of spending on national defence.
Sources: ZGTJNJ (1995: 140, 219, 628); ZGTJNJ (1987: 798); ZGTJNJ (1990: 762); ZGTJNJ (1996: 142, 229–30, 670); ZGTJNJ (1997: 155, 241–2, 682).

Pudong, have certainly played a role. So, too, has the transfer of assembly operations by many manufacturing companies from Hong Kong to south-east China; one indicator of this is the fall in the share of industry in Hong Kong's GDP from 32 per cent in 1980 to 25 per cent in 1991 (Ash and Kueh, 1993: 739). Moreover, a substantial number of joint ventures have been set up since 1978 ranging from hotels and soft drinks to cars, computers, and consumer electronics. Quantifying the scale of the transfer is difficult, partly because some of the transfers—from Taiwan and South Korea via Hong Kong—were not officially recorded. However, the Ministry of Foreign Economic Relations and Trade records the value of technology imports[12] as rising from an annual average of US$1.9bn. in 1981–4 to $3.5bn.

in 1988 (Simon, 1991: 575). Another way of looking at the scale of transfers is to look at data on the degree to which investment in technical updates and transformation has been financed from foreign sources. Here, the data show foreign investment rising from a very modest 555m. *yuan* in 1985 to 2.6bn *yuan* by 1988 and to 21.29bn *yuan* in 1994 (ZGTJNJ, 1995: 160).

Finally, it is worth noting that the re-emergence of private industry after 1984 also helped to accelerate the pace of technological advance. Although many of the new private industries lacked the financial resources and qualified personnel to produce path-breaking new technologies, they were remarkably effective in expanding product variety and in improving existing methods of production. Wenzhou is of course the classic example. There, examples of 'heroic' Schumpeterian entrepreneurship abounded in the late 1980s, ranging from the use of leftover acrylic fibre to pattern blankets, carpets, and clothing to the production of a vast range of new types of badges, labels, and brooches (Li, S., 1990).

The findings of these studies (rising TFP and accelerating technological progress), taken together, strongly suggests a rise in productivity growth during the transition era. This is not to say that there is unanimity of opinion. There are two particular areas of debate. One concerns the path of TFP in the *early years* of the transition. Although most of the studies reported in Table 10.3 have TFP rising up to 1984/5, the McGuckin, *et al.* (1992) estimate has productivity declining. This estimate is less convincing in terms of its theoretical foundation than the others because McGuckin, *et al.* proxy marginal products in the production function by income shares, a remarkable procedure given that one would be hard put to think of an economy further removed from perfect competition than the China of the early 1980s. However, their results are supported by those obtained by Hay, *et al.* (1994):

> Leaving out 1985, it is hard to avoid the conclusion that total factor productivity due to exogenous technical level fell over the entire reform period . . . [p. 166] Total factor productivity change was negative over the period 1980–7 as alleged by Lin (1988). In detail, factor productivity shows a fluctuating pattern. Enterprises experienced a slight fall in total factor productivity in the period 1980–83, an improvement in 1983–5, but suffered a severe setback after 1986 [pp. 178–9].

Whether these results are any more reliable than those of McGuckin, *et al.* is a moot point. The sample was restricted to 386 enterprises, with large firms in the ferrous metal industry overrepresented (Hay, *et al.*, 1994: 461, 468). More seriously, the data for 1980 are not likely to be very reliable because the first proper census of Chinese industry was not carried out until 1985. Nevertheless, there is nothing inherently implausible about the results obtained by Hay, *et al.* and McGuckin, *et al.* Almost all the other studies (the exception being Chen, *et al.*, 1988*b*) show slow TFP growth in the early phase of transition. Moreover, and perhaps more significantly, we know that enterprise reform had barely begun even in 1984, that the TVE sector was still extremely small and that the extent of competition from either imports or the products of joint ventures was also negligible. In those circumstances, and assuming that TFP growth was affected by these supply-side factors, one would not expect to see much by way of an acceleration of productivity growth in the early years of transition.

The second area of debate concerns how much progress has been made in the state sector since the mid-1980s. Friedman (1990: 8) has expressed doubts:

> . . . as long as industrial enterprises are government-owned, there are severe limits to the ability of politically sensitive managers (bureaucrats) to respond effectively to market pressures. The most serious limitation is on flexibility, that is, on the willingness or ability of managers in state-owned enterprises to be venturesome, to undertake risky projects that are likely to fail but have a real, if small, chance of spectacular success.

Sachs and Woo (1994: 119) are more precise, claiming that the growth of TFP calculated by Jefferson, *et al.* (1992b) is too high because the growth of intermediate inputs is underestimated. The same point has been made by Fan, *et al.* (1996: 269, 276–8), Woo, *et al.* (1994; 1997), and Huang and Duncan (1997). The reason for the debate concerns the trend in the value-added deflator used in the Jefferson, *et al.* series. That series shows a decline in the deflator over the transition period which the critics argue is implausible given the upward trend in other prices (Woo, *et al.*, 1997: 35, 305). It is also very widely claimed that TFP levels in SOEs are well below the optimum, that their TFP growth has lagged behind that of TVEs and that many of them continue to make large losses (Sachs, 1995; World Bank, 1995: 66, 189; Broadman, 1995: 28–9; Woo, *et al.*, 1997). Sachs (1995: 471–2) states his pessimism thus:

> The East Asian two-track strategy would be a more convincing model for EEFSU if we could find evidence that China's gradual state enterprise reforms had in fact restored vitality to the state enterprise sector. Unfortunately, in this area of most importance for EEFSU, there is little sign of progress in the Chinese reforms, despite ten years of effort at state enterprise reform.

Fan, *et al.* (1996: 276) go further, claiming that 'there has been a decline in total factor productivity during 1984–8 . . .', and many Chinese reformers are not especially positive about performance either (Putterman, 1995: 1057).

Yet the pessimistic analysis offered by the likes of Woo and others is not especially convincing. It may well be that some sectors of state-owned industry have not performed particularly well. Lo (1997), for example, shows that small-scale state-owned enterprises have done much less well in terms of productivity growth that their medium and large-scale cousins (mainly because state ownership restricts the flexibility that is so essential for effective performance). This may help to explain why many local governments sold small-scale SOEs to the private sector in 1996. But on the whole, the arguments and evidence assembled by the critics are not compelling. The privatization of small SOEs in 1996—3,700 enterprises were privatized in Sichuan in 1996, Xinhua has claimed (SCMP 9 Aug. 1997)—was driven primarily by a desire to raise revenue, not by concerns over technical efficiency. More generally, the samples used to evaluate SOE performance are too small[13] and the time periods considered are often too short; several of the studies, for example, consider only 1984–8 and the evidence for 1988–92 (which in the Jefferson, *et al.* (1996) series shows slower TFP growth) is necessarily misleading because of cyclical factors. Moreover, it is not obvious that the value added deflator should necessarily have increased if the SOE sector was making significant efficiency gains. Indeed the issues raised by the critics concerning the data and method of estimation have all been rejected by those who have been working on these issues for over a decade (Jefferson, *et al.*, 1996). Although small SOEs have not done especially well, large and medium SOEs have performed almost as well as COEs, despite the much lower base from which the COE sector began its explosive growth.

Even more importantly, it is as well to remember—especially given the number of estimates of state-owned enterprise TFP growth that have been, and continue to be, published—that the data and methodological problems are so acute that the debate over SOE efficiency is not likely to be resolved by TFP estimates alone. Far more important is the existence of a plausible theory, and in this respect the 'optimists' have a much more convincing case. To argue there was no productivity growth in China's state sector at a time when new technology was being introduced from overseas, when the state sector was being rationalized by mergers (Nolan, 1996), when many of China's best scientists were being rehabilitated after the Cultural Revolution, and when the SOE sector was facing growing competition from rural and private industry is simply unconvincing. It would only make sense if one could show that TFP growth is *impossible* in enterprises still under state control (irrespective of the competitive environment within which they operate). However, this view that private ownership—not competition—is central to enterprise performance is a fallacy; it is refuted by evidence drawn from countries as far removed as Britain, Taiwan, and South Korea.[14] Of course Chinese SOEs were inefficient in any absolute sense; one estimate made in the mid-1990s put the degree of overstaffing at 30 million workers (Lin, 1996: 240 n.). Moreover, even those writers who have argued most powerfully that TFP has risen in the transition period, make no bones about the fact that there remains considerable unexploited potential (Jefferson, *et al.*, 1996: 171). But this is not the point; all enterprises in all countries routinely operate some way below their (notional) production frontier. In the Chinese case, the problem is compounded by the fact that SOEs perform a social/welfare function as well; and while transferring these functions to local government will raise absolute TFP in the SOE sector in an accounting sense, this is no more than a trick involving smoke and mirrors. The key point remains that the bulk of the statistical evidence, and economic theory both point overwhelmingly in the direction of a significant increase in state-sector TFP after 1978. More generally, the fact that Chinese writers have increasingly criticized the performance of SOEs in the mid-1990s has much more to do with a political agenda—justifying privatization, which started to occur on a significant scale in 1996–7 mainly for budgetary reasons—than with any realistic assessment of performance. In short, to claim that the transition process has done nothing to improve the 'efficiency' of the key SOEs stretches the bounds of credulity.

1.3. Labour Productivity in Industry

This theoretical presumption is supported by trends in labour productivity. The case for using labour compared to total-factor productivity as a measure of 'efficiency' is not clear a priori; in principle, an economy might be able to boost its labour productivity by increasing the available capital stock per worker. This possibility is predicated upon the standard neoclassical conclusion of continuous substitution possibilities between labour and capital; that is, it is typically assumed that a factory director chooses from a book of blueprints, each of which combines labour and capital in varying proportions to produce a given level of output. If one further assumes than the marginal productivity of capital used to raise labour productivity is low, it follows that a country may be better served by reducing its investment and savings, and raising consumption instead. However, if reducing investment also reduces output, it is evident that income will fall and therefore total consumption also. In other words, a country with a high rate investment may not be able to raise consumption simply by cutting back on supposedly 'unproductive' investment projects. Everything will depend on whether the marginal productivity of investment is high or low; in a developing country, it is likely to be rather high even if one takes no account of the possible embodiment effects of investment on technical progress.

The second reason why labour productivity is a better measure than TFP is that the difficulties involved in measuring the latter are far greater than those involved in computing the former. There are, to be sure, difficulties in estimating effective labour supply; strictly, one needs to adjust for differences in skill levels, and it is rarely easy to find reliable data on hours worked. However, the computation of TFP requires not just that these problems are overcome but also that the capital stock is accurately measured—a problem long recognized to pose great difficulties. These difficulties go far towards explaining why estimates of TFP for the same country vary dramatically, as was noted in Chapter 4, and provide good cause for looking at labour productivity.

Estimates of trends in labour productivity in state-owned industry are given in Table 10.5. These results show a sustained and significant rise in labour productivity over the transition era. The NVIO data—in principle the better data to use because they allow for fluctuations in intermediate input use—are probably best put to one side because of the unreliability of the value-added figures. This treatment tends to be the norm in much of the literature, although the potential for misleading results is great if the ratio of value-added has been declining significantly over the transition period.[15] As for the GVIO data, these show a significant rise in labour productivity over the period 1980 to 1995. It is true that the growth rate is slower after 1987, but this is largely explained in terms of two factors. First, the fiscal and monetary contraction of the late 1980s and early 1990s reduced labour productivity; as is invariably the case, labour productivity moves procyclically. Second, the slow growth of the post-1992 period reflects the tendency of a significant number of the most dynamic state enterprises to be reclassified as 'other' enterprises.

TABLE 10.5. *Labour productivity in state-owned industrial enterprises, 1980–1995* (annual real percentage growth rates; 1990 prices)

Period	NVIO per worker	GVIO per worker
1980–7	4.5	5.1
1987–95	2.8	3.4
1980–95	3.0	4.3

Notes: NVIO is calculated from current price GVIO data which, for the state sector, have been significantly revised following the Third Industrial Census of 1995 (ZGTJNJ, 1997: 413) and therefore the series breaks in that year. Gross output value is deflated using the recently constructed official index of industrial producer prices (ZGTJNJ, 1996: 271) that supersedes the older implicit price deflators; these new data are available only for 1980 onwards. Constant price GVIO data are converted to NVIO using the official value-added ratios for the GDP measure of industrial output. The value-added ratios for the NDMP measure of industrial output—the only value-added data available pre-1992—have been converted to a GDP basis using the ratio of the GDP measure of value-added to the NDMP measure in 1992. Employment data are as published by the State Statistical Bureau. These have not been adjusted as per Jefferson, *et al.* (1996) because it is not self-evident that the so-called 'unproductive' workers they exclude—employed mainly in providing health and other social services within enterprises—are any less or more productive than other workers.

Sources: ZGTJNJ (1990: 410; 1991: 392; 1992: 404; 1994: 388; 1995: 396; 1996: 102, 271, 403, 422; 1997: 412); ZGGYJJTJNJ (1990: 133; 1991: 133; 1992: 142; 1993: 142); Zhongguo tongjiju (1989*a*: 43).

Sometimes this has been because of investment from overseas firms—the Sichuan Glass Company, for example, converted itself into a foreign-funded stockholding company in 1994, with a significant Singaporean shareholding—but more generally it is because many SOEs have turned themselves into shareholding companies after the 1993 Congress. A significant number of SOEs were quoted on the Hong Kong stock exchange by the late 1990s—for example, Ma'anshan Iron and Steel, Shanghai Petrochemicals, and Qingdao Breweries. Thus in the electronics industry, 19 of the top 100 enterprises in 1996 (measured by sales turnover) were shareholding enterprises (CD, 3 April 1997). In other words, one is not comparing the same firms in 1992 and 1995. If all these 'other' companies were to be included in the state-owned category, the rate of growth of GVIO per worker would rise from 0.6 per cent per annum for 1992–5 to 2.4 per cent.[16]

One of the reasons for the post-1978 rise in SOE labour productivity has been the redeployment of labour from relatively low- to relatively high-productivity industries *within* the state-owned sector. An indication of the trends over the transition period is given in Table 10.6. Not surprisingly, there is no precise correlation between the rate of growth of employment, and productivity levels in these data. It is apparent, for instance, that some of the industries with high productivity levels have not seen significant increases in the their labour forces. Chemicals, ferrous-metal smelting, transport equipment, electronics, and electrical equipment were all industries where labour productivity exceeded 10,000 *yuan* per worker in 1992—substantially above the industrial median of 7,200 *yuan*. However, employment growth in all these industries was below the median, and dramatically so in the case of transport equipment.

TABLE 10.6. *Employment growth and productivity levels in state-owned industry by sector, 1980–1992* (ranked by labour productivity)

Sector	Annual growth in employment, 1980–92 (% per annum)	Labour productivity, 1992 (*yuan* per worker at 1990 prices)
Tobacco manufacture	6.9	107,689
Petroleum extraction	5.8	36,395
Petroleum processing	7.5	32,399
Chemical fibres	9.2	27,222
Power generation	5.5	20,515
Pharmaceutical products	7.0	17,936
Electronic equipment	4.0	14,648
Ferrous-metal smelting	3.8	13,777
Non-Ferrous metal smelting	4.9	13,438
Rubber goods	5.0	13,259
Beverage manufacture	8.0	12,792
Forage manufacture	22.8	12,447
Chemicals	4.4	12,059
Salt mining	2.1	11,727
Water supply	0.7	11,136
Transport equipment	2.5	10,691
Electrical equipment	4.5	10,544
Plastic goods	5.3	9,009
Instruments and meters	1.4	7,943
Food manufacture	4.1	7,294
Non-Ferrous metal mining	3.8	7,195
Machine building	2.0	7,185
Paper making	5.2	6,952
Printing	3.3	6,883
Ferrous-metal mining	3.1	6,780
Cultural and sporting items	6.7	6,720
Metal products	2.4	6,577
Other	4.7	6,558
Building materials	3.6	6,439
Textile manufacture	6.0	6,368
Clothing	4.6	6,146
Logging	0.7	5,849
Arts and crafts	7.3	5,823
Leather and fur	5.2	5,811
Non-Metal mineral mining	2.4	5,664
Other mineral mining	8.7	5,451
Furniture manufacture	–0.3	4,804
Coke and coal gas	8.3	4,551
Timber processing	4.2	4,208
Coal mining	3.0	4,179
Median	4.6	7,245

Notes: These statistics are for independent-accounting enterprises of all types at the *xiang* level and above. No data are available for 1981–3. Labour productivity data are in 1990 *yuan* and measure net output value by sector.

Source: ZGGYJJTJNJ (1993).

Nevertheless, there is a clear correlation for the sample as a whole between sectors of high labour productivity and employment growth. Of the seventeen industrial sectors with labour productivity of 10,000 *yuan* or greater, ten of them experienced above-median employment growth. The top six industries in terms of labour productivity levels all enjoyed employment growth in excess of the median; the bottom three industries all enjoyed below median employment growth. Three notable examples of the process whereby labour increasingly shifted to high productivity industries are coal mining, petroleum extraction and processing, and tobacco. Coal was the industrial sector with the lowest level of labour productivity in the early 1990s, partly because of inadequate investment during the transition era, and partly because the price of coal products was kept low by the state. However, the coal sector saw employment growth of only 3 per cent per annum on average between 1980 and 1992 (and cuts in employment thereafter). This sector's poor performance therefore served to depress the overall level of productivity by a declining amount. By contrast, the petroleum extraction and petroleum-processing industries boasted productivity level of nearly five times the industrial median. As a result, the fact that their workforces increased by 5.8 and 7.5 per cent respectively provided a powerful stimulus to overall industrial productivity. This reflected the progressive development of new oilfields, notably in Xinjiang and in the Yellow River delta (the Shengli oilfield). The same process of employment expansion is equally apparent in the case of the tobacco industry. However, the impact on overall industrial productivity was even greater because labour productivity in the tobacco sector was 3 times high than in petroleum, and almost 15 times the industrial median.[17]

2. Productivity Growth in Agriculture

Many writers, in some cases even those schooled in the master discourse, have accepted that productivity improvement in agriculture was one reason for the surge in output after 1978. The incentive structures newly-introduced after 1978 generated both static and dynamic gains. On the one hand, they successfully raised productivity levels by motivating firms and farm households to use their existing labour and capital inputs more productively. Justin Lin (1992) interprets the (de facto) privatization of farming in just this sort of way, arguing that the household responsibility system was the main reason for the output surge. On the other hand, it is alleged, the new incentive structures promoted innovation and thereby enhanced the productive potential of the economy, a point again stressed by Lin. This section evaluates these types of claim. Is it true that there was no productivity growth under Mao? Was agricultural output growth after 1978 caused merely by the productivity enhancing effects of decollectivization?

2.1. Agricultural Productivity in Maoist China

It is well known that that the yields of a number of key crops increased during the Maoist era. Grain is the most obvious example. During 1952–7, the yield increased annually by 2.3 per cent (Nongye bu, 1989). After the Great Leap Forward, the rate of increase seems to have accelerated, registering 3.2 per cent for the years between 1965 and 1978. Nevertheless, the consensus in the literature is that productivity growth was exceptionally low, and perhaps even negative, after 1957. Measured at 1990 prices, labour productivity stood at 1,003 *yuan* in 1957. By 1965, however, it had fallen back to 848 *yuan*, and on the eve of Deng's accession in 1978, labour productivity registered only 918 *yuan*.[18] This seems to imply that the improvement in land productivity was achieved primarily by increased applications of labour to an essentially unchanging area of cultivated land, an involutionary process that had been occurring since at least the middle of the Qing (Huang, 1990; Perkins, 1969).

A second reason for the pessimistic conventional wisdom on agricultural productivity trends in the late Maoist era is the evidence on total factor productivity. Some estimates of TFP growth are summarized in Table 10.7.[19]

TABLE 10.7. *Estimates of total factor productivity growth in Chinese agriculture, 1952–1978* (per cent per annum)

Estimates by:	1952–7	1965–78
Tang	+0.8	−1.1
Lin	+0.7	−0.7
Hayami and Ruttan	+0.4	−1.7
Wiens	+0.4	−1.3
Wong	+0.2	−1.5

Notes: These estimates collected by Wen use an identical methodology and identical data on input growth. The reason for the differences in TFP growth is that the studies use different weights to aggregate inputs (land, labour, capital, and current inputs) into total factor input growth. For example, Lin's analysis gives a weight of 0.54 to land, whereas that of Hayami and Ruttan uses a weight of only 0.10. (Putterman (1993: 202 n.) regards Lin's weights (to be precise, these are the weights used in Lin's 1992 paper rather than those in Lin's 1990 paper cited by Wen, but the two sets are not very different) as 'plausible' in that they give a high weight to land. This accords with the Putterman data for Dahe township.) As cultivated area grew very slowly, this goes far towards explaining why the reduction in TFP between 1957 and 1978 recorded by Lin was much less that that recorded by Hayami and Ruttan.

Source: Calculated from Wen (1993: 37).

The most important feature of these results is that the conclusion of declining TFP in the late Maoist period appears insensitive to changes in factor weights. In every case, the growth rate of TFP between 1965 and 1978 was negative.

Again, the precision of these calculations disguises their shaky foundations. In the case of Maoist agriculture, the TFP approach is flawed in theory and in practice. It is flawed in practice because we have no data on the numbers of hours worked, or on the size of the agricultural labour force employed in farm production; the estimation of a *general* production function for agriculture as a whole (i.e. farming plus forestry, fisheries, livestock, and sideline industries) is a nonsense. There are no good data on the use of non-chemical fertilizer, or its quality. There are severe problems in the aggregation of capital inputs; it is common to measure it in terms of horsepower but the limitations of this definition are obvious. Additionally, we know too little about the number of draught animals—to say nothing of the extent to which they were used in farm production—to attach much weight to the aggregate in any case. Irrigation poses special problems of its own (see also Chapter 6). The real difficulty is to determine its impact upon yields, something about which we know very little. In sum, Wen (1993: 22) is naive in claiming that:

> There should be little controversy involved in calculating an output index and individual input indexes once official data become available and accepted as better than alternative unofficial sources.

The growth-accounting approach is also flawed in theory. One great difficulty for agricultural estimates is the complementarity of inputs. For example, improvements in irrigation typically led to the use of more fertilizer and improved seed varieties. It is therefore virtually impossible to isolate the impact of irrigation.[20] It is the *package* of technology that is crucial:

> Among all the indicators associated with progress in agricultural development, only three are indispensable to rapid and prolonged growth in yields at the initial stage: improved water control; abundant supplies of fertilizers; and high-yielding seed varieties responsive to these inputs. While the introduction of one or more of these three normally provides some growth in average yields, there are much greater returns when all three are applied appropriately. These are the fundamental ingredients of the 'green revolution'. (Stone, 1988*a*: 767)

This problem of complementarity of inputs is dwarfed only by that of prices. In order to aggregate output and inputs, prices have to be used. But this makes sense only if prices reflect relative scarcity, i.e. if they are equal to marginal costs. In other words, only if the economy is in general equilibrium do prices accurately reflect costs of production. Wen (1993) uses 1952 prices 'as if' these are general equilibrium prices on the grounds that research shows that the pre-war economy operated efficiently and that, by 1952, recovery to pre-war output (and therefore price) levels was complete. Even though these implicit assumptions feature prominently in the work of Brandt (1985, 1989) and Rawski (1989), it is hard to take them very seriously. These writers seem to have little conception of the very special assumptions that need to be made to prove the existence of a general competitive equilibrium (Huang, 1991). In concrete terms, the biggest problem with the use of 1952 prices it that chemical fertilizer is overvalued relative to farm output.[21] Although Ishikawa (1967) has argued that 1952 is a 'good' base year, a number of Chinese economists have pointed out that the price of agricultural products relative to manufactures in that year was about 30 per cent lower than it had been in 1936/7. Moreover, relative agricultural prices had actually declined in the decade prior to 1936/7 (Sheng, 1992: 22). In other words, it easy to argue that the relative price of fertilizer in 1952—in common with that of manufactures—was well above its relative marginal cost.[22] The use of 1952 prices therefore has the effect of overstating the rate of growth of current inputs (and therefore total inputs) in the Maoist period. This in turn means that the decline in TFP is exaggerated. It is probably a step too far to claim that the Maoist record on agricultural TFP growth was impressive. Even with substantial revision to the data and to the methodology, it is very unlikely that one can show in any plausible fashion that TFP growth was better than extremely modest. But that does not alter the fact that the precision offered by growth accounting is spurious. One might just as well rely on a more qualitative evaluation of the Maoist record.

Part of any such qualitative evaluation should be a discussion of the pace of technical progress. If the hypothesis of slow TFP growth is to stand up, we need to be able to show either that technical progress was negligible, or that it had only minor effects on output. On the first count, some have argued that technical progress was indeed slow and that any innovations that occurred were offset by negative technical progress. Certainly there are examples of the latter. The famous double-wheel double-bladed plough (too heavy) is a case in point. So, too the universal introduction of double rice cropping (the growing season is too short in many parts of China unless plastic sheeting is used to prevent frost damage).

But it is increasingly well recognized that China made significant progress in developing new seeds during the late Maoist period (Barker, *et al.*, 1985, ch. 5; Stone, 1988*a*; Hussain, 1989; Nongye bu, 1990; Lin, 1994). According to Stone (1988*a*: 795):

> . . . HYV extension progress for all major cereal crops during the final two Maoist decades was exceedingly rapid, culminating in 1978 with hybrids covering 60 per cent of corn area, 12.6 per cent of rice area and around 40 per cent of sorghum area. Even more rapid progress with other short-stature, fertilizer responsive non-hybrid varieties was at least of equal importance. Semi-dwarf rice (including hybrids) covered no less than 80 per cent of rice area, and semi-dwarf wheat covered 40 per cent of spring sown wheat area, and perhaps a comparable proportion of over-wintering wheat.

Rice is perhaps the best example. Modern semi-dwarf varieties were developed by 1964—*before* International Rice Research institute varieties were released in the rest of Asia (Barker, *et al.*, 1985: 60–1). Over the next decade, dwarf and semi-dwarf varieties spread throughout the bulk of China's rice-growing region (Nongye bu, 1990: 419). This rate of diffusion compares very well with diffusion rates in other Asian economies with only the Philippines and Sri Lanka coming close to matching China's record (Table 10.8).

TABLE 10.8. *Rice area planted to modern varieties, 1965–1980* (percentage of rice area)

Country	1965/6	1973/4	1976/7
China	14	80	80
Indonesia	0	37	48
South Korea	0	12	44
Philippines	0	63	68
Thailand	0	5	11
India	0	25	36
Sri Lanka	0	55	63

Sources: Barker, *et al.* (1985: 63); Stone (1988*a*: 792).

These varieties raised yields by over 50 per cent in some parts of China (Nongye bu 1990: 200; Bramall, 1995*a*).[23] In the 1960s, too, pioneering research on higher yielding hybrid rice began under the direction of Yuan Longping (Zhu, 1992: 579), and successful dissemination began in 1976. Moreover, some of the new varieties pioneered in China were so effective that they were successfully adopted by other countries. One example of this is 'Purbachi' semi-dwarf rice. Purbachi was exported to Bangladesh in the late 1960s and, although it received none of the promotion that accompanied other new IRRI varieties in Bangladesh, the variety remains popular even in the 1990s (Anderson, *et al.*, 1991: 264–5). This type of evidence explodes the notion that there was little successful technical progress in agriculture during the Maoist period.

Nevertheless, it is fair to point out that Maoist technical progress was probably not fully reflected in terms of productivity growth. Hybrid varieties were not available until 1976, and their effects were therefore apparent only at the end of the 1970s and during the 1980s. At least as significantly, the full yield potential of the semi-dwarf varieties introduced in the 1960s was not exploited because of shortages of nitrogen fertilizer (Stone, 1988*a*). As these new varieties were extremely responsive to nitrogen, it is not surprising that yields did not rise rapidly until the 13 synthetic ammonia urea plants purchased from abroad in the early 1970s came on stream. Stone (1988*a*: 808) summarizes the importance of nitrogen as follows:

> With nitrogen deficiencies throughout Chinese farm soils, and with the rapid introduction of fertilizer (primarily nitrogen-) responsive crop varieties, this meant the agricultural system remained severely nitrogen-constrained through the 1960s and 1970s. This situation began to change much more rapidly when the large synthetic ammonia/urea complexes purchased in 1973–74 went into production in the late 1970s.

It is also probable that the nature of collective farms played a role in reducing the productivity gains from new varieties. As is well known, Chinese collectives suffered from substantial incentive problems (Liu 1991*a*; Putterman, 1988; Nolan, 1988). There is little evidence that this slowed the diffusion of technology; on the contrary, rates of diffusion were probably faster than they would have been under private farming because of risk-pooling. But the weak link between effort and remuneration on the Chinese collective, and the growing disaffection of the population as a result of both the famine of the early 1960s and the repeated campaigns of the subsequent decades (Chan, *et al.*, 1984; Siu, 1989; Potter and Potter, 1990), probably ensured that the rural economy was operating inside its production-possibility curve. In other words, those technological opportunities which did exist in the 1970s were not being exploited to the full. It is therefore quite possible to reconcile evidence of slow productivity growth with evidence of substantial technical progress. As Wen (1993: 34–5) says:

> . . . deteriorating supply was not caused by lack of technological progress. On the contrary, modern technology was readily available and modern inputs were eagerly adopted and accumulated under the commune system with its compulsory saving mechanism and modernization impulse. Yet, under the commune system, modern technology did not have

the opportunity to demonstrate its worth . . . the technological progress embodied in the modern inputs was overshadowed by the rampant inefficiency of the commune system.

2.2. Agricultural Productivity after 1978

Whatever the trend prior to 1978, there is little doubt that productivity in agriculture rose sharply thereafter. A plethora of studies on total factor productivity point to this conclusion (Table 10.9).

Table 10.9. *Estimates of total factor productivity growth in Chinese agriculture, 1978–1989* (per cent per annum)

Estimates by:	1978–84	1978–89
Tang	7.4	6.2
Lin (1990)	8.0	6.6
Hayami and Ruttan	6.7	5.2
Wiens	7.9	6.7
Wong	7.7	6.3
Feng	3.4	1.3
Lin (1992)	3.5	2.8[a]
McMillan, *et al.*	5.7	n/a
Putterman	8.9[b]	n/a

[a] 1978–87.
[b] 1980–5.

Sources: The first five estimates come from Wen (1993: 37) and refer to the entire agricultural sector; the same is true of McMillan, *et al.* (1989). Feng's (1990: 48) methodology is not explained. The Lin (1992) study looks only at TFP in the crop sector, as does Putterman (1993). The latter's TFP estimate comes from Dahe township in Hebei province; it is adjusted for changes in the relative prices of inputs and outputs.

The range of estimates of TFP growth for 1980–4 in this table is of course wide. At the top end is the 8.9 per cent estimated by Putterman; this is, however, for the single township of Dahe in Hebei province. Moreover, the years chosen (1980–5) probably give the estimate an upward bias because 1980 was a year of low yields because of poor weather; the grain yield was 15 per cent below its 1979 level and 9 per cent below the average yield for 1974–9 (Putterman, 1993: 88). At the bottom end is the estimate of Lin (1992). This is lower than the others largely because they include fast-growing sectors (such as animal husbandry and household sidelines) in their definition of agriculture; these subsectors started from a low base in the late 1980s largely because of state suppression ('the tails of capitalism'). By contrast, Lin looks exclusively at the crop sector. The mainstay of crop production (grain) had been the centre of Maoist agricultural development, and because it had reached quite a high level in the 1970s, there was less scope for explosive growth of either output or productivity. But despite the variation in estimates, the overall picture of rapid TFP growth is clear.

It needs of course to be repeated that these estimates of total factor productivity are not especially reliable, for the methodological reasons already discussed. However, neither the difference in the estimates of TFP growth in the early 1980s, nor the rather unreliable nature of the magnitudes involved for the estimates as a whole, is especially important for our purposes here.[24] The key point is that all show a strongly positive productivity growth rate—in marked contrast to the results for the late Maoist period. To be sure, the growth rates for the whole post-1978 period are slower than for the initial reform period of 1978–84. But the difference between even these rates and those of pre-1978 is very sharp. This general evidence of a significant rise in total factor productivity after 1978 accords with what we know of the pace of technical progress. Perhaps the most significant development was the introduction in the mid-1970s of hybrid varieties of rice, corn, and cotton (the *sanza* or 'three hybrids') (Bramall, 1995*a*).[25] In other words, much of the growth in agricultural output during the transition period was driven by the diffusion of farm technology developed in the Maoist period.

An indication of the pace at which new varieties were adopted by farmers is provided by Table 10.10 which illustrates the case of hybrid rice. Starting from zero in the mid-1970s, around one-third of rice area was sown to hybrid rice by 1987. Much the same was true for hybrid corn. In 1973, hybrids accounted for about 40 per cent of corn-sown area. By 1985, however, the figure exceeded 70 per cent (Stone, 1988*a*: 792) and by 1994 it had climbed further to reach 83 per cent (ZGNYTJZL, 1994: 36).

TABLE 10.10. *Spread of hybrid-rice varieties*

Year	Area sown to hybrid rice (m. *mu*)	Hybrids as % total rice area
1976	n/a	neg.
1977	n/a	6
1978	n/a	13
1979	75.45	15
1980	70.56	14
1981	76.76	15
1982	84.25	17
1983	101.24	20
1984	132.65	27
1985	104.62	26
1986	134.15	28
1987	n/a	33

Sources: Nongye bu (1989: 350); Stone (1988*a*: 792).

This rapid pace of diffusion largely reflected two factors. First, a willingness on the part of Chinese farmers to adopt technologies which raised yields. According to Lin (1994: 392–3), hybrid rice raised yields by about 17 per cent in Hunan for a given level of inputs. This is not very different from IRRI estimates with rice hybrids, which suggest that they raise yields by about 20 per cent (Barker and Herdt, 1985: 61).[26] Secondly, the system of agricultural extension developed during the Maoist period continued to be very effective in forcing farmers to adopt new technology whether they liked it or not (Delman, 1992). Although most farmers were not entirely enamoured of this coercive approach to innovation, they recognized that the system was comparatively effective in introducing new and effective technologies.

3. Productivity in the Transport Sector

Finally, a word about productivity in the transport sector. During the Maoist period, productivity growth rates were modest (Table 10.11). As the data show, rail productivity in both freight and passenger sectors grew less quickly after 1965 than it had done in the previous 15-year period. This may have been because of greater utilization of the road network, for certainly road productivity growth rates rose substantially after 1965. Indeed the efficiency of freight movements by road actually declined between 1952 and 1965, compared to an annual increase of 4.2 per cent after 1965.

More interesting, however, is the acceleration of productivity growth after 1978. As was seen in Chapter 6, one of the characteristics of the post-1978 period was the slow growth of the road and rail networks. In consequence, the only means by which the vast increase in demand for transport services could be met was by increased productivity. The dimensions of this increase are set out in Table 10.11.

TABLE 10.11. *Productivity growth in the transport sector, 1952–1995* (growth rates of productivity; per cent per annum)

Period	Railway productivity		Road productivity	
	Passenger-km	Tonne-km	Passenger-km	Tonne-km
1952–65	4.5	6.3	1.9	−0.1
1965–78	3.8	3.3	4.2	4.2
1978–95	6.6	5.2	n/a	n/a
(1984–95)	(3.7)	(4.4)	(8.4)	(7.9)

Notes: Productivity is measured here as passenger-km per km of road and rail, and tonne-km per km of road and rail. The road transport data are not precisely comparable across periods; from 1984 onwards, private transport is included. More generally, there must also be grave doubts about the accuracy of data on movements of passengers and freight by road in a market economy.

Sources: ZGTJNJ (1983: 299–309); ZGTJNJ (1985: 385–96); ZGTJNJ (1995: 467–73); ZGTJNJ (1996: 502–4).

As these data show, rail productivity growth accelerated markedly in the transition era. The growth of freight productivity rose from 3.3 per cent per year during 1965–78 to 5.4 per cent annually during 1978–94; and the increase in passenger productivity was even more dramatic. The productivity acceleration in road transport was equally marked; during 1984–94, the productivity of road movements of freight and passengers grew at more than 8 per cent, approximately double the rate achieved in the late Maoist period.

It is of course true that the measures of productivity given in Table 10.11 are only partial measures. They neglect trends in employment and in the availability of vehicles. For example, one of the reasons why rail productivity was able to increase more quickly after 1978 was the greater availability of rolling stock. Whereas the rail network increased by only 11 per cent between 1978 and 1994, the number of passenger coaches increased by 109 per cent (ZGTJNJ, 1995: 467, 474). The number of freight cars in operation also increased by 66 per cent. Furthermore, there were 2.20 million workers employed on China's state-owned railways by 1994 (ZGTJNJ, 1995: 90) compared to only 1.68 million in 1981 (ZGTJNJ, 1983: 131). Even so, the fact that passenger-km travelled per km of track increased by almost 200 per cent during 1978–94—and freight movements by 130 per cent over the same period—suggests that total factor productivity on the railways was increasing significantly during the reform period.

4. Conclusion

Trends in total factor productivity are impossible to measure with any degree of precision. This conclusion is true for agricultural and industrial sectors, just as it is true for developed and underdeveloped countries. Nevertheless, the available information for China during the transition era points to a significant rise in agricultural and industrial productivity. There are two pieces of evidence. First, many studies have tried to estimate productivity directly and the majority of these have found evidence of significant rises. The second piece of evidence documents the extent of technical progress, often seen as a key precondition for sustained productivity growth, in agricultural and industrial sectors. Some of the new technologies introduced came from abroad, but the existence of extensive invention, innovation, and diffusion throughout the Chinese economy is undeniable.

The growth of the Chinese economy during the transition era was driven, therefore, by more than simply factor accumulation and favourable initial conditions. Productivity growth was especially fast in rural industry, and in agriculture in the early 1980s. But even in state industry, one of the largest sectors of the economy in terms of output value, productivity growth was occurring, and it would have been impossible for economy-wide output growth to have occurred without substantial increases in the productivity of the transport sector. That productivity growth was so fast, and occurred across the entire economy, goes far towards explaining why the pace of Chinese economic growth was so rapid after 1978; factor accumulation by itself would have brought about growth, but not on the scale that was seen.

11

Differences in Prefectural Growth Rates

It was argued in previous chapters that China's principal achievement during the era of transition—rapid economic growth—reflected in large measure the favourable legacies of the Maoist period. These ranged from a well-developed transport infrastructure and an extensive irrigation network to high levels of human capital. China was not unusual in possessing these attributes, but was remarkable amongst LDCs in combining them with low levels of per capita income. It was this combination that helped facilitate the dramatic growth of the Dengist era. In addition, the growth rates of the transition era depended upon the maintenance of a high rate of investment—in agriculture, industry, and in human capital. Furthermore, and at least as fundamentally, growth was spurred by productivity growth based upon technical progress within agriculture and industry alike.

This chapter tests these arguments more fully by looking at local data; more precisely, it asks whether differences in growth rates at the *county level* in four of China's prefectures can be explained in this way. It was seen in Chapter 2 that per capita GDP (in 1990 prices) grew at 13.5 per cent per year in Suzhou between 1980 and 1996, substantially faster than the rates attained in Wenzhou (11.8 per cent for 1980–95) and Wenjiang (11.7 per cent for 1982–96), and almost double the rate achieved in Liangshan (7.8 per cent for 1982–96), deep in the mountains of south-west China.[1] If the argument outlined in the previous chapters is correct, one would expect to find that fast-growing Suzhou prefecture was well favoured in terms of initial conditions, factor accumulation and productivity increases, and that slow-growing Liangshan was constrained by its limited social and physical capabilities, a deficient transport infrastructure, low rates of investment and slow productivity growth.

1. Initial Conditions

1.1. The Agricultural Inheritance

As has been previously noted, agricultural yields are sensitive not so much to any single component of the 'green revolution' technology but to the package as a whole. That is, when chemical fertilizer is applied to high-yielding varieties grown on well-irrigated land in areas where there is abundant sunlight, and when plastics are also available (to protect against frost damage), the impact on crop yields can be very substantial. But although the availability of such preconditions varied considerably, between the four prefectures of Suzhou, Wenjiang, Wenzhou, and Liangshan at the beginning of the transition era (Table 11.1), these variations in irrigation and chemical fertilizer use seem to be inadequate explanations of the pattern of yields.

If one compares Suzhou and Wenzhou, for example, it is evident that irrigation and fertilizer use were much higher in Suzhou, yet grain yields in the two regions were virtually identical. Similarly, the counties of the Chengdu plain used more fertilizer and were better irrigated than those of Wenzhou but their yields were significantly lower. It is only when allowance is made for the impact of climatic differences, the importance of irrigation and fertilizer use becomes clear. For although Wenzhou was disadvantaged in terms of input use, it enjoyed the massive advantage of an average temperature some 15 per cent higher than in Suzhou and the Chengdu plain, and 50 per cent more rainfall. These advantages were so significant for farming that they outweighed Wenzhou's other handicaps.

TABLE 11.1. *Irrigation and fertilizer use in 1980*

Prefecture	Fertilizer used (kg per *mu*)	Irrigated area (%)	Average temp. (°C)	Average rainfall (mm)	Grain yield (kg per *mu*)
Suzhou	26	92	15.5	1,073	346
Wenjiang	18	84	15.6	1,071	296
Wenzhou	14	68	17.7	1,664	341
Liangshan	3	22	14.4	1,000	170

Notes: Data are for chemical fertilizer use only. The figures for fertilizer use and irrigated area refer respectively to inputs per unit, and shares in, cultivated area. The temperature and rainfall figures are annual averages for the post-1949 period. Grain yield is per unit of sown area. Grain yield data for Suzhou are for 1979 (the grain-sown area figures used are for 1980) because the weather in 1980 was extremely poor (Huang, 1990: 224, 235–6). The same is true to some extent for Wenjiang; the data provided in the available *xian zhi* suggest that 1980 grain yields were about 1 per cent lower than in 1979. Allowing for underlying growth, this implies that the 1980 yield might have been as much as 5 per cent higher if the weather had been good. But given that this would not alter the rankings of the regions, and that we have no comprehensive data for 1979, 1980 yields are given in the table. No data are directly available for Liangshan, but we know that 1980 grain output in Sichuan's ethnic minority areas was 1.5 per cent down on its 1979 level (SCTJNJ, 1990: 507). As Liangshan was by far the most important grain-producing ethnic minority area in the province, it is reasonable to conclude from this that 1980 yields were depressed. Note that Wenzhou's 1980 grain yield, in contrast to both the other three regions and to Zhejiang as a whole, was extremely good: it was 17 per cent higher than in 1978 (Wenzhou tongjiju, 1985: 18; LSTJ, 1990: 384).

Sources: ZGFX (1989); Jiangsu tongjiju (1989: 401); Wang (1987: 182–4); LYZG (1985: 335–66); JSSXGK (1989).

This conclusion is reinforced by considering the case of Liangshan. This region was triply disadvantaged. First, its climate is not especially good for farming. Although rainfall is on a par with that for the Chengdu plain, the average annual temperature is more than a degree lower. Moreover, the Liangshan average disguises very wide temperature differences. In mountainous areas such as Butuo and Ganluo, the average annual temperature is only about 10 °C compared to about 17 °C at Xichang. Secondly, fertilizer use was only about one-tenth of the level in Suzhou. This reflected low levels of production, but also the inability of the region's (poor) farmers to purchase modern farm inputs. Thirdly, only a comparatively small fraction of the region was irrigated, compared to almost universal irrigation in Suzhou.

This conclusion is emphasized by looking at Xichang county, one of the few parts of Liangshan where conditions were favourable. With an average temperature of 17 °C, an irrigated area of 81 per cent and chemical fertilizer inputs of 15 kg per *mu*, this county was able to achieve a grain yield of 356 kg in 1980—higher than the Suzhou average. Econometric analysis tells the same story about the importance of climate, irrigation, and chemical fertilizer use. If a regression is run with chemical fertilizer use, the share of cultivated area that is irrigated, average temperature and average rainfall, the coefficients for fertilizer, rainfall, and irrigation are all significant. The temperature coefficient has the right sign, but is not significant. The R^2 is 0.89.

From a growth perspective, of course, what matters is the extent to which initial input use was out of line with yields. Regions with high yields and high input levels would not be expected to grow quickly; the same applies to regions with low yields and low inputs. The region in which one would expect to see rapid growth would therefore be the one in disequilibrium; that is, a region where high input levels coincided with low yields. The data here suggest that only Wenjiang of the four was poised to experience a rapid increase in grain yields in the early 1980s. In Suzhou and Wenzhou, input levels were high but these were already reflected in their high yields. In Liangshan, inputs were much lower—but so too were yields. In Wenjiang, however, yields were somewhat lower than one would expect given its input levels. However, the 'yield gap' between it and both Suzhou and Wenzhou was not very great, and therefore one would not have expected explosive yield growth on the basis simply of these preconditions. To see what actually happened must be deferred until we have examined the rate of input *growth* in the 1980s. At this stage, it is enough to conclude that agricultural conditions in 1978 do seem to often a partial explanation of differences in prefectural performance during the transition era.

1.2. Inherited Industrial and Transport Infrastructure

Before looking at input growth, we need to note the enormous differences between the four prefectures at the end of the Maoist era in terms of the industrial and transport infrastructure that had been established, and these differences also go some way towards explaining post-1978 growth differentials.

In the case of Liangshan, the economic geography of the region had been transformed between the Revolution and the late 1970s. The road network, for example, increased from 408 km in 1952 to 3,613 km in 1970 and reached 6,978 km by 1980 (LYZG, 1985: 245; SCTJNJ, 1986: 214). Perhaps even more significantly, one important by-product of 'Third Front' construction was the building of a railway linking Chengdu with Kunming. This passed through Liangshan via Xichang, and at a stroke greatly improved its transport links with the rest of China. Furthermore, the pace of industrialization in the prefecture after 1949 was also fast. Gross industrial output value, measured at 1980 prices, rose from 12m. *yuan* in 1952 to 81m. by 1965, and to 316m. by 1978—amounting to an annual growth rate between the two endpoints of 13 per cent (SCZL, 1990: 376–7). In large measure, this process of industrialization was based upon the exploitation of Liangshan's abundant natural resources. The raw material/semi-finished processing industry accounted for a further 14 per cent of total GVIO in 1978 and, within light industry, 78 per cent of output in 1978 was based upon the use of agricultural inputs. Even more remarkable was the growth of mining. In 1952, mining accounted for only about 0.2 per cent of GVIO. By 1978, and as a result of an annual growth of 37 per cent during the preceding 26 years, the share of the mining sector had climbed to reach one-third of the total.

Nevertheless, Liangshan's physical infrastructure lagged well behind the other three prefectures. The position in respect of transport is set out in Table 11.2. These data are difficult to interpret because of definitional problems. It is rarely the case that a 'road suitable for vehicles' is properly defined in Chinese publications.[2] For some counties, narrow unmetalled routes are no doubt included and in others they are probably excluded, while the difference between the quality of the modern carriageways increasingly constructed in areas like the Chengdu plain in the 1980s and the mountain tracks of Liangshan is too obvious to require discussion. In addition, it is not clear whether every road—including dirt tracks linking communes to the main roads—is included in the data. In any case, the density measure adopted in this table is manifestly a crude one; and the data are not properly comparable because they refer to different years.[3] Nevertheless, Liangshan's backwardness in the early 1980s is plain. With 9 square km of area for every 1 km of road, the density of the network was well below the figure for every other area listed. Moreover, these figures probably understate the degree of backwardness of Liangshan's road network. The official data suggest that in 1980, for example, only 547 km of road were metalled in the prefecture and around one-third of communes were still not connected to the prefecture's road network (LYZG, 1985: 245). Furthermore, many of these routes were anything but safe; 150 people died and four villages were transformed into a sea of mud as the result of a landslide in Meigu county in June 1997 (SCMP, 10 June 1997).

TABLE 11.2. *Road transport density in the 1980s*

Prefecture	Surface area (km^2)	Road network (km)	Ratio
Liangshan (1980)	63,000	6,978	9.0
Wenjiang (1991)	9,806	3,958	2.5
Wenzhou (1980)	11,784	1,795	6.6
Suzhou (1984)	13,138	2,191	6.0

Notes: Inconsistencies have been removed wherever possible but (as discussed in the main text) it is extremely unlikely that the definition of what constitutes a road is consistent across locations. The Wenjiang figure of course exaggerates the position in the early 1980s but data are hard to obtain. By way of direct evidence, the ratio of area to roads for Guanghan—one of the most developed counties—was 3.7 in 1977 (*Guanghan xian zhi*, 1992: 1, 206). This suggests that the road density for the prefecture in total must have been between 4 and 5 in 1980.

Sources: *Wenzhou cidian* (1995: 626); Wenzhou tongjiju (1985: 13); Jiangsu sheng jingji dili (1993: 350); SCTJNJ (1993: 134–5); LYZG (1985: 1, 245).

More significantly for economic development, road transport was the only practical form of transport for goods in most parts of Liangshan (the main exception was the Anning valley, which was served by the Chengdu–Kunming railway). By contrast, other prefectures could rely heavily on water transport. In Wenjiang prefecture on the Chengdu plain, water transport has long been important even though the area is outside what Skinner (1964–5) called the province's central riverine zone. In both Wenzhou and Suzhou, much freight and passenger traffic is carried by water. Of Wenzhou's nine counties, six are coastal and a seventh (Yongjia) is on the Oujiang River which divides the prefecture in two. As for Suzhou, the length of the road network is thoroughly misleading as a guide to the extent of the transport network. The prefecture can not only rely upon a vast network of canals, water transportation across Lake Tai and the main railway line between Nanjing and Shanghai, but also upon the great Yangzi waterway. In many of these counties, the network of waterways was as extensive as the road network; even Wujiang, which is not on the Yangzi, shipped 90 per cent of freight by water in the mid-1980s (JSSXGK, 1989: 517). None of these options exist in Liangshan, where navigable waterways are scarce; in particular, only short stretches of the Jinsha River are navigable west of the town of Xinshi. In fact, the only significant 'export' trade of the prefecture was in timber, which was either transported north along the Anning valley or overland to Xinshi *zhen* and then via the Yangzi River.[4]

Liangshan's industrial infrastructure in 1980 was also limited compared to Wenjiang, Wenzhou, and Suzhou, at least if its level of per capita production is any indication (Table 11.3).[5]

TABLE 11.3. *Per capita industrial output by prefecture in 1980*

Prefecture	NVIO per capita (1990 *yuan*)
Liangshan	92
Wenzhou	164
Wenjiang	181
Suzhou	517

Notes: Industrial output is on a GDP basis. 1980 population for Wenjiang and Liangshan estimated by back projecting the 1981 natural growth rates reported in the 1982 Population Census. The output data are somewhat problematic because officially reported Chinese figures at the county and city level frequently omit the output of enterprises managed directly by national ministries and the provincial government. For example, the county data given in SCZL for 1988 omit about 36 per cent of total provincial GVIO. Fortunately, this problem is far more significant for China's large cities—where most of these omitted enterprises are to be found—than for counties. Nevertheless, these omissions make comparisons between prefectures imprecise.

Sources: SCZL (1990); Wenzhou tongjiju (1985: 126); Jiangsu tongjiju (1989: 394); Population Census Office (1987).

At 92 *yuan* per capita in 1980, Liangshan's industrial output lagged well behind the 164 and 181 *yuan* figures recorded by Wenzhou and Wenjiang respectively. Compared to Suzhou, where industrial production averaged over 500 *yuan* per head, Liangshan was massively underdeveloped. Perhaps more significantly, as noted previously, total industrial output in Wuxi city alone was over five times higher than in the whole of Liangshan.[6]

To be sure, these sorts of comparisons exaggerate the industrial underdevelopment of Liangshan. In particular, it is reasonable to question the quality of the extensive industrial base that was inherited by Suzhou (in particular) in 1980. Although it is true that the figures on GVIO are impressive, it is more questionable whether the prices used to value the output are a reasonable proxy for the (social) marginal cost of production. This problem was particularly acute in the *wuxiaogong* (five small industries). A considerable proportion of these were inefficient in both economic and technical respects, and many were closed in a national programme of restructuring in the early 1980s (Wong, 1982; 1989; 1991*a*; 1991*c*; Ho, 1994). In Kunshan county, for instance, only 11 of the 59 larger *xiang* and *cun* enterprises operating in 1987 had been founded before 1976, a clear indication of the difficulties encountered by many of the early rural industries (*Kunshan xian zhi*, 1990: 302–15). In Wuxi, 40 per cent of factory equipment stood idle in 1980 (*People's Daily*, cited in Leeming, 1985: 116).

Even so, it is hard to believe that these considerations should lead us to conclude that the 'object gap' between Suzhou and Liangshan prefectures was an illusion. Although rural industry was 'inefficient' on a number of criteria, there is some evidence that the problem was less acute in Suzhou than elsewhere in 1980. In Wuxi county, for example, the number of *cun* industries dropped by only about 8 per cent between 1980 and 1982 (the nadir of the restructuring programme) and the number of *xiang*-level industries actually rose over the same period. Furthermore, and despite the closure programme, *cun* GVIO (at current prices) increased by 12 per cent over the same period in Wuxi (WXGY, 1990: 28–9). In other words, the problems of rural industry in Suzhou were not deemed so acute as to warrant wholesale closure of the enterprises. In short, the essential conclusion remains: an immense gulf existed in capital stock between the most prosperous areas of eastern China and the prefectures of the western hinterland in 1980. Moreover, given the transport problems that afflicted areas like Liangshan, the scope for rapid industrialization in such prefectures was manifestly limited in the 1980s whatever the best intentions of local government.

1.3. Inherited Human Capital

Liangshan was also constrained at the beginning of the 1980s by its limited endowment of human capital. This is very apparent from the 1982 Census data on literacy rates (Table 11.4).

TABLE 11.4. *Literacy rates by prefecture in 1982*
(illiterates aged 15 and over as a percentage of total population aged 15 and over)

Prefecture	Illiteracy rate
Liangshan	36.6
Suzhou	22.0
Wenjiang	17.8
Wenzhou	26.5

Note: To be classified as literate, a person needed to know 1,500 characters, be able to read a newspaper, and be capable of writing a short note in either Chinese or their own language.
Source: Population Census Office (1987).

With an illiteracy rate of about 37 per cent, Liangshan was obviously disadvantaged compared to the other prefectures. Although this figure may exaggerate illiteracy because of Census procedures—it remains unclear whether ethnic minorities literate in their own language, but not in standard Chinese, were classified as literates or not[7] —there is no doubt that Liangshan lagged well behind. Moreover, these data probably understate the true level of disadvantage faced in poor areas of western China because they take no account of the technical and other skills possessed by the workforce. This is particularly true for Suzhou. Although the literacy rate there was rather low at the beginning of the 1980s given the high level of per capita income, the levels of skills possessed by the workforce was relatively much higher. This was because of the long history of industrialization in the Suzhou area.[8] Handicraft and proto-industry was well established there in the late Ming and early Qing periods (Xu and Wu, forthcoming; Li, 1986). After 1895, modern industry also began to be established, producing goods such as cotton, silk, and cigarettes. Wuxi county is of course the best example of this early rural industrialization. By 1930, 315 factories existed and its industrial production (nearly 2 per cent of the *national* total) was second only to Shanghai and Guangzhou; as a result it gained the sobriquet 'little Shanghai' (WXGY, 1990: 5). By the 1930s, about 12 per cent of the workforce was employed in modern industry; there were 170 modern factories in Wuxi county alone, employing 60,000 workers on the eve of the 1932 depression (JIH, 1933: 107). The majority of these workers (37,000) were employed in silk filatures and a further 14,000 were employed in cotton spinning. In neighbouring Suzhou county, modern industry was much less well developed; however, proto-industry was well established with some 10,000 workers employed in the county's famous embroidery sector alone (JIH, 1933: 47, 114–15).

From the perspective of the 1980s, what was important about this early industrialization in Sunan was not the plant and equipment that was set up, but rather the body of skills that were acquired in the process and which could be handed down to later generations. Of course some of this human capital was lost during

World War II, and many of the capitalists fled to Hong Kong or Taiwan. Nevertheless, the base was extensive enough to make it a comparatively easy matter to resurrect rural industry during the Maoist era; even in 1949, and despite the exodus, there were 1,353 industrial enterprises in Wuxi (WXGY, 1990: 5). Furthermore, the advantages of a family tradition in handicraft production were evident in the 1980s. One estimate suggests that women from traditional silk-weaving families in the silk centre of Shengze picked up the skills needed to go into independent production four or five times faster than those with different backgrounds (Ju and Wu, 1986: 305). Finally, many rural enterprises acted as subcontractors for large urban enterprises in Shanghai and this placed a higher premium on product quality than would otherwise have been the case.[9] In some towns, the proportion of rural enterprises linked in this way was around 70 per cent in the late 1970s (Lee, 1991: 142).

In Wenzhou, too, there was a history of modern industrialization dating back to the designation of the town (then called Yongjia) as a Treaty Port in 1876. Hand in hand with this industrialization came a corresponding legacy of skills. It is true that the bulk of the industrial workforce in the 1930s was employed in proto-industry. The straw-mat industry, for example, employed about 70,000 workers in the late 1920s, and the straw-hat industry employed a further 65,000; a further 8,000 workers were employed in paper production and, although the level of employment is not known, the rattan and bamboo products sector produced about one-third of provincial output (ZIH, 1935: 635–6, 685–7, 705). The production of paper umbrellas was also centred in Wenzhou; output was over 50 per cent of the provincial total. Other important proto-industries in Wenzhou in the inter-war years included candle making, knitted goods, lace, rice milling, wine, tea, and sugar. But, and very significantly, many of these enterprises were *genuine* proto-industries in that their production was increasingly orientated towards national and even international markets; for example, Wenzhou exported no less than 3.4 million umbrellas in 1931 alone. The prefecture's increasingly export orientation had of course much to do with the growth of the port of Wenzhou, which was handling more trade than either Ningbo or Hangzhou in the late 1930s (ZIH, 1935: 63, 708–11, 720).

Perhaps even more importantly, some relatively modern industries had begun to establish themselves in Wenzhou by the late 1920s. Power plants had been set up in four of the prefecture's counties by 1928, a telephone system was in operation and, crucially, about 80 modern factories were operating there. Of these, the 18 cotton mills were perhaps the most important; they employed some 1,250 workers. Yet what is perhaps most remarkable was the relative diversity of the modern industrial base. China's first condensed-milk factory was established in Rui'an county in 1924, and this was but one part of the region's canning industry. Four factories specialized in machinery production, and although straw-mat production was dominated by proto-industry, over 1,000 workers were employed in modern factories, a figure far in excess of anywhere else in the province. Other important modern industries in Wenzhou included matches, and the bleaching, dyeing, and printing of cotton fabrics (ZIH, 1935: 131, 489, 517–18, 607, 612, 665, 671).

It is of course easy to exaggerate the importance of this skills legacy in Suzhou and Wenzhou. To repeat, a considerable proportion of workers died during World War II,[10] and some skills atrophied during the Maoist era. Furthermore, there is no necessary link between proto-industrialization and the emergence of modern industry; the European evidence in particular suggests that a vibrant proto-industrial sector was neither a necessary still less a sufficient condition for an industrial revolution (Ogilvie, 1993).[11] Nevertheless, it is hard to believe that this pre-revolutionary industrial legacy did not contribute to the rapid industrialization of the 1980s in China's eastern provinces. Although western regions like Liangshan did possess handicraft industries, they produced a narrow range of goods and did no more than supply the needs of local markets.[12] In particular, there was no modern industry nor any manufacturing apart from food processing. Perhaps more importantly, the industrial skills that had been acquired in Wenzhou and Wuxi were by no means destroyed during the Maoist era. To be sure, the pattern of industrialization changed, and Maoist proscriptions against private services and commerce undoubtedly led to an erosion of some of the skills important to the functioning of a market economy. Nevertheless, the emphasis placed throughout the period between 1949 and 1978 on the development of industry ensured the availability of a large industrial workforce in parts of eastern China. What the Maoist development strategy did not do—despite the resources channelled into the Third Front—was to create an industrial proletariat in many of the regions of western China.

TABLE 11.5. *The share of industrial employment in total employment by prefecture, 1982* (per cent)

Prefecture	Median industry share	Highest county	Lowest county
Suzhou	33.3	Wuxi city (68.0)	Kunshan (21.8)
Wenzhou	32.9	Wenzhou city (63.7)	Taishun (21.9)
Wenjiang	8.6	Shifang (15.9)	Pujiang (4.9)
Liangshan	3.2	Xichang city (29.7)	Jinyang (1.0)

Note: Data are taken from the 1982 Population Census results.
Source: Population Census Office (1987).

As Table 11.5 illustrates, the gulf between regions like Wenzhou and Wuxi on the one hand and even the prosperous agricultural areas of western China such as Wenjiang in terms of the share of industrial employment was vast. While only about 9 per cent of Wenjiang's working population was employed in industry in 1982, the figures recorded in Suzhou and Wenzhou both stood at 33 per cent. In Liangshan, the position was even worse. Industrial employment amounted to only 3 per cent of the total; in three counties, it was below 2 per cent. This limited industrial workforce inevitably made it difficult for Liangshan to begin the transition to industrialization.

1.4. The Role of Culture in Liangshan

It is also important to consider whether cultural factors help to explain Liangshan's poor growth rate. Liangshan is, for example, very different in cultural terms from the other three prefectures in having a large ethnic minority population. Extensive in-migration by Han Chinese settlers has occurred throughout the post-1949 period. This led to a large concentration of Han Chinese in the Anning river valley (especially around Xichang) and at Dukou; this latter, associated with the development of coal and steel production at Panzhihua, led ultimately to the creation of a separate municipality. There was also substantial migration into some of the counties in the eastern part of Liangshan, notably Leibo; as a result, Han Chinese were a majority in the prefecture by the 1980s. Nevertheless, a very large fraction of the population was still ethnic—44 per cent according to the 1982 Census (Liu, 1988: 324). The figure was much higher in some counties; in Meigu, there were only 5,500 Han out of a total population of 130,000 (LYZG, 1985: 354, 363), and the comparable figure was 14,000 out of 185,000 in Zhaojue.[13] By contrast, Wenzhou, Suzhou, and Wenjiang are almost exclusively Han regions.

Many Chinese writers have argued that the Yi culture found in Liangshan was a constraint on economic development; this is very obvious in the titles of some of the ethnographies of the region (for example, 'Emerging from Primitivity') and the use of the word *Lolo* (barbarian) to describe the Yi.[14] These arguments derive from the (alleged) persistence of slavery in the early twentieth century, religious superstition, opposition to commerce, high levels of alcohol consumption, and the comparative isolation of the region from the impact of modernity that affected so much of eastern and central China. More generally, there is a perception in most of the Chinese literature that the economic problems of ethnic minority areas throughout China (including Tibet) are primarily cultural in origin, rather than a consequence of resource constraints or transport deficiencies; a classic text in this respect is Wang and Bai (1991). All these Chinese writers have been heavily influenced by Stalin's ideas on ethnic minorities, the Marxist notion of historical materialism, and the writings of Morgan and Engels. Their theories have therefore been firmly teleological. There is a basic assumption that the economies of ethnic minority regions will inevitably make the transition from the slave social formation to socialism. However, because these areas lag behind Han regions, the extent of their progress will depend upon the degree to which they assimilate the values of Han civilization. Liangshan's problem from this perspective is therefore the lack of willingness of the Yi to accept Han values. As Harrell (1995: 82) points out: 'according to official histories, Liangshan was still in the slave stage of society in 1950 while Yi areas in Yunnan and Guizhou had passed into feudalism hundreds of years ago.' But this perspective is not confined exclusively to Han Chinese writers; it was also the norm amongst Western visitors to the region before 1949 (Harrell, 1995: 71):

> . . . in the accounts of scientists, natural and social, we find an explicitly racialist paradigm, one that derives more from the scientific impulse of generalization and systemization than

from the intimate knowledge and desire to describe accurately that seems to have motivated the missionaries. For these scientists, beginning with Legendre and in rudimentary form even with Baber, the History of the Yi is the history of a race, built on a series of unexamined assumptions, probably part of the 'habitus' of Western culture, about the nature of ethnic or social groups.

It is of course immensely difficult to get to the bottom of the role played by inherited cultural factors in Liangshan's slow growth in the transition era. There is probably an element of Han chauvinism in many Chinese studies of Liangshan, as well as a willingness to engage in some rewriting of history; official Chinese proclamations about the status and history of Tibet make that very clear. Nevertheless, it is hard to escape the conclusion that the culture of Liangshan was much more resistant to the ideas of modernity than the culture of Han Chinese areas to the east.[15] Modernity was associated in the minds of ethnic minorities with Han colonization—and therefore summarily rejected in many cases. The result was that explosive ethnic tensions persisted throughout the 1980s and 1990s in the prefecture. Rightly or wrongly, the mistrust that exists between Han and Yi makes it very difficult to develop the long-distance trading links that are essential for economic growth. Yi children in Leibo, for example, take great delight in stoning buses filled with Han Chinese travelling through the area. That hardly facilitates trade, and without the regional specialization that trade makes possible, it is hard to see how Liangshan can exploit those economies of scale that exist.

These Han–Yi ethnic tensions are compounded by the absence of ethnic homogeneity amongst the non-Han population itself. Han Chinese ethnographers have long categorized the Yi as a distinctive racial group; indeed the Yi have the status of a national minority (*minzu*). But this neglects the profound cultural and linguistic differences between those labelled Yi, yet living in different communities across south-west China. In particular, there is no common Yi language. The main language is spoken by between 20 and 42 per cent of the population, but there are five other main dialects, and all are mutually unintelligible (Harrell, 1995: 63). This does not act as much of a barrier to short-distance trade where a common language is the norm, but long-distance trade is an entirely different matter. Moreover, many of those people categorized by Han ethnographers as Yi do not see themselves as having much in common. The *shuitian* people of Panzhihua, for example, see themselves as very different from the 'barbarian' Yi who live in the Zhaojue area (Harrell, 1995: 65). The same is true for other ethnic groups in south-west China. Thus those people living in the Yongning-Lugu Lake area are officially classified as Naxi *minzu* but regard themselves as Mosuo and therefore as very different from the Naxi people of Lijiang (McKhann, 1995: 53–62). More generally, the ethnic diversity of those living in counties on the fringes of Tibet like Muli is dramatic; the cultural differences between (say) the Yi, Pumi, and Tibetan populations cannot simply be ignored in thinking about the promotion of economic development in these areas.

Liangshan society was also very different from that of Han areas before 1949. There was a distinct hierarchy running from the Black Yi (nobility) through the White Yi (farm owners), Ajia (farm labourers) to the Xiaxi (slaves), with the latter making up more than 50 per cent of the population (Bramall, 1993: 230–1); income differentials between these groups were enormous, perhaps in the order of 100 to 1. The persistence of slavery marked Liangshan out from the comparatively more 'advanced' Han areas. A third problem is that modernization in eastern China in many respects left the culture of Liangshan (and many other isolated ethnic minority areas) untouched. In large measure, this reflected the geographical isolation of the region (as has been seen). The region was not untouched by the Maoist drive towards modernization. Urban intellectuals and youth were 'sent down' to live in areas like Muli and Shimian during the Cultural Revolution, and built schools whilst they were there. Many convicts found themselves despatched to labour camps in Liangshan, and employed there in infrastructural construction, especially those associated with the development of agricultural production in the Anning river valley (Endicott, 1988). But the impact of modernization was exceptionally slow because of the absence of transport links and electrification. Moreover, collectivization—the Maoist institutional innovation most destructive of traditional cultures—occurred very late in western Sichuan. Land reform was not completed there until 1957, and collectivization proper did not occur until the mid-1960s (Bramall, 1993: 300). As a result, its impact was necessarily transient.

In short, there is some evidence that culture factors help to explain differences in growth rates between Chinese prefectures after 1978. The limited impact of capitalism before 1949, the relatively limited impact of the Maoist modernization drive, and extensive Han in-migration all served to slow Liangshan's economic development.

2. Surplus Labour

We have noted earlier that Sachs and Woo (1994) explain China's unusual achievement in generating rapid growth during the transition period in terms of the abundance of surplus labour to be found in the People's Republic in the late 1970s. It was argued in Chapter 7, that this argument was not very convincing. Surplus labour was created by the transition policies, and that which was absorbed by rural and urban industry, may actually have depressed industrial productivity. Moreover, in so far as labour was absorbed by the industrial sector, it was absorbed by low-productivity industrial sectors. To what extent does this conclusion also apply in the case of the four prefectures? Does surplus labour and its release help to explain the difference in the growth rates of the prefectures?

2.1. Surplus Labour in Suzhou

In fact, the Lewis model does not carry much conviction as an explanation of the relatively faster growth rate achieved in Suzhou because of the wealth of evidence suggesting that the extent of surplus labour in that region was limited—such that, if anything, growth was *constrained* by labour shortages. Some evidence on this is presented in Table 11.6.

TABLE 11.6. *Proximate indicators of surplus labour, 1982*

Prefecture	Share of labour in agriculture (%)	Participation rate (%)	Labour productivity (*yuan*)
Suzhou	49	65	985
Wenjiang	82	57	483
Wenzhou	53	40	528
Liangshan	86	51	316

Notes: The participation rate is the share of the workforce aged 15 and over in total population. Data on labour productivity are median values for real NVIAO per worker in 1980 constant prices.

Sources: Population Census Office (1987).

Three indicators of surplus labour are provided in this table, and by all three Suzhou fares badly. As was argued earlier, surplus labour is typically found in the agricultural sector. However, the share of agricultural in total employment in Suzhou during the late 1970s was much smaller than on the Chengdu plain, Wenzhou, or Liangshan prefecture. By Chinese standards, in fact, the Suzhou region was highly industrialized. The participation rate tells a similar story. Whereas only 40 per cent of Wenzhou's population was employed, the figure for Suzhou was an exceptionally high 65 per cent. This was well above the Chinese average of 52 per cent (Population Census Office, 1987: 90). Moreover, if one expresses the working population aged fifteen and over as a percentage of the population aged 15 and over (rather than as a percentage of total population), the level of participation in the Suzhou region was truly remarkable. For the nine counties and two cities that comprised the region, the average participation rate was 85 per cent. In Changshu county, the rate was 90 per cent and in Taicang it was 92 per cent. Furthermore, this calculation makes no allowance for the inability of a considerable proportion of the population aged over 65 to work at all due to age-related disabilities. In other words, the data for Suzhou suggest that almost the entire population aged 15 or over and capable of work was in fact working. Nor do the data on labour productivity suggest an abundance of surplus labour in Suzhou; by Chinese standards, industry was operating at high levels of productivity, and land productivity in the prefecture was impressive even by world standards. For example, the average rice yield in Songjiang in 1975–9 was 5.2 tonnes per hectare (Huang, 1990: 224), not far below the Japanese average of 5.7 tonnes for 1976–80 (Barker and Herdt, 1985: 47). In Kunshan, rice yields were even higher at 6.6 tonnes per hectare (*Kunshan xian zhi*, 1990: 195).

However, the argument is not that there was *no* surplus labour in Suzhou in the early 1980s, only that its extent was actually rather limited. That it existed is clear for a number of reasons. In deciding on whether Suzhou had surplus labour, the key issue is not whether its agricultural labour force was fully mobilized or (notionally) fully employed but, in W. A. Lewis's words, whether its marginal productivity was 'low, zero or even negative'. We have seen in Table 11.6 that agricultural labour productivity was high by Chinese standards, but the far more relevant question is whether Suzhou's agricultural sector was efficient in an absolute sense; that is, was it operating close to—or well below—its production possibility frontier? One clear piece of evidence that Suzhou was well *below* this frontier comes from the fact that a large proportion of the workforce was employed in triple cropping (Huang, 1990: 222–8; Leeming, 1985: 110–14; Powell, 1992: 102–10). Triple cropping typically involved two crops of rice grown between late April and mid-November, combined with a winter crop of wheat, barley, or rapeseed. It was pioneered in some parts of Suzhou during the 1950s, but was promoted with messianic zeal only after the late 1960s. This increase in the multiple cropping index led to a direct increase in labour demand for tasks such as rice transplanting and fertilizing. The shift to triple cropping increased the demand for labour for another reason. It is true that triple cropping is technically feasible; the growing season in the Suzhou area is 165 days, and the varieties of the late 1970s needed between 160 and 170 days to be grown successfully. But the schedule was remarkable tight and therefore it was absolutely imperative that the entire labour force was mobilized for the task.

The increase in the demand for labour as a consequence of triple cropping was considerable. According to data cited in Leeming (1985: 113), the input of labour days after the introduction of triple cropping rose to 12,540 per 100 *mu* compared to 7,150 under double cropping. According to Powell (1992: 109), the demand for labour increased by about 46 per cent per *mu* between 1966 and 1978. Zu (1985: 242) gives an increase of 45 per cent in the volume of labour days required to produce 50 kg of rice for Jiangsu as a whole between 1965 and 1977. Moreover, between 1965 and 1977, the volume of required labour inputs per *mu* increased from 41 to 66 labour days (Zu, 1985: 246). In fact, the increase in labour demand was so large that it was only the introduction of labour-saving technology—the tractor—that made double cropping of rice a possibility. According to Huang (1990: 225):

> The double-cropping of rice was not tried on a large scale again [CMB: in Songjiang county] until tractor plowing was introduced in the mid-1960s. Just as in North China, it was a labor-saving device, ironically, that permitted further labor intensification in the form of increased frequency of cropping.

In short, it was the introduction of triple cropping in Suzhou which had the effect of ensuring a participation rate of close to 100 per cent for the able-bodied workforce by the late 1970s.

The problem, however, with triple cropping in the particular case of Suzhou was that it used labour in a very inefficient and low-productivity way. Although triple cropping spread rapidly during the 1970s, it was not very popular, and for the good reason that it required greater inputs of labour and of fertilizer. To be sure, the combined yield of early and late rice was typically 20 per cent higher than that of a single crop of middle rice, but this yield differential was not large enough to make the shift to triple cropping profitable. The clearest evidence on this comes from the decline in the value of a labour day. Figures given in Leeming (1985: 113) suggest a decline of 17 per cent in Songjiang county between 1966 and 1976. Huang

(1990: 239) gives a not dissimilar trend. All this is reflected in the popular sayings of farmers during these years on the relative merits of double and triple cropping. In Kunshan, the usual refrain was 'three times three is nine, which is inferior to two times five equals ten' (*sansan de jiu, bu ru erwu de shi*) (*Kunshan xian zhi*, 1990: 194). Further evidence of the unpopularity of triple cropping comes from the events of the early 1980s, by which time the initial rural reforms of the late 1970s had given the population much greater latitude over cropping patterns. In Jiangsu in general, and in Suzhou in particular, the result was a sharp decline in triple cropping. Labour inputs per 50 kg of rice declined by 11 per cent in Jiangsu between 1975–7 and 1978–80 alone (Zu, 1985: 243). For Suzhou as a whole, the area given over to triple cropping declined by 26 per cent between 1976 and 1981 (Powell, 1992: 110). In Kunshan county, triple cropping had been virtually abandoned (*wuji*) by 1984 (*Kunshan xian zhi*, 1990: 194).

In short, labour productivity in triple cropping was low. There was a positive yield effect, but only at the expense of a reduction in the average value of the labour day. Crucially—this being the calculation made by Suzhou's farmers at the beginning of the 1980s—the marginal productivity of labour engaged in triple cropping fell well short of the marginal productivity of labour employed in other agricultural activities or in rural industry. Furthermore, the balance was tipped even further in the direction of the non-farm sector by the arduous nature of the work involved in rice production.[16] All this seems to be confirmed by the explosion of non-farm employment during the 1970s and (especially) the 1980s, when the rural population of Suzhou opted in increasing numbers to abandon grain production. The demands of triple cropping did not prevent the expansion of the industrial sector in the 1970s. In Wuxi county, for example, the industrial workforce in all types of industry totalled 46,521 in 1970. By 1978, and despite the spread of triple cropping, the industrial workforce had risen to 120,778, an annual rate of increase of 12.7 per cent; after 1978, the process accelerated.

This conclusion that the productivity of labour employed in triple cropping was low in Suzhou is not materially altered by the fact that the prices paid by the Chinese government for procured grain were well below their shadow price before 1979. Now there is no doubt that shadow prices were higher than procurement prices in the late 1970s. As many have argued, the intersectoral terms of the late 1970s were systematically skewed against agriculture. To put the situation more concretely, the price of chemical fertilizer (the main input) was 'too high' and the price of grain (the chief output) sold to the state was 'too low'. The increase in procurement prices in 1979 reduced the extent of this unequal exchange, but it was not eliminated entirely. Only the use of an increasingly large proportion of the profits made by rural industry to subsidize agriculture (the policy of *yigong punong*) ensured that the net level of resource extraction from agriculture was held down. As Sheng (1993: 170–1) says:

> There were persistent resources extracted from agriculture into non-agriculture through [the] price mechanisms throughout the period 1952–83; meanwhile, there were persistent net financial transfers from non-agriculture to agriculture in 1956–83. These transfers partly returned

> the extracted resources to agriculture. In the period 1979–83, the returned resources may compensate for a large part of the extracted resources.
>
> Though changes in the terms of trade were in favour of agriculture throughout the period 1952–83, the state purchase price of agricultural products had been lower than the real price. In other words, the improvement is not as big as required . . . the Chinese government has repeatedly attempted to correct the distorted price structure in recent years, but such efforts have not been successful.

One can also very reasonably argue that there were high social benefits (positive externalities) from increased grain production in the context of the 1970s. On the one hand, it is clear that there remained a need for raising per capita production. To be sure, direct consumption demands were essentially satisfied by the early 1980s, but there remained an urgent need to increase output in order to expand the production of dairy and meat products. On the other hand, China could not afford to rely upon grain imports. The strategic 'threat' posed by the United States had diminished following Nixon's visit in the early 1970s, and the progressive normalization of relations. But heavy grain imports would shift the terms of trade against China. That did not matter in the sense that it was possible for China to generate the required export earnings by increasing her production of light consumer goods. But the strategy involved clear potential costs in that it would make China exceedingly vulnerable to both fluctuations in world grain production and to any drift towards protection measures directed against Chinese manufactured exports. Much the same argument applies to chemical fertilizer production.

It follows from this analysis that the prevailing late Maoist price structure made little sense except as a way of financing defence industrialization (Bramall, 1993). The price paid for grain by the state was below both the world and Chinese market price when, in fact, there was a case for paying a price above the market price because of the positive externalities generated by grain production. In other words, the shadow price for grain was well above the actual price in the late 1970s. Additionally, if this price is used to calculate the marginal productivity of labour in rural Suzhou, one obtains a rather different result from that discussed above; a lower chemical fertilizer price and a higher grain price clearly increases the marginal productivity of labour. The importance of prices is obvious from the impact of the abrupt shift in the intersectoral terms of trade in 1979. This had the effect of delaying the abandonment of what was the inferior technology of triple cropping; by raising farm profits (and therefore the value of the labour day), the shift in the terms of trade made triple cropping more profitable than it would otherwise have been. It is perhaps for this reason that, although the proportion of area given over to a single crop of middle rice rose in Songjiang county from 3.2 per cent in 1977 to 22 per cent in 1981, it fell back thereafter to only 17 per cent in 1984 (Huang, 1990: 226–7).

Nevertheless, even after making due allowance for the 'distorted' late Maoist price structure and the likelihood of positive externalities in grain production, it remains hard to argue that Suzhou's agricultural labour force was operating at anything close to its potential productivity under the triple cropping regime. Triple cropping only made sense if the prices paid for grain sold to the state were far above those that prevailed in Jiangsu even in the early 1980s.[17] Labour productivity (and income) was still far higher in the non-farm sector, and this led to a growing exodus from the grain sector in Suzhou (and also in both Wenjiang and Wenzhou).

Furthermore, Suzhou's agriculture suffered from the same incentive problems as other Chinese regions. One can argue about the relative importance of the price structure and collective farming in adversely affecting labour productivity in agriculture, but few claim that price changes *of themselves* would have entirely eliminated the problem of weak incentives. As even supporters of the collective farm have admitted, Chinese farmers had an incentive to maximize their time allocation (and thus maximizing their workpoint earnings) but not their effort allocation. Philip Huang's work suggests that a low level of labour intensity was very much the norm in the counties of the Yangzi delta despite the gradual absorption of labour by rural industry in the 1970s. This 'loitering work' (*langdong gong*) typically meant that jobs took about a third longer to complete in the late Maoist period than they did in the 1980s (Huang, 1990: 219–21). Nevertheless, and as was noted earlier, much of Suzhou's labour was not surplus in the sense that it could be removed from the countryside during the entire year. According to Huang (1990: 214):

> In brigade enterprises close to home, workers typically work only five to seven hours a day; in the busy farming periods, they spend four hours a day on agriculture. In commune enterprises farther away, workers typically work eight-hour days and spend only two or three hours in agriculture during the busy periods.

We should nevertheless be clear that the productivity of Suzhou's agricultural labour force was not zero. Accordingly, the transfer of labour out of farming and into rural industry could have raised *total* GDP, but only at the cost of lower grain production. This is confirmed by the trend in production in Suzhou after 1978 (Table 11.7). In almost all of these counties, grain output shows a trend decline between 1978 and 1996. Only in Suzhou city was the increase significant, but much of that reflected boundary changes and, in any case, the city's contribution to overall output was so small that the increase had no more than a trivial effect upon the output of the region. In consequence, the data for the region as a whole show an annual output decline of about 0.3 per cent per year after 1978. To be sure, the trend was gradually being reversed at the end of the 1980s. Output was well above the nadir of 1981 (when it fell to 3.5m. tonnes), and the reversal would be more apparent but for the impact of severe flooding on the 1991 harvest. However, the resumption of rapid growth after 1991 had adverse effects on grain production with the result that output was about 10 per cent lower in 1994 than it had been in 1990. Even as a result of the modest rises in production seen in 1995 and 1996, total grain output in 1996 was still below the level achieved in the late 1970s. The *best*, therefore, that can be said of grain production in Suzhou prefecture over the course of the transition era is that it stagnated. That this is in such marked contrast to the clear rise in production that occurred in the 1970s reflects the positive contribution of the rural labour force to grain production during that decade.

TABLE 11.7. *Grain production in Suzhou, 1978–1996*

County	Grain Output (000 tonnes)						Growth rate (% p.a.)
	1978	1982	1986	1990	1994	1996	1978–96
Wuxi city	35	23	11	8	5	58	−1.4
Suzhou city	35	25	20	49	49	141	+8.7
Jiangyin	553	467	426	445	418	458	−0.6
Yixing	542	648	656	579	547	576	−0.1
Xishan	632	582	529	508	476	455	−1.7
Zhangjiagang	346	311	323	310	302	354	neg.
Changshu	564	512	529	511	491	521	−0.1
Taicang	298	271	276	281	281	300	+0.4
Kunshan	467	456	455	474	424	455	neg.
Wuxian	707	683	661	677	526	557	−0.8
Wujiang	527	553	519	533	456	463	−0.7
TOTAL	4,704	4,530	4,405	4,374	3,976	4,370	−0.3

Note: County outputs do not sum to the total because of rounding. The sharp rises in output in Wuxi and Suzhou cities reflect boundary changes.

Sources: Jiangsu tongjiju (1989: 401–2); ZGFX (1991: 55–9; 1992: 55–9); Jiangsu tongjiju (1992: 49–50); ZGNCTJNJ (1994: 468–70; 1995: 446–8); Suzhou tongjiju (1996: 469, 473); JSTJNJ (1997: 352–3).

In summary, the extent of surplus labour in Suzhou at the end of the 1970s was probably not very different from elsewhere in China. The expansion of rural industry and, far more importantly, the propagation of triple cropping in the late Maoist period had led to exceptionally high participation rates and to the disappearance of open unemployment, with virtually the entire able-bodied population employed in some form of economic activity. It is therefore possible to argue that Suzhou's farm labour force was not 'surplus' at all in the mid-1970s if one believes that a very high shadow price should be attached to grain production to reflect China's strategic isolation and a level of grain production little better than subsistence—hence providing a justification for triple cropping. But the dwindling of the external threat in the late 1970s, increases in grain production stemming from the use of chemical fertilizer and new seed varieties, and the shift in the internal terms of trade towards agriculture in 1979 make that line of argument untenable by the early 1980s. With Suzhou suffering from the same problem of shirking under the commune system as other parts of China and full employment only ensured by triple cropping, it is clear that a substantial labour surplus did exist.

But where Suzhou did differ from the rest of China was in having a much faster rate of growth of demand for labour in *xiangzhen* enterprises. In fact, the evidence suggests that Suzhou's growth was increasingly constrained as the transition era wore on by labour shortages. To be sure, there was enough labour to facilitate considerable rural enterprise growth. For example, Wuxi county expanded its industrial workforce from 120,778 in 1978 to 370,604 by 1988, a rate of increase far above that of population. By that time, some 60 per cent of the entire rural workforce was employed in *xiangzhen* industry (WXGY, 1990). But eventually, labour shortages set in. Indeed, these shortages had become so acute by the end of the 1980s that some 88,000 of Wuxi's workers came from outside the county (WXGY, 1990: 15, 28, 30). As Ho (1994: 67) notes:

> We have no reliable measure of underemployment in rural Jiangsu but the evidence suggests that while some rural underemployment continued to exist into the late 1980s, underemployment was much reduced. In fact, after a decade of rapid employment growth, labour was in short supply in some parts of rural Jiangsu.

In other words, surplus labour did exist in Suzhou in the early years of transition but not in sufficient quantities.[18] As a result—and very much contrary to the Sachs–Woo approach—the growth of the prefecture may have been constrained by labour shortages. These shortages were not a matter of grave concern; it was after all comparatively straightforward to attract migrants to Suzhou from other parts of China. But Suzhou's experience does cast a critical light on those theories which routinely assume that surplus labour always exists in developing countries.

2.2. Surplus Labour in Liangshan

Can we argue that Liangshan's growth was also constrained in the transition era by a lack of surplus labour? On the face of things, it seems not. As the data in Table 11.6 show, the region entered the reform era with all the advantages of backwardness. Her labour force participation rate was only 51 per cent, well below that for Suzhou. No less than 86 per cent of her population was employed in agriculture, where underemployment was widespread. Moreover, average labour productivity in agriculture and industry combined in 1982 was only 316 *yuan* per person, far below the level reached in Suzhou and not much more that half the level of labour productivity achieved in Wenzhou and on the Chengdu plain.

However, some of these indicators are misleading. Although growing conditions in the Anning river valley area of Liangshan are good, the region for the most part is characterized by poor soils and difficult, mountainous, terrain. These conditions inevitably depressed yields to levels well below those achieved in the rest of the province. For example, the grain yield in 1977 along the Anning valley was 351 *jin* per sown *mu* compared to a provincial mean of 376 *jin*. The yield for the remainder of Liangshan prefecture averaged only 277 *jin*, lower than the provincial mean and far below the norm on the Chengdu plain of 485 *jin* (ZKCDY, 1980: 139). In conditions such as these, it was inevitable that labour productivity in agriculture was much below the norm in and around Suzhou. Similarly, the mountainous topography of the Liangshan region imposed high costs on industry and thereby reduced industrial productivity. In a very real sense, therefore, labour productivity in Liangshan was low because of adverse physical geography, rather than because the labour force was being used inefficiently. The participation rate also says very little concrete about surplus labour. To be sure, it was well below Suzhou's but a rate of 51 per cent was barely to be distinguished from the national mean of 52 per cent. Moreover, this Chinese average—especially bearing in mind that this figure measures the workforce aged 15 and over as a percentage of the total population and therefore understates the true participation rate—is remarkably high by international standards and indicates an extensive degree of mobilization of the female population. In other words, the scope for increasing the labour force by pushing up the participation rate was limited in much of China by the late 1970s.

In point of fact, there is some evidence that suggests only a small labour surplus in Liangshan. The 1980 *Agricultural Geography* (ZKCDY) claimed, for example, that the area's population was too small relative to the area of arable land being cultivated (ZKCDY, 1980: 207):

> The region's population is small, its labour-power deficient and industry and transportation are backward—these are the major constraints on agricultural development. The rural population totals only 1.559 million and therefore each agricultural worker bears a heavy burden, being responsible for 4.64 *mu* of arable land and 3.6 animals, 55.7 per cent and 1.2 fold respectively higher than the provincial average. . . . quite a large proportion of communes and brigades still lack road communications and rely mainly on transportation by humans and animals, which uses a tremendous amount of agricultural labour power.

Moreover, an arable land supply per capita of 4.64 *mu* was in fact very close to what was regarded as optimal for the province in the mid-1980s (4.5 *mu*); in other words, the pervasive underemployment of labour caused by a high ratio of population to arable land in the rest of China did not apply in Liangshan. The need to use labour for transportation instead of farming was therefore a clear problem, not least because labour was being used to transport indispensable commodities such as water. In Leibo county, for example, there were some 80 production teams suffering from desperate water shortages at the end of the 1970s. In order to obtain enough drinking water for themselves and their livestock, some 49 per cent of the labour force was employed solely in the task of carrying water (LYZG, 1985: 201). Across Liangshan, but especially in counties close to Leibo such as Jinyang, Huili, and Meigu, some 148,000 people were in similar straits.

This evidence of labour shortages is supported by the efforts made by the provincial government to promote in-migration in the Maoist period. Liangshan was a significant beneficiary (Liu, 1988: 168–71). During the period of Third Front construction, and largely in order to construct the new Chengdu–Kunming railway, there was a substantial influx of workers into the region. By the end of September 1964, for example, 53 new construction organizations had been set up employing over 48,000 workers. A further indication of labour shortages in Liangshan comes from the number of labour camps established there. There were four large camps run by the province within the region, as well as other camps run directly by Liangshan prefecture; many factories also used prison labour. The number of 'criminals' sent to Liangshan is given as more than 20,000 between 1951 and 1983 (Wenshi ziliao weiyuanhui, 1993: 38, 45–6). For some, this proved a blessing in that they were spared the starvation that affected eastern Sichuan during the early 1960s (Endicott, 1988: 61–4).

None of this is to imply that there was *no* surplus labour in Liangshan by the early 1980s. In some ways, in fact, the reality in Liangshan was not so very different from that in Suzhou. On the one hand, communal incentive systems depressed labour productivity. On the other hand, the labour force was misallocated. In Suzhou, too much of it was employed in multiple cropping; in Liangshan, it was mis-employed in transport. As soon, therefore, as collectives were abandoned and transport modernization began, the labour force was no longer even notionally employed. As a result, *surplus* labour was seen to be one of Liangshan's advantages in the early 1980s (Zhu, 1992: 170):

> Following the introduction of the production responsibility system, Liangshan has an abundance of surplus labour . . . This is a great boon (*da youshi*) for Liangshan and a source of great hope.

Nevertheless, the evidence does suggest that there was probably less surplus labour in Liangshan than in Suzhou. Much of the high demand for labour in the latter during the late 1970s derived from the use of the inappropriate technique of multiple cropping. It was an easy matter to abandon this technology and, once that had been done, the existence of surplus labour was very apparent. In Liangshan, as has been seen, it was no easy matter to reduce the demand for labour. Decollectivization of course helped by raising labour productivity. But it was exceptionally difficult (i.e. expensive) to modernize transport networks in order to release labour. Moreover, and given that transport problems precluded the development of industry (which might have used less labour than agriculture), the low ratio of population to arable land meant the lion's share of rural labour would have to be employed in farming in the foreseeable future. In the end, this left comparatively little surplus labour.

Whether this disadvantaged Liangshan very much remains a moot point. It certainly did not prevent the development of *xiangzhen* industry. The data on this show current price gross output value rising by 25 per cent per year between 1978 and 1985, which was not so very much below the provincial growth rate of 31 per cent (*Sichuan xiangzhen qiye shinian*, 1988: 84). Moreover, and as has been argued earlier, the transfer of labour to rural industry may have been a mixed blessing in that it depressed industrial productivity. The general conclusion, however, is clear. As with Suzhou, the case of Liangshan points up the limitations of the labour surplus model.

3. Investment in Physical and Human Capital

3.1. Investment in Agriculture

The interaction of input and yield *levels* was discussed earlier in the chapter; that discussion concluded that Wenzhou (lower yields than justified by its input levels) was best placed to grow quickly. This section turns to a discussion of input *growth* and the way in which levels and growth rates jointly determined yield growth.

Some evidence comes from Table 11.8, which shows that spatial differences in yield growth were indeed the joint product of input levels and input growth rates. Consider first Liangshan, where grain yields increased by some 34 per cent between 1980 and 1990. This impressive performance was certainly not because Liangshan enjoyed favourable preconditions; as we saw earlier, irrigation and chemical fertilizer use was much less widespread than in the other three prefectures. Rather, yield growth in Liangshan can be traced directly to a massive increase in input use. Over the period 1980 to 1990, inputs of fertilizer and water from irrigation networks multiplied apace: fertilizer use doubled, and the share of irrigated area increased by 4 percentage points. In contrast to Wenjiang, Liangshan entered the reform era with a combination of low yields, low fertilizer inputs, and a primitive irrigation infrastructure. Fertilizer use, for example, was only a quarter of the levels on the Chengdu plain and in Wenzhou, and only a sixth of the Sunan level; the development of irrigation also lagged far behind. In short, the underlying problem faced by Liangshan in 1980 was that too little of its land was irrigated and that too little chemical fertilizer was being used. These problems were not properly addressed in the Maoist period; only when these key constraints are removed will yields in Liangshan begin to approach those in other areas of China. Nevertheless, the partial lifting of these barriers served to generate a dramatic increase in yields in the 1980s. With fertilizer use increasing by well over 100 per cent, and the irrigation ratio rising by 15 per cent, it is not surprising that yields also rose significantly. The Liangshan of the early 1990s was by no means rich as a result of this growing use of modern inputs; many of its Yi ethnic minority were still heavily reliant upon state handouts in the early 1990s. Moreover, grain yields there did not increase very much more quickly than in Wenjiang (34 per cent compared to 30 per cent in total) despite proportionately greater input application. Nevertheless, the prefecture had seemingly embarked upon the road to greater material prosperity, and that in itself was testimony to the efficacy of the modern agricultural package of irrigation, new seed varieties, and chemical fertilizer.

TABLE 11.8. *Growth of input use and grain yields, 1980–1990* (total percentage increase)

Prefecture	Irrigation ratio	Chemical fertilizer use	Grain yields
Suzhou	8	38	12
Wenjiang	4	31	30
Wenzhou	9	79	3
Liangshan	15	123	34

Notes: The irrigation ratio is the proportion of cultivated land that was irrigated. Grain yields were severely depressed by poor weather in Wenzhou in 1990. Data on 1991 grain yields are therefore used (from ZJTJNJ, 1992: 530–1, 490–1). 1990 was a good year in both Jiangsu and Sichuan.

Sources: ZGFX (1989; 1992).

Yield growth was also impressive in Wenjiang. Unlike Liangshan, however, Wenjiang did not enjoy especially rapid input growth; irrigation and fertilizer use grew no more quickly than in Suzhou and Wenzhou. The explanation lies instead in preconditions. First, the weather. 1980 saw flooding on the Chengdu plain, which inevitably depressed yields. By contrast, 1990 was a year of very good weather. This combination inevitably imparted an upward trend to yield growth. Secondly, as we saw earlier, yields were substantially lower than justified by input levels; as result, there was substantial scope for catch-up.

As for Wenzhou, it is evident from the table that yields grew slowly. That is perhaps surprising given that chemical fertilizer inputs grew more quickly than in Wenjiang or Suzhou. But one needs to remember that Wenzhou was not especially favoured by its preconditions. The climate was favourable, but grain yields were already extremely high in the prefecture in 1980, especially given that much of its terrain is hilly and therefore far less conducive to grain production than the paddy fields of Suzhou (Bramall, 1990). As a result, there was only modest scope for yield improvements in the transition era. Finally, Suzhou enjoyed neither favourable preconditions (in the sense that yields were below the level implied by input use) nor rapid input growth. Chemical fertilizer was already in extensive use, and the irrigation network was essentially complete (Huang, 1990; Leeming, 1985). Indeed the yields attained in both Wenzhou and in Suzhou by 1980 were very high by both Chinese and world standards. The national average for 1980 was only 183 kg per *mu*, barely 50 per cent of the Suzhou and Wenzhou figures. By 1990, the national figure was up to 262 kg (ZGTJNJ, 1993: 371), but this was still far below the Wenzhou-Sunan figures for 1980. In other words, it was extremely difficult to increase yields any further without a new burst of technical progress.

3.2. Industrial Investment

As for the impact of industrial investment, it is instructive to look at the contrasting fortunes of counties drawn from two very different prefectures in Sichuan province: prosperous Wenjiang and poverty-stricken Liangshan.[19] Consider Wenjiang first. In view of its favourable location on the Chengdu plain—good transport links and easy access to the provincial capital itself—one would expect to see an impressive industrial growth rate registered over the 1980s, and that is what one finds (Table 11.9). Measured at constant prices, median net industrial output grew at 10.1 per cent per year between 1978 and 1988.[20] Moreover, there is no doubt that high rates of investment played a central role in this process of growth. In the two counties where the capital stock grew most quickly (Wenjiang and Qionglai), the rate of growth of industrial output was substantially above the mean. In the two counties where capital stock growth was slowest (Shifang and Pengxian), NVIO growth was well *below* the mean. Nevertheless, the relationship is far from precise. For example, of the six counties where capital growth exceeded the mean, only in three cases did NVIO growth also exceed the mean. In Xinjin, Guanghan, and Xindu, high rates of investment were not reflected in rapid industrial output growth.

TABLE 11.9. *The growth of industrial output and capital in Wenjiang, 1978–1988* (annual percentage growth rates; current prices)

	Net industrial output	Gross capital stock	Employment
Wenjiang	23.6	27.1	15.0
Pixian	21.4	18.7	9.3
Xindu	16.0	21.0	12.5
Guanghan	16.6	22.9	n/a
Shifang	15.8	12.6	10.0
Pengxian	15.0	7.8	6.9
Guanxian	17.0	15.6	8.3
Dayi	12.7	14.8	7.0
Qionglai	20.8	25.0	n/a
Xinjin	17.6	19.6	24.1
Median	17.6	18.7	9.7

Notes: Independently accounting industrial enterprises administered at the level of the *xiang* and above.
Source: SCZL (1990).

Indeed NVIO growth in Xindu (16 per cent per annum) was barely above that achieved in Pengxian (15 per cent)—even though the capital stock grew almost three times faster in the former. Nor does including employment growth as an independent variable in a regression alongside capital stock growth improve the quality of fit.[21] The coefficient on capital is barely significant, the coefficient on employment is negative and the adjusted R^2 is only 0.32.

In fact, industrial investment was much more important for growth in the case of the poor prefecture of Liangshan (Table 11.10). Despite its poverty—perhaps because of it—Liangshan achieved an annual rate of real industrial growth of 9 per cent between 1978 and 1988, not much less than the rate attained by Wenjiang. Investment seems to have played a critical role in this. Of the eight counties which achieved above-median capital stock growth, only one (Butuo) experienced below median growth in NVIO. Furthermore, of the three *xian* where capital grew at less than 10 per cent annually, two also registered very slow (negative in the case of Jinyang) industrial output growth; the exception here was Leibo, which enjoyed industrial output growth of over 16 per cent at current prices despite its capital stock growing by only 6 per cent. Moreover, and in contrast to Wenjiang, the fit of the regression for Liangshan is much better. Although the employment coefficient is again insignificant (though at least it is positive), the capital coefficient is strongly significant and the adjusted R^2 is a rather more respectable 0.45.

Yet perhaps the most interesting aspect of this comparison is that the growth rate of industrial output was lower in Liangshan than in Wenzhou despite the much smaller industrial base in Liangshan (and therefore the scope for catch-up); as was seen in Table 11.3, real GVIO per capita in 1982 was less than 50 per cent of Wenjiang's. The explanation for the disparity in industrial growth rates must therefore lie in two factors.[22] First, the growth of the capital stock was lower in

TABLE 11.10. *The growth of industrial output and the capital stock in Liangshan, 1978–1988* (annual percentage growth rates; current prices)

County	Net industrial output	Gross capital stock	Employment
Xichang	18.5	14.4	5.9
Muli	44.5	59.9	2.9
Yanyuan	31.0	28.9	6.2
Dechang	19.3	15.4	4.2
Huili	12.2	10.2	4.7
Huidong	11.1	13.0	0.2
Ningnan	10.8	14.2	7.6
Puge	26.1	14.9	2.3
Butuo	4.3	22.0	8.5
Jinyang	−0.6	4.6	−2.5
Zhaojue	4.0	2.3	−7.2
Xide	21.2	22.1	7.8
Mianning	19.2	14.9	−1.0
Yuexi	11.9	14.5	0.7
Ganluo	20.0	19.2	7.6
Meigu	16.1	11.8	−1.3
Leibo	16.4	6.0	1.4
Median	16.4	14.5	2.9

Notes: Independent-accounting industrial enterprises administered at the level of the *xiang* and above.
Source: SCZL (1990).

Liangshan. Secondly, there were other obstacles to industrial growth aside from low physical investment; as a result, the returns to investment were comparatively low. The failure, therefore, of data on investment to fully explain spatial differences in industrial growth is as one would expect. One can hardly hope to explain growth rates without reference to the base level of output, the role of other inputs (human capital, technical progress, and mineral resources in parts of Liangshan), the level of demand, or transport constraints. Indeed the most obvious difficulty faced by many parts of south-eastern Liangshan is locational: the roads are few, the distances long, and the topography extremely difficult. If the Yangzi were navigable by steam craft so far inland it might be a different story. But as it is, *xian* such as Leibo and Meigu are always going to be handicapped by their physical geography. Nevertheless, what does seem clear is that investment in physical capital offers at least a partial solution to these problems of underdevelopment. It is because of the acceleration in capital stock growth after 1978 that poor prefectures like Liangshan have embarked on the path to prosperity.

3.3. Investment in Human Capital

The level of investment in human capital also helps to explain regional differences in growth rates. The relationship between the growth of NVAIO per capita in the four prefectures and their literacy rates is shown in Table 11.11.

TABLE 11.11. *Literacy rates and per capita income growth by prefectures*

Prefecture	Literacy rate (%)		Growth of Literacy (% p.a.)	Growth of GDP per capita (% p.a.)
	1982	1990	1982–90	1982–91
Suzhou	78	84	0.9	10.3[a]
Wenjiang	82	87	0.7	8.9
Wenzhou	74	81	1.2	8.5[a]
Liangshan	64	62	–0.3	6.7

[a] 1980–91

Notes: Literacy rates are for the population aged 15 and over. Growth rates are annual percentage increases. GDP per capita growth is at 1990 constant prices and is calculated along the lines explained in the notes to Table 2.11.

Source: Population Census Office (1987); ZGRKTJNJ (1992).

There is nothing precise about the relationship between growth and education in Table 11.11. That is hardly surprising in view of the many other influences upon the growth rate. Nevertheless, the positive contribution of education is clear. The two regions (Suzhou and Wenjiang) which grew most quickly had the highest literacy rates in both 1982 and 1990. Although literacy grew more quickly in Wenzhou than in either Suzhou or Wenjiang, this reflects the fact that Wenzhou started from a lower literacy base. It was therefore 'easier' (at least in a statistical sense) for that region to raise its literacy rate than it was for either Wenjiang or Suzhou. Accordingly, the fact that Wenzhou's growth rate was slow despite the relatively rapid increase in its literacy rate does not cast doubt on the positive nature of the growth–literacy relationship.

This relationship is borne out by the path taken by Liangshan over the course of the 1980s. Liangshan, it appears, was doubly disadvantaged. On the one hand, its literacy rate in 1982 was well below the rate achieved in the other three regions. It therefore entered the reform era with a weak human-capital base. In fact, the extent of illiteracy amongst Liangshan's Yi population was higher than amongst any other ethnic minority in Sichuan; 76 per cent of Yi living in the province and aged 12 and over were illiterate in 1982 compared to 31 per cent of Han Chinese. Of Yi women aged 12 or over, 90 per cent were illiterate (compared, for example, to 84 per cent of Tibetan women) (Liu, 1988: 342). On the other hand, Liangshan's literacy rate not only failed to grow over the course of the 1980s but actually declined, falling from about 64 per cent in 1982 to less than 62 per cent in 1990. This reflects in large measure falling numbers of children attending school. In 1979, there were 465,765 children attending primary school in Liangshan. By 1991, this had fallen to only 341,800. Moreover, the decline cannot be explained by any fall in the size of the cohort of school age. In 1979, for example, the primary school enrolment rate was 89 per cent. By 1991, it was down to only 73 per cent (LYZG, 1985: 295; Zhu, 1992: 228).

In short, Liangshan's record over the reform decade in terms of human-capital formation was dismal (Table 11.12). Although the literacy rate rose in four of the prefecture's counties, it fell in no less than twelve (and was virtually unchanged in Ningnan). Furthermore, and equally significantly, it was in the counties where literacy rates were already high that improvement took place. In Xichang (76.5), Dechang (69.9), and Mianning (65.1), the 1982 literacy rates were in each case above the prefectural average of 63.4 per cent. Only Ganluo, where the 1982 rate (63.2) was marginally below the average, was exceptional, and in this case the rise in the literacy rate was only modest. The reasons for growing illiteracy in Liangshan are several. For one, there was considerable hostility amongst the Yi ethnic minority to learning Chinese and to any association with Chinese culture. Inevitably this Han–Yi antagonism translated into comparatively limited demand for education on the part of Yi households. The situation was not helped by the comparatively small proportion of Yi teachers. The 1982 Census for Sichuan records that 1.8 per cent of the province's employed Han population were working in education. By contrast, the percentage for ethnic minorities was only 1.3 per cent and for the Yi it was even lower at 0.8 per cent (Liu, 1988: 337).

TABLE 11.12. *Literacy rates in Liangshan, 1982 and 1990*

	1982 (%)	1990 (%)	Growth rate, 1982–90 (% p.a.)
Xichang city	77	80	0.6
Muli	58	55	−0.6
Yanyuan	60	57	−0.5
Dechang	70	73	0.6
Huili	66	63	−0.7
Huidong	61	57	−0.8
Ningnan	68	68	0
Puge	63	60	−0.6
Butuo	58	51	−1.6
Jinyang	57	56	−0.2
Zhaojue	62	58	−0.7
Xide	64	59	−1.1
Mianning	65	69	−0.7
Yuexi	66	60	−1.0
Ganluo	63	64	0.1
Meigu	56	54	−0.5
Leibo	67	67	−0.1
Liangshan	63	62	−0.3

Note: These are literacy rates for the population aged 15 and over.
Source: ZGRKTJNJ (1992).

A second problem appears to have been declining educational provision. In Zhaojue, the number of middle and primary schools apparently fell from 413 in 1978 to 169 in 1982. Not surprisingly, the number of pupils dropped over the same period from 20,285 to 8,795 (Zhang, 1985: 9), and in Liangshan as a whole, the number of primary schools dwindled from 5,656 in 1979 to only 3,827 in 1991 (LYZG, 1985: 295; Zhu, 1992: 228). In part, of course, the problem was lack of funds. The prefecture's revenue in 1991 was only 375m. *yuan* compared to expenditure of 618m. (Zhu, 1992: 222). However, Liangshan's financial position had actually improved considerably compared to the late 1970s. In that period (1977–80), expenditure averaged 145m. *yuan* per year and income 47m. *yuan* (LYZG, 1985: 274). In other words, income increased by almost 21 per cent per year during the reform decade whereas expenditure increased at an annual rate of only 14 per cent. The deterioration of educational provision during the 1980s thus reflected the changing priorities of local government rather than any decline in funds.

Yet irrespective of the reasons for Liangshan's poor record on human-capital formation over the course of the 1980s, it is clear that the prefecture's failure to invest hampered its economic development. Although its literacy rate over the course of the 1980s remained well above the notional 30 per cent development 'threshold', the prefecture's capacity for rapid economic growth was enormously hampered and this is reflected in its slow rate of economic growth.

4. Conclusion

It is evident from our discussion of these four prefectures that the factors considered in previous chapters go far towards explaining differences in local growth rates. Liangshan's growth rate was the slowest of the four prefectures considered, and this reflected a number of factors. First, its legacy from the Maoist era was small. Its irrigation networks were underdeveloped, the industrial base was small, and transport infrastructure was woefully inadequate. Moreover, its literacy rate was low and Yi culture was not especially receptive to the ideas of modernity. Second, surplus labour arguments are not very convincing. They do not explain why growth in Liangshan was slower than in Suzhou because neither prefecture had abundant surplus labour relative to demand. In Suzhou, labour demand grew so quickly that it could only be satisfied by importing labour. In Liangshan there was comparatively little surplus labour; most of its labour force was needed in agriculture and in transport. Thirdly, Liangshan's investment record after 1978 was not especially good. To be sure, it was not disastrous; the rapid increase in chemical fertilizer inputs and irrigated areas alongside high investment rates in industry allowed the prefecture to achieve a growth rate that was perfectly respectable by international standards. Nevertheless, given the scale of investment needed, the effort was inadequate. This was especially so in the sphere of education, where literacy rates actually declined between 1982 and 1990. Against this backcloth, it is not hard to see why Liangshan's growth rate was no more than modest by Chinese standards.

By contrast, Suzhou was privileged in most respects. It inherited a well-developed transport, human-capital, agricultural, and industrial infrastructure from the Maoist period; indeed some of this infrastructure dates from the Republican era. There was also some surplus labour available for use in rural industry once triple cropping and collective farming were abandoned (though its release may have worked to depress industrial productivity growth). Finally, Suzhou made the most of its initial advantage by high levels of investment in industry (especially in the rural sector) and by improving its literacy rate still further. The prefecture could have done better. Its literacy rate by 1990 was still low by the standards of Taiwan and South Korea; and investment in agriculture rather lagged behind. Nevertheless, its many obvious advantages go a long towards explaining why its growth rate exceeded 20 per cent per annum, whereas Liangshan's was barely one third of that.

Part IV

The Growth-Promoting State and Its Origins

12

The Master Discourse and the State

A central part of the analysis offered by the master discourse is that the respective contributions of initial conditions, factor accumulation, and technical progress to economic growth will vary enormously across countries. It does not, in other words, offer a theory of universal applicability when it comes to the sources of growth. The key issue for its proponents is therefore to identify what factors determine the composition of growth. Why, for example, has factor accumulation rather than productivity improvement driven East Asian growth?

The answer offered by the master discourse to this question is that the extent of technical progress will depend upon the willingness of a country to establish a market-based economy. To be sure, heavily regulated economies are capable of growth. Singapore and the USSR, for example, did manage to grow over a long period of time because even their highly interventionist economic systems were capable of generating very high rates of factor accumulation. However, if they—or any other LDCs—wish to complete the transition to the status of a developed country, marketization is essential. Only the market system can generate the innovation without which growth will cease in a mature economy. The deeper explanation of the economic success of those countries which have caught up is therefore their reliance upon the market system.

1. Thinking about the State

The view that state-induced price distortions and state-led industrial policy can be successful is at odds with the view held by the Washington Consensus. This master discourse, built as it is on the foundation of neoclassical theory, derives essentially from the work of Arrow and Debreu in the 1950s. Their work demonstrated the conditions under which markets would lead to efficient outcomes in terms of resource allocation. That analysis has in turn been modified and informed by the work of the Austrian school (the main obstacle to centralization is the gathering and processing of information), public choice theorists such as Buchanan and Tullock (the state is malevolent), economists trained in Eastern Europe such as Kornai (there is no resting place between the free market and state socialism), and new institutional economists like North (the state must secure private property rights). There is only limited scope for government intervention, which should be designed to correct the more egregious market failures; some public goods must be provided (and financed by lump sum taxes and transfers), and the worst externalities should be dealt with by market mechanisms (internalization, pollution permits, etc.).[1] The upshot is the doctrine espoused by international agencies such as the IMF and the World Bank, and promoted by successive American administrations during the 1980s and 1990s.[2] The 'Washington consensus', as Williamson calls it, advises all LDC governments to follow a strategy which:

> . . . emphasizes fiscal rectitude, competitive exchange rates, privatization, undistorted market prices, and limited intervention (save for encouraging exports, education and infrastructure). Faith in the desirability and efficacy of these policies unites the vast majority of professional economists in the developed world who are concerned with issues of development. (Rodrik, 1996: 9)

One should perhaps add to this list that the state has long been seen as the only check on the abuse of monopoly power, although this is not usually given great emphasis because of empirical research showing the size of Harberger triangles to be small. But in essence the vision here is of a minimalist state presiding over a growth process led by the private sector in an environment characterized by intense competition between foreign and domestic firms. Redistributive taxation is akin to theft; by infringing upon property rights, it adversely affects investment and innovation.[3]

An integral part of the orthodoxy is also an instrumental view of democracy (Fukuyama, 1995; Barro, 1996; Mauro, 1995). Just as individuals are best able to judge their own economic interests, so individual citizens are in the best position to decide upon the form their government should take. Conversely, authoritarianism has adverse economic consequences. A characteristic of any authoritarian regime is unclear property rights; the assets of private-sector agents are subject to arbitrary confiscation. Uncertain property rights in turn have adverse consequences for investment. Rural enterprises will live in fear of predatory local government. Farm households live in the shadow of land confiscation. Foreign firms will also be reluctant to risk investing in a country with an authoritarian and arbitrary government. There is one paradox in this advocacy of democracy: a constitutional monarch or president may be better able to raise tax revenue than a despot (Eggertsson, 1990; McGuire and Olson, 1996). The point is that if the ruler is deprived of the right to make arbitrary interventions, property rights will be more secure. Investment and therefore the tax base will be greater. Moreover, if financiers see that a ruler has a large and stable source of revenue, they will be more willing to lend. According to Eggertsson (1990: 348):

> . . . credible commitment by the state to stable property rights both promotes private investments and lowers the transaction costs to the state of raising revenue. In modern nation states, such commitments seem to require an effective separation of powers.

This separation of powers, North and others argue, explains why Britain was the first industrial nation. It resolved the early modern revenue crisis faced by the British crown via a credible commitment (executing King Charles I in 1649) to democracy. Democracy thus has instrumental as well as intrinsic value.

It needs, however, to be emphasized that the master discourse is not monolithic. On a theoretical plane, the views of neoclassical economists, the Austrians, and public choice theorists on the reasons for state failure are very different in their emphasis. Furthermore, even amongst neoclassicals, there is significant disagreement. For example, and as is well known, Jeffrey Sachs has been extremely critical of the failure of the IMF and the World Bank to provide adequate aid to enable Eastern European economies in the process of making the transition to a market economy to reduce some of the social costs involved. Furthermore, a number of those who were in power during the process of transition have either attempted to introduce a more authoritarian style of government (such as Yeltsin ruling by decree) or have argued in retrospect that their task would have been easier without democracy (Balcerowicz, cited in Rodrik, 1996: 36). Sachs has taken a similar view, arguing that the government—once elected, and in the period before the next election—must be allowed to rule in an authoritarian way (Rodrik, 1996: 33).

A further qualification is that the orthodoxy does not claim that unfettered market forces will bring about a general competitive equilibrium that is efficient, stable, and unique; to some extent, therefore, critics of the pure Arrow-Debreu framework like Stiglitz (1994) are tilting at windmills. The best practitioners of the art of neoclassical economics (the Austrians go further) all recognize that the existence conditions needed for a general equilibrium price vector are plainly falsified; the world is characterized neither by perfect information, nor a continuum of seriatim contingent future markets. Externalities are commonplace. But this in itself does not mean there is a case for state intervention. That only follows if it can be shown that market failure will not be displaced by state failure. As it is, argues the master discourse, we cannot regard the state as either omniscient or benevolent; in fact, state failure is far more pervasive than market failure. The implication is therefore that a market economy is *second-best*; both resource allocation and the pace of innovation will be suboptimal, but a market economy will be more efficient than an economy characterized by widespread state intervention actually designed to correct market failures. Only in very special circumstances is state intervention likely to work, and the probability of these conditions being fulfilled in a developing country are often seen as particularly remote (Krugman, 1993*a*).

Perhaps the best illustration of this type of reasoning is the treatment of industrial ownership. The orthodoxy here claims that the state cannot make SOEs efficient without privatizing them. There is in fact no prospect of the state making SOEs 'efficient' because the state is vulnerable to capture by rent-seeking coalitions and hence to the allocation of subsidies to inefficient firms. The second element in the orthodox story stresses the consequences of inefficient SOEs. First, state ownership of enterprises provokes rent-seeking behaviour; this entails deadweight losses for the economy. Secondly, because SOEs are inefficient, they are a claim on—rather than a contributor to—state revenue. What follows is in effect a crowding-out argument. Lower revenue compels the state either to raise taxes or to accept the higher interest rates entailed by the need to make additional bond sales to the private sector. The result is that private-sector investment is crowded-out by higher interest rates or higher taxation.[4] In short, therefore, state ownership of enterprises will usually impose a series of efficiency costs on the economy that would not otherwise be incurred. Although there may in theory be a case for industrial policy, governments are advised not to be tempted by the siren voices who are its advocates because the costs of government failure will exceed those of market failure (Krugman, 1993*b*; 1994).

The case against this master discourse is predicated on two arguments. First, the state even in the Third World may sometimes be benign rather than malevolent. It is therefore important not to generalize about the prospects for intervention; we need to look at the political sphere and to identify whether the conditions needed for successful economic intervention hold in each specific case. It is argued in Chapter 13 that these conditions did hold in the case of China after 1978, and this is why state intervention was especially successful. The second argument is that the orthodoxy consistently underestimates the extent of market failure, and therefore the range of interventions that need to be undertaken to offset that failure. Provided the state is effective, its intervention in the economy can in fact lead to dramatic improvements in performance. There has been some recent recognition of this by new institutional economists which has begun to influence the orthodox prescriptions. Indeed it is particularly striking (and more than a little paradoxical) that many recent orthodox accounts seem to accept without demur the proposition that the state can be effective in securing property rights, even though the state is seen as worse than ineffectual when it comes to (say) an interventionist industrial policy.

A way of thinking about the potential for state intervention is offered by Stiglitz (1995). Suppose that externalities are pervasive, and that positive feedback is the rule. Then in such an economy, multiple equilibria will exist; some will be at low levels of output and others at high levels of output. For example, the demand for telephones will be high only if there is a large number of existing owners, i.e. the demand for telephones will rise as ownership rises, at least up to a point (positive feedback). Alternatively, the economy may settle at a point where telephone ownership is low; there is no incentive to acquire a new telephone precisely because there is hardly anyone to talk to. Stiglitz argues that, following David and Arthur, the equilibrium in which a real market economy will settle is largely a matter of luck: 'history matters'. Moreover, there can be no expectation that the economy will move automatically over time from the 'low' to the 'high' equilibrium because of limited information and market failure.[5] In particular, there is no reason to expect price signals to produce an optimal configuration of institutions which would ensure transition to the 'high' equilibrium. The market may produce some institutions, but there is likely to be a coordination problem such that only an incomplete set is ultimately created. Real market economies are therefore characterized by path dependence; there is no reason to expect convergence on the efficient equilibrium. According to this sort of analysis, the role of government is to move the economy from an inefficient to an efficient equilibrium (by subsidies, the creation of institutions, etc.). In effect, government is seen as correcting market failure. Stiglitz (1995: 60) summarizes his argument thus:

> The persistence and pervasiveness of externalities and the related consequences of multiple equilibria, path dependence and myopia help explain the differing circumstances in which different countries find themselves: some countries may be 'trapped' in a low level equilibrium. This can provide a rationale for government intervention.

This is of course just one way of thinking about the case for government intervention and it is predicated upon the assumption that states can solve coordination problems. One might equally well focus on the problem of static resource allocation, and the inconsistencies in the neoclassical approach. For example, if information is perfect and transaction costs close to zero, it is hard to explain why firms and money exist (or one can resort to the more obvious empirical critique: information is decidedly imperfect and transaction costs are high). An alternative line of criticism of the orthodoxy is that market economies are characterized by endemic macroeconomic coordination failures of the sort emphasized by economists working within the Keynesian tradition. Once unemployment has been created (by a collapse in exogenous investment), there may exist no mechanism whereby prices can change; these are the small menu cost and coordination problems stressed by new Keynesian theorists. Or one can simply invoke the debt and Fisher effects outlined in chapter 19 of the *General Theory*; even if prices fall, the impact on corporate debt may well depress investment even further (Tobin, 1980; Trevithick, 1992). But whether one invokes path dependence, static resource allocation, or macroeconomic coordination arguments, these critiques amount to saying the same thing: economies are characterized by pervasive market failures, and there is thus a strong prima facie case for state intervention.

The main debate amongst the critics of the orthodoxy is therefore not about whether market failure is pervasive but about how much state intervention is required by way of remedy, and what form it should take. One influential strand within this heterodoxy is what might be called *market socialism* (Nove, 1983; Bardhan and Roemer, 1992; Bardhan and Roemer, 1993; Roemer, 1994; Stiglitz, 1994; Roemer, 1996). Its theoretical basis is the Lange–Lerner–Taylor idea that the central planning body (CPB) can set and manipulate prices, mimicking market forces along the way to achieve an equilibrium even in the absence of private property. The role of the state is to 'get prices right', i.e. ensure that demand equals supply; but it also needs to devise non-market means of allocating investment because that requires the forecasting of future demand. Public ownership of property ensures that wealth and income are distributed fairly. In this way, the market-socialist approach can achieve both efficiency and equity objectives. In essence, and as Stiglitz (1994) says, this is done by taking advantage of the second fundamental theorem of welfare economics: any Pareto-efficient allocation can be achieved by the market irrespective of whether property is privately or state-owned.

However, market socialists have recognized that *complete* ownership of the means of production is likely to discourage (*inter alia*) innovation; recent market-socialist writings have taken to heart the Hayekian critique that the CPB, however well-intentioned, cannot resolve all the informational problems that need resolution when the means of production are entirely under public ownership. In this sense, recent developments have moved on from the older Lange–Lerner–Taylor approach; they start off from the Hayekian view that the chief merit of capitalism is not so much its effectiveness as a mechanism for static-resource allocation, but instead the way in which private-property rights spur innovation. In concrete terms, this has led to market socialists advocating a dualistic ownership structure; whilst heavy industry and utilities are owned by government, many consumer goods and services are left to the province of the private sector. The inspiration for this type of market socialism is provided by the writings of Bukharin and by the practice of Soviet New Economic Policy in the 1920s; see, for example, Nolan (1988). Kornai's *early* work provided additional inspiration, and it is widely recognized that Hungary and the former Yugoslavia have sought to adopt a broadly market-socialist strategy. The same is true of China in both the early 1950s, and since 1978. A variant on the market socialism theme is the idea of coupon socialism (Roemer, 1994). This involves issuing every adult male a coupon representing a share in the value of industrial companies; these coupons can be traded in exchange for other coupons, but cannot be sold for cash. This, Roemer argues, serves two purposes. First, it creates a system of genuine public-rather than state-ownership of companies. Secondly, it eliminates those inequalities derived from profit-based income (which serves little real incentive function in capitalist economies because it accrues essentially as rent to shareholders—Roemer, 1994: 6).

The second strand in the heterodox tradition is a belief in what Robert Wade has called the *governed market*.[6] Many of the advocates of the governed market have conducted empirically orientated work on East Asia (Amsden, 1989; Amsden, *et al.*, 1994; Bowles and Dong, 1994; Chang, 1993*a*, 1993*b*; Chang and Nolan, 1995; Fishlow, 1994; Nolan, 1993, 1995*a*; Wade, 1990; Weitzman and Xu, 1994); Stiglitz, whose approach is more orthodox, also writes admiringly of the role played there by government. These writers have in common a critical view of the extent of state ownership of property implied by market socialism, and tend instead to advocate other forms of intervention such as loans, subsidies, and the appointment of state nominees to head private banks. This argument is not predicated on any simplistic notion that private firms are qualitatively different from state-owned enterprises; because of the distinction between ownership and management in modern corporations, the principal-agent problem in state and private enterprises is essentially the same (Vickers and Yarrow, 1988; Stiglitz, 1994; Roemer, 1994: 5). Nevertheless, it is still generally argued that private firms will tend to be more efficient in resolving these principal-agent problems because they have greater freedom in designing incentive systems (Stiglitz, 1994: 179–81, 199–202). The commitment to greater equality under market socialism, for example, is an obvious constraint on the design of such systems. It follows, therefore, that most property needs to be privately owned.

However, there is no suggestion in the governed market analysis that economic activity can be left to the market; as with all the critics of the Washington consensus, market failures are viewed as pervasive. To be sure, price determination should in the main be the province of the private sector. Nevertheless, a wide variety of interventions will be needed in respect of interest rates, taxes, wage setting in SOEs, and subsidies (some admittedly may only need to be transitional); in this approach, there is no virtue in 'getting prices right' if those prices do not promote growth.[7] Under the governed market, innovation is generated in part by a competitive private sector, and in part by state mobilization of funds for research; in this last respect, the governors of the market stress the superiority of bank-based (as opposed to stock market-based) systems of industrial finance (Zysman, 1983; Bardhan and Roemer, 1992, 1993). This is in large measure because dissatisfaction is expressed in more bureaucratic financial systems (Germany, France, Japan) via voice rather than exit; this tends to promote long-run investment and risk-taking as opposed to short-termism (Pollin, 1995). Furthermore, institutional structures which conflict with the aim of efficient static-resource allocation are seen as desirable if they promote growth. The classic neo-Schumpeterian example here is oligopoly; the output level under monopoly in the short run will be suboptimal, but the supernormal profits made by monopolistic firms (quasi-rents) will serve both to finance investment/innovation and to spur on new innovation. For the perfectly competitive firm, there is no reason to innovate because the firm is unable to capture the quasi-rents that are generated by innovation; those rents are rapidly dissipated by new entrants into the market. This very insight is of course the foundation of much of the new neo-Schumpeterian economics of growth and provides a rational for an industrial structure which is not perfectly competitive (Romer, 1994; Grossman and Helpman, 1991, 1994).

The governed-market approach has little to say about the need to ensure equality; its primary commitment is to growth and it is stretching the term much too far to call it a socialist approach. Although it is a commonplace to argue that the post-war development of Taiwan, South Korea, and Japan has been associated with a comparatively equal distribution of income, the best studies in the governed-market approach acknowledge that this is not true, except perhaps in the case of Taiwan. Initial land reform did much to reduce pre-war inequalities, but since then industrial growth has tended to produce wide wage differentials and pervasive gender inequalities. As Amsden (1990: 30) says of South Korea, 'Wage discrimination against women in Korea and Japan is the worst in the world; in this area traditional patriarchal forms have, so far, been successfully adapted to modern capitalism.' Nevertheless, it is not clear that Amsden is implying (or others in the governed-market tradition) that the approach adopted in East Asia could have been improved upon. Her view seems to be that inequality was not extreme by Latin American standards and that it was a necessary price to pay for rapid growth.

The other main heterodox position is an egalitarian Marxist-Leninist perspective that is critical of the neoclassical orthodoxy, the governed market and market socialism alike. Despite their many disagreements, these egalitarian Marxists agree on one essential point: the need for much more emphasis on redistribution, and less on growth.[8] This point is largely neglected in the governed-market approach, and the same is true of market socialism. Thus Roemer's coupon-based socialism eliminates profit-based income differentials, and he also favours a more general system of wealth taxation (Roemer, 1994: 119). However, he is quite open in arguing that attempts to secure greater equality of wage income are likely to have harmful effects on incentives. Accordingly, the extent of redistribution should be limited:

> In a market economy, I think people tend to believe they have earned, in the moral sense, what they receive through selling their talents on the market. . . . If so, this places a limit on the degree of redistribution that can be accomplished by social-democratic methods: an economic mechanism, at least in a democracy, cannot be stable if it rewards people in disproportion to what they believe they deserve . . . The limited degree of equality that I think market socialism can achieve is due in the main to my skepticism concerning the existence of alternatives to a competitive labor market for allocating labor in an efficient manner. (Roemer, 1994: 119–20)

The overriding preoccupation with inequality on the part of traditional socialists in turn reflects two ideas.[9] First, the strongly held view that equality is ethically desirable; by contrast, market socialists and advocates of the governed-market place more weight on the need to reduce absolute poverty. The second preoccupation of egalitarian Marxists centres on the instrumental value of equality: inequality undermines the capacity of the state to intervene in ways that promote the well-being of the bulk of the population. In that sense, the case for socialist equality and participation in decision-making is that it ensures democracy (Bowles and Gintis, 1986; Block, 1992). That is, the emergence of substantial inequalities—inevitable in any economy with a large market sector—allows a small number of individuals to exercise an inordinate level of power via industrial corporations and the media, and which may even allow them to 'capture' the state. Only by reducing the economic power of this new capitalist class via expropriation of their assets and continuous progressive taxation to prevent them from acquiring new capital can the state serve the needs of the many rather than the greed of the few. In other words, the egalitarian Marxist perspective challenges the assumption of market socialists that the state autonomy they see as necessary for effective intervention is possible in circumstances of high income inequality. Clearly, progressive taxation (especially of wealth) offers a way to increase state autonomy, but this issue of the nature of the state requires a full discussion; this is deferred until Chapter 13.

In sum, these various heterodox approaches perceive market economies as characterized by pervasive failures which need to be corrected by state intervention. But there is no universal heterodox presumption that rapid growth requires state *ownership* of the entire industrial sector; most interpretations of the experience of the USSR have put paid to that. The role of the state must be extensive, but cannot be all-embracing if economies are to generate an adequate rate of innovation. In addition, the heterodoxy is at pains to emphasize the need for state intervention to redistribute income. Although there is much disagreement between market socialists and governors of the market on the one hand, and egalitarian Marxists on the other, it is characteristic of heterodox writers that they reject the notion that almost all forms of income redistribution are akin to theft or have extremely damaging incentive effects.

2. International Evidence on the Role of the State

The master discourse interprets the evidence as saying that fast-growing economies are largely market-orientated or that intervention, where it has taken place in a high-growth economy, has been market-conforming.[10] In economies where government intervention has led to price distortion, growth rates have been much slower. From this perspective, the OECD countries are alleged to be affluent because they have market economies. The rise of East Asia reflects its commitment to undistorted prices, secure property rights and export orientation, especially in second-wave newly industrializing countries such as Indonesia, Thailand, and Malaysia (World Bank, 1993*a*). However, the World Bank has modified its position somewhat in the 1990s. First it acknowledged that there was extensive intervention in the North-East Asian NICs; this signalled a move away from the sort of views expressed by Little (1979) and the World Bank's own *World Development Report* (WDR, 1991), which both deny the fact of intervention.[11] Nevertheless, in arguing that these interventions were at best neutral and at worst harmful, the Bank remained true to the orthodoxy. This is evident from the 1997 *World Development Report* (WDR, 1997) which, although it acknowledged the role of industrial policy in South Korea, continued to assert that countries must 'get prices right' (de facto short-run marginal-cost pricing)—despite Amsden's (1989) well-known conclusion that South Korea grew quickly by getting prices wrong. The crisis of 1997–8 allowed the Bank to go the whole way. Following the growth slowdown in East Asia, it was able to argue that widespread interventions occurred all the time and that the crisis was the ultimate result.

The orthodoxy accepts that those previously interventionist economies which embraced the transition orthodoxy (Poland and Chile) suffered in the short run. However, the macroeconomic crisis they faced when transition began made these costs unavoidable, and the long-run prospects are very rosy (Lipton and Sachs, 1992; Sachs, 1993*a*, 1993*b*; Bosworth, *et al.*, 1994). The Polish economy grew quickly after the mid-1990s, as did Chile after the crisis of the early 1980s. Other economies which began to make the transition along the lines prescribed by the orthodox view also started to see the benefits by the 1990s (Brazil, Argentina, Peru). By contrast, those planned economies which embarked half-heartedly upon the transition path (Russia, Ukraine, and Hungary) or avoided transition at all (much of sub-Saharan Africa, Cuba, and North Korea), did badly during the 1990s. These failures of gradualism are interpreted as evidence supporting Kornai's view that market socialism is an unsustainable path (Kornai, 1992).

But the orthodox interpretation of this evidence is entirely implausible. One problem is that the short-term costs of transition are typically understated. For example, the impact of marketization on poverty (and on resulting life expectancy, which fell sharply in Russia in the 1990s)[12] has been so dramatic that many of the losers may not be alive to see the promised land. In other words, the problem from the perspective of the neoclassical orthodoxy is that even if the market delivers the goods, there are only likely to be net gains in the very long run. It is therefore entirely unsurprising that the imposition of shock therapy on Eastern Europe has been portrayed by some as imperialism (Gowan, 1996).

Nevertheless, much of the debate about transition is misconceived. The main issue is not the speed of transition but rather the long-term objective. To be sure, the pace of transition does matter; for example, dual-track price systems allow a gradual transition to a fully-fledged market economy, but the disadvantage is that they encourage corruption and intertemporal speculation. However, these issues pale in significance compared with the question of whether interventionist economies outperform market-orientated ones in the medium and long run. If this proposition is true, it makes no sense at all to follow the orthodoxy.

On this central issue, the evidence is against the master discourse. In the cases of Chile and Poland, for example, it remains debatable whether their long-run futures are secure; Chilean development is based upon rates of investment that are low by East Asian standards, persistently low real wages, and the exploitation of limited natural resources to generate export earnings.[13] Secondly, variations in growth rates (as opposed to levels)[14] across the OECD are typically less in interventionist economies like Japan and Germany than in more market-orientated regimes like the UK and the USA.[15] To argue that there is a devastating crisis in store for Japan or Germany just around the corner—as many of those in the orthodox tradition do—is either mere speculation or based upon an over-interpretation of ephemera (the collapse of the property boom in Japan, or German unification). Rather, it is the economies of the USA and the UK that stand on shaky foundations (extensive and rising absolute poverty, and low investment).

A third problem with the orthodoxy lies in its interpretation of the East Asian experience. It is clear that these economies have succeeded with authoritarian governments or peculiar forms of democracy (one-party rule in Japan for decades). That demonstrates rather obviously that democracy is not a necessary condition for rapid economic growth.[16] Even the World Bank's management were unable to entirely suppress the views of the *East Asian Miracle*'s authors that institutional and policy factors played a positive role in some respects. As Wade (1996: 28, 30) points out, there were enough concessions in the final version to appease MITI's Industrial Policy Bureau and still to persuade Argentina's executive director at the World Bank to call it an 'apologia for interventionism'. The need to appeare MITI was not surprising given the wealth of evidence demonstrating that pervasive state involvement was remarkably effective in promoting growth (Johnson, 1985; Amsden, 1989; Wade, 1990; Chang, 1993a; Amsden, *et al.*, 1994; Rodrik, 1995, 1996).[17]

The more general evidence on ownership and on macroeconomic policy casts further doubt on the view put forward by those advocating gradual—but eventual—transition to a market economy.[18] Countries such as Germany, Japan, Taiwan, Singapore, and South Korea have performed extremely well over a long period of time even though their economies have been heavily 'distorted' by state intervention. Industrial organization theory suggests overwhelmingly that privatization is not essential (Vickers and Yarrow, 1988). It is hard to argue that interventionist trade policies have damaged the East Asian economies given their success in exporting to the West. And the case for conservative financial policies (balanced budgets and tight monetary control) has been undermined by a sustained and successful attack on the theoretical foundations of the NAIRU and new classical economics, as well as the failures of such policies in both UK and USA (Coen and Hickman, 1987; Cross, 1995; Eatwell, 1996; Hargreaves Heap, 1992; Michie and Grieve Smith, 1994,

1995; Rowthorn, 1995; Stiglitz, 1997; Tobin, 1980; Trevithick, 1992). Nobody doubts that large and sustained fiscal deficits or exceptionally fast monetary expansion are undesirable, or that the crisis affecting Latin America in the 1980s was one of macroeconomic/stabilization policy (Rodrik, 1996); as a long-term perspective, the orthodox view that deficits are unambiguously bad for growth (Easterly, *et al.*, 1994) is plausible if by that is meant a unbalanced budget on average over a long period of time. As Rodrik (1996: 15) says:

> . . . the generalized debt crisis . . . was a dramatic confirmation of the importance of prudent macroeconomic policies . . . it was evident that the crisis affected only those countries that did not respect budget constraints. India, the import-substitution country par excellence, managed to escape the debt crisis during the 1980s, thanks to its tradition of conservative monetary and fiscal policies.

But that is very different from the entirely unsubstantiated claim—a central tenet of the orthodoxy—that contra-cyclical monetary and fiscal policy should always be avoided.[19] Indeed the evidence on the 1980s and 1990s suggests that European unemployment reflected general demand deficiency (Malinvaud's notion of Keynesian unemployment) and inadequate investment, rather than labour market failures (classical unemployment).[20]

The desirability from a growth-promoting perspective of having an interventionist state is also demonstrated by the historical evidence. This evidence seems to suggest that those economies which have retained 'feudal remnants'—that is, institutional structures through which the state is able to intervene—have tended to perform better than economies which made a rapid transition to capitalism. It has frequently been argued in recent years that the (relative) decline of the British economy was a consequence of incomplete transition from feudalism to capitalism. That is, Britain failed because it retained too many feudal structures—the monarchy, an aristocracy and House of Lords, a culture of 'gentlemanly capitalism' (Wiener, 1981) that abhorred engineering and manufacturing. This analysis is associated with a diverse group of writers including Clark (1986), Nairn (1988), and Anderson (1987), and in some ways its diagnosis underpinned the Thatcherite project of the 1980s which sought to revive the economy by sweeping away these residues of the past. However, as Ellen Wood (1991) observes, it is more sensible to see the failure of Britain as resulting from the abolition of the key feudal structures and traditions. By making an incomplete transition to capitalism, the state in countries as diverse as Wilhelmine Germany and post-war South Korea retained the capacity and legitimacy for intervention. But in Britain (and the USA), the completeness of the transition to capitalism after the abolition of the Corn Laws made it exceptionally difficult for the state to intervene, except during wartime. Thus Chamberlain's attempt to convert the Conservative Party to the cause of protection as an instrument of industrial policy failed in the first decade of the twentieth century; the City of London regulates itself rather than relying on the state; and the attempt to set up a Ministry of Economic Affairs with an avowedly interventionist brief in the mid-1960s foundered on the intransigence of the Treasury. All this is very different from the way in which (say) the Japanese government is able to exercise enormous influence over the entire industrial and financial system, or the modern German system of state-regulated apprenticeships (a clear feudal remnant if ever there was one).

Britain's problem was thus the completeness of its transition to capitalism. The capitalist class that emerged in the mid-nineteenth century was a capitalist class in the true sense of the word. That is, its aim was to maximize profit—not to maximize growth. It is true that capitalism will tend to develop the forces of production—that is, the productive potential of the economy—but, and as Marx pointed out, the priority of capitalism is profit maximization:

> Once set in train, the dynamic of capital accumulation was bound to transform production, but only in ways that were profitable, in the short term, to individual capitals. Corrective pressures, from the state in particular, have been required to push capital beyond its limited, short-sighted and often self-defeating 'rationality' . . . [p. 165] capital's essential commitment . . . is not to production as such but to profit-maximization. If there is an obstacle to the revitalization of British industry, according to this view, it has less to do with Britain's institutional anachronism than with the predatory impulses of capital itself. It is not (as Martin Wiener has suggested) the gentility of British capitalism that has hindered its development but, on the contrary, its unbridled rapacity [p. 167]. (Wood, 1991)

In other words, and contra Nairn, Anderson, and others, the British problem is capitalism itself, not the persistence of pre-capitalist structures and institutions.

> Britain's early and unrivalled evolution as a capitalist power left it bereft of the means to reverse the decline once set in train, while other European capitalisms were, at least for a time, better equipped. Early English capitalism never faced the need to establish institutions and practices to enhance or accelerate development [p. 15] . . . there may be circumstances in which the survival of archaic forms can promote, rather than impede, capitalist development—for instance, the availability of bureaucratic state-forms whose interventions can override the inherent contradictions of 'pure' capitalism [p. 16]. (Wood, 1991)

The difficulty for Britain and other market-orientated economies such as the USA is therefore to devise institutional structures that will promote growth instead of profit maximization. In Stiglitz's phrase, the USA and Britain have become stuck in a low-level equilibrium by virtue of historical chance (a complete transition to capitalism); the role of the state must be to shift them out of this low-level equilibrium trap, and into a higher equilibrium. States that have managed to do this, and it has arguably been easier for late industrializers such as South Korea precisely because they did not destroy all their traditional institutions, have grown much more quickly in the post-war era. Notwithstanding the economic problems of the 1990s, Japan in 1998 continued to close on the USA and may ultimately surpass US GDP per capita. Indeed it is arguable that Japan has not yet done so only because of the vast range of natural resources available to the US, which enable it to hold down food and other commodity prices.

Finally, even the evidence on the effects of planning in socialist countries is difficult to interpret. The conventional conclusion that growth in these economies was slower than in East Asia is probably robust, data problems notwithstanding. But it remains a matter of some debate whether slow growth reflects systemic failure. It is not difficult to argue that their isolation, and the associated military threat posed to their existence by the West, forced economies like China and the USSR to allocate the lion's share of their 'surplus' to the military sector and to defence industrialization, rather than to more productive sectors (Carr, 1980). Moreover, it is increasingly clear that China had every cause to be concerned about US intentions in the 1960s. Recently released Pentagon and State Department papers show that Kennedy and Johnson secretly considered an attempt at destroying China's nuclear capability in 1964 using bombers or commandos, and even hoped to involve the USSR in such action (the *Guardian*, 26 July 1997). There is sense, in which Trotsky was right in denying the possibility of 'socialism in one country' because of such threats. Furthermore, it is at least arguable that some of these state-socialist countries did not aim to maximize economic growth. The relentless commitment of Mao to egalitarianism probably did have adverse short-run incentive effects and stood in the way of growth promotion. In that sense, one ought perhaps to 'judge' the performance of such countries using a different set of criteria from those habitually used by the neoclassical orthodoxy. If growth promotion had been the over riding aim in state-socialist countries, it is entirely possible that the outcome would have been significantly different.

3. Perspectives on the Chinese State in the Transition Era

The literature on the role of the state in China since 1978 mirrors the general debates outlined above. The orthodox view of China's success is that rapid growth was down to the introduction of market forces into many parts of the economy; the meteoric growth of agriculture and rural industry are seen as classic illustrations of the liberating influence of the market. By contrast, in those sectors of the economy where state ownership persisted, productivity levels and growth rates were poor because of limited competition, insecure property rights, and soft budget constraints (Kornai, 1989; Sachs and Woo, 1994; Woo, *et al.*, 1994; Sachs, 1995; Fan, *et al.*, 1996; Woo, *et al.*, 1997). This assessment is shared by a large number of Chinese economists based in China; the views advocated by Hua Sheng, Dong Fureng, and Chen Yizi in the 1980s were especially pro-market, and were reflected in the policy pronouncements of (*inter alia*) Zhao Ziyang, Hu Yaobang, and Wan Li.

A different view of the sources of Chinese growth is that the state has played an important and positive role since 1978, but that the scale of its intervention needed to be reduced by the time of Deng's death. Many Western China specialists take this stance (McMillan and Naughton, 1992; Rawski, 1994; Wong, 1994; Naughton, 1995*a*, 1995*b*; Jefferson, *et al.*, 1996)[21] but so also do a number of Chinese academics (Lin, 1996). This group, and especially Naughton, see state involvement as an essential *transitional* factor in the transformation of a state-socialist to a market economy. 'Gradualism' is preferable to 'shock therapy' because it avoids the enormous social costs associated with mass unemployment and the break up of the welfare system:

Big bang transitions inevitably involve large short-run adjustment costs, generally including discontinuous changes in the price system and sharp increases in unemployment. By contrast, the Chinese leadership has acted as if it were constrained to maintain both inflation and open urban unemployment within fairly narrow limits. The Chinese have acted as if minimizing short-run adjustment costs (at the expense of prolonging the overall adjustment process) were an important argument in their overall transition strategy. (Naughton, 1995*a*: 19)

To be sure, these writers acknowledge that 'big bang' reform strategies will generate large efficiency gains (especially in terms of enterprise performance); however, these gains will be offset by the welfare costs of privatization.[22] Moreover, Naughton and others see the argument tilted further in favour of the gradualist strategy adopted in China by the abundance of evidence showing that that the Chinese state improved SOE performance by adopting measures which fell well short of privatization. The lesson from China is thus argued to be that SOEs, operating under a reformed regime of state ownership which provides only conditional subsidies (a 'hard' state), will still be inefficient compared to private enterprises. However, SOEs will be more efficient than if the state makes no attempt at all to make them operate efficiently; thus the worst-case scenario is that of the (Maoist) soft state providing unconditional and open-ended subsidies. The argument is essentially one of second best; SOEs operating under a hard state will still perform suboptimally compared to private enterprises but they will be more efficient than SOEs operating under a soft state. The particular characteristics of the hard state that Naughton (1995*a*: 311–17) has in mind here are competition from the private sector and foreign firms, greater security vis-à-vis profit retention and use, and pressure from local and central government to maximize state revenue.

Nevertheless, the Naughton view is crushingly orthodox in its appraisal of the strategy China should adopt in the long run; neither he nor other gradualists take issue with the idea that capitalism represents 'the end of history'. There is no suggestion that the Chinese state should be permanently interventionist; rather, the goal should be to create an Anglo-Saxon capitalist economy modelled on the USA and its imitators (UK, Canada, New Zealand, and Australia). Short-run efficiency gains can be made by hardening the state, but in the long run nothing short of a market economy will suffice if efficiency improvements to be fully realized. Thus Naughton (1995*a*) identifies a number of problems continuing to bedevil enterprises in the China of the early 1990s:

For the past ten years, in spite of the overall improvement in the incentive environment, China has been building and expanding factories that will ultimately turn out to be unviable and will have to be closed. That is, the very gradualness of the transition path on which China has embarked has implied the maintenance for many years of the set of incentives that lead to wrong and wasteful investment choices [p. 321]. . . . In a broader sense, China's reforms have failed to establish clearly demarcated property rights, both in the state sector and in the rural enterprise sector. Ownership remains extraordinarily vague for a surprising number of Chinese firms. Privatization of existing firms has contributed almost nothing to Chinese performance, and even entry of strictly private firms has been of distinctly secondary importance [p. 322].

Naughton's view is therefore that China at the time of Deng's death needed to proceed with a wide-ranging privatization programme. In his view, large efficiency gains can be expected from such a programme, and there is no justification for avoiding it (Naughton, 1995*a*: 324–5).[23] For him, the transition to a fully functioning market economy is a sine qua non in the long run and, as with the neoclassicals, the creation of democratic political structures is also essential. In the short term, China has got by, but in the long term 'The dysfunctional political system might prevent the Chinese people from quickly building the kind of future economic system they would prefer; it might even jeopardise the achievements of recent decades' (Naughton, 1995: 310). Others amongst this group (e.g. Wong, 1994) argue that the limits to gradualist reform have been reached. Accordingly, an accelerated pace of reform is not an option but a necessity.

A more heterodox view is offered by those adopting the 'governed-market' perspective (White, 1991; Nolan, 1995*a*; Blecher and Shue, 1996; Lo, 1997). These writers argue not only that the state has been 'developmental' during the transition period but also that there is scant reason to curtail its interventions in the immediate future. Rather, China should follow in the footsteps of South Korea and Taiwan and continue to intervene where there is evidence of market failure. Nolan (1995*a*, 1996) argues that the positive role played by large firms in the Chinese economy was brought about by a wave of merger and rationalization driven by central government, planners, local authorities, and the more successful enterprises themselves; its most obvious manifestation has been the growth of giant industrial 'enterprise groups'. By contrast, Blecher and Shue (1996) have emphasized the key role played by local government in promoting growth in areas including industry, town planning, infrastructure, and water conservancy. As a result, the role played by local government in China probably increased during the 1980s:

> Even as late as 1990, Shulu government cadres, unlike officials in many other Chinese localities, apparently saw little need to distance themselves from many of the developmental values and goals they thought of as Maoist. Of course they were duly critical of the excesses of radical policies, especially the extremism of the Cultural Revolution. But they did not spend much time disparaging their own past. They were as likely to point out accomplishments made using Maoist policies and methods as accomplishments made under reform [p. 42]. . . . This developmental orientation of state activity, where the state stays above the competitive fray while helping to keep that fray vibrant, fits comfortably within a paradigm of 'market socialism' or 'planned commodity economy', a model now thought by many observers of Eastern Europe to belong on the scrap heap of history [pp. 211–12].

The very fact that growth rates have been slower in those parts of China where local government has not been interventionist[24] reinforces their view that an activist state is a necessary condition for rapid growth.

4. Summary

The international evidence reviewed in this chapter largely refutes the analysis offered by the master discourse on the role of the state. The costs incurred in the transition to market economies in Eastern Europe, Poland, and Chile have been so high that even the high priests of the neoclassical orthodoxy acknowledge they are unlikely to be recouped except in the very long run. The more market-orientated (predominantly Anglo-Saxon) OECD countries have done less well than their interventionist cousins. The rise of East Asia reflects pervasive intervention rather than 'getting the prices right'. Britain's historical record suggests that it is the complete transition to capitalism that is likely to cause slower growth, not the persistence of 'feudal remnants'. Finally, it is not obvious that even in the most clear-cut case of failure—the slow growth rates achieved in state-socialist countries—that their leaders actually aspired to maximize growth.

As for China, three distinctive views of the role played by the state since 1978 have been identified. There are, of course, others but the majority of China scholars can be classified under one or other of these headings. The argument in this book is closest to the third of the assessments of the Chinese state given above. This 'state-centred' explanation of growth is controversial but it will be shown that it is nevertheless the most plausible explanation for China's swift growth after 1978. By boosting aggregate demand, the state pushed the economy on to a higher growth path. Growth was strengthened by continued state involvement in agriculture (Chapter 14), and by the commitment to acquire foreign technology within an interventionist trade regime (Chapter 15). And the Chinese state played a crucial role in improving the performance of the industries owned by the ministries of central government, partly by promoting rationalization, but mainly by allowing local governments to develop industries of their own, thereby promoting inter-industry competition (Chapter 16). This is not to say that Chinese state policy towards the economy was ideal: its neglect of transport infrastructure and many aspects of human-capital formation both served to constrain the pace of economic growth. Furthermore, it would be wrong to ignore the positive impact of the private sector and foreign capital after 1978; the growth rate achieved in the Dengist era was not a product of planning alone. But it is hard to imagine that the pace of growth would have been anything like as fast if the task of growth promotion had been left to the forces of the market.

The discussion proceeds by considering in turn the possible arenas for state intervention, and the extent to which the Chinese state has been successful in each. It begins with macroeconomic policy, which occupies Chapter 13. Chapter 14 shifts the focus to agriculture and Chapter 15 to foreign trade, both areas in which it is often alleged that the impact of the market was decisive. Chapter 16 concludes this evaluation of the economic role of the Dengist state by shifting the focus to industry and infrastructure.

13

Aggregate Demand and Relative Prices

This chapter, along with Chapters 14 to 17, probes the *underlying* reasons for the rapid growth of the Chinese economy in the transition era. In particular, it is argued that the proximate explanations for growth outlined in previous chapters—the favourable Maoist legacy, the high rate of investment in physical and human capital, and economy-wide productivity growth—can themselves be explained in terms of the role played by the Chinese state. This chapter begins that discussion by looking at the way the state boosted aggregate demand, and altered the internal terms of trade.

1. Levels of Government in China

The post-1978 Chinese state was not monolithic. However, it is hard to make a simple distinction between local and central government. For example, industrial enterprises were owned by every level of the Chinese state: central government ministries, the provinces, large municipalities (especially the provincial capitals), urban districts, and counties. Of the 109 million staff and workers employed in state enterprises in 1994, 21 per cent were employed in enterprises owned by central government, 17 per cent in provincial-level enterprises, 26 in prefectural-level enterprises and 39 per cent at the county level and below (ZGTJNJ, 1995: 90). In Sichuan province in 1988, the ownership of industrial enterprises was distributed as given in Table 13.1. However, even this disaggregation does not do justice to the complexity of the situation because it only considers ownership. As Blecher and Shue (1996) note, five types of industry operated in Shulu county at the time they studied it, each functioning in a different way.[1] Local state industries (*difang guoying*) were notionally managed by county governments, but their profits accrued to those higher levels on whose behalf management was exercised. Secondly, some industries were officially designated as collectively owned, but as they were run by the county's Second Light Industry bureau (which received the bulk of their profits), they were essentially locally run state industries. But even here the position was complicated because the cadres employed by the county in its Second Light Industry Bureau were accountable to higher officials in the same industry. Thirdly, not all the state-owned enterprises notionally run by county bureaux were actually under the control of the county government in Shulu; most were, but not all. The fourth Shulu category comprised industries that fell outside the state plan. These were clearly local industries because they were controlled by the county government, to whom the profits accrued (after partial retention by the enterprises themselves). Finally, there were industries both owned and run by high level authorities; these were completely outside the control of the Shulu government. All this demonstrates, in short, that even industries operating at the county level defy easy generalization. They varied enormously in terms of who owned them, who managed them and to whom profits accrued. In addition, of course, no analysis of the role of the state would be complete without mentioning that township and village governments played a key role in managing and regulating the operations of those enterprises that were collective in little more than name (the *xiangzhen qiye*).

TABLE 13.1. *Ownership of state-owned industrial enterprises by level of government in Sichuan, 1988*

Government level	Number of enterprises	Total GVIO (bn. 1990 *yuan*)	GVIO per enterprise (m. 1990 *yuan*)
Central	374	12.75	34.09
Provincial	194	3.04	15.67
Municipality	1,246	18.85	15.13
City	362	1.40	3.87
County	4,472	7.76	1.74
District	279	0.44	1.58
Unidentified	347	2.37	6.83

Note: 'Municipality' refers to cities under the jurisdiction of the province (*shengxiashi*) and 'city' to (smaller) cities under the jurisdiction of prefectures (*dixiashi*).
Source: SCZL (1990: 24).

With these considerations in mind, it is evident that no discussion of the role of the state at all these various levels can be exhaustive. Accordingly, this chapter, and those which follow, focuses on the role played by central government. However, when industry (in particular) is discussed, some attempt is made to distinct between the performance of state and *xiangzhen* industries. Fortunately, Chinese data tend to divide industry into two categories: all industries owned by county governments or above (including industries notionally styled collective) and those operating at the level of the township or below (*xiangzhen qiye*). This distinction is therefore generally followed here, except where it is possible to distinguish clearly between the roles played by county and higher levels of government.[2]

2. The Expansion of Aggregate Demand

2.1. The Macroeconomics of Demand

One of the key contributions made by the central Chinese state to the acceleration of growth after 1978 was its willingness to allow the expansion of aggregate demand. In an economy operating at close to full capacity, such an approach would have been folly. Although there is abundant international evidence of a Kaldor–Verdoorn relation between demand growth and productivity growth (dynamic economies of scale), 'populist' growth strategies of the sort implemented in Latin America in the 1960s, 1970s, and early 1980s that interpreted this relationship too literally were inflationary because of short-run supply-side bottlenecks. However, the Chinese economy was not operating at full capacity in 1978.[3] Its industry and transport infrastructure had been expanded in the three decades after 1949, but the incentive structures needed to fully utilize that infrastructure were not in place. The same was true of agriculture, which had seen a big increase in irrigated area and where increased supplies of chemical fertilizer were to be forthcoming as the plants imported from the West and Japan came on stream during the 1970s. The failure to fully utilize this available capacity was largely a consequence of the Maoist pursuit of defence industrialization. But it was also a consequence of a macroeconomic stance that was unduly conservative in its approach to fiscal and monetary policy. All that changed with a marked increase in aggregate demand in the first years of Dengist rule.

It is not clear what role was envisaged for financial policy (that is, fiscal and monetary policy) by the Dengist regime in the late 1970s. Yabuki (1995: 111) claims that 1978 marked the transition to a more activist approach:

> During the Mao Zedong era, great efforts were made to maintain a balance of government receipts and outlays. Basically, government expenditures were adjusted to remain within fiscal revenues. . . . By contrast, the Deng Xiaoping era brought a change to an activist fiscal policy of issuing government debt and borrowing from abroad and, when the growth of fiscal receipts slowed in consequence of economic reform, of consistently running huge fiscal deficits.

But this analysis is not very convincing. Chen Yun, who exercised a great influence in economic policy-making between 1978 and 1984, had made a name for himself in the early 1950s in helping to devise ways of eliminating hyperinflation. Chen had also opposed the Great Leap Forward. Accordingly, he was not very enthusiastic about uncontrolled fiscal or monetary expansion. More generally, the idea that government revenue should fall short of expenditure on a regular basis was hardly compatible with Chen's devotion to the idea of economic planning.[4]

A different analysis is offered by Naughton (1995*a*). He argues that the Chinese leadership after 1978 was bent upon reversing Hua Guofeng's Ten Year Plan and sought therefore to reduce the growth rate by contractionary financial policy:

> One of the initial objectives of economic reorientation was to create 'slack' in the economy by reducing the pressure of excess demand on available resources [p. 92] . . . planners were most decidedly not aiming at acceleration of the growth rate in the short term. Quite the contrary. They believed that the measures they were taking would reduce the short-run growth rate [p. 94].

More generally, Naughton argues that the Chinese government has not been able to use fiscal policy as a macroeconomic tool during the post-1978 period. This is because decentralization has gradually reduced central government control over tax revenue. Accordingly, the central government has been saddled with a persistent fiscal deficit and therefore has had no option but to manage this deficit by gradually reducing its expenditure:[5]

> Policy-makers don't have the revenue available to reduce the deficit, and they don't dare run a larger deficit for fear that this would signal economic difficulties. Budgetary authorities have therefore been forced to resign themselves to simply managing the decline in revenues and expenditures in an orderly fashion. Previously, only fiscal policy was important; since reform, fiscal policy has been rendered impotent. (Naughton, 1995*b*: 1,086–7)

However, this analysis is not very convincing either. There is no evidence that the Chinese leadership aimed at a contractionary financial policy in the late 1970s. This is not surprising because there was little evidence of general excess demand in the economy; the inflation rate in 1978 was low, surplus labour in agriculture was manifest by the early 1980s, and there was an urban unemployment problem as those exiled to the countryside during the Cultural Revolution returned to the cities. Rather, the aim of macroeconomic policy was *readjustment*: the reallocation of resources from investment and heavy industry towards light industry, agriculture, and consumption against the background of an unchanged macroeconomic stance. Macroeconomic contraction only occurred after 1980 when it became clear that it had proved much easier to increase spending on agriculture (via price subsidies) than to reduce spending on heavy industry. As to the issue of fiscal impotence, it is important to distinguish long and short run. A long-run fiscal deficit is unsustainable, but it is quite possible to combine long-run budget balance with activist fiscal policy in booms and depressions. Furthermore, it is important in assessing the scope for fiscal activism to adjust the deficit for the phase of the cycle (the constant employment fiscal deficit); a deficit of 2 or 3 per cent in a depression is much less of a cause for concern than a deficit of that magnitude in a boom. Accordingly, Naughton's claim that the *average* deficit was too high in China for fiscal policy to be used as a policy instrument in the short run is not very plausible because the average unadjusted deficit is meaningless.[6]

Yet whatever the *intentions* of the policy-makers, it is clear that in practice one of the key contributions of the Chinese state to post-1978 economic growth was the raising of aggregate demand in the early years of Dengist rule. The strategy adopted by the Chinese reformers was to raise demand by means of an increase in credit expansion which took the form of an increase in agricultural profits. The scale of the fiscal and monetary expansion is summarized in Table 13.2. To put the deficits of the Dengist era in context, the Chinese government ran a budget *surplus* in almost every year of the late Maoist period (in this sense, Yabuki's view cited earlier is an entirely accurate description of trends in the deficit). The only exceptions to this were 1967 and 1974–6, and in each case the deficit was caused by a fall in revenue. This was not a result of deliberate economic policy, but was caused by a decline in tax revenue which reflected the disruption to industrial production caused by the Cultural Revolution. In 1967, for example, government revenue fell by 25 per cent compared to 1966, mainly as a result of a 30 per cent fall in the surpluses made by state-owned industries (ZGTJNJ, 1993: 215, 216).

TABLE 13.2. *Monetary and fiscal expansion, 1978–1996*

Year	M0 growth (% p.a.)	M2 growth (% p.a.)	Government spending (bn. *yuan*)	Government revenue (bn. *yuan*)	Government deficit (% of GDP)
1978	n/a	n/a	112.2	113.2	−0.3
1979	26	27	128.2	114.6	3.4
1980	29	27	122.9	116	1.5
1981	15	23	113.8	117.6	−0.8
1982	11	19	123	121.2	0.3
1983	21	20	141	136.7	0.7
1984	49	31	170.1	164.3	0.8
1985	25	17	200.4	200.5	0.0
1986	23	29	220.5	212.2	0.8
1987	19	24	226.2	219.9	0.5
1988	47	22	249.1	235.7	0.9
1989	10	18	282.4	266.5	0.9
1990	13	28	308.4	293.7	0.8
1991	20	27	338.7	314.9	1.1
1992	37	31	374.2	348.3	1.0
1993	35	24	464.2	434.9	0.8
1994	24	34	579.3	521.8	1.2
1995	8	29	682.4	624.2	1.0
1996	12	25	793.8	740.8	0.8

Notes: M0 = notes and coins in circulation. M2 = M0 + enterprise deposits + investment deposits + institutional deposits + rural deposits + peasant sight deposits + worker sight deposits + worker time deposits. Up to (and including) 1993, Chinese accounting practice classified state borrowing at home and abroad as government revenue (Hsiao, 1987: 46–50; ZGTJNJ, 1995: 215–16). A consistent series for government revenue excluding borrowing was published in 1997 for the first time (see ZGTJNJ, 1997: 231–2) and this is given above. The deficit based on this data is expressed in the final column as a percentage of nominal GDP (this latter is taken from Zhongguo tongjiju (1998) and is slightly different from the figure given in ZGTJNJ (1997: 42) for 1996). A minus sign indicates a surplus.

Sources: Yang, 1988: 9 (pre-1985 monetary data); Ma and Sun (1995: 186) (1985–94 monetary data); ZGTJNJ (1993: 31, 215, 227); ZGTJNJ (1994: 544); ZGTJNJ (1995: 32, 215–16, 572); ZGTJNJ (1997: 235); Zhongguo tongjiju (1998: 12, 66).

From this perspective, it is clear that the fiscal policy pursued in the 1980s signalled a clear break with late Maoist practice. Moreover, the break began right at the beginning of the transition era when big deficits were run in 1979 and 1980 (and only a part of the increase in expenditure was down to the war against Vietnam, as will be discussed below). Fiscal policy was comparatively less expansionary in the years that followed, but it is significant that central government ran a deficit in every year after 1981. These deficits were by no means small by the standards of OECD countries (Table 13.3), though differences in accounting practices make accurate comparisons rather difficult. The official data used in Table13.2 suggest that the average Chinese fiscal deficit over the 1978 to 1996 period was 0.9 per cent of GDP, below even that of West Germany in the 1980s. However, IMF estimates are much higher. According to these data, the budget was in deficit in every year between 1979 and 1994. Over this period, the average deficit was 2.3 per cent, by no means unusual by OECD standards. Furthermore, the peak Chinese deficit—5.8 per cent in 1979—was equally normal.

TABLE 13.3. *OECD fiscal deficits, 1970–1990*
(average annual fiscal deficit as per cent of GDP)

Country	1970–80	1980–90	Peak deficit
Germany	1.0	1.5	3.6 (1975)
Japan	4.0	5.1 (1980–9)	6.7 (1983)
UK	3.8	2.4 (1980–9)	7.4 (1975)
USA	2.2 (1972–80)	4.0	6.0 (1983)
China	n/a	2.3 (1979–94)	5.8 (1979)

Note: Chinese figures are IMF estimates.
Sources: WT (1992); World Bank (1996: 94).

It is of course true that the deficits in the second half of the 1980s were recorded despite the best efforts of central government. As a number of writers have pointed out (Wong, 1991*b*; Shirk, 1993; Wong, 1994; Huang, 1996), the late 1980s marked a period of growing fiscal crisis for central government. The centre was able to exercise very little control over the expenditure of local government, and the policies of enhanced fiscal autonomy for the localities—especially for Shanghai and Guangdong, both of which provided a large proportion of pre-1978 central revenue—that had been pursued during the 1980s made it increasingly difficult for central government to raise enough revenue to balance the budget. This policy of 'playing to the provinces' (as Shirk calls it) has undoubtedly complicated fiscal policy. Particularly important here was the introduction of lump-sum revenue-sharing arrangements whereby provinces were required to hand over a fixed sum to the central government and were allowed to keep the remainder. Most of the subsequent local-level expenditure was financed out of this retained revenue; nevertheless, persistent deficits remained the norm and there was little that the state could do to check the profligacy of provinces such as Sichuan, Shandong, Jiangsu, and Guangdong. In Sichuan, for instance, there was a budget surplus in 1980 of 0.4 per cent of NDMP but by 1985 that had become a deficit of 1.1 per cent and it rose further to 3.9 per cent in 1986. Nationally, income raised by local governments increased by 34 per cent between 1981 and 1985 but over the same time period expenditure increased by nearly 97 per cent (SCTJNJ, 1987: 613, 619; ZGTJNJ 1989, 673). These difficulties were summarized by Xue Muqiao (CD, 24 Dec. 1989) as follows:

> In implementing the Party's strategy of economic reform, our over-eagerness to see quick accomplishments has wrought serious mistakes. When a new infrastructure, in which economic levers such as prices, taxes and credits work to regulate the economy, was yet to be instituted, the central government's managerial power in economic planning, finance, monetary affairs and foreign trade were tremendously whittled. Over-centralization became over-decentralization overnight.

Fiscal decentralization has also had the unintended consequence of making the provinces increasingly unwilling to collect tax revenue for the sole purpose of passing it on to central government (Wong, 1994). In addition, the revenue from state-owned enterprises grew much more slowly than either GNP or central-government expenditure. As a result of all this, government budget revenue declined from about 35 per cent of GNP in 1978 to perhaps 20 per cent by the late 1980s (Shirk, 1993: 151–2). This has had important political and economic consequences. As Shirk (1993: 190) concludes:

> The cumulative effects of the economic and political incentives structured by post-1980 fiscal and administrative decentralization was dynamic economic growth distorted by shortages, inflation and deficits as well as by local protectionism [CMB: by which local governments try to maximize local revenue] and administrative meddling. These economic maladies provided ammunition for conservative CCP leaders, who wanted to stem the tide of marketization and restore central financial control.

Nevertheless, even though the deficits in the latter years of the transition era reflected problems of fiscal control, the rise in the deficit in 1979 and 1980 was very much discretionary. Expenditure increased by about 32 per cent in 1978 but this did not result in a deficit because of a similar surge in government revenue. In 1979, however, expenditure rose by a further 15 per cent, and revenue fell slightly. Expenditure fell back slightly in 1980, and this had the effect of closing the deficit somewhat; further cuts in expenditure in 1981 and 1982 also reduced the deficit to a more manageable level (ZGTJNJ, 1993: 215). The detailed reasons for the emergence of a large deficit in 1979 become clear from the data in Table 13.4.

TABLE 13.4. *Sources of the Chinese fiscal deficit, 1977–1980* (billions of current *yuan*)

	1977	1978	1979	1980	1981
Sources of deficit:					
Military spending	14.9	16.8	22.2	19.4	16.8
Farm price subsidies	n/a	5.1	12.4	16.9	19.6
Impact on deficit:					
Military spending	n/a	+1.9	+5.4	−2.8	−2.6
Farm price subsidies	n/a	+5.1	+7.3	+4.5	+2.7
Joint impact	n/a	+7.0	+12.7	+1.7	+0.1
Net change in deficit	n/a	+2.1	+19.6	−3.5	−7.2

Notes: A plus sign in the panel of the table 'Impact on deficit' indicates an increase in the deficit. 'Farm price subsidies' exclude subsidies paid on agricultural means of production of approximately 1.4bn. *yuan* in 1980. The value of this category changed little in the period 1978–81.

Sources: ZGTJNJ (1993: 217, 221). Data on subsidies from SSQ (1984: 714), which gives much more complete figures than ZGTJNJ (1993: 231); the order of magnitude given in ZSSWY (1984) is similar to that given in Zhonggong zhongyang xuanchuanbu xuanchuanju (1988: 46). The reason for the low figures in ZGTJNJ (1993) is probably because part of the cost of subsidies is reflected in the national accounts by a the fall in income from commercial enterprises. They made a profit of 13.7bn. *yuan* in 1978 but this fell sharply to only 5.2bn. *yuan* in 1979.

Two major changes occurred in 1979. First, there was a sharp increase in military spending caused by the war against Vietnam. Secondly, the Chinese government began to provide large subsidies to its Ministry of Commerce in order to hold down the price of key consumer goods—grain, vegetable oil, and cotton—for urban consumers. In all, the government provided subsidies of 73bn. *yuan* between 1979 and 1982 (inclusive) to the Ministry of Commerce to cover its losses. Of this, 23.2bn. *yuan* was due to above-quota sales (Shangye bu, 1984: 400–1). These subsidies were a direct consequence of the abrupt shift in the intersectoral terms of trade in favour of agriculture in 1979; their impact is discussed more fully in the next section.

The expansionary fiscal policy of the early 1990s is also worth noting. In 1989, the fiscal deficit stood at around 2.4 per cent of GDP, not an especially high figure given that this was a period of (comparatively) slow growth. By 1992, however, the deficit had increased to 3.4 per cent of GDP, this time against the background of an acceleration in economic growth (which would in itself reduce the deficit by increasing tax revenue). In other words, once adjusted for the phase of the cycle, the fiscal stance moved from being mildly expansionary (and perhaps even neutral) in 1989 to being strongly expansionary in 1992. Not surprisingly, this fiscal stimulus was reflected in a substantial increase in the growth rate; by 1994, 'overheating' was the norm. Nevertheless, the fiscal stimulus had helped to pull the economy out of the doldrums of 1989–90. These episodes of fiscal expansion during the early 1980s and again in the early 1990s suggest that the central government—whether intentionally or not—did use fiscal policy as an effective tool of economic management.

Monetary growth was also fast during much of the 1980s (Table 13.4). The reasons for this monetary increase were several. First, as has already been discussed, fiscal policy was expansionary. As increases in government spending could not be financed out of taxation, and as the market for government securities in China was relatively rudimentary (though growing), much of the deficit had to be funded by monetary means. Secondly, and more importantly, bank lending grew very quickly during the early 1980s. Regions in the forefront of reform such as Wenzhou spawned a plethora of quasi-banks which lent to relatives and kinship groups, essentially on the basis of trust. In that this enabled them to maintain lower reserve asset ratios than the formal banking system, their expansion led to a much faster rate of growth of lending than would otherwise have been the case. Thirdly, the operation of the banking system itself was only loosely controlled. The underlying problem by the mid-1980s was that soft budget constraints were as much a feature of the functioning of the banking system as they were of state-enterprise activities. Following the greater devolution of power to branch banks that has occurred during the 1980s, the capacity of the People's Bank of China, the reserve bank, to restrict or supervise loans has declined. Indeed the Bank came to function almost as a lender of first, rather than last, resort for the banking system. Thus the willingness of the Bank to provide funds during periods of monetary relaxation enables branch banks to build up reserves. Reserve asset ratios in the mid-1980s typically exceeded

20 per cent when the legal minimum was only 10 per cent (Zhao and Zhang 1988: 30). In consequence, when monetary policy was tightened, local banks could continue to lend simply by drawing down their reserves.

This pattern of movement in the reserve ratio was especially evident in 1985 and 1986:

> The grass-roots banks' hunger for credit volume and the credit allocation measures have led to 'funds stockpiling' on the part of the grass-root banks. An analysis of the quarterly reserve balances of these banks show an obvious 'counter-cyclical' tendency: when the money supply relaxed, bank reserves increase and when the money supply is tightened, the reserves decrease. This flow preference on the part of the banks can only serve to reduce the effect of the central bank's regulatory policies and render it difficult for the monetary policy to achieve the expected results. (Microresearch Department, 1988: 54)

These monetary difficulties were compounded by the authorities' lack of willingness to use interest rates as a tool of monetary policy. Interest rates were no longer fixed by the end of the 1980s, but they still did not reflect market pressures. In any case, because interest payments are included in enterprise costs, they reduce an enterprise's liability to pay tax revenue to the Ministry of Finance. The result was (and is) that monetary contraction is offset by fiscal relaxation.

It is clear from this discussion of financial policy that China's central government—partly by accident and partly by design—was pursuing a policy of rapid fiscal and monetary expansion over the course of much of the 1980s and early 1990s. In conjunction with the economic slack that existed in rural areas at the beginning of the transition, this increase in the level of aggregate demand led to extremely rapid output growth. The late Maoist economy was characterized by enormous supply-side slack, and the balanced budgets of the period had done nothing to eliminate it. In other words, the situation inherited by the Dengist regime was akin to one of Keynesian unemployment, and therefore demand expansion offered an obvious means to unlock the economy's economic potential.

2.2. Weak Inflationary Pressures

Yet one of the most remarkable feature of China's experience is that demand expansion did not trigger any significant inflation until the late 1980s (Table 13.5). The inflation rate did accelerate in 1980 to over 7 per cent in urban areas. However, this was quickly checked, and inflation in the early 1980s was a modest 2 per cent per annum or so. Further, although the inflationary surges of 1985–6 and 1988–9 were marked in the context of what had gone before, these increases had much to do with once-and-for-all price changes and, in any case, swift remedial action by government ensured there was little likelihood of the hyperinflation so characteristic of Latin America or Eastern Europe. Even the inflationary episode of 1993–5—when the retail price index registered a peak annual rate of increase of 21.7 per cent, the highest recorded during the transition period—was brought under control by 1996 without reducing the growth rate of the economy much below 10 per cent.

TABLE 13.5. *Inflation rates in China, 1978–1996* (annual percentage rate of increase)

Year	National retail prices	Urban consumer prices
1978	0.7	0.7
1979	2.0	1.9
1980	6.0	7.5
1981	2.4	2.5
1982	1.9	2.0
1983	1.5	2.0
1984	2.8	2.7
1985	8.8	11.9
1986	6.0	7.0
1987	7.3	8.8
1988	18.5	20.7
1989	17.8	16.3
1990	2.1	1.3
1991	2.9	5.1
1992	5.4	8.6
1993	13.2	16.1
1994	21.7	25.0
1995	14.8	16.8
1996	6.1	8.8

Sources: ZGTJNJ (1993: 237); ZGTJNJ (1995: 233); ZGTJNJ (1997: 267).

These low rates of inflation in China during the early years of reform are rather surprising. One would expect any economy undergoing extensive structural change to experience inflation in the short run; this has been one outcome of reform in Eastern Europe. Why, then, was the Chinese experience been different? The standard explanation is that monetary growth has been accompanied by a marked reduction in the velocity of circulation (Sachs and Woo, 1994; World Bank, 1996: 9; Aghevli, 1996: 291–2). According to Sachs and Woo (1994):

China managed these large deficits without an explosive inflation, principally because Chinese households substantially increased their real money balances during the 1980s: seigniorage was collected without inflation. While the ratio of money to GNP collapsed in Russia, it rose sharply in China [p. 128] . . . The Chinese government maintained positive real interest rates on household bank balances through most of the period . . . Overall Chinese saving rates have been extraordinarily high, more than 30 per cent of GNP in the 1980s rising to nearly 40 per cent in the early 1990s. Much of household saving was held as money balances in the state banking system [p. 129].

In other words, and in terms of the quantity theory of money, a part of the increase in the money supply was absorbed in the form of higher output, and much of the rest (in classic Kaldorian fashion) by a fall in the velocity of circulation. Only a very small part of the increase translated into a rise in prices.

There are two other reasons for China's comparative success. First, and as was seen in Chapter 2, the prices of a wide range of commodities were still set by the state during the 1980s. As a result, inflationary pressures tended to be 'repressed', taking the form of queues and shortages rather than increases in the retail price index. Secondly, and more importantly, the supply of consumer goods rose substantially in the short term. This is apparent in Table 13.6. For each of these major five consumer goods, production was rising during the 1970s and did so at an increasing rate during the early 1980s. The increase in grain production in particular—5 per cent per year—was especially marked. Together, these substantial increases in output did much to hold in check the inflationary pressures of the early 1980s.

TABLE 13.6. *Production of consumer goods, 1977–1984*

Year	Grain (m. tonnes)	Cloth (bn. metres)	Bicycles (million)	Watches (million)	Sugar (m. tonnes)
1977	282.7	10.2	7.4	11.5	1.8
1978	304.8	11.0	8.5	14.1	2.3
1979	332.1	12.2	10.1	17.5	2.5
1980	320.6	13.5	13.0	22.7	2.6
1981	325.0	14.3	17.5	29.1	3.2
1982	354.5	15.4	24.2	33.1	3.4
1983	387.3	14.9	27.6	34.8	3.8
1984	407.3	13.7	28.6	38.1	3.8

Sources: ZGTJNJ (1993: 364, 444–5).

None of this is to suggest that, fiscal and monetary policy was ideal over the course of the Dengist era. The inflationary episodes of 1985, 1988–9, and 1994–5 are an indication that financial policy was sometimes too expansionary. By the middle and late 1980s—when much of the slack that existed in the late 1970s had been taken up—monetary and fiscal expansion translated into inflation as well as output growth. In these circumstances a rather more conservative macroeconomic policy was called for. To be sure, the real growth rates of 1989 and 1900—3.9 per cent in each year—were too slow given the potential of the Chinese economy; some expansion was called for. But the rate achieved in 1992 (14.2 per cent) was far too fast, and reflected an unduly expansionary financial policy. To aim at a growth of about 10 per cent per year—the avowed ambition of the planners after the inflationary debacle of 1994–5—was rather more sensible. Nevertheless, and despite these mistakes, it is hard to avoid the conclusion that the shift towards a more expansionary financial policy after 1978 played an important role in the acceleration of economic growth in the Dengist era. This was one of the key contributions of central government to China's economic success.

3. The Shift in the Internal Terms of Trade towards Agriculture

As was noted in the previous section, one of the main reasons for the increase in aggregate demand that occurred in China in the late 1970s was the shift in the intersectoral terms of trade towards agriculture. As the state was unwilling to pass on the full extent of this price rise to the urban sector, it could only be financed by allowing the budget deficit to rise. Did this change in relative prices stimulate agricultural production, thus holding down inflationary pressures by raising the supply of wage goods like grain and cotton?

Many recent studies have cast doubt on the idea that the pattern of resource flows was systematically biased against agriculture in the late Maoist period (Ishikawa, 1967, 1988; Nakagane, 1989; Karshenas, 1995). These have suggested that agriculture was a net recipient of resources because of rising prices paid by the state for farm products, falling rates of farm taxation, and fiscal transfers from local government. Only in the early 1950s (and perhaps in the middle of the 1960s) was agriculture a net exporter of funds. It has also been suggested that even the impetus for the growth of local industry in the early 1970s, previously thought to have been a classic example of the much-vaunted Maoist policy of rural self-reliance, was provided by central government in the form of subsidies (Wong, 1991*c*).

However, the whole issue of the direction of intersectoral flows is bedevilled by a triple problem: how to account for services (invisible flows), how to define sectoral boundaries and—most fundamentally of all—how to value goods. In a (hypothetical) market economy in general competitive equilibrium, this last point poses no particular difficulty: prices reflect social marginal costs and therefore relative scarcity. However, in 'actually existing' market and planned economies alike, there is no simple relationship between prices and marginal costs. Market economies are never in general competitive equilibrium. Moreover, planners in state-socialist economies have always sought to manipulate prices to serve broader welfare objectives on the grounds that competitive equilibria may be 'efficient' but are unlikely to involve a just distribution of income.

For these sorts of reasons, most Chinese economists have concluded that the prices observed in the Maoist economy diverged from their equilibrium values. The price paid by the state for agricultural commodities purchased from the peasants was too low. More importantly in view of the decreasing returns to 'traditional' farm inputs encountered during the 1970s (which meant that communes were increasingly forced to resort to the use of 'modern' chemical-based inputs), the price of plastics and chemical fertilizer supplied to the agricultural sector was very high by world standards. Moreover, and despite rapid productivity growth in the industrial sector, the prices charged for these modern inputs did not decline markedly over time. As a result, the double factorial (internal) terms of trade show a very different pattern to that charted by the unadjusted terms of trade. In consequence, the extent of 'unequal exchange' between the two sectors increased during the late Maoist period from 23 per cent in 1952 to an average of more than 50 per cent for 1959–73 (Chen and Buckwell, 1991: 106). According to another study by Li (1985: 233), the degree of unequal exchange peaked at 30 per cent in 1965, but even in 1978 (when it reached 25 per cent), it was still 4 percentage points higher than its level in 1952. Yan's (1990: 67) analysis yields a similar result, and a particularly clear conclusion along these lines is that of Sheng (1993).

Of course, the absolute numbers cited in these calculations are of little significance. Such exercises are based upon the notion that the value of a commodity is determined by the volume of labour used in its production, a Marxian approach that is difficult to make operational (how much 'dead' labour is embodied in a particular piece of machinery?). The trend, however, is far from implausible. We know that vast sums were invested in the programme of Third Front construction begun in the Chinese interior in 1965 in an attempt to create an industrial base less vulnerable to either US or Soviet attack. Although much of this was financed in accounting terms by the profits made in the industrial sector, these profits were themselves a direct consequence of the relatively high prices charged for goods sold in the rural sector, i.e. they resulted from unequal exchange. Furthermore, the Chinese leadership of the late 1970s was adamantine in its belief that the intersectoral terms of trade were biased against agriculture, not least because the production of many farm commodities was increasingly unprofitable.

3.1. Increases in Relative Agricultural Prices in 1979

As a result of this perception of continuing 'urban bias', the first major policy initiative of the new government was to raise farm procurement prices in 1979 (Sicular, 1989; Han and Feng, 1992) in the hope that this would revitalize the agricultural sector. On average, procurement prices rose by 22.1 per cent in 1979; for vegetable oil, cotton, and live pigs, the increase was closer to 27 per cent. The average margin between the quota and the above-quota price was increased from 30 to 50 per cent, and the state began to buy increasing quantities of commodities at negotiated prices (a price pegged to the market price, but generally higher than the above-quota price) (Oi, 1989: 158). A further 7 per cent increase in procurement prices occurred in 1980. Over this same period, the rural retail price of agricultural means of production increased by a mere 1.4 per cent between 1978 and 1980 (ZGTJNJ, 1993: 251).

This shift in the intersectoral terms of trade had the effect of increasing profitability in farming. This is plain from the available data on profits (*shouyi*) per *mu* by crop type (Table 13.7). In the case of rice production, earnings quadrupled; for wheat the losses of 1977 and 1978 became profits, and for corn the meagre profits of the mid-1970s became substantial. The same marked turnaround is clear also for 'economic' crops; for example, vegetable oil production became profitable and the profitability of cotton production soared. At the same time, central government acted to prevent any cut in urban incomes. In September 1979, it announced that the retail price of grain, vegetable oil, cotton, and sugar would remain unchanged. The retail prices of beef, pork, mutton, fowls, eggs, fish, vegetables, and milk were raised from 1 November, but urban workers received a 5 *yuan* monthly subsidy (8 *yuan* if they lived in pastoral areas where meat consumption was assumed to be higher) (Zhonggong zhongyang xuanchuanbu xuanchuanju, 1988: 230; Ma, 1990: 406). The resulting losses incurred by state-owned commercial enterprises were financed by subsidies and inevitably caused an increase in the fiscal deficit.

TABLE 13.7. *Trends in profits by crop type, 1975–1980* (*yuan* per *mu*; current prices)

Year	Rice	Wheat	Corn	Vegetable oil	Cotton
1975	1.6	–3.2	2.3	–8.8	10.4
1976	1.4	–4.2	–2.3	–3.9	–2.8
1977	6.4	–11.4	1.3	–11.4	–1.2
1978	6.1	–2.6	0.5	–2.6	12.8
1979	25.0	6.7	12.7	10.9	29.3
1980	23.3	5.7	15.7	10.5	54.0

Note: Profit here is per *mu* after the deduction of material and labour costs, and taxation. Fluctuations in profits primarily reflect variations in yields and the impact of price changes.
Source: Han and Feng (1992: 506–12).

The conventional wisdom is that the 1979 price increase did have a positive effect on output. In part, this presumption is based upon theoretical considerations: one would expect rational farm producers to respond to a price increase by both raising production and the amount marketed. To be sure, it is theoretically possible for production and marketing to fall; that would be the case if the income effect of the price increase outweighed the substitution effect. However, the bulk of the international evidence points to a positive role for relative price increases (WDR, 1986; Mellor and Ahmed, 1988; Sicular, 1989; Behrman, 1993: 176). It also suggests that the output response tends to be greater in the long run because there is then more scope for the relaxation of supply-side constraints. But if supply-side slack exists in the short run—as was most emphatically the case in China in 1979—there is every reason to expect a more or less immediate positive-output response. One would also expect a positive-supply response in the Chinese context because increases in farm profits made possible increased purchases of modern inputs such as chemical fertilizers and plastics, and (arguing along standard 'efficiency wage' lines) they also allowed farmers to spend a part of their higher income on food, thus improving their nutrition and therefore their labour productivity.

The evidence on China broadly supports this contention. According to Stone (1988*b*: 147–8):

> Of course it is virtually impossible to sort out the effects of the price changes alone in the presence of such sweeping reforms. It is quite possible that they would not have been so effective without the other important changes in rural incentive structure allowing farmers to keep most of their increased output or to sell it profitably in the free markets. But it is also clear that without the price changes, the additional application of fertilizers indispensable to such a massive increase in yields might not have been possible.

These arguments are recognized in many studies of the sources of agricultural output growth in the early 1980s (Nolan, 1988; Lin, 1992; Putterman, 1993). Although there are debates about the precise significance of the relative price changes, there is no attempt to dispute the positive effects on output. This conclusion is strongly supported by one recent study on the price elasticity of the marketed grain surplus (Du, 1995). Elasticities were generally low in rich coastal provinces like Guangdong and Zhejiang because higher prices could not offset the much greater incomes to be made from participation in rural industry. However, in the bulk of China, rural industrialization had proceeded much less quickly and therefore grain production was still attractive at higher prices.

The importance of the relative price structure has been reaffirmed by developments in the 1980s and 1990s. In the early 1980s, farmers were paid the quota price for mandatory sales of commodities to the state, and a higher (above-quota) price for deliveries that exceeded the quota. In 1985, however, the two prices were amalgamated into a single 'proportionate' price. In practical terms, this 'shift to proportionate pricing, although designed to maintain the average prices paid for deliveries to the state, effectively lowered marginal prices' (Sicular, 1991: 353); this was because the proportionate price was below the above-quota price. Even after substantial price increases in 1988, the contract price remained no higher than the above-quota price of 1985 at a time when inflation was having a powerful upward impact on market prices. It is therefore not surprising that the period 1985–8 was one of sluggish agricultural growth, and the importance of reversing this trend by altering the terms of trade in agriculture's favour was gradually recognized by both academics and the Chinese government (Ash, 1991; Watson, 1989*b*) (see Table 13.8).

TABLE 13.8. *The internal terms of trade, 1978–1996* (price indices; 1978 = 100)

Year	P_A	P_A/P_I	$P_A/P_{I(PROD)}$
1978	100.0	100.0	100.0
1979	122.1	122.0	121.6
1980	130.8	129.7	129.0
1981	138.5	135.9	134.3
1982	141.5	136.8	134.6
1983	147.7	141.2	136.5
1984	153.6	142.7	130.3
1985	166.8	150.2	135.0
1986	177.5	154.8	142.1
1987	198.8	165.3	148.8
1988	244.5	176.7	157.5
1989	281.2	170.9	152.3
1990	273.9	159.2	140.6
1991	268.4	151.5	133.9
1992	277.5	152.0	133.5
1993	314.7	154.0	132.7
1994	440.3	183.8	152.7
1995	527.9	192.2	143.7
1996	550.1	188.6	138.1

Notes: P_A is an index of the procurement price paid by the state for agricultural products. Before 1985 it is an average of quota and above quota prices; thereafter it is the contract price. P_I is the retail price of industrial products sold in rural areas. $P_{I(PROD)}$ is the retail price of agricultural producer goods sold in rural areas.

Sources: ZGTJNJ (1994: 239); ZGTJNJ (1995: 233, 245); ZGTJNJ (1996: 255, 267); ZGTJNJ (1997: 267, 278–9).

The internal terms of trade shifted in favour of agriculture to the tune of 34 per cent between 1978 and 1981. But between 1981 and 1988, the increase was a more modest 17 per cent; and, as Sicular points out, this change in average prices disguises the decline in the marginal agricultural price in 1985. Even more significantly, and despite CCP rhetoric stressing the importance of agriculture, the terms of trade actually shifted against agriculture by about 15 per cent between 1988 and 1991. The decline in the relative price of grain sold to the state was even more dramatic after 1988. In conjunction with the tendency of local government to pay farmers using IOUs instead of cash, this helps to explain the rural discontent of the early 1990s.

Renewed emphasis on boosting farm prices appears to have been triggered by the 1994 grain harvest of 445m. tonnes, significantly down on the 1993 figure of 457m. tonnes (ZGTJNJ, 1996: 352). This spurred a government response which paralleled the actions of 1979 and 1985: a substantial increase in the procurement price. In 1993, agricultural procurement prices had increased by 13.4 per cent, only about 0.2 per cent more than the rise in the national retail price index. In 1994, however, the price increase was a massive 39.9 per cent, far above the (substantial) 21.7 per cent increase in the RPI. The same pattern was repeated in 1995, when the agricultural procurement price rose by 19.9 per cent compared to a general RPI increase of 14.8 per cent. Price increases on this scale were unsustainable; the cost to the exchequer was too high, and this was reflected in the modest 4.2 per cent increase in procurement prices registered in 1996 (State Statistical Bureau, 1997). But there is little doubt that the policy worked in the short run. From the 1994 nadir of 445m. tonnes, grain output rose to 467m. tonnes in 1995 and soared to 490m. tonnes in 1996—which far surpassed the original forecast of 470m., and even the higher revised forecast of 480m. (SCMP, 5 April 1997; State Statistical Bureau, 1997; ZGTJNJ, 1996: 352). Accumulated stocks were therefore high enough to allow the economy to weather the sharp fall in output in 1998 caused by extensive flooding along the Yangzi valley.

Yet despite this evidence on the positive role of price stimuli, a negative assessment is offered by Hua, *et al.* (1993: 208–9). They dismiss the role of the internal terms of trade in China's rapid growth over the course of the 1980s:

> . . . it is certainly wrong . . . to attribute the growth of grain production to the increased government procurement price instead of the moving back to family farming. . . . because the high self-consumption rate which has characterized Chinese grain production made the increase in state procurement price less appealing to both successful and unsuccessful collectives. For the former, the margin was too small. For the latter, there was no surplus for sale. What is more, the evaluation of grain by the peasants, as expressed in the 'free' market price, was still much higher than the increased state price.

This type of approach accords with their view that privatization rather than price reform was the best way of improving enterprise performance put forward during the debates of the mid-1980s.[7]

However, this dismissal of the role of relative prices is unconvincing for two reasons. First, Hua, *et al.* are correct in noting that the state price for grain in the early 1980s remained below the market price even after the procurement price increase. But at the margin—and it is that, rather than average levels, that matters—the relative increase in the state price must have affected the decisions of farmers. This is because grain sales allowed farmers to acquire cash that could be spent on other commodities. The same argument applies to the volume of sales. Even if the rate of 'self-consumption' was high in poor areas, a price increase would have both raised incomes and provided an incentive to raise production. The analysis would only fail to hold if farmers sold nothing at all to the state (in which case their income would be unchanged) or if there was a binding supply-side constraint which prevented them from increasing production.

3.2. Evidence on the Role of Rising Agricultural Prices

A second reason for being sceptical about the claims of Hua, *et al.* lies in the empirical evidence. Now it is important to tread carefully here. As will become evident, a good deal of information is needed to show that prices did play a positive role in promoting production, and much of this information is not available. Nevertheless, a variety of pieces of local evidence suggest that Hua, *et al.* are incorrect. One such piece comes from the data on the changing structure of grain sales after 1979. If the Hua approach is right, one would not expect to see any sign of increased voluntary sales to the state after the price rise. However, this diagnosis is contradicted by the evidence on Sichuan (Table 13.9).

Table 13.9. *Grain sales to the state in Sichuan, 1975–1981* (billion *jin*)

	1975	1976	1977	1978	1979	1980	1981
Grain tax	2.59	2.73	2.88	2.80	2.50	2.38	2.23
Quota sales	4.01	3.94	4.26	4.18	4.05	4.06	4.04
Share of compulsory sales (%)	92	90	86	82	73	64	60
Above-quota sales	0.57	0.72	1.17	0.98	2.07	2.68	2.83
Negotiated sales	neg.	neg.	neg.	0.56	0.38	1.02	1.36
Share of 'voluntary' sales (%)	8	10	14	18	27	36	40

Notes: Grain volumes in *maoyiliang* (processed grain) one *jin* = 0.5kg.
Source: ZSSWY (1984: 559–60).

These data show that the proportion of grain sales that can be classified as compulsory (tax plus quota grain—often called *zhenggou renwu*) declined between 1975 and 1978. This reflected the long-term trend decline in the grain tax but also the temporary relief granted to producers to enable them to cope with the poor harvests of 1975 and 1976. After 1978, however, the fall in the share of compulsory grain deliveries was dramatic. By 1981, the sum of above-quota and negotiated sales was fully 40 per cent of procurements—five times higher than its share in 1975; and this despite the poor harvests of 1980 and 1981, which would have made farmers less willing to sell grain to the state. In other words, this evidence of rising 'voluntary' grain sales suggests that farmers in Sichuan responded extremely positively to the changes in the relative price structure that were made in 1979.[8]

One might of course argue that this is not a very good test of the Hua hypothesis. After all, poor though Sichuan was in the late 1970s, its counties still marketed a substantial proportion of their output. On a provincial level, therefore, one would expect higher grain sales. A better test would be whether the 1979 procurement increase benefited poor *counties*. In other words, it is important to consider whether Hua, *et al.* are correct in claiming that poor prefectures and counties did not market grain and other agricultural commodities and therefore gained nothing from price changes.

A way of evaluating this proposition is to look at the case of Sichuan's Liangshan prefecture. As noted in earlier chapters this was Sichuan's poorest region, and indeed one of poorest areas in the whole of China in the late 1970s. If the Hua, *et al.* proposition is correct, one would expect to find evidence for it in Liangshan. To give Hua, *et al.* their due, some of the evidence for Liangshan does seem to support their view that poor areas did not gain from the 1979 prices. One of Liangshan's problems was the area's mountainous topography. This restricted the ability of the region to increase production in response to price stimuli. This was especially true for grain output. For although the state did in fact procure (*zhenggou*) 6.19bn. *jin* of grain between 1952 and 1980, this was almost entirely offset by sales of 5.92bn. *jin* (LYZG, 1985: 267). Moreover, the region depended upon grain imports in years of comparatively poor harvests. For the 1952–80 period, imports totalled 1.04bn. *jin* and of these 0.54bn. *jin* were imported during 1966–76 (Liangshan gaikuang, 1985: 268). Of course (although the point seems to be ignored by Hua, *et al.*), the 1979 price increases applied to more than merely grain. However, there is some evidence that the volume of a wide range of procured products actually fell in Liangshan during the late 1970s (Table 13.10). Although the total for items such as tobacco and sugar rose, it is significant that there were substantial declines for many animal products. As the value of tobacco and sugar procurements were not especially high, these declines had a depressing effect upon the overall level of procurements. In 1978, the total value of agricultural procurements for Liangshan was 76.3m. *yuan* (Zhu, 1992: 219). This was well above the 1980 level of 42.6m. *yuan* (LYZG, 1985: 256). Moreover, the increase in tobacco procurements cannot be attributed to higher prices; the tobacco price was not changed from its 1965 level until 1981 (ZSSWY, 1984: 710).

However, none of this is decisive in showing whether Liangshan was a beneficiary of the 1979 price increase because of the many problems involved in trying to interpret the data. For one thing, changes in the volume of procurements depend upon supply conditions and policy as much as they do upon prices. We know that there were four successive good harvests during the late 1970s in Liangshan and this ought to imply rising procurements. (LYZG, 1985: 268). However, we also know

TABLE 13.10. *Volume of procurements in Liangshan, 1976 and 1980*

	Unit	1976	1980	Increase (%)
Pigs	head	219,000	205,600	−6
Cattle	head	64,300	48,700	−24
Sheep	head	6,900	3,000	−57
Sugar	tonnes	7,130	14,621	+105
Tea	*dan*	7,826	9,774	+25
Tobacco	*dan*	37,219	43,641	+17
Cow hides	number	34,045	27,820	−18
Sheep skins	number	514,600	645,652	+25
Other hides	number	35,191	38,902	+11

Source: LYZG (1985: 258, 268).

that a policy (*tiyang shengxi*) of reducing the procurement burden in poor areas throughout the province was being pursued by the provincial government in the late 1970s (Bramall, 1995*a*). In other words, a decline in the volume of procurements cannot be taken as signifying a failure to respond to price incentives. The second problem in analysing the procurement data is that it is unclear how much of the procurement burden was taxation. Terms like *shougou* and *zhenggou* are often used to refer to the combined volume of taxation and procurements. However, the two cannot be treated in the same way because taxation—in contrast to procurements—is an unrequited transfer. It follows that Chinese data showing a fall in either *zhenggou* or *shougou* could reflect a decline in the tax component which offsets the increase in the true procurement total. Finally, the data on the value of procurements cited above are uncertain. Although the *Liangshan gaikuang* (LYZG, 1985) gives a value of procurements for 1980 of 42.6m. *yuan*, the 1986 *Sichuan Economic Yearbook* (SCJJNJ, 1986: 214) gives a figure for the same year of 94m. *yuan*. If true, this latter implies a substantial increase on the 1978 total (if that is itself correct) of 76.3m. *yuan*.

Given all these data problems, the most useful evidence on the impact of the 1979 rise in procurement prices is the direct evidence, namely an explicit statement by the compilers of LYZG (1985: 265) that the price rise 'increased the incomes of the prefecture's farmers by 15m. *yuan*, an average per capita increase of 5.6 *yuan*.' This does not sound like a very large sum. However, one does well to bear in mind the fact that average per capita income for the prefecture was only 120 *yuan* in 1978 (Zhu, 1992: 201), and that rural purchasing power per capita even in 1980 was only 86 *yuan* (LYZG, 1985: 255). Furthermore, in the four poorest counties, per capita income levels had barely reached that level even in 1983; the figure in that year for Meigu was only 114 *yuan* and for Butuo it was 121 *yuan* (Yin, 1986: 145). Moreover, it also needs to be remembered that much of the income of the farm population was in kind. The income increase derived from selling commodities to the state was in cash, and doubly valuable in that—as was the norm throughout

China—the sale of commodities to the state earned the sellers preferential access to farm inputs such as fertilizer. In an economy where cash did not always buy goods because of rationing, this was a great boon. The importance of the 1979 procurement price rise is underscored by the increased volume of sales of agricultural inputs (principally fertilizer). In 1979, the volume of sales was only 18.26m. *yuan*. In the following year, however, it leapt to 35.01m. *yuan* (LYZG, 1985: 259). Without the increase in procurement prices, this increased demand for inputs would simply not have occurred. On balance, therefore, there is evidence here that even poor prefectures like Liangshan benefited from the shift in the intersectoral terms of trade towards agriculture in 1979.

In one sense, the spirit of the Hua, *et al.* approach seems correct: the 1979 price rise undoubtedly benefited those areas which marketed a large proportion of their output more than areas which did not. This is clear from the direct evidence on the varying value of price subsidies paid to enterprises engaged in grain commerce across China. One indication of the impact of the price rises is given in Table 13.11.

TABLE 13.11. *The rise in the value of price subsidies per capita, 1978–1979*

	Net farm income per capita in 1978 (*yuan*)	Increase in subsidy in 1978–9 (*yuan*)	Increase in subsidy (%)
China	134	9.2	6.9
Sichuan	117	5.7	4.9
Liangshan	120	5.6	4.7

Notes: Per capita subsidies are calculated as the total subsidy paid to commercial enterprises divided by the total rural population in the region. These data exclude subsidies paid by the state on agricultural inputs.

Sources: 1978 incomes—ZGTJNJ (1993: 313); value of price subsidies—ZSSWY (1984: 714), LYZG (1985: 265); rural populations—ZGTJNJ (1993: 81), SCTJNJ (1990: 57).

These figures show that the per capita increase in income was much greater for China as a whole than it was for either Sichuan or for Liangshan. Nevertheless, this approach is not especially reliable. These estimates of subsidies are based upon the losses made by commercial enterprises—and hence the decline in government income—as a result of the price change of 1979. However, there is no reason to suppose that the change in the profits of commercial enterprises is a good measure of the impact of the price change on farmers. Profitability may have been boosted by the increased volume of commodities procured following the price rise, and it is not clear to what extent fluctuations in profits reflect changes in internal enterprise efficiency. The figure also ignores sales of commodities to state industrial and other non-commercial departments, and to non-agricultural dwellers.

A better approach is to look at the impact of the price change on the value of agricultural 'exports' to non-agriculture (*shougou*). The *shougou* is the sum of agricultural taxes in kind (*zhengshou*), sales to state commercial departments, sales to other state departments (e.g. industry) and sales to non-agricultural residents (Sheng, 1993: 122–3; Nongye bu, 1989: 396–7; LSTJ, 1990: 26). This is not an ideal measure of the income received by farmers because it includes agricultural taxes, an unrequited transfer; moreover, although data on the *zhengshou* are available nationally, provincial data are hard to obtain. Fortunately, however, this does not matter much because the size of the *zhengshou* by the late 1970s was small. In 1979, its value was 2.95bn. *yuan*, significant in absolute terms but only 4.1 per cent of the *shougou* (Nongye bu, 1989: 397). The *shougou* data are therefore good proxies for the incomes earned by farmers from commerce. As the impact of 1979 price increase by province is known, we can calculate the impact of the price rises on farm incomes by dividing the value of the *shougou* in 1979 by the percentage price increase between 1978 and 1979. The result is a measure of the value of 1979 sales that can be attributed to the price increase alone. In other words, it is the actual value of the 1979 *shougou* less what the *shougou* in 1979 would have been at 1978 prices. We can therefore calculate the impact of the 1979 price rise for provinces. The results are given in Table 13.12.

TABLE 13.12. *Impact of the 1979 procurement price rise on per capita income*

	Per capita value of price rise (*yuan*)	Net farm income per capita in 1978 (*yuan*)	Rise in income due to price rise (%)
Shanghai	44	290	+15
Zhejiang	26	165	+15
Jiangsu	24	152	+16
Sichuan	13	117	+11
Anhui	11	102	+11
Gansu	6	98	+6
Yunnan	6	124	+5
Guizhou	5	108	+4
China	16	134	+12

Note: As explained in the text, the inclusion of the agricultural tax in kind in the value of 'sales' means that the value of 1979 price rise is slightly exaggerated. Per capita values are calculated on the basis of the rural (*xiangcun*) population.

Sources: LSTJ (1990); ZGTJNJ (1993: 313) for per capita incomes.

The values here are considerably larger than those in Table 13.11. However, the spatial pattern suggested by the data on the value of subsidies is replicated in this table. In other words, those parts of China which sold a large proportion of their agricultural output benefited far more than poor areas. The difference is reduced if the impact of the 1979 price rise is expressed as a percentage of farm income; in the case of Shanghai, the 44 *yuan* that accrued from the price rise was smaller in relation to per capita farm incomes than the 24 *yuan* received by Jiangsu farmers. Nevertheless, it is clear that even in percentage terms, rich parts of China benefited much more than the poor provinces of the West such as Guizhou, Gansu, and Yunnan. Precisely because these latter marketed only a small proportion of their agricultural output, the farmers in the three provinces enjoyed an income increase of only about 5 per cent.[9]

We can adopt the same sort of approach at a regional level by comparing Suzhou and Liangshan. The precise data needed for this are not readily available. However, on the basis of the 1980 Liangshan *shougou* of 94m. *yuan*, the gain per Liangshan farmer was 7 *yuan*, or about 6 per cent. This is similar to the figures given in Table 13.12 for Yunnan and Guizhou, which is not surprising in view of the similarities in the degree of commercialization and topography between Liangshan and these two. For Suzhou, it is reasonable to assume that the impact of the price rise must have been very similar to that seen in Jiangsu and Shanghai, namely 15 per cent.[10] This is a far from insignificant difference. The rate of expansion of the non-farm sector was much faster in Suzhou precisely because the 1979 price rise caused a much greater increase in the investible surplus. In Liangshan, the price rise allowed farmers to purchase more farm inputs and raise yields. It also played a role in raising demand for the products of rural industry.

It is also important to note that, even *within* Liangshan, some counties did better than others from the 1979 price increase. The main counties to gain were those located in the Anning and lower Yalong river valleys where grain production per member of the rural population in 1980 was actually 7 per cent higher than the provincial average. These counties were the main suppliers of grain to other areas of Liangshan, both urban and rural. In fact, the counties of Xichang, Mianning, Dechang, Huili, Puge, Miyi, and Yanbian (these last two falling within the jurisdiction of the Panzhihua municipality) had been designated a commodity grain base and, on average, sold between 16 and 21 per cent of their output or about 140m. *jin* in the 1970s The region was thus 'second only to the flatlands in the western part of the Sichuan basin' (SAG, 1980: 65). Moreover, the supply of grain to the state for sale in urban and deficit rural areas appears to have increased in the late 1970s. Of the total grain quota of 223m. *jin* for the prefecture in 1980, 183m. *jin* (82 per cent) were procured from the Anning region (LYZG, 1985: 268, 269). The counties of the Anning area also benefited from the increase in the procurement price for non-grain products. Tobacco and sugar were important products of these counties, and sold at a comparatively high price; the counties of Miyi, Dechang, Yanbian, Ningnan, Huidong, and Huili had even been designated a commodity base for sugar-cane production (SAG, 1980: 82). Pig breeding was also an important source of income, although the predominant breed was much smaller than was the norm in the Sichuan basin, where the 'Neijiang' breed was about 80 per cent heavier than its 'Liangshan' counterpart (Zheng, 1985: 123).

By contrast, the other counties of Liangshan gained far less from the procurement price increase because they were much poorer, and much less market-orientated. In the nine counties of eastern Liangshan—where average temperatures are lower and the topography more mountainous—grain output per head of the rural population was about 12 per cent lower than in the Anning valley and 5 per cent below the provincial average. Moreover, the average grain ration (*kouliang*) for the four poorest counties in Liangshan (Butuo, Meigu, Zhaojue, and Leibo) was only 633 *jin* even in 1983, still below the level achieved for farmers in and around Xichang city in 1980 of 641 *jin* (Yin, 1986: 145; Peng and Zou in Minzu Yanjiu, 1988: 24).

In view of this poverty, the counties of eastern Liangshan relied to no small extent upon grain provided by the central government during the late Maoist period. Between 1955 and 1980, the nine received in total 748m. *jin* of grain from the state. Nevertheless, 58m. *jin* of grain were procured (*zhenggou*) in 1979 even from this poor area, presumably for resale to the relatively small urban population (LYZG, 1985: 269). The effect of the rise in grain procurement prices in 1979 on incomes even in this area was therefore probably positive, although we do not know to what extent the *zhenggou* for these poor counties was comprised of taxation. The fact that the *zhenggou* was reduced from 58m. *jin* in 1979 to 40m. *jin* does suggest that the burden on the area was very considerable. This was probably partly offset by the increase in income derived from the increase in the procurement price of non-grain agricultural products such as livestock and skins.

4. Conclusion

This chapter has considered one of the ways in which the state intervened in the Chinese economy during the 1980s: increasing aggregate demand. The evidence discussed shows that this intervention had a positive effect on the growth rate (although probably at the cost of increasing spatial inequality). On the one hand, the increase in aggregate demand provided a general stimulus to the level of economic activity. As this increase did not coincide with any supply-side crisis (as had happened during the Great Leap Forward, when China ran a large deficit), the inflationary consequences were negligible. On the other hand, the specific form that the increase in demand took (a shift in the terms of trade towards agriculture) helped to generate a large rural-sector surplus that was to supply the finance for the dramatic growth of rural industry. It also, via its substitution effects, provided a direct stimulus to farm production. In that the relative shift of prices towards agriculture tended to benefit the affluent regions (Suzhou) more than poorer regions (Liangshan), it contributed to the rising spatial inequality of the transition era.

14

The Chinese State and Agriculture

It has often been suggested that Chinese growth was driven above all by the decollectivization and marketization of agriculture. This chapter argues that this is misleading. Decollectivization and marketization played a role, but their influence has been exaggerated. In the process, the part played by the Chinese state has been largely overlooked.

1. Marketization and Privatization

The obvious riposte to the 'governed market' conclusion that the state played the key role in the rapid growth of the Chinese economy after 1978 is to point instead to the part played by the decollectivization of agriculture. This process, one of privatization and marketization par excellence, has often been viewed as the source of the agricultural miracle and—because agriculture provided the capital to launch it—the emergence of rural industry.[1]

We do know that the pace of change in agriculture was much faster than in urban industry in the early years.[2] After 1976, controls on the extent of the rural private sector were gradually removed in provinces like Sichuan, where privately operated land increased from some 5 per cent of arable area to between 10 and 15 by the end of the decade (the 15 per cent ceiling was formally approved nationally in March 1981—Central Committee, 1991: 113). This, however, was merely the beginning. As the Communiqué of the Third Plenum made clear, agricultural development was central to economic modernization:

> The plenary session holds that the whole Party should concentrate its main energy and efforts on advancing agriculture as fast as possible because agriculture, the foundation of the national economy, has been seriously damaged in recent years and remains very weak on the whole. (Central Committee, 1991: 13)

By late 1978, experiments had been launched in Sichuan which decentralized farm operations from the production team to the work group in the hope of establishing a much closer link between remuneration and work done, and the process accelerated in the province during 1979. In Anhui (notably in Feixi and Guzhen counties), however, the programme was more radical in that it sought to transfer decision-making into the hands of farm households.[3] Initially, most experiments took the form of the *baochan dao hu* system (contracting output to the household), a scheme in which households were given land to manage as they thought fit but which still required them to hand over any surplus output for distribution by the production team. However, this system gave way in time to the much more radical *baogan dao hu* (contracting everything to the household), which turned not only land management over to the peasantry but also distributed amongst them draught animals and farm equipment. Moreover, once they had met their procurement quota and paid the agricultural tax, households were allowed to retain any surplus for their own use. By the end of 1983, decollectivization was virtually complete with the household re-established as the principal organizational form in the farm sector in Anhui, and across the whole of China.

The process of agricultural transition, however, encompassed more than decollectivization. The early 1980s also saw the reintroduction of rural markets and the abolition of the commune as a unit of local government; from the mid-1980s onwards, the administrative functions of the commune were formally vested in reinstated *xiang* (township) government. Equally dramatically, the controls over cropping patterns of the Maoist era, which were designed to promote self-sufficiency in grain production, were gradually removed, and localities were encouraged instead to exploit their comparative advantage. Perhaps even more fundamentally (as we saw in the previous chapter), the internal terms of trade were shifted decisively towards agriculture in 1979 when state procurement prices were increased by an average of 22.1 per cent and the margin between the quota and the above-quota price paid by the state was raised from 30 to 50 per cent (Sicular, 1989). By providing an immediate boost to farm profitability, this alteration in the structure of relative prices paid a key role in promoting farm-sector output growth.

Nevertheless, the 1979 price changes did not resolve the pricing problem. Two particular pricing problems remained by the mid-1980s. First, procurement prices for farm products remained under state control; although farmers were allowed to sell surplus production on free markets, the bulk of grain, edible oil, and cotton production was subject to mandatory procurement quotas and prices. Furthermore, despite increases in the procurement price in 1979 and at regular intervals during the 1980s, Chinese procurement prices remained below international levels. Secondly, the price at which procured farm products were sold in urban areas remained well below the procurement price. This meant in effect that urban consumers were being subsidized by the state to the extent of the difference between procurement and urban retail prices, with adverse consequences for the state budget.

These problems were apparent in 1984–5, and since then the Chinese government has gone a substantial way towards rectifying them. Nevertheless, and although this process of moving towards (world) market prices has been styled the 'third revolution' in the Chinese countryside[4] (Garnaut, *et al.*, 1996), the process was extremely slow. In 1985, in a change widely heralded in the West as the introduction of market-based price determination, it was announced that contracts would replace mandatory procurements for grain and cotton products. However, this proved to be a false dawn; poor harvests in 1985 led to the reimposition of mandatory quotas in 1986 (Sicular, 1991: 352–4; Sicular, 1995: 1023). Nevertheless, the policy of shifting towards a more market-orientated system was never abandoned, not least because of the cost of subsidies to the state budget. The late 1980s therefore saw a f experiments in different parts of China in which grain sales in urban areas ..idized prices (via the grain coupon system) were reduced or in which all urban grain sales were made at prices much closer to market prices (Tang, 1996: 91–3). Urban residents received partial compensation for the price rises in the form of a monthly cash payment. However, in the context of the more general inflationary pressures in 1988–9, and the popular discontent associated with it, these experiments were not pushed to their logical conclusion and for a while the process of price liberalization stalled.

By 1991, however, it was widely held that economic circumstances were much more propitious, largely because fiscal and monetary contraction had brought a halt to inflationary pressures. Over the two years that followed, the opportunity to introduce more sweeping changes was seized in two ways. First, in measures adopted nationally in May 1991 and April 1992, the grain sale and purchase prices were equalized; this was achieved by urban grain price increases of around 60 per cent in 1991 and 45 per cent in 1992 (World Bank, 1993*b*: 18). Although the urban population again was partially compensated in the form of cash payments, the net result was a modest reduction in (current price) state subsidies for grain, cotton, and vegetable oil from 26.7bn. *yuan* in 1991 to 20.2bn. *yuan* in 1994 (ZGTJNJ, 1994: 224). In real terms, the reduction was of course much bigger. The retail price index increased by 21.7 per cent in 1994 alone, and to have kept pace with inflation between 1991 and 1994, price subsidies would have had to be increased to 38.8bn. *yuan* (ZGTJNJ, 1995: 233). In other words, the real value of subsidies was reduced by about 50 per cent over this period. Secondly, in a process completed by mid-1993, grain prices were substantially liberalized and the use of coupons in urban areas largely abandoned (Tang, 1996: 94–5; Sicular, 1995: 1024). Although this process was partially reversed because of low levels of production and very rapid general inflation in 1993–4 (indeed the need for greater stability and control over prices was emphasized by Li Peng at the NPC in March 1995), there is no doubt that China has come a long way in terms of agricultural pricing since 1985. By late 1994, Chinese and international farm prices had essentially converged (Garnaut, *et al*., 1996: 188–93).

2. The Process of Decollectivization

Despite the range of changes that occurred in agriculture during the transition era, it is the process of decollectivization which has received most attention. It has been viewed as crucial in removing the shackles from the Chinese peasantry and thereby allowing full scope for their creative talents. This perspective is very clear from much of the language used to describe decollectivization; Zhou (1996) calls her book *How the Farmers Changed China: Power of the People*, Wang, *et al.* (1985) entitled their book *Smashing the Communal Pot*, Garnaut, *et al.* (1995) speak of a 'second revolution', and Kueh (1985) of a 'second land reform'.

However, three characteristics of the process of decollectivization are still not fully appreciated. First, it was not really a classical process of privatization. To be sure, farm machinery was sold to farm households during 1982–3. However, farmers gained only management, not ownership, rights over their land. Further, the new organs of local government established after 1983—the *xiang* and the *cun*—continued to play an extremely important management role in many parts of China (Nee and Su, 1990: 18–21; Oi, 1990; Sicular, 1991; Judd, 1992, 1994; Zhu and Jiang, 1993). For example, the *xiang* continued to redistribute land from household to household in response to demographic change. It allowed successful farm households to manage more land if, and only if, they were prepared to make a disproportionate contribution to the *xiang*'s procurement quota and land tax burden. In parts of north-east China, local government encouraged households to amalgamate their holdings into large 'plots' so that the land could be harvested mechanically, and to cooperate over irrigation.[5] Furthermore, although investment in irrigation was suboptimal in most areas during the 1980s, management of water conservancy by local government was not abandoned. In analytical terms, therefore, the agricultural settlement of the 1980s fell far short of satisfying the conditions of the classic property-rights model first put forward by Coase. The ownership rights of farm households were not secure; they could not freely buy or sell land. Their profits from farm production were not secure against predation by local government and their labour could still be 'conscripted' for infrastructural projects. Additionally, their freedom to move about the country remained heavily circumscribed. For all these reasons, many China specialists have been wary of describing the decollectivization process as privatization (Lin, 1988; Rozelle, 1994). According to Andrew Watson (1992: 194):

> The problem facing China's leaders is that the trend of economic development now requires some clear decisions about fundamental issues of ownership and control. Sleight of hand is no longer possible. . . . If the problems of the relationship between local government and economic enterprises, systems of ownership, village management, and cooperative organization are not resolved, distortions will continue.

According to Lin (1988: 196), progress had been made, but the process of marketization/privatization was still incomplete by the late 1980s:

> Most barriers for factor market transactions which existed before the household responsibility system reform have been cleared. Land can be leased out for rent. Interest can be charged for credit. Labor can be hired with a limitation that is not enforced. However, transactions in land, labor, and credit markets are still not very active. The main reason may be due to the fact that a lender's right is not protected by the government; therefore, lenders have to charge high interest rates to offset the risks of default.

The second feature of the decollectivization process was its comparative slowness. Despite the claim made by Sachs and Woo (1994: 114–15) that the process was 'breathtakingly rapid' and that it 'essentially took place in the three years 1979–81', the process is far better described as gradual. For China as a whole, the pace of rural reform is shown in Table 14.1 Essentially, there were three phases. In the first period (1977 to the end of 1980), the most actively promoted system was *baochan daozu* because it remain closest to the system of collective farming. The second phase saw a growing radicalization of the process as the emphasis shifted away from contracting responsibility for production to groups and instead towards households (*baochan daohu*). The process only amounted to decollectivization proper when full responsibility was delegated to households (*baogan daohu*) during 1982–3.

TABLE 14.1. *The pace of rural reform*
(percentage of production teams using each system)

Date	*Baochan daohu*	*Baogan daohu*	*Baochan daozu*
January 1980	4.1	0.02	24.9
December 1980	18.5	5.0	23.6
June 1981	26.6	38.0	10.8
October 1981	26.6	38.0	10.8
June 1982	19.7	67.0	2.1
December 1982	8.7	70.0	neg.
December 1983	neg.	94.0	neg.

Note: The *baochan daohu* category includes the categories identified in Su (1992) as *lianchan daolao* (contracting output to labourers) and *bufen baochan daohu* (partial contracting of output to households) on the grounds that these forms of contracting were very similar to *baochan daohu*. *Baochan daozu* is often called *lianchan daozu* (as in Su).

Sources: Su (1982: 6); Kueh (1985: 125); Wang, *et al.* (1985: 46). Kueh's figures for *baochan daozu* after June 1982 seem inconsistent and therefore are not given here.

There were also substantial variations in the pace of decollectivization at the provincial level. Decollectivization began in the late 1970s in Anhui. 71 per cent of teams there had adopted *baogan* by the end of 1981 (Yang and Liu, 1986: 121) and the figure reached 98.8 per cent by the end of 1982 (HNH, 1990: 539). Other provinces in the van of rural reform were Sichuan, Guizhou, Henan, and Gansu. It is not coincidental that these were the provinces which had suffered most loss of life during the Great Leap Forward. If one measures the intensity of the famine by the ratio of the average crude death rate in 1958–61 to the crude death rate in 1957 (i.e. before the famine), Sichuan heads the list with a ratio of 3.2 : 1. Anhui was second (2.9 : 1), Guizhou third (2.6 : 1), Gansu fourth (2 : 1) and Henan was seventh (1.6 : 1) (Bramall, 1993: 293). These provinces were administered by officials both sympathetic to the views of Deng Xiaoping and willing to experiment (to at least some extent) with rural reform (Hua, *et al.*, 1993: 44). Nevertheless, even in provinces in the vanguard of reform, decollectivization was much slower than in Anhui. In Sichuan, for example, rural reform emphasized the work group (*baochan daozu*) as the basic unit of account until the end of 1980—when *baochan daohu* still accounted for only 10 per cent of production teams. By the end of 1981, 71 per cent of teams had adopted *baogan* in Anhui (as we have seen) but the figure for Sichuan was only 31 per cent (Bramall, 1995*a*). Even in Anhui itself, the pace of decollectivization slowed down after the more sceptical Zhang Jingfu replaced Wan Li as Party secretary in February 1980.

Decollectivization was especially slow in prosperous areas, suggesting that not all of China's farmers viewed collective farming in a negative light. On the Chengdu plain, for example, *baogan* was not generally introduced until 1982/3 (Bramall, 1995a). Tie Ying, the Zhejiang party secretary was unenthusiastic and in Jiangsu, too, there was considerable resistance, especially in the Suxichang area (Liu, 1991*a*; Zweig, 1997). In Shandong's prosperous Yantai prefecture, decollectivization was also very slow because it was seen as interfering with the goal of mechanization. This objection was even more manifest in north-east China. The figures for the adoption of *baogan* for Liaoning (early 1982) and Jilin (October 1982) of 31 per cent and 29 per cent respectively were far below the all-China figure of 38 per cent in October 1981 (Zhongguo nongmin bao, 1983: 44; Bramall, 1993). Even at the end of 1982, when the all-China figure had reached 70 per cent, the percentages for Liaoning and Jilin were only 35 and 30 per cent respectively (Nongye bu, 1985: 71). Heilongjiang, however, is the most extreme case. There the pace of decollectivization was glacially slow (Table 14.2). In the spring of 1982, for example, the extent of *baogan daohu* in Heilongjiang was barely one-eighth of the national average.

TABLE 14.2. *Decollectivization in Heilongjiang province*
(percentage of production teams using each system)

Date	*Baochan daohu*	*Baogan daohu*
September 1981	50.4	0.3
May 1982	n/a	8.7
February 1983	10.0	73.0
October 1983	3.8	87.1

Note: The figure for *baochan daohu* includes *lianchan daolao*.
Sources: HNH (1990: 492, 546, 555); Zhongguo nongmin bao (1983: 44).

The third respect in which the literature on decollectivization is often misleading is in suggesting that decollectivization was a grass-roots movement rather than one engineered by the state. Many Chinese writers have emphasized the former, and this view has been taken by Watson (1984). According to Zhou (1996: 15):

> the Chinese farmers' movement of 1978 to the present as analyzed here is a spontaneous, unorganized, leaderless, non-ideological, apolitical movement (SULNAM) that has succeeded longer and more broadly than any comparable unorganized movement. China offers an extraordinary case in which farmers leached away the economic dominance of an authoritarian government and replaced it with a phenomenal real growth rate, powered almost entirely by farmers' initiative and ingenuity.

This type of argument has been made about the beginnings of the process in Anhui (Kelliher, 1992: 55–64), but also about its propagation even in the north-eastern provinces. According to Hua, *et al.* (1993: 51), decollectivization occurred there in the spring of 1983 as a result of 'tremendous pressure from peasants and cadres at the grass-roots level as well as from central government'. A similar account appeared in *Zhongguo nongmin bao* (1983: 44) in 1983 in which cadres are portrayed as having 'emancipated their thinking' and 'eliminated their misapprehensions'. Other writers, however, have attributed a much larger role to local and central government in the process (Unger, 1985–6; Hartford, 1985; Endicott, 1988; Hinton, 1992; Judd, 1992); even for Anhui, a good deal of credit has been awarded to Wan Li, the provincial party secretary (Wang, 1988; Fewsmith, 1994: 49).

The problem with the argument that decollectivization was a process led from below is twofold. First, it is hard to believe that farmers in Anhui could have organized themselves to overthrow the collective in the way suggested. It is not impossible for private households to solve what Olson calls the 'collective action problem' but it happens extremely rarely. Most revolutions, for example, occur because of a combination of state weakness, an organized and disciplined opposition, and widespread unrest (Skocpol, 1979), not through any single element in this trinity. In the case of China, it is especially implausible to portray the farmers as 'spontaneously' banding together to overthrow the collective precisely because, if they had been capable of such cooperative behaviour, collective farming would have been a great success; cooperation would have obviated the need to provide incentive systems and to supervise the workforce. The best explanation of decollectivization in Anhui is that local and provincial leaders took advantage of peasant resentment to encourage a return to family farming. The degree of opposition to collective farming may have been higher there than in other parts of China (because of the intensity of famine after the Great Leap Forward and very slow growth thereafter); there was also the collective memory of the 'responsibility fields' of the early 1960s as a guide to how successful family farming could be. But it would be wrong to neglect the role of leadership even in Anhui.

Secondly, the evidence in other parts of China shows that there was considerable resistance at a grass-roots level to the decollectivization movement, which meant that ultimately it had to be imposed. According to Kelliher (1992: 105):

> Yet without question a significant number of communities opposed this division of land, sometimes bitterly. For reasons of wealth, ideology, topography, farm mechanization, and market access, these communities had deep misgivings about family farming. They preferred the collectives, but were helpless to resist family farming once the government mandated it.

In Sichuan, most of the counties on the Chengdu plain did not decollectivize until the autumn of 1982—even though group contracting originated in that very region (in Guanghan county) as early as 1977—because it was not seen as offering very much to relatively prosperous collectives (Endicott, 1988; Bramall, 1995*a*). Not surprisingly, there was resistance to decollectivization in Dazhai and in other parts of Shanxi. In the case of Heilongjiang, decollectivization occurred especially late, as we have seen. In part, this reflected the hostility of provincial officials (notably Yang Yichen, the provincial Party Secretary). But, and at least as importantly, it also reflected the nature of production. Precisely because Heilongjiang was both a wheat-producing area and (partly as a result) relatively highly mechanized, there was very little enthusiasm for decollectivization.[6] In Xiaji village (Shuangcheng county), there was opposition because, despite severe shortages during the Leap, the village had successfully mechanized production and was thus one of the richest in northern China. Nevertheless, this did not stop the privatization of farm machinery during decollectivization in 1983 (Yan, 1996: 31).[7]

3. Decollectivization and the Growth of Agricultural Output

The key question about decollectivization—which, despite being pushed by the state, clearly amounted to a reduction in the role played by the state in the rural economy—is whether it played an important role in the substantial rise in agricultural output in the early 1980s.

On this question, few scholars have argued that decollectivization raised output in every part of China. In many parts of Gansu, the absence of water supplies was a binding constraint. In the most advanced areas of Jiangsu, yields were already above the Japanese average by the late 1970s (Huang, 1990). Nevertheless, even in these areas, decollectivization had merit: arid Gansu and technologically advanced Jiangsu benefited because decollectivization released labour that could be redeployed to the non-farm sector. In general terms, however, the case for decollectivization rests on two pillars. First, the performance of collectivized agriculture during the late Maoist period was poor because of the weak incentive structure within the communes and because of the insecure nature of Maoist property rights. Secondly, there is econometric evidence which suggests that the bulk of agricultural growth in China during the period between 1978 and 1984 can be attributed to decollectivization. We explore these arguments in turn.

The Failure of the Maoist Collective

The conventional wisdom in the literature is that Maoist yields were substantially below potential because of the impact of the commune and the system of property rights it embodied (Watson, 1983; Nolan, 1988; Putterman, 1988; Selden, 1988; Friedman, *et al.*; Putterman, 1993). Although farmers had an incentive to participate in collective work (because they accrued workpoints in doing so and because notionally competitive private-sector employment opportunities were very limited), on-the-job shirking was the norm. In the main, this was because exhortation (or what one might call the ideological motivation of 'building socialism') was increasingly ineffectual in motivating the rural population, and because the value of workpoints was dependent upon the efforts of other commune members such that the direct link between effort and remuneration was severed. Neither of these failures would have mattered much if it had been possible to properly supervise farm work, but in the event that proved virtually impossible. As Liu (1994: 113) points out, supervision is the key issue:

The critical factor here is work supervision or effort monitoring. When a member's effort could not be properly monitored, there then existed incentives, and scope, for him to shirk, since he could then secure the same number of workpoints while not having to put in the required amount of effort. Putting in more effort could raise total collective production, but he would himself be entitled to only a very small share . . . This is, of course, a typical free-rider case. It is this aspect of the commune, or the effort-saving phenomenon widespread under it, that I think people really have in mind when they now deride the commune as a 'big public pot'.

But successful mutual supervision was ruled out because the commune was as much a social unit as a unit of production; any farmer criticizing the poor quality of the work carried out by a neighbour was likely to face social ostracism and therefore it was easier to keep quiet. Moreover, the low value of the workpoint, and the limited differential between workpoint earnings per task, did little to encourage cadres to supervise effectively (Nee and Su, 1990: 8). Furthermore, the very nature of farm work—spatial-dispersed, weather-sensitive, and generating a product that could not be 'disaggregated' into its component parts for the purpose of identifying the causes of poor quality—made supervision an immensely onerous task even for a committed cadre.

Hua, *et al.* (1993) summarized the failings of Maoist agriculture thus:

. . . to most peasants in rural areas, socialism, which was believed to be a Garden of Eden, turned out to be an unbearable nightmare [p. 39] . . . the immediate consequences of collectivization in China were no less disastrous than in Russia. Tens of millions of people died of starvation during the period 1959–61. . . . When the radicals and the military took over the administration of the rural economy, the movement ['in agriculture, study Dazhai'] turned out to be forced labour on a huge scale. Tens of millions of peasants were exhausted by working 365 days a year . . . They had to cultivate the land, which nominally belonged to them, on the orders of the cadres, no matter how ridiculous the orders might be [pp. 40–1] . . . In 1978, before the reform, there were more than 150 million peasants still suffering from hunger. Annual consumption of coarse food grain was less than 150 kilograms per capita on average. More than half the Chinese peasants were worse-off than they had been in the mid-1950s, and some were even worse off than they had been before the communist revolution [p. 41].

By contrast, family farming would not only eliminate the coercive aspects of the commune but also improve incentives by providing a direct link between effort and farm income. The logical corollary was of course that yields could be raised by abolishing the commune and by reinstating family farming. Some of these gains would inevitably be one-off. However, in so far as the restoration of family farming would raise farm profits and provided these profits were reinvested in the farm sector, there would be dynamic gains as well. Moreover, these could be enhanced by the introduction of a proper system of formal property rights to land. In this way, family farmers would be provided with an incentive to invest in their land and its improvement. In large measure, these were the aims of rural policy in China during the 1980s and early 1990s.

To be sure, not even the most vehement critics of the Maoist development strategy believe that every collective failed. The case of Dazhai (a production brigade in Shanxi's Xiyang county) in particular has attracted enormous controversy.[8] Dazhai was regarded as a 'model' brigade during the late Maoist period because of the way that its workforce was galvanized by its leader (Chen Yonggui) to build dams, terrace hillsides, and more generally raise grain yields to a level on a par with communes operating in South China—where rainfall was much more abundant. In the language of the 1960s, Dazhai 'crossed the Yangzi river'. All this was achieved by self-reliance; despite catastrophic flooding in September 1963 (which destroyed many new fields and most of Dazhai's houses), Dazhai was still able to meet its procurement targets without any state aid. After 1975, however, Dazhai achieved the unusual distinction of being criticized both by Jiang Qing (and other members of the Gang of Four) and by the Dengist regime.[9] It has, for example, been suggested that Dazhai received covert state aid, that its success was due to the income generated by its coal mines or that its grain yields were simply fabricated—charges refuted by Dazhai's (many) defenders. As a result, the reality of Dazhai's achievements have been hopelessly obscured. Nevertheless, the point about Dazhai for many of the critics of collective farming is that, even if successful, Dazhai and others like it were exceptional; in the majority of cases, Chinese farmers preferred family farming (Kelliher, 1992: 105). It has never been doubted that inspired leadership could overcome the deficiencies of the communal incentive system and perhaps, it is argued, Chen Yonggui provided exactly that in Dazhai. But this was not the norm across the People's Republic. Ultimately, and in the absence of Chen's charismatic leadership in other Chinese production brigades, the only way to overcome the mutual distrust of the peasantry was to restore family farming.

The Econometrics of Decollectivization

The case for decollectivization has also been argued on the basis of the econometric evidence. The approach generally adopted is to run a regression in which gross output is the dependent variable. The independent variables are factor inputs (land, labour, capital, and chemical fertilizer), product prices (to capture the impact of changes in the intersectoral terms of trade), the non-grain crop share, the multiple cropping index, a time trend (to capture technological progress), and the proportion of teams using the responsibility system.

The results of this type of growth accounting for China during the early 1980s are shown in Table 14.3. The conclusion of these growth-accounting exercises is clear. Output growth was caused by a combination of factors, but the roles played by greater inputs of chemical fertilizer, changes in the intersectoral terms of trade, technical progress, and—crucially—decollectivization stand out. As for productivity growth, in all but Kim's study it is decollectivization that was the crucial factor.

TABLE 14.3. *Econometric studies accounting for the rise in agricultural output, 1978–1984* (percentages)

Independent variables	Lin 1978–84	McMillan 1978–84	Kim 1981–4	Fan 1965–85
Output growth due to:				
Land	–2	–1	neg.	neg.
Labour	5	6	1	8
Capital	11	6	12	19
Fertilizer	32	7	–1	31
Prices	—	—	–11	—
Decollectivization	47	71	33	27
Multiple cropping	–2	—	—	—
Non-grain share	4	—	7	—
Residual	6	11	40	16
Productivity growth due to:				
Decollectivization	87	78	36	63
Prices	—	22	–12	—
Multiple cropping	–4	—	—	—
Non-grain share	7	—	7	—
Technical progress	10	—	45	37

Notes: The non-grain share is the proportion of area given over to non-grain crops. The shift away from Maoist emphasis on grain self-sufficiency is alleged to have raised output by allowing regions to exploit their possible comparative advantage in non-grain production. Prices refers to the ratio of above-quota prices to the price of industrial products in rural areas. The contribution is negative in Kim's study because of the time period he uses, which excludes the dramatic price change of 1979. The McMillan study uses national data, Lin uses provincial data, and Kim uses figures from the single township of Dahe (Huailu county, Hebei). Prices do not enter Lin's growth-accounting approach as an independent variable; the impact of price changes is instead reflected entirely by changes in factor inputs. The introduction of the HRS is assumed not to change the volume of input use, but only their productivity. In order to estimate the impact of price changes, Lin (1992) estimates a 'supply response function'. This approach yields the result that changes in the intersectoral terms of trade accounted for 16 per cent of output growth. Dashes in the columns indicate that this independent variable did not feature in the analysis.
Sources: McMillan, *et al.* (1989: 794–5); Fan (1991: 273); Lin (1992); Putterman (1993: 199).

4. Towards a Reassessment of the Maoist Collective

The critique of Maoist collective farms outlined in the previous sections is overdone. In most accounts, a straw man is set up in which an ideal family farm is contrasted with 'actually existing' communes. Implicit here is the notion that capitalist family farms employ labour up to the point where the real wage rate is equal to the marginal productivity of labour. As a result, workers and family members are powerfully motivated because they are paid their marginal product. The distribution of income is therefore 'just' and there is no need to monitor performance. But nowhere in this account is there any place for the exploitation of workers by their employers, or female family members by male heads of households. To be sure, collective farms did not eliminate problems of intra-family distribution but, by giving female members of the family an independent source of income via work on the collective, they did do something to alter the balance of power within households.

The 'straw man' approach is also apparent in some of the property rights literature on China, which contrast the insecure property rights of the Maoist era with the secure ones of the 1980s. According to Nee and Su (1990: 22):

> By establishing a contractual relationship between state and market, thereby limiting the arbitrary power of the state in directly intervening in economic activity, the state has sought to specify and define a new set of norms, or operating procedures, that have redrawn the boundaries among state, society and economy. Taking the state out of direct control over agricultural production and economic transactions has lowered transaction costs and paved the way for consolidating property rights that are more favourable to economic growth.

But as we have seen, it is hard to argue that property rights were secure, or that the 'arbitrary power' of the state was circumscribed after 1983. Local government played a key role in levying taxes and fees, requiring labour services for water conservancy, and in redistributing land between households; a good illustration of a pro-developmental interventionism is the role played by the county government of Shulu in Hebei (Blecher and Shue, 1996). Additionally, central government continued to impose both procurement quotas and prices for most key crops throughout the 1980s. If anything, growing inequality in the countryside increasingly led to the 'capture' of local government by richer rural entrepreneurs, who were able to influence policy to suit their own objectives.

In addition, too many accounts of decollectivization ignore the way in which economies of scale are lost in small-scale family farming because of boundaries and the small average size of plots. Minute farms have become almost universal in China since 1983; these farmily farms averaged less than 10 *mu* in size and, to ensure the allocation of land of roughly equal quality to each family, the decollectivization settlement broke up these holdings into eight to ten non-contiguous plots. Indeed decollectivization was strongly opposed in many of the wheat- and corn-growing areas of northern China precisely because of these adverse implications for mechanization (Kelliher, 1992: 106; Hinton in Qin, 1995). As a result, there have been many calls for farmland consolidation programmes; the importance of these programmes is underlined by the fact that consolidation has actually been carried out in Taiwan since the 1960s (Bain, 1993). Moreover, it is revealing that even J. L. Buck (1947: 34) —no admirer of collective farms—was fiercely critical of the larger Chinese farms of the pre-1949 period on the grounds that they were too small:

> In China, at least 80 per cent of the farms are too small to be economic units and studies made by the Department of Agricultural Economics, University of Nanking, have shown that profits from farming increase with size of farm, until the most economic unit is reached.

A similar argument has been made using Buck's data by Chinn (1980) who shows that cooperation in principle allowed greater crop specialization and fewer seasonal labour constraints in northern China compared to pre-war family farming.

Finally, one must remember the luminous record of the collective in promoting the development of irrigation as noted in Chapter 6. For example, the remarkable drainage tunnels built under the roads of rural Suzhou in order to maximize arable land availability were built by China' collectives. From all this, it is clear that collective farms did offer a number of advantages which were lost after the transition to *baogan* in 1982–3.

5. The Evidence on Decollectivization and Agricultural Growth

The empirical evidence on the role played by decollectivization in the surge of agricultural production in the early 1980s is also less than compelling because of the problems which afflict the existing econometric studies. First, the level of analysis. McMillan, *et al.* (1989) construct an all-China production function, but that makes little sense in view of vast regional variation (especially between the predominately wheat-producing north and the predominantly rice-producing south). Kim's work suffers from the opposite problem; it is unwise to draw any conclusion about the national picture from a single township in Hebei.[10] Lin's (1992) provincial study is a compromise between these two extremes, and therefore has at least something to recommend about it. Even so, and in view of the enormous regional variation within provinces, it remains less than convincing; the level of disaggregation ought to be that of the county.

A second problem concerns the measurement of inputs. For some inputs, the problems are trivial. For example, although the area of cultivated land is under-reported in the official data, we know that it changed comparatively little in the early 1980s. Under the heading of fertilizer, Lin ignores organic fertilizer but this probably matters little. Although transport improvements may have allowed farmers to increase the use of night-soil produced in urban areas, it is hard to believe that this was very significant, Moreover, the pig stock was virtually constant in the early 1980s, thereby producing little change in the supply of pig manure. As for capital, Lin rightly avoids the valuation problem in an economy where prices differ markedly from marginal costs by measuring it in terms of horsepower. However, the very fact that Lin considers only tractors and draught animals severely circumscribes his analysis because it ignores the role of transport (increased supplies of trucks and bicycles), plastics (for buckets and crop protection), and pumps (for irrigation). The most serious problem vis-à-vis inputs concerns the measurement of labour. McMillan, *et al.* avoid this problem by looking at the gross output value of agriculture as a whole. As labour force data are available on this, measuring labour inputs is a simple matter. Unfortunately, this gain is more than offset by the impossibility of estimating non-labour inputs for subsectors such as sidelines and forestry. It is not sensible to estimate a production function for agriculture as a whole when agriculture is defined in standard Chinese fashion to include forestry, sidelines, and aquatic production as well as cropping.

Lin's study is undoubtedly the best of the published econometric studies. It uses the available data with considerable care, and sensibly estimates a production function for crop production rather than agricultural output as a whole. Nevertheless, Lin's work remains unconvincing because of the underlying problems with the data, especially those on labour inputs. The problem is that there is no reliable way in which to allocate either the rural or the agricultural workforce by subsector. We simply do not know how much labour was supplied by either the main or the subsidiary (children and the elderly) labour force to the crop sector. Lin, who admits that 'data on the labour force in the cropping sector are not directly available', uses the share of crops in gross agricultural output as a proxy. But that leads to a clear bias, as is clear from the data given in Table 14.4.

TABLE 14.4. *Shares of the crop sector in agricultural employment and output* (percentages)

Province	1980			1985			Change,
	Employment	Output	Ratio	Employment	Output	Ratio	1980–5
Jiangsu	97.6	68.6	0.70	89.9	60.5	0.67	−3
Zhejiang	75.7	66.1	0.87	71.2	51.1	0.72	−15
Guangxi	85.1	81.2	0.95	85.3	73.2	0.86	−9
Ningxia	96.7	68.5	0.71	94.9	73.1	0.77	+6
China	91.9	67.7	0.74	89.2	55.4	0.62	−12

Note: The final column is the change in the ratio of output and employment shares between 1980 and 1985. Agricultural output here is gross output value at current prices. These data come from a labour-force survey of 222 *cun* drawn from ten provinces and Shanghai, and covering 189,000 workers.

Source: Yu (1989: 6, 19, 66, 82, 88, 105, 226, 242, 248, 265).

In the case of each of the four provinces given here, and for the sample as a whole, it is clear that the employment and output shares of the crop sector did not move hand-in-hand during the period between 1980 and 1985. In general, the two moved in the same direction, with the importance of the crop sector tending to decline as reform unleashed a process of agricultural diversification. However, the decline in the output share was far more dramatic than that of employment. In Jiangsu in 1980, for example, the bulk (98 per cent) of agricultural labour was employed in the crop sector, but that sector provided only 69 per cent of output. By contrast, the employment and output shares were very similar to each other in Guangxi. In other words, using output as a proxy for employment understates the contribution of labour to agricultural output growth in production functions.

In addition, a remarkable omission from the econometric studies is the role of irrigation. The expansion of irrigated area was one of the major achievements of the collective era, and it contributed to the growth of the late 1970s and 1980s in a critically important way. But the impact was lagged. Only after the mid-1970s, when chemical fertilizer became more generally available (and could be afforded by Chinese farmers following the 1979 price rises) and new high-yielding varieties began to make an appearance, did irrigation help to raise yields. As Hussain (1989: 238) rightly says:

> . . . a large credit for the rates of growth since 1978 must go to technical change, interpreted broadly to include increased application of inputs made possible by the introduction of HYVs in the past. The shift over to family farming has indeed led to a more efficient utilization of technical possibilities, but it was the introduction of HYVs and the massive investment in irrigation that created those possibilities in the first place.

However, because irrigated area itself expanded little in the late 1970s and early 1980s, its importance in the growth process is completely missed in the econometric studies.

The final problem with the econometrics lies in its treatment of fluctuations in output induced by good and bad weather, a factor which in essence is ignored (Putterman, 1993: 202 n. 17). In Lin (1992: 17), for example, weather only matters in so far as it has 'region-specific' effects; it can therefore be dealt with by the use of provincial dummies. There is no effort in any of the studies to smooth out the agricultural output to remove weather-induced fluctuations, still less any attempt to use weather as an independent variable. This would not matter so much if the economy had been highly industrialized, or crop output had contributed only a small share of output value. But this was not the case for China, where farming contributed 77 per cent of gross agriculture output value in 1978 (LSTJ, 1990: 11). Furthermore, Chinese agriculture remained sensitive to the impact of the weather, which tends to bias econometric analysis in favour of decollectivization as follows. 1976–8 were generally years of poor weather, although it suits many admirers of the Dengist regime to argue that output was depressed because of the Cultural Revolution. 1980 and 1981 were also in general rather poor years. By contrast, there was remarkably good weather in the three successive years beginning in 1982. The effect of the weather is therefore to magnify the impact of decollectivization on output in 1982–4, and to mask the positive impact of the change in the terms of trade and other reforms that occurred in the late 1980s (and which will be discussed shortly).

Two examples of the role played by the weather will help to make this clear. First, 1981 saw an extremely bad harvest in Sichuan. The summer saw the worst flooding of the century in Tuo and Jialing river valleys. 18m. *mu* of arable land were inundated across the province and over 1,000 people died. Furthermore, much of the damage (and 200 deaths) occurred on the key Chengdu plain (Guojia kewei quanguo zhongda ziran zaihai zonghe yanjiuzu, 1993: 263). Agricultural output on the Chengdu plain was still higher in 1981 than it had been in 1980 (Chengdu shi renmin zhengfu jingji yanjiu zhongxin, 1987: 651). Nevertheless, for the province as a whole, real net agricultural output value in 1981 grew by only 4 per cent; it had grown by 9 per cent in both 1979 and 1980 (SCTJNJ, 1990: 31). By contrast, and fuelled by the return of good weather in 1982, agricultural output in that year rose by 12 per cent. The effect of all this in terms of the econometrics is to mask the impact of the 1979 shift in the intersectoral terms of trade and *baochan* on output in 1980 and 1981, and to exaggerate the impact of *baogan* in 1982–4. Another example comes from the north-east (Bramall, 1993: 290–1). In Heilongjiang province, where decollectivization did not really begin before 1983, real net agricultural output did surge in 1983 by no less than 23 per cent (LSTJ, 1990: 281), but it was no coincidence that 1983 saw the best weather of the decade, whereas that for 1981 and 1982 was poor. Again the impact of the initial reforms was masked by poor weather, and the effect of subsequent decollectivization markedly overstated.

In sum, therefore, the econometric evidence showing that decollectivization was decisive in promoting agricultural growth is thoroughly misleading. Too many of the studies use all-China production functions. The acute problems involved in measuring input use are ignored. The role of irrigation is invariably omitted. And the treatment of weather in these studies is decidedly suspect.

6. An Alternative Explanation: Group Contracting and Readjustment

There can be no denying that 'actually existing' Maoist collective farms did fail in a number of ways. For instance, the workpoint differentials between jobs and between commune members was too narrow. As a result, the more gifted and the more industrious of the workforce were inadequately rewarded and this adversely affected labour productivity. The workpoint system was also remarkably sexist in the way that it operated: the most talented women could almost never earn as much as the most incompetent men even when doing the same task. Potter and Potter (1990: 120–1) present data showing that 83 per cent of men in the Zengbu area of Guangdong were classified as first-class workers—compared to only 25 per cent of women. Furthermore, the workpoint rating of a fourth-class male worker (9.1) was significantly higher than that of a first-class female worker (8.3).

Perhaps most fundamentally of all, and especially during the early 1970s when the campaign to 'learn from Dazhai' was in full swing, farmers were often rewarded for what might be called their 'ideological enthusiasm'—their willingness to participate actively in political work and to show a positive attitude towards Maoist policy. For example, mere attendance at political study classes brought an award of two work points in Anhui during the early 1970s (Wu, 1993: 295). A further problem with the Dazhai system was that the workpoint ratings assigned to individuals were based upon assessment at public meetings. In practice, and in order to avoid recrimination, it was easier for farmers to avoid criticizing each other. As a result, there was a tendency for almost all able-bodied workers to receive high ratings, irrespective of their merits. Finally, strict post-1957 controls on migration and over the types of work that farmers could engage in contributed (not least over the size of private plots) to feelings of alienation by restricting choice.

It follows that simply reforming the mode of operation of collective farms might have led to big increases in agricultural output and productivity. This is precisely what happened after 1976 across China. The process of institutional change did not involve any sudden replacement of collectives with family farms, but rather the gradual reform of the collective system. The initial changes took the form of the restoration of the workpoint systems that had operated in the mid-1960s before the 'learn from Dazhai' movement. These systems typically combined two elements. First, there was a piece-rate system. This was the labour-contract or work responsibility system (*baogong zhi*) under which workers were paid workpoints in return for the completion of a specific task, e.g. sowing; ploughing. Secondly, a time-rate system was used for other jobs (such as carrying water). Under this system, each worker was given a workpoint rating per labour day, and was awarded that rating irrespective of the task undertaken. Thus a woman with a workpoint rating of eight would be awarded eight workpoints for every day spent weeding or carrying water. If she spent a day carrying out a task for which piece-rate payments applied, she might earn more than that, e.g. eleven workpoints for ploughing a distant field. Although the precise remuneration system varied from location to location, the use of piece-rate systems was increasingly the norm during the late 1970s (Potter and Potter, 1990: 120).

But the restoration of the workpoint system did nothing to resolve the problem of monitoring the quality of performance. As a result, the late 1970s saw the gradual introduction of output responsibility systems (*lianchan zhi*) that involved the linking of remuneration with the actual output produced by a group (*lianchan daozu* or *baochan daozu*) or by a household (*baochan daohu*). This reduction in the size of the accounting unit served to tie income much more closely to output per head. In parts of Guangdong, this system was launched in 1979 (Potter and Potter, 1990: 167). In Sichuan, it began during the summer and autumn of 1977 (Bramall, 1995*a*). The system of group contracting does not appear to have spread especially quickly. By January 1980, some 24 per cent of production teams were using this system across China, a considerable rather than a massive proportion. Nevertheless, the system was comparatively popular in some areas. By the end of 1979, for example, the percentage of teams using the system of *baochan daozu* reached 25 per cent in Beijing, 29 per cent in Inner Mongolia, 42 per cent in Guangdong, 52 per cent in Guizhou, 58 per cent in Sichuan, and 62 per cent in Anhui (Wang and Zhou, 1985: 44).

The reason for the comparatively slow diffusion of *baochan* may be that the system was simply a compromise between collective and genuine family farming. The *baochan* systems sought to combine the positive incentive effects of small-scale, family farming with the mobilizational capacity of the collective and continued collective control over income distribution. Thus *baochan* centred around the retention of the production team as the unit of account. Although groups and households received additional workpoints for overfulfilment of their contract, the value of these workpoints was dependent upon the performance of other groups or households within the production team. Nevertheless, the awarding of workpoints in the late 1970s on the basis of output generated powerful incentive effects compared with both the task-based and Dazhai workpoint systems. It was the decentralization of production to households and groups that made this new system possible; collective workers in the Maoist era moved between jobs during the year and were therefore never responsible for seeing a single crop through from beginning to end. However, these positive incentive effects were weakened by the continuation of the collective system of distribution, which made workpoint value dependent on the performance of others. The *baochan* decentralization also created problems of its own (Potter and Potter, 1990: 166–72). It multiplied administration because newly created groups and households were now required to keep accounts.

Collective solidarity was undermined even though it was still needed for team-, brigade-, or commune-wide projects. There were conflicts between groups over the allocation of means of production, and over the assignment of individuals to groups. Furthermore, the problem of how to allocate income within groups remained (although it was much easier to monitor and control performance within a small group compared to a team).

The impact of the systems of group contracting is difficult to judge. Potter and Potter (1990: 170) summarized their findings as follows:

> The economic results of Zengbu's experiment with small groups were inconclusive: some teams did better and others worse than before . . . [But] As a system, it had certainly failed to lift Zengbu out of economic stagnation. . . . at the small group level, the Zengbu teams had reached the point of diminishing sociological returns; the small groups cost more in terms of reduplicated leadership, increased accounting costs, and conflicts and dissatisfaction amongst the team members, than they were worth in terms of whatever minimal increased production they might have facilitated.

This conclusion is mirrored in the writings of many Chinese economists. According to Wang, *et al.* (1985: 20), 'it may only mean a change from very careless work to somewhat less careless work and from "sharing food from the big pot" to sharing food from a smaller pot, and the problem of firing the enthusiasm of commune members will still not be properly solved.' Moreover, to the extent that the switch from group to household contracting was voluntary, the fact that group contracting declined after 1980 does tend to support this view.

Yet there is by no means agreement on this. In particular, it has been argued by Liu (1994) that *baochan daohu* was a superior system to both collective and family farming. On the one hand, the contracting of output to households provides a clear incentive to raise production and thus avoids the effort allocation problems that afflicted the commune. On the other hand, the maintenance of the workpoint system and the institution of the commune ensured that labour could be mobilized for the infrastructural projects which were carried out so effectively by the commune (of which more below). Moreover, collective control over the distribution of income also meant that a part of the profits made by households could be readily siphoned off to finance infrastructural projects. As for the rapid transition to the *baogan* system in the 1980s, that simply reflects the failure on the part of policy-makers at that time to recognize the adverse long-run implications of *baogan* for irrigation and other public works. Liu (1994: 122–3) summarizes the case thus:

> *Baochan* is thus a system that can combine advantages both of the commune and the present *Baogan* system while avoiding their respective shortcomings. This feature of *Baochan*, however, was not recognised in the earlier phases of the reform. By the early and certainly the mid-1980s, the rural reform in China settled on *Baogan*. The perception of the commune then was simply one of a 'big public pot' providing few incentives for members to work hard.

As importantly, there is a substantial body of evidence from the experience of Sichuan province in the late 1970s and early 1980s that suggests that the *baochan* systems were effective (Bramall, 1995*a*). Sichuan's agriculture had reached a nadir in the mid-1970s. Although a net exporter of grain in the early Qing and again in the early 1950s, the *tianfu zhiguo* ('granary of heaven', the classical name for the Sichuan basin) became a significant net importer in 1975, and imported around 600,000 tonnes in 1976. Thereafter, however, growth was swift, with gross agricultural output value (at 1990 prices) rising annually by 3.5 per cent for the 1975–96 period (Table 14.5).

TABLE 14.5. *Growth of agricultural production in Sichuan, 1975–1996*

Year	Growth rates (% p.a.)		Teams using *baogan daohu* (%)	Weather
	Crops	Agriculture		
1976	−3.0	−5.4	0	Very bad
1977	7.4	6.0	0	Very good
1978	17.7	18.0	neg.	Good
1979	2.8	8.5	neg.	Good
1980	5.1	7.8	neg.	Bad
1981	1.5	3.6	31	Very bad
1982	13.3	11.4	94.3	Very good
1983	5.3	7.6	99.7	Good
1984	5.2	7.4	100	Good
1975–82	5.7	6.8	n/a	n/a
1982–96	2.4	4.2	n/a	n/a
1975–96	3.5	5.3	n/a	n/a

Note: The *baogan* figure given for 1982 is actually for spring 1983, but there is little reason to suppose that it had changed much compared to the end of 1982. The data on weather are based largely on local accounts rather than official 'cultivated area affected by natural disaster' figures which give no real indication of the intensity of (for example) the worst flooding of the century in the summer of 1981. Crop and agricultural growth rates refer to the increase of gross output value at 1990 constant prices, and are based on the boundaries of the new province of Sichuan (i.e. old Sichuan less the Chongqing municipality). Agricultural growth rates for new Sichuan are not yet available for 1975 to 1978; the annual rates in this table are those for old Sichuan.

Sources: Bramall (1995*a*: 734–5); Nongye bu (1985: 167); ZGNMYYTJZL (1986: 10–11); SCTJNJ (1997: 273–4).

Furthermore, the structure of agricultural output diversified dramatically as a result of the exceptionally rapid growth of cash crops. Yet the truly significant piece of empirical evidence is that the overall agricultural growth rate in Sichuan averaged 6.8 per cent between 1975 and 1982, well above the average for the transition era as a whole. This is crucial because decollectivization proper (that is, the introduction of *baogan*) did not occur until after the summer harvest of 1982; as late as November 1981, only about 30 per cent of teams had adopted *baogan*, and these were found mainly in the western part of the province and in the mountainous areas on the fringes of the Sichuan basin. In fact, and in contrast to Anhui, the dominant system of farming up to 1982 was *baochan daozu*. Thus the surge in output that occurred in 1982 was largely a product of the old system; *baogan* was introduced only after the main summer harvest.

It is also crucial to recognize that the *baochan* systems were just part of a more general *package* of policy changes that were introduced in the province under the direction of Zhao Ziyang after 1976. The second crucial element in the package was the supply of modern inputs. Second generation varieties of dwarf wheat, hybrid corn, and (critically) hybrid rice not only made their appearance in Sichuan in the mid-1970s but were planted on around 50 per cent of sown area by 1982–3. These new varieties were supplemented by growing supplies of chemical fertilizer, some of it produced in Sichuan's 'five small industries', some of it imported, and the lion's share of the remainder produced in two state-of-the-art imported synthetic ammonia plants installed in the province in the spring of 1974. As a consequence, chemical fertilizer production grew by 31 per cent in each year between 1975 and 1980, compared to 12 per cent between 1970 and 1975 and 2 per cent between 1980 and 1985. Sichuan was not alone in demonstrating the importance of increased use of chemical fertilizer in boosting output. Some idea of the extent of increased availability is given in Table 14.6, and this led to increased use throughout China. Whereas the median growth of fertilizer use in Sichuan was 6.6 per cent between 1978 and 1985, its use grew at 19.3 per cent in Anhui and 11.8 per cent in Henan (Table 6.7, above). Although both were in the van of institutional reform, it was surely no accident that their rapid agricultural growth was accompanied by a dramatic increase in the application of chemical fertilizer.[11]

TABLE 14.6. *Production and imports of chemical fertilizer, 1978–1996*

Year	Production (m. tonnes)	Imports (m. tonnes)	Imports as per cent of output
1978	8.693	1.54	18
1979	10.654	1.763	17
1980	12.319	2.104	17
1981	12.389	1.954	16
1982	12.781	2.334	18
1983	13.789	3.448	25
1984	14.602	4.597	31
1985	13.221	7.61	58
1986	13.597	5.10	38
1987	16.722	10.90	65
1988	17.402	14.71	85
1989	18.025	13.93	77
1990	18.797	16.27	87
1991	19.795	18.18	92
1992	20.479	30.04	147
1993	19.563	14.79	76
1994	22.728	19.38	85
1995	25.481	19.91	78
1996	28.09	18.57	66

Note: Output measured in 'effective' terms (i.e. at nutrient weight).

Sources: ZGTJNJ (1994: 410, 509); ZGTJNJ (1995: 414, 540); Nongye bu (1989: 325); ZGTJNJ (1987: 601; 1989: 643; 1991: 627; 1993: 645; 1994: 410); ZGTJNJ (1997: 449, 601).

These figures show that imports of chemical fertilizer were by no means insignificant in the early years of transition; a share of around 18 per cent of production was not trivial. Furthermore, the importance of chemical fertilizer increased very substantially in the second half of the transition era. By 1987, the share had reached 65 per cent, and it rose further to reach 147 per cent by 1992. In other words, more than half of the chemical fertilizer used by China's farms was coming from abroad in that year. Moreover, much of the increase in Chinese production of chemical fertilizer—as in Sichuan—in the 1970s, which laid the foundations for the revival of agriculture in the late 1970s and early 1980s, was due to imports of *capital equipment*. More precisely, it reflects the decision taken in January 1973 to import 13 pairs of synthetic ammonia plants from Japan, the United States, and Western Europe (Yang, 1990: 173). As a result of this decision (and the expansion of small-scale chemical fertilizer plants in the late 1960s and early 1970s), capacity and production increased rapidly. In Sichuan, for example, output grew annually by 12 per cent between 1970 and 1975, accelerating to 31 per cent during 1975–80—compared to only 2 per cent between 1980 and 1985 (Bramall, 1995*a*).

The third element in the reform package introduced in Sichuan during the late 1970s is best described as deregulation—the removal of many of the more debilitating policies pursued during the Cultural Revolution. The policy of *fangkuan zhengce* (relax government controls) increased the size of private plots, phased out double rice-cropping, allowed rural markets and greater scope for the production of non-grain crops, and removed some of the restrictions on rural sideline production. The policy of *tiyang shengxi* (recuperate and multiply) froze the tax and procurement burden for Sichuan, and cut it sharply in poor parts of the province.

Taken together, these three policies—an increased supply of modern inputs, deregulation and the introduction of the *baochan* systems—in conjunction with the 1979 national decision to raise the procurement prices paid by the state for agricultural products by over 20 per cent led to a massive boost to agricultural production. Whilst these policies were demonstrably a retreat from those pursued during the Cultural Revolution, it is hard to see this package as the introduction of a market economy. Furthermore, given that the household remained heavily circumscribed in its freedom for manœuvre by the group, the production team, the brigade, and the commune, the economic system operating in Sichuan during 1977–82 was much more 'socialist' than (say) New Economic Policy in the USSR in the 1920s.

However, it has still been argued that the dynamic force behind agricultural growth in Sichuan in these years was decollectivization. Despite the multifaceted nature of the reform package, it is said, agricultural growth was led by those poor counties where *baogan* was introduced early. In fact, however, there is no evidence to support the hypothesis. It seems that those counties where *baochan* was the norm up until 1982 grew at least as fast as those counties where *baogan* was introduced early in the proceedings. This can be seen from Table 14.7. As these data show, the growth rate of grain yields was the same in both categories of counties between 1977 and 1982. Furthermore, the introduction of *baogan* in the 'late' counties after the 1982 summer harvest did nothing to produce a spurt in growth rates; yields grew less quickly in these counties under *baogan*—even though the weather on the Chengdu plain (where most of the counties in the late sample were to found) was generally better. If we look at GVAIO, a broader measure of economic performance—on the grounds that *baogan* would have both made it easier for households to develop the product of non-grain crops and to redeploy household workers from agriculture to more lucrative industrial pursuits—these data again show that the late counties did at least as well, and probably better, than the counties that adopted *baogan* early.

TABLE 14.7. *Growth rates of grain yields and GVAIO in counties which decollectivized early and late in Sichuan* (per cent per annum)

	Growth of grain yields		Growth of real GVAIO
	1977–82	1982–5	1975–82
Late counties	5.9	1.2	9.6
Early counties	5.9	2.0	8.1
Sichuan	5.3	2.9	9.1

Notes: 'Late' refers to counties where *baogan daohu* was introduced by a majority of teams in the autumn of 1982 or later. The late sample comprises sixteen counties; the early one consists of four. GVAIO is measured at 1980 constant prices.

Source: Bramall (1995*a*: 750).

We should be wary of claiming too much. It may be that too many of the GVAIO data are at current rather than constant prices. The county gazetteers from which these data are drawn may not provide an accurate report of when *baogan* was introduced; *baogan* was formally illegal in the late 1970s, and its use was not officially allowed even in poor counties until the publication of Document no. 75 on 27 September 1980 (Kueh, 1985: 124; Zhonggong zhongyang xuanchuanbu xuanchuanju, 1988: 241). Only Document no. 1 of January 1982 approved its universal introduction (Kelliher, 1992: 59). Many of the counties which introduced *baogan* late were in a much better position—the Dujiangyan irrigation system, the fertile soil of the Chengdu plain, proximity to the provincial capital (a market and a source of inputs), and higher literacy rates—to generate growth than those located in mountainous areas.[12] Differences in growth rates may simply reflect these other factors, rather than the impact of institutional change. Nevertheless, these data are anything but a ringing endorsement of the hypothesis that the Chinese agricultural revolution of the early 1980s was down to the introduction of private farming. Rather, they suggest that the 'conservative' reform package of the late 1970s centring around the *baochan* system was primarily responsible.

7. The State and Chinese Agriculture in the 1990s

The Chinese state, far from ignoring agriculture after the completion of decollectivization in 1983, also played a crucial role in resolving some of the agricultural problems that emerged during the transition period. These were seen as being particularly acute at the end of the 1980s and in the early 1990s, when both the CCP and academics saw Chinese agriculture as being close to crisis. There were two obvious symptoms of crisis. First, as discussed in Chapter 9, the irrigation system was showing signs of neglect. Second, there was a fall in grain production in China's coastal provinces compared with the late 1970s. In Jiangsu's Wuxi municipality (Wuxi city, Jiangyin, Yixing, and Jinshan), grain production in 1990 was 1.54m. tonnes, well down on the 1978–9 level of 1.8m. tonnes and peak 1984 output of 1.88m. tonnes (Wuxi tongjiju, 1997: 106). In Guangdong as a whole, grain production rose throughout the 1980s to reach 19m. tonnes in 1990, compared with 16m. tonnes in 1977 (LSTJ, 1990: 628; ZGNCTJNJ, 1995: 190). But thereafter production declined: total output was down to 16m. tonnes in 1994 (ZGNYTJZL, 1994: 46). The main reason for this was a sharp decline in output in the Pearl River delta. The delta had seen almost continuous declines in grain output after the early 1980s as cultivated land was used for other purposes; the annual rate of decrease in the delta was 1.35 per cent per year between 1980 and 1990 compared with 0.85 per cent for Guangdong (Lin, 1997: 113). This decline was evident in spectacular falls in output in many of the delta counties. In Zhuhai, 1992 grain output was only 78 per cent of its peak level (1980), and the corresponding figures for some of the other counties were 62 per cent for Shunde (1971 to 1992), 75 per cent for Nanhai (1980 to 1992), 66 per cent for Dongguan (1977 to 1992), and only 19 per cent for Shenzhen (1977 to 1992). Large declines were also recorded for Panyu (1980 to 1992) and Jiangmen (1978 to 1992); the 1992 figures were, respectively, 66 and 18 per cent of peak (Guangdong sheng difang shizhi, 1996: 451–507).

By 1988–89, the Party was aware of these problems. According to Li Peng's 'Work Report' of March 1989 (Central Committee, 1991: 786–7):

> Agriculture stands out as the weakest link in the economy at present . . . Though we are to reduce expenditures and currency issue this year, the State Council has decided that the central financial authorities put more money into agriculture, including forestry and water conservancy. . . . To resist natural disasters and ensure good harvests, it is imperative to emphasize agricultural capital construction, water conservation and harnessing of the rivers, especially the major ones, to prevent floods.

CCP rhetoric did translate into concrete action. By 1991, state investment in water conservancy was running at an annual level of 5.016bn. *yuan*, more than double the total in 1988 (ZGTJNJ, 1992: 161). As a result of this, and continued state investment in the 1990s, the losses in irrigated area during 1978–88 were more than made good. As Table 9.5 shows, irrigated area increased significantly after 1988. The annual rate of increase was a respectable 1.4 per cent between 1988 and 1996, and substantial rises were recorded in the relatively backward agricultural regions of the south-west and north-west. Moreover, only four provinces recorded a decline in this period.[13] As a result, irrigated area for China as a whole rose by 0.6 per cent per year between 1978 and 1996, a reasonable achievement in the end.

Nevertheless, the decline in grain output in many coastal areas continued: according to one agricultural specialist 'the performance of the south and centre-east —notably Guangdong, Fujian, and Zhejiang—has mostly been dismal (Ash, 1997: 41).

Indeed, as we have seen, it was only *after* 1990 that total grain output in Guangdong started to decline. As a result of these perceived failures, much more extensive state intervention was initiated in 1994. Three types of policies were implemented. First, the price paid by the state for agricultural products was raised. As a result, the internal terms of trade improved from 152 in 1991 and 1992 (1978 = 100) to 192 in 1995 (Table 13.8, above). Second, the 'governor rice-bag system' was introduced during 1995 in a palpable attempt to return to the Maoist approach of encouraging provincial self-sufficiency in grain production (OECD, 1997; Crook, 1997). Third, strenuous attempts were made to end the practice (prevalent in 1992, when government funds were diverted to finance industrial and infrastructural investment) whereby farmers were paid for grain sales to the state in IOUs rather than cash; these had largely succeeded (as a result of both additional funding, and explicit instructions from central to local government to end the practice) by early 1993 (Wedeman, 1997).

Taken together, these policies appear to have been successful—at least as expedients to resolve the immediate agricultural 'crisis' of the early 1990s. In Guangdong, for example, grain production recovered from 16m. tonnes in 1994 to 18.4m. tonnes in 1996 (ZGNYNJ, 1997: 301). And for China as a whole, grain production increased by a massive 8 per cent in 1996. If we accept that it was in China's interests to raise grain production (and the dangers inherent in reliance on world markets are transparent), it can only be concluded that the actions of the state were a decisive success.

8. Conclusion

The role played by the restoration of household farming in raising agricultural output in China after 1978 has been exaggerated in much of the literature. Decollectivization probably played a part. But the impact of three years of extremely good weather between 1982 and 1984 was important. So, too, the decision by the state to shift the intersectoral terms of trade in favour of agriculture in 1979. Equally significant, however, were other actions taken by the state. These included support for a scaling-down of the size of collective units of organization (whereby group replaced team farming), the relaxation of procurements quotas and the introduction of the modern technological package of chemical fertilizer (produced mainly in state-owned plants), improved irrigation systems (created by communes and county governments) and new HYVs (developed in state-run research institutes). As a result, agricultural output began to rise quickly in almost every part of China in 1977—well before decollectivization.

To be sure, decollectivization heralded an era of reduced commitment to agriculture by the Chinese state. Nowhere was this neglect more obvious than in the sphere of irrigation. But the continuing capacity of the state to intervene remained undiminished, as was shown by its wide-ranging response to the perceived crisis of the early 1990s. Belated that intervention may have been, but its effectiveness is undeniable.

15

The Open Door

The process of economic transition in China in a strict sense dates from 1972, when Nixon visited the People's Republic.[1] The gradual improvement in Sino-American relations which followed enabled foreign trade to grow, so much so that the development strategy proposed by Hua Guofeng in 1976–7 involved a marked break with the late Maoist development strategy in its greatly enhanced reliance upon imports, foreign capital, and technology.

The process of integration into the world economy was given further fillips by the re-establishment of diplomatic relations between China and the USA from 1 January 1979, Chinese membership of the World Bank and the IMF, and the progressive devaluation of the currency, especially against the US dollar. Yet the most tangible sign of China's engagement with the world was the announcement of an 'open-door policy' in December 1978. This took the concrete form of the establishment of Special Economic Zones (SEZ) in Shenzhen, Shantou, and Zhuhai in Guangdong province after July 1979, developments which received official sanction in August 1980. A further SEZ was created in Xiamen in Fujian province in October 1980. Perhaps rather surprisingly in view of its central role in the Chinese economy before 1949, SEZ status was not granted to Shanghai.[2]

The purpose of the open-door policy was to attract direct foreign investment and technology transfer (and ultimately to promote the growth of exports) by a combination of state investment in infrastructure and low tax rates. To that end, for example, a law on Sino-foreign joint ventures was passed in July 1979 and massive infrastructural investment was directed towards Shenzhen in particular in the early 1980s. The open door widened further as the 1980s progressed. In May 1984, fourteen coastal cities were open up to foreign investment (for the rationale, see Central Committee, 1991: 379–90). In 1985, the Xiamen–Zhangzhou–Quanzhou triangle in southern Fujian, Zhujiang (the Pearl River), and Yangzi deltas, as well as the Liaodong and Jiaodong peninsulas, were designated open coastal economic areas (Central Committee, 1991: 440–7). In April 1988, the programme went a stage further when 288 counties and county-equivalents (such as small municipalities)[3] along the coast were opened up and the newly created province of Hainan island was granted SEZ status.[4] Between 1988 and early 1992, the pace of liberalization slowed markedly following the post-Tiananmen purge of Zhao and the resurgence of a more 'conservative' faction within the CCP. In 1991, however, the process of liberalization began anew, albeit very slowly. Three areas (two in Shenzhen and one in Shanghai) were exempted from customs duties in 1991. In July and October of the same year, China participated in UNDP-sponsored conferences on developing the Tumen river basin (bordering North Korea, Russia, Mongolia, and north-east China) along with Russia, North Korea, Mongolia, Japan, and South Korea. Furthermore, the growth of the Pudong development zone in Shanghai continued to gather momentum in 1990 and 1991, partly driven by growing direct foreign investment.

In 1992, the rate of integration into the world economy accelerated dramatically. The catalyst here was Deng Xiaoping's 'spring tour' to south-east China, the underlying themes of which were crystallized into Central Committee Document no. 4, issued in June 1992.[5] This document contained three key decisions. First, a whole series of border cities and counties were opened up to foreign trade and investment; the areas targeted were on the border with Russia in Heilongjiang-Jilin and Xinjiang-Nei Menggu, and on the border with Burma and Vietnam in Yunnan and Guangxi. The clear intention was to broaden the scope of the coastal development strategy of the 1980s to include China's inland borders as well. The second element of Document no. 4 was to open up all the provincial capitals. In part this was because many of these were closely linked in economic terms to the newly opened border regions. In part, it also seems to have reflected the view that the provincial capitals were a central focus of provincial economic growth. The third element of the 1992 strategy was perhaps the most important in that it focused on the opening up of the 'dragon': the Yangzi River corridor between Chongqing in Sichuan, and Pudong in Shanghai, the 'dragon's head'. This third decision therefore involved the opening up of five Yangzi cities, and a sixth was added in March 1993. This links in with the decision to commence the building of the controversial dam in the Three Gorges of the Yangzi River.[6] In the long run, it is hoped, the raising of water level will greatly ease the shipments of goods along the river, as well as producing much-needed electricity and perhaps even allowing the diversion of water to the parched areas of northern China. By the end of 1996, as a result of these various post-1992 initiatives, no less than 48 Economic and Technology Development Zones existed in the People's Republic.

As has been seen, one of the main intentions of the open door was to encourage foreign investment and technology transfer with a view to the future growth of exports. Some Chinese economists close to Zhao Ziyang (such as Wang Jian) even argued during 1987–8 that development should be based upon her comparative advantage in labour-intensive products and therefore be in essence export-led (Hsu, 1991: 138–42), and it was this that prompted the extension of the open door to virtually the whole of the coastal region in early 1988. The form that the policy took—in particular, its emphatic concentration on opening up the coastal region rather than the interior—reflected a view that economies of scale would accrue from the concentration of foreign investment and, moreover, that the policy would be more attractive to overseas (and especially Hong Kong) investors by virtue of the coast's locational advantages. It was hoped, however, that the coastal development strategy would also lead in due course to the enrichment of the interior via migration, backwards linkage effects, and the use of a part of the surplus accruing to the coast to finance fiscal transfers to the indigent provinces of the west.

1. Theory and Literature

It is often argued, especially by those adhering to the master discourse, that the open door policies outlined above were decisive in bringing about the acceleration in the growth rate after 1978. That is not entirely surprising given the emphasis in the literature on the notion of a causal link between export orientation and economic growth. Nurkse's (1961) classic statement of the role of trade in driving economic growth—export-led growth, as it has come to be known—was in essence simply restating Ricardo's analysis of comparative advantage.[7] Moreover, and especially after its formalization by Heckscher and Ohlin, the link between exports and economic growth has been an integral part of neoclassical analysis. Early neoclassical approaches tended to stress static issues. That is, trade was desirable because it allowed countries to exploit differences in sectoral marginal productivity even if there were no economies of scale by specializing in the production of those goods where factor productivity was relatively high. Alternatively, free trade was seen as a mechanism whereby an economy suffering from allocative inefficiency could be shifted on to its production possibility frontier.

More recently, the merits of outward orientation have been boosted within the neoclassical tradition by the analysis of rent-seeking (Krueger, 1974). Perhaps even more importantly, neoclassical economists have increasingly emphasized the dynamic advantages which stem from trade (Krueger, 1985). More precisely, free trade is seen as a means of promoting competition and hence a determinant of productivity growth. As a result, much recent empirical work has sought to establish a link between either the degree of openness of an economy or its rate of export growth, and its rate of growth of total factor productivity (Balassa, 1989*a*; Balassa 1989*b*; Dollar, 1992; Edwards, 1993; Page, 1994). This all leads to the conclusion that Soviet-type economies are inefficient on the static criteria of rent-seeking and allocative inefficiency, and on the dynamic criterion of failing to promote rapid productivity growth.

Some Marxists have taken a similarly positive view of the role of trade in explaining the emergence of capitalism. Although many have embraced the *dependencia* tradition (Baran, 1957; Frank, 1967; Emmanuel, 1972; Amin, 1976; Wallerstein, 1974, 1979), it has been argued by some that Marx himself saw imperialism—whatever its short-run effects—as a pioneer of capitalism in the long run (Warren, 1980). Such an interpretation is not surprising. There are very clear passages to this effect in the *Communist Manifesto*, and many of Marx's writings on British India suggest this same conclusion. The phrase 'neo-Smithian Marxists' (Brenner, 1977) is therefore by no means inapposite as a description of those, such as Paul Sweezy, who stress the long-run benefits to be derived from the introduction of capitalism by foreign powers into a low-income economy. It is also worth noting that even new trade theorists such as Paul Krugman (1993*a*) argue that selective protection is extremely difficult to carry out in a developed country, still less an LDC. For the latter, therefore, free trade will generally be the best policy.

The emphasis placed on the role of the open door in China's post-1978 success is also unsurprising in view of the extremely rapid increase in the value of exports that has occurred during the 1980s. Over the period 1979 to 1993, exports grew by 17 per cent and imports by 15 per cent per annum. This growth was accompanied by a marked change in the structure of exports. In 1980, food accounted for 18 per cent of exports, and fuels a further 22 per cent. By 1990, the combined share of these two items had fallen to 16 per cent. Over the same interval, the share of manufactures rose from 47 to 80 per cent; most of that growth occurred after 1985. Not surprisingly, the textile subsector—which provided 29 per cent of export value in 1990—was the key subsector in the rise of manufacturing (World Bank, 1994*c*: 1, 5).

The precise share of exports in China's GDP is difficult to estimate. This reflects the peculiar treatment of exports in Chinese statistics (World Bank, 1994*c*: 8 n.) but more importantly the underestimation of GDP relative to exports because of the continuing use of domestic prices which diverge markedly from world levels (World Bank, 1994*c*: p. xvii; Lardy, 1992).[8] Nevertheless, the sheer magnitude of China's export growth after 1980 has persuaded some writers to conclude that China's growth has been export-led. According to Lawrence (1996: 1), for example, 'China, the world's most populous country, has enjoyed the most rapid growth by embracing a strategy of export-led growth driven by foreign investment.' Sachs and Warner (1995: 45–6) argue that initial conditions played a key role in China's rapid growth, but suggest that trade played a decisive part in raising the growth rate of the fast-growing coastal provinces above the mean. Finally, Wei (1995: 95) looks at the performance of Chinese cities and, concludes that their growth was positively related to both exports and foreign investment—the latter being especially important in the late 1980s.

By contrast, those China specialists who have interpreted growth as a product of gradualism have been more circumspect. Lardy (1992: 14), for example, suggests that 'Like other liberalizing import substitution regimes, expanded foreign trade led to, *or at least coincided with*, a spectacular increase in the growth of China's economy' (emphasis added). Furthermore, although he argues that export revenue financed the import of modern equipment and machinery, Lardy suggests that further domestic liberalization is needed to sustain China's initial success and to reap further reward (Lardy, 1992: 144). Hsu (1989: 26) goes further. He argues that, prior to 1985, the growth of exports was caused by the growth of output, thus reversing the usual assumption of causality: 'In summary, China's foreign trade expansion during the period between 1979 and 1985 was growth-led. The expansion of exports was made possible by the smooth growth of GNP.' Naughton (1997: 280) offers a not dissimilar view, arguing that foreign direct investment followed domestic-policy changes, and that FDI has had a major impact on the domestic economy only since the mid-1990s. Moreover, Susan Shirk (in a view echoed by Lardy and in a number of World Bank publications) stresses that China's degree of integration into the world economy even in the mid-1990s remained very limited. As Shirk says (1994: 3): 'Even now, however, although its volume of foreign trade and investment has increased dramatically, China's economy is only shallowly integrated into the world economy.'

This caution is not surprising. For despite all the changes that had taken place, China was a comparatively inward-orientated economy throughout the main part of the transition era. As even a recent World Bank study (1997*b*: 14) has acknowledged, the weighted average tariff rate in the People's Republic barely changed between 1980–3 (when it stood at 31.9 per cent) and 1991–3 (30.6 per cent). This inward orientation only began to change to a significant extent in the mid-1990s. The People's Republic did not commit itself to joining GATT until 1986; at that time, its average nominal tariff rate was about 33 per cent (compared to 53 per cent in 1950), and it actually rose during the late 1980s to reach 43 per cent in 1992. Thereafter, however, the rate steadily declined; it stood at 23 per cent in April 1996. Measured as tariff revenue as a percentage of import value, the tariff rate has also declined during the 1990s. In 1978, the real tariff rate stood at 15.4 per cent, and rose to 16.6 per cent in 1984. By 1990, however, it was down to 6.8 per cent and it had fallen further to 3.3 per cent by 1994 (*China in Brief* (1996: 2, 3, 15)). As for the exchange rate, progress was very gradual. Foreign exchange certificates operated in parallel with renminbi throughout the 1980s, and the exchange rate only became fully convertible on the current account in July 1996. Moreover, the pattern of industrial ownership illustrates the shallowness of China's integration into the world economy even in the mid-1990s. For example, in the key dynamic industrial sector of electronics, only 21 of the top 100 companies in early 1997 were Sino-foreign joint ventures; the largest enterprise was the state-owned Sichuan Changhong Electronics Group, which produces TVs (CD, 3 April 1997).

More generally, the alleged theoretical link between trade and growth is uncertain. Despite numerous attempts by the master discourse to interpret East Asian growth as being export-led, very many economists hold a strikingly different view. Nurkse's original idea of export-led growth was criticized, as is well known, by Kravis (1970). For him, it was more sensible to see exports as a 'handmaiden' rather than an 'engine' in the growth process. Others have pointed to the catastrophic effects of integration into the world economy for Latin America and sub-Saharan Africa in the 1980s. For while it may be the case that the well-known Prebisch-Singer hypothesis of a secular decline in the terms of trade of developing countries is overstated, the collapse of primary commodity prices in the 1980s illustrate the dangers of integration into the world economy.[9] It is also worth noting that the World Bank, in its analysis of African depression in the 1980s, came to the conclusion that internal factors were primarily responsible for the debacle:

> Although the worsening terms of trade hindered growth, they were not decisive in Africa's stagnation and decline. If an annual income loss of 1 percentage point from declining terms of trade reduces the annual rate of growth by no more than 0.8 percentage points, then the falling terms of trade can account for no more than 10 per cent of the reduction in growth rates between the early 1970s and the mid-1980s. (World Bank, 1994*b*: 27)

In other words, although the Bank is a firm advocate of export orientation, this is not usually seen as the *key* factor in promoting rapid economic growth.

Most importantly of all, Alice Amsden (1989) and Robert Wade (1990) have demonstrated that East Asian economic success stems from factors largely ignored by writers in the neoclassical tradition. First, the degree of openness 'enjoyed' by Taiwan and South Korea after their 'liberalization' in the early 1960s has been exaggerated. Second, there is a great deal of evidence which shows that industrial policy has been very successful in a number of key sectors; much the same is true of Japan, which served as the model for late starters. In other words, economies can grow very successfully despite 'getting prices wrong' (Amsden). Thirdly, in so far as trade has played a role in East Asian success, imports of capital goods have been pivotal. That is, the East Asian economies have not been successful because of the competition in consumer good markets provided by imports: in practice, there has been very little in many of the key sectors. Rather, imports have been important because they have embodied new technology.[10] In Amsden's phrase, East Asian growth has been a process of 'industrialization by learning'. Inevitably, the empirical evidence on East Asia is difficult to interpret; it will not be resolved by mindless multiple regression, not least because of very basic data problems (Srinivasan, 1995).[11] Furthermore, the counterfactual proposition beloved of the master discourse—that East Asian growth would have been yet faster without state intervention—falters in the face of a lack of empirical evidence to show that an economy can grow faster than the 10 per cent rate achieved by Japan, South Korea, and Taiwan over a sustained period of time.

Much historical analysis also suggests that export-led growth is unusual.[12] Robert Brenner's (1977; 1985*a*; 1985*b*; 1986; 1994) long-run analysis of the emergence of capitalism in Britain places the emphasis firmly on internal factors. While Brenner's explanation, centred as it is on the leading role played by class struggle, is controversial even within Marxist circles, there are few who would now seek to explain the rise of Britain primarily in terms of external trade. Furthermore, there is little inclination on the part of those working on Britain's Industrial Revolution to ascribe much weight to the role of trade. Harley (1994: 306) estimates that self-sufficiency would have cost Britain only about 6 per cent of its national income even in 1860. Although such calculations are necessarily heroic, and though many earlier writers saw foreign trade as a *sine qua non* for industrialization (Harley, 1994: 301), the general result is by no means implausible even for a relatively small country.[13]

Much the same is true for Japan. There have been attempts to portray Japanese growth after 1868 as export-led (Shinohara, 1962; Blumenthal, 1972), and although Huber (1971) claimed that Japan's entry into the world economy increased its GNP via the terms of trade effect by over 60 per cent, the bulk of Japan specialists have viewed external trade as at best a handmaiden of growth.[14] Its effects were more important in terms of technology transfer than in terms of generating rapid export growth. Nevertheless, and as Morris-Suzuki (1994: 85–6) notes, there was more to Japanese growth than Western technology:

> Technological change in Meiji Japan was not confined to state-owned enterprises, nor to the handful of embryonic zaibatsu who possessed close links to the government . . . Much of it, indeed, was not imported technology at all, but incremental improvement of techniques developed in the Tokugawa period.

Indeed, and as is well known, Meiji agricultural growth was driven primarily by the spatial diffusion of indigenous technology pioneered during the Tokugawa era (Smith, 1959, 1988; Nakamura, 1965, 1966; Francks, 1984, 1992; Hayami and Yamada, 1991). The only countries where growth might be said to have been export-led are the small city states of Hong Kong and Singapore, or countries where the export of raw materials contributes the bulk of GDP (most notably some of the OPEC economies). Given all this evidence, it seems unlikely a priori that post-1978 Chinese growth could have been export-led. Raw material exports do not contribute the bulk of Chinese GDP. World trade grew comparatively slowly during the 1980s, and one would not in general expect growth in an economy as large as China's to be export-led.

2. The Notion of Export-Led Growth

Before looking at the evidence, it is important to be more precise about the issues, not least because much of the literature is rather vague about the meaning of export-led. Broadly, there are four issues. The first question is whether exports were a leading sector in the sense that the rate of growth of export value (measured at current prices to allow for terms of trade effects) was greater than the rate of growth of current price GDP. This is, to be sure, a simple way of thinking about the notion of a leading sector, but it does capture the key idea of leadership: a sector growing faster than the rest of the economy. The second issue centres on the importance of exports. Even if exports were a leading sector in the sense defined, it does not follow that they were of crucial importance in the growth process unless their role was greater than that of other sectors. That is, it is entirely feasible for two leading sectors to exist at any given time. It may be, for instance, that both exports and investment increased their share in GDP simultaneously. Both would therefore classify as leading sectors, and the key issue would be determine the relative importance of each. Thus if exports contributed only a very small proportion of GDP, one would be justified in concluding—even if the export share was rising—that their role was less than pivotal.

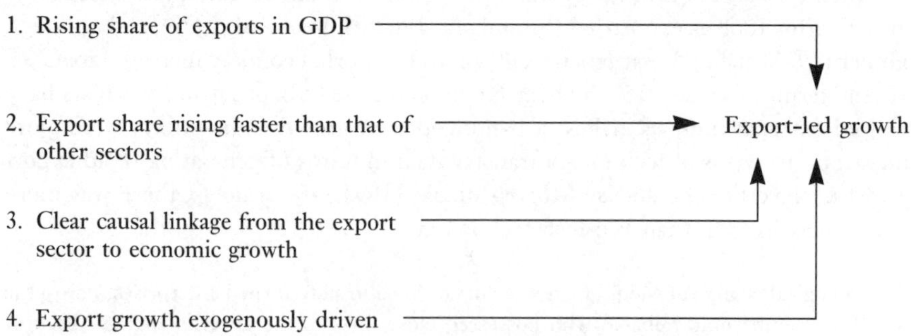

FIG. 15.1. The preconditions for export-led growth

The third issue centres more directly on the key issue: accounting aside, can a causal link be traced out from exports to GDP growth? In the development of Japan, for instance, the most plausible theory of the role of exports sees them as essentially a response to domestic industrialization. Thus the first stage of Akamatsu's classic 'wild geese flying' pattern of growth in Meiji Japan involved the importation of machinery and raw materials (financed by the export of raw silk and tea). The second stage is one of import substitution; in Japan's case, this involved on the development of a cotton textile industry in the period 1885–1904. In the third stage, domestic industry begins to sell to international markets. As exports are the final—rather than the initial stage—in the cycle, this process of growth is often seen as one of growth-led exports (Yamazawa, 1990; Howe, 1996). This Japanese story is of course susceptible to several interpretations. Precisely because exports of raw silk and tea were critical in the early stages of the process, and because these exports grew more quickly than GDP, it could be argued that growth was export-led. However, the problem with this view is that it is hard to see the development of the cotton textile sector as an endogenous response to raw material exports; the linkage effects from silk and tea to cotton textiles were far too weak. For that reason, most Japan specialists are reluctant to call this type of growth process export-led.

The fourth issue concerns the determinants of export growth. Even if exports increase their share, have quantitative significance and have backward and forward linkages to the rest of the economy, the notion of export-led growth carries with it the additional idea that exports are exogenous. In the Japanese case, it has been argued by many economists that import substitution—and therefore the export growth that ultimately derived from it—was a product of state agency rather than 'market forces'. In this view, it was the Meiji state which played the crucial role in promoting import substitution in that the state used its foreign exchange to establish pilot cotton textile plants (Smith), and thus laid the foundation for the great textile boom which began in the late 1880s. Was this also the case in China after 1978, or should we point to foreign direct investment as the prime mover in the creation of an export-orientated industrial base?

3. Exports as a Leading Sector in Chinese Growth

The best way to begin the analysis is to look at the share of exports in Chinese GDP over time. Some evidence on this is presented in Table 15.1, which looks at the relationship between export growth and GDP growth at the provincial level. Both exports and GDP are measured in US dollars, and growth rates are given separately for 1978–92 and 1992–6. This is done to see if there is any evidence that Deng's southern tour of early 1992—during which the emphasis was firmly on the need for greater economic liberalization—led to a surge in Chinese exports.

To be sure, these export data are not entirely reliable. Many of the provincial series show abrupt jumps in the early 1980s and again in the early 1990s. It is not beyond the bounds of possibility that these are genuine. However, for the early 1980s, the leap is almost certainly explained by the splicing of two different series, namely

TABLE 15.1. *The growth of exports and GDP in China's provinces* (annual rates of growth in US$, current prices)

Province	1978–92		1992–6		1978–96	
	Exports	GDP	Exports	GDP	Exports	GDP
Anhui	33.7	4.3	19.9	17.0	25.0	6.0
Beijing	11.4	3.6	29.3	9.7	16.0	4.7
Fujian	21.4	7.4	21.6	20.2	24.5	10.5
Gansu	17.8	1.8	4.1	8.5	15.9	2.9
Guangdong	21.2	8.5	17.1	15.1	25.8	10.1
Guangxi	8.2	4.3	13.2	16.3	10.5	7.3
Guizhou	31.5	4.5	17.9	7.4	26.1	4.9
Hebei	12.3	3.8	16.6	14.0	10.0	6.1
Heilongjiang	34.6	1.4	−7.1	14.6	27.8	3.8
Henan	17.1	4.4	16.4	16.3	14.4	6.2
Hubei	16.6	3.8	6.9	14.2	13.3	5.6
Hunan	12.9	3.3	5.5	13.8	11.8	5.2
Jiangsu	15.5	4.8	29.5	15.1	17.5	7.3
Jiangxi	18.8	3.2	9.1	13.4	14.4	5.0
Liaoning	4.0	3.4	17.4	6.8	4.4	5.0
Nei Menggu	33.7	4.6	−1.2	9.9	23.7	5.8
Ningxia	9.0	4.0	16.2	10.3	9.7	5.2
Shaanxi	40.1	3.7	17.4	7.8	31.5	4.8
Shandong	10.2	5.7	25.3	14.9	11.8	7.8
Shanghai	4.3	−0.5	18.7	12.8	7.8	2.4
Shanxi	44.3	2.7	23.4	9.4	35.2	4.2
Sichuan	39.6	3.5	12.8	13.1	29.1	5.3
Tianjin	4.2	1.4	21.5	14.0	7.4	3.4
Xinjiang	35.5	6.5	−3.1	9.8	23.2	7.8
Yunnan	15.8	5.1	19.2	10.5	17.6	7.0
Zhejiang	23.0	6.7	23.8	17.8	23.5	8.9
China	14.7	4.6	17.8	12.7	15.3	6.2

Notes: Inadequate data are available for Hainan, Jilin, Qinghai, and Tibet. The exchange rate used is the renminbi value of (imports + exports) relative to the dollar value of (imports + exports).
Sources: LSTJ (1990); ZGTJNJ (1995: 33, 60, 552); ZGTJNJ (1997: 43, 45, 70, 603).

data collected by the Ministry of Foreign Trade on the one hand and Customs on the other. Thirdly, the export intensity of the inland provinces is probably understated for the pre-1992 period. In part, this reflects illicit border trade between Yunnan and Burma, and between Guangxi and Vietnam. More importantly, it is not easy to determine the source of exports in the case of exports trans-shipped from the interior via one of the eastern provinces, especially if value is added (processing) in the administrative unit that does the actual exporting. In the pre-1990 statistics at least, a considerable proportion of the products of the inland provinces were exported via agencies (foreign trade corporations) operating from coastal provinces (Sung, 1995: 98–9). As a result, goods originating in (say) Sichuan often end up classified as exports from Shanghai. It is not wrong to attribute them in part to Shanghai because the agency operating out of the city is generating income streams in the process for the city; a large proportion of the goods are re-exports (i.e. exports which are processed and then exported by Shanghai) rather than merely transshipments.[15] But it is plainly wrong to ignore their province of origin. The relationship between (say) Shanghai and Sichuan is analogous to that between China and Hong Kong. Of China's exports in 1989, 41 per cent were indirect, i.e. routed via Hong Kong (Sung, 1991: 144–5). But the fact that these exports went via Hong Kong did not make them any less China's exports. As a result, the data on the regional location of exports undoubtedly overstates the export volume of the coastal provinces and understates the export-orientation of the interior; for this reason, the more recent data on provincial exports given in the statistical yearbooks distinguish clearly between the province of origin, and the province that actually dispatched them. An additional statistical problem relates to trade between the People's Republic and Taiwan and South Korea. Data on this only began to appear officially in 1992[16] and this causes substantial complications in trying to assemble consistent data for (in particular) Heilongjiang, Liaoning, Fujian, Zhejiang, and Guangdong provinces.

Yet despite these data problems, the evidence in Table 15.1 is very clear. As far as 1978–92 is concerned, the national data show that exports were growing about three times faster per year than GDP. At the level of the province, the evidence is even more telling: not in a single case did the growth of GDP exceed that of exports. In several instances—Heilongjiang, Shanxi, and Shaanxi, for example—export growth was over ten times faster than that of GDP. For the sub-period 1992–6, there is little evidence that Deng's intervention heralded a rapid acceleration in export growth. On the contrary. Exports were still very much a leading sector, but the gap between export and GDP growth was very much less than it had been before 1992. Thus national export growth averaged less than 50 per cent more than the growth rate of GDP, and there were nine provinces where exports did not play the role of leading sector. This was especially the case for Xinjiang, Heilongjiang, and Nei Menggu, all of which recorded declining export values. Nevertheless, despite these caveats, it is overwhelming clear that exports were a leading sector in an accounting sense throughout the transition period.

4. The Quantitative Significance of Exports in the Growth Process

Having established that exports grew quickly relative to GDP, we next need to consider next whether exports were of quantitative significance in the growth process. The evidence here is much less positive because it appears that exports contributed only a small share of Chinese GDP even at their peak in 1994 (Table 15.2). Indeed the data in Table 15.2 are remarkable in two respects. First, the export shares of the interior provinces were exceptionally low by international standards despite two decades of the open door. The interior median for China is below the median for all the other countries in this table and even the most open interior provinces (excluding Beijing) were barely more integrated into the international economy than the

TABLE 15.2. *Share of exports in purchasing-power parity GDP, 1994*

	Export share in GDP (%)		Export share in GDP (%)
China: Interior provinces		*China: Coastal provinces*	
Beijing	6.4	Guangdong	22.8
Heilongjiang	3.2	Shanghai	9.1
Jilin	3.1	Tianjin	7.6
Shanxi	2.3	Fujian	6.5
Guangxi	2.0	Zhejiang	4.4
Shaanxi	1.8	Liaoning	3.6
Hebei	1.6	Jiangsu	3.1
Yunnan	1.6	Shandong	3.0
Hubei	1.5	Hebei	1.6
Ningxia	1.4	Coastal median	4.4
Gansu	1.3		
Hunan	1.3	*Other countries*	
Nei Menggu	1.3	South Korea	19.4
Xinjiang	1.2	France	18.9
Jiangxi	1.1	United Kingdom	18.1
Sichuan	1.0	Italy	16.5
Guizhou	0.9	Japan	14.0
Henan	0.9	Chile	8.0
		United States	7.3
Interior median	1.5	Brazil	4.6
China	4.9	Kenya	4.2
		India	2.0

Notes: The table shows the share of exports in GDP for China's provinces in 1994 (the year during the transition period in which the export share peaked). Exports are at current prices and converted from dollars to *yuan* using the 1994 exchange rate. GNP is revalued from current prices to GNP at purchasing power parity. This calculation is based on the ratio of official exchange rate GNP per capita to purchasing-power parity Chinese GNP per capita in 1993 as estimated by the World Bank (WDR, 1995). For comparative purposes, the export shares of a number of other countries are given as well; these are exports as a percentage of purchasing-power parity GNP. The figure for Taiwan, based upon the official exchange rate, was 39 per cent in 1993 (calculated from ZGTJNJ, 1994: 694, 700).

Sources: ZGTJNJ (1995: 33, 537); WDR (1995: 162–3, 186–7, 220–1).

least open country (India). Secondly, and perhaps more significantly, even China's coastal provinces were not very open by international standards even in 1994. Guangdong, to be sure, fares well by international standards. Its export share of nearly 23 per cent was higher than that of any of the countries in this sample. But other provinces which were open by Chinese standards—such as Shanghai and Tianjin—were essentially closed by the standards of medium-sized OECD economies: none of these provinces registered a double-digit export share.

In fact, the export shares achieved in coastal provinces like Fujian (6.5 per cent), Zhejiang (4.4), Jiangsu (3.1), and Shandong (3.0) were remarkably low. This reflected the fact that their principal products—textiles and processed food—were aimed at the home rather than the overseas market. Take Zhejiang. Agricultural exports amounted to $US0.310 billion in 1991, or 1.652 billion *yuan* at the official 1991 exchange rate (ZJTJNJ, 1992: 295; ZGTJNJ, 1994: 506). But agricultural production (current prices) in the province in that year was 24.042 billion *yuan* (ZJJNJ, 1992: 25). In other words, agricultural exports accounted for only 6.9 per cent of agricultural production in 1991. It is true that, if one repeats the calculation for industry, the result is very different: exports account for 31.4 per cent of industrial production. However, this ignores the purchasing-power parity problem. As is well known (see, for example, Lardy, 1992) China's prices are on average well below world prices and this is not fully reflected in the exchange rate. As a result, China's GDP and NDMP are seriously undervalued relative to its exports. Thus the purchasing-power parity estimate of Chinese GDP per capita for 1993 was $US2,330 compared to only $US490 at the official exchange rate (WDR, 1995: 162, 220). Using this conversion factor reduces the share of agricultural exports in agricultural production in Zhejiang to 1.4 per cent, and that of industrial exports in industrial production to 6.6 per cent. In other words, even Zhejiang—one of the most open provinces in the People's Republic—exported an extremely small proportion of her production. In short, China's provinces may have been more geared towards selling on the international stage in the mid-1990s than they had been in 1978 but one is hard put to call them international in their orientation.

The rather limited role of exports even in Zhejiang's rapid post-1990 growth is also clear from the nature of growth in that province in the 1990s (Table 15.3).

TABLE 15.3. *The share of investment and exports in GDP in Zhejiang province, 1990–1996* (percentages)

Year	Share of exports in GDP (based on $US values)	Share of investment in GDP (based on *yuan* values)
1990	13.0	28.1
1991	15.8	31.1
1992	14.9	39.1
1993	13.4	47.2
1994	20.4	44.5
1995	20.1	50.1
1996	17.4	49.1

Note: The exchange rate used is the *yuan* value of (imports + exports) relative to the dollar value of (imports + exports); from Zhongguo tongjiju (1998: 133).

Sources: Zhongguo tongjiju (1998: 24); ZGTJNJ (1997: 603); ZJTJNJ (1996: 22, 326).

The share of exports did indeed increase substantially in Zhejiang after 1990. If the trough of 1990 is compared with the peak of 1994, the export share rose by slightly more than 7 percentage points; exports were thus playing the role of a leading sector and their contribution was by no means insignificant. Nevertheless, their role pales when compared with that of investment. The trough-to-peak comparison here of 1990 to 1995 shows an increase in the investment share of no less than 22 percentage points, three times greater than the rise in the export share. This stark contrast places in perspective the contribution of exports even in one of China's most open provinces during the 1990s.

Things might have been very different if Zhao Ziyang had retained his position as CCP secretary. For Zhao had become a convert to the 'great international cycle' theory, first put forward by Wang Jian and Pei Xiaolin in August 1987. Wang and Pei's basic idea was that China should accelerate its growth rate by promoting export-orientated rural industries—exploiting China's abundance of cheap labour—located in the coastal provinces. The attraction of this idea was strong. It would allow the coastal provinces to break free from their dependence on the interior for supplies of key raw materials; they could be imported instead. Additionally, the development of labour-intensive industries would allow the absorption of surplus rural labour. Furthermore, and doubtless one of the reasons why it appealed to Zhao, it would allow the state sector to be increasingly supplanted by a vibrant private sector geared towards world markets.[17] Zhao's fall in the summer of 1988 effectively brought an end to the idea that Chinese development should *primarily* be outward orientated.

5. The Causal Links between Export and Economic Growth

The discussion in the two preceding sections lends somewhat equivocal support to the notion of export-led growth in China. To be sure, exports were a leading sector in accounting terms, growing as they did much more quickly than GDP. However, apart from the instances of Guangdong, Tianjin, and Shanghai, the quantitative significance of exports for the vast majority of Chinese provinces was rather slight. Despite the rapid pace of international liberalization during the transition era, China at the time of Deng's death was not a very open economy by world standards. Nevertheless, if we accept that the export-led hypothesis is supported so far, to what extent did the growth of exports promote that of GDP?

5.1. Linkage Effects: The Composition of Exports

On the face of things, it appears that exports did have strong linkage effects with the domestic economy. Although some provinces specialized in the export of primary commodities—Heilongjiang, China's main oil-exporting province,[18] is perhaps the best example—the bulk of Chinese exports by the mid-1990s were manufactures. In 1992, for example, manufactures accounted for 80 per cent of the dollar value of US exports; by 1996 that figure had risen to 85 per cent. This compared to 50 per cent in 1980 (ZGTJNJ, 1997: 589). In some of the coastal provinces, the role of primary commodities was even smaller; in Zhejiang no less than 22 per cent of exports were heavy industrial products (ZJTJNJ, 1996: 326), a figure more typical of a high-income economy than China.

However, the problem with many of China's manufactured exports is that they have a high import content and therefore generate few linkage effects to the rest of the economy. This is because the bulk of exports from the People's Republic are based on processing or assembly of imports, an area of activity which exploded after 1984, when tariffs were removed from imported goods destined to be used for export purposes. The main products involved here are clothing, toys, and electronics, and the import content was very high; according to the World Bank (1994*c*: 11–12), imports for processing may have accounted for as much as 77 per cent of export value.

In some ways, the best example is the case of Dongguan in Guangdong, where many of the industries were involved primarily in processing materials imported via Hong Kong. As Lin (1997: 173) notes:

> the arrangement requires Hong Kong to supply raw materials, components or parts, and models for what is to be processed, while the Chinese provide labour, land, buildings, electricity, and other local utilities necessary for production

In consequence, the backward linkage effects to other Chinese industrial sectors and agriculture were very weak—as was the case with the Japanese silk and tea industries during the Meiji period. In addition, most of the new jobs created by the export sector were filled by young migrant women, who remitted a large part of their incomes to the home village to which they returned after living for several years in Dongguan. The growth of demand in the municipality was therefore far less than implied by its output growth, and this almost certainly acted as a constraint upon the development of other industries.

5.2. Linkage Effects: Provincial Analysis

One of the most salient features of the transition period in China was the rapid growth achieved by the coastal provinces. It is tempting to view this acceleration as providing powerful support for the idea that exports *caused* economic growth. Precisely because the coastal provinces were more open than those of the interior, one might argue, their growth rate was faster—thus providing support for the notion of strong linkage effects from exports to economic growth.

Now, output growth in China's coastal provinces was certainly faster than in the interior provinces after 1978. To be more precise, however, it is first necessary to categorize China's provinces into coastal and interior categories. Into the coastal category go Liaoning, Hebei, Beijing, Tianjin, Shandong, Jiangsu, Shanghai, Zhejiang, Fujian, and Guangdong. All the other provinces are classified as belonging to the interior. Two points are worth noting about the coastal list. First, the inclusion of Beijing. Although China's capital is not coastal, it is located within the coastal province of Hebei and—more to the point—its status as national capital meant that a large share of foreign trade crossed its boundaries. In other words, it is logical to include Beijing within the coastal region. Secondly, the exclusion of Guangxi. One could take issue with this on the rather obvious grounds that Guangxi does have a coast line. But that coastline is small, and the province's border with Vietnam contributed to slower rather than to faster growth. In other words, Guangxi is best regarded as a province of the interior.

The coastal provinces were, not surprisingly, much more export orientated than those of the interior (Table 15.4). The top nine provinces in terms of exports per capita in 1996 were all coastal (apart from Beijing, which was of course rather special), and the poorest performing of these—Shandong—still generated a per capita export level three times the national median. Only Hebei of China's coastal provinces is not in the top ten, but this largely reflects the fact that its two most obvious trading outlets—Beijing and Tianjin—classify as separate independent provincial units. If Beijing and Tianjin are incorporated into Hebei, then its level of exports per capita would rise very substantially. By contrast, the provinces of the interior feature well down the list; and there is some evidence that exports per capita are correlated with distance from the coast. Moreover, even though some of the

TABLE 15.4. *Exports per capita, export growth rates and the growth of GDP in China's provinces, 1978–1996* (provinces ranked by exports per capita)

Province	Exports per capita, 1996 ($US)	Growth of exports (% p.a.; current prices)	Growth of GDP (% p.a.)	
			Current prices	1990 prices
Shanghai	925	7.8	13.7	8.7
Guangdong	862	25.8	22.4	13.6
Tianjin	493	7.4	14.8	8.0
Beijing	402	16.0	16.2	8.8
Fujian	259	24.5	22.7	12.4
Zhejiang	200	23.5	21.0	12.0
Liaoning	177	4.4	16.7	8.7
Jiangsu	168	17.5	19.2	11.3
Shandong	114	11.8	19.8	11.2
Heilongjiang	81	27.8	15.4	5.9
Shanxi	56	35.2	15.7	7.8
Hebei	37	10.0	17.9	9.6
Ningxia	31	9.7	16.8	9.2
Guangxi	30	10.5	19.7	9.0
Shaanxi	28	31.5	16.5	9.2
Yunnan	25	17.6	18.9	9.5
Hubei	24	13.3	17.2	9.1
Anhui	22	25.0	17.8	9.7
Xinjiang	22	23.2	19.7	10.7
Hunan	21	11.8	16.8	8.6
Nei Menggu	21	23.7	17.6	8.7
Jiangxi	19	14.4	16.7	9.6
Sichuan	16	29.1	16.9	8.9
Henan	15	14.4	18.0	9.8
Gansu	11	15.9	14.3	9.4
Guizhou	11	26.1	16.4	8.8
Median	31	16.8	17.1	9.2

Notes: Exports are classified by province of origin. Inadequate GDP data exist for Jilin, Qinghai, Tibet, and Hainan. No export data are readily available for 1990 and 1991.

Sources: LSTJ (1990); ZGTJNJ (1995: 33, 60, 552); ZGTJNJ (1997: 43, 45, 70, 603).

interior provinces did achieve rapid export growth, they were still far behind the coastal provinces. Despite growth of around 30 per cent per annum, neither Sichuan nor Shaanxi province surpassed the median provincial level of per capita exports even by 1996.[19]

Using this coastal–interior distinction, the most striking feature of the data provided in Table 15.5 is that the mean growth rate of the coastal provinces was higher than that of the interior provinces in *all three* periods.

TABLE 15.5. *Growth of net domestic material product in China's interior and coastal provinces, 1952–1992* (% growth rates; provinces ranked by growth rate between 1978 and 1992)

	1952–78	1965–78	1978–92
Interior provinces			
Xinjiang	4.3	2.7	10.1
Yunnan	3.8	4.4	9.2
Henan	3.6	5.0	9.0
Ningxia	5.3	6.2	8.7
Jilin	3.7	4.5	8.7
Nei Menggu	4.4	4.6	8.6
Anhui	3.3	4.6	8.5
Guizhou	1.9	2.9	8.2
Gansu	5.0	8.1	8.2
Hubei	3.3	4.3	8.0
Sichuan	2.4	3.5	8.0
Jiangxi	3.4	3.6	8.0
Shanxi	4.4	3.7	7.8
Shaanxi	3.8	4.7	7.8
Guangxi	4.4	6.3	7.3
Hunan	3.4	4.7	7.0
Heilongjiang	5.5	5.6	6.3
Mean	4.1	5.0	8.2
Coastal provinces			
Guangdong	4.0	4.5	11.3
Zhejiang	3.6	4.4	10.9
Fujian	2.4	4.4	10.5
Jiangsu	4.6	5.9	10.3
Shandong	4.2	6.4	10.3
Beijing	8.1	10.4	8.6
Hebei	3.2	5.1	8.3
Liaoning	4.3	7.1	7.5
Shanghai	6.1	6.4	7.5
Tianjin	5.7	7.1	7.1
Mean	4.2	5.7	9.3

Notes: Growth rates are of NDMP calculated from output data at 1990 constant prices. Incomplete data are available for Tibet, Qinghai, and Hainan; these provinces are therefore excluded.

Sources: LSTJ (1990): ZGTJNJ (1992: 37–8, 79); ZGTJNJ (1993: 41); ZGRKTJNJ (1991: 359–63); ZGTJNJ (1994: 38–9).

For the Maoist period as a whole (1952–78), coastal China grew at 4.6 per cent per year, a rate significantly higher than the 3.9 per cent recorded by the interior. Shanghai—despite the high level of taxation imposed on it by central government to fund development in the Chinese interior—was still the fastest-growing coastal province during 1952–78. Overall, however, Beijing was the fastest-growing province in the country for the Maoist period, and the slowest growing province (Guizhou) grew at only about a quarter of Beijing's rate. Fujian also did rather poorly, presumably because of the enforced severing of many of its historic trade links with Taiwan after 1949.

In the *late* Maoist period (1965–78), the lead of the coastal provinces was rather greater in terms of growth rates than for 1952 to 1978 as a whole. Despite the programme of Third Front construction designed to increase the industrial capacity of the Chinese interior, the inland provinces managed a growth rate of only 5.0 per cent. This was admittedly higher than for the whole 1949–78 period, and in that sense the Third Front programme did achieve something. However, the gap of 0.7 per cent sustained over 13 years was not insignificant, and, of the interior provinces, both Guizhou and Xinjiang lagged for behind.

After 1978, however, the lead of the coastal region was more marked even though the actual growth rate in the interior rose by more than 3 percentage points. The provinces along the Pacific coast achieved a phenomenal average growth rate of 9.3 per cent, and of the six provinces which recorded rates in excess of 10 per cent, only Xinjiang was to be found in the interior. Zhejiang, Guangdong, and Fujian all achieved growth rates well over double their late Maoist rates of advance; Fujian in fact grew no less than 4 times faster than it had between 1952 and 1978. Yet not every coastal province did well; Tianjin's growth was very unusual by Chinese standards in that it did not rise after 1978. Nevertheless, taken as a whole, the average growth rate of the interior was slower than that of the coastal provinces at 'only' 8.2 per cent. Heilongjiang did especially poorly; this province fell to bottom place after 1978.

This comparison of provincial growth rates over the entire period between 1952 and 1992 therefore illustrates the continuity in the Chinese growth process after 1949. For, as we have seen, the coastal region grew more quickly than the interior provinces in *each and every time period*—and not just after 1978. In other words, it appears that the superior growth performance of coastal China after 1978 reflects not the open-door policy or some fundamental difference between economic policy in Maoist and transition periods (though there were, of course, enough of these), but simply the locational and historical advantages of the coastal region, advantages that were as important during the Maoist period as they were in the reform era.

This conclusion is confirmed by looking at the *changes* in provincial growth rates that occurred after 1978 (Table 15.6). If there were powerful linkage effects running from the export sector to economic growth, one would expect to see the more integrated coastal provinces reaping the benefit in terms of much faster growth. By contrast, one would expect to see the interior provinces registering an increase in their growth rate—after all, one would expect other transition policies to have

TABLE 15.6. *Changes in provincial NDMP growth rates, 1952–1992* (provinces ranked by change in growth rate during 1978/92 compared to 1965/78)

Province	Change in Growth rate (ratio)		NDMP per capita *(yuan)*
	1978/92–1965/78	1978/92–1952/78	1978
Xinjiang	3.7	2.4	546
Guizhou	2.8	4.3	323
Guangdong	2.5	2.8	680
Zhejiang	2.5	3.0	609
Fujian	2.4	4.4	524
Sichuan	2.3	3.3	451
Jiangxi	2.2	2.4	454
Shanxi	2.1	1.8	529
Yunnan	2.1	2.4	422
Jilin	1.9	2.4	625
Nei Menggu	1.9	2.0	507
Hubei	1.9	2.4	571
Anhui	1.9	2.6	420
Henan	1.8	2.5	395
Jiangsu	1.8	2.2	641
Shaanxi	1.7	2.1	498
Hebei	1.6	2.6	583
Shandong	1.6	2.5	537
Hunan	1.5	2.1	532
Ningxia	1.4	1.6	505
Shanghai	1.2	1.2	2,481
Guangxi	1.2	1.7	449
Heilongjiang	1.1	1.2	874
Liaoning	1.1	1.7	1,053
Gansu	1.0	1.6	493
Tianjin	1.0	1.3	1,598
Beijing	0.8	1.1	1,684
Coastal	2.4	1.7	967
Interior	2.2	1.8	571
Overall	2.3	1.8	703

Note: The change in the growth rate is calculated as the annual percentage growth rate during 1978–92 (see Table 15.5) divided by the annual percentage growth rate during 1952–78 and during 1965–78. NDMP per capita at 1990 constant prices.

Sources: As for Table 15.5.

generated a growth boost—but only by a rather small amount, precisely because very few parts of the Chinese interior benefited either from a massive influx of foreign capital or extensive trade links with the world economy.

Yet there is nothing in Table 15.6 to support this hypothesis. Consider first the comparison between 1952–78 on the one hand, and 1978–92 on the other. The growth rate of the coastal provinces was on average 2.4 times faster after 1978 than before, clear evidence of the impact of transition on growth rates. But a similar effect is apparent for the inland provinces; their growth was 2.2 times faster in the transition period than during the Maoist era. In other words, this similarity in performance suggests an underlying continuity in the regional impact of economic policy.

This analysis is supported by a second comparison, this time between the post-1978 period and the late Maoist era, i.e. 1965–78. This is probably the better comparison; many of the growth rates for 1952–78 are affected by the massive but extremely variable trough associated with the Great Leap Forward. Moreover, the second comparison gives a more direct indication of the growth boost provided by transitional policies. This second comparison if anything suggests that the inland provinces actually benefited *more* from transition than did their coastal cousins. For whereas the inland provinces grew on average 1.8 times faster after 1978 than in the late Maoist era, the coastal region grew only 1.7 times faster. Moreover, of the ten provinces which recorded the highest change in their growth rate between 1965–78 on the one hand and 1978–92 on the other, no less than seven came from the interior. Indeed it is particularly interesting that Guizhou—China's poorest province by some distance in 1978—benefited so much from the reform process compared to the late Maoist period, being ranked second only to Xinjiang. Almost equally interesting is the fact that some of the most prosperous coastal districts received only a relatively modest boost; obvious examples here are Liaoning, Tianjin, Shanghai, and Jiangsu. In other words, even though a province like Jiangsu did extremely well after 1978 by Chinese standards, it had done even better in relative terms in the late Maoist period.

To be sure, it is important not to make too much of this conclusion that the interior seems to have gained just as much from the open door as coastal China. Part of the reason for the modest acceleration in the growth rate of the coastal region was that many of these coastal provinces had already reached a comparatively high level of per capita output by 1978. Shanghai, Beijing, Tianjin, and Liaoning are the most obvious examples of the phenomenon; all four had a level of per capita income of more than 1,000 *yuan* per capita in 1978, a time when only one other province (Heilongjiang, at 874 *yuan*) exceeded 700 *yuan*. Given their relatively high base, it is not entirely surprising that the coastal post-1978 growth rate was comparatively slow. Conversely, many of the interior provinces were still extremely underdeveloped in 1978, especially those of the north- and south-west; there was accordingly abundant scope for rapid growth once the transition package had been put in place. Obvious examples are the provinces of Sichuan (where the growth rate after 1978 was 3.3 times faster than during 1952–78), and Guizhou (where the differential was even higher at 4.3); in both cases, per capita NDMP was less than 50 per cent of Liaoning's (and only about one-fifth of Shanghai's) at the beginning of the transition era.

This hypothesis of catch-up is confirmed by the records of Zhejiang and Fujian. Although both were coastal provinces, their levels of development were still comparatively low in 1978. As a result, the acceleration in their growth rate was much greater than in (say) Liaoning, with Fujian growing 4.3 times faster than it had during 1952–78 and Zhejiang growing more than 3 times faster. Indeed the very fact that Zhejiang and Fujian virtually matched Sichuan and Guizhou respectively in their growth acceleration despite starting from a higher level of NDMP per head (609 and 524 *yuan* in Zhejiang and Fujian compared to 452 and 323 *yuan* in Sichuan and Guizhou respectively) illustrates the potency of the open door even in comparatively prosperous regions. That Shandong and Hebei did rather less well than other coastal areas—despite being poor (with per capita income standing at 537 and 583 *yuan* respectively in 1978) and located in coastal China—in turn suggests the importance of the role played by Taiwan, Hong Kong, and the special economic zones in promoting growth in Zhejiang, Fujian, and Guangdong.

This comparison of the growth records of China's coastal and interior provinces also shows that the open door was by no means a necessary condition for rapid economic growth in the Dengist era.[20] Provinces such as Sichuan, Guizhou, and Yunnan were able to achieve dramatic increases in their growth rates after 1978 even though they were much less affected by the open door than the coastal region of the People's Republic. This was all the more remarkable when it is remembered that one of the reasons why their output growth was comparatively respectable in the Maoist era was the impact of the Third Front programme, which involved a massive injection of resources into western China. That boost to economic activity was largely terminated after 1978. Yet these provinces were still able to grow quickly.

The common-sense explanation is twofold. First, the Third Front yielded a significant long-run infrastructural legacy. Many parts of western China had negligible industrial capacity before World War II, and no railways worth speaking of. The very fact that the Third Front led to the creation of a rudimentary infrastructure paid great dividends after 1978 even though that infrastructure was not extended. Secondly, the principal dynamic in the early years of the transition period was provided by agriculture. Precisely because many of the reforms began in agriculture, and agriculture was such a dominant component of the economies of western China, the growth rates achieved in the Chinese interior were comparatively impressive. By contrast, the more industrialized provinces of the coastal region benefited rather less. Where growth did accelerate quickly (as in Zhejiang and Fujian), the key reason was the dominance of agriculture in the economy, rather than the impact of the open door.

Furthermore, an indication of the very limited role of international trade can be observed from the slowdown of economic growth that occurred in China in the late 1980s. This slowdown occurred as a result of deliberate government fiscal and monetary policy designed to reduce the rate of inflation. The policy was launched in 1988 and plunged the national economy into recession in 1989 and 1990. Now if China's provinces had been dependent primarily on international trade, these cuts in domestic demand would have left them largely unaffected because of the importance of export markets. In other words, the domestic market is of little importance if most of one's sales are directed overseas. This hypothesis about the role of the open door in the late 1980s can be evaluated by comparing provincial growth rates during 1984–92 with those achieved during the course of the entire 1978–92 period (Table 15.7).

TABLE 15.7. *Growth rates of NDMP in interior and coastal China* (per cent per annum at 1990 prices)

	NDMP growth			Change in growth rate (ratio)	
	1965–78	1978–92	1984–92	1984/92–1965/78	1984/92–1978/92
Coastal	5.7	9.3	7.8	1.46	0.83
Interior	5.0	8.2	6.8	1.51	0.83

Sources: As for Table 15.5.

These data show the ratio of economic growth during 1984–92 to the growth rate in both 1965–78 and 1978–92 in the coastal and interior provinces. If one first compares the growth rate after 1984 with that of the late Maoist period, it is evident that economic growth was still much faster in the second half of the 1980s—the recession of the period notwithstanding. More interesting, however, is the comparison between coastal and interior provinces. One would have expected the coastal provinces to have done rather better than the interior provinces in this type of comparison because of their high level of integration into the world economy. In other words, the recession of the late 1980s should have hit the interior harder because the interior provinces were more reliant upon domestic demand. But the data show that the increase in the growth rate achieved in the interior between 1984–92 on the one hand and 1965–78 was significantly greater than in the coastal provinces. Doubtless catch-up played a role in this. After all, despite its rapid growth during 1978–84, the Chinese interior was still far behind the coastal region in 1984 and therefore could continue to grow rapidly after that date. Nevertheless, the comparatively poor performance of the coastal provinces suggests that they continued to be dependent primarily upon the Chinese rather than the foreign market even after 1984. They were therefore hit just as hard by the recession as the interior.

A second comparison is also made in Table 15.7. This compares growth rates during 1984–92 with 1978–92 as a whole. If external markets were the critical element in economic growth, one would not expect to see any obvious slowdown after 1984.[21] It is therefore interesting that, of the 27 provinces listed in Table 15.6, only Gansu increased its rate of growth after 1984 compared to 1978–92 as a whole, and Guangdong maintained the same rate. With Gansu's acceleration largely unrelated to external factors, that leaves us with only Guangdong significantly dependent upon external markets. That is not surprising. Guangdong's links with the world economy, and especially with Hong Kong, increased apace over the course of the late 1980s. As a result of the relocation of Hong Kong manufacturing companies in Guangdong and increasing trade via Hong Kong, the province—in sharp contrast to China's other provinces—was able to ride out the recession. Furthermore, if the open door was the key element in the growth process, one would expect to see the coastal provinces—which were obviously more affected by the policy—riding out the recession rather better than the interior provinces. But this was not the case. The coastal provinces grew at about 83 per cent of the rate they achieved post-1978 in total during 1984–92. But the interior provinces did equally well. In other words, these data suggest—with the exception of Guangdong—that the recession took its toll equally in the interior and along the coast. Even fast-growing provinces such as Zhejiang and Fujian were significantly affected by the growth slowdown.

This analysis as a whole therefore suggests that the coastal region benefited at best comparatively little from linkage effects between its export sector and the rest of its economy. The reasons for this are probably several. First, the coastal provinces lost as well as gained by being open to foreign trade and investment because their openness exposed them to an additional source of instability: fluctuations in foreign demand and investment. This was a particular problem in 1989 following the Tiananmen massacre. Many Western governments responded by imposing restrictions on investment in, and trade with, China. Furthermore, and irrespective of the extent of formal restrictions, the massacre raised doubts about the long-term stability of the Chinese economy and therefore adversely affected the expectations of Western (and Hong Kong) companies. As a result, those provinces that were more closely integrated into the world economy suffered a significant loss of trade and investment in the late 1980s.

6. Was Export Growth Exogenous?

The final part of the hypothesis of export-led growth is the notion that export growth was driven primarily by exogenous factors. In the case of China, however, it is clear that the country faced a peculiar mix of exogenous advantages and constraints on the eve of transition in seeking to successfully implement an open-door policy.

The main advantage was the proximity of overseas Chinese sources of capital which might be tapped to finance foreign direct investment, or which might buy into Chinese companies floated on the Hong Kong stock market. Hong Kong, of course, was China's 'window on the world' during the Maoist era and was an important source of foreign technology as well as the gateway for international trade. The British colony could undoubtedly have been annexed by China in the late 1940s, or flooded with migrants in the 1960s. That the People's Republic did neither is perhaps the strongest indication of its perceived usefulness. Nevertheless, the potential benefits from the Hong Kong connection would be much greater if overseas Chinese could be persuaded to invest in the mainland. That was of course a realistic prospect given that many of Hong Kong's leading industrialists had been born in Shanghai or in the coastal provinces, and had migrated to the colony in the 1940s. Moreover, the links between Hong Kong and China were strong even in the late 1970s; for example, there were 2.1m. visits to China by Hong Kong residents in 1978 (Sung, 1991: 23). There were also legitimate expectations of Taiwan. Taiwan and Fujian had been part of the same province during the Qing period and there was every reason to expect significant investment (albeit via Hong Kong to start with) if Taiwan's industrialists could be offered suitable incentives.

There were also important complementarities between the economies of Taiwan, Hong Kong, and coastal China (Chen and Ho, 1994). Hong Kong's economy was service-orientated and it was a key financial centre. Taiwan's strength was in manufacturing. By contrast, the mainland could offer land and low-cost labour in abundance. In retrospect, it is obvious that there was a 'South China Growth Triangle' of great potential here. This allowed, to take but one example, the share of manufacturing in Hong Kong's GDP to fall from 42 per cent in 1980 to 28 per cent in 1990 as manufacturing companies relocated to Guangdong, and as the service sector expanded in response to increased demand from South China (Chen, 1994: 87).

It is evident in fact that many features of the open-door policy were specifically tailored to the perceived needs of potential investors in Hong Kong and Taiwan. Thus the special economic zones were located in Guangdong and in Fujian, and equipped with considerable infrastructure (as will be seen below). Indeed, Shenzhen was set up in very close proximity to Hong Kong. By reducing travel time and costs, and by minimizing the language barrier, the locational logic behind the SEZs was clear. The fact that Shanghai was not given SEZ status may well have been a move designed to appease Hong Kong interests, fearful of the competitive threat. The 1984 decision to offer tax rebates on goods imported from Hong Kong for use in the processing and assembly industries was also designed to appeal to overseas Chinese investors.

Nevertheless, the benefits to be reaped by China from the South China Growth Triangle were partly offset by the slow growth of world trade. In this respect, China was in a much more difficult position to expand its exports than Japan, Taiwan, and South Korea had been in the years between 1950 and 1973. The main reason was the slowdown in growth in the large OECD economies; per capita GDP growth in the G7 countries declined from 4.5 per cent between 1959 and 1970 to 2.2 per cent between 1974 and 1989 (UNCTAD, 1997: 79). This slowdown was reflected in the declining pace of growth of world exports. Between 1958 (by which time all exchange controls on current-account transactions in the G7 countries had been removed) and 1971—the height of the 'golden age'—world exports of goods and services increased by over 7.5 per cent per annum. But between 1978 and 1985, the rate of growth was only 2.8 per cent, and the figure of 3.7 per cent recorded for 1985–95 was little better (Brenner, 1998: 212). Although China's main market—the USA—grew reasonably quickly due to the 'military Keynesianism' initiated by Reagan and largely continued by Bush until the end of the Gulf War, the slower growth of the world economy inevitably conditioned the degree to which China could rely on exports as an engine of growth. Of necessity, therefore, the main source of demand for Chinese products had to be domestic.

6.1. Foreign Direct Investment, Exports and Economic Growth

One of the most important aspects of China's export growth in the transition era was the important role played by foreign direct investment (Zhan, 1993; Lardy, 1995; World Bank 1997*b*; Yeung, 1998). Averaging only about $400m. per year during 1979–92, the volume of FDI rose to about $2bn. by 1985. The Tiananmen massacre did have some effect and in 1990 FDI—at $3.7bn.—was barely above its 1988 level. Thereafter, however, FDI increased very rapidly. By 1992 it had reached $11.3bn. and in 1996 $42bn. of FDI was recorded (Zhongguo tongjiju, 1998: 138).[22] As is well known, the bulk of this investment came from overseas Chinese; Hong Kong alone contributed some 50 per cent in 1996 (ZGTJNJ, 1997: 605–8).

The other key characteristic of FDI into China was that much of it generated export growth precisely because the bulk went into industries that were explicitly export-orientated. In the case of Guangdong, for instance, about 50 per cent of all exports were FDI-related as early as 1992 (Kueh and Ash, 1996: 176); since then, the figure has undoubtedly increased. Nationally, 29 per cent of exports were produced by foreign-funded firms[23] (including firms funded from Hong Kong, Macao, and Taiwan). That figure had risen to 32 per cent in 1995 and to 41 per cent by 1996.[24] The figure for Guangdong in 1996 was even higher at 52 per cent (ZGTJNJ, 1997: 604).

But for all this seemingly impressive growth, it is not clear that FDI was the catalyst for either export or more general economic growth across the People's Republic. First, FDI was spatially concentrated. In 1996, $US35bn. of the $US42bn. received in 1996 was accounted for by the nine coastal provinces,[25] with 25 per cent of the national total going to Hong Kong alone (ZGTJNJ, 1997: 608). As one of the main features of post-1978 Chinese growth was that it was countrywide, it is clear that FDI was by no means a necessary condition for achieving rapid growth. Guizhou, for example, received only $US31m. in FDI in 1996, which was in itself far more than the province received in the mid-1980s—only $US2.5m. was invested in 1987 (LSTJ, 1990: 745). Yet despite this measly injection, Guizhou achieved a real growth rate of almost 9 per cent between 1978 and 1996.

A second problem with the hypothesis that Chinese export growth was FDI-driven is that the figures involved were simply far too small throughout the 1980s. Despite the rapid increase that occurred in the total invested, FDI still accounted for only 1.1 per cent of nominal GDP as late as 1991 (Table 15.8).

TABLE 15.8. *The share of FDI in GDP, 1979–1996* (percentages)

Year	FDI/GDP	Year	FDI/GDP
1979	0.2	1988	0.9
1980	0.1	1989	0.8
1981	0.2	1990	1.0
1982	0.2	1991	1.1
1983	0.3	1992	2.3
1984	0.4	1993	4.6
1985	0.6	1994	6.3
1986	0.8	1995	5.4
1987	0.8	1996	5.2

Notes: FDI and GDP are both measured in nominal terms in $US. FDI data are actual (realized) and include commercial credit. The figures for 1979 to 1982 are calculated by annualizing the total for 1979–82.

Source: Zhongguo tongjiju (1998: 12, 133, 138).

It is very hard to believe that, even at the margin, FDI on the very limited scale of the 1980s could have galvanized the economy into achieving very fast growth, either by the promotion of exports or via some other route. That is especially so given that growth was driven by the agricultural sector until at least 1984 and that agriculture received less than 3 per cent of the limited FDI that was flowing into China. Moreover, it is equally hard to envisage FDI creating powerful linkage effects in the mid-1980s to the industrial sector when it is known that at least a third (almost 50 per cent in 1986) of that investment was being directed into land and public utilities (Sun, 1991: 88).

The more interesting questions centre on the role of FDI in the national economy after 1991, and in Guangdong throughout the Dengist era. By 1993, FDI accounted for 4.6 per cent of Chinese GDP, and it climbed to 6.3 per cent in 1994 before falling back to 5.2 per cent in 1996. By international standards, these were very high figures; an FDI/GDP ratio of 3.5 per cent would have placed China in the top ten countries for FDI during 1990–94. They suggest that the impact of FDI in the People's Republic during the mid-1990s cannot have been insignificant—and, as we know, it was FDI that played a crucial role in promoting exports in the 1990s. Yet, even so, it is hard to escape the conclusion that FDI was still not very important for the national economy. For one thing, it is almost universally accepted that China's GDP is underestimated if one uses the official exchange rate (as these FDI/GDP ratios do). It is quite plausible that Chinese GDP is at least 3 times higher when measured at purchasing-power parity (see, for example, Ren 1997: 128). If true, that would reduce the FDI/GDP ratio to less than 1 per cent and significantly alter assessments of the importance of FDI to the Chinese economy.[26] A second qualification is that most FDI was still concentrated in the south-east and along the coast—and yet the Chinese interior provinces continued to grow at rates that were remarkable by international standards. The figures here are compelling: between 1991 and 1996, real per capita GDP grew annually by 7.5 per cent in Guizhou, 9.1 per cent in Yunnan, 9.2 per cent in Gansu, and 10.5 per cent in Sichuan. These provinces may have grown faster if they had received more FDI—Guangdong's per capita GDP rose by 15.1 per cent per year over the same period—but it can hardly be claimed that FDI was necessary for rapid growth.

Although there is little evidence that the acceleration in the overall rate of Chinese growth can be attributed to FDI, it is worthwhile considering whether the growth of Guangdong province was driven primarily by its links with the world economy and in particular with Hong Kong. On the face of it, this does not seem an unreasonable proposition. It has, for example, been argued earlier that Guangdong was little affected by the domestic recession of the late 1980s—suggesting a high degree of reliance on the international economy. Secondly, we know that Guangdong's economy grew at 13.6 per cent per year between 1978 and 1996, considerably above the national average of 9.9 per cent. In other words, if national growth was impressive, Guangdong's growth was exceptional. That view is reinforced by looking at the growth rates of industrial production. For although China achieved an internationally spectacular rate of 11.1 per cent, Guangdong's industrial production grew by an incredible 17.2 per cent.[27] It follows that we ought to look for some additional 'special factor' to explain these growth differential. Thirdly, in looking for an explanation of Guangdong's success, the open-door policy is a natural candidate. Three of the original four Special Economic Zones were founded in Guangdong and there were strong links between the province and Hong Kong, with the result that by 1991 85 per cent of exports went to the British colony (and 74 per cent of imports came from it) (Ash and Kueh, 1993: 724). There is a sense in which Hong Kong and Guangdong can be regarded as two parts of the same economy, with Guangdong the home to agriculture and industry, while Hong Kong supplied most of the services.

In addition, it is clear from the outset that FDI was anything but trivial in relation to Guangdong's economy (Table 15.9).

TABLE 15.9. *The share of FDI in Guangdong's GDP, 1979–1996* (percentages)

Year	FDI/GDP	Year	FDI/GDP
1979	0.7	1988	4.1
1980	1.3	1989	3.8
1981	1.5	1990	5.2
1982	1.5	1991	5.8
1983	2.2	1992	8.9
1984	3.3	1993	13.5
1985	3.4	1994	19.2
1986	4.3	1995	15.0
1987	3.4	1996	15.0

Notes: FDI and GDP are both measured in nominal terms in $US. FDI data are actual (realized) and include commercial credit. The figures for 1979 to 1982 are calculated by annualizing the total for 1979–82.

Sources: Pre-1990 Nominal GDP and FDI: LSTJ (1990);1993–6 GDP: ZGTJNJ (1996: 43); 1990–2 GDP: ZGTJNJ (1994: 35); pre-1990 FDI: LSTJ (1990: 637); 1991–2 total FDI: ZGTJNJ (1993: 650); 1990–1 FDI: ZGTJNJ (1992: 643); 1995–6 FDI: ZGTJNJ (1997: 608); 1994 FDI: ZGTJNJ (1996: 600); 1993 FDI: ZGTJNJ (1994: 530).

By 1985, FDI already accounted for over 3 per cent of GDP and by 1991 that had risen further to reach 5.8 per cent. Thereafter, growth was incredibly rapid with the result that the ratio hit 19 per cent in 1994, stabilizing at around 15 per cent in 1995–6. Even allowing for the underestimation of GDP already mentioned, these figures make Guangdong a very open economy by international standards in the mid-1990s. Moreover, they provide prima facie evidence that growth was led by FDI in the 1990s. The main reason for the inflow of FDI was the progressive reallocation of manufacturing production from Hong Kong to Guangdong where labour costs were much lower. Dongguan municipality, located between Guangzhou and Shenzhen, offers the classic example (although the Pearl River (Zhujiang) delta as a whole has grown very fast). This was a very poor rural area by Chinese standards in the late 1970s. However, Dongguan was unusual in that its population had more relatives per head living in Hong Kong than most other parts of Guangdong. Partly as a result of exploiting this link, Dongguan began to grow extremely fast in the late 1980s and early 1990s via the development—based on FDI from Hong Kong—of a large export-processing industry (Lin, 1997; Yeung, 1998).

Yet even in Guangdong's case, the impact of FDI is by no means clear-cut. For example, the growth rate achieved by Guangdong during 1991–6 was obviously very fast at 15.1 per cent. However, Zhejiang managed a rate that was faster still (17.4 per cent) and did so even though FDI accounted for only 3.7 per cent of GDP at its 1994 peak. In other words, there is scant evidence that Guangdong achieved a faster growth rate as a result of its greater foreign direct investment. And although it is of course impossible to adequately normalize for differences between the two provinces, it is hard to argue that Zhejiang was growing faster because it started from a much lower base; per capita GDP was lower in Zhejiang (2,265 *yuan*) than in Guangdong (2,680 *yuan*) in 1991, but hardly by enough to explain Zhejiang's faster growth.

This is not to say that Guangdong did not benefit from its greater FDI. Although Zhejiang was able to grow faster, it seems that it was able to do so only by increasing its investment share from 31 per cent of GDP in 1991 to a quite remarkable 50 per cent in 1995 (ZJTJNJ, 1996: 22). By contrast, no such heroics were needed in Guangdong precisely because of the volume of overseas investment being received (Table 15.10).

TABLE 15.10. *Investment in Zhejiang and Guangdong, 1991–1996* (percentages)

Year	Share of FDI in GDP		Share of Gross Fixed Capital Formation in GDP	
	Guangdong	Zhejiang	Guangdong	Zhejiang
1991	5.8	0.5	n/a	31.1
1992	8.9	1.1	n/a	39.1
1993	13.5	3.1	48.0	47.2
1994	19.2	3.7	46.7	44.5
1995	15.0	3.0	41.5	50.1
1996	15.0	3.1	41.7	49.1

Notes: GDP is nominal and converted to $US using the official Chinese exchange rate.
Sources: ZJTJNJ (1996: 22); Zhongguo tongjiju (1998: 24); ZGTJNJ (1995: 38; 1996: 48; 1997: 48).

The benefit to Guangdong from its FDI therefore came in a much higher share of consumption in GDP. In 1995, for instance, Guangdong's investment share was only 41.5 per cent (ZGTJNJ, 1997: 48), well down on Zhejiang's 50.1 per cent. To be sure, the comparison is not quite so clear-cut as the 1995 data imply. In both 1993 and 1994—even though the province received 19.2 per cent of its GDP in the form of FDI in the latter—Guangdong was still using 46.7 per cent of its GDP in the form of investment. Nevertheless, in 1995 and 1996 Guangdong's investment share was well below that of Zhejiang, and this more than offset the initial consumption 'losses' in 1993–4. There was then a real pay-off to Guangdong's ability to attract FDI, but it is still rather surprising that there was not more of an effect upon the growth rate vis-à-vis Zhejiang.

6.2. Exports and the Realization Problem

The main problem with the hypothesis of FDI-driven exports is that it neglects the impact of processes at work within China itself. One such endogenous factor was the role played by the state, and this will be discussed in the next section. However, an alternative endogenous explanation for the growth of exports is that they were driven by the need to solve the realization problem.[28] It is certainly possible in principle that either downward pressure on urban real wages caused by in-migration (as mentioned in Chapter 7), or rising income inequality, could have led to a situation in which consumption growth lagged behind the growth of output. Even if aggregate demand as a whole increased at the same rate as production due to investment, this increased demand for capital goods would not solve the problem of excess supply of consumer goods. As a result, China's export drive after 1978 could in principle have been motivated by the desire of the producers of consumer products to find a market for their goods.

To be sure, some of the evidence suggests that this was unlikely. For example, there is little evidence of any stagnation in national consumption growth (measured using the GDP measure of household consumption). For the whole period 1978–96, current-price household consumption spending rose by 15.6 per cent annually, compared to GDP growth of 17.8 per cent. For 1992–6, the gap was even more narrow; consumption rose by 27.5 per cent per annum and GDP by 28.3 per cent (ZGTJNJ, 1997: 46–7). Moreover, real wages also increased dramatically during the transition era.

However, the fact that income inequality rose after 1978 lends some support to the idea of an enforced reliance on export markets caused by the higher marginal propensity to save of the affluent. Although the data on the distribution of income are very unreliable (Bramall and Jones, 1993; Griffin and Zhao, 1993; Khan and Riskin, 1998), there is no doubt that inequality rose at least as sharply as suggested by the data in Table 15.11.

Moreover, there is substantial evidence of a realization problem in some of the coastal provinces. This seems especially true of Guangdong, perhaps because a large proportion of the wages paid to migrant workers were remitted to their home village. The data for example show household consumption rising annually by 20.8 per cent between 1985 and 1996, whereas GDP grew by 25.9 per cent. This gap did not close during the 1990s (consumption grew at 25.2 per cent and GDP by 30.3 per cent between 1990 and 1996), but neither does it seem to have widened (Zhongguo tongjiju, 1998: 77; LSTJ, 1990; ZGTJNJ, 1994: 35; ZGTJNJ, 1997: 43). The problem in Zhejiang was even more serious. Between 1990 and 1995, the ratio of consumption to GDP fell from 53 to only 35 per cent. This was because the growth rate of (current price) per capita consumption was only 20.9 per cent, compared to a per capita GDP growth rate of 31.8 per cent—a massive difference (ZJTJNJ, 1996: 18, 23). Although much of this increase in GDP was driven by rises in investment, this ensured only a big increase in demand for capital goods.

TABLE 15.11. *Income inequality in China, 1978–1996*

Year	Rural gini	Urban gini	Overall gini
1978	0.21	0.16	
1978 (AS)	0.22	0.17	0.32
1979	n/a	n/a	
1980	0.24	0.16	0.28
1981	0.24	0.16	
1982	0.23	0.15	
1983	0.25	0.15	
1984	0.26	0.16	
1985	0.26	0.19	
1986	0.28	0.19	
1987	0.30	0.20	
1988	0.30	0.23	
1988 (GZ)	0.34	0.23	0.38
1989	0.32	0.23	
1990	0.31	0.23	0.36
1990 (WB)	0.30	0.22	0.34
1991	0.31	0.24	
1992	0.31	0.25	
1993	0.33	0.27	0.38
1994	0.32	0.30	
1995	n/a	0.28	0.41
1995 (WB)	0.33	0.28	0.39
1995 (KR)	0.42	0.33	0.45
1996	n/a	0.28	0.39

Notes: The data here are official State Statistical Bureau estimates unless otherwise identified. AS—Adelman and Sunding; GZ—Griffin and Zhao; WB—World Bank; KR—Khan and Riskin.

Sources: (1) Rural: 1978–91 Bramall and Jones (1993: 45); 1978 (AS)—Adelman and Sunding (1987: 163); 1988 (GZ)—Khan, *et al.* (1993: 61); 1992—Ma and Sun (1995: 259); 1993 and 1994—ZGNCTJNJ (1995: 4); 1995 (WB)—World Bank (1997*c*: 17); 1995 (KR)—Khan and Riskin (1998: 237). (2) Urban: 1978–96—Wang and Lu (1997: 34); 1978 (AS)—Adelman and Sunding (1987: 163); 1988 (GZ)—Khan, *et al.* (1993: 61); 1995 (WB)—World Bank (1997*c*: 17); 1995 (KR)—Khan and Riskin (1998: 242). (3) Overall: 1978 (AS)—Adelman and Sunding (1987: 163), excluding subsidies; 1980—Yabuki (1995: 232); 1988 (GZ)—Khan, *et al.* (1993: 61); 1990—Yabuki (1995: 232); 1993, 1995, 1996—Wang and Lu (1997: 186); 1990 (WB)—World Bank (1997*c*: 12); 1995—World Bank (1997*c*: 8); 1995 (KR)—Khan and Riskin (1998: 247).

In principle, provinces such as Zhejiang and Guangdong could have found markets for their goods in other provinces, where consumption growth was more closely aligned with GDP growth. However, this type of strategy was constrained by high transport costs, not least in the form of barriers to cross-provincial trade such as transit taxes. For the producers of consumer goods, increasingly the TVE sector in Zhejiang and Guangdong, the only way to sell many of their products was therefore on the export market.

6.3. Exports and the Role of the State

The hypothesis that export growth was FDI-driven and therefore exogenous is also problematic because it neglects the critical role played by the Chinese state in the process, especially in Guangdong.

As Kueh and Ash (1996: 167–8) note, this seems to be an unlikely interpretation because of a general perception that Guangdong was in the van of marketization during the transition process. There is some truth in this; some of the reforms were pioneered in Guangdong. However, the reality remains that the really important reforms—agricultural decollectivization, the 1979 shift in the intersectoral terms of trade, and the removal of restrictions on collective and household industry in 1984—were applied nationally. Furthermore, the growth of the non-state sector was little more advanced in Guangdong at the end of the 1980s than it was elsewhere in China. It is true that only 36 per cent of gross industrial output value in Guangdong in 1991 was provided by the state sector, substantially less than the national figure of 51 per cent (ZGTJNJ, 1992: 409, 415). It is also true that the size of the state sector did fall quickly in the province; from a figure of 68 per cent in 1978, it was down to 38 per cent by 1989 (LSTJ, 1990: 629).[29] Nevertheless, the state subsector remained a key component of the industrial sector in the early 1990s. Kueh and Ash rightly point to the fact that the share of the state sector in gross investment rose up to 1992, even though it declined in China as a whole. This reflected heavy state investment in infrastructure, and the fact that most of the joint ventures in Guangdong actually involved SOEs.

6.3.1. The Fiscal Treatment of Guangdong

In fact, the most plausible explanation for Guangdong's relative success lies in its treatment by the state. Prior to 1980, Guangdong had been a significant contributor to the national treasury along with other rich provinces such as Beijing, Shanghai, and Jiangsu. The revenue thus raised was used to subsidize the provinces of western China, where expenditure ran regularly ahead of income. In order to promote Guangdong's development, a decision was taken in 1980 to change revenue-sharing arrangements. Under the new system, Guangdong agreed to make a payment of 1bn. *yuan* to the central government irrespective of its income. Any extra revenue raised by the province could be retained (Shirk, 1993: 166–8; Vogel, 1989: 89–90; Goodman and Feng, 1994: 186; Li, 1997). This in effect amounted to the introduction of a system of lump sum taxation: very strong income effects and no substitution effects. In other words, the province was given a massive incentive to raise revenue confident in the knowledge that, at the margin, every *yuan* raised could be used for reinvestment within Guangdong. Even more importantly, the tax rate was not especially onerous; although Guangdong's contribution to the centre was below the 1bn. *yuan* mark in 1979, the figure had been comfortably exceeded in 1978. Guangdong was thus being given a privilege denied to most of China's other affluent provinces, namely the right to retain and spend surplus revenue on the promotion of the economy. This was clear from the attitude of other provinces. Shanghai in particular felt discriminated against, and not without cause: its remittance rate averaged 72 per cent of revenue during 1980–92, compared to 31 per cent for Guangdong (Li, 1997: 790).[30] Perhaps Shanghai might have performed as well as Guangdong if it had received Guangdong's fiscal privileges (Shirk, 1993: 141 n.). This jealousy led to a concerted attempt to persuade Li Peng to treat Guangdong less preferentially; as a result, a new system of revenue-sharing came into effect in 1988.

Quite how much Guangdong benefited from the 1980 agreement is difficult to determine because of the complexity of the Chinese fiscal system.[31] For example, Guangdong's low notional contribution to the state treasury was partially offset by the levying of a forced loan on it of 1.6bn. *yuan* in 1981 and again in 1982 (Shirk, 1993: 173 n.).[32] However, some indication of the impact of fiscal decentralization can be seen from the data on provincial revenue and expenditure. In general, the rich provinces ran surpluses of income over expenditure, and this surplus can be seen as their contribution to central funds. Conversely, poor provinces ran deficits—implying they were net recipients of state funds.

From our point of view, what is of interest is the trend over the course of the 1980s in the scale of contributions made by various provinces. These are summarized in Table 15.12.

TABLE 15.12. *Fiscal surpluses of provincial governments, 1978–1989* (fiscal surplus as a percentage of revenue)

Year	Guangdong	Shanghai	Jiangsu	Zhejiang	Guizhou	Gansu
1978	31	85	54	37	−97	30
1979	19	84	46	31	−103	23
1980	31	89	54	44	−89	−7
1981	31	89	62	50	−110	−15
1982	24	88	63	49	−96	−3
1983	19	86	56	48	−71	−43
1984	6	82	48	38	−89	−60
1985	7	75	43	36	−62	−46
1986	−4	67	33	26	−79	−52
1987	3	68	37	33	−47	−39
1988	−7	59	32	26	−39	−46
1989	−3	56	28	24	−43	−31

Note: The fiscal surplus here is government revenue less expenditure as a percentage of revenue. This is a *very* approximate measure of fiscal transfers to central government. A minus sign indicates that a province's expenditure exceeded its income; in other words, it was receiving a subsidy from central government. No data are available for post-1989.

Source: LSTJ (1990).

The most relevant feature of these data is the speed with which Guangdong's contribution to central funds declined during the early 1980s. In 1978, some 32 per cent of its revenue was surplus (and therefore, by implication, transferred out of the province). The lump-sum tax system initially maintained it at this level in 1980 and 1981, but thereafter the decline was sharp. By 1985, Guangdong was making a surplus of less than 500m. *yuan* and in the late 1980s it actually moved into deficit. This is a remarkable result. Despite its rapid growth and high level of income, Guangdong seems to have become a net recipient of central funds at the end of the 1980s. One does not have to look much further for an explanation for Guangdong's growth.

This conclusion is strengthened by looking at state revenue and expenditure in other provinces. In this respect, Shanghai is especially interesting. In 1978, no less than 85 per cent of its revenue was transferred; in absolute terms, this was ten times the sum remitted by Guangdong.[33] In 1984, its contribution was virtually unchanged at 82 per cent, and even in 1989 it stood at 56 per cent. This was soon to change with the launching of the new Pudong development zone, and Deng Xiaoping's admission that Shanghai should have been given SEZ status in the late 1970s. But in the late 1980s, the extent to which Shanghai acted as a milchcow in financing national development was remarkable—especially when compared to Guangdong. The same is true of the experiences of Zhejiang and Jiangsu provinces which in essence mirror those of Shanghai. For although the contributions of these two were much smaller than for the great metropolis, both continued to make very substantial contributions to the state treasury in the late 1980s. Thus in 1989, the combined contribution of Zhejiang and Jiangsu was 5.7bn. *yuan* at a time when Guangdong was contributing nothing. In fairness, this almost certainly underplays the contribution of Guangdong in that the data in Table 15.12 refer to budgetary revenues and take no account of extra-budgetary revenues or forced loans. According to Yang (1994: 86–7), Guangdong contributed 3.83bn. *yuan* to the centre in 1990. But even when allowance is made for this, the degree of fiscal autonomy granted to Guangdong compared to other provinces at the beginning of the 1980s was astonishing. It was this fiscal autonomy, and the right to retain revenue that it conferred, that played an instrumental role in Guangdong's growth.

The importance of *domestic* investment can be illustrated in microcosm by considering the case of the Shenzhen Special Economic zone. Now there is no denying that output in Shenzhen grew quickly after it became an SEZ in 1979. Between 1980 and 1991, in fact, Shenzhen's real GNP grew at 38 per cent per annum. This was far greater than the rate achieved in Xiamen SEZ (23 per cent), and especially Guangzhou (13 per cent) (Ash and Kueh, 1993). Equally, it cannot be denied that the motor for some of this growth was foreign investment. Guangdong received some $US8.9bn. between 1985 and 1991, but Shenzhen alone received $US2.1bn.—virtually double the sum received by Fujian (Ash and Kueh, 1993: 730).

But a key factor, and one which some accounts of the rise of Shenzhen seem to ignore, is that there was also substantial investment by the Chinese government in the SEZ. This was especially true in the early days of Shenzhen's SEZ status; between 1979 and 1986, only 20 per cent of capital construction investment was funded from foreign capital. The remainder came from Chinese sources, mainly bank loans and local government. In addition, no less than 25,000 engineers and construction workers were provided by central government (Kleinberg, 1990: 58–9). The scale of infrastructural development was probably inadequate, at least to judge by the extent of bottlenecks in the late 1980s (Yeung, 1994). But without it the likelihood is that little FDI would have been attracted. Two other points need to be made about the impact of foreign investment. First, much of the foreign investment went either into low technology assembly projects as Hong Kong firms shifted their manufacturing operations from the (high-wage) British colony to the (low-wage) mainland, or into property speculation. Secondly, about 60 per cents of inputs were imported (Kleinberg, 1990: 63). In consequence, the linkage effects between foreign investment and both local and national economies were rather weak and limited. The skewed pattern of investment did not prevent Shenzhen from growing; the GDP growth rate of more than 30 per cent is proof of that. But given the exceptionally low base from which the SEZ started, and the massive injections of funds (from all sources) that occurred, one might even argue that the growth rate was disappointing.

6.3.2. *Depreciation and Export Growth*

A more general difficulty with the view that export growth was exogenous is the fact that the Chinese currency depreciated substantially after 1978. In contrast to the approach of many Latin and Central American countries—alike in being committed to an overvalued exchange rate in order to hold down the price of imported goods—the Chinese state has been willing to preside over a sustained currency depreciation (Table 15.13).[34]

Of course, exchange rate devaluation does not offer a long-term solution to the problem of slow growth. Yet the international evidence points overwhelmingly to the conclusion that, when the exchange rate is fundamentally misaligned, devaluation works by promoting export growth. Two key assumptions are needed for this to hold: that export demand is price-elastic and that the economy has spare capacity.[35] The first assumption ensures that export value increases, the second that the depreciation is not offset by rising domestic prices. Both these assumptions held for China in the transition period and in consequence there is little doubt that depreciation contributed significantly to export growth—not least because the growth of its main markets in USA and Japan in both the 1980s and 1990s was not very rapid.[36] For example, the sharp depreciation of the exchange rate in 1994 heralded a massive surge in exports just as the appreciation of the currency in 1995 and 1996 was associated with poor export performance. Similarly, exchange rate stability in 1987–9 was associated with rather slow export growth.

TABLE 15.13. *The devaluation of the renminbi*

Year	*Yuan* per US dollar	*Yuan* per 100 Yen
1978	1.7	n/a
1979	1.6	n/a
1980	1.5	n/a
1981	1.7	0.8
1982	1.9	0.8
1983	2.0	0.8
1984	2.3	1.0
1985	2.9	1.2
1986	3.5	2.1
1987	3.7	2.6
1988	3.7	2.9
1989	3.8	2.7
1990	4.8	3.3
1991	5.3	4.0
1992	5.5	4.4
1993	5.8	5.2
1994	8.6	8.4
1995	8.4	8.9
1996	8.3	7.6

Sources: Lardy (1992: 148); ZGTJNJ (1997: 588).

6.3.3. The State and Import-Led Exports

More generally, the Chinese state contributed to the growth of exports by its policy on imports—the aim of which was to promote import substitution industrialization, rather than to satisfy consumer demand. Indeed, one of the key features of the Chinese economy in the 1980s has been the limited scale of imports of non-essential consumer goods. In so far as China has imported, those imports have been firmly biased towards capital and intermediate goods. As a World Bank report (1994*c*: 17) noted:

> China's import structure thus clearly reflects a conscious import strategy, which has been to ensure the supply of key raw materials and to acquire embodied technology through the import of capital goods, while imports of consumer goods have been regarded as a residual. . . . What is significant is the relative openness of China, like Korea, Taiwan (China) and Malaysia to the imports of capital goods. . . . this is what sets China and the East Asia NIEs apart from other large developing countries such as India and Brazil, where the share of capital goods imports is significantly smaller.

Looking at the structure of imports in more detail, in 1984, food accounted for 10 per cent, intermediate goods about 54 per cent (principally steel, chemicals, and crude materials) and capital goods a further 34 per cent; consumer goods contributed a mere 2 per cent. By 1990, the share of food had changed little, and that of consumer goods had risen only to 5 per cent. However, imports of increasingly less essential intermediate goods had declined to 39 per cent—whereas capital goods had increased to 44 per cent (World Bank, 1994*c*: 16). Furthermore, the structure of China's imports was palpably different from that of South Asia in the early 1990s (WDR, 1993: 266). 41 per cent of China's imports consisted of machinery or transport equipment, but the respective figures for India (18 per cent), Bangladesh (17 per cent), and Pakistan (28 per cent) were much lower. This Chinese figure was also in excess of the average for low-income countries (32 per cent). In many respects, this approach mirrored that taken in Japan in the late Meiji and inter-war period (Yamazawa, 1990).

China's ability to resist the wholesale importation of consumer goods reflected deliberate state policy: continued restrictions on the use of foreign exchange by the state-owned enterprises, provincial governments and the private sector. It also reflected a system of selective protection which penalized purchasers of non-essentials. Thus non-essential foodstuffs typically have tariffs of between 20 and 50 per cent (around 150 per cent for tobacco products) but foodstuffs deemed essential face a tariff of less than 10 per cent. This approach is repeated for other commodities. Thus textiles and footwear bear tariffs of 60 to 80 per cent, but minerals are taxed at 11 per cent, chemicals at 15 per cent, and machinery at 28 per cent. Some idea of the range is given in Table 15.14.

TABLE 15.14. *Tariff rates by import category, early 1990s* (percentages)

Category	Weighted tariff rate
Wood pulp	2.0
Cereals	3.0
Fertilizer	5.0
Railway rolling-stock	9.9
Iron and steel	13.9
Electrical machinery	30.6
Cotton	48.0
Coffee	51.0
Photographic equipment	53.2
Footwear	70.4
Beverages and spirits	88.2
Tobacco	143.4

Source: World Bank (1994*c*: 51–2).

It is also interesting to note that many of the coastal provinces have, if anything, increased the proportion of capital goods which they imported over the course of the 1980s. Take Jiangsu. In 1981, producer goods accounted for about 60 per cent of imports (with machinery and equipment alone comprising 13 per cent of all imports); the remaining 40 per cent consisted of consumer goods (*shenghuo ziliao*). For 1989–91 on average, however, the producer goods share had risen to a remarkable 97 per cent (JSTJNJ, 1994: 220).[37] This illustrates the way in which Chinese policy towards imports changed. In the late 1970s, imports were geared towards satisfying consumer demand in certain key areas.[38] By the early 1990s, the primary purpose behind buying imports was to promote economic development.

All in all, the Chinese approach to imports reflected a conscious effort to 'industrialize by learning'. The strategy has focused on importing those goods which were deemed essential for exports, and for economic growth, rather than those which satisfied consumer demand. A key example was the 1994 decision (and which began operation in April 1995) to provide rebates on the indirect taxes paid for imported goods which were later exported (Lardy, 1992: 48–50); as has been noted earlier, this played a key role in promoting FDI in processing and assembly production. In that the transition era focused on the promotion of industrialization, the economy remains truer to its Maoist antecedents than is sometimes recognized. More generally, however, there are clear parallels between the Dengist route to modernity and that embarked upon by Taiwan and South Korea in the early 1960s. Liberalization has taken place, but the Chinese economy remained heavily protected and geared towards promoting domestic production—rather than the aspirations of Western multinationals.

7. The Open Door and Export-Led Growth: A Summary

The evidence discussed here suggests that the export-led growth hypothesis offers a poor explanation of Chinese economic growth. The share of exports in GDP did rise dramatically over the transition period, but it remained rather low by international standards in all but a handful of coastal provinces. The notion of a causal link running from exports to GDP is not compelling; many of China's export industries were based upon the processing and assembly of imported components, and there is not much evidence that the coastal provinces received much of a boost to GDP from their openness compared to those of the interior. It was their location, rather their involvement in the international economy, that seems to explain the historically faster rate of growth of the coast compared to the interior.

The fourth element in the export-led hypothesis suggests that the source of export growth is primarily exogenous. There is something in the evidence to support this: a large proportion of Chinese exports originated in enterprises financed by foreign direct investment, and this is especially true of Guangdong province. Nevertheless, the hand of the state in initiating and accelerating the process of export growth is all too apparent. It granted Guangdong favourable fiscal treatment, which allowed it to invest heavily in the basic infrastructure necessary to both promote industrialization and to attract FDI. Almost all of the basic infrastructure in the Shenzhen special economic zone was financed by the state. FDI was also actively encouraged after 1984 by tax rebates on imports destined for use in export products. And in the macroeconomic sphere, sustained devaluation helped to make exports profitable. Finally, the import regime of selected tariffs promoted industrialization, rather than the satisfaction of consumer demand, and this was instrumental in facilitating production for export markets.

To be sure, the 1990s saw a drive to exploit export markets. This was (endogenously) initiated by the producers of consumer goods in provinces like Zhejiang and Guangdong, where the growth of GDP easily outstripped the growth of consumer demand. The realization problem faced by these producers could only be resolved by selling abroad, instead of to the congested home market. As a result, exports played an important role in coastal economic growth after 1978. However, not even in Guangdong is the hypothesis of export-led growth fully substantiated. For all the role of exogenous factors, it was active intervention by the state across a range of areas which was crucial, especially during the early years of transition. Paradoxically, it may even have been the failure of the Chinese state to prevent growing income inequality which provided an important boost to the search for export markets during the 1990s.

16

The State, Industry, and Infrastructure

Chapters 13, 14, and 15 discussed the way in which the Chinese state promoted economic growth by raising the level of aggregate demand, by continuing to regulate foreign trade, and by restructuring agriculture in a manner which was far removed from any simple process of privatization. This chapter continues this discussion by looking at the role played by the state in promoting industry and infrastructural development. It is in this last area that the role played by the Chinese state was least positive.

1. Industry Owned by Central Government

China's central government played a key role in the rejuvenation of industrial state-owned enterprises (SOEs) after 1978. It did that in two ways. First, it reallocated investment towards fast-growing industries, towards industries supplying inputs to the agricultural sector and towards industries geared towards the production of consumer goods. Secondly, the Chinese state was instrumental in ensuring a sustained and significant increase in the productivity levels of SOEs. Competition *may* also have helped these industries to become more 'efficient', but the evidence on this is not very clear—restructuring of the ownership system by central government may have been more important.

1.1. Structural Change: The Reallocation of Investment

One of the most important functions of the post-1978 central government in China was to reallocate investment within the state sector. This reallocation was crucial because it was the state sector that provided the bulk of Chinese industrial output throughout the Dengist era. The shift in investment was achieved by a number of instruments. These included the use of the state budget to allocate surpluses made in one enterprise for use in another, and the negotiation of different rates of profit remittance across industries; by varying what amounted to a profits tax, the central government could easily prioritize a sector by increasing its retained profit. In addition, central government could make it easier or more difficult for enterprises to borrow from the banking system.[1]

The resulting sectoral allocation of investment within the state sector is shown in Table 16.1.[2]

TABLE 16.1. *Growth rates of NVIO and gross capital stock by ISIC disaggregation, 1980–1992* (annual percentage growth rates)

Industrial sector	Nominal gross capital stock	Real net value of industrial output
Coal mining	11.2	5.6
Petroleum extraction	19.5	4.9
Ferrous-metal mining	7.7	4.6
Non-ferrous metal mining	10.9	6.5
Non-metal mineral mining	11.9	6.5
Salt mining	12.0	0.8
Other mineral mining	15.4	12.8
Logging	5.1	−0.9
Water supply	16.1	4.5
Food manufacture	17.0	8.3
Beverage manufacture	24.5	12.2
Tobacco manufacture	31.2	11.1
Forage manufacture	44.3	54.8
Textile manufacture	19	4.6
Clothing	23.0	9.7
Leather and fur	18.8	7.6
Timber processing	16.0	2.1
Furniture manufacture	13.1	1.8
Paper-making	14.8	5.3
Printing	14.7	5.4
Cultural and sporting items	18.0	7.4
Arts and crafts	23.2	10.0
Power generation	13.5	6.5
Petroleum processing	19.8	1.5
Coke and coal gas	21.4	8.6
Chemicals	12.3	7.9
Pharmaceutical products	19.6	11.5
Chemical fibres	20.5	14.3
Rubber goods	15.1	3.7
Plastic goods	22.6	10.2
Building materials	14.9	5.8
Ferrous-metal smelting	12.6	5.2
Non-ferrous metal smelting	11.2	5.1
Metal products	13.9	3.6
Machine building	8.3	6.0
Transport equipment	9.8	9.6
Electrical equipment	16.2	9.3
Electronic equipment	16.5	12.1
Instruments and meters	8.9	3.9
Other	20.7	9.6
Median	15.7	6.3

Notes: These statistics are for independently accounting enterprises of all types at the *xiang* level and above. No data are available for 1981–3. The capital stock data are at current prices; deflators are not available for individual subsectors, and to deflate all sectors by the machine-building deflator—though logical—is pointless. The NVIO data are in constant prices. The current price data have been deflated using the 15 producer price deflator indices given in ZGTJNJ (1995: 249). In most cases, the assignment of a deflator to a subsector is straightforward; textile manufactures are deflated by the textile deflator, petroleum extraction by the petroleum deflator, and so forth. For less straightforward subsectors, the following deflators have been used: non-metal mineral mining, salt, coke and coal gas, and other mineral mining—use the coal deflator; water supply, forage, and other—use the average deflator; beverages and tobacco—food; timber processing, and furniture—building materials; printing—paper; arts and crafts—cultural products deflator; pharmaceuticals, chemical fibres, rubber, and plastics—chemicals; transport, electrical, electronics, and instruments—machine building.

Source: ZGGYJJTJNJ (1993).

It is clear from these data that a number of sectors were promoted much more than others in the sense that their capital stock growth exceeded the median. Energy is a case in point, with investment in oil extraction, oil processing, and gas all growing quickly. However, investment in coal production languished as the state attempted both to reduce Chinese dependence upon coal, and to restructure the state-owned sector of the industry to make it more profitable. This became especially marked after 1992, when a conscious attempt was made to trim the size of the coal sector. Employment, standing at 3.7 million in 1992, was reduced by almost 900,00 by early 1997 and the process of restructuring continued thereafter with the aim of creating an industry employing only around 1 million workers. Moreover, there is considerable evidence that this restructuring programme was successful. While output continued to increase (at least until early 1997), the cuts in employment allowed the industry to register a profit for the first half of 1997—after losses for the preceding seven years (SCMP, 23 Aug. 1997). This a clear illustration of the capacity of the Chinese state to restructure industrial production without having recourse to privatization.

A second subsector promoted was traditional manufacturing; all the subsectors in the table between food and timber show capital stock growth in excess of the median. A third promoted subsector was chemical products (though not chemicals itself); indeed the growth rates of the capital stock in chemical fibres, pharmaceutical products, and plastic goods were well above the median (20.9 per cent on average for these three against a median of 15.7). The fourth broad subsector promoted was electronic and electrical goods, although the capital stock there grew only modestly above the median.

These trends suggest that the Chinese central government adopted a policy of investment allocation that was firmly geared towards the economy's perceived needs in the transition era. There were significant shortages of consumer manufactures of all types at the end of the 1970s; much post-1978 investment therefore was firmly directed towards consumer manufacturing. There were crippling energy shortages, which investment in petroleum and gas sought to rectify. It is true that coal mining languished, but the principal problem there was a shortage of rolling stock rather than production; extensive stocks of coal in Shanxi province were a feature of the 1980s because of the limited capacity of the railway system. Thirdly, Chinese industry at the end of the Maoist period was very traditional in terms of its products. A strenuous effort was made to put this right via investment in chemical products and both electrical and electronic equipment.

The data presented in Table 16.1 also suggests that the Chinese state was relatively successful in that many of the industrial sectors which received investment priority also experienced output growth in excess of the median. Many of the traditional manufacturing subsectors experienced above-median output growth, as did electrical and electronic equipment. Pharmaceutical products, plastics, and chemical fibres also grew quickly. It is true that, of the subsectors where investment growth exceeded the median, five experienced below-median output growth during 1980 to 1992. However, this is less telling than it appears. Of the five, four (oil extraction, oil processing, water supply, and timber processing) were natural-resource constrained. For example, despite extensive offshore exploration, oil finds off the Chinese coast have been relatively disappointing. Similarly, China's timber resources are very limited except in Heilongjiang and parts of the south-west. Additionally, much of northern China suffers from severe water shortages (which is one of the justifications offered for building a dam in the Yangzi gorges). It is therefore not especially surprising that output growth was comparatively slow relative to the level of investment. As for the fifth sector, the slow growth of textiles almost certainly reflects its size. It was the largest single industrial sector in China in 1980 in terms of its output value. Accordingly, investment increases faltered somewhat in the face of diminishing returns in the key textile centres in eastern China, and the result was a rather modest (by Chinese standards) industrial growth rate of about 4.6 per cent per year.

Finally, it is worth noting the changing priority given to investment in those sectors producing inputs for the agricultural sector. Agriculture had long been a source of concern to Chinese economists, and one particular problem identified was an inadequate supply of modern inputs (Xu, 1982). The response to this was a growing allocation of investment to the chemical fertilizer industry. For although much of the capacity invested in during the early and mid-1970s came on stream at the end of the decade (ZGTJNJ, 1983: 349), there was still perceived to be a widespread shortage of fertilizer—which was, after all, the key farm input. By contrast, the need for agricultural machinery capacity diminished. This was in part political; Hua Guofeng's gradual loss of power to Deng Xiaoping led to the steam going out of the 'learn from Dazhai' campaign.[3] With that went less emphasis on agricultural mechanization. This was reinforced by the parcellization of land that occurred during decollectivization (which led to reduced demand for large tractors). What is interesting about these two trends is that the Chinese government responded to these changing needs by increasing state investment in chemical fertilizer and reducing it in agricultural machinery capacity. This is shown by data on basic construction investment during 1981–4 (Table 16.2). In other words, the system of investment allocation was very flexible. It simply was not the case that the investment patterns of the past continued unabated during the early 1980s in the face of changing needs.[4]

TABLE 16.2. *Basic construction investment in the chemical fertilizer and agricultural machinery industries, 1981–1984* (m. current *yuan)*

Year	Chemical fertilizer capacity	Agricultural machinery capacity
1981	427	147
1982	563	99
1983	631	74
1984	919	63

Sources: ZGTJNJ (1983: 331); ZGTJNJ (1985: 429–30).

1.2. Institutional Change and SOE Productivity Growth

Important though the reallocation of investment within the state sector was, most Western specialists have argued that the key contribution of the central government in the industrial sphere was to introduce a number of policies which improved the efficiency—faster growth of total factor productivity—of the state enterprises. This interpretation suggests that privatization is not even a necessary condition for improvements in efficiency, and is reflected in the writings of a wide variety of specialists:

> There is substantial evidence that China's second-stage reformers have been successful, even without state industry. Thus far, available evidence strongly supports the hypothesis of changed behaviour and improved performance [p. 242]. . . . reforms have created significant changes in behaviour in state-run firms, and significant gains in economic efficiency [p. 233]. (Naughton, 1995*a*)

> China's reform experience shows that privatizing state enterprises has not been essential for the near- to medium-term success of its industrial reform program. Expanding managerial autonomy and incentives and ending the state's monopoly over industry have, to a substantial degree, substituted for the privatization of state enterprises. (Chen, *et al.*, 1992: 222)

> China has deployed an unorthodox strategy of industrial reform to great advantage. An initial round of partial reforms opened the door to growing competition involving old and new forms of public enterprise. During the 1980s, competition emerged as a powerful force for beneficial change in all segments of China's semi-market industrial system. As a result, this episode of partial reform raised the level of industrial output and enhanced the economic welfare of China's factory work force. (Jefferson and Rawski, 1994: 67)

> Whether deferring privatization has retarded China's economic growth is a much debated question. . . . I am nevertheless drawn to the conclusion that . . . it is doubtful that a more economically liberal regime could have produced a significantly better overall record of growth. (Putterman, 1995: 1064)

This positive assessment is based upon two pillars. First, as was discussed in Chapter 10, there was an increase in the rate of growth of total factor productivity in the state-owned industrial sector after 1978. Secondly, a number of important institutional and policy changes were introduced by the central government over the course of the Dengist era which can plausibly account for this acceleration in productivity growth.

These institutional changes occurred relatively slowly. Most prices were set by the state but, from September 1979 onwards, industries and localities could vary the prices of their products by about 20 per cent from the centrally determined price in response to industry and locality-specific demand and supply factors.[5] In addition, the prices of a number of non-strategic commodities were given over almost entirely to 'market forces'. The aim of these and subsequent price reforms was to shift gradually towards a system of market-based price determination in the hope that prices would thereby be brought into line with marginal costs of production. Prices would then act as indicators of relative scarcity, leading to the 'efficient' allocation of factors of production across sectors. After January 1985, the pace of price reform accelerated when enterprises were allowed to charge 'market floating prices'

(prices that were only marginally below market prices) for output sold by the enterprises themselves after fulfilling the requirements of the central plan. This introduction of a 'dual-track' pricing system progressed gradually such that, by the end of 1988, only about 25 per cent of prices were set by the state. These prices were themselves very different from those that prevailed in 1978, as adjustments were made to serve a variety of social and economic objectives.

The inflation that appeared during 1988 and 1989 was in part a result of relative price changes announced well in advance. During April–June 1988, the Party lifted price controls on a number of non-basic foodstuffs, notably vegetables, eggs, pork, and sugar. It further announced, largely thanks to an initiative from Deng himself (Shirk, 1993: 325–7) that there would be a rapid transition to market determination of prices for almost all commodities. Although the effect of these rises was meant to be cushioned by the payment of an income subsidy, the announcements caused large-scale panic buying and hoarding during August. As a result, the urban inflation rose to more than 30 per cent during the autumn. These very unwelcome developments effectively forced the Party to shelve further price reform, and persuaded it (at the 3rd Plenum in September 1988) to begin a programme of macroeconomic contraction designed to bring inflation down (You, 1991; Naughton, 1991*c*). In the early 1990s, however, price reform continued and was increasingly extended to include most basic urban consumer goods. In May 1991, for example, the urban price for grains was increased by 60 per cent, and it rose by a further 45 per cent in 1992 (by which time the ubiquitous grain coupon, in use since the 1950s, had been abandoned in many parts of China). As a result, the price paid by the state to farmers for grain was essentially equalized with that charged by the state to urban consumers. The price of vegetable oils also increased by over 150 per cent in May 1991, and both energy and rail prices have seen sharp increases during the first half of the 1990s. Although these price rises were in many respects far more dramatic than those of the mid-1980s, the programme was comparatively successful. In part this was because the increase in the key grain price in urban areas in the spring of 1991 was accompanied by an income subsidy to the urban population, and because the price increase was announced only a few days in advance, which made large-scale hoarding difficult. In addition, these price changes took place against a background of muted inflationary pressure, in sharp contrast to the situation in the summer of 1988. As a result, the relative price changes of 1991 did not precipitate any significant urban unrest.

Industrial reform in urban China extended well beyond mere price adjustments. Policies designed to raise productivity were launched in Sichuan in October 1978 with the introduction of a scheme whereby state enterprises were allowed to keep a proportion of their profits instead of handing them over to the state (Lin, 1980; Ren, *et al.*, 1980). By the early 1980s, this type of autonomy had been granted to most state enterprises. Enterprises were also granted much more control over wage payments (Walder, 1987; Chow, 1989). As a result, the wages paid to state employees were increased, thus ending a freeze which had lasted from 1963 to 1977. With enterprises also given the right to pay wages on a piece-rate basis, and to institute bonus schemes (both to be financed out of newly retained profits), patterns of remuneration were virtually transformed during the early 1980s.

In May 1984, the urban reforms were carried a stage further with the introduction of the Factory Directory Responsibility System which had as its objective an increase in the power of factory directors relative to enterprise party committees (Naughton, 1995*a*: 204–20).[6] First, the power of managers was increased by reducing the influence of the Party secretary, who often lost office as well as the power to make appointments. With no other countervailing influence present in the workplace—unions had powers that were no more than notional—the power of the factory director was effectively absolute. Secondly, the newly independent factory director was allowed greater latitude in wage and employment decisions than had been permitted even the enterprise's Party secretary during the Maoist period. For example, the factory director of the late 1980s was allowed to pay wages that were significantly out of line with those paid in other enterprises, and to make bonus payments that were related to enterprise profits. After 1986, new workers were employed on five-year contracts rather than permanently. It was also made easier to fire incompetent workers (Chevrier, 1990). Thirdly, the proportion of profits remitted to the state was set for a period of years, rather than negotiated afresh every year. This allowed factory directors to plan ahead—especially in respect of investment decisions—with more confidence than had previously been the case. Fourthly, and tied up with the introduction of longer-term contracting arrangements between state and factory director, some directors were required to bid in a competitive auction for the right to manage their enterprise over the period of the contract. In effect, the right to manage—and with it the right to the control of monopoly rents—was auctioned off to the highest bidder. This type of contest was admittedly rather rare; the majority of managers selected were appointed rather than determined by competitive bidding (Naughton, 1995*a*: 215–18).

As a result of these various policy initiatives, directors and workers in state enterprises came under increasing pressure to improve performance. Although there was little danger of either bankruptcy or takeover, managers of SOEs were in an increasingly difficult position. Unless they could increase the wages paid to their workforces at the same rate as their competitors, they would suffer a gradual haemorrhage of skilled labour. Furthermore, the profitability of enterprises was increasingly indicative of the effectiveness of enterprise management.[7] Managers could no longer easily hide behind excuses such as a distorted price system or interference by the Party secretary. As the state was increasingly prepared to dismiss (or at least not reappoint) managers deemed to be incompetent, there was real pressure on them to perform well. The same was true for workers. Their job was less secure because of five-year contracts and greater penalties for slacking. More positively, their income was increasingly related to the performance of the firm.

Nevertheless, as Chevrier (1990: 129) points out, progress in many of these areas was at best fitful: 'a strong party at the top and established party elites at the local level defended existing power and gained control over new wealth.' For example, the new Bankruptcy Law (first mooted in 1986) was rarely used over the next decade.

Moreover, a proposal to create joint-stock enterprises—first put forward by Li Yining and involving joint share ownership by state and enterprise—was rejected by the NPC in 1986. Only at the 3rd Plenum of the CCP in September 1988 was the idea approved, and even thereafter—as will be seen below—the pace of implementation has been slow (Sun, 1995: 71, 78). More generally, 1985–6 saw a furious debate on the question of whether price reform or ownership reform (and in particular privatization) should come first. The former position was closely associated with Wu Jinglian, and the latter with Li Yining, Dong Fureng, and Hua Sheng. The merit of price reform was that the abolition of the dual-track pricing system (and hence arbitrage possibilities) would greatly reduce the scope for corruption, thus serving a political as well as an economic purpose. This may have been why Deng supported this approach in 1988 (Fewsmith, 1994: 220–4).[8] The problem with price reform was that it was bound to have very general political consequences, unlike privatization (the effects of which would have been largely restricted to employees in state enterprises). Perhaps more importantly, if firms were granted the right to set prices without any attempt by the state either to harden budget constraints or reduce their monopolistic power, the consequence of price reform would be high rates of inflation (as was the case in Russia in the early 1990s).

Industrial transition did eventually accelerate during the 1990s. This acceleration was heralded by the establishment of stock markets in Shenzhen (spring 1991) and Shanghai (summer 1991), and the emergence of joint-stock companies following the 1988 legislation. However, this process was not especially dramatic. The number of companies traded on these exchanges was very small at the time of Deng's death, and the bulk of joint stock companies in existence in the mid-1990s had sold their shares solely to their employees rather than to the general public (Naughton, 1995*a*: 299). Accelerating transition also saw the emergence of relatively large private-sector enterprises. The capital value of the top 500 private firms, for instance, amounted to over 46 times that of the private-sector average. Nevertheless, the top 500 were still rather small by western standards; on average, they employed only 395 workers each (BR, 39/8–9, 1996).

In addition, the Chinese government sought to set up enterprise groups (*jituangongsi*) via the merger of existing SOEs, and by converting SOEs into joint-stock companies, with a view to eventual privatization. The enterprise groups envisaged seem rather similar to South Korean *chaebols*; they will reduce administrative duplication (by, for example, creating a single board of directors) and promoted managerial specialization. Vertical and horizontal mergers were also enforced with the aim of reaping the benefits of economies of scale (Nolan, 1996). As the transition era progressed, greater emphasis was placed on this type of industrial restructuring; it was, for example, the main focus of industrial restructuring in 1996 (as Li Peng's 'Report on the Work of Government' made clear), which centred on the 1,000 largest enterprises, and on 57 enterprise groups (BR, 40/13: 10). Enterprise restructuring also involved a willingness to bail out strategic SOEs which were making losses, especially in the wake of the recession of 1989–92. One example of this was the Shougang corporation. By 1996, Shougang was a large enterprise group with 27 wholly-owned subsidiaries, including trading, banking, and electronics companies; 4 of these subsidiaries were listed in Hong Kong. The core steel operation made profits of 966m. *yuan*, although group net profits were lower (324m. *yuan*) because of losses in its construction, mining, and machinery divisions. Moreover, the extent of diversification and restructuring had gone so far that only 50,000 of Shougang's 220,000 workers were employed in steel production.[9]

A second major development in the 1990s followed from one of the decisions (the Fifty Articles) made at the 3rd Plenum of the 14th Central Committee (November 1993) to establish a 'socialist market economy'. This Article allowed the conversion of SOEs into joint-stock companies. This was the way in which privatization proceeded in Russia, and was seen as presaging wholesale privatization in China (Putterman, 1995: 1062)—with some justification in the light of the privatization of small-scale county-level SOEs in 1996. However, it is by no means certain that this will be the case. The Fifty Articles themselves state that the extent of private ownership should vary across industries, but that key products and industries would remain firmly under state control (Yabuki, 1995: 235). Moreover, many prominently placed members of the CCP continued to insist that privatization was not the solution for poor enterprise performance, arguing that the aim of creating joint-stock companies should be to allow them access to other forms of capital and to give them greater autonomy from the state. But whatever the long-term intent, comparatively few share-holding companies had been established by the end of 1996.

A further important type of institutional change presided over by the state was the introduction of competition. The argument went as follows. Productivity grew quickly during the 1950s when the state sector was both relatively small and faced at least some competition from private enterprises. By contrast, the late Maoist period saw the abolition of private ownership and the creation of a monolithic state-owned industrial sector. Furthermore, there was no competition from imports because the economy was effectively closed. Both factors combined to ensure very low productivity growth, with output increases stemming from the increased employment of inputs (notably capital). The best way, therefore, to improve performance was to reintroduce competition—in the form of foreign firms, imports, encouragement for private enterprises, and the promotion of enterprises owned by local government. During the initial phase of transition (1978–84) the degree of competition that enterprises faced in their product and input markets was still comparatively small. As a result, the acceleration in productivity that occurred in the early 1980s was modest. After 1984, however, competition in product markets and for skilled labour rapidly intensified as rural industry began to grow quickly and as some of the barriers to imports were removed. Furthermore, gradual price reform meant that prices in many markets moved closer to marginal costs such that factory managers became increasingly aware of the true opportunity costs involved in many of their production decisions. In addition, the extent of competition within the SOE sector also accelerated, with positive effects on productivity. For example, lower prices induced the Changchun First Automobile company to switch to the Baoshan Iron and Steel Company (Baogang) as its supplier, instead of relying upon the Anshan

Iron and Steel Company (Angang) as it had done in the past. Partly as a result, Angang made a loss in late 1994. Angang's response was to reduce its output of redundant products—some 40 per cent of steel output had been stockpiled in 1994—and to develop a marketing/sales department for the first time in its history (CT, May 1997).

It is evident from this discussion that the steps taken by the central government to invigorate its enterprise were introduced very gradually. Indeed, the pace of industrial transition—despite the acceleration of the 1990s—has been glacially slow compared with events in Poland, the former USSR, and Chile, where strong emphasis was placed on privatization and allowing unprofitable private enterprises to fold right from the start. Some 44 per cent of Chinese state enterprises were still loss-making in 1996; they received subsidies to the tune of 61.6bn. *yuan*, 30 per cent higher than in 1995 (SCMP, 4 March 1997). To be sure, the number of SOEs allowed to go bankrupt each year in China increased as the 1990s progressed; there were, for example, 50 bankruptcies in 26 experimental cities in the first four months of 1996 (Zong in BR, 40/12: 1). More generally, the Bankruptcy Law passed in 1988 has begun to facilitate industrial restructuring; 6,232 firms of all types went bankrupt in 1996. Yet the gradual nature of Chinese industrial transition is never better exemplified than by pointing out that the 1996 bankruptcy total was greater than the total for the entire 1989–95 period of 5,395 firms (SCMP, 29 Jan. 1997).

Nevertheless, the pace of transition was accelerating at the time of Deng's death, with the privatization of state-owned enterprises begun in earnest in 1996 in some parts of Guangdong, so often the pacemaker during the transition era. In Shunde prefecture (in the Pearl River delta), the privatization programme was announced to be no more than converting state-owned enterprises into joint-stock (or shareholding) companies for fear of offending Beijing. But in practice, the process was undoubtedly one of privatization. For one thing, these enterprises were no longer granted state loans; and thus faced a hard budget constraint. For another, government typically retained only 30 to 40 per cent of the shares of the new companies. Although in principle a shareholding of this size still allows state control, in practice the management was able to exercise a decisive influence over company operations by buying worker shares (SCMP, 18.vi.97). Nevertheless, the key point about places like Shunde was their exceptionalism even in the mid-1990s. In the overwhelmingly majority of locations in the People's Republic, privatization was only being talked about in 1996.

1.3. The Impact of Institutional Change on SOE Productivity

It seems hard to believe that this package of policies, taken as a whole, had no effect on the growth of enterprise productivity. However, it remains unclear which element in the package was decisive. Particular doubts surround the role played by competition. To be sure, there was a growing presence of foreign companies and private firms in the Chinese industrial sector after 1978.[10] Competition from imported products was also more marked. But the competitive threat to SOEs

—both those run by counties and by national ministries—came principally from enterprises owned by townships and villages (TVCEs). These latter were most emphatically state-owned; the reality of China in the 1980s was that collective industry was in essence *local*, rather than centrally owned, state industry. As a result, the Chinese industrial landscape was characterized by a competitive contest for rents between centrally and locally owned state enterprises presided over by central government. To call this market-based competition is at best a distortion.

The evidence, however, does not really show that competition, whether from private, TVCE or urban collective industry, was especially important in improving productivity in SOEs after 1978 (Table 16.3).

TABLE 16.3. *The growth of labour productivity in state-owned industrial enterprises and the rise of the non-state sector, 1978–1989* (ranked by growth of labour productivity)

Province	Labour-productivity growth	Growth of non-state share in GVIO	Share of non-state sector in GVIO, 1989
Yunnan	8.3	3.5	28
Xinjiang	7.3	6.1	21
Fujian	6.6	8.0	60
Hubei	6.5	5.6	40
Zhejiang	6.4	6.1	75
Shandong	4.0	6.0	62
Gansu	3.3	8.4	22
Liaoning	3.1	8.6	43
Mean	5.7	6.5	44

Note: Labour-productivity growth is based on GVIO per employed worker in state-owned independent accounting industrial enterprises at 1980 constant prices. The share of the non-state sector is total GVIO (at constant prices), minus state-sector GVIO, as a percentage of the total. The non-state sector is thus the sum of urban collective, urban private, TVE, and other enterprises. Growth of the non-state share is calculated by logs between the 1978 and 1989 endpoints only; the 1978 share is based on 1970 constant price data and the 1989 share is based on 1980 constant prices.

Source: LSTJ (1990).

Three types of data are presented here. First, the rate of growth of labour productivity in state-owned independent accounting industrial enterprises measured in constant prices. Although a partial productivity indicator, this has the merit of circumventing the problems of measuring the capital stock and specifying the type of production function. The trend here is clearly upward, averaging close to 6 per cent per year for the sample of provinces. The second column of data shows the growth of the non-state sector share (mainly urban collective enterprises and TVEs) in gross industrial output value, again at constant prices. This is a measure of the extent to which marketization/competition increased during the Dengist era; it is not a measure of the size of the private sector, which contributed only a small proportion of both urban and rural output value in the late 1980s. These figures show a dramatic increase in the size of the non-state sector; typically, the share of the non-state sector doubled in every province between 1978 and 1989. The third and final indicator in the table is the actual share of the non-state sector in 1989. This gives an indication of the absolute magnitude of the competitive threat to the state sector. It is important to include this in the analysis as well as the growth rate; even if the non-state share had grown quickly, it would not have posed much of a competitive challenge but for its relatively large market share.

These data are not ideal. The time period is shorter than one would like. Net output would be better than gross output as the numerator in the estimation of labour productivity. It would be preferable to have data on output per hour worked rather than merely per worker. The data on productivity may not in every case be at constant prices. Industrial SOEs in some provinces may have faced extensive competition from non-state industries located outside its borders—Anhui's industry had to compete with local state enterprises based in neighbouring Jiangsu, for example. In that sense, the share of provincial non-state production is a poor proxy for the true degree of competition. Additionally, the share of private and local enterprises may be underestimated because of under-reporting. The sample size is also rather small.[11] Finally, provincial differences in productivity growth may reflect differences in the composition of industrial output; the scope for productivity growth was clearly greater in some industrial sectors than in others.

Nevertheless, the table is startling in showing little correspondence between the growth of labour productivity in state-owned industrial enterprises, and either the growth of the non-state sector or the absolute size of the non-state sector. In Liaoning, for example, the growth of labour productivity is well below the sample average. Yet its non-sector sector grew faster than that of any other province and its absolute magnitude was average. In other words, here is a province which quickly diversified into non-state production of industrial goods—but reaped little benefit in terms of labour-productivity growth.[12] Conversely, Xinjiang and Yunnan both recorded exceptionally fast labour-productivity growth in their state industrial sectors. Yet in both cases, the non-state share of output was very low and the relative growth rate of the non-state sector was below average.[13] Note also that the table suggests exposure to foreign capital and trade played little rolc in determining productivity growth. Interior provinces such as Xinjiang and Yunnan did at least as well as coastal provinces like Zhejiang and Fujian. Of course, Gansu did much less well—but that is counterbalanced by the case of Shandong.

The clear conclusion is that the new conventional wisdom offered by Naughton, Rawski, and others—that competition from local government enterprises was crucial in improving SOE productivity performance—is not yet fully substantiated.[14] This conclusion seems rather more in accord with the view of Jeffrey Sachs that marketization is not very important. It is also in line with the evidence from some other countries. In Hungary, for example, the market-socialist economy was poor at generating significant productivity growth in the 1970s and early 1980s, despite the introduction of marketization (and especially foreign competition) under Kadar, and its intensification after 1988 under Grosz. However, Sachs' view that privatization is essential for improved efficiency is equally unconvincing. As was noted in Chapter 10, there is much evidence that total factor-productivity growth accelerated after 1978. This is supported by the data in Table 16.3 showing impressive growth in labour productivity. If competition from TVE or private enterprises was not the decisive factor, then the reforms to enterprise management and the promotion of mergers to create enterprise groups must have been critical. Moreover, perhaps the faster rate of growth of demand—along Kaldor–Verdoorn lines—also played a role as suggested in Chapter 10. Given the explosion of per capita rural disposable income following the agricultural revolution, it would have been hard even for a comparatively 'inefficient' enterprise to meet growing product demand in the short term without any improvement in its productivity. But one way or another, China's central government seems to have played a central role in improving the performance of its industrial enterprises during the Dengist period.

2. Rural Industry and Local Government

Central government played a key role in the acceleration of Chinese industrial growth in the Dengist era. Yet even more remarkable was the positive role played by local government in the promotion of rural industrialization. Indeed, perhaps the best-known feature of the post-1978 era in China has been the exceptionally rapid growth of the rural non-farm (TVE) sector. The traditional Chinese rural economy had always been based upon a dualistic foundation of handicraft industry and farming, and product diversification occurred during the Great Leap Forward (1958/9) when iron and steel production was actively promoted. Nevertheless, the low profitability of the farm sector hampered the capacity of the Maoist collective to promote rural diversification. The famine of the early 1960s saw the collapse of most rural industrial production and, although the process began anew after 1965, no more than a fledgling non-farm sector existed by the mid-1970s.

This changed dramatically during the transition era.[15] The expansion of farm-sector profits during the early 1980s allowed local government to invest some of the proceeds in developing rural industry, construction, transportation, and commerce. The growth of the TVCE sector was also encouraged by a series of legislative provisions which granted tax holidays of three years to most such enterprises (and five-year 'holiday' periods to industries in very poor areas) and by a reduction in the rate of enterprise taxation. Rural diversification was further promoted by leasing arrangements, which encouraged private-sector investment in enterprises that continued to be owned by local government, and by growing access to the banking sector for industrial finance. Much of the subsequent growth of the *xiangzhen* sector —in particular its TVCE component—was superintended and directed by local government which, as a number of writers have pointed out (Oi, 1990; Blecher, 1991; Shue, 1990; Shue and Blecher, 1996), was strengthened rather than emasculated by the decollectivization of farm production because it broadened the tax base. Some township and village governments used this revenue to set up and run new non-farm enterprises; virtually all reinvested some of the proceeds in the farm sector, and (crucially) invested in new non-farm enterprises that were subsequently leased out to the private sector for management.

The 1980s also saw the growth of the private non-farm sector.[16] Such enterprises were not legalized until 1984, and even then many classified themselves as collective (*jiajiti*) as a tax shelter with the connivance of local government (Zhou, 1996: 120–7). The growth of the non-farm private sector followed naturally from the initial agricultural reforms because they allowed peasant households to diversify away from crop production and specialize instead in other types of agricultural production. Propelled by the same constellation of factors which gave rise to the rapid growth of TVCEs, and helped by the difficulties faced by local government in taxing such a vibrant and dynamic sector, the growth of the private sector—especially in the spheres of commerce and services—was meteoric (Nolan and Dong, 1990; Odgaard, 1992*b*; Young and Yang, 1994). With a structure of relative prices during the 1980s that ensured far higher rates of profit outside the farm sector, it was inevitable that many rural households would seize the opportunities open to them.

This growth of the TVE sector in China has been extensively discussed in the literature and there is little point in repeating such discussions. But the exceptionally fast pace of growth does bear emphasizing (Table 16.4).

TABLE 16.4. *Growth of real value-added in rural industry, 1978–1994* (at 1990 constant prices)

1978–84	13.9
1984–90	11.6
1990–4	34.5
1978–94	18.1

Sources: As for Table 2.9.

The overall pace of growth—18 per cent per year—was remarkable by any standard, and the fact that rural industry grew annually by nearly 12 per cent between 1984 and 1990 says something about the depth of the 'recessions' of 1985–6 and 1989–90. As for the post-1990 growth rate of 34.5 per cent, that can only be described as extraordinary.[17] In fairness, these estimates are not beyond suspicion. The means by which real net output value has been calculated for Table 16.4—using value-added data for *xiang*-level enterprises only and the all industry producer price index—is far from ideal. Perhaps more importantly, and as Field (1992) cautions, there are many inconsistencies in the data and the method of data collection. Even so, large errors in the estimates shown in this table would not undermine the essential conclusion that the growth of rural industry was extremely swift after 1978.

Local government was instrumental in the process of rural industrialization. The main reason was financial. As is extensively documented, the bulk of set-up capital for TVEs (and especially for TVCEs) was provided by local government and even though retained profits gradually grew in importance, the significance of external sources of finance was enormous (Byrd, 1990; Wang, 1990; Ho, 1994; Yuan, 1994).

Some of this capital came direct from the coffers of local government. Much of the remainder came from the Rural Credit Cooperatives (RCCs) and from the Agricultural Bank of China;[18] these funds in turn were provided out of the household savings deposited with the RCCs in growing quantities following the upsurge in agricultural production in the early 1980s. Although the RCCs were notionally independent, they were de facto under the control of local government, which was able to direct lending activities towards favoured projects which did not always meet strict banking criteria for loans. According to Yuan (1994: 108–9)

> . . . local governments also imposed political pressures on banks to fund local projects. Hence, although proposed banking reforms focused on making banks more commercial, banks still found it difficult to become independent arbiters in the allocation of financial resources [p. 108]. . . . In the absence of sound regulations, the banks had no effective measures to supervise loan repayments or to secure the debt should the enterprise go bankrupt. In some ways, therefore, loans to township and village enterprises were almost like gifts [p. 109].

The best indicator of the activist role played by local government in rural China is therefore the explosion of bank lending to TVEs in the early 1980s. On this, there is a good deal of evidence available in the various *xian zhi*.[19] In Kunshan county in Jiangsu, lending to *xiangzhen qiye* rose from 5.55m. *yuan* in 1978 to 39.72m. yuan in 1983 and to 199.07m. *yuan* in 1987, an average annual rate of increase of 49 per cent (*Kunshan xian zhi*, 1990: 433). In Jiangshan in Zhejiang, lending increased annually by 50 per cent between 1984 and 1987 (*Jiangshan shi zhi*, 1990: 317). In Linhai (Zhejiang), the volume of bank loans rose more modestly, but still managed a heady 25 per cent annual growth rate between 1980 and 1985 (*Linhai xian zhi*, 1989: 476). In Tonglu, also in Zhejiang, *xiangzhen* lending rose from 10.16m. *yuan* in 1979 to 76.61m. *yuan* in1985, an annual growth rate of 40 per cent (*Tonglu xian zhi*, 1991: 385). In Guanghan, the county in Sichuan in which rural industry developed most quickly, lending rose from 3.57m. *yuan* in 1978 to 55.22m. in 1985, an annualized rate of increase of 48 per cent (*Guanghan xian zhi*, 1992: 323).[20] Even in poor counties—such as Wushan in the Yangzi Gorges—lending to TVEs increased swiftly in the early 1980s (*Wushan xian zhi*, 1991: 312). At a provincial level, the explosion of lending to the *xiangzhen* sector is even more apparent. In Jiangsu, lending by RCCs increased by 48 per cent per year between 1978 and 1985, and by a further 26 per cent annually between 1985 and 1993; bank lending to TVEs increased annually by 21 per cent during this latter period (JSTJNJ, 1994: 234–5). But once again, lending to TVEs increased substantially even in poor provinces. In Henan, for instance, bank lending rose annually by 33 per cent during 1979–84 and RCC lending by 27 per cent between 1978 and 1984 (Henan yanjiushi, 1987: 591 and 594). Not surprisingly given the relatively low income level (and therefore lower savings), this growth of lending was slower than in Jiangsu but it was an impressive rate of increase all the same.

Despite these common patterns, one should be wary of over-generalization because of marked regional variation in the relationship between TVCEs, local government and financial institutions. For one thing, the role of local government in financing rural industrialization in Sunan has been more marked than elsewhere, probably because of both the relative prosperity of agriculture and the obstacles to further growth in farm production (Huang, 1990). By contrast, the TVCE sector in Wenzhou has been relatively underdeveloped; there, private enterprises have predominated and, because of the problems involved in providing collateral to secure loans from formal financial institutions, they have relied heavily on funding from the informal credit market. In Fujian and Guangdong, an approach often styled the Jinjiang model, the major source of investment has been remittances from overseas Chinese. Additionally, enterprises in suburban areas have often relied heavily upon urban corporations to provide finance (Yuan, 1994). A further distinction is that made by Blecher (1991) between 'entrepreneurial' and 'developmental' local government. Thus Blecher argues that some local governments in China have been entrepreneurial by creating and managing TVEs themselves whereas others have been more developmental—that is, they have granted greater autonomy to managers. One famous example of the entrepreneurial state is Daqiuzhuang village near Tianjin.[21] The exact opposite is offered by Nanjie village (in Linying county, Henan), which demonstrated its continued commitment to state intervention by erecting a new statue of Mao in 1993. In Dazhai, that most famous of all Maoist villages, there is a Dazhai Economic Development Corporation to oversee industrial development managed by the Party Secretary Guo Fenglian, who first came to fame for her espousal of self-reliance in the aftermath of the floods of 1963. A similar example is presented by Blecher and Shue (1996), who draw attention to the role of local government in Shulu county in Hebei. The county leaders there continued be preoccupied with many of the concerns of the late Maoist era—the need for co-operation and to avoid the emergence of large income inequalities, for example—and showed little interest in amassing personal fortunes.

The more important question in assessing the role exercised by local government lies not in describing the growth of rural industry or in identifying local variation, but in determining whether its role was benign. Although there can be no doubt that TVE expansion in the 1980s was rapid and that activist local government played a key part in this process, it has been argued that the TVCEs inherited from the Maoist period, and newly established in the early 1980s, were remarkable for their inefficiency. The logical corollary is that TVCE expansion was very much a second-best policy: it did create an extensive network of rural industries, but China would have been better served if this growth had been left to the private sector. One of the leading critics of Chinese policy in this regard has been Christine Wong (1982, 1991*a*, 1991*c*). According to her, the bulk of local industries established in the late Maoist era were funded by central government rather than out of local resources; the notion of a self-reliant industrial development strategy in rural China is therefore a myth. Furthermore, many of the 'five small industries' established after 1958 were hopelessly inefficient, producing second-rate products using antiquated capital stock, and consuming valuable raw materials in the process.[22] As a consequence, the losses of rural enterprises amounted to 50 per cent of those of all SOEs in 1978 (Wong, 1991*a*: 25). She therefore concludes that:

> Although some of the investment funding for rural industry was raised locally, outside of the state sector, available aggregate statistics show the share of total investment financed by state funds to have been surprisingly large . . . By showing that state funds were readily available for use in investment, I argue that this 'easy money' fed excessive growth in the programme so that, by the mid-1970s, rural industries had expanded beyond optimal scales and local supply capabilities, creating enormous technical, supply and financial problems. (Wong, 1991*a*: 184–5)

It is further argued that not much changed after 1978, largely because of the persistence of Maoist views amongst local officials (Wong, 1994: 49). As local government aimed to maximize tax revenue rather than profit, it was not overly concerned by the growth of loss-making industries. There was also far too much emphasis on employment, to the detriment of efficiency (Wong, 1989: 48). A further problem often remarked upon was the tendency of *some* local governments to use TVCEs as a milch cow to finance prestige projects which did little to promote local economic growth. Whereas local government in Shulu county (Hebei) eschewed conspicuous consumption and reinvested heavily in public goods, local government in Guanghan county (Sichuan) used TVCE revenue to finance the construction of new hotels and the acquisition of high-quality Japanese cars (Blecher, 1991: 288).[23] Finally, the enthusiasm with which local government has embraced TVCE development has also been reflected in a good deal of parochialism. For example, local governments across China during the 1980s and 1990s protected their own industries against imports and tried to prevent outflows of raw materials in order to maximize their tax base. The result has been the creation of formidable obstacles to trade and the duplication of production (Yuan, 1994). This may be one reason why some studies have found that regional specialization and the extent of internal trade actually dwindled over the course of the 1980s (Kumar, 1994). The final criticism of what might be called the Dengist model of rural industrialization is that the property rights that underpin it are unclear, and that short-termism and suboptimal investment levels are the results. According to Kornai (1989: 90):

> The most important change needed is to give a clear, stable framework both to private business and to the government officials who deal with the private sector. It must be clear what is permitted and what is prohibited. Rules must not be changed capriciously. Hungarian experience shows that ambiguity, improvisation, and unpredictable steps forward and backward create the feeling of uncertainty in the formal private sector.

A (typically) clear statement of this view for China comes from Sachs and Woo (1994: 130–1), who argue that even the 'successful' TVCEs of Jiangsu were debt-ridden and 'facing financial difficulties' in 1992.

It is debatable whether there is much truth in these criticisms of post-1978 rural industrialization. Wong's charge that Maoist rural enterprises were 'inefficient' is not so much wrong as misdirected. Although many of these enterprises did make losses, it is not very surprising. Most of China's communes lacked personnel trained in industrial production and thus were at the very beginning of the learning curve. More importantly, it is not sensible to judge the success of these enterprises in terms of their profitability. The Maoist development strategy was very much geared towards providing inputs to the farm sector at minimum cost; the bulk of China's investment and skilled labour was instead directed towards Third Front construction and rural enterprises were required to make do with whatever resources were available locally. Whether the enterprises made a profit in the process was largely irrelevant provided they mobilized local resources that previously would not have been tapped to produce usable evidence; only at the height of the Great Leap Forward was this objective unfulfilled. The key point is that an extensive industrial base had been established across rural China, and that a large number of local officials had become familiar with basic industrial techniques in the process.

As for the 1980s, it is often forgotten that the rural enterprise sector was deliberately restructured at the beginning of the period as part of the 'readjustment' programme. The aim was to shift away from the production of basic farm inputs. With the lifting of the American strategic threat, these inputs, chemical fertilizers in particular, could be better made available from larger (imported) state-owned plants or via imports of the finished product. Instead, rural industry was to switch towards the production of consumer goods. In other words, the rural industrial sector was restructured to meet the perceived demands of the new development strategy. The scale of this programme of restructuring *xiangzhen* enterprises is apparent from the data. In Hunan province for example, 224 projects were halted and the number of enterprises was reduced by 18,100 between 1979 and 1983 (Hunan sheng nongye quhua weiyuanhui, 1989: 83–4). Furthermore, the structure of industrial production changed dramatically; while the output of machinery produced in *xiang* enterprises was falling by 20 per cent and that of coal rising by only 10 per cent between 1978 and 1982, electricity production was up by 166 per cent, textiles by 238 per cent, and food processing output by 368 per cent. Although it is true that the restructuring of smaller enterprises was partly a consequence of decollectivization as Wong (1988: 8–9) claims (there were few buyers amongst the peasantry for unprofitable enterprises), that was hardly true of commune enterprises which remained firmly under the control of *xiang* government. Furthermore, the bulk of the restructuring occurred *before* 1982, the year in which decollectivization really got under way. In Sichuan, the story is much the same. Between 1978 and 1980—well before decollectivization—the number of TVCEs involved in food processing fell significantly, but overall output increased. The number of firms producing alcoholic drinks increased from 264 to 3,734, with a corresponding leap in output. By contrast, firms producing farm tools fell in number from 12,695 to 3,261; real output value also fell by about 30 per cent (*Sichuan xiangzhen qiye shinian*, 1988: 70). As to the national picture, the total number of *xiang* and *cun* enterprises fell from 1.52 million in 1978 to 1.35 million in 1983 (Nongye bu, 1989: 290–9). This reduction was principally amongst *cun*-level agricultural enterprises; the number of industrial companies barely changed. Nevertheless, the production of rural industry was dramatically restructured. Whereas output in the grain processing, agricultural tools, and chemical fertilizer subsectors declined, production in the cement, food processing, and electricity subsectors increased significantly. Even in Wuxi county in Suzhou, where one might reasonably have expected enterprise performance to have been better (after all, modern industry had been established there as early as 1895), the number of *cun*-level industrial enterprises fell from 1,848 in 1980 to 1,695 by 1982 (WXGY, 1990: 28). In sum, then, local government was capable not only of creating new enterprises but also of closing down unwanted companies.

None of this is to pretend that enterprise control by local government is ideal. The principal–agent problem that affects the management of state-owned enterprises in all countries has also been seen in China. The officials (cadres) responsible for the management of TVCEs are an obvious target for manipulation by local vested interests able to exploit family ties. In order to solve this problem, it was decided in 1993 to implement a new cadre appointment system whereby officials were only allowed to act as cadres outside their own township. However, this gave rise to a new problem, namely a lack of accountability. As the new cadres were no longer local, they were less concerned with managing TVCEs effectively and one consequence was that many township enterprises were sold to raise money to finance short-run projects. This appears to have been a particular problem in Zhejiang and Jiangsu in 1995–6 (SCMP , 13 June 1997). More generally, the early 1990s saw an endless series of disputes between TVCEs and local government over performance targets, tax payments, and retained profits. Nevertheless, all these problems need to be kept in perspective because there is little doubt that the performance of TVCEs over the transition period has been impressive in terms of productivity growth. Even after adjusting the official data to allow for over-reporting of output, TFP growth was swift. As Jefferson, *et al.* (1996: 155) have shown, *xiang*-level TFP grew by 7.2 per cent per annum between 1980 and 1992 according to official data, but still managed 3.4 per cent per year even after allowing for output over-reporting. By any standard, that was an impressive record, and it demonstrates that the agency problems associated with local state control should not be exaggerated.

It remains to consider whether private industry would have outperformed TVCEs during the transition era. One way of doing this is to compare the performance of enterprises in Wenzhou (where private industry dominated) and Suzhou (where industrial TVCEs were the mainstay).[24] If private industry outperformed collective industry, one would expect to see a faster *overall* rate of industrial growth in Wenzhou than in Suzhou; not only would private industry itself grow quicker but also one would expect to see the growth of the private sector placing competitive pressure on both state and collective industry, thereby forcing them to improve their performance as well. By contrast, this hypothesis would imply slower growth in Suzhou due to a smaller private sector and less competition.

Some evidence on these issues is presented in Table 16.5. The first part of the table shows that the industrial growth rate achieved in Suzhou was slightly less than attained in Wenzhou. However, Suzhou started from a much higher base; per capita industrial output was over three times higher than in Wenzhou in 1980. The very fact that the Wenzhou rate only slightly exceeded the rate achieved in Suzhou despite its low base suggests strongly that private industry would not have generated a faster pace of industrialization than was actually attained in areas like Suzhou where TVCEs dominated. This is clear if we normalize for the initial (1980) level of per capita industrial output. As the second half of Table 16.5 shows, those counties in Suzhou that started at around the same level of industrialization as those in Wenzhou grew if anything somewhat faster. Yixing grew slightly faster than Yueqing from an almost identical base; Kunshan grew considerably faster than Rui'an, even though it started from a higher base. In short, there is no evidence here that the Sunan model was inferior to the Wenzhou one—and the very fact that Wenzhou progressively downgraded household industry after 1989 supports that hypothesis.

TABLE 16.5. *Industrial growth rates in Suzhou and Wenzhou, 1980–1996*

	Net industrial output per capita in 1980 (1990 *yuan*)	Growth of net industrial output (% p.a.) (1990 prices)
Suzhou	517	18.4
Wenzhou	164	21.4
Suzhou:		
Yixing	177	22.6
Wuxian	193	21.5
Kunshan	187	26.6
Wenzhou:		
Yueqing	172	22.3
Rui'an	157	24.5

Notes: The Wenzhou growth rates are for 1980–95. For the methodology, see the notes to Table 3.6.
Sources: Wenzhou tongjiju (1985; 1989); ZJTJNJ (1988; 1989; 1990; 1991; 1992; 1993; 1994; 1995; 1996). Jiangsu tongjiju (1989; 1992); JSTJNJ (1994; 1997); Suzhou tongjiju (1996).

We nevertheless need to probe more deeply because of the difficulties inherent in making this sort of comparison between two different regions (Bramall, 1990). For one thing, there was no rigid distinction between the types of industries involved. TVCEs in Suzhou may have been owned by local government, but most were leased out to be privately managed. Furthermore, in Wenzhou—as elsewhere in China—the legal system gave scanty protection to private owners of enterprises; to say that property rights were muddy would be understating the case. In practice, this meant that private enterprises were subjected to all manner of management fees and levies by local government (Odgaard, 1992*a*; 1992*b*). Accordingly, it is hard to characterize private enterprises as being independent of government intervention in the way that they would be in a Western economy. A second problem is locational. Wenzhou differs from Suzhou in terms of its geography, and this inevitably led to differences in industrial performance between the two areas which had nothing to do with the nature of industrial enterprises. Most obvious in this regard was the proximity of the great municipality of Shanghai which offered both an enormous market for Suzhou's industrial products and a source of technical expertise via cooperation with state-owned industrial enterprises. Furthermore, if local government in Suzhou adopted a more predatory attitude towards private industry than in Wenzhou, differences in performance between the two areas would reflect government policy rather than the intrinsic merits of the type of industrial enterprise. Additionally, it is hard to normalize for enterprise size and output composition. The size of industrial enterprises differed between the two regions; if one makes the usual assumption of economies of scale in industrial production, that would give Suzhou an advantage that again had little to do with the nature of industrial TVCEs per se. Similarly, the composition of industrial output differed between the two. If the underlying rate of technical progress varied across industrial subsectors (which it unquestionably did), that too must have played a role in influencing the regional growth rates. Finally, comparisons of growth rates say little about efficiency; we need some measure of productivity if we are to try to say anything helpful about the underlying merits of the two types of industry.

For all these reasons, it is worth attempting a different test of the hypothesis that private industry would have outperformed industry owned by local government in the 1980s by normalizing for the regional dimension. A way of doing this is to compare the growth rates of different types of industry within the same administrative unit. Consider Zhejiang and Jiangsu provinces (Table 16.6).

TABLE 16.6. *Growth of labour productivity in industrial enterprises in Jiangsu and Zhejiang, 1985–1993*

	Jiangsu			Zhejiang		
	Productivity level in 1985 (*yuan*)	Productivity level in 1993 (*yuan*)	Growth rate, 1985–93 (% p.a.)	Productivity level in 1985 (*yuan*)	Productivity level in 1993 (*yuan*)	Growth rate, 1985–93 (% p.a.)
Xiang	8,216	67,989	27.8	6,125	43,685	25.8
Cun	6,140	59,694	30.3	3,321	33,662	31.8
Private	3,066	20,420	24.8	3,011	26,718	31.4

Note: Labour productivity is GVIO (current prices) divided by employment. Private (*geti*) excludes team, cooperative, and joint-household enterprises (*hezuoqiye* or *lianhu*) which is sometimes included under the heading of private (Young and Yang, 1994).

Sources: JSTJNJ (1994: 180–1); ZJTJNJ (1994: 192–3, 226–8).

The data show the rates of growth of labour productivity in three types of industry: *xiang*, *cun* (both are owned by local government), and *geti* (de facto private) over the period since the emergence of private industry on a significant scale after 1984. But the results are very difficult to interpret. In Jiangsu, it appears that TVCEs outperformed private industry; labour productivity growth was faster in both *cun*- and *xiang*-level industry. But in Zhejiang, the picture is more complex. *Cun* industrial productivity grew faster than in the private sector but the difference is hardly significant. Moreover, because private industry did much better than *xiang* industry, private industry productivity grew faster than the rate achieved by *xiang* and *cun* industry combined.

Nevertheless, there is little in Table 16.6 to suggest that private industry outperformed TVCEs. This is because of the very significant disparity in base levels of productivity, and the resulting scope for catch-up enjoyed by the private sector. As the table shows, the level of *xiang* and *cun* labour-productivity was much higher in 1985 than in the private sector; one would expect faster growth in the poorer sector.[25] Accordingly, the very fact that private industry grew (on the most generous interpretation of the data) no faster despite its low base suggests that there was little opportunity cost involved in the extensive involvement of local government in Chinese industrialization in the 1980s. In these circumstances, it is not surprising that Weitzman and Xu (1994: 539) concluded thus:

> The driving force in the Chinese model is the so-called TVE [CMB: strictly, TVCEs] . . . The TVE is essentially what might be called a 'vaguely defined cooperative'. A TVE is basically a communal organization very far removed from having well-defined property rights. The typical TVE has a vaguely defined ownership and reward structure in whose operation the community government is deeply involved. The legal system related to the TVE is also ill-defined. The typical TVE seems almost the exact opposite of the type of private organization at the centre of the East European model, since the TVE seem to go almost completely against the grain of standard property rights theory.
>
> Yet the Chinese model is in fact enormously successful, much more successful so far than any actual applications of the East European model. So we have on our hands an enormous paradox. why does a model based on vaguely defined cooperatives seem to be significantly outperforming a model based on well-defined private property?[26]

This favourable conclusion on the role played by local government is of course anathema to economists schooled in the master discourse. Nevertheless, a number of econometric studies have reached a similar conclusion. A study by Dong and Putterman (1997:197) for ten provinces between 1984 and 1989 concluded 'we find that enterprises owned by township and village governments were at least as productive as those owned privately.' Furthermore, it is not especially difficult to explain why it is that Chinese local government has been so effective in creating efficient industry. As has been widely noted (Byrd and Gelb, 1990; Yuan, 1994; Oi, 1995), a key reason for local government's success in the owning of industrial enterprises is fiscal. Local government is expected to collect a number of taxes on behalf of central government, and in more prosperous areas it receives little or nothing by way of subsidies from the state budget; in effect, local government faces a hard budget constraint. All local governments wish to engage in local infrastructural projects, subsidize poor households and invest in agriculture; local democracy in China is still 'underdeveloped', but the ability of local leaders to retain power does depend upon their ability to win and retain popular support. Furthermore, local leaders have clear personal incentives in that their pay, perks, and career prospects are all affected by their ability to successfully run local industries; promotion to central government, for example, is one reward for successful local leaders. The net effect is that local leaders are forced to finance their expenditure from local sources to gain promotion. In practice, this means they need to create efficient local industries which can either be taxed (or required to pay a management fee) or which can be required to remit their profits. Of course, these incentive structures are not ideal. The goals of tax revenue maximization and profit maximization will rarely be identical; as a result, inefficient local enterprises may be kept open if they generate substantial tax revenue. If all *xiang* governments wish to run their own township brewery (and many do), economies of scale will be lost. But there is little in the evidence to suggest that the private sector would do any better. Above all, investment levels (public and private combined) will tend to be higher with local government ownership. Given the importance of investment in the growth process, this more than anything else helps to explain the impressive performance of industrial TVCEs.

3. State Infrastructural Failure: Irrigation, Transport, and Education

For all the successful growth-promoting interventions of local and central government, there were also failures. One such was the comparative neglect of irrigation, transport, and education infrastructure. As was seen in Chapter 9, one of the principal failings of the Dengist era was inadequate investment in infrastructure; total investment in irrigation and in transport infrastructure was wholly inadequate, in terms of need and in comparison with the scale of investment in the Maoist period.

3.1. The Neglect of Irrigation

Perhaps the main reason for the neglect of transport and irrigation was inadequate investment by central government.[27] Inadequate state spending on transport was especially damaging because the externalities involved make transport provision by the private sector infeasible. The same theoretical considerations apply to irrigation. Here the trend in state investment is summarized in Table 16.7. These data show clearly how real state investment in irrigation declined sharply after 1978 from 6.5bn. *yuan* to only 2.3bn. *yuan* in 1981. In the seven years that followed, there was little improvement; investment by the state continued to hover at around 3bn. *yuan*, only 50 per cent of the levels of the late 1970s. Moreover, it is hard to argue convincingly that substantial state investment in irrigation was no longer needed. Of course, many of the more obvious programmes had been completed by the late 1970s, and spending by farmers and local government may have compensated for reduced investment by central government. But the revival in basic-construction investment after 1988 gives an indication of the perceived adequacy of the scale of investment as far as the state was concerned. Even so, the 1978 level of investment was not regained until 1995.

TABLE 16.7. *Basic-construction investment by the State in irrigation, 1978–1996* (in billion *yuan*)

Year	Nominal basic construction	Real basic construction
1978	3.46	6.53
1979	3.50	6.36
1980	2.71	4.68
1981	1.36	2.30
1982	1.75	2.98
1983	2.11	3.54
1984	2.07	3.29
1985	2.02	2.90
1986	2.29	3.13
1987	2.70	3.51
1988	2.36	2.72
1989	2.95	3.11
1990	4.07	4.07
1991	5.02	4.71
1992	6.83	5.94
1993	8.16	6.19
1994	9.82	6.24
1995	14.25	8.00
1996	20.66	10.79

Note: Current price data have been deflated using the GDP deflator; this gives real basic-construction investment at 1990 prices.

Sources: ZGNCTJNJ (1995: 115); Nongye bu (1989: 384); ZGTJNJ (1996: 159); ZGTJNJ (1997: 171).

3.2. INADEQUATE STATE INVESTMENT IN TRANSPORT

Just as investment by the state in irrigation after 1978 was inadequate, so too was investment in the transport sector. As was seen in Chapter 9, the rail and road networks were expanded only slowly after 1978. The primary reason again was inadequate state investment. This is not immediately obvious from the data (Table 16.8). Real basic-construction investment by the state in transport and communications (at 1990 prices) grew at 13.1 per cent between 1978, substantially *faster* than GDP. For 1978–90, the two grew at about the same rate (GDP by 9.7 per cent per year, basic construction in transport and communications by 9.3 per cent). Naughton (1995*b*: 1091) makes the point more strongly:

> China has experienced extremely rapid rates of overall economic growth, which would have been inconceivable without generally adequate provision of infrastructure. Although bottlenecks have repeatedly re-emerged under the pressure of rapid growth, government investment has generally been sufficient to overcome them and prevent growth from faltering. Adequate provision of infrastructure must be considered the second key element of successful Chinese growth policy.

There is undoubtedly something in this.[28] However, a more detailed examination shows a number of deficiencies. First, state basic-construction spending fell sharply in the first years of transition; investment in the transport and communications sector halved between 1978 and 1981. Only in 1983 was the real level of 1978 restored; as a result, the rapid economic growth of the early transition period owed nothing to increased investment in transport. Secondly, and even though there was a clear upward trend in spending after 1983, state spending fluctuated violently. Between 1985 and 1988, the level of investment stagnated at around the 25bn. *yuan* mark and, not surprisingly given that it is easier to sacrifice investment than consumption, the recession of the late 1980s saw investment fall to 18bn. *yuan* in 1989, and 21bn. in 1990. Only after 1990 did the Chinese state begin to recognize the deficiencies of its transport and communications infrastructure; as a result, spending in 1994 was more than four times higher than it had been in 1990. And, after falling back in 1995, the 1996 level was almost eight times higher in real terms than it had been at the beginning of the transition era. Nevertheless, given the long gestation periods involved in infrastructural projects, this spending did very little to promote economic growth in the early 1990s.

The third problem with state investment in transport and communications was that it was increasingly directed away from railways. The budgetary cutbacks at the

TABLE 16.8. *State basic-construction expenditure on transport and communications* (in billion *yuan*)

Year	Nominal	Real
1978	6.80	12.84
1979	6.41	11.64
1980	6.23	10.75
1981	4.05	6.86
1982	5.72	9.73
1983	7.80	13.09
1984	10.85	17.27
1985	17.81	25.54
1986	18.81	25.75
1987	19.54	25.38
1988	21.63	24.90
1989	17.02	17.97
1990	21.10	21.10
1991	34.02	31.89
1992	45.76	39.78
1993	90.12	68.38
1994	137.29	87.17
1995	68.07	38.22
1996	184.71	96.50

Note: Real basic construction is at 1990 prices; it has been deflated using the GDP deflator.

Sources: ZGTJNJ (1985: 425); ZGTJNJ (1995: 147); ZGTJNJ (1996: 167); ZGTJNJ (1997: 171).

beginning of the 1980s reduced the share of state basic-construction spending on railways to 36 per cent of the total (ZGTJNJ, 1983: 333). That did recover to 46 per cent in 1982 and to 54 per cent in both 1983 and 1984 (ZGTJNJ, 1985: 431). Thereafter, however, the share of state investment in the rail network steadily declined. By 1993, only 35 per cent of the total was in railways (ZGTJNJ, 1994: 149), and by 1996 that had fallen further to 25 per cent (ZGTJNJ, 1997: 159). This neglect of railways can be justified in three ways. First, the decline in the share of state investment going to railways was not as bad as it appears because the proportion of traffic carried by railways also declined. Between 1978 and 1994, for example, the proportion of passenger-kilometres provided by the rail system declined from 63 per cent to 42 per cent (ZGTJNJ, 1995: 468). Secondly, foreign investors were willing to invest in railway construction; for example, the Jinhua–Wenzhou railway owed its revival to the enthusiasm of a Hong Kong-based entrepreneur. State funding was therefore less necessary. Thirdly, and more generally, the decision not to invest more in the railway network during the early and mid-1980s may have been rational. The reluctance of the planners to extend the railway network at the beginning of the transition era is explained in part by their view that the modernization of existing routes was much more important (Huenemann, 1991: 457); that in turn seems to imply that the existing capacity of the rail network was deemed adequate. Indeed one might argue that this conscious decision to increase the 'efficiency' of the network—in the sense of passengers and freight carried per kilometre of track—was eminently sensible. If resulting Chinese utilization rates were higher than in other countries, that merely reflected 'inefficient' usage elsewhere rather than any Chinese failure. Moreover, it was in any case more logical for short-haul freight to be moved by road rather than by rail, and hence some excess demand could be diverted on to the roads without any decline in efficiency. Much the same was true of long-distance passenger transport; the expansion of the civil aviation sector was perhaps a more appropriate response than massive railway investment.

By the late 1980s, however, the limits of this strategy of greater reliance upon non-rail transport had been reached. The railway network was saturated and so, increasingly, was the road network. As was seen in Chapter 9, the intensity of use of the railway system was far in excess of the norm in other large countries such as India, the USSR, and the USA. In consequence, the Chinese planners began to realize the importance of remedial action. This took two forms. First, there was a big increase in passenger fares in late 1989 to choke off demand in the short run.[29] Second—and as is apparent in the figures in Table 16.8—the state decided upon a big increase in spending on transport, with a number of new major projects included in the Eighth Five-Year Plan (1991–5). The very scale of these remedial actions testifies to the crisis affecting the railway system at the end of the 1980s.

This argument that the Dengist state did comparatively little to promote infrastructural development does not mean that the Chinese state deserves no credit for infrastructure construction, but rather that the credit must go to the Maoist state (Bramall, 1993). It was during the Maoist era that the infrastructure—transport, communications, and irrigation—so vital to post-1978 growth was created. The efficiency with which that infrastructure was being used in the late 1970s was low, but the fact remains that efficiency gains were only possible precisely because the infrastructure existed in the first place.

3.3. The State and Educational Failure

The reversal of some of the educational achievements of the Maoist era was perhaps the greatest state failure of the transition era. This failure is not very apparent on the surface. On the contrary. The Chinese state has continually re-emphasized its commitment to compulsory education. The State Education Commission in 1994 reaffirmed its determination to achieve the 'two basics' of literacy for young and middle-aged adults and nine years of compulsory education, publishing a list of those counties and districts which had been successful (ZGJYNJ, 1995: 164–8). Project Hope, an attempt to encourage school drop-outs in poor rural areas to return to education (partly by refurbishing existing schools), has been financed by a combination of central government and external funds; it apparently returned 466,000 drop-outs to school in 1994 (ZGJYNJ, 1995: 910), and a further 237,000 in 1995 (State Statistical Bureau, 1996). Moreover, there was a clear increase in the level of real educational spending by the Chinese state after 1978 (Table 16.9). This increase was not small; on average, real state spending on education rose by nearly 10 per cent between 1978 and 1995.[30] Finally, expressed as a percentage of GDP, state spending rose from 2.1 per cent in 1978 to 2.7 per cent by 1983.

However, these data are misleading. For one thing, the bulk of the increase in state spending went on teachers' salaries. These needed to be raised in order to maintain a modicum of comparability between them and wages in the private and TVE sectors, thus limiting any significant exodus of teaching professionals; between 1978 and 1987, in fact, the salaries of teachers employed by the state increased more quickly than the state-sector average (Zhongguo tongjiju, 1989*a*: 136). Even so, state educational spending as a percentage of GDP fell back after 1986 and as a result took up a smaller share of GDP by 1995 than it had in 1978. Moreover, in international terms, state educational spending was unusually low by the mid-1990s. According to UNESCO, Chinese educational spending as a proportion of GDP in 1993 stood at 1.9 per cent, significantly less than in Bangladesh (2.3 per cent), India (3.7), Pakistan (2.7), and the Philippines (2.4). It lagged even further behind the rapidly growing economies of Thailand (4.0 per cent), South Korea (4.2), and Malaysia (5.1) (UNESCO, 1995). Although this poor Chinese performance partially reflects demographic trends (fewer children of primary school age), it is also indicative of increasing reliance on fees as a way of financing educational provision. For example, after experimenting in 1994, the State Education Commission decreed that higher education colleges and universities would not provide free tuition after 1997 but instead charge fees of between 1,200 and 1,500 *yuan* per annum (CD, 28 Feb. 1997). Against this background, it is not surprising that even a World Bank report (1996: 53–4) concluded that state spending on education needed to increase substantially.

TABLE 16.9. *State spending on education, 1978–1995*

Year	Real State spending on education (bn. 1990 *yuan*)	Share of State spending on education in total State expenditure (per cent)	Share of State spending on education in GDP (per cent)
1978	14.18	6.7	2.1
1979	16.93	7.3	2.3
1980	19.70	9.3	2.6
1981	20.80	10.8	2.6
1982	23.40	11.2	2.7
1983	26.05	11.0	2.7
1984	28.79	10.6	2.5
1985	32.52	11.3	2.5
1986	37.61	12.5	2.7
1987	38.17	13.0	2.5
1988	41.06	14.3	2.4
1989	43.54	14.6	2.4
1990	46.25	15.0	2.5
1991	49.91	15.7	2.5
1992	54.05	16.6	2.3
1993	57.28	16.3	2.2
1994	64.69	17.6	2.2
1995	67.04	17.5	2.0

Note: Real state spending on education is at 1990 prices and includes both budgetary and extra-budgetary expenditure; calculated by using the GDP deflator.
Source: ZGTJNJ (1997: 244).

Perhaps even more significantly, the Chinese government pursued a policy of cutting back on secondary education (especially in rural areas) after 1977. In essence, the aim of the educational restructuring of 1977–82 was a return to the 'golden age' of the early 1960s on the grounds that secondary education was wasted on the bulk of the rural population and that the money could be better spent on improving the quality of upper-level secondary schools and higher education. The products of the secondary sector were seen as unsuited to productive employment and therefore their education was a waste of state resources (Lo, 1989: 573). The new approach of the 1980s therefore amounted to recreating high quality 'keypoint' schools, reducing the number of general secondary schools (especially in rural areas), and placing greater emphasis on vocational education for the rural population. In other words, the aim was to replace the mass educational system of late Maoism with an elitist system. All this was set out in a secret 1977 directive (Pepper, 1996):

In 1977, according to interviewees, the Education Ministry began circulating internally the recommended reduced proportions of elementary and junior middle graduates who should be allowed to pass on to the level above. These controlled pass rates were preparatory to implementing the more important decision to curtail rural senior secondary schooling and drastically reduce enrolments at that level in urban areas as well [p. 481].

> Too provocative to be publicized at the time or later, this directive explicitly overturned the education revolution's most sacrosanct aim by exonerating the traditional divisions between mental and manual labour. . . . The 1977 directive argued that schooling was unnecessary for many different occupations and that universalizing secondary education at the mass level was too expensive—hence the decision to restrict enrollments [p. 494].

The 1977 directive aimed to reduce the number of those going on from primary to middle schools from 94 per cent in 1976 to about 66 per cent, and the proportion going on from junior to senior middle school was cut from over 70 per cent to closer to 30 per cent. As the data show (Table 16.10), these aims were certainly achieved by the early 1980s.

TABLE 16.10. *Enrolment rates in the secondary sector, 1976–1996*

Year	Primary school graduates (millions)	New junior secondary school enrolment (millions)	Ratio (per cent)
1976	24.90	23.44	94.1
1977	25.74	23.68	92.0
1978	22.88	20.06	87.7
1979	20.88	17.28	82.8
1980	20.53	15.51	75.5
1981	20.76	14.13	68.1
1982	20.69	13.63	65.9
1983	19.81	13.17	66.5
1984	19.95	13.03	65.3
1985	20.00	13.49	67.5
1986	20.16	13.87	68.8
1987	20.43	13.94	68.2
1988	19.30	13.41	69.5
1989	18.57	13.09	70.5
1990	18.63	13.70	73.5
1991	18.97	14.11	74.3
1992	18.72	14.65	78.3
1993	18.42	14.79	80.3
1994	19.00	16.16	85.1
1995	19.62	17.52	89.3
1996	19.34	17.61	91.1

Sources: ZGTJNJ (1991: 688, 690); ZGTJNJ (1995: 588); ZGTJNJ (1997: 639–40).

Although the ratios began to rise again in the late 1980s, the staying-on rate even in 1996 was still less than it had been in 1976–7. This shift of emphasis towards vocational education was bitterly resented in many of China's rural areas at the end of the 1970s. Many rural cadres and teachers were keen to upgrade educational quality in rural schools, but the narrow sort of education offered by vocational schools was not seen as the way to do it (Pepper, 1996: 502). Rather, the new system was a reversion to the more traditional approach of the Chinese educational professionals.

To argue that the changes that occurred in the late 1970s and early 1980s were merely a response to reduced demand for education as opportunities to earn higher private-sector incomes was enlarged (Paine, 1994) is misleading. Most of the changes occurred during the late 1970s, well before the rural non-farm private sector was liberalized, and were pushed through despite powerful local resistance.

These cuts were felt in rich and poor areas alike. In poor Wushan county in eastern Sichuan, the number of middle schools was cut from 65 in 1978 to only 23 in 1981; these cuts were confined entirely to the *minban* sector, which saw the abolition of upper middle-school education in 1979 (*Wushan xian zhi*, 1991: 470). But it was not just poor areas that suffered as a result of the cutbacks of the late 1970s and early 1980s. For example, in prosperous Guanghan county on the Chengdu plain, the number of students graduating from middle schools fell from 17,180 in 1979 to only 5,409 by 1981.[31] Total numbers enrolled in middle school fell from over 36,000 in 1978 to only 20,000 by 1984 (*Guanghan xian zhi*, 1992: 479). In Pujiang, the proportion of primary school graduates going on to lower middle school declined from 82 per cent in 1979 to 51 per cent in 1982 and had only recovered to 70 per cent by 1985 (*Pujiang xian zhi*, 1992: 638).

By 1993–4, the Chinese educational system was in crisis as rural schools were deprived of state funds and teachers' salaries were unpaid (Paine, 1994: 131–8: Pepper, 1996: 535). It was this that accelerated the transition towards tuition fees and self-funding that became increasingly the norm in the mid-1990s as schools were forced to operate like enterprises. Nevertheless, the crisis continued. In 1996, only 66.4 million students—no better than in 1978—were enrolled in the secondary system compared to 136 million enrolled in the primary sector (ZGTJNJ, 1997: 639). Although the government (rightly) claimed that about 91 per cent of primary-school graduates continued their education in 1995, the fact remained that the legacy of the cutbacks of the 1980s was still being felt in terms of total enrolment numbers. The problem was especially acute in poor rural areas, where local government was simply unable to raise the funds required to fund even a minimal level of provision.

17

Origins of the Growth-Promoting State

The development record of the People's Republic during the Dengist era was tarnished. Human rights violations were legion. Inequality soared. Catastrophic damage was inflicted on the environment.[1] Yet amidst all this, China's growth was impressive by historical and international standards; her remarkable record has rightly attracted the attention of numerous economists. Two further conclusions are equally clear from the discussion of the previous chapters. First, growth was driven by a range of economic factors: by productivity increases (driven by diffusion and systemic reform), by the accumulation of capital, and by the exploitation of the physical and social capability bequeathed by late Maoism. Of these, productivity growth and the Maoist legacies were much more important than has been acknowledged in recent years. Second, the responsibility for the post-1978 development record rests squarely on the shoulders of government. It is the Chinese state that is to blame for deliberately encouraging a rise in income inequality, and for acquiescing in high rates of female infant mortality. From this perspective, it is evident that the Dengist state was not 'developmental'.[2] Yet, and to the exclusion of everything else, the Chinese state assuredly, and successfully, followed a growth-promoting agenda. Whether that should be seen as outweighing developmental failures in the scales of justice is a moot point, but the fact that the state encouraged swift growth brooks no denial.

In a sense, the transition to a phase of rapid growth in the People's Republic was simply a consequence of the adoption of the 'right' economic strategy by the Dengist state. Whereas Russia, Poland, and Pinochet's Chile destroyed the institutions of central planning, China modified and supplemented them.[3] In Russia, the process of transition to a market economy was swift; over the period between January 1992 and June 1994, privatization was largely completed. In China, the changes were much slower. Private enterprises were not allowed in the countryside until 1984, and the most dynamic enterprises in the rural economy were those owned by local government (TVCEs).[4] No more than a handful of centrally owned industrial enterprises had been closed by the mid-1990s, and Chinese stock markets promote mergers in very rudimentary fashion. The exchange rate was not fully liberalized even in the mid-1990s; as late as December 1993, a system of parallel currencies existed (Shirk, 1994: 65–7). Price reform was not initiated until 1985, and even then took the form of a 'dual-track' approach rather than an immediate transition to market determination. Furthermore, price controls on a number of key commodities (e.g. rice) were not lifted until 1993, and were reimposed in late 1994. Property rights were insecure throughout the 1980s; the protection offered by 'the law' to private individuals was little more than derisory. In view of all this, it stretches credulity to suggest that China was a well-functioning market economy in the Dengist era. Rather, the People's Republic succeeded in generating rapid growth precisely because its leaders ignored the policy prescriptions offered by the master discourse. Instead of embracing the 'Washington consensus' or Anglo-Saxon model of capitalism, China followed the path taken earlier by Japan, South Korea, and Taiwan.

Yet as an explanation of rapid economic growth, this is inadequate because it tells us nothing about *why* China successfully adopted the governed-market approach after 1978. This is a very general analytical problem in explaining economic growth. The narrowly economic terrain of the debate centres on which economic strategy to follow in order to promote growth; the argument of this book, which is of course in line with much recent research on East Asia, is that the state must go well beyond a mere securing of property rights. But at a deeper level, the debate is about the conditions under which the state can play this role. Why has the state-centred approach not been more widely implemented given its appeal to a wide range of heterodox thinkers? Why are successful growth-promoting states not universal in the developing world?

There are three basic answers.[5] First, a state may wish to promote growth, but does not know which economic strategy to follow. In particular, it may not be clear about the respective roles for planning and markets. This source of failure may be termed 'myopia'. Second, the state may have an 'alternative agenda' to growth. It might, for example, aspire to military security or to the promotion of equality, either as alternatives to growth or as objectives to combine with growth. In such circumstances, one can hardly criticize a government for failing to achieve electrifying growth; its performance must be judged against the objectives it sets for itself. In other words, it is not for academics—still less foreign governments—to impose any definition of development upon a country and its people.[6] Countries must make their own development choices, and select their governments accordingly. Third, the state may want to promote rapid growth, and be aware of the economic strategy that needs to be adopted to achieve that growth. But it may be unable to create the necessary institutions, or to make them function effectively. In other words, the state may be constrained. In such circumstances, the governed-market approach will be pointless; it simply will not work. The objective of economic growth will then probably be better served by implementing the 'Washington consensus' relying upon market forces to provide the growth dynamic.

It follows that to explain rapid growth in the People's Republic after 1978, it is necessary to explain why the Chinese state began to function in a manner very different from that seen in early periods of Chinese history, and in other countries. Should we contrast the far-sighted vision of the Dengist regime with the myopias of the late nineteenth century Qing government, Chiang Kaishek's Republican regime, and the Maoist state? Did Mao, Chiang, and the Qing Emperors aspire to a set of developmental objectives other than growth? Or was it simply that the Dengist state was free of the constraints that hampered Maoist China and the state in other poor countries?

1. Myopia and the Lessons of Chinese History

As far as an explanation for Chinese growth based on the absence of state myopia is concerned, it has long been recognized by economic theorists that mistakes by economic agents (including the state) are commonplace. For instance, the debate on the new classical economics ultimately spawned a considerable literature on learning as a way of explaining why monetary contraction would not lead to a rapid fall in the inflation rate; learning procedures may be closer to adaptive rather than rational expectations, and therefore convergence on the rational expectations equilibrium may not occur (Hargreaves Heap, 1992). Furthermore, it has been argued that the failure of early modern European economies to emulate the creation of efficient institutions and carefully specified property rights that was a feature of England during the period between 1500 and 1750 was down in large measure to myopia. For example, it has been argued that the French crown mistakenly pursued a policy of short-run revenue maximization, rather than long-run growth promotion (North and Thomas, 1973). Moreover, the governments of poor countries are myopic precisely because they follow the Washington consensus. The sway of the master discourse over the hearts and minds of governments in these countries is strong, and is the result of its assiduous promotion by the World Bank and the American establishment even though the master discourse is not supported by the evidence as being the optimal economic strategy. In other words, state myopia is at least in part induced by international agencies. By contrast, the Japanese 'governed-market' model is either denigrated (it cannot be sustained) or misinterpreted. Arguably the only reason for the absence of myopia in East Asia is that most policy-makers there were not trained along neoclassical lines and were therefore less prejudiced against a dirigiste approach.

However, the imperfect information argument does have its problems, and therefore we need to be very careful before casually concluding that leadership myopia is the key to explaining poor growth performance in every case. The essential difficulty is that myopia is not much of a *general* theory, especially in the last decade of the twentieth century when the growth record—and, more importantly, the growth-orientated institutional structures—of a wide variety of countries is increasingly well-known. Even if policy-makers do sometimes err, it is hard to understand why they do not learn from their mistakes over time: development is not a one-shot game (Rodrik, 1996: 23). More generally, myopia does not seem to explain why countries have failed to achieve rapid growth despite adopting the 'right' strategy (Khan, 1995). After all, a wide range of countries—post-1947 India, Pakistan, and much of Latin America come to mind—have in the past aimed at similar goals, and even pursued similarly interventionist strategies to those pursued in East Asia. They have eschewed free markets, but at the same time the degree of intervention has fallen well short of central planning. For example, the Soviet model was influential in India in the 1950s, but to describe the growth strategy as Stalinist would be absurd. Streeten (1996) makes the same point.[7] In other words, slow growth cannot always be explained in terms of a failure to select the right strategy:

> Pakistan in the 1960s, for instance, had an interventionist state quite similar in its modernizing motivation to the one in South Korea. . . . Its economic performance was initially promising, but not good enough to satisfy all demands and the experiment ended with civil war and the dismemberment of the country in 1971. (Khan, 1995: 77)

Nevertheless, imperfect information does have obvious intuitive appeal. To argue, for example, that ideas are universally available across the world—the view routinely advanced by advocates of human-capital augmented Solowian growth theory like Mankiw—is much less plausible than the Romer (1995) view that ideas are not a public good. Moreover, in the *specific context* of post-1949 China, there is something to the myopia argument. One can argue that rapid growth occurred under Deng Xiaoping—but not during late Maoism (1965–78)—partly because Deng (and the CCP leadership more generally) knew how to promote growth, whereas Mao did not. Maoist failures had taught them wisdom, and this disappearance of myopia explains the comparative success of the Dengist era.

There are several pieces of evidence on this. First, the relative efficacy of various growth strategies was much better known by the early 1980s than in the mid-1960s. In explaining why Mao failed to adopt a 'governed-market' approach in the 1960s and 1970s, it is easy to simply assert that Mao was myopic. Perhaps he was misled by the apparent success of the USSR into believing that central planning was the way forward. If so, that should not come as any great surprise; as Krugman has recently reminded us, the conventional wisdom in the 1960s was that we should learn from the success of the Soviet Union. Moreover, there was a great deal of uncertainty about the way forward for China, and this is particularly evident from the debates that occurred during 1955–8 and which centred on agriculture. For example, it had been made clear to Mao that there was an alternative to the saltationist socialism of the Leap and the 'Third Front', namely the strategy offered by Chen Yun (Lardy and Lieberthal, 1983). As is well known, Mao and others argued that agricultural growth was too slow; these arguments are set out in Mao's speech on cooperatives in July 1955. However, this line was opposed by Deng Zihui, Deng Xiaoping (at least initially), and Liu Shaoqi (Riskin, 1987; Selden, 1988; Teiwes and Sun, 1993). Even the disaster of the Leap did not settle the debate; it was still open to argument as to whether the famine reflected the pace of collectivization and the gigantism of the commune, or collectivization per se.

By the late 1970s, however, it was increasingly clear that growth in the USSR was slowing down, and that collective farming there had not been a conspicuous success. Furthermore, it was also very evident by then that late Maoism had not generated rapid growth. To be sure, growth performance was not disastrous. As noted in Chapter 2, the growth rate of real per capita NDMP averaged 2 per cent between 1957 and 1978 despite the disastrous impact of the Great Leap Forward and the disruption of 1967–8 and 1976. Moreover, the growth strategy had achieved remarkable things in western China as a result of the sheer scale of investment in 'Third Front' projects. Still, the growth rate was less than miraculous, and the most obvious indication of this was enduring material poverty in rural China: despite respectable growth and radical income redistribution, as many as 200 million Chinese farmers may have been living below subsistence in the late 1970s.

Second, it was increasingly obvious by the late 1970s that there was an alternative to both the Anglo-Saxon and Soviet growth models. In the early 1960s, the Japanese economic miracle was in its early stages and those in Taiwan and South Korea had not yet begun. In such circumstances, the Chinese Communist Party could be excused for not adopting the East Asian approach. By 1980, however, the success of East Asia was plain. Japan had caught up with many European countries, and both South Korea and Taiwan were moving unambiguously in that direction. Furthermore, the East Asian growth model was very obviously different from its competitors, involving as it did a proactive state. It was the obvious place for China to look for an alternative—and successful—growth strategy, and it was an option that had not been open to Mao in the 1960s.

China's own historical experience also offered a number of pointers as to what might work. That Chinese transition began by following the 'Leninist' path ('readjustment') advocated by Chen Yun—which involved little more than a reallocation of investment towards heavy industry supplying civilian producer goods, towards light industry and towards agriculture—was due in considerable measure to historical precedent. For while it makes little sense to characterize the CCP as following a transition *strategy*, the Chinese transition path after 1978 was undoubtedly conditioned by the (perceived) success of the Chinese economy during 1952–6 and again during 1961–5.[8] In these successes, markets played an important role, and Deng Xiaoping was prominent.[9] The early 1950s have even been called Mao's 'Bukharinist phase' (Kalain, 1984).

Integral to the impressive Chinese growth record in the early 1950s and from 1961/2 to 1965 was the important macroeconomic role played by the state. During these periods, the combination of small-scale private farming (especially after land reform had been completed), state ownership of the key industrial sectors, and state control of internal trade in key consumer goods had been sufficient to allow net domestic product to grow at about 14 per cent. But more importantly, the institutions and performance of agriculture in periods when collective farming did not exist provided the best illustration of the possibilities there existed in the late 1970s. For example, Chinese agricultural output grew quickly between 1952 (the completion of land reform) and July 1955 (the start of collectivization). This success was one of the reasons why Deng initially opposed Mao's desire to introduce rapid collectivization (though the primary conflict in 1955 was between Deng Zihui and Mao). It also helps to explain the reversion to a system akin to private farming during 1961–5 in the aftermath of the Great Leap Forward. More precisely, the household responsibility system that underpinned the rural reforms of the early 1980s was not pioneered in Anhui in the late 1970s, but in early 1957. Some areas of China adopted it then because of the coincidence of a relaxation in the campaign for uniform transition to socialism (the 'Hundred Flowers') with the slowdown or even fall in some types of farm output that occurred following collectivization in 1955–6.[10] In other words, the adoption of the responsibility system was in some ways a response to crisis, and so it was again in the early 1960s. The reversal of Great Leap Forward began in September 1960 when the slogan 'readjusting, consolidating, filling out and raising standards' was first put forward.[11] The eight characters which made up this slogan led to it being called the Eight Character Policy (*bazi fangzhen*) (Zhongguo shehui zhuyi zhengtai jingjixue sishi nian, ii, 1991: 78 n.). The policy assumed slightly more concrete form at the 9th Plenum of the 8th Central Committee in January 1961, which decreed that:

> The whole country must concentrate efforts on strengthening agricultural work, implementing the policy of taking agriculture as the foundation, and going in for agriculture and grain production in a big way. (Liu and Wu, 1986: 272)

Nevertheless, the real turning point was provided by the 'Rules Governing Work in the Rural People's Communes (draft)' (May 1961). These comprised six main elements (Liu and Wu, 1986: 273–5). First, the egalitarianism of the Leap was abandoned. The communal canteens were closed, private plots and rural markets were restored, and incomes made dependent entirely upon work done. Secondly, the assets seized from production teams by the communes were restored. Third, the agricultural tax and the grain procurement quotas were substantially reduced. Fourth, the quota price for grain paid by the state was increased by 20 per cent; prices for other crops also increased. Fifth, industry was instructed to produce greater quantities of agricultural producer goods. Finally, many of the industrial enterprises established during the Leap were closed, and the bulk of peasants who had moved to the cities during the Leap (perhaps 29 million people) were relocated to the countryside. This reform programme gathered further momentum following a work conference organized by the Central Committee and attended by about 7,000 cadres in January 1962. The whole process culminated in the 'Rules Governing Work in the Rural People's Communes (revised draft)' adopted by the 10th Plenum in September 1962 (Liu and Wu, 1986: 282, 297). This made the production team, rather than the brigade, the basic unit of account, and authorized the creation of temporary and even permanent work groups.

An indication of the effectiveness of the programme is provided by Tables 17.1 and 17.2. Both outline trends during 1957 to 1965 in China and in the three provinces hit hardest by the famine. The former looks at total output (NDMP), the latter agricultural output (NVAO).

TABLE 17.1. *Trends in NDMP, 1957–1965*

	Growth rates (% p.a.)		Total NDMP (bn. *yuan*)	
	1957–61	1961–5	1957	1965
China	−5.5	+10.0	268.1	304.8
Sichuan	−13.0	+12.5	25.8	24.5
Anhui	−10.7	+11.8	12.1	11.9
Guizhou	−9.5	+11.6	5.7	5.7

Note: Total NDMP is at 1990 constant prices.

Source: LSTJ (1990).

TABLE 17.2. *Trends in NVAO, 1957–1965*

	Growth rates (% p.a.)		Total NVAO (bn. *yuan*)	
	1957–61	1961–5	1957	1965
China	−10.1	+10.3	193.8	198.3
Sichuan	−18.7	+13.7	20.4	17.5
Anhui	−15.4	+13.2	10.2	9.0
Guizhou	−13.2	+13.9	4.7	4.7

Note: Total NVAO is at 1990 constant prices.
Source: LSTJ (1990).

Table 17.1 shows the scale of the collapse in output caused by the Leap. Nationally, NDMP fell by over 5 per cent per year. In the worst hit provinces, the decline was even more spectacular (about 10 per cent). From the nadir of 1961, however, recovery began. For China as a whole, the period was not only one in which the 1957 peak was regained but of new growth. As a result, total output in 1965 was 13 per cent higher than it had been 8 years earlier. The same was true even for poor provinces like Guizhou. This gives some indication of the potency of the NEP-style package. To be sure, the process of recovery was by no means complete in the famine-devastated provinces of Sichuan and Anhui even in 1965. In Sichuan, where some 15 million had died, NDMP was still about 5 per cent below its 1957 level. In Anhui, where the death toll was around 7 million, NDMP was still 2 per cent down. In the agricultural sector, and as Table 17.2 shows, the output decline was precipitate. Indeed it is not hard to see why there was a famine of such intensity in Sichuan: there, agricultural output had fallen by an *annual* average of nearly 19 per cent over a four-year period. Even a comparatively well-off country would find it difficult to shrug off such a decline; in Sichuan, by no means China's poorest province but undoubtedly below the average, it was impossible. Furthermore, it is also apparent from Table 17.2 that recovery was by no means complete in 1965. To be sure, national agricultural output was about 2 per cent higher than it had been in 1957. In Sichuan, however, output was still about 14 per cent below its pre-Leap peak.

Nevertheless, even though the recovery process was slow, it is clear that the package introduced in 1961 proved very effective in raising production. Indeed, even though Chen Yun and Deng Zihui were both sacked in 1962 for clashing with Mao over the degree of marketization to be allowed, there was no real policy reversal until military priorities became all-consuming after 1965 (Teiwes, 1988: 28).[12] As a result, rural output showed sustained recovery. In Sichuan, Guizhou, and Anhui, agricultural production grew on average by more than 13 per cent per year between the trough of 1961 and the eve of the Cultural Revolution. Although grain output per head in the three provinces remained below the 1957 level even in 1965, it was in each case above the national average.[13] Furthermore, grain availability was higher than it had been in the late 1950s. That was especially true for Sichuan because the heavy procurement burden imposed by the central government—the province was a net 'exporter' of grain during the First Five-Year Plan (1953–7)—had been greatly reduced. Indeed, and largely as the result of the catastrophe, Sichuan was never again to be a significant grain exporter during the Maoist era.

But the most interesting features of the rural reforms of the early 1960s is that they were repeated almost verbatim in the late 1970s. Still more interestingly, the *provincial variations* that existed in the early 1960s were also repeated in the late 1970s. Anhui, one of the provinces worst hit by the famine, is a good example. Famine conditions reigned between 1959 and the first half of 1961; as the 1962 government work report acknowledged, high levels of morbidity were widespread and this resulted in mass emigration and unusually high levels of mortality (Lu, 1992: i. 169–70). Such extreme conditions called for extreme remedies; in Anhui's case, Zeng Xisheng (the Party secretary) decided that arable land was to be allocated to households on an experimental basis in the spring of 1961. Furthermore, Zeng gained Mao's approval for this *zerentian* (responsibility field) system at a meeting in Guangzhou on 15 and 16 March. Mao is reported to have said: 'You experiment. If it goes badly, write a self-criticism. If it goes well, you will be able to raise grain output by one billion *jin*, and that will be a great thing' (Lu, 1992: i. 171). With this high-level backing, the 'responsibility fields' were actively promoted from 27 March onwards. At that time, something in the order of 39 per cent of land was already being farmed by households. By August, the figure was 75 per cent, and it peaked in February 1962 at 85 per cent (Lu, 1992: i. 172–3).[14] Some other provinces followed suit and also allowed the reintroduction of private farming, e.g. in central Hebei (Friedman, *et al.*, 1991: 252–5) and in south-east Shanxi (Hinton, 1983: 285). But none went as far as Anhui.

To be sure, Anhui's deviation from the national line came to an end in the spring of 1962. By the end of 1961, in fact, Mao seems to have decided that decollectivization had gone too far in that province. Although Liu Shaoqi and Deng Xiaoping fully supported household quotas at the Xilou Conference in February 1962 (Lieberthal 1997: 120), Mao seems ultimately to have got his way. Zeng was transferred out of Anhui and a programme of rectification was launched in March 1962. This aimed to restore the system of team-based production by the end of the year. The target was more or less achieved (Wang, 1988: 15–20). Nevertheless, the radical nature of agrarian reform in Anhui in the early 1960s was repeated in the province in the late 1970s, when Anhui was again the pace-setter in rural reform. By the end of 1978, 1,200 production teams had already adopted the system of *baochan daohu*, and this had risen to 38,000 (about 10 per cent of the total) by the end of 1979. By the end of 1980, *shuangbao* (*dabaogan* and *baochan daohu* combined) covered 67 per cent of teams. In the most 'advanced' part of the province—Chuxian prefecture—3,688 teams out of 22,641 had already adopted the system of *dabaogan* by October 1979 (Lu, 1992: i. 186, 188).

Other provinces lagged far behind Anhui in both the early 1960s and the late 1970s. For example, the rural reforms of the early 1960s and late 1970s were far less radical in Sichuan. Even though the famine had claimed some 15 million lives, the province adopted the 'reform package' no more quickly than was the rule elsewhere in China. If anything, Sichuan may have been slower in implementing the package because of the resistance of Li Jingquan, the Party secretary, to what he saw as 'revisionism' (Goodman, 1986: 154–6) Those *xian zhi* (county records) that are available show that Sichuan's counties did not move towards abolishing communal canteens until May 1961. Additionally, there is little evidence that any of them moved towards household farming; most did not make the production team the basic unit of account until March/April 1962 following the national '7000 cadre' conference. It is true that some of Sichuan's counties did authorize private plots quite early. In Nanchong, for example, 95,000 *mu* of cultivated land was allocated to private plots in response to drought in the autumn of 1961 (*Nanchong xian zhi*, 1993: 31). Nevertheless, this amounted to only about 7 per cent of arable area—as prescribed by central government. The same was true elsewhere. In Kaijiang, the allocation was 5–6 per cent (*Kaijiang xian zhi*, 1989: 31). In Wushan, it was just under 7 per cent (*Wushan xian zhi*, 1991: 111, 113) and the same was true in Qianwei (*Qianwei xian zhi*, 1991: 141). In Anyue, however, the allocation was only 5 per cent (*Anyue xian zhi*, 1993: 175) and in Mianzhu it was barely 4 per cent (*Mianzhu xian zhi*, 1992: 260, 299). Some *xian zhi* (e.g. Kaijiang *xian zhi* (1988: 22)) talk of the adoption of *dabaogan* (contracting all responsibilities), the name often used to refer to household farming in the early 1980s. But it is clear that the relevant unit to which responsibility was contracted was merely the production team instead of the commune.

The rather cautious approach adopted in Sichuan in the early 1960s set the tone for the province in the late 1970s. Whereas Anhui pressed ahead with household farming, even those counties in Sichuan which were in the van of reform (e.g. Guanghan) emphasized decentralization of decision-making to work groups (*baogan daozu*) rather than to households (Bramall, 1995*a*). As a result, although 66 per cent of Sichuan's teams had adopted group contracting by August 1980, only 10 per cent had made the transition to *baochan daohu* by December of the same year and the proportion using *baogan* was negligible. By that time, as we have seen, the Anhui figure for *shuangbao* was 67 per cent. Furthermore, many counties in Sichuan vigorously opposed decollectivization until the winter of 1982–3. Sichuan's experience was in fact much closer to the Chinese norm than that of Anhui. Indeed Anhui is the only Chinese province that systematically promoted household production in the early 1960s. For instance, in Nanyang prefecture in Henan—another province hard hit by the famine—private plots were only authorized in the autumn of 1961 and accounted for no more than 5 per cent of arable area (Ma, 1991: 99–100). Clearly, therefore, the experience of the early 1960s remained a critical influence on the plans of the reformers in the late 1970s. The 'rural package' adopted in the late 1970s was remarkably similar to that of the early 1960s, and those provinces in the van of reform in 1961–2 led the way in the late 1970s. Those, like Heilongjiang and Jiangsu, that were least adventurous in the late 1970s also experimented little in the early 1960s.

This historical evidence makes the adoption of a variety of NEP-style packages after 1978 less surprising. These packages were obviously successful in the aftermath of the Great Leap Forward, to which the agricultural crisis of the late 1970s was sometimes likened. Moreover, the presence of two of the three who had presided over the post-famine recovery—Deng Xiaoping and Chen Yun—in leadership positions at the pinnacle of the CCP in the late 1970s must also have played a large role. Of course, the 'objective' situation inherited by the reformers was far more propitious than in the early 1960s; Anhui's crude death rate was less than 5 per thousand in 1978 compared to almost 69 per thousand in 1960. Nevertheless, there was a widespread view that the late Maoist economy was underperforming, and a clear sense that the NEP package had worked in the early 1960s, and that it could work again. The existence of this vision of an alternative growth-promoting approach undoubtedly facilitated the task of transition.

This discussion suggests that the leaders of the CCP knew in 1978 which type of strategy was likely to bring about rapid economic growth.[15] The weak Qing state had presided over stagnant levels of per capita income, and the even weaker Republican state had done little better; that seemed to rule out a laissez-faire option. But equally, the debacle of the Great Leap Forward and late Maoism illustrated the dangers inherent in central planning. The New Economic Policy of the governed market, the middle way, offered the obvious alternative to the twin myopias of the past. Not only had it worked in the 1950s and early 1960s, but the alternative growth strategies had been discredited. In a sense, therefore, successful growth of the 1980s may be seen as the product of collective learning; the 'reformist' wing of the CCP can be portrayed as having learnt by 1978 from the mistakes and the successes of China's past. Indeed Deng Xiaoping said as much in 1979:

> Despite our errors, in the past three decades we have made progress on a scale which old China could not achieve in hundreds or even thousands of years. Our economy has achieved a fairly high rate of growth. Now that we have summed up experience and corrected errors, it will undoubtedly develop more rapidly than the economy of any capitalist country, and the development will be steady and sustained. (Central Committee, 1991: 44)

Still, for all the plausibility of these arguments, we need to be cautious. To argue that Mao was simply unaware of how to maximize growth in the mid-1960s is a very strong conclusion, and one that is open to challenge precisely because he had presided over the rapid growth of 1949–57, and the recovery of 1962–5. Perhaps he was myopic, and genuinely uncertain about which growth strategies were best. But there is an alternative interpretation: Mao did not believe an NEP-type strategy could succeed given the constraints which faced China in the 1960s and which had not been present in the 1950s. It was therefore the absence of constraints which allowed transition after 1978. To there issues we now turn.

2. The Growth-Promoting Agenda, Ideology, and External Constraints

Some of the best-known phrases of the Dengist era stress the importance of increasing per capita income. It was Deng who resurrected Zhou Enlai's slogan 'The Four

Modernizations' and set the aim of these modernizations as the quadrupling of Chinese GDP by 2000. It was Deng who made it clear in his phrases 'poverty is not socialism' and 'take the lead in getting rich' that growing inequality was a price worth paying if it led to a faster pace of economic growth. It was Deng who was willing to accept a rate of inflation during the 1980s and 1990s—the inevitable concomitant of rapid economic growth and structural change—that would have been regarded as anathema by the governments of the European Union, and was so regarded by the IMF and World Bank. Finally, it was Deng who de facto ordered the resumption of rapid economic growth during his 'southern tour' in 1992 after the recession of 1989–90. Finally, Deng's own writings make it clear that rapid economic growth was at the top of his agenda:

> the fundamental task for the socialist stage is to develop the productive forces. The superiority of the socialist system is demonstrated by its faster and greater development of the productive forces than that of the capitalist system. Speaking of our shortcomings since the founding of the People's Republic, one was negligence in developing the productive forces. (Central Committee, 1991: 2)

The definitive Party statement of the importance of growth promotion is set out in the CCP Resolution on 'Questions of Party History' issued in 1981:

> . . . the principal contradiction our country has had to resolve is that between the growing material and cultural needs of the people and the backwardness of social production. It was imperative that the focus of Party and government work be shifted to socialist modernization centring on economic construction and that the people's material and cultural life be gradually improved by means of an immense expansion of productive forces. In the final analysis, the mistake we made in the past was that we failed to persevere in making this strategic shift. . . . All our Party work must be subordinated to and serve this central task—economic construction. (Liu and Wu, 1986: 629)

By contrast, the Maoist agenda placed much more emphasis on the primacy of class struggle, on egalitarianism, and on nationalism, as China under Mao sought to avoid the dictates of *pax Americana*.[16] It was not that the CCP lacked the information to formulate a plausible growth strategy; rather, its abiding goal was to avoid the instability and external interference that marked the Qing and Republican eras. Those who survived the massacre of Nanjing and other Japanese atrocities were at one in clamoring for security against occupation, and the capacity of the CCP to embrace this nationalist cause was perhaps the key reason for its ultimate success in overthrowing the Kuomintang in 1945–9 (Bianco, 1971; Johnson, 1962).

Alternatively, one might contrast the differing agendas of Deng Xiaoping and the nineteenth century Qing government. One can argue that the late Qing state ultimately recoiled from following the modernizing logic of the self-strengthening movement and the Tongzhi restoration to its logical conclusion because of what was implied for the old order. As Wright (1957: 312) concluded: 'The T'ung-chih Restoration failed because the requirements of a modern state proved to run directly counter to the requirements of the Confucian order. . . . To the makers of the T'ung-chih Restoration, adjustment that yielded . . . on the essentials of the Confucian society, was no alternative to extinction, but extinction itself.'

The difficulty with this type of approach, in which economic outcomes reflect differing ideologies formulated by sociocultural factors, is its neglect of the possibility that agendas are themselves the product of economic and political factors—that is, the agenda may be merely part of a superstructure which is the product of the economic base and the international environment. In other words, ideology has no independent existence. Of course ideology is important in its own right; Skocpol (1979), for instance, is surely wrong in not giving more weight to the role of Marxist and Enlightenment ideals in her explanation of the French, Russian, and Chinese Revolutions. But agendas and ideologies are not formulated in a vacuum. Consider the failures of France and Spain to establish growth-promoting institutions between 1500 and 1700. In a sense, the problem was ideological; the primary aim of the state was short-run revenue maximization rather than growth promotion. However, as North and Thomas (1973: 100) point out, the short-run time horizon of the state was a product of the insecurity of successive rulers. As they say 'survival was at stake' and therefore a long-run time horizon was a luxury the rulers of France and Spain could ill-afford. North and Thomas did not take this insight through to its logical conclusion. Their analysis—as North (1990: 7) admits—saw inefficient institutions as little more than an aberration; ultimately, efficient institutions would emerge as a result of price signals and incentives. But more recently, North (1990) has recognized the path-dependent nature of economic organizations, and that it usually takes a revolution—the removal of the underlying political and cultural constraints that push an economy along a slow growth path—to establish a state with a growth-promoting ideology. As he says (North, 1990: 112): 'Reversal of paths (from stagnation to growth or vice versa) . . . will typically occur through changes in the polity.'

Alternatively, consider the failure of the self-strengthening movement in China in the nineteenth century. One could argue that the abandonment of modernization by the Qing government was not driven by the conflict between it and Confucianism (if that were true, why was self-strengthening ever attempted in the first place?) but by opposition from vested interest at home, and the catastrophic defeat in the Sino-Japanese war of 1894–5 (which shattered the credibility of the regime). Or, consider the Taiping rebellion. The quasi-Christian doctrine advanced by Hong Xiuquan was inspirational to thousands of farmers (Spence, 1996). But that ideology was itself a product of the impact of the West, which provided the Bibles; and Hong's followers were inspired as much by the negative message (state weakness, as revealed by the defeat of the Qing government in the first Opium War by the British) as by the positive aspects of Hong's creed. From the perspective of both neo-Smithian Marxism and modernization theory, it is the external shock which is crucial in changing ideology and perceptions of what is possible in poor economies.

This sort of 'externalist' approach is increasingly popular as a way of explaining the emergence of the growth-promoting state in East Asia. Kohli (1994) emphasizes the way in which Japanese colonialism paved the way for the emergence of the developmental state in South Korea. More recently, Campos and Root (1996) argue that East Asian states sought legitimacy by promoting 'shared growth' in the face of the alleged Chinese Communist 'threat'. The possibility of conquest forced these regimes to carry out land reform and increase spending on education in order to ensure regime stability. Now it is moot point whether the East Asian countries really did see themselves as threatened given the strong support they received from the USA. Indeed, it is surely arguable that—in so far as a military threat was perceived—this led to the adoption of a more 'Stalinist' approach to growth and excessive 'unproductive' military spending, the result being the slow growth experienced in South Korea and Taiwan in the 1950s. The transition to a growth-promoting strategy in the early 1960s arguably had more to do with US pressure and (if anything) the waning of the Chinese threat than the converse. Furthermore, cold war warriors like Campos and Root can hardly use their thesis of a *Communist* threat as the spur to growth given its limited relevance in the cases of the late-starting Asian economies such as Thailand, Malaysia, and Indonesia—to say nothing of China itself in the 1950s and after 1978! It is also worth noting that some writers (e.g. Grabowski, 1994) have been critical of the externalist explanation of East Asian success for its neglect of internal factors.[17]

Nevertheless, even though the *detail* of the externalist arguments is rather unconvincing, it is hard to dismiss the notion that external factors have had considerable influence on China's choice of development strategies. Perhaps the most obvious example is the Maoist development strategy itself. To be sure, late Maoism did indeed emphasize egalitarianism, autarkic development, and class struggle. However, that had not been the case during the 1950s. We can in fact pinpoint an 'epistemological break' in Maoist thought in 1956–7 and the ending of Mao's 'Bukharinist phase' (Schram, 1989). Mao's speech 'On the Correct Handling of Contradictions among the People' (27 February 1957) stressed the importance of economic growth, and the same was true of many of his speeches in the spring of 1957. Indeed some of them would not have been out of place in the early 1980s. One such was 'On Ideological Work':

> We now find ourselves in a period of transition, a period in which the old struggle—class struggle, has basically ended, has basically been completed. . . . we now find ourselves in a period of change: from class struggle to the struggle against nature. to improve living conditions we must promote construction. (MacFarquhar, *et al.*, 1989: 322–3)

However, by the autumn, Mao's tone had changed decisively; now class struggle was declared to be the main task facing China:

> . . . the contradiction between the proletariat and the bourgeoisie, between the socialist road and the capitalist road, is undoubtedly the principal contradiction in contemporary Chinese society . . . The resolution of the Eighth Congress makes no mention of this question. It contains a passage which speaks of the principal contradiction as being that between the advanced socialist system and the backward social productive forces. This formulation is incorrect. (Schram, 1989: 159)

Nevertheless, it is at least arguable that external factors—the break with the Soviet Union—forced a different developmental agenda on the Maoist regime. Schurmann (1974: 275–6, 299–301) puts the argument very clearly:

> Although the Chinese (like the Russians and the Americans) wrote and talked about economic planning as if it had no relationship to foreign policy, the fact is that estimation of the external environment was the basis of all planning. Was the environment to be peaceful or hostile?—that was the key question. . . . China plunged into the Great Leap Forward with both an evangelistic sense of moving from socialism to communism and another sense of desperate urgency to ready the country for a new international conflagration. . . . while small-scale industry was being developed throughout rural China and communes were being formed, Mao also ordered the rapid development of village militias in the summer of 1958.

The reason for this shift was largely to do with events. The USA deployed missiles (with a range of 600 miles) in Taiwan in May 1957, and this was followed by an inflammatory anti-China speech by Dulles in June 1957. As for the initiation of the Third Front in the mid-1960s, that had much to do with the growing American build-up in Vietnam.

From this 'externalist' perspective, the rural egalitarianism of the Leap and late Maoism can be seen as no more than an attempt to share out the scanty resources available in an equitable fashion whilst using the bulk of the 'surplus' to finance urban-based defence industrialization. Even the Cultural Revolution can be seen as an attack on 'the enemy within', an attempt to purge the Party machinery of those elements sympathetic either to the West or (especially after the demise of Lin Biao) to the Soviet Union. Perhaps, therefore, it is not so ludicrous to argue that the initial Maoist development aim was output maximization, but that this had to be abandoned. Unfashionable though it is to say so, it may well be that the Maoist development strategy was not a product of myopia or ideology, but imposed by circumstance.

This discussion is of course tentative; the more exhaustive analysis that undoubtedly is required lies well beyond the scope of this book. But it does illustrate a general point; even if a regime has a growth maximizing agenda and knows what the strategy should be, growth is by no means assured. Translating the goal into a policy and institutional framework is not a simple task. In explaining the success of some states in achieving rapid economic growth, we need to look at constraints are well as ideologies.

3. An Autonomous Dengist State?

Perhaps the most remarkable feature of the Dengist era is in fact the limited range of constraints faced by the Chinese state in implementing its growth-promoting agenda. This relative absence of constraints made the task of governance in China altogether easier than in other countries desperately trying to create growth-promoting institutions. As will become apparent, it is not the Dengist attempt to use the state to promote growth that marks post-1978 China out as unusual; the People's Republic was merely emulating the growth strategies pursued in many other developing countries. Rather, China is unusual in that its state was successful; and the Dengist state, it seems, was successful precisely because it did not face the kind of crippling constraints that prevented rapid economic growth in (for example) the Soviet Union under Gorbachev or contemporary South Asia. In other words, the Dengist state was unusual in that it enjoyed a high measure of autonomy.

3.1. The Theory of the Autonomous State

Three broad theories of the state are identifiable. First, there are those which see the state as autonomous, but functioning in a way that is parasitic; here, the state is predatory and maximizes its own income at the expense of all other groups and therefore at the expense of GDP growth. Nozick's (1974) work views the state in this sort of way, as do those of Hayek and Friedman. Some of Marx's early and late writings (on, for example, the Asiatic mode of production) also fall under this heading, as does Gates' (1996) view of the Imperial and twentieth-century Chinese state as a break on peasant initiative. In all these writings, it is recognized that the state is needed to secure the property rights of private individuals, but grave fears are expressed about the likely impact if the state becomes a Leviathan and expands its role beyond these confines.

A second, and this time 'society-centred', view of the state is the orthodox Marxist 'class theoretical' interpretation in which the state is little more than an instrument of the capitalist class. This is to be found in Marx's *Critique of Hegel's Philosophy of the State* (1843), but more especially in the writings of Engels (1972) and Lenin:

> According to Marx, the state could neither arise not endure if it were possible to reconcile classes. According to Marx, the state is an organ of class rule, an organ for the *oppression* of one class by another. [p. 9]. . . . A democratic republic is the best possible shell for capitalism, and therefore, once capital has got control of this excellent shell . . . it establishes its power so securely, so firmly, that no change of individuals, of institutions or of parties in the bourgeois-democratic republic can shake this power. [p. 14]. (Lenin, 1918)

Miliband's (1969) writings fall within this same tradition, as do some of Gramsci's writings (although his emphasis was more on the way the state elicits consent via cultural and ideological hegemony instead of via coercion).

A third, this time a 'state-centred', view has gained adherents in recent years The key idea in this neo-Weberian approach is that the state has a substantial degree of autonomy from civil society, and is able to exploit this autonomy to promote growth. The state does so via economic policy; for example, by promoting high rates of investment in physical and human capital. It also fosters growth by the creation of growth-promoting institutions which reduce transaction costs. This view of the state as autonomous and progressive has a long history. Hegel, for instance, portrayed the state as ruling in the interests of society as a whole. More significant are Weber's writings on Wilhelmine Germany (although, as we will see, Weber was in two minds on whether the autonomous state would be progressive). According to his justly famous analysis, a bureaucracy might obtain a position of effective independence:

> The power position of a fully developed bureaucracy is always great, under normal conditions overtowering. The political 'master' always finds himself, vis-à-vis the trained official, in the position of a dilettante facing the expert. This holds whether the 'master', whom the

bureaucracy serves, is the 'people' equipped with the weapons of legislative initiative, referendum, and the right to remove officials; or a parliament elected on a more aristocratic or more democratic basis and equipped with the right or *de facto* power to vote a lack of confidence; or an aristocratic collegiate body, legally or actually based on self-recruitment; or a popularly elected president or an 'absolute' or 'constitutional' hereditary monarch. (Weber, 1956: ii. 991)

Some Marxists have also stressed that states may have a high degree of autonomy. According to Engels (1972: 160), for example, the state would usually represent the interests of the dominant class but might acquire a position of independence if the 'warring classes' were evenly matched. Poulantzas (1968) and Offe (1974) also argue that the state should be seen as promoting the long-run viability of capitalism as a whole. It might, for example, create a welfare system rather pursue the short-term interests of the dominant class. The state is able to do this precisely because capitalism—as distinct from feudalism—did not require the exercise of direct coercive power. This was because workers were free to leave their particular employment, and to exercise their freedom under the law.[18] The essential thrust of Poulantzas's argument is summarized as follows by Robert Bates (1983: 145):

Other scholars impute a more independent role for the state. Rather than acting as the passive agency of particular interests, they argue, the state stands relatively independent of such interests and thereby facilitates the attainment of otherwise unattainable objectives. . . . Capitalism, they stress, contains an inherent contradiction; it requires accumulation for its reproduction, but accumulation generates class antagonism. The state, acting out of the interests of capitalism, must therefore stand apart from the dominant class and compel it to lower its rate of accumulation; only by exacting such concessions can it placate the lower classes, secure the reproduction of labor power, and thereby guarantee the reproduction of the capitalist order.

One of the first accounts to stress the importance of a 'hard' state in the development process was Myrdal (1968: i. 66). He characterized the states of South Asia as 'soft'; that is, 'policies decided on are often not enforced, if they are enacted at all, and . . . the authorities, even when framing policies, are reluctant to place obligations on people.' It was, Myrdal (1968: i. 67) argued, essential for economic growth that the state was hardened:

. . . our investigation has convinced us that the success of planning for development requires a readiness to place obligations on people in *all* social strata to a much greater extent than is now done in any of the South Asian countries. It requires, in addition, rigorous enforcement of obligations, in which compulsion plays a strategic role.

In the 1970s and 1980s, the state-centred approach became increasingly influential, and is perhaps best epitomized by the idea of 'bringing the state back in', the title of the book by Evans, Rueschemeyer, and Skocpol (1985). The modern state-centred approach has been influenced in particular by the work of Skocpol (1979; 1994) on revolutions, Olson (1965; 1982) on collective action, and Mann (1993) on the nineteenth-century European state. Skocpol's key contribution was to show that state weakness—rather than the voluntary actions of groupings within civil society or the ideologies associated with Marx and the Enlightenment—was decisive in bringing about the social revolutions which ended the *ancien régimes* in France (1789), Russia (1917), and China (1911–49). Revolution:

> . . . was *not* because of deliberate activities to that end, either on the part of avowed revolutionaries or on the part of politically powerful groups within the Old Regimes. Rather revolutionary political crises, culminating in administrative and military breakdowns, emerged because the imperial states became caught in cross-pressures between intensified military competition or intrusions from abroad and constraints imposed on monarchical responses by the existing agrarian class structures and political institutions [p. 285].

Mancur Olson's work has been even more influential. In showing how special interest groups would increasingly solve their own collective action problem in a stable society, Olson demonstrated the need for an autonomous state, a state 'hard' enough to resist pressure from these groups and therefore able to rule in the national interest. Thus war and occupation allowed the emergence of autonomous states in post-war Germany and Japan by destroying interest groups:

> . . . it follows that countries whose distributional coalitions have been emasculated or abolished by totalitarian government or foreign occupation should grow relatively quickly after a free and stable legal order is established. This can explain the post-war 'economic miracles' in the nations that were defeated in World War II, particularly those in Japan and West Germany. (Olson, 1982: 75)

But an autonomous state might also emerge endogenously; Thatcherism, for example, has been seen by Olson (1996) as demonstrating how the existence of special interest groups in a democratic society might ultimately lead to the recreation of state autonomy. The same was true of political trends in Australia and New Zealand in the 1990s. Finally, Michael Mann's (1993) study of eighteenth- and nineteenth-century states takes this type of analysis of the role of the state a stage further by making an important distinction between infrastructural and despotic power. Although many of these states were despotic (able to redistribute resources in their own favour), none possessed much by way of infrastructural power ('the institutional capacity of a central state, despotic or not, to penetrate its territories and logistically implement decisions'—Mann, 1993: 59). They lacked the bureaucratic capacity to intervene decisively in the functioning of civil society; state strength therefore went hand in hand with state weakness.

This neo-Weberian work has in turn spawned research on the reasons for state successes and failures in developing countries. Shue (1988; 1990) has argued that the 'reach' of the Maoist state in China was weak, and its intentions increasingly frustrated by local communities. Kohli (1987; 1994) adopts a similar tack in analysing India. Whereas the parliamentary-communist regime in West Bengal has been able to initiate redistributive programmes because of the effectiveness of its party bureaucracy, the power of central government has increasingly declined as the capacity of Congress to implement policy via village elites has dwindled in the face of increasingly well-organized peasant and middle-class opposition. Although Indira and Rajiv Gandhi were still able to gain power by adopting a populist agenda,

Congress was entirely unable to implement its anti-poverty programme. More generally, Haggard (1990: 45) sees a direct causal link between the degree of state autonomy and economic growth:

> . . . I argue . . . that democracies and polities organized on the basis of clientelistic networks are less insulated than corporatist regimes and those authoritarian regimes which limit autonomous political organization and public contestation. As a result, economic policy in liberal-democratic and clientelistic systems is more likely to be explained by coalitional and rent-seeking pressures and less likely to be consistent and internally coherent.

The notion of the autonomous state has also been extensively used to explain economic growth in East Asia, and especially in Taiwan and South Korea. Haggard (1990; 1993) has for example stressed the role of internal factors in destroying interest groups, and especially both the charismatic leadership of Park and the bureaucratic capacity of the Korean military. The same is true of Chang's (1993*b*: 151) work; 'calculated political moves and institutional innovations' by Park Chung Hee were 'as much, if not more' important than 'historical conditions and culture'.

3.2. The Theory of the Autonomous State: A Critique

For all the appeal of the idea of an autonomous state, it has long been apparent that an exclusively state-centred analysis will not do because the notion of a fully autonomous state promoting economic growth is little more than a convenient fiction. Weber himself was ambivalent about both state autonomy and.(if realized) its likely economic impact. There was a danger of 'uncontrolled bureaucratic domination' but this might be offset by charismatic or Caesarist leadership. Moreover, state autonomy in the guise of bureaucratic rule was in itself no guarantee of economic growth. In a passage explicitly entitled 'The Indeterminate Economic Consequences of Bureaucracy' in his *Economy and Society*, Weber argued that:

> In political and especially in state formations, too, bureaucratization and social leveling with the associated breaking up of the opposing local and feudal privileges have in modern times frequently benefited the interests of capitalism or have been carried out in direct alliance with capitalist interests . . . But, on the other hand, there is also an effect of bureaucratization that meets the petty-bourgeois interest in a safe traditional 'living' or even a state-socialist effect that strangulates opportunities for private profit. (Weber, 1956: ii. 989–90)

In the light of these sorts of antecedents in Weber's own writings, it is not entirely surprising that much of the best theorizing in this area has eschewed the notion of full state autonomy and instead combined (Marxist) society-centred and (neo-Weberian) state-centred ideas. For example, Skocpol's (1979) work on revolutions gives centre stage to state weakness, but in true Althusserian fashion, she resists the temptation to replace one type of determinism with another; her theory is as much society-centred as it is state-centred. Similarly, Migdal, *et al.* (1994) argue that we need to focus on 'the state in society'. The state is not monolithic nor is it a Leviathan; very rarely—if ever—has the state been able to effect a total transformation of society. Not even the Maoist regime aimed at, still less achieved, that result; as Gates (1996) has rightly argued, many traditional aspects of Chinese culture served it well. For example, maintaining the status quo in terms of gender enabled the Maoist state to consolidate its support amongst men. Finally, the notion of 'embedded autonomy' (Evans, 1995) seeks to embed the state in society. That is, it rules successfully only by virtue of cooperation between itself and private sector interest groups.

A second problem with the state-centred approach is that much of the empirical research that underpins it is less than convincing. For example, Kohli's (1987) work on West Bengal is problematic because in fact the ruling coalition there has been far less successful in reducing poverty than he seems to be suggesting (Mallick, 1992). As Drèze and Sen (1995: 56) say:

> While issues such as land reform have received high priority in the programme of the Left Front coalition. . . . public policies concerned with health, education and related matters have been comparatively neglected. Correspondingly, the improvement of living conditions in West Bengal in recent years has remained relatively slow. An important opportunity has been missed here, since the skills of popular mobilization of the West Bengal government (amply demonstrated in other fields) could have been used with good effect to a achieve a real transformation in the fields of education and health [p. 56].

Shue's (1988) work on China is also problematic. Her claim that the central government was increasingly 'thin'—that is, unable to implement its policies—is largely contradicted by the absence of local-level deviance. For example, there is little apart from a few anecdotes to suggest that private farming survived at a local level in China between 1963 and 1977. Moreover, Zhou's (1996) work suggesting that the decollectivization movement was spontaneously 'led from below' rather than encouraged by provincial elites is equally unconvincing. In both cases, the difficulty is the same: how were Chinese peasants able to solve the 'collective action problem' and thereby resist central government policy? Even more importantly, if they were able to solve the problem, why did collective farming suffer from incentive problems at all? The work of Robert Bates (1981; 1989) on Kenya is also unconvincing. In particular, it is hard to see how Moi—who lacked any significant power base—was able to undermine the allegedly growth-promoting and quasi-autonomous state that existed under Kenyatta. An alternative reading of the evidence would be that Kenyatta's policies were driven by the sectional agricultural interests of the Kikuyu, with the result that industrial investment was far too low. Once the easier catch-up possibilities had been exhausted in the two decades after independence, and in the face of depressed world commodity prices, the Kenyan economy simply stagnated in the 1980s. In part, of course, all these country-specific questions indicate that much of the empirical work is in its infancy. Nevertheless, the fact remains that a great deal remains to be done to make the theory convincing.

A third problem with the state-centred approach is that too many writers within this tradition have tended to casually equate the desirability of state autonomy with a need for authoritarian rule.[19] This idea that authoritarianism leads to rapid economic growth is especially true of the writings on East Asia. One emerging conventional wisdom here is that only an authoritarian state led by a charismatic leader will be able to ward off the rent-seeking behaviour invariably associated with interventions and push through the sort of transaction-cost reducing policies that are required. This type of explanation is common currency amongst many admirers of the East Asian model, most of whom dismiss the widely held view that democracy is a necessary condition for rapid economic growth (Chang, 1993*a*; Nolan, 1995*a*). Furthermore, Japanese economists and political scientists often argue that Japan's experience shows both the desirability of a strong state in the early stages of development (pre-World War II) and the way in which the rise of living standards led to the gradual emergence of democracy after 1945 (Yabuki, 1995: 227).[20] Nevertheless, advocates of this type of approach argue that an authoritarian state can exist only in the early stages of development because rising per capita incomes will lead ultimately to democratic government (Nolan, 1995*a*: 67–8). This argument is rarely made explicit but it seems to be as follows. First, authoritarianism leads to rapid per capita income growth. Second, once a certain threshold income level is reached, democratic demands will start to be voiced. Third, any resulting move to democracy will reduce the growth rate of income, but as long as the *level* of income remains above the threshold, democracy itself will not be imperilled. It is presumably in this sense that the phrase 'democracy is a luxury that only affluent countries can afford' is intended.

Now there is perhaps something in this view that strong leadership is essential for growth and fundamental economic restructuring. Perhaps the reform of American health care in the 1990s failed because of the incompetence of Hillary Rodham Clinton. Perhaps the Keynesianism pursued by Francois Mitterrand in the mid-1980s foundered because of his overweening ambition rather than the impossibility of pursuing such an expansionary programme in France against a background of European recession. Perhaps, conversely, the success of East Asia can be attributed to the visionary statesmanship and charismatic leadership of Lee Kuan Yew in Singapore, General Park in South Korea, and Chiang Kaishek in Taiwan.

But ultimately, the idea of a functional relationship running from authoritarianism to rapid income growth and, later, to democracy is not very compelling. First, few of those who intone the mantra of the 'strong state' understand the difficulties involved in defining whether a state is strong or not. As Michael Mann (1993) says, it is important to distinguish between the despotic and infrastructural power of the state. There is a tendency to cite the examples of Britain and America in the nineteenth century as showing that authoritarian rule 'works', but this falls foul of the point that the British and American states were remarkably lacking in infrastructural power compared to many of the states of the twentieth century:

> Whoever controls these [modern] states has infinitely more control over me than agrarian states had over my ancestors. As Huntington (1968: 1) observed, the British, US and Soviet (before 1991) states were more similar to one another than either were to historic states or to many states in developing countries. (Mann, 1993: 61)

In that nineteenth-century European states all lacked the capacity to intervene in the lives of individuals, one can argue that these countries were far more democratic than their twentieth-century successors. By contrast, all high-income late twentieth-century states are able to exercise enormous control over the lives of their citizens, whether despotic or democratic. As for the much quoted example of post-1947 India, one can argue about whether it is democratic. Vanhanen's (1997: 252, 260) index of democracy—which is based upon both the extent to which elections are competitive and the extent to which the adult population participates in them—shows India in the 1950s to have been more democratic than the UK in the first decade of the twentieth century. However, this is clearly a very narrow definition of democracy in that it takes no account of the infrastructural power of the state or the degree to which the distribution of economic resources allows effective participation in decision-making.[21]

A second problem with the authoritarianism hypothesis is that it is unclear whether rising per capita incomes will ensure democracy in the long run. To be sure, a number of scholars have concluded that there is a long-run causal relation running from per capita income to democracy. The idea was first put forward in a famous article by Lipset (1959) and it has been extensively discussed since (Lipset, 1993; Fukuyama, 1995). Perhaps the most powerful recent restatement has been by Diamond (1992), who found a strongly positive relation between democracy on the one hand, and both GNP and the HDI on the other. But many other writers have cast doubt on this proposition, arguing that average income or capability measures offer little by way of explanatory power. Some, for example, have argued that what matters is the emergence of a capitalist class; this is seen as enlarging both the size and organizational capacity of the working and middle classes, whilst weakening the landed elite (Huber, *et al.*, 1993). A more general hypothesis is offered by Vanhanen, for whom the emergence of democracy is most likely when 'power resources have become so widely distributed that no group is any longer able to suppress its competitors or maintain its hegemony' (Vanhanen, 1997: 5). In other words, it is the dispersion of power—rather than the level of development—which is critical for the emergence of democracy.

A third problem for the authoritarian approach is that the theoretical arguments linking the type of government with the pace of economic growth are inconclusive (Przeworski and Limongi, 1993). It is not clear whether democracy or dictatorship is best for property rights; democracy may prevent the exercise of arbitrary power by a dictator (North and Weingast, 1987) but it does not necessarily protect the population against either the workers or a dispossessed peasantry. It is true that, because an autocratic government will have an encompassing interest (that is, its income may be increased by reducing the tax rate and increasing public spending in so far as these raise GDP), it may adopt policies that promote growth; as McGuire and Olson (1996: 94–5) say, this provides one rationalization of the success of strong states in East Asia. However, a strong argument for democracy is that authoritarian regimes maximize their *revenue* rather than total output.[22] Although autocrats have an incentive to hold taxation down (the deadweight loss incurred by a higher marginal tax rate may, by reducing the tax base, reduce the autocrat's total income), democracies tend to do better because the governing majority receives income from both taxation and from market activities. A high tax rate therefore affects adversely both their tax revenue and their market-based income (McGuire and Olson, 1996). Additionally, the mere act of maintaining autocracy may dictate a high level of expenditure on the 'apparatus of repression'—the police and the military. Moreover, although economic policy in a democracy runs the risk of being dictated by powerful interest groups (interest groups have a narrower interest than an autocrat and therefore have less incentive to avoid high general tax rates), interest groups can sometimes be encompassing. Sweden provides the classic example. Centralized wage bargaining creates an encompassing interest by giving unions a strong incentive to consider the national interest; though they can increase their income by pushing for a higher share of national income, the centralized nature of wage bargaining makes it clear that any agreement they reach will significantly affect the inflation–unemployment trade-off (Olson, 1982). They may therefore find that their interests are best served by negotiating in such a way as to promote economic growth.

Fourthly, the empirical evidence on the link between authoritarianism and growth is at best equivocal. Przeworksi and Limongi (1993: 60–1) report twenty-one studies; of these, eight found for democracy, eight for authoritarianism and five reached no clear conclusion. In other words, every successful authoritarian regime is complemented by one ruled by a dictator who keeps corpses in his refrigerator; the records of Bokassa of the Central African Empire, Amin in Uganda, Ceaucescu in Romania, Pol Pot in Kampuchea, Duvalier in Haiti, and Marcos in the Philippines amply demonstrate the frailties of the charismatic leader. Furthermore, there is no guarantee that higher per capita incomes lead inexorably to the expansion of the sway of democracy; the emergence of the 'new authoritarianism' in the middle-income countries of Latin America in the 1960s is clear proof of that. Furthermore, even the evidence that OECD countries are both rich and democratic is not conclusive. Dictatorships may be better at promoting growth than democracies, but they often collapse because they are bad at handling economic crises, or because of reasons unconnected with their growth record (corruption, military defeat, environmental failures, or extremely inegalitarian income distribution). For these reasons, only democratic regimes tend to survive. In other words, one cannot infer that OECD governments are democratic because this type of government is best suited to growth promotion (Przeworski and Limongi, 1993). Bates and Krueger (1993) arrived at the same conclusion that there is no causal link running from authoritarianism to growth in their analysis of eight developing countries.[23]

Finally, the emphasis placed by some of the advocates of state autonomy on the charismatic leadership of a single (invariably male) individual is not very convincing. China's growth accelerated after 1992 despite Deng Xiaoping's near-total incapacity. More generally, the charismatic leadership hypothesis seems to imply either that the process is a matter of luck, or that some cultures are more able to produce leaders than others. If the emergence of charismatic leaders is simply a question of luck, it is difficult to explain why a horde of such leaders suddenly emerged in post-war East Asia—and nowhere else. It is also rather difficult to explain Chiang Kaishek's career in this way. On the one hand, he contrived to 'lose' China—one of the more remarkable achievements of the century given the fervent Chinese nationalism (a product of Western imperialism and Japanese invasion) of the late 1930s, ripe for exploitation by the leader of a party that even called itself Nationalist, and which received massive military assistance from the USA. On the other hand, Chiang later succeeded in transforming Taiwan into one of the most successful economies of the late twentieth century. The alternative view—some cultures (especially those of East Asia) are better at producing 'leaders of men' than others—is equally unappealing. For one thing, to assert that South Korea can produce charismatic leaders, but Bangladesh cannot, is little better than racism. More generally, history warns us that the search for the 'definitively superior' economic culture is illusory. It used to be thought that only the West and its Protestant work ethic were capable of modern economic development (Weber, Marx, Tawney)—until the rise of Japan. Then it was argued that Japanese culture was different from those of other East Asian countries (Morishima)—until South Korea, Taiwan, and China followed in Japan's footsteps. In the next stage of the retreat, it was East Asian culture that was special (Singapore's experience could be explained in terms of its having been occupied by Japan during World War II and having therefore fallen under the influence of Japanese culture)—until it was pointed out that Japanese culture was detested in many parts of East Asia (and especially in South Korea and China) and that rapid economic growth was also beginning to be seen in Thailand, Malaysia, and Indonesia. Finally, if culture is the most important determinant of whether transition is successful or not, it is hard to explain why countries can move *suddenly* to a growth-promoting regime. Culture is not immutable (as discussed in Chapter 6),[24] but it does not change quickly. It is simply implausible to explain the transition from Maoist to Dengist development strategies in China within two years in terms of a change in culture.

We may conclude from this discussion that a state-centred explanation of economic growth is not convincing unless there is incorporated into it a proper explanation of the origins of state autonomy. This is largely because there is a good deal of evidence that powerful special-interest groups often serve as a constraint by weakening the capacity of the state to create growth-promoting institutions and policies. But there is little doubt that autonomy is an essential prerequisite for effective state action. Myrdal has written eloquently of the weakness of the state in South Asia:

> The inauguration of the 'strong state'—which in principle, of course, could be democratic—is handicapped not only by the attitudes and institutions in the villages, but also by the inhibitions of the rulers. Moreover, no South Asian country has an administration prepared to enforce new rules, even when these rules are not very revolutionary. Corruption, rampant at least on the lower levels even in colonial times, is generally increasing and takes the edge off commands from the central government. (Myrdal, 1968: ii. 898–9)

These ideas that state autonomy matters are reinforced by the historical evidence. For example, Olson's (1982; 1983) view that the poor post-war performance of

Britain—as compared to the impressive records of West Germany and Japan—reflects the growth of interest groups in the former is well known. He also argues that the declining economic performance of the USSR can also be explained in terms of interest groups which distort the flow of information to the central planners (Murrell and Olson, 1991; Olson, 1996). Furthermore, although Bates' work on Kenya is not entirely convincing, there is no doubt that the weakness of indigenous capital in the 1960s and 1970s helps to explain the relative freedom of manœuvre enjoyed by Kenyatta's government. Finally, Alice Amsden (1989) has rightly emphasized the way in which war, occupation, and land reform paved the way for a strong centralized state in South Korea by destroying interest groups:

> The Korean state was able to consolidate its power in the 1960s because of the weakness of the social classes. Workers were a small percentage of the population, capitalists were dependent on state largesse, the aristocracy was dissolved by land reform, and the peasantry were atomized into smallholders. (Amsden, 1989: 52)

The same emphasis is to be found in Robert Wade's (1990) work on Taiwan.

In short, an approach which centres on state autonomy seems to offer the key to explaining the growth records of successful developing countries; it unlocks the performance riddle in a way that none of the other theories can. It does so by bringing together ideas drawn from Weber (the need for an efficient bureaucracy), Schumpeter (the 'best' economic institutions are those which promote growth rather than static efficiency), Coase's theorem (institutions are needed to reduce transaction costs), the Althusserian rejection of all forms of determinism, and Marx's emphasis on the influence of class interest on government. The very fact that it appeals to a wide range of left-of-centre opinion is an indication of the power of the approach.

But can the approach explain why the Dengist state has been successful in China? Were interest groups much weaker there relative to the state at the end of the 1970s and beginning of the 1980s than in less-successful developing countries? Was the Dengist state really so powerful, and if so why?

4. Breaking the External Constraints: The Rapprochement with the USA

The answer to the last question is undoubtedly in part that the waning of the external threat to the Chinese revolution strengthened the Dengist state. It is widely recognized that a state may be powerless to implement policy if it is confronted by a powerful external threat.[25] As some of the more recent theories of revolution have suggested, the collapse of the old order is precipitated not so much by the existence within civil society of anger/relative deprivation or of a 'vanguard' communist party but rather the weakness of the state itself in the face of both internal and external forces (Skocpol, 1979). The collapse of Russian power in 1917, brought about in no small measure by the loss of legitimacy which followed its catastrophic handling of World War I, is the classic example. But there are many others, not least in the Chinese context. The late Qing state, for example, was fatally undermined by its inability to resist imperial incursion and its poor showing in the war of 1894–5 against Japan; it was this shattering defeat that brought to an end the resurgence of Qing power that followed the Tongzhi Restoration (Wright, 1957). The same was true for the Nationalists in the 1940s. The sheer incompetence of Chiang's war effort when contrasted with that of the Communists became increasingly apparent both at home and abroad (Tuchman, 1970). This is not, of course, to suggest that the state is always helpless in the face of the 'foreign threat'. External pressure may in the long run strengthen the domestic state by unleashing nationalist fervour, as indeed it did in China during the twentieth century; the revolution of 1949 was not simply a triumph for nationalism but it did play a key part in the process (Johnson, 1962; Bianco, 1971). According to Bianco (1971: 166), 'Chinese nationalism is first and foremost the triumphal assertion of Chinese nationalism. It is a nationalism of explosive vitality, as aggressive as it is vigorous, as often ill-considered as profound.'

But nationalism does constrain policy in that it forces the state—if it wishes to remain in power—to respond to the external threat. In retrospect, it is clear that it was the combination of the American (and later Soviet) threat and resurgent Chinese nationalism that dictated Chinese economic and strategic policy under Mao. This perception of an external threat on the part of the Chinese leadership was far from being paranoia. Relations between China and the USA collapsed following the decision of the USA to support Chiang Kaishek during the Chinese civil war. They remained at a low ebb throughout the next two decades, largely because of the readiness of successive US administrations to view China as a threat to world peace. The intransigence of the USA towards China is evident in its foreign policy.[26] Throughout the 1950s and 1960s, the USA provided significant financial and military aid to Taiwan, and protected the country against invasion by its readiness to move its Seventh Fleet into the Straits of Formosa. A string of US bases were constructed and maintained in Japan, Korea, the Philippines, and Taiwan itself. US military intervention in Korea, Vietnam, and Cambodia was designed to hold China in check by providing as a clear signal that the advance of communism in Asia would not be tolerated. Moreover, attempts by China to improve diplomatic relations with the USA—by Zhou Enlai in the mid-1950s, for example—were rebuffed. To be fair, China contributed to her own isolation. The bombardment of Quemoy in 1958, Chinese criticism of the USSR for backing down over Cuba, and China's war with India in 1962, did little to convince either the US administration or China's friends in America that the intentions of the People's Republic were wholly peaceful. Nevertheless, the notion in some American circles that China's aims under Mao were primarily expansionist was more than a little fanciful. For example, China provided no more than material aid to Vietnam; it did not deploy ground troops. Maoist China was not bent upon building the 'blue water' navy needed to invade Taiwan or to establish naval supremacy in the western Pacific. Even the guidance systems being developed for its nuclear missiles were primitive—thus ruling out any notion that China was trying to develop a precision, first-strike, nuclear capability.[27]

Moreover, irrespective of American perceptions of Chinese intentions, the strategic position of the People's Republic was further weakened by the breakdown of relations with the USSR. The end of the Sino-Soviet alliance of the early 1950s reflected growing disagreement between Khrushchev and Mao over both foreign and domestic policy. Khrushchev's tentative steps towards improving Soviet relations with the USA infuriated Mao, as did Soviet criticism of the Great Leap Forward. These disagreements culminated in the withdrawal of Soviet technicians from China in the middle of 1960. Nevertheless, the Soviet Union was not seen as especially threatening until the late 1960s when a series of border disputes escalated into full-blown crisis. Border classes occurred in Manchuria in March 1969, and in Xinjiang in August. Thereafter, the Soviet Union was seen as every bit as serious a threat to China as the USA.

The unremitting hostility of the USA towards China, and the breakdown of friendly relations with the USSR, necessarily conditioned economic policy in the People's Republic. The inward-looking industrialization strategy of the Great Leap Forward was in no small part a recognition that China could not rely upon foreign trade; as a result, Chen Yun's alternative proposals for the Second Five-Year Plan were quickly rejected (Lardy and Lieberthal, 1983). A more significant response to China's isolation was its nuclear-weapons programme, which was begun in the 1950s. Although handicapped by the withdrawal of Soviet specialists, the programme was brought to a triumphant conclusion by the detonation of a nuclear device in October 1964. Nevertheless, this explosion by no means guaranteed Chinese military security. This security depended both upon China's capacity to construct a satisfactory launch vehicle for its new weapon and, equally importantly, to ensure that its launch vehicles would survive any 'first strike' by either the USA or the USSR. Given that China lagged well behind in developing submarine-launched ICBMs in the 1960s, the only option was to develop well-hidden underground launch facilities. Two other military considerations were at work in the mid-1960s. First, there was a need to develop a more spatially diversified industrial sector. China's industrial heartlands in Shanghai and Liaoning were both extremely vulnerable to both nuclear and conventional attack. The best way to circumvent this vulnerability was to create a new industrial base in the west of China. Secondly, in order to help counter American encroachments in Indo-China, there was a case for establishing new heavy industrial plants in south-west China. From there, it would be much easier to channel supplies to Vietnam. Out of all these various considerations was born the Third Front, the vast programme of defence industrialization in western China (Naughton, 1988; 1991; Gu, 1985; Lin and Gu, 1985). The programme was launched by the Central Committee in 1964 and was explicitly cast in terms of preparation for war. However, it did not really get under away in some provinces until the end of the 1960s, probably because deteriorating Sino-Soviet relations at that time gave the programme new impetus; in Hunan, for example, it only began in earnest in 1969 (Liu, 1990). Not surprisingly, the Third Front led to the wholesale diversion of investment resources from civilian purposes towards militarily-orientated heavy industry.

But what the Third Front did was to give China the capacity to deter nuclear aggression. By the mid-1970s, its nuclear launch sites were well hidden in western China and gave the People's Republic the capacity to reply to even a heavy nuclear attack. Similarly, China's industrial base was so diversified by the end of the 1970s that even a massive conventional attack could not destroy its industrial capacity. Accordingly, the vulnerability of China to either American or Soviet aggression was much reduced by the time of Mao's death. The final piece of the jigsaw slotted into place at the end of the decade: the development of suitable launch vehicles (Lewis and Xue, 1988: 210–15). By 1966, China had deployed its medium range DF-2 missile, capable of hitting targets in the USSR and US bases in Japan and the Philippines. The longer range (4,800 km) DF-4 came into service in 1971, but it was not until 1979 that China's first genuine ICBM, the 13,000 km DF-5, was deployed.

The development of this launch vehicle, as well as the success of the Third Front, meant that China was no longer seriously threatened by the USA at the beginning of the 1980s. To be sure, the People's Republic was still no more than a middle-ranking nuclear power. Its DF-5 was not tested at full range until 1980 and its launch vehicles were few in number. Nevertheless, it possessed a formidable capacity to respond to any first strike, and its industrial structure was far too diversified to make it especially vulnerable in a conventional war. Furthermore, the American threat had itself diminished in importance by 1980. Nixon had visited China in 1972; this, in conjunction with US withdrawal from Vietnam and Cambodia, led to a steady improvement in diplomatic relations between the USA and the People's Republic, and culminated in diplomatic recognition for China in 1979. All this meant that, by 1980, the need for further defence industrialization along the lines of the Third Front had disappeared. China was able to reorientate its development strategy, and out of this was born the transition policies of the Dengist era. Had China's strategic vulnerability persisted into the 1980s, it is very unlikely that late Maoist development strategy would have changed so markedly. Chinese nationalism remains as virulent as ever, but its capacity to influence economic policy is much more limited precisely because China's strategic vulnerability is a thing of the past.

5. The Internal Determinants of State Autonomy

5.1. The Legitimacy of the Communist Party

The most important question that needs to be answered about China's transition is why the authority of the Communist Party remain largely unchallenged even though it had presided over two decades (1957–78) of stagnant material living standards, a devastating famine in which 30 million died, and a 'cultural revolution' that went far towards the destruction of China's intellectuals. The logical corollary ought surely to be that the Chinese state of the late 1970s was much more *feeble* than states elsewhere in East Asia. Yet the evidence points to the conclusion that the Chinese state was if anything stronger.

This strength did not derive from the support of the military; indeed, it would be quite wrong to see the Dengist state as little more than a military dictatorship. To be sure, Deng Xiaoping had strong links with the upper echelons of the PLA from the 1930s. Indeed much of his reputation in the early years rested on the role he played as political commissar in the Second Field Army alongside Liu Bocheng in the late 1940s (Yang, 1993: 454–6). The power of the military is also illustrated by the protection they gave to Deng Xiaoping in Guangdong after his third fall from grace in 1976, and by the arrest of the 'Gang of Four' on 6 October 1976 by units of the PLA. Nevertheless, it is hard to see either state socialist countries in general, or China in particular, as being under the control of the military. In the USSR, for example, Stalin's ability to eliminate Trotsky, Zinoviev, and Kamenev, and Bukharin, Rykov, and Tomsky—and thereby seize power—owed little to support from the military. Moreover, Stalin was even able to liquidate the leadership of the Red Army in the bloody purges of 1937–9 (Volkogonov, 1991). The assumption of power by General Jaruzelski in Poland in 1981 was the exception that proved the rule. As for China, the military were undeniably powerful in the late 1960s. This reflected the threats posed to the independence of the Chinese nation state by the USSR and the USA, and the key role played by the PLA in suppressing the Red Guards in January 1967. Both factors enhanced the status of the military as the only force capable of safeguarding the Chinese Revolution, and made Lin Biao, the Defence Minister, the only real choice as Mao's successor. But even at the zenith of Lin's power, the military remained subordinate to the Party. For example, Lin's attempt to seize the Chairmanship of the CCP at the 2nd Plenum of the 9th Central Committee (at Lushan in August–September 1970) was easily defeated by Mao. Moreover, Lin's attempted coup in September 1971 was a dismal failure which (probably) ended in the crash of his aircraft in Mongolia as he fled from the People's Republic.

The dominance of the Party over the military was even more marked at other times. Peng Dehuai, the Defence Minister, was summarily dismissed at Lushan in 1959 when he criticized Mao over the Great Leap Forward and his attitude to the professionalization of the army. Peng favoured closer military links with the USSR and a more professional army, whereas Mao wanted China to have an independent nuclear capability, more emphasis on guerrilla tactics, and a larger militia. But although Mao's vision antagonized many sections of the military, they were unable to prevent Peng's dismissal.[28] There are other examples of the relative impotence of the PLA. Many senior members of the PLA were concerned that Deng's rehabilitation after 1976 would lead to their own dismissal because of the role they had played in supporting the terror of the Cultural Revolution. But although they (notably Ye Jianying) tried to prevent Deng's return by supporting Hua Guofeng, they were unsuccessful (MacFarquhar, 1993: 311–16). Another example of the weakness of the military is the ease with which defence cuts were imposed in 1980 and 1981; the decision to make cuts was of course helped by the army's dismal performance in the war with Vietnam in early 1979. Army numbers were further reduced in 1984/5, and a number of senior officers were retired at the same time without precipitating a military coup. Furthermore, it is hard to see either the suppression of the Red Guards in January 1967, or the Tiananmen massacre of 1989, as military coups. Yang Shangkun had played a key role in the latter and, with Deng close to death, appeared as an increasingly likely successor; yet Yang and his faction were successfully purged in 1993. In any case, the suppression of the Democracy movement was ordered by Deng, rather than being an independent act of will by the PLA. The same is true of the intervention of the PLA in the Cultural Revolution in January 1967, when it was simply acting upon Mao's instructions. As Harding (1993: 198) says:

> . . . the main beneficiaries of the seizure of power was the PLA, as the country fell under military rule. But military intervention in Chinese politics in early 1967 occurred at the behest of civilian authorities in Beijing, not in defiance of them. If the events of January 1967 in China amounted to a revolution, in other words, it was a revolution from above; and if they resulted in military rule, then that outcome reflected the decision by one civilian faction to use military force to overthrow another, rather than a military coup against civilian authority.

In other words, the authority of the CCP in China did not rest on support from the military, probably because the armed forces themselves were disunited—never more obviously in how to deal with the student-worker protests of 1989.

The legitimacy of the CCP seems instead to have rested upon its historical record. To be sure, average levels of material consumption had probably increased little compared to the 1930s, and the devastation wrought by both the famine of the early 1960s and the Cultural Revolution could not easily be forgotten. But on the other side of the scales, the CCP had won the Revolution. It had safeguarded China against the foreign threat and had resisted the imperialist encroachments on Chinese soil that had marked the late nineteenth and early twentieth centuries. Perhaps above all, the CCP had raised the living standards of the bulk of the rural population. Land reform and nationalization had ensured that the distribution of consumption was far more equal even though average per capita incomes improved but little, and the Maoist regime had presided over an unprecedented rise in life expectancy and in literacy. To be sure, the record since 1958 was less good. Despite the successful development of nuclear weapons and continuing improvements in education and health, the famine of the early 1960s and the instability associated with the height of the Cultural Revolution (1966–8) had weakened the hegemony of the CCP. Nevertheless, its legitimacy was not really in question at the end of the 1970s, not least because it was a simple matter to blame many of the failures of late Maoism on the baleful influence of Lin Biao and the Gang of Four.

5.2. The Authority of Deng Xiaoping

As important as the continuing legitimacy of the Communist Party in forging the autonomy of the Chinese state was the political stature of Deng Xiaoping. Indeed, one of the key reasons for the successful implementation of the gradualist transition within China as opposed to the Soviet Union and Eastern Europe was the respective standings of Deng Xiaoping and M. S. Gorbachev. Gorbachev was a newcomer to the Soviet stage. He had no luminous war record, and the days had long passed when Soviet leaders could point to the role they had played in the Revolution. He had only been brought to Moscow in 1978, having previously been the First Party Secretary in lowly Stavropol. This contrast between China and the USSR reflected the fact that Stalin's purges were infinitely bloodier than China's Cultural Revolution. Stalin's' victims were invariably executed, whereas many of Mao's survived. In fact, the Soviet equivalent of Deng would have been Nikolai Bukharin, and Bukharin would have been younger at the time of Stalin's death than Deng was when Mao died in 1976. But Bukharin had been executed in March 1938. By contrast, Deng Xiaoping was very much alive.[29]

As a result, the generational difference between Deng and Gorbachev meant that Deng enjoyed far greater prestige. He had gone to France in 1920 at the age of 16, and had played an important role in producing the improbably-named *Red Light*, journal of the Communist Youth League. Back in China, his career went into apparent eclipse following the rout of the Seventh Army (of which he was political commissar) and his disagreement with the Comintern line that revolution in China in the early 1930s would be 'premature'. This latter led to Deng losing all his leadership positions in May 1933 (Yang, 1998: 75). However, Deng was doing no more than supporting Mao Zedong in disagreeing with the Comintern view and this helped him to win the friendship and support of Mao, a friendship that probably saved him from death during the Cultural Revolution. Furthermore, the Comintern line was discredited by the military defeats suffered by the Red Army in 1934, and which ultimately forced it to begin the Long March west and north to escape Chiang Kaishek's troops. This allowed Mao to gradually assume control of the Party, and with his triumph at the Zunyi meeting of the Politburo in January 1935 (at which Deng took the minutes), Deng's promotion was assured.[30]

This involvement in the early stages of the rise of the Chinese Communist Party was instrumental in Deng's assumption of power in the late 1970s. His association with Mao conferred upon him a degree of legitimacy; whatever Mao's failings, the Party decreed that his achievements outweighed his mistakes even in the revisionist atmosphere of the late 1970s (Central Committee, 1981). Deng had participated in the Long March, something which was almost a sine qua non for leadership in the 1980s.[31] He had also been heavily involved in the activities of the Red Army (as political commissar of the Eighth Route Army's 129th Division) during the war against Japan. This gave him important contacts and prestige within the army in the years after 1949.

At the same time, Deng could portray himself as a critic of the worst excesses of Maoism. The point should not be exaggerated. Deng played a key role in orchestrating the Anti-Rightist campaign of 1957 which put an end to the 'Hundred Flowers', and seems to have voiced little opposition to the Great Leap Forward (MacFarquhar, *et al.*, 1989: 18; Shambaugh, 1993: 485; Goodman, 1994: 58).[32] Nevertheless, Deng was by no means a Maoist puppet. He took that view that the pace of collectivization was too fast in the mid-1950s (Teiwes, 1993: 508).

Deng also became increasingly critical of the Great Leap Forward after 1960 (Shambaugh, 1993: 467).[33] He was perhaps fortunate to be absent from the crucial meeting at Lushan Plenum (July–August 1959)—at which Peng Dehuai was consigned to oblivion for his temerity in criticizing the Leap—because of a broken leg.[34]

More importantly, Deng was purged twice during the Cultural Revolution. In September 1966, and having been General Secretary of the Party for the previous decade, he was an obvious symbol of the Party bureaucracy. As he had also played a key role in the market-orientated policies of 1962–5, Deng was also vulnerable to the accusation of being a 'capitalist roader'. He was therefore an early victim of the Cultural Revolution and lived in an isolated house in Zhongnanhai between early 1967 and October 1969 (Yang, 1998: 168–9). Deng was sent to live in Xinjian County, Jiangxi in October 1969, and remained there until February 1973, when he was rehabilitated and returned to Beijing. However, he was purged for the third time in the spring of 1976 by the Gang of Four following the death of Zhou Enlai and Deng's implicit support for demonstrations against the Gang in Tiananmen Square in April.[35] Deng was therefore very much a victim of the Cultural Revolution. He suffered much less than did some; Liu Shaoqi, for example, died in November 1969. Nevertheless, Deng's status as victim, veteran of the Long March and accomplished administrator made him the most credible candidate as Mao's successor.

Furthermore, his authority was cemented by the centrist line he adopted in the 1980s. Despite the emphasis that has been placed in the literature on the way in which Deng advocated the pursuit of profit and entrepreneurship, many of his speeches make plain his dislike of unbridled self-interest. His speech at the 2nd Pleaum of the Twelfth Central Committee in October 1983, in which he attacked the literary establishment for its pursuit of material advantage, is one example of this. Furthermore, the standing committees of the Politburo in the 1980s tend to balance the views of the liberals and conservatives within the Party. The September 1982 standing committee balanced party veterans Chen Yun, Li Xiannian, and Ye Jianying against Hu Yaobang and Zhao Ziyang, with Deng as the sixth member; the November 1987 standing committee comprised conservatives such as Li Peng, Qiao Shi, and Yao Yilin alongside the 'liberal' Zhao Ziyang and Hu Qili (MacFarquhar and Fairbank, 1987: 536–7). Moreover, in the spiritual pollution campaign of 1983, Deng was careful to hold in check the attacks of Deng Liqun on Hu Yaobang. It is this centrist stance adopted by Deng that helps to explain the governed-market approach to economic growth adopted in China during the transition period; neither markets nor planning were allowed complete control. Only with Deng's incapacity after 1992 did the CCP begin to swing decisively in favour of privatization.

Deng's accession in the late 1970s owed much to the Chinese tradition of one-man leadership. Elite politics within the People's Republic has often been interpreted as a 'two-line struggle' between right and left in which Mao was never able to exercise real dominance until the mid-1960s. For example, the economic policies of 1962–5 have often been seen as reflecting the temporary ascendancy of Deng Xiaoping and Liu Shaoqi following the debacle of the Great Leap Forward.

Teiwes, however, has strongly disagreed with this interpretation. The title of his book *Politics at Mao's Court* gives the flavour of his essential conclusion: that Mao should be seen as de facto Emperor:

> . . . in any elite debate, when Mao chose to assert himself, he got his way. The Chairman was the pivot of leadership politics, and the nature of conflict had much more to do with winning Mao over to one's favored position than with opposing him. Opposing Mao in the policy sense—once Mao's position was clear—was rare; opposing Mao in the political sense was unheard of. (Teiwes, 1993: p. xv)

David Goodman has taken the same view. According to him, the notion of extensive disagreement between Deng and Mao before 1966 is 'easily exaggerated' (Goodman, 1994: p. viii). Moreover, the events of 1962–5 broadly support Teiwes' view. For example, Mao was on the opposite side to Liu Shaoqi and Deng Xiaoping in early 1962 on the question of household quotas in famine-stricken provinces such as Anhui. Mao's triumph, however, in this debate was never in doubt.

Perhaps even more remarkably, Deng was able to exercise an hegemony as absolute as Mao's once he had shifted Hua Guofeng and his supporters to one side after 1978. Deng was instrumental in suppressing the demonstrations of 1989, purging Zhao Ziyang in the aftermath of Tiananmen, and in purging Yang Shangkun and Lin Biao in 1992–3. He injected new momentum into the transition process during his 'southern tour' of February 1992. Even on his deathbed, the Chinese leadership candidates dared not act. In other words, Chinese politics after 1949 were characterized in essence by personal rule, first by Mao and later by Deng. According to Teiwes (1993: p. lxiii):

> . . . [the] impulse to obedience was reinforced by both the authoritarian traditions of the international Communist movement and China's 'feudal' past, both of which created pressure for ideological conformity and veneration of the top leader . . . a political culture of submissiveness existed at both high and low levels within the CCP. While the formal quasi-democratic norms corresponded to real leadership values and expectations, ultimately they were less powerful than the need to have someone 'in charge' (*zhuchi*), a need naturally growing out of the search for dynamic leadership of the perilous revolutionary enterprise yet fully compatible with and influenced by traditional culture.

Goodman (1994: 86) puts even greater emphasis on the strength of Deng's position in the late 1970s:

> Deng's position, despite being formally outside the leadership, was almost impregnable. From the moment Mao died Deng Xiaoping was considered the leader in exile, and from the moment the Gang of Four was arrested, Deng was the leader in waiting. . . . Deng had been closer to Mao Zedong and those who supported him in the leadership—and particularly those who supported him well before he Cultural Revolution—for considerably longer than any of those in the Gang of Four, or even the group that supported Hua Guofeng. His claim to leadership was firmly grounded in his relationship to Mao. . . . At the same time, Deng had decades' worth of organizational and political associations which he could, and did, mobilize for political support, as for example from his time in the CCP Secretariat before the Cultural Revolution and his work as a Vice-Premier since his return in 1973.

This ascendancy was reinforced by the rapid growth of the economy after 1977, and by the successful decollectivization of agriculture. Once established in that position, Deng's power was close to absolute.

5.3. The Distribution of Power and the Weakness of Civil Society

Yet perhaps the key reason for the hegemony of the CCP was not so much the weakness of intra-Party factions opposed to transition, but rather the weakness of *civil society*, and in particular the absence of factions within civil society possessing significant economic power (interest groups).

In recent years, the (related) notion that an equitable distribution of *income* provides the conditions for the establishment of a growth-promoting state has gained currency. The basic idea in much of the literature is that there is a positive relationship between equality and economic growth. It is not so much that income equality per se is good for growth, but rather that equality makes it easier for governments to implement growth-promoting development strategies. According to Persson and Tabellini (1994: 600):

> . . . incentives for such productive accumulation hinge on the ability of individuals to appropriate privately the fruits of their efforts, which in turn crucially hinges on what tax policies and regulatory policies are adopted. In a society where distributional conflict is more important, political decisions are likely to result in policies that allow less private appropriation and therefore less accumulation and less growth.

In other words, income equality breeds political stability, which in turn promotes higher investment. More generally, Rodrik (1996: 20–1) gives three arguments linking equality and growth. First, the governments of egalitarian societies do not have to deal with powerful interest groups.[36] Of all the arguments on offer, this is surely the most convincing because there are many examples of high-income groups blocking growth-promoting strategies. The main obstacle to health-care reform in the USA in the 1990s was not Hillary Clinton but rather the financial power of the tobacco and private health-insurance lobbies.[37] Japanese imperialism in the 1930s was—at least in part—a product of the desire of *zaibatsu* to increase their profitability; land reform was blocked by Japanese landowners in the same decade (despite the clear-trend deterioration in agricultural performance over time). Land reform in China during the 1930s was impossible for the Kuomintang because many of its most influential supporters were landowners. Pressure for land reform in Brazil in the early 1960s led to a military coup aimed at preserving the unequal distribution of land ownership. In the Soviet Union, the urban elite had much more by way of entrenched economic and financial privilege than in China, largely because of the unremitting attack on privilege in the latter in the 1960s. It was correspondingly much more reluctant to see the break-up of the old order. This does not mean that interest groups have never been overcome without bloodshed. Daniel arap Moi, for example, was able to redirect Kenyan economic policy after 1978 even though this conflicted with the interests of the economically powerful Kikuyu tribe in export-orientated agriculture and who had enjoyed a largely unchallenged position during the Presidency of Kenyatta (Bates, 1989: 137). The Corn Laws were repealed in Britain in 1846 despite the opposition of landed interests. Nevertheless, it is clear that the absence of powerful vested interest makes the task of transition much easier.

The second argument suggested for the link between equity and growth is that there is less political pressure to redistribute income more equitably in such societies; if one assumes that there is a trade-off between redistribution and accumulation, this implies a higher investment rate and therefore faster growth. In other words, it is not that inequality per se hinders growth but the policies adopted to reduce it. In fact, the argument and evidence presented by Persson and Tabellini (1994) is quite the contrary. They show that for authoritarian regimes there is a correlation between growth and *inequality*. Authoritarian regimes are much less susceptible to political pressures arising out of inequality than democracies and in narrowly economic terms a high profit share encourages investment, both because it is seen as a rent and because it provides the finance for accumulation. In fact, the Persson–Tabellini argument is essentially that initial equality is desirable because it allows the income distribution to become more *unequal* (which, they assume, is what growth requires) without significant social pressures building up.[38] This notion that equality is desirable because it allows more inequality must be one of the more bizarre results to emerge from the literature in recent years.

The third argument linking growth with equity is that, in the absence of a distributional 'problem' in need of urgent remedy, governments are able to focus all their (bureaucratic) attention on generating rapid growth instead. If one makes the assumption that effective civil servants are usually in short supply, this argument makes sense. Without a focus on growth, states may be forced to draft in expertise from the army, as happened in South Korea under Park and Chile under Pinochet. Whilst that may alleviate the problem in the short run, the involvement of the military in politics runs the risk that policy will bc subordinated to military objectives—with disastrous long-term results. One thinks of the obsession of the Argentine military with the recovery of the Falkland islands at the end of the 1970s, and the influence of the Japanese military in the 1930s.

The appeal of an approach linking rapid growth to income equality is not just the intrinsic desirability of equality but also that the idea has been supported by a number of empirical studies. Several of these have reported that inequality is negatively related to average national life expectancy, primarily for psychological reasons; moreover, the life expectancy of those on middle and high incomes is reduced by inequality, not just the life expectancy of the poor (Wilkinson, 1994). There are also several studies which show that countries where income is distributed more equally tend to grow more quickly (Alesina and Perotti, 1992; Alesina and Rodrik, 1994; Persson and Tabellini, 1994; Corry and Glyn, 1994; Rodrik, 1995). Even the World Bank reached this conclusion in its study of the rapid growth achieved in East Asia (1993*a*: 29–32).[39]

Perhaps even more importantly, one of the great appeals of this emphasis on a high degree of equality as a desirable precondition for successful transition to a growth-promoting regime is that it offers an explanation of the success of the 'governed-market' model in East Asia. That is, Japan, South Korea, and Taiwan were all characterized by a low level of inequality in the early years of their development such that the fruits of growth were comparatively widely shared in the initial years of growth. According to Rodrik (1996):

> . . . in all of them [CMB: the East Asian economies] the distribution of income and wealth around 1960 was exceptionally equal by cross-country standards [p. 20] . . . [more generally] the initial level of income equality around 1960 is shown to be robustly and positively correlated with growth over the next three decades, controlling for other initial conditions such as per capita income and educational attainment [p. 21].

The key element in each case was a thoroughgoing land reform, which broke up large estates and transferred the land to small-scale family farmers. In Japan, the Allied forces of occupation under MacArthur carried out reform between 1946 and 1950. All holdings in excess of one hectare were purchased by the government and sold to tenant farmers. This reduced the share of land under tenancy from 45 per cent in 1945 to 9 per cent in 1955 and, to prevent the re-emergence of landlordism, a ceiling of 3 hectares on subsequent land holdings was enforced (Hayami and Yamada, 1991: 84–5). The collaboration of South Korean landlords with the Japanese, and the elimination of landlordism in the North, undermined their own position. As a result, land reform was launched by the American occupying forces in 1948; this redistributed the land formerly held by Japanese landlords to their tenants. An agrarian reform law was passed in March 1950, setting a 3-hectare ceiling. However, the temporary occupation of South Korea by the North led to more radical redistribution and, with this precedent to hand, post-war land reform was also more radical and culminated in average landholdings per household of about 1 hectare (Sobhan, 1993: 30–1). As Hart Landsberg (1993: 131) notes:

> Perhaps somewhat ironically, it was this revolutionary land reform [CMB: which followed invasion by the North] that finally broke the power of the large South Korean landowners and made possible Syngman Rhee's own much more modest post-Korean war land redistribution programme.

In Taiwan, land reform occurred in three phases (Yager, 1988; Selden, 1988; Bain, 1993). First, a 37.5 per cent rental ceiling was imposed in 1949 (compared to an average pre-war rent of about 50 per cent). Secondly, the land formerly owned by the Japanese government and landlords was sold off during 1948–53; most of these sales, which amounted to about 20 per cent of arable area, were made in 1951. Third, the 'Land-to-the tiller' programme of 1953 imposed a 2.9-hectare ceiling on landholdings. The government purchased the excess by issuing low-yield bonds to landowners, and sold the land to tenant farmers at a low price. These major reforms effectively eliminated land ownership as a primary source of inequality. In addition, Taiwan in particular pursued a relatively labour-intensive industrialization strategy. This may have increased inequality initially (only a comparatively small number of agricultural workers were able to move to higher-income industrial occupations) but the scale of employment creation was so vast that the bulk of the rural workforce was absorbed into the industrial sector comparatively quickly. In other words, the 'Kuznets process' (Anand and Kanbur, 1993) was truncated by the intensity and nature of the industrialization process.[40]

This type of approach does seem to offer a key explanation for China's successful post-1978 transition because the position of the People's Republic at the time of Mao's death was similar to that in these East Asian NICs at the start of their industrialization drives. As is well known, the Chinese income distribution was comparatively equal by the standards of other developing countries, although it has certainly become much less equal since 1978 (Table 15.11). This reflected the land reform of 1947–52, the nationalization of industrial assets, restrictions on the private sector, and curbs on wage and workpoint differentials.

The data on the Chinese distribution should not be taken to mean that inequalities were insignificant at the end of the 1970s because this ignores the urban–rural income gap. This was the principal outstanding type of stratification remaining in 1978 and the urban population were conscious of their position as a group receiving substantial subsidies: housing, transport, health, education, and meals. Moreover, any attempt to reduce the well-being of the urban population was high risk. Mao had done so by stripping cadres of their posts and despatching them to the countryside. Many urban youth had suffered a similar fate. But the post-1978 leadership did not possess the prestige enjoyed by Mao at the height of the Cultural Revolution. The very fact that the urban population had been able to acquire a whole raft of privileges during the 1950s and early 1960s for itself was an indication of its capacity to promote its own interests. The Chinese revolution may have been made by the peasantry, but it was no easy matter to remove urban privileges—not least because many of the peasant leaders of 1949 had become the urban cadres of 1978. Conversely, the rural population was keen to improve its position; not for nothing was the urban residency permit an object of desire. The political and economic problem faced by Deng Xiaoping, Chen Yun, and those in the higher echelons in the CCP was therefore to devise a development strategy that raised the living standards of the rural population without reducing the incomes and privileges of the urban population.

Nevertheless, the urban–rural income differential was not as significant as it appears.[41] For one thing, the urban–rural gap in China was less apparent than the gap between the urban rich and poor, and rural rich and poor, in other LDCs; as a result, demands for its eradication were relatively low key. There was still a latent threat to the regime if rural living standards continued to stagnate, but there is little evidence that the rural population was disenchanted enough to wish to launch a second revolution. Secondly, the Chinese urban population faced a collective action problem, composed as it was of very disparate elements, ranging from the 'eight bad elements' to high-ranking cadres. It was not easy for them to make common cause to protect their living standards, and therefore in principle it was possible for the government to reduce their real incomes somewhat without risking a revolt.[42]

Thirdly, it was not too difficult for the state to devise a strategy which raised the incomes of the rural sector without markedly affecting those of the urban population. In fact, the strategy adopted in the early 1980s fitted these requirements admirably. On the one hand, the shift in the terms of trade towards agriculture had an immediate effect on rural incomes. On the other hand, precisely because the retail price of food in urban areas was held more or less constant, the urban population suffered no loss of income. This circle could only be squared by the payment of subsidies, which in turn meant the government had to be willing to tolerate a significant budget deficit. In retrospect, it is clear that the 1978 inheritance was crucial for the success of Deng's programme. If the CCP had inherited an economy operating at full capacity with a substantial fiscal deficit—the norm after all in much of Latin America in the late 1970s—the Chinese growth strategy might well have foundered on the rock of hyperinflation. As it was, Deng inherited not only budget balance but also an infrastructural legacy. By increasing aggregate demand, this supply-side slack could be put to good use in raising rural incomes. In other words, the problem of low incomes in the countryside was resolved by growth—which made redistribution possible. Nevertheless, this strategy would not have worked but for the fact that the urban–rural gap, though quite large by LDCs standards, was not impossible to bridge. Indeed the six years of growth achieved up to 1984 was quite enough to precipitate grumbles of discontent from the urban population, who saw their relative position being eroded by the rising incomes of 'peasant bumpkins'.

In summary, and despite the urban–rural income differential, the similarity between the income distribution in China at the end of the 1970s and the East Asian NICs at the beginning of their 'miraculous' growth is striking (Table 17.3).

TABLE 17.3. *Income inequality at the start of rapid East Asian growth* (gini coefficients for pre-tax income)

Country	Year	Gini coefficient
Japan	1956	0.31
Taiwan	1964	0.32
South Korea	1965	0.34
China	1980	0.28

Notes: Although earlier data exist for Taiwan, the 1964 estimate is the first calculated from a large sample. The figure for China in 1980 is an official estimate by the SSB; the calculation by Adelman and Sunding (1987: 163) for 1978, which uses a much higher estimate of the urban–rural gap, was 0.32.

Sources: Yabuki (1995: 232–4); Tseng and Mao (1994: 268); Hart-Landsberg (1993: 199); Wada, 1975 (cited in Minami, 1998).

Nevertheless, we need to be wary about accepting the notion that it is easy to create a growth-promoting state by income and asset redistribution.

The main problem is that asset redistribution is not a simple task, and yet asset redistribution is usually a sine qua non for growth.[43] Even an apparently innocuous measure such as the formalization of property rights in law has a distributional implication because it limits the ability of powerful groups to exercise their power in an arbitrary manner. In a feudal economy, the main problem is that land is held by a class which has conspicuous consumption rather than accumulation as its aim. In nineteenth-century Tokugawa Japan, for example, much of the 'surplus' (output less necessary consumption) was used up in financing attendance at Court by the *daimyo* (nobility) for six months in every year. Economic growth required that this surplus was redistributed to those who worked the land and who would reinvest it. According to Dore (1965), there was a need in 1868 for a land reform which would transfer land from Type I (feudal) to Type II (capitalist) landlords. A second rural problem commonly encountered in feudal regimes is that the average size of farms is large; this is disadvantageous because of diseconomies of scale in farm production (at least beyond a certain point). In such circumstances, there is a case for a land reform designed to achieve something closer to the optimal size of farm. Of necessity, this implies a substantial redistribution of income and wealth. Redistribution of assets may also be essential in the industrial sector. Many slow-growing economies are characterized by the high degree of monopoly power exercised by a comparatively small number of affluent families. Although large firms do have many scale advantages, growth promotion may still require reductions in industrial concentration.[44] One thinks here of Germany under Bismarck and late Tsarist Russia. The governments of Eastern Europe and the USSR after 1989 were also confronted with the need for redistribution. In order to provide the resources for investment in excess demand subsectors, it was necessary to transfer resources away from machine building, metallurgy, and defence towards consumer goods. In other words, the sectors and interests long prioritized in the Soviet industrialization drive had to be cut back.

The urgency of such redistribution brings the incoming government into conflict with those vested interests which stand to lose out from the redistribution. An election victory is by itself not enough to ensure legitimacy in the face of such powerful opposition; a stark example of this comes from Allende's Chile. One way out of this dilemma is for the government to make side payments (pay compensation) to those groups who will lose out from income redistribution. This was, for example, the route adopted by the Meiji government in Japan after 1868 (Beasley, 1990; Jansen and Rozman, 1986; Ramseyer and Rosenbluth, 1995). The main losers from the Meiji restoration, the *daimyo* (nobility) and the *samurai* (gentry), continued to be paid stipends. After 1876, the salaries paid to the *daimyo* were converted into bonds with a capital value of five years' worth of income and paying interest at 5 per cent. In effect, they received full compensation under the new regime. Indeed even the *shogun*, though deprived of his title, retained a large estate and was given the highest rank in the new Japanese peerage. The *samurai* were not so fortunate. The bonds they received in 1876 did not provide full compensation, and this played a key role in precipitating the Satsuma rebellion in 1877. However, the fact that partial compensation was paid helped to reduce the scale of the rebellion. Moreover, the *samurai* also gained from the Meiji political settlement in that previous restrictions on their employment were removed. Most importantly, the generosity of their treatment in the early days delayed rebellion until nine years after the restoration, thus allowing the new regime to consolidate its grip on power.

However, none of this is especially useful as a general policy prescription that can be offered to (say) sub-Saharan African countries. The basic difficulty is of course that it is usually hard to make side payments. One problem is organizational; there are substantial transaction costs involved. It is often difficult to identify precisely the losers from any new political settlement; in that sense, Meiji Japan was unusual because the losers were readily identifiable as those receiving stipends by the previous Tokugawa regime. Transaction costs are also likely to be high because of the problem of credibility—how can one persuade the losers from any political settlement that they will be fully compensated? How does one convince potential beneficiaries that they will indeed be better off?[45] This is of course a particular problem for democratic regimes where the opposition party must convince potential losers that they will be adequately compensated if that opposition is to win power. This was precisely the difficulty that confronted the Democrats in the USA and the Labour Party in Britain in the early 1990s. New revolutionary regimes self-evidently do not face this problem in seizing power, but they must still offer credible compensation packages if policy changes are to be accomplished without bloodshed. The second problem with side payments is that a real resource cost is involved. If the aim is to ensure that one group is better off without any other group being worse off (a Pareto improvement)—which is the only way in which the new political settlement is likely to win a measure of consent—the new regime must be able to generate an increase in real per capita output in the short run. Alternatively, the new regime can borrow from abroad. This is exactly what Japan did in the early 1870s, and post-1989 Russia too has received significant loans from the IMF to ease the process of transition. But again the problems speak for themselves. It is not easy to borrow from international agencies or other governments, nor is it easy to generate growth in the short run.

In practice, there are two implications. First, an incoming government must simply hope that it inherits a high degree of income equality. It was not the growth-promoting regime itself that was primarily responsible for the high degree of equality in post-war Japan, Taiwan, and South Korea; one cannot view equality in these three as endogenous. In South Korea, rapid growth began only after the successful coup of 1960 which brought General Park to power. Redistribution occurred earlier; land reform, for instance, was a product of the Japanese occupation, the war with North Korea, and US pressure. In Japan, the break up of the *zaibatsu* and land reform were policies effectively imposed by the US occupying forces. In Taiwan, it is true that Chiang Kaishek presided over the land reform of the 1950s. However, prior Japanese occupation undermined the traditional landlord class and land reform was in essence imposed by the USA via the JCRR. Only after 1958–61 did growth-orientated policies really begin.[46] The unpalatable conclusion, at least from the viewpoint of those who advocate a heterodox explanation of East Asian success, is that the growth miracles of Taiwan, South Korea, and Japan were largely down to 'luck'—if war and occupation can be so described. The same seems true for China. From this perspective, the much-vaunted success of the Dengist regime relied not on the merits of its leader, its strategy or even its (narrowly defined) economic preconditions, but nothing more than chance.

The other implication is that, because side payments are so difficult to arrange, the only way to create the longed-for hard state is by means of revolution—which obviates the need for side payments. If a government has sufficient power, it can simply liquidate the vested interests; one thinks here of the annihilation of the landlord classes accomplished in Russia between 1917 and 1921, in China between 1947 and 1952, and in Cambodia in the 1970s. The disadvantages of this type of 'revolutionary' strategy are self-evident; even putting the morality of such a policy aside, the new regime is likely to lose international support and necessarily incurs a loss of significant human capital. But for most countries, there is probably no alternative but the seizure of power by armed struggle. Yet even this is of little comfort. Just as there is a collective-action problem in arranging side payments, so there is a collective action problem in creating a revolution. Peasants can be revolutionary; the case of pre-war China is proof enough of that. But at best it is a long, drawn-out, and difficult process. One can hardly see it featuring at the top of a World Bank policy menu.

The general hypothesis that income equality is the key precondition for growth is also rather suspect because it is not clear that equality of *income* is what is needed. The theory is contradicted most obviously in the case of Eastern Europe and the former Soviet Union, where all the data on the income distribution suggest a degree of equality comparable with that seen in China and in East Asia at the onset of rapid growth. To be sure, this conclusion is rather stark. Perhaps the official data on EEFSU do exaggerate the degree of income equality because they take no account of the extensive privileges enjoyed by the *nomenklatura*. Yet one would be hard put to claim that there was a high degree of inequality by international standards at the time of Gorbachev's accession, no matter how creative the accounting.

Rather, the key to explaining the divergent paths of EEFSU on the one hand, and East Asia (including China) on the other is the equitable distribution of *power*. As Amsden (1989: 52) rightly says of South Korea:

> The Korean state was able to consolidate its power in the 1960s because of the weakness of the social classes. Workers were a small percentage of the population, capitalists were dependent on state largesse, the aristocracy was dissolved by land reform, and the peasantry were atomized into smallholders.

The distribution of income is of course a major determinant of the distribution of power, especially in a market economy, but it is only one factor. The dominant characteristic of late Maoist China was that a variety of factors, of which income equality was but one, ensured that remarkably few powerful interest groups existed. But the main reason for that was the Cultural Revolution.

5.4. The Institutional Legacy of the Cultural Revolution

It is impossible to explain the autonomy of the Dengist state in terms either of the CCP or the political stature of Deng himself. Far more important was the weakness of the interest groups that opposed the transition to the growth-promoting institutional structures of the 1980s. In this respect, the damage wrought to the Party bureaucracy during the Cultural Revolution played the decisive role. Trotsky (1937) had long anticipated the need for this type of movement in order to prevent bureaucratic ossification in Soviet-type systems,[47] and Olson (1996) has argued that the Cultural Revolution did have this effect:

> in the absence of organizationally destructive events like China's cultural revolution, the theory predicts that the economic performance of stable Soviet-type societies deteriorates over time [p. 77].
>
> The only Communist or once-Communist country that has enjoyed an economic miracle is the one that suffered the cultural revolution (and after this revolution China was ruled by a pragmatic dictator with an encompassing interest in a productive domain) [p. 78].

Deng's ability to preside over an effective transition to growth-promoting institutions in fact owed much to the effects of the Cultural Revolution (1966–76). The scope of the Revolution was enormous; perhaps as many as half a million people died (Harding, 1993: 244). Many of the victims were ordinary citizens. Many were persecuted by the Red Guards. Others were Red Guards themselves who perished in a vain attempt to resist the efforts of the PLA to restore order in 1967. But many were prominent members of the party bureaucracy. Deng himself, as has been seen, was purged twice after 1966. Liu Shaoqi was hounded to death in 1969. In addition, Zhu De was demoted from the Standing Committee of the Politburo, and Lin Biao died in mysterious circumstances in September 1971. In other words, only Mao and Zhou Enlai out of the seven-man Standing Committee of the Politburo in office in 1965 retained their position during the early years of the Cultural Revolution.[48]

Other high-ranking members in the Party were also removed from power. Peng Zhen fell in 1966. Peng Dehuai, purged in 1959, died in 1974. Other members of the Central Committee who were purged included Yang Shangkun (purged 1966), Chen Yun, Luo Ruiqing (chief of staff to the PLA; purged 1966), Nie Rongzhen, Chen Yi (died January 1972), Bo Yibo (purged 1968), Ye Jianying, He Long (purged 1966, died June 1969), Tao Zhu (purged December 1966, died 1969), Lu Dingyi (purged along with Peng Zhen in 1966), and Zhu De (Central Committee, 1981: 601–2; Zong, 1989: 131, 139, 142, 146, 291; Harding, 1993: 163–5, 189). Of the 170 full and 109 alternate members of Ninth Central Committee (elected in April 1969), only 53 had been members of the Eighth Central Committee (Zong, 1989: 147).[49] All this was very different from (say) the 1956 Congress, at which virtually the entire 1945 Central Committee was re-elected, the only obvious exceptions being Gao Gang and Rao Shushi, purged in 1953–4 (Teiwes, 1988: 11). Harding (1993: 242) summarizes the impact of the Cultural Revolution as follows:

> In the central organs of the Party, the purge rate was about 60–70 per cent. Only 9 Politburo members out of 23, 4 secretariat members out of 13, and 54 CC members out of 167 survived the Cultural Revolution with their political position intact. Only about half of the fifteen vice-premiers and forty-eight cabinet ministers remained on the State Council at the end of the movement.

The removal of so many prominently placed members of the Party bureaucracy had the effect of fatally undermining its ability to resist the restructuring of the 1980s, and the Cultural Revolution reinforced the Chinese tradition of personal rule. The bureaucracy did no more than rubber-stamp the decisions of the paramount leader, and one of the characteristics of the Cultural Revolution was that the bureaucracy could be readily circumvented. Once Deng had consolidated his position by 1980, there was no effective check on his authority. The norms of Party government had been destroyed during the Cultural Revolution, and they were not to be easily restored. The checks on personal rule that had been created in the Soviet Union after the death of Stalin simply did not exist in China (Shirk, 1993; 1994). According to Harding (1993: 247):

> the devastating impact of the Cultural Revolution on the CCP, all in the name of preventing revisionism, weakened the Party's ability to resist a restructuring of the political and economic order that went far beyond that which Mao had found so objectionable in the Soviet Union. In short, had there been no Cultural Revolution, it is unlikely that reform in the post-Mao period would have gone as far or as fast.

This impact, and the enormous personal prestige that Deng enjoyed, was the foundation of transition in China after 1978. Indeed, the clearest evidence that China's institutions were different from those of the USSR was the way the new Chinese constitution of December 1982 effectively restored that of 1954—itself imported from the USSR. In other words, the very attempt to restore 'socialist legality' in the early 1980s testifies to just how far such legality had been abandoned in the late Maoist years.

The transition process may also—paradoxically—have been helped by the *xiafang* campaign that was one of the core elements in the Cultural Revolution. Many young urban exiles resented immensely their enforced sojourn in the countryside. But some learned a great deal about rural China in the process, a knowledge that they could not have come by via a conventional urban education. Above all, their exile brought home to them the extent of poverty in the countryside. This imbued some with a fierce desire to bring prosperity to rural areas, and one consequence of this may have been the decision of a number of the young exiles to form one of the key think-tanks of the early 1980s, the Rural Development Group. This organization played an important role in promoting decollectivization as a way of raising agricultural output in the early 1980s. Although the group had little formal power, it was well connected and was therefore able to lobby with considerable success for *baogan daohu* (Fewsmith, 1994: 34–5).

The institutional legacy of the Cultural Revolution in retrospect is plain: it ensured that any leader of obvious legitimacy would face scanty opposition in implementing a programme of transition emulating those pursued elsewhere in East Asia. The privileged groups in the late Maoist era were those associated with the great ministries of heavy industry—especially the 'petroleum faction'—and centred around both the Gang of Four and Hua Guofeng. Nevertheless, these groups possessed very little economic or financial power. In contrast to the Soviet Union, where Stalin's purges were very much a thing of the past, the Cultural Revolution in China cut a giant swathe through the ranks of the elite that had emerged by the early 1960s. Those occupying positions of power in the Ministries had not been there long enough to have amassed anything approaching a fortune. Furthermore, the power of the Gang of Four and Hua Guofeng (and supporters of his like Chen Yonggui) rested on nothing more than their association with Mao. After Mao's death in 1976, their power base collapsed. The Gang of Four were arrested, whilst Hua, Chen, and the rest were gradually moved to one side with barely a whimper of protest.

The military, of course, offered a potential source of opposition. But transition directly weakened its economic position because one of the ways in which price subsidies to the urban population were financed was by cutting the military budget. As it transpired, however, the military did not resist this erosion of its privileges. In part this was doubtless because the privileges of the military were rather limited; the Chinese officer corps enjoyed few opportunities for self-aggrandisement especially after the purge which followed the death of Lin Biao. In part it was also probably because the officer class saw the transition programme as enhancing their prestige. One of Deng's commitments in the 'four modernizations' was to the modernization of the army, and the foreign exchange that could only be earned via the open door offered a plausible means by which the PLA could be modernized. In the eyes of many officers, the Maoist idea of a 'people's war' was redundant in the nuclear age. This view was underlined by the dismal performance of the army in the war against Vietnam in the late 1970s. In any case, the developing rapprochement with USA and China's development of its own ICBMs made a strategic defence system like the hugely manpower-intensive Third Front unnecessary.[50]

The absence of powerful interest groups also eased the path of local government in the People's Republic. In rural areas, few households had a vested financial interest in the old order. The most lucrative 'possession' from the Maoist era was a job in a non-farm enterprise, and it was clear to all concerned in the late 1970s that employment in these enterprises would expand rather than contract in the years ahead; that, indeed, had been the aim even of Mao. Furthermore, decollectivization itself held the prospect of the acquisition of farm capital and, for former rich peasants and landlords, perhaps even the recovery of their former estates. The absence of concentrations of income and wealth also meant that local government was not vulnerable to what might be called 'cooperative capture'—that is, the capture of cooperative institutions by landlord interests and the manipulation of those institutions to suit their own ends. This, of course, is precisely what had happened before 1949, when local government was controlled by the landlord class. This class was therefore able to use the power of local government (the militia and the police) to control and divert water—the lifeblood of every Chinese agricultural community—to imprison and expropriate debtors, and to enforce the more dubious of their property rights via a tame judiciary. This problem of cooperative capture, so common in LDCs, is precisely the reason why the combination of local government and an unregulated private sector will lead to suboptimal off-farm investment in comparison to collective farms. The leaders of production teams and brigades certainly did have some power in the late Maoist era, but their position was weak compared to that of wealthy landowners in other countries precisely because of Maoist egalitarianism. Indeed, as inequality has increased in China during the 1980s and early 1990s, so the ability of local government to act in the interests of the whole community has dwindled. The central government tried to prevent this by requiring after 1993 that township cadres were 'outsiders' (that is, permanently resident elsewhere); however, this has created a different problem in that these outsiders have less interest in serving the needs of the communities they govern.

The absence of significant concentrations of economic and financial power in late Maoist China thus made it much easier to introduce growth-promoting institutional structures. In essence this seems to have been because of the absence of powerful interest groups rather than some of the more fanciful theories relating to income equality previously discussed. For example, Rodrik's view (mentioned earlier) that initial equality allows the bureaucracy to concentrate its energies on growth promotion is not very relevant because the Chinese bureaucracy largely ceased to exist during the Cultural Revolution. Moreover, the Persson-Tabellini idea that equality meant there was less need for redistribution, and therefore that investment was higher than it otherwise would have been, is not very plausible. The acceleration in the Chinese growth rate in the 1980s was not due primarily to an increase in the overall rate of investment. On the contrary: the readjustment programme of the early 1980s reduced investment. Moreover, decollectivization and the attempt to confer at least minimal property rights on the rural population did very little to stimulate agricultural investment. In fact, the force driving both the rate and the allocation of investment in the China of the 1980s was the government itself, and not the private sector agents at the heart of the Persson–Tabellini conceptualization of the growth process.

18

Conclusion

It is incontestable that the Chinese economy grew rapidly between the death of Mao Zedong in 1976, and that of Deng Xiaoping in 1997. Much of the growth that occurred in the first two years was driven by cyclical factors; this was a period of recovery from the agricultural depression of 1975–6, and the industrial disruption of 1976. After 1978, however, it is plain that the Chinese economy moved on to a new growth path as a result of the initiation of a gradual process of transition to a market economy that was very different to, and altogether more successful than, the programmes of shock therapy implemented in much of Eastern Europe and the Republics of the former Soviet Union.

In its early stages, the transition towards capitalism was cautious. Launched under the banner of 'readjustment', it drew inspiration more from the halcyon days of Chinese Bukharinism in the 1950s, and Japan's development trajectory after 1868, than from the market economies of the West. Increasingly, however, the goal of reform came to displace that of readjustment, before in turn giving way to a messianic faith in the 'master discourse' of Anglo-Saxon capitalism. Nevertheless, even in the late 1990s, the triumph of the master discourse was not complete. To be sure, the wholesale privatization of state-owned enterprises had been placed on the agenda by the end of 1996 and had been accomplished in some parts of south-east China. Yet growing unemployment forced Jiang Zemin and Zhu Rongji to rein back the privatization programme by late 1998, and the impact of the Asian economic crisis of 1997–8 served to harden their commitment to capital controls. In short, and despite the extent of systemic change after 1978, China's economic transition remained incomplete at the turn of the century, let alone at the time of Deng's death. It was this that allowed it to ride out the Asian crisis relatively unscathed

The Growth Process

The process of Chinese economic growth in the Dengist era was not smooth. Regional inequalities widened, and the economy experienced periods of breakneck growth in 1984–5 and 1992–4 as well as phases of slow growth in 1979–81, 1986, 1989–90, and 1995–6. Genuine doubts also remained in the mid-1990s over the nature and sustainability of the growth process. The official data released by the State Statistical Bureau have long exaggerated the growth of rural industry, and the level of agricultural production in the late 1970s was undoubtedly under-reported, thus inflating agricultural growth rates during 1978–84. Furthermore, much of the acceleration in agricultural growth that did occur would have happened anyway as heavy Maoist investment in chemical fertilizer production, high-yielding crop varieties, and irrigation bore fruit. And, given the low base from which China began its transition, the growth rates attained by the People's Republic were arguably not as impressive as those achieved by many other East Asian economies. State-owned industry continued to operate within its production-possibility frontier, farm output remained vulnerable to poor weather, and China's gastronomic transition means that the demand for grain continued to run ahead of domestic supply. The very fact that the controversial and high risk 'Three Gorges' dam project was launched testified to pervasive energy and (in northern China) water shortages. Additionally, the lives of China's workers and peasants were blighted by the re-emergence of the sort of income stratification last seen in the Republican era. In parts of poor provinces like Yunnan, real rural incomes may even have declined after 1986. This is therefore no time for panegyrics on the Chinese development 'miracle'. There has not been a miracle, nor will there be until the Chinese Communist Party remembers that the opulence of the few has been built upon the exploitation of the many.

Yet for all that, the success of the transition policies in raising the pace of economic growth is undeniable. Deng Xiaoping presided over an economy which grew at around double the rate achieved in the late Maoist era. The growth rate surpassed even that achieved in the 1950s, and was not far below the rates achieved in the most successful East Asian economies. China was particularly successful in increasing agricultural output in the early 1980s, and in creating a sea of new rural industrial enterprises producing consumer goods for a vast domestic and a lucrative export market. Even state enterprises managed to shake off the torpor of the Maoist years and effect significant improvements in labour and capital productivity. Although growth did falter in the late 1980s, the very fact that output increased at around 10 per cent per year between 1992 and 1996 suggests that the 'crisis' of Chinese transition was not at hand at the time of Deng's death.

The bulk of GDP growth during the period 1978–96 was contributed by the industrial sector. Indeed, those areas of the People's Republic which grew most quickly during the transition era did so because of large rises in industrial output. In that sense, it is not inaccurate to talk of an industrial revolution in China in the years after 1978. Furthermore, the industrial growth of the 1980s and 1990s did not merely replicate the pattern of growth in the Maoist era. Rather, the structure of Chinese industrial production changed dramatically. Rapid growth took place in 'traditional' light industry such as food and textiles, long in the doldrums because of Maoist emphasis on defence-orientated heavy industry. But, and more significantly, the transition era also saw the emergence of fast-growing new industries such as pharmaceuticals, chemicals, and electronic engineering. By the mid-1990s, indeed, there was even considerable over-capacity in television production—not of great significance in itself, but symbolizing just how far China had moved down the road towards satisfying consumer demand in less than two decades. Even in poor areas like Liangshan, deep in the mountain fastness of south-west Sichuan, industry was the leading sector in the transition era; and in more prosperous regions like Suzhou, the industrial growth of the Dengist era was both quantitatively and qualitatively different from the Maoist decades which had preceded it.

Nevertheless, and as in the 'classical' cases of Japan and Britain, agriculture played a key role in the Chinese growth process. In purely accounting terms, agriculture contributed as much to GDP growth as did services and industry during 1978–84; indeed, the share of agriculture actually rose above its 1978 value in a majority of provinces in the early 1980s. Furthermore, it was the performance of agriculture that was decisive in raising material living standards in poor regions between 1978 and 1984, as exemplified in areas like Xiangxi prefecture in Henan, Gansu's ethnic minority prefectures, and in mountainous parts of Wenzhou. In every one of China's seven poorest provinces, indeed, agriculture contributed more to output growth than did industry during 1978–84. It is therefore accurate to describe growth as agriculture-led in the early days, and the significance of agriculture throughout the Dengist era is reinforced when one looks at its broader contribution to economic growth. Not only did agricultural production rise in order to meet growing demand without recourse on any significant scale to imports, but also agriculture's linkage effects were instrumental in facilitating the growth of the light industrial and construction sectors. It is no exaggeration to say that Dengist economic growth would have foundered but for the massive contribution made by the agricultural sector.

Theoretical Perspectives

At the heart of the master discourse on economic growth assiduously promoted by the World Bank and other Washington agencies is the Solowian view that economic growth is driven by the interaction of initial conditions and capital formation (broadly defined) in poor countries. A recent accounting treatment of Chinese economic growth is typical of this approach; of China's annual GDP growth of 9.3 per cent between 1979 and 1993, 1.3 percentage points at most were due to 'genuine' (total factor) productivity growth[1] whereas 4.9 per cent were due to capital accumulation (Woo, 1998: 33). This illustrates a general theoretical proposition: whilst the capital–labour ratio remains below its steady state value, factor accumulation will dominate. To be sure, the master discourse acknowledges that technical progress will become progressively more important as a country develops, if only because the scope for factor accumulation declines. That is especially so once the country joins the ranks of the exalted (the OECD). But technical progress cannot explain differences in growth rates between countries by assumption. The underlying pace of world technical progress is exogenous, and all countries are assumed to have perfect information on available technologies; the inability of some to 'industrialize by learning' from more technologically advanced countries simply reflects inadequate physical and human capital.

This emphasis on capital accumulation is very convenient. It explains both the rise of the USSR, powered by the defence industrialization launched by Stalin and continued by his successors, and its subsequent fall as the iron law of diminishing returns to capital set in with a vengeance. Even if the 1997–8 Asian crisis proves to be no more than a cyclical downturn, the very fact that growth was driven by capital accumulation implies that East Asian growth will peter out before these economies have attained the per capita income levels enjoyed in the (resource rich) USA. Furthermore, and as a corollary, there is no need to modify the master discourse in the light of the East Asian experience. There is no need to learn from East Asia precisely because its pre-crisis growth has been so conventional in its sources.

The analysis offered by the contemporary master discourse is certainly an improvement on Solow's pioneering work of three decades ago. The emphasis placed on human capital in recent neo-Solowian models deepens our understanding of the growth process. The stress laid on initial economic conditions, both physical infrastructure and social capability, has led to a developing recognition that rapid growth is path-dependent, that history matters. Whether for good or ill, the Maoist era has left an indelible mark on the Chinese economy. All this undoubtedly serves as a good starting point for an analysis of Chinese economic growth in the Dengist period.

Nevertheless, the master discourse is thoroughly pernicious because its approach is so narrow. Three areas of neglect stand out. First, although it cannot be denied that capital accumulation matters, it is hard to believe that neither innovation nor diffusion played any role in driving the growth process in post-war East Asia and the USSR. Some of the attempts at growth accounting have reached this conclusion, but the methodology is so flawed that these results are hard to take seriously; the very fact that all manner of estimates of TFP can be found in the literature serves only to reinforce the point. Even a cursory examination of the evidence shows that the East Asia of 2000 was different from the East Asia of 1950 because it had capital of a superior quality, not simply more capital. In other words, technological change has played a crucial role in transforming the economic landscape of so many Asian countries. This is not to pretend that technical progress occurs in isolation. Plainly it does not. None of the great theorists of the past ever sought to deny the proposition that capital formation matters, and it is a characteristic of the best work on growth that it sees capital formation and technical progress as interdependent. Thus Kaldor emphasized investment's role in embodying technical progress (thereby generating dynamic economies of scale), and Paul Romer stresses the way in which Schumpeterian quasi-rents both finance and reward spending on research and development. But in all these accounts, technical progress is central to the story, and not peripheral as it is in so many orthodox accounts. Accordingly, we cannot adequately explain economic growth in China if we ignore technical progress.

The second problem with the master discourse is that it pays too much attention to the part played by the release of labour in the growth process. To be sure, it is a characteristic of many developing countries that labour productivity in agriculture is lower than in industry. This seems to imply that total output can be increased by the sectoral redeployment of labour. However, this type of analysis—and it features strongly in Sachs and Woo's (1994) explanation of Chinese growth—is fundamentally unconvincing. It downplays the adverse effect on agricultural production of redeployment. It ignores realization problems. It omits to consider the adverse effect of an increasing reserve army of labour on investment in new technologies. And it neglects the adverse impact of labour transfers on industrial productivity; labour is not merely a commodity, to be transferred at will between economic sectors.

The final limitation of the master discourse lies in its superficiality. By focusing its attention on capital formation in particular, and the proximate sources of growth in general, it neglects those factors which offer a deeper explanation of economic success and instead simply argues that 'market forces' are ultimately the key (despite the failure of many market economies across the globe to generate rapid growth). In fairness, this has begun to change in recent years as greater emphasis has been placed on the institutional foundations of economic growth. That the World Bank, for example, devoted much of its 1997 *World Development Report* to the role of the state is indicative of the scale of the shift brought about by Stiglitz in the late 1990s. Nevertheless, the master discourse is never state-centred in its explanation of economic growth. At best, the function of the state is to provide the conditions that will allow private sector accumulation to flourish—namely, secure property rights, the promotion of competition, and the provision of public goods. The role of the state is not, however, to produce; that must be left to the private sector except in extremis.

It should be emphasized, however, that there is little common ground amongst the critics of the master discourse on the role for the state in promoting development. One perspective is that offered by market socialists, which emphasizes the critical importance of state *ownership* of the 'commanding heights' of the industrial sector. A second view is that of the 'governed-market' school in which the need for industrial policy is accepted, but not the need for state ownership. Finally, there is the view of the orthodox Marxist-Leninists, for whom one function of the state is to reduce inequalities in asset ownership on both instrumental and intrinsic reasons. The East Asian states, post-1978 China included, have all neglected this issue and a raft of other developmental issues.[2] For that reason, it is thoroughly misleading to call these states 'developmental'.

Yet whatever the disagreements amongst the critics, they are assuredly right in their charge that the exponents of the master discourse persistently underestimate the pervasive nature of market failure. Of course capitalist economies are capable of faster growth than feudal ones; few heterodox economists—from Marx onwards—have sought to deny that simple proposition. Moreover, capitalist economies have arguably outperformed state socialist economies, if only because the latter have been forced to adopt strategies of defence industrialization in the face of external threats; the historical record does indeed suggest that 'socialism in one country' is unattainable. But there are manifest limits to the capitalist road. The very completeness of the transition to capitalism in nineteenth-century Britain—and with it the abandonment of the institutions through which the state could effectively intervene—made it vulnerable to countries unwilling to accept free trade in its purest form. By the end of the nineteenth century, Britain had been passed by the USA, and many other countries followed in America's footsteps as the twentieth century unfolded. Yet the completeness of the transition to capitalism in the USA made it vulnerable in turn to more interventionist 'late industrializers'. For although the natural resource base of the USA has enabled it to maintain a higher level of (purchasing-power parity) GDP per capita than its rivals, Japan and Western Europe are closing fast, and neither Taiwan nor Singapore are far behind; and all this despite desperate attempts by the USA to impose an Anglo-Saxon capitalist model on these followers. By contrast, those developing countries which have sought to catch up by making a more complete transition to capitalism have not been especially successful. To be sure, some—Malaysia, Thailand, and Indonesia—grew rapidly during the 1980s and early 1990s, but growth was not sustainable precisely because so much of it was driven by the sort of footloose foreign capital that deserted these countries when a better short-run opportunity presented itself.[3] South Korea's liberalization in the early 1990s made it equally vulnerable.

The Maoist Legacy, Investment, and Productivity Growth

The pace of growth during the era of transition was in no small measure a product of the favourable inheritance of the Dengist regime. To be sure, Chinese urban and rural elites suffered during the Maoist era, and many have given vent to this suffering in their autobiographies. The devastation wrought by the famine of the early 1960s is well known. Not perhaps surprisingly, therefore, the accounts of the period rarely acknowledge the economic progress made in the countryside during the first three decades after the Revolution as a result of the consistently high rates of investment that were undertaken. One tangible sign of the scale of this investment drive was the expansion of the irrigated area, which tripled between 1952 and 1978.

Equally significantly, the Maoist era was one during which an extensive transport and industrial infrastructure was created in some of the most inhospitable parts of the People's Republic. Progress was perhaps most apparent in rural areas, and it was here too that the expansion of the educational system had its principal impact. Although elite education suffered, the spread of literacy in rural China was one of the greatest achievements of the Maoist era, and this helped to pave the way for rural industrialization in the 1980s. In other areas also, the Maoist legacy was a favourable one. In contrast to many of the nations of Eastern Europe (especially Hungary and Poland), China entered its transition era with no external debt, and with legitimate hopes of tapping into the capital of the overseas Chinese. Chinese culture, too, was no longer as inimical to modernization as it had been in the late Qing period. The impact of Western imperialism in the nineteenth and early twentieth centuries served to undermine many of the old certainties, and the Maoist attack on traditional village and urban elites served to enlarge the process of creative destruction.

The Dengist regime continued to follow the high accumulation strategy initiated under Mao. Driven by investment hunger at a local level, and acquiesced in by the central government, the investment share increased: during the transition era it averaged around 33 per cent of GDP, a figure comparable with the rate elsewhere in the fast-growing nations of East Asia. Investment was especially high in the industrial sector, and it was this that undoubtedly played an important role in the exceptionally fast rates of output growth that were achieved after 1978. Nevertheless, it is hard to explain the accelerating growth of the transition era purely in terms of a surge in investment. Not only was the increase in the investment share rather modest, but also there were a number of significant failures. Investment in irrigation, for example, was far too low throughout the 1980s, and this contributed to the slowdown in agricultural growth between 1984 and 1993. The transport and energy sectors, if not quite denuded of investment, received far too low a priority, and this neglect contributed to the bottlenecks and inflationary pressures that were increasingly felt after 1988. Perhaps even more importantly, the expansion of rural secondary education that had been the hallmark of the late Maoist period was abandoned as China returned to the more elitist urban-centred educational system it had set up in the 1950s. Moreover, even the effectiveness of primary education declined because of rising drop-out rates amongst girls and in poor parts of western China. Of course one can easily exaggerate these problems, and ignore some of the achievements—such as improvements and university education, and the continued fall in the rate of illiteracy between 1982 and 1990. Nevertheless, it is one of the most remarkable features of the transition in China that illiteracy rates exceeded the national average in two of its fastest growing provinces (Jiangsu and Zhejiang). It seems fair, therefore, to conclude that investment in human capital made rather a modest contribution to economic growth in the Dengist era.

China's transition-era growth has in fact owed as much to large increases in productivity as it has to factor accumulation, although the respective contributions of the two are impossible to measure accurately. Some of the productivity surge reflected intrasectoral redeployment of labour in agriculture and industry. In the former, as the need for single-minded emphasis on grain diminished in line with the waning of the American and Soviet military threats, workers moved away from the production of grain, and towards the production of dairy products, sidelines, meat, and fish. Within industry, the emphasis shifted away from low productivity sectors such as coal and basic metallurgy, and instead towards oil, tobacco, and consumer electronics. All the while, productivity rose.

Nevertheless, Chinese productivity growth in the transition era stemmed from more than simply the reallocation of labour: technological diffusion also played a pivotal role. In agriculture, a key factor behind growth was the diffusion of new seed varieties which had been successfully developed in the Maoist era, and which began to come on stream in the mid-1970s. This process was facilitated by the importation of chemical fertilizer plants from Japan, Europe, and the USA—well before 1978. In industry, too, technical progress was considerable. Despite a number of desperate attempts by some to prove the contrary, there is now a large body of evidence showing that even state-owned industry generated increases in both labour and total factor productivity. This weight of evidence is now so considerable that the defenders of the citadel of the master discourse have been forced to argue not that productivity has been absent—but rather, and in the absence of any evidence, that it is modest and will ultimately peter out.

The Sources of Growth: A Regional Perspective

The plausibility of a heterodox argument in which the growth of the Dengist era was driven by factor accumulation the legacies of the past and by productivity is supported by the experience of a number of China's regions. Liangshan prefecture, spanning the mountains of south-western Sichuan, was one of the slowest-growing regions in the People's Republic after 1978. The prefecture's problem was, to some extent, an inadequate rate of investment; as a result, both its literacy rate and stock of physical capital increased only slowly. But at root, the prefecture was a prisoner of its economic geography which was little affected by the Maoist development strategy. Despite substantial investment in irrigation and transport during the Maoist era, Liangshan entered the 1980s with an infrastructure signally inadequate given its poor soil, and mountainous terrain. The underlying problem was that Panzhihua received the lion's share of Third Front investment in Sichuan during the 1960s and 1970s, and much of what remained went to the rocket-launching site near Xichang, Liangshan's capital. Such an allocation was largely unavoidable given what was perceived to be the American (and later the Soviet) threat to the very existence of the People's Republic, but it did mean that Liangshan's rural hinterland received next to nothing. Liangshan also possessed very little surplus labour. Not only was population density low, but also the bulk of its labour force was perforce employed in the transport sector. Even with the best will in the world—and transport was low on the agenda of the Dengist regime—a colossal investment programme was needed to achieve the level of transport modernization that would have freed Liangshan's workforce for industrial production.

By contrast, Suzhou prefecture laboured under no such handicaps. Its well-watered land ensured high yields, and had been exploited to the full by the expansion of irrigation networks between 1949 and 1978. The agricultural surplus thus generated had in turn allowed investment in rural industry during the 1960s and 1970s. This process was facilitated by one of the legacies of the Western intrusion of the nineteenth century: a sophisticated light-industrial sector, serviced by a comparatively skilled labour force. As a result, and even though the Third Front had passed it by every bit as thoroughly as rural Liangshan, Suzhou entered the Dengist era in a formidably good position to exploit the opportunities that soon opened up. It was, for example, a comparatively simple matter to raise labour productivity. For one thing, the prefecture was a magnet for the inflow of new ideas and technology—the bulk provided by the overseas Chinese, some of whom had been born in the region and forced to flee in the late 1930s and 1940s. Furthermore, the high rate of investment maintained throughout the Dengist era help to embody this technology in new machinery.

Wenzhou and Wenjiang prefectures lay in between these two extremes. Wenjiang faced few of the almost insurmountable physical obstacles that stood in the way of prosperity in Liangshan, and its fabled Dujiangyan irrigation system made possible the exploitation of the new high-yielding seed varieties that became available in the late 1970s. Wenjiang's new-found agricultural prosperity in turn allowed the development of rural industry; for example, the rise of Shifang—Sichuan's fastest-growing county—was based upon the development of its tobacco sector. Nevertheless, Wenjiang grew less quickly than Suzhou because it lacked the latter's inherited industrial infrastructure, and because the skills of its workforce were significantly inferior. By contrast, Zhejiang's Wenzhou prefecture lacked neither skills nor industrial infrastructure, and there was a well-developed history of industrialization; Wenzhou city (Yongjia), for instance, had even been a Treaty port. However, grain yields at the end of the 1970s were already high by international standards, and therefore the scope for big increases was limited. Moreover, the illiteracy rate was higher than in either Wenjiang and Suzhou and, perhaps crucially, the level of investment in education after 1978 was comparatively low. As a result, Wenzhou was unable to move into high productivity industries as quickly as Suzhou.

Bringing The State Back In

The problem with an explanation of Chinese economic growth in terms of the Maoist legacy, productivity growth, and factor accumulation—the approach taken in Part II of this book—is its limited scope. Such an explanation identifies the proximate sources of growth, but it does not address the more fundamental question of whether the acceleration in growth was driven by the introduction of 'market forces', or led by the state.

A substantial proportion of the literature on the economy of the People's Republic in the Dengist era has suggested that the state played a key role in the growth process. Some writers, to be sure, have offered a narrowly neoclassical explanation in which growth is attributed almost entirely to 'market forces' and in which the state is seen as an obstruction to a yet faster growth rate. But the dominant refrain even from those schooled in the precepts of the master discourse has been that the Chinese state played a positive role in the Dengist era. In the long run, most argue, it is imperative to create a fully-fledged capitalist economy, but the likes of Naughton and Jefferson have acknowledged the contribution made by the state to China's rapid growth. A few writers have gone further even than this, arguing that China should aim to realize one of the competing heterodox visions in the long run by combining markets with a powerful industrial strategy on a permanent basis.

The evidence on the economic role played by the Chinese state in the Dengist era discussed in this book points to the positive economic impact of the state. Its financial policy was broadly expansionary. The money supply expanded rapidly in the long run, but without a major inflationary crisis; this reflected rapid real output growth as well as declining velocity. The inflation rate did threaten to get out of hand in 1985–6, 1988–9, and again in the mid-1990s. But in each case, the state was able bring the rate down without having to engineer a major depression; there is scant evidence that the Chinese state was ever unable to exercise macroeconomic control. Expansionary fiscal policy also played a role in promoting growth; that was especially true for 1979–80 and again during 1989–92. Perhaps equally importantly, the state had a decisive impact on the economy by transferring expenditure away from the defence sector, and towards agriculture in 1979. The form that this took—a shift in the internal terms of trade towards agriculture—played an important role in promoting agricultural growth, although the richer, more commercialized, regions benefited most. Significantly, state-engineered price rises also helped to boost dramatically the level of grain output in 1995 and 1996—a clear sign of the continuing importance of the Chinese state.

However, the positive role of the Dengist state encompassed more than merely macroeconomic policy. Aside from relative price changes, one of the reasons for the swift rise in farm output *before decollectivization* was the reform of agricultural institutions and in particular the introduction of group contracting; reduced procurement quotas in poor areas also helped. Decollectivization may have played an important role, but agricultural growth pre-dated the dismantling of the commune; and output in those areas which decollectivized early grew no faster than in latecomers. Moreover, even after the completion of decollectivization in 1983, the agricultural sector was far short of operating along market lines; local government has periodically redistributed arable land, made some effort to maintain the irrigation network it inherited from the communes and promoted cooperation amongst farm households (particularly in mechanized, wheat-growing, areas).

As for the foreign sector, it is clear that the aim of the state was to carefully control China's entanglement with the world economy; its integration was shallow, not deep. To be sure, trade and foreign investment along the eastern seaboard grew exceptionally quickly and there is a clear correlation between this 'opening up' and the pace of GDP growth. But the coastal region grew faster than the interior even during the Maoist period, suggesting its advantage was due more to basic economic geography (notably high-yield agriculture, low transport costs and a historical legacy of skilled labour) than to international trade. Moreover, the Chinese state did not embrace free trade in the Dengist era; tariff barriers, though declining, were high. As a result, and with the probable exception of Guangdong after 1992, Chinese economic growth was not led by foreign trade or investment during 1978–96. Even the growth of the Shenzhen Special Economic Zone owed much to state investment in basic infrastructure in the late 1970s and early 1980s. As for the interior, the impact of the foreign sector was important at the margin, but growth was led by domestic factors. The hypothesis of export-led growth can therefore be rejected, though exports did help to resolve the realization problem in the mid-1990s and thus *sustain* growth.

The key source of growth in the People's Republic was industrialization. This in turn had much to do with those industries owned by central government. These SOEs not only provide the bulk of industrial output even in the 1990s, but also generated sustained productivity growth. In all of this, central government played a critical role. By shifting state investment away from metallurgy and machine building towards energy, traditional manufactures, chemicals, electrical and electronic products, and agricultural inputs, the structure of industrial output was markedly altered, and with it went a faster rate of industrial growth. In addition to this (heterodox) structural adjustment, systemic change also occurred; the Chinese state promoted mergers, encouraged competition, allowed the payment of bonuses, and granted more authority to factory directors. As importantly, the Dengist era was one of rapid rural industrialization, a process led by enterprises that were notionally collectively-owned but in reality were creations of local government. These enterprises seem to have performed at least as well as private enterprises, a conclusion which confirms a truth increasingly acknowledged in the literature; privatization is neither a necessary nor sufficient condition for the rapid growth of an 'efficient' industrial sector.

All this having been said, the Chinese state failed in a number of areas during the transition era. The failures were most apparent in the sphere of infrastructure. State investment in irrigation was allowed to decline, the failure to expand the railway network led to pervasive transport bottlenecks in the late 1980s and early 1990s, and the decision to cut the secondary school enrolment rate in 1977 was a remarkably short-sighted attempt to recreate the elitist educational system of the 1950s. Many of these deficiencies were starting to be made good in the 1990s, but the systematic neglect of the 1980s undoubtedly constrained the pace of economic growth. The implicit counterfactual of faster growth is not implausible; greater investment in infrastructure probably could have been financed by reducing Chinese military spending. Average GDP growth of around 10 per cent per annum in the Dengist era was impressive, but it could have been faster (especially if the official data overstate the true rate of advance). For example, Japan grew as fast during 1950–70 even though its scope for catch-up was much less (higher base level of output and less of a backlog of technology). South Korea grew by 9.4 per cent per annum during 1980–90, despite a very much higher base level of GDP per capita than in China; even in 1994, South Korea GDP per capita at PPP was four times higher than China's (WDR, 1996: 189, and 209).

Yet it is hard to write convincingly of 'failure'. That China was able to grow at a rate almost unprecedented outside East and South-East Asia in a decade characterized by economic crisis in Latin America and sub-Saharan Africa, as well as slow growth in world trade, suggests that state intervention served to increase output growth. Dengist China may not be a model of state intervention (its record on infant mortality, human rights, and inequality makes that word a misnomer) but its record provides further support for the proposition that capitalism is not the best engine of economic growth. The Dengist state was not 'developmental' in the true sense of the word, but it certainly was growth-promoting.

Origins of the Growth-Promoting State

It would be easy to conclude from the experience of China and East Asia that rapid economic growth is merely a matter of the state following the 'right' strategy, and suggest that the countries of (say) sub-Saharan Africa should reject the policies of structural adjustment recommended to them by the exponents of the master discourse and instead pursue selective protection, the promotion of agriculture by relative price changes, reduced military spending, and (crucially) selective industrial policy.

This is the wrong conclusion. The lesson from transition-era China is rather that selective interventionism can work—but only if the state is 'strong'. If the state is weak, then an interventionist strategy is bound to fail because the state will be captured by a series of rent-seeking coalitions pursuing their own interests, rather than the goal of growth promotion. That is precisely what has happened to interventionist governments in Latin America, sub-Saharan Africa, and South Asia. But 'hardening' the state is no simple task. Dictatorship does not offer a simple panacea; on the merits of democracy versus dictatorship, the international evidence is equivocal. Even charismatic leadership will not succeed in the face of implacable interest groups. Nor is the creation of a strong state merely a matter of attacking trade unions, paring down the state bureaucracy, and privatizing public enterprises. This sort of approach is flawed because it focuses only on the obstacles to capitalist accumulation. Such an approach will serve only to reduce a *part* of the inequality of income, wealth, and power that constitutes the real obstacle to the introduction of a state-centred, growth-promoting, strategy. Indeed, the principal opposition to intervention will come from wealthy landowners and both industrial and financial capital; any attack on trade unionism is likely merely to enhance existing inequalities. As a result, a radical and effective land reform coupled with an assault on private industrial capital are necessary preconditions for the implementation of successful state intervention in a developing country. Even then, continued policies of redistribution will be needed in order to prevent the re-emergence of growth-retarding interest groups.

The suppression of growth-retarding interest groups was one of the main achievements of the Maoist era. Land reform, collectivization, and nationalization destroyed the power of landed and industrial capital, and ensured that it could not re-emerge during the 1960s and 1970s; the clearest evidence of that is the relative equal distribution of income in 1978. Moreover, the sustained attack on the Party machine during the Cultural Revolution prevented the emergence of a growth-retarding bureaucracy. Deng Xiaoping's position was immensely strong in 1978 precisely because domestic interest groups were so weak. His legitimacy sprang in part from the pivotal role he had played in the Chinese Communist Party for so long. But it also rested upon the absence of any challenge to his authority, either from within the Party or from without.

This analysis has a number of uncomfortable implications. For one thing, it suggests that the dynamism of the Chinese economy will diminish as income inequality increases, wealth becomes more concentrated, and the power of certain party-based interest groups is enhanced by the abandonment of redistributive policies. These trends have served to make the Chinese state increasingly 'soft', and the willingness of the CCP to embrace (partial) privatization and rapid integration into the world economy after Deng's death is the clearest sign of a willingness to capitulate to the interests of a resurgent capitalism at home and abroad. Secondly, and following on, it will be no simple matter to recreate China's growth-promoting state.

The weakening of the state has already gone so far that tinkering will be of no avail. Without a new revolution, or war and occupation, it is difficult to see how the growing power of China's domestic interest groups can be checked. Both privatization and integration into the world economy will merely strengthen their hand. China has done well in terms of growth since 1978 but, by allowing income inequality to rise almost unchecked during the transition, its growth is unlikely to be sustained. Despite the rapid growth of the Dengist era, the likelihood of China catching up with the West remains slight.

Notes

Chapter 1. Introduction: The Dengist Restoration

1. The term 'East Asia' as used in this book refers to Japan, South Korea, and Taiwan; as will become evident, the role played by the state in China during transition is very similar to that played in these three. The city states of Hong Kong and Singapore are thus excluded from the definition of East Asia, as are the much more outward-orientated economies of South-East Asia (Indonesia, Malaysia, and Thailand).
2. This discourse will also be referred to as the 'Washington consensus', or simply 'the orthodoxy' below. The master discourse is at root little more than the notion that growth is best promoted by the Anglo-Saxon brand of capitalism. The doctrine is assiduously promoted by the World Bank, the IMF, the OECD, and the Economics departments of most universities in the USA and Europe. Its populist organs include *The Economist*, *The Wall Street Journal*, and the *World Development Report*. Wade and Veneroso (1998) call the doctrine the Wall Street–Treasury–IMF complex. The attempts by Stiglitz, chief economist at the World Bank in the late 1990s, to forge what he called a 'post Washington consensus' did little to change the analysis offered by the master discourse.
3. Three motives can be identified in the attack on the East Asian model. First, as mentioned, an attempt to undermine the theoretical basis of the developmental state. Second, a recognition that there was no longer a need to promote industrialization in East Asia in the aftermath of the Soviet collapse. US hegemony in the Far East was no longer threatened by the USSR but rather (potentially at any rate) by the growth of East Asia. As Cumings (1998: 45) points out: 'South Korea and Japan have been sheltered economies, indulged in their neo-mercantilism and posted as engines of economic growth, because of the great value they had in the global struggle against communism. . . . The deeper meaning of the Asian crisis . . . lies in the American attempt to bring down the curtain on "late" development of the Japanese-Korean type.' The third motive is the world crisis of overproduction and excess competition in Western markets which has driven down the rate of profit. The attack on organized labour in the 1980s and 1990s has failed to restore profit margins to the levels seen in the early 1960s during the 'golden age'. The only way to restore these margins is to destroy the industrial base of East Asia, thus reducing global overcapacity (Brenner, 1998).
4. The bulk of the data used in this book to estimate growth rates span the years between 1978 and 1996.
5. This is arguably the reason why the privatization of Chinese SOEs has been actively encouraged by so many visiting Western economists. The abandonment of industrial policy will not only move China closer to the market paradigm but also the resulting unemployment will help to undermine a regime which is the only check on American power in the Pacific.
6. Much has been made of the contribution of surplus labour by the orthodoxy (Sachs and Woo, 1994; World Bank, 1996; 1997*a*; Woo, 1998), but their growth accounting shows that labour transfers contributed no more than about one-sixth. Investment is seen as much more important, typically contributing about half of all output growth.

7. The relatively positive tone of this report doubtless reflects the input of Barry Naughton —who has consistently found evidence of state-sector total factor productivity growth after 1978—as consultant to the World Bank team.
8. As Wright points out, the term *chongxin* (renewal) as applied to the Tongzhi Restoration is rather different in meaning to *weixin* (modernization or reform), the term usually used to describe the 1868 Meiji Restoration in Japan.
9. Although the growth-accounting treatments show little evidence of this; productivity growth plays only a modest role even after 1978.
10. The much larger 1997 study (World Bank, 1997*a*: 5, 107, 113) found that 46 per cent of growth between 1978 and 1995 was unexplained by factor accumulation. Of this, 15 percentage points were attributed to economies of scale and a further 15 points or so to factor reallocation between sectors. This leaves 'genuine' TFP contributing only 15 per cent of growth (somewhat over 1.5 percentage points) to China's annual growth rate of 9.4 per cent between 1978 and 1995. This estimate is very much in line with the IMF study of Borensztein and Ostry (1996: 226–7), who suggest that TFP growth may have been negative between 1979 and 1990 and that underlying TFP growth is 2 per cent per year at best. See also Woo (1998) for similar results.
11. Privatization was promoted in the sense that the state allowed private-sector industry and commerce to flourish free of the restrictions that were the norm in the 1960s—even though little was done to privatize large, state-owned, enterprises.
12. This was especially evident in South Korea, where the removal of capital controls associated with the desire to become a member of the OECD in the early 1990s, fatally weakened the ability of the economy to resist speculative attacks against its currency.

Chapter 2. The Process of Economic Growth

1. The events of this interregnum are discussed in Sun (1995).
2. The 'Two Whatevers' (*liangge fanshi*) group consisted primarily of Hua (Mao's anointed successor) and the 'Little Gang of Four' (Wang Dongxing, Chen Yonggui, Chen Xilian, and Wu De).
3. As well as Deng, whose resumption of office was blocked by the 'whatever' faction until July 1977, the 'practice' faction was based around Hu Yaobang and the provincial leaders Zhao Ziyang (Sichuan) and Wan Li (Anhui). Its growing ascendancy reflected the increasing support offered to it by many highly placed Long March veterans (e.g. Marshals of the PLA); the Guangzhou military command was particularly important in supporting Deng.
4. It took longer to repudiate 'Take class struggle as the key link', the key slogan of the Cultural Revolution. Not until January 1979 was it first suggested (by Hu Qiaomu) that class struggle was no longer the main contradiction, a view accepted by the National People's Congress in July 1979. This enabled the CCP to shift the focus of its work from political to economic issues.
5. For these provincial reforms, see Shapiro (1981), Shambaugh (1982), Wang, L. X. (1988), and Hinton (1990).
6. In more analytical terms, the changes that have occurred since 1978 can be divided into four categories: changes affecting urban state-owned enterprises; agricultural readjustment, marketization, and decollectivization; the promotion of the rural non-farm sector; and the opening-up of China to foreign trade and investment. These changes, and their impact on the economy, are discussed in Part IV of this book.

7. See, for example, the collection of articles edited by Xu (1982). For the views of Chen Yun (the most prominent economist in the CCP) on the priority of readjustment as distinct from reform, see Bachman (1986), and Lardy and Lieberthal (1983).
8. The principals of the Petroleum faction included Xu Xiangqian, Yu Qiuli, and Kang Shi'en. It was not ousted from office until August 1980 (Sun, 1995: 57). The faction was so called because many of its members had risen to power by virtue of their involvement in the successful development of the Daqing oilfield. It also regarded the expansion of oil output as the key to Hua's Ten-Year Plan because oil would generate both the export revenue needed to finance machinery imports and the energy needed to operate those plants (Naughton, 1995*a*: 69–73). As it transpired, the second OPEC oil price rise was more important in raising export revenue than in expanding the volume of oil exports. The dollar value of Chinese exports almost doubled between 1978 and 1980 (LSTJ, 1990: 27).
9. Although one can in general identify the economists based at the State Planning Commission and RenDa with readjustment, and those based at CASS with reform, there were exceptions. The reformist Xue Muqiao was economic adviser to the State Planning Commission, whereas Wang Jiye and Wu Kaitai—both 'readjusters' in that they saw China's economic success in the early 1950s as an affirmation of the effectiveness of planning—were based at CASS.
10. Deng's position during the 1980s was rather ambivalent. His commitment to transition is clear from the 1992 *nanxun*, and he had been largely responsible—in the face of opposition from most Chinese economists—for pushing the radical price reforms of 1988 which aggravated inflationary pressures (Fewsmith, 1994: 220–1). However, Deng made little attempt to sustain either Hu Yaobang or Zhao Ziyang in office when their desire to accelerate the transition process came under criticism. This suggests that the opposition to transition within the CCP was (and perhaps remains) formidable.
11. See for example Nolan (1993; 1995*a*), Naughton (1995*a*), and McMillan and Naughton (1992). The role of the state in Chinese growth is discussed in Part IV.
12. This slogan was coined by Chen Yun at the Central Work Conference of December 1980 (Fewsmith, 1994: 39). This phrase is usually contrasted with Vaclav Havel's 'it is impossible to cross a chasm in two leaps' to distinguish between the transition paths taken in China on the one hand and Eastern Europe on the other.
13. This protocol broke down when Hua Guofeng's Ten Year Plan was largely abandoned after the autumn of 1978, and also because China was unable to meet its target for oil exports; it was hoped that oil output would reach 250m. tonnes by 1985, but even in 1990 production stood at no more than 100m. tonnes.
14. For example, the deflation of the 1920s (ostensibly designed to allow Japan to return to the Gold Standard) was half-hearted; and the programme of monetary and fiscal expansion launched by Finance Minister Takahashi after 1931 was unparalleled in its magnitude outside Germany.
15. At least, Japan succeeded if we regard World War II as an aberration—and not an inevitable product of the process of pre-war development.
16. All growth rates in this book (unless otherwise indicated) are calculated by least squares via the equation: $\ln Y_t = \alpha + \beta_t + u_t$.
17. The contrast is less dramatic if one uses 1952 instead of 1990 constant prices because 1990 prices give a higher weight to agriculture relative to industry than do those of 1952. 1990 constant prices depress the growth rate of NDMP in all three sub-periods because agriculture generally grew much less quickly than industry. However, this procedure

tends to reduce the growth rate of NDMP for 1957–78 much more than that for 1978–93 because agriculture grew exceptionally slowly relative to industry in the late Maoist period. By contrast, and although it still grew less quickly than industry, agriculture's growth was much more impressive after 1978.

18. This is the usual index number problem for developing countries making the transition from an economic structure based on agriculture to one based on industry. The use of a Paasche index (1990 prices) reduces growth rates compared to those derived by the use of a Laspeyres index (1952 prices) by giving a lower weight to the fast-growing industrial sector. 1980 relative prices, which give a lower weight to agriculture than 1990 prices but a higher weight than 1952 prices, offer a compromise between these two.
19. NDMP data are probably preferable to GDP on the grounds of reliability if one wishes to make long-run comparisons. This is because newly published data on gross national product are not especially reliable because so little information was collected before the early 1980s on the size of the unproductive service sector. Nevertheless, GDP data are used wherever possible in this book because they are a more comprehensive measure of income than NDMP data. More significantly, the SSB has abandoned the use of NDMP; the series is not given in ZGTJNJ from the 1995 edition onwards. The use of GDP also of course conforms to international usage, and therefore allows international comparisons to be made more readily. Nevertheless, as a comparison between Tables 2.1 and 2.2 makes clear, the difference in growth rates between NDMP and GDP for the post-1978 period is not especially great.
20. The estimates put forward by Yeh (1979: 104)—which are much more plausible than those of Rawski (see, for example, Huang, 1991)—suggest a GDP growth rate of 1.1 per cent during the Republican period, or about 0.33 per cent per capita.
21. According to Sachs (1993*a*: 140), 'The lack of clarity in China's property rights remains the greatest risk to the Chinese economy.'
22. The idea that living standards have declined in Eastern Europe is denied by Sachs (1993*a*: 145): 'But contrary to widespread misunderstanding, there is simply no evidence of a sharp drop in living standards in Eastern Europe.' The data on rising rates of mortality in particular makes this claim hard to sustain.
23. At the provincial level, total gross industrial output in Jiangsu was overstated by 17 per cent in 1995, and output of collective enterprises by 20 per cent. In Guangdong, the gross output of the *geti* (individual) sector was over-reported by 40 per cent. Compare the data in ZGTJNJ (1996: 404–5) with those in Disanci (1997: 3–5).
24. Chinese data problems are discussed in Naughton (1997), World Bank (1994*a*), and Field (1992).
25. Compare ZGTJNJ (1997: 413) and ZGTJNJ (1995: 377).
26. Even if Maddison's (1998*b*: 56) estimates are accepted, GDP growth for 1978–95 (7.5 per cent) is still far above the figure for 1952–78 (4.4 per cent). In terms of per capita GDP growth, the rate achieved during the transition era is getting on for three times greater than it was during the Maoist period (6 per cent compared to 2.3 per cent).
27. The obvious objection to this interpretation is of course that transition-era China was on balance disadvantaged by its Maoist inheritance. However, as Chapter 6 will show, this line of argument is not very convincing.
28. This counterfactual is not implausible given the evidence that the later a country starts its modern economic growth, the faster it can grow because the gap between LDCs and the world leader has increased over time. Thus Britain's growth rate during the Industrial Revolution was comfortably exceeded by Germany and the USA in the late

nineteenth century. These rates were in turn easily surpassed by Japan, South Korea, and Taiwan after 1950. Thailand's experience since 1985 offers further support for this hypothesis; its growth rate of GDP per capita between 1985 and 1994 was 8.6 per cent per year (WDR, 1996: 188–9), significantly higher than the rate of about 6 per cent per annum achieved by Taiwan and South Korea in their golden age.

29. Although poor weather in 1980 and 1981 meant that agriculture grew considerably less quickly than envisaged. The net value of agricultural output fell by 2 per cent in 1980 (ZGTJNJ, 1992: 34).
30. Hua's Ten-Year Plan (1976–85) was officially announced in February 1978. Its cornerstone was the construction of 120 new large-scale projects and the popularization of the Dazhai model throughout rural China. Most Chinese economists (for example, Liu and Wu, 1986: 432) subsequently condemned it as overly ambitious, and certainly the targets set were high; for example, steel production was set to increase to 60m. tonnes by 1985 (actual steel production in that year was 47m. tonnes—ZGTJNJ, 1989: 299). It should be noted, however, that the grain target set for 1985 of 400m. tonnes was actually surpassed in 1984.
31. These rates are calculated in the same way as those given in Table 2.2, i.e. by rebasing the components of GDP at 1990 prices and aggregating.
32. Mexican real GDP fell by 4 per cent in 1983 and by the same amount in 1986. In Chile there was a fall of no less than 14 per cent in 1982 (WT, 1992: 180–1, 416–17).
33. Chinese definitions of the scope of agriculture have changed during the 1980s (Field, 1988). In essence, however, agriculture includes forestry, fisheries, animal husbandry, and household sidelines (including handicrafts) as well as farming. Households specializing in handicraft or industrial production were classified as part of the industrial sector after 1984.
34. This has long been the Chinese practice, and is another example of the tendency for units of volume, weight, and measure to be used in a way very different from in the West. In the Republican era, for instance, the number of *li* in a journey depended upon whether it was uphill or down (the *li* was therefore in effect a measure of time rather than distance). Similarly, the amount of land owned by a Sichuan household in the 1930s was typically measured in terms of its total output rather than its size; for example, 20 *mu* of hillside might be recorded as a landholding of only 5 *mu* (that is, equivalent in its total productive capacity to 5 *mu* of land on the plain). See Bramall (1989: 12) for a discussion.
35. But to put this in perspective, grain yields in 1978 were far higher than they had been in the mid-1960s. Growth in the 1980s was dependent upon raising yields to entirely unprecedented levels, and this helps to explain why output growth was not spectacular.
36. Rawski (1989: 330) puts the growth rate of agriculture during the same period at between 1.4 and 1.7 per cent per year.
37. Nakamura's more pessimistic revisions of Meiji growth rates suggest an annual rate of only 1.2 per cent at best (Nakamura, 1965; 1966). In fairness, the comparison between late nineteenth century Japan and China in the 1980s is biased because of the extent of technical progress in the intervening years. The application of modern technology based upon the 'green revolution' package of modern varieties and chemical fertilizers allows explosive rates of 'catch-up' in late developers.
38. Lee Travers has, for example, argued that there was considerable under-reporting of output, particularly in Sichuan province, and William Hinton has long been a critic of the officially recorded data on grain production in the early 1980s.

39. It is not entirely clear that Kueh's use of official data on the area affected by natural disasters as a weather proxy is appropriate. The series he presents on weather deviations from the 1952–84 mean (Kueh, 1995: 299) implies that every year between 1976 and 1984 was worse than average. That conclusion is very hard to accept given a general perception throughout rural China that 1982–4 were extraordinarily good harvest years. Nevertheless, Kueh's conclusion that the weather in 1984—whatever its relation to the post-1952 average—was far better than in 1978 accords with all the evidence; there is therefore no reason to doubt the notion that the 1978–84 comparison of agricultural output is biased.
40. Other estimates of food consumption suggest a more dramatic increase from an average of 2,034 kcals in 1955–7 to 2,272 kcals during 1976–8 (Riskin, 1991: 24). However, this is probably rather optimistic. Riskin's figures are based upon an earlier and subsequently revised study by Piazza (1983).
41. For the performance of Chinese agriculture under Mao, see Perkins and Yusuf (1984), Walker (1984), Nolan (1988), Selden (1988), Oi (1989), Huang (1990), and Riskin (1991). For recent accounts of output growth after 1978, see also Aubert (1990), Wakashiro (1990), Yu and Buckwell (1991), Ash (1992), and Kueh (1995).
42. The largest decline occurred in 1959, when production was 21 per cent lower than it had been in 1958. However, the decline in production during the Leap occurred not just in one year but over four successive years. As a result, grain production during the trough of 1961 was 39 per cent below its level in 1958 (LSTJ, 1990: 416).
43. Instability actually increased during 1978–84. Kueh (1995) not unreasonably concludes that this was largely due to the magnitude of the agricultural policy changes that occurred during these years. It probably also had something to do with the gradual shift towards more reliable reporting of crop data, as noted earlier.
44. For the Western literature on agricultural problems in the late 1980s and early 1990s, see Watson (1989*a*), Watson (1989*b*), Aubert (1990), Crook (1991), Ash (1991; 1992), Watson (1992), and OECD (1997). For some of the Chinese literature, see Zhu (1991*b*) and Zhu and Jiang (1993).
45. This refers to the provincial governor responsibility (or 'rice bag') system introduced in 1995–6 (OECD, 1997).
46. It has been argued by some that it is simply not feasible for China to meet grain demand from domestic production in the long run given continued population growth, growing levels of environmental damage, acute water shortages in north China, and the high yield levels already recorded in the early 1990s (Brown, 1995). This rather apocalyptic view probably understates the scope for yield improvements in many parts of south-central and south-western China. It is clear, however, that to realize the agronomic potential of these regions will require high levels of investment in water conservancy, transport networks, and fertilizer production—and that the private sector is unlikely to perform this function.
47. Such 'over-industrialization' will also make sense from an efficiency viewpoint if there are external economies of scale to be exploited.
48. For a summary of these debates, see Hsu (1991: 138–41).
49. The official Chinese post-1978 definition of industry includes mining and utilities. It excludes transport, communication, and construction.
50. The industry share for 1952 is defined as the sum of factory, handicraft, mining, and utility output as a percentage of GDP measured at 1952 prices. The estimate for the 1930s also defines industry to include mining and utilities, and the share is derived from 1933 constant price data.

51. For some of this burgeoning literature, see Wong (1988), Nolan and Dong (1990), Byrd and Lin (1990), Odgaard (1992*a*; 1992*b*), Oi (1990), Zweig (1991), Ho (1994), and Findlay, *et al.* (1994). The abbreviation TVE (township and village enterprise) is used in this book to include all rural industry. TVCE (township and village collective enterprises) refers only to those rural enterprises owned by township and village government. The coverage of the TVCE category thus excludes (team) *dui*, cooperative (*lianying*), and private (*geti*) enterprises. This usage follows that of Byrd and Lin (1990).
52. This series is not consistent because of the definitional changes made in 1984 and noted in the footnote to Table 2.8. In addition, the removal of legal restrictions on private enterprises in the mid-1980s almost certainly encouraged the reintermediation of 'underground' enterprises into the formal economy (see Odgaard, 1992*b*, Appendix 1).
53. See, for example, Nolan and Dong (1990), Odgaard (1992*b*), and Young and Yang (1994).
54. For the literature on SOE productivity growth, see Chen, *et al.* (1988), Jefferson (1989), Jefferson, *et al.* (199), Jefferson, *et al.* (1992*a*), Jefferson, *et al.* (1992*b*), Jefferson and Rawski (1994), Jefferson, *et al.* (1996), and Woo, *et al.* (1997).
55. The share of state enterprises in 1996 cannot easily be compared with 1991 because many SOEs have been reclassified as joint stock enterprises.
56. Measured in *yuan*, the value of Chinese exports increased by a factor of 10.5 between 1978 and 1988 (ZGTJNJ, 1992: 627). The slower growth of the (US) dollar value of exports reflected the steady depreciation of the currency.
57. A Chinese prefecture (*diqu* if predominantly rural, *shi* if predominantly urban) is a group of counties. It corresponds to a Western European region.
58. This provides a sample of 49 counties with a total population of about 27 millions in 1996. GDP per capita data are available, or can be estimated, for all these counties between 1980 and 1996. This chapter offers no more than a brief discussion of the growth of the four prefectures during the years after 1978: Chapter 11 addresses the way in which the growth processes of the transition era played themselves out in these very different geographical contexts.
59. The slowest growing county in the 4-prefecture sample was Butuo in Liangshan, where incomes rose by only 1.7 per cent per annum. Even this was a perfectly respectable performance by the standards of sub-Saharan Africa and South Asia.

Chapter 3. The Sectoral Contributions of Industry and Agriculture

1. Manufacturing will promote agricultural growth by supplying wage goods to the rural population and by providing inputs for farm production. The latter has a direct effect, and the former will encourage the production of a marketed surplus.
2. This latter might seem an implausible argument given the allegedly low quality of heavy industrial goods. But in fact the prices of many heavy industrial products were held below their marginal cost in the 1970s and 1980s because they were key inputs for other industries; obvious examples include machinery, trucks, chemicals, and fuels (though not petroleum, which earned hard currency).
3. Note that, because the planners used heavy industrial prices which were below probable heavy industrial shadow prices to value output, the slower growth of the heavy industrial sector is not properly reflected in the overall industrial growth rate. In other words, heavy industry is assigned price weights which are too low in the Chinese accounts, and therefore slower heavy industrial growth after 1978 wrongly translates into only a modest decline in overall industrial growth. Nevertheless, this distortion to output growth

was probably not very great (because, though it slowed after 1978, heavy industrial production still grew very quickly by world standards).

4. It is not possible to extend the data beyond 1992 because of the introduction of a different type of industrial disaggregation; see for example ZGGYJJTJNJ (1995).
5. For energy production in China in the 1980s, see Fridley (1991).
6. The same conclusion was reached by Lo (1997), although he used gross output value data.
7. Industrial production in Wuxi city alone was higher in 1980 than in the whole of Liangshan in 1996. Even so, its 11 per cent industrial growth rate was hardly unimpressive.
8. Although the inflation rate in Liangshan was probably below the provincial average whereas the converse applied to Suzhou.
9. Allen (1994: 102); Clark (1993: 237).
10. However, the question of whether the Tokugawa period created the preconditions—invention of new agricultural technologies, the construction of irrigation networks and the development of human capital—for subsequent growth remains more open. It is here that the revisionist case is most persuasive.
11. Agriculture contributed almost nothing to growth in the large urban centres, for obvious reasons.
12. It is true that the current-price share of agriculture in both national income and GNP does rise between the late 1970s and the mid-1980s. According to the World Bank (1990*a*: 107), agriculture's share of GNP at current prices rose from 33 per cent in 1978 to 40 per cent by 1984. Official Chinese data on the share of agriculture in national income show exactly the same trend (ZGTJNJ, 1992: 32). However, this trend is due to the shift in the internal terms of trade between agriculture and industry that occurred in 1979. It is reversed once 1990 constant prices are used.
13. The share of agriculture in NDMP is expressed in every case here at 1990 constant prices. Note that some of the declines occurred in the burst of industrialization of 1992 and beyond; in the cases of Beijing, Tianjin, and Xinjiang, the 1991 share of agriculture in NDMP was no lower than in 1978.
14. Tianjin is the (rather insignificant in agricultural terms) exception; there, the agriculture share peaked in 1991 instead of in the early 1980s.
15. There are no GDP data by county for the early years of transition in Wenzhou. NDMP data have therefore been used instead.
16. In fact, Xiangxi prefecture was one of the centres of Third Front construction. The programme began between 1965 and 1967 with the initiation of 19 large and medium-sized projects, and reached a peak between the first half of 1969 and the end of 1970. During this latter stage, some 35 large and medium-sized projects were launched, and at a cost of about ten times that spent on the projects launched in 1965–7. With some 2 million workers deployed in the prefecture, it is scant wonder that Xiong (1990: i. 163) commented that the programme was 'unprecedented in the history of economic construction' in the province. But in the process, agriculture was neglected.
17. The 1990 input–output data are not disaggregated by the agricultural subsector in the source used here. However, if we assume farming is a good proxy for agriculture, it is striking that the linkage effects between agriculture and industry were similar to those calculated for 1981. According to the 1990 data, 33 per cent of agricultural output was used as inputs by industry, and only 5 per cent was used for accumulation. Consumption (private and public) again constituted the principal use of agricultural output (40 per cent). Net exports, however, took up 3 per cent of gross output; this was arguably the biggest change compared to 1981 (ZGTJNJ, 1995: 42–3). This and the reduced claim

of consumption testify to the successful increase in agricultural output over the 1980s; a significant proportion of production could now be exported, rather than required for home consumption.

18. Calculated from data in LSTJ (1990) and ZJTJNJ (1992).

Chapter 4. Theories of Growth

1. Respectively, Hahn and Matthews (1964), and Arrow and Hahn (1971).
2. For surveys of the evolution of growth theory, see Romer (1991; 1994), Abramovitz (1993), Fagerberg (1994), Solow (1996), Crafts (1997), and Aghion and Howitt (1998). The term 'new growth theory' refers to both endogenous theories of technical progress and the neoclassical extensions of the Solow model (augmented Solowian models) which largely retain Solow's assumptions and results (diminishing returns to broad capital, exogenous technical progress and conditional convergence).
3. The word 'institution' is used to refer to organizations as well as the laws and rules that theorists such as North mean when they use the word.
4. This fourth possibility is superficially similar to the growth of an economy driven by a rise in its savings rate. For that reason, it is discussed under capital accumulation below. But strictly, the two are very different in analytical terms.
5. In later works, social capability is defined to include social attitudes (Abramovitz, 1989, ch. 1; Abramovitz and David, 1996), and efficient capital markets (Abramovitz, 1994: 98).
6. However, as will be seen below, British technical progress was based primarily around innovation (especially in cotton textiles) rather than simply diffusion. Britain's debt to France was more in terms of invention than innovation.
7. To amplify, Britain's modest literacy rate probably did not matter as much as the more general skill level of its population. According to Mitch (1993: 293–4), literacy was not very useful in 50 per cent of male occupations and 'possibly useful' in only a further 26 per cent in 1841. Only in 5 per cent of occupations was it necessary. For female workers, the comparable figures were 25, 68, and 2 per cent respectively. It is also worth noting that contemporary India has had little difficulty in introducing Green Revolution technology since the 1960s despite low literacy rates. These may have made the illiterate members of the rural population more risk-averse and slower to adopt the technology, but it has certainly not proved a serious obstacle—probably because of the population's well-developed informal agricultural skills.
8. The usual source given for this is Dore (1984), who estimated male literacy at 43 per cent and female literacy at 10 per cent by 1868.
9. According to Kiyokawa (in Minami, 1995: 85): 'These days it is beyond dispute that one of the main factors responsible for the rapid and sustained development of the Japanese cotton industry was the continuous introduction of western technological innovations.'
10. This figure is for 1929–40. The inclusion of the years of depression at the beginning of the decade reduced the rate somewhat, as did the start of war with China in 1937.
11. Drèze and Sen (1995: 5) probably go too far in asserting that 'India's literary achievements today are also very much lower than what South Korea, Thailand, and the other newly industrializing Asian countries had already achieved by 1960, when they moved ahead with their rapid economic growth.' With an overall literacy rate of 52 per cent by 1992, India was very similar to Singapore and Taiwan in 1960. This is not to say that India's educational system in the early 1990s was excellent; clearly it was not (Drèze and Sen, 1995, ch. 6). But the India of the 1990s did not lag much behind the East Asian newly industrializing norm in 1960.

12. The potential importance of underemployed rural labour was discussed at some length in Rosenstein-Rodan (1943) and many other dualistic models appeared in the 1960s, notably those of Jorgenson (1961) and Fei and Ranis (1964).
13. As will be seen below, this is the basis for the Sachs and Woo (1994) view that Eastern Europe and the former Soviet Union could not have emulated the pace of growth achieved in China in the 1980s because they lacked surplus labour. The impact of labour reallocation on growth can be expressed more formally (Sachs and Woo, 1997). In a Cobb–Douglas framework (without human capital), output growth is the (weighted) sum of labour force growth, capital accumulation, labour reallocation and residual TFP growth. This differs from the usual neoclassical formulation because here conventionally measured TFP growth is divided into a labour reallocation and a residual component. This disaggregation allows Sachs and Woo to show that much conventionally measured TFP growth in China was no more than a one-off sectoral reallocation effect.
14. Krugman's analysis is based on the work of Murphy, *et al.* (1989).
15. The absolute level of agricultural employment probably increased slightly up to the Napoleonic Wars (Crafts, 1980, 1985; Clark, 1993; Allen, 1988; Campbell and Overton, 1991). However, the longer-run data compiled by Allen (1994: 107) show agricultural employment falling from 1.55 million in 1700 to 1.52 million in 1851.
16. This fall is over and above the reduction in marginal productivity caused simply by diminishing returns. That is, alienation will cause the industrial marginal productivity of labour curve to *shift* towards the origin.
17. The outcome will depend upon whether the income effect (higher profits and therefore greater investment) will outweigh the substitution effect (lower relative cost of labour and therefore less investment).
18. This debate is summarized in McCombie and Thirlwall (1994: 181–4).
19. As with the other classical economists, Marx did not expect this process of accumulation to continue in perpetuity if all other factors within the economic system remained unchanged. Accumulation would tend in the long run to raise the organic composition of capital and hence depress the rate of profit (Marx, 1894: 212–13). The process of economic growth would therefore come to an end unless this tendency could be offset by either an increase in the rate of surplus value, or by a reduction in the cost of capital (Marx, 1894: 232–40). But unlike the other classical economists, Marx argued that technical progress could reduce the cost of capital per unit of output. As a result, even though the volume of capital relative to labour might tend to increase over time, the *value* of capital (the organic composition of capital is measured in terms of its value) might remain the same or even fall. As Cullenberg (1994: 40) says: 'It is entirely possible that while the mass of capital goods . . . increases with accumulation, the unit value of the capital goods could fall sufficiently so that the overall effect would be a fall instead of an increase in constant capital. Thus, accumulation could conceivably lower the organic composition of capital instead of increasing it.'
20. It is arguable that the Feldman assumptions were more plausible in the contexts of Maoist China and the USSR than in most other countries. Authoritarianism meant that demands for big increases in material consumption could be held in check in the short run, whilst the political and diplomatic isolation of both made extensive foreign trade a risky undertaking—so that the closed economy assumption did more or less hold.
21. The Harrod model is discussed by many writers, notably Solow (1956), Hamberg (1977), and Asimakopulos (1991). Although the Domar model is often linked with Harrod's, the two were very different. Domar did not distinguish between full capacity utilization

and full employment of the labour force (Pasinetti, 1974: 95) and there was no role for expectations in his theory of investment; the relationship between capital and output was purely technological (Marglin, 1984: 73–4, 533).

22. Solow's own views on his 1956 model are to be found in Solow (1970; 1996).
23. Though few economies will progress this far because the cost of raising the investment rate beyond a certain point is lower per capita consumption even in the long run.
24. The total factor productivity residual is often identified with technical progress. However, it is recognized that a part of that residual may also reflect economies of scale and errors in measurement, as well as the factor reallocation effects already discussed.
25. Note, however, that the studies of Abramovitz (1956), Solow (1957), Kendrick (1961), and Denison (1967; 1974) all found that TFP was a key factor in explaining post-war US growth.
26. Even Romer (1993: 548) in his critique of De Long and Summers does not deny that LDCs may suffer from object as well as idea gaps—not least because imported capital goods embody new ideas.
27. It is necessary to introduce human capital in this way because the original Solow model (which assumes exogenous technical progress) implies that differences in income per head between countries can be explained in terms of differences in physical capital per head. But given diminishing returns to physical capital, this would imply that an income 'gap' of (say) 10 to 1 between countries would require a gap in terms of capital per head of at least 100 to 1. Although this is not impossible, such a gap in capital per worker would also imply a massive difference in marginal capital productivity and hence profit rates between countries. That in turn would imply than there ought to be capital flows from rich to poor countries on a scale far greater than is observed. In order to retain the essential structure of the Solow model (diminishing returns to factors of production and exogenous technical progress), the only way to proceed is to somehow broaden the concept of capital to include human as well as physical capital. For a discussion, see D. Romer (1996: 23–4) and Mankiw (1995).
28. Not all the evidence points to this conclusion. Schofield's (1973) data show the literacy rate for grooms rising from 60 per cent in 1780 to 65 per cent in 1830; for brides, the comparable figures are 40 per cent and 50 per cent (Mitch, 1993: 275).
29. Although it is impossible to measure the true social benefits which accrue from education. These estimates almost uncertainly understate the real picture.
30. Although, of course, no country is likely to have a lead in every area of technology. In that sense, the USA can still grow by exploiting technologies developed in Japan. More importantly, countries can grow by diffusing technologies developed in a previous time period. The growth of agricultural output in Meiji Japan, for example, was driven to a significant extent by invention and innovation during the Tokugawa period.
31. One reason for much of the debate about the role of technical progress is that it has been thought about in different ways. The neoclassical notion is much closer to the idea of invention; some inventions (at least historically) can be explained as exogenous shocks and thereby largely unrelated to systematic expenditure on R&D. The notion of technical progress in endogenous growth theory is much closer to innovation; ideas are important only in so far as they can be translated into mass-produced machinery suitable for country-specific environments.
32. The Solow equation takes the (general) form $Y = F(K, AL)$, rather than $Y = AF(K, L)$ or $Y = F(AK, L)$ because Harrod-neutral or labour augmenting technical progress is a necessary condition for a steady state to exist (Barro and Sala-i-Martin, 1995: 54–5;

D. Romer, 1996: 7). Most attempts to apply the Solow model use a Cobb–Douglas production function of the form $Y = K^{1-\beta} A(t) L^{\beta}$.

33. Writing technical progress in this way also implies that it is Hicks-neutral, i.e. the marginal rate of substitution of inputs is constant.
34. However, the structure of the Arrow model is such that higher saving does not in the long run lead to faster per capita growth (Romer, 1991: 90).
35. If one denotes the sum of research, human capital, and physical capital as *K*, these models are essentially of the von Neumann linear form $Y = F(K) = AK$. Romer (1995: 316) summarizes all these models as follows: 'Early versions of the endogenous growth models let *A* vary because of spillover effects from investment in physical capital or human capital. More recent models have proposed more complicated mechanisms for producing variation in *A*, such as research and development, or trade in intermediate inputs in production.'
36. 'To act with confidence beyond the range of familiar beacons and to overcome . . . resistance requires aptitudes that are present in only a small fraction of the population and that define the entrepreneurial type as well as the entrepreneurial function' (Schumpeter, 1943: 132).
37. Weber's theory of bureaucracy and the role of the charismatic leader is discussed in Giddens (1995).
38. He knew very well that the threat of competition under capitalism were difficult to ignore even for a monopolist: 'For, especially in manufacturing industry, a monopoly position is in general no cushion to sleep on. As it can be gained, so it can be retained only by alertness and energy' (Schumpeter, 1943: 102).
39. Moreover, and explicitly contra to the Marxist view, there was no tendency for the rate of profit to fall over time (Kaldor, 1961: 231).
40. As Kaldor (1966: 290) points out, the two equations say the same thing: 'The results are summarized in two regression equations, productivity on output, and employment on output—which are two different ways of looking at the same relationship . . .'
41. Meaning a market-orientated economy.
42. An important qualification to this story is that particular innovations may have only a minor impact on growth in the short run. This is a point that has often been made about the extremely rapid pace of technological change in the 1980s and 1990s. Nobody would deny the extent of this change; the explosion in ownership of personal computers is the most obvious example. Yet there is little evidence that any of this has been reflected in a marked increase in productivity. It is as if 'the US has been throwing its computers down a big black hole, and presumably other countries are doing so as well' (Gordon, 1992: 419–20). In part this may be because of measurement problems which understate true product growth (Gordon 1992: 420). More likely, however, the growth slowdown reflects diminishing returns to the cluster of new technologies introduced in the early post-war decades combined with the inevitable lag between introducing personal computers and their revolutionizing productivity. Krugman (1994: 60–2) concurs: 'Economic historians have observed that it often takes a very long time before a new technology begins to make a major impact on productivity and living standards. . . . The reason for these long lags is that a technology often does not have its full impact when it is used in isolation; it is only when it becomes broadly applied and interacts with other technologies that its true potential can be exploited (p. 60). . . . simply adding computers to an office organized in traditional fashion may add little to productivity . . . [it may be that] the computer doesn't realize its full potential in an office designed around

the flow of paper, in the same way that electric power didn't realize its full potential in factory buildings designed for machines powered by steam' (p. 62). The major problem with Krugman's account is that it takes too little account of the way changes in the world economy have impinged upon the resumption of the growth seen in the West during the 'golden age' of 1950–73 (Brenner, 1998). The growth of LDC competition and a failure to boost aggregate demand (because of the overarching importance accorded to reducing inflation) suggest that the slowdown in productivity may be more than simply a temporary phenomenon.

43. 'Between 1966 and 1990, the Singaporean economy grew at a remarkable 8.5 per cent per annum . . . This achievement seems to be a kind of economic miracle. But the miracle turns out to have been based on perspiration rather than inspiration: Singapore grew through a mobilization of resources that would have done Stalin proud' (Krugman, 1996: 175).
44. According to Yamamura (1986: 201): 'the Japanese economy in the rapid growth period would have achieved much of what it accomplished even without industrial policy. . . . There, indeed, is much truth in an observation an economist friend of mine once half-jokingly made: "Even had all MITI officers been graduates of third-rate universities, the economy would have grown very rapidly".' Chalmers Johnson (1985) offers, of course, a much more positive view of MITI's contribution.
45. The data used here are revised figures based on the work of Selyunin and Khanin in 1987 (Aslund, 1995; Shmelev and Popov, 1990: ch. 2, 298–9). These figures are generally regarded as reliable; in any case, they show the same basic trend as the official data in the post-war period. They are probably least reliable for the period 1928–40 when Khanin's 3.4 per cent figure for NMP is well below the 5.5 per cent rate for GNP estimated by Bergson for 1928–37 or the 6.2 per cent figure estimated by Moorsteen and Powell for the same period. According to Harrison (1994: 44): 'Khanin emphasized agricultural setbacks and the falsification of product growth as factors in poor Soviet inter-war economic performance, but it is not clear whether these justified such a depressing assessment of the achievements of the period.'
46. This is not to imply an absence of technology transfer. As has been extensively documented, many of the innovations diffused across the Soviet economy originated in the West (Vander Elst, 1981; Sutton, 1973).

Chapter 5. The Maoist Legacy and the Literature

1. The impact of institutional reform, because it was engineered by the state, is covered in Part IV of the book. The specific reforms considered there are decollectivization, changes to agricultural prices, and the reforms to the management of state-owned enterprises.
2. A variant on this theme is that Maoist China did no better than Republican China (1911–49). According to Rawski (1989), 'The return of domestic peace and political integration for the first time in forty years produced a growth spurt in the 1950s that largely reflected the unfulfilled potential of China's pre-war economy . . . despite the modest capital formation proportions of the 1930s, the powerful and effective intervention of China's post-1949 central planning apparatus has failed to push investment performance beyond the trend lines established during the prewar decades' (pp. 348–9).
3. Data on the service sector in Eastern Europe do not as yet exist and therefore it is impossible to calculate shares in GDP.
4. Just as the well-known work by Young (1995) showing low TFP growth has allowed the master discourse to argue that there was no miracle in the East Asian economies after World War II (Krugman, 1996).

5. The problem with the argument is that a good deal of Western technology had already diffused to Russia by the late 1980s. By contrast, because China's economy had been more isolated under Mao and because the economy lacked the social and physical capability to take advantage of Western technology until the 1970s, there was much more scope for shifting the production function outwards. The difference in per capita income says it all; GDP per head in Russia in 1978 was (in 1990 international prices) $6,500, whereas in China it was only $977 (Maddison, 1998: 13).
6. Though not all. Chen Yizi, one of the more radical reformers of the 1980s and closely associated with Zhao Ziyang, argued that two-thirds of capital construction investment in state enterprises between 1958 and 1978 was wasted (Sun, 1995: 79). Chen's hostility to Maoism was hardly surprising in view of his background; his father was a Qing official and Chen himself suffered *xiafang* for a 'rightist' letter sent in 1958 (Fewsmith, 1994: 33). 1988–9 in particular was a period during which a number of radicals despaired of China. Emblematic of this despair was Sun Xiaokang's 'River Elegy' TV series, and the claims by some that China would have been better off if Japan had triumphed in World War II (Sun, 1995: 206).
7. The Dazhai movement was based upon the practice of the Dazhai production brigade in Xiyang county, Shanxi. Xiyang only adopted the Dazhai approach after 1965, when Chen Yonggui (Party Secretary in Dazhai) took over. The radicalization of the county is evident from the increase in brigade-level accounting, which rose from 5 per cent in 1966 to 100 per cent in 1968, and the abolition of private plots, down from 24,041 *mu* in 1966 to 1,215 *mu* in 1969 and zero in 1970 (Chen, *et al.*, 1993: 431, 435–6).
8. However, as Misra (1998: 97) points out, this notion of three stages (primary stage of socialism, secondary phase of socialism, and communism) was to be found nowhere in the writings of Marx or Lenin. Marx's idea of a transitional phase applied to the entire period of socialism and not just to a part of it. In effect, Su's theory amounted to no more than calling capitalism the primary stage of socialism.

Chapter 6. Social Capability and the Capital Stock at the End of the Maoist Era

1. Other types of modern fixed capital are much less important in terms of raising yields. The Indian evidence on tractorization, for example, suggests that tractors increase profitability by saving labour but have little direct effect upon yields (Gaiha, 1985). It is also of course true that the mechanization of rice production is an extremely difficult process (Bray, 1986).
2. A rather belated recognition of this was the renaming of Guanxian as Dujiangyan *shi* in the 1980s.
3. The extent of under-reporting allegedly varied from 17 to 37 per cent depending on the commune; the figure for Dazhai commune is given as 31 per cent; detailed data are given in Chen, *et al.* (1993: 446–7). A figure of 24 per cent is given in Zhonggong zhongyang xuanchuanbu xuanchuanju (1988: 239) for the whole of Xiyang county.
4. Qin (1995, ch. 39) refutes these criticisms.
5. The only systematic statistical data in the entire book—the source for which is not given—are on Xiyang. The very precision of these data, and the general tone of the analysis, suggests that much of it is fraudulent.
6. If one accepts Kueh's (1995) analysis (see Chapter 2), the weather for the 1970s as a whole was far worse than in the 1950s and 1980s. By implication, the natural disasters recorded in the 1970s were due to poor weather rather than poorly constructed or mismanaged late Maoist irrigation systems.

7. Kueh (1995) does, however, argue that official data on disaster-affected areas do accurately reflect the impact of poor weather.
8. Hinton (in Qin 1995: 602 n.) is utterly dismissive of their claims, arguing that Friedman, *et al.* did no more than repeat some of the accusations made against the Dazhai movement: 'Without these two books [CMB: two attacks on Dazhai in the 1980s] the outrageous attack on Mao's whole rural policy contained in *Chinese Village, Socialist State* by Friedman, Selden and Pickowicz, could never have been launched. The three Americans authors follow every twist and turn of the original polemics, and especially the slander that under socialism only massive State aid can bring prosperity to any rural community.'
9. Red Flag Canal was an ambitious water diversion scheme, located in Lin county in Henan province. It started in 1960 and was completed in 1969. For a discussion, see Lin (1974).
10. Even the Central Committee evaluation of Dazhai (published as Document no. 83 on 23 November 1980) acknowledged the achievements of Dazhai before the Cultural Revolution and confined its criticisms to the 'Learn From Dazhai' campaign, essentially on the (technological) grounds that the Dazhai approach was not suitable for the majority of Chinese counties. This 'verdict' seems to have been accepted by Chen Yonggui (Qin, 1995: 583–5). The full text of Document no. 83 can be found in Zhonggong zhongyang wenxian yanjiushi (1982: 562–72).
11. This classification of industrial sectors is something of a simplification. Although the chemical and machine-building sectors produced goods that were primarily 'heavy', they did produce some light-industrial goods as well. In fact, about one-third of the (gross) output value of the chemical sector was classified as light-industrial products in 1978; the corresponding figure for machine building was 19 per cent (Zhongguo tongjiju, 1985*a*: 29, 34–5).
12. Data on the shares of heavy and light industry are at 1990 constant prices.
13. These figures on physical output mirror those on output value. This suggests that value data on industrial production give a reliable indication of relative sectoral growth rates, even though the relative prices used to estimate the value of industrial production have always been viewed with some suspicion by western economists.
14. All the output data in this paragraph are at 1980 constant prices (SCZL, 1990: 336–77).
15. These figures on enterprise production capacity come from ZGTJNJ (1985: 443).
16. This figure is for railways operated by central government only. The time series data provided in the Statistical Yearbooks exclude locally managed track; compare Tables 12–2 and 12–3 in ZGTJNJ (1992: 508–9) for 1991. For a more detailed discussion in the case of Guangdong province, see Harral (1992). The fact that railways were managed by different authorities severely affected the efficiency of the system because it led to the use of different gauges. In Guangdong, the gauges of local lines varied between 0.702 and 1.055 metres, compared to the national gauge of 1.435 metres.
17. A list of railways completed during 1966–75 is given in Yabuki (1995: 39). This shows that 2,784 km of track were completed during 1966–70, and a further 3,025 km were completed during 1971–5.
18. If a double-tracked kilometre of track is counted as two km, the growth rate rises to 3.3 per cent per year (ZGTJNJ, 1989: 396).
19. US and Indian data are for the mid-1980s.
20. The best account is that of Pepper (1996).
21. The reliability of these accounts is questionable. Almost all these writers have an incentive to exaggerate their experiences (especially when their accounts have been translated

into English), there is little independent corroboration of their tales, and the ability of these storytellers to remember dialogue from twenty years ago is remarkable. Still, they undoubtedly give an accurate flavour of the attitude of many of those exiled to the countryside in the late Maoist period. The other noteworthy feature of this literature is that it ignores the 'sending down' on Deng's instructions of those who were associated with Hua Guofeng in the late 1970s and early 1980s. In this, as in many other cases, the history is the history of the victors.

22. The usual World Bank/UNDP criterion for literacy looks at those aged over 15. A '15 and over' definition was used in China's 1990 Census.
23. This figure is calculated as the number of those enrolling in junior secondary school as a percentage of those graduating from primary school in the same year.
24. This neglect of the independent impact of culture on the economy is something that unites the master discourse and the heterodoxy. Both sets of writers are agreed that (for example) an explanation of the rise of East Asia is not be found in the cultural realm.
25. As Greenblatt puts it (Veeser, 1989: 3), Jameson's position was that 'once we were whole, agile, integrated; we were individual subjects but not individuals, we had no psychology distinct from the shared life of the society; politics and poetry were one. Then capitalism arose and shattered this luminous, benign totality.'
26. In one sense, this 'pluralism run amok' fractures the opposition, promotes quietism and thus makes it difficult to organize political struggle against the status quo. But on the other hand, it enlarges the constituency of the opposition; and in any case, from the perspective of Kristeva amongst others, the site of liberation may be as much the psychoanalyst's couch as the formal political arena.
27. Jiang Qing's role in the late Maoist period remains an enigma. She has been vilified in almost every Chinese text as well as by the Dengist leadership, but this may simply be a product of gender bias; there is a well known Chinese tendency to attribute the more dramatic instances of economic and social failure in China to malevolent women (writings on the Empress Wu and the Dowager Empress Cixi are the most obvious examples).

Chapter 7. The Role of Surplus Labour

1. Wang (1998: 71) cites estimates of the surplus ranging from 10 to 50 per cent of the national rural workforce.
2. The gap is less if GDP is measured at current prices because of the rise in relative agriculture prices during the transition period. In 1996, the secondary- to primary-sector productivity gap was 5.2 compared to 6.4 at constant prices.
3. There was also widespread disguised unemployment in the industrial sector in China in the late 1970s. As is well known, most workers in the urban, state-owned, sector were effectively guaranteed jobs for life and overmanning was widespread. If industry had been operating closer to its production possibility frontier, it seems extremely likely that the sectoral productivity differential would have been even greater. This is confirmed by the evidence on sectoral-labour productivities for developing countries as a whole, which suggests a productivity differential of almost 10 to 1 in 1980 compared to 2.2 to 1 for market economies (Bhaduri, 1993: 173); modern industrial enterprises in many LDCs are typically much less overmanned than in China.
4. It will, however, be argued below that industrial employment turned out to be just as alienating as farm work—despite the expectations of many farm workers.
5. For example, Huang's (1990: 239) data on Jiangsu show the value of the labour day varying between 0.8 and 1.1 *yuan* over the period 1965–78.

6. A number of attempts (for example, Hughes and Senik-Leygonie, 1992) have been made to estimate value-added and profitability in the Soviet Union and Eastern Europe in the late 1980s using world shadow prices for inputs, outputs, and wages (the consumption basket is typically revalued at world prices to calculate this last variable). These studies typically find high rates of value-added and profit for energy and capital-goods sectors but extreme negative value-added and profitability in food processing. However, such studies are hard to take seriously. The use of world prices invokes the assumption that the world economy is in general competitive equilibrium, a wildly implausible notion. Furthermore, the results fly in the face of a mass of Chinese and Soviet studies which point to low rates of return in metallurgy and machinery subsectors, not light industry. This is reinforced by the high rates of profit made in the market-orientated rural *light* industrial sector in China since 1978.
7. Although the process was by no means linear. At the height of the agricultural 'miracle' in 1984, there was an absolute release of labour. By contrast, the recession of the late 1980s saw a rise even in the share of the labour force employed in agriculture as the CCP responded to what it perceived as neglect of agricultural production.
8. The terms absolute and relative labour release are as used by Crafts (1980).
9. In view of the limitations of the TFP estimates, the discussion here focuses exclusively on labour productivity.

Chapter 8. The Rates of Saving and Investment

1. From a neoclassical perspective, the Soviet Union in 1989 can be thought of as having virtually completed the transition to its steady state. The savings rate was increased in the late 1920s, and remained high thereafter. Over the following half century, this high savings rate allowed the capital–labour ratio and per capita income to rise. By 1989, therefore, both the capital–labour ratio and per capita incomes were substantially higher in the USSR than they were in China in 1978; China was still in the process of moving towards its steady state.
2. Data on gross domestic investment as a percentage of GDP do not exist prior to 1978 for China. However, the accumulation share—accumulation (*jilei*) as a percentage of net national material product (*guomin shouru shiyonge*)—is a good proxy; it understated the ratio of gross domestic investment in GDP by only about 2 percentage points in 1978 (36.5 compared to 38 per cent; see Zhongguo tongjiju, 1998: 21).
3. The 1978 figure of 36.5 per cent was probably not sustainable; it fell back to only about 30 per cent in the early 1980s.
4. Raiser (1995: 141) argues that 'in spite of the systematic terror that had governed China in 1966–76, most Chinese retained their faith in the ability of the old administrators to get the economy running again, once the vendettas of the Gang of Four were put to an end.'
5. Calculated from LSTJ (1990) and ZGTJNJ (1991).
6. Measured at 1990 constant prices, agricultural output in Sichuan rose by 6 per cent in 1977, 18 per cent in 1978, 10 per cent in 1979, and 7 per cent in 1980. Per capita output in 1980—a year of rather poor weather—stood at 294 *yuan*, about 9 per cent higher than the average for 1955–7. This growth had little to do with decollectivization; only 10 per cent of production teams had reverted to household farming by December 1980 (Bramall, 1995*a*).
7. In accounting terms, $I = S + (T - G) + (M - X)$. Overseas Chinese funds meant that China was able to run a capital account surplus to help in financing investment.

8. Exports of pork also imposed a significant consumption cost (Eckstein, 1964: 138).
9. In this context, it is significant that Sichuan did not export grain (even to other Chinese provinces) after the Great Leap Forward. This was in marked contrast to the role she had played in the 1950s (Walker, 1984).

Chapter 9. Capital Accumulation after 1978

1. In 'stock-market' economies such as the USA or the UK, a firm prone to very high levels of investment would necessarily tend to pay lower dividends. Accordingly, its shareholders would be likely to welcome a takeover bid.
2. Investment by the *state* in the subsector of heavy industry producing inputs—tractors, chemical fertilizers, etc.—for use in agriculture is discussed in Chapter 16. The discussion here therefore looks only at the purchase of inputs by the agricultural sector.
3. However, that is not surprising; part of the reason for the spectacular growth in fixed capital was simply the very low base of the mid-1970s. It would hardly be reasonable to expect the capital stock to have grown consistently at 20 per cent or more over a period of 15 to 20 years.
4. This is the nominal capital stock for farming, forestry, animal husbandry, and fisheries combined deflated by the GDP deflator to give the real capital stock in 1990 constant prices.
5. Nevertheless, as Kueh (1995: 251–2) rightly points out, the events of 1991 show how far agriculture had developed over the post-1931 period. Despite weather comparable in its severity to the disastrous years of 1959–61, the impact on crop yields was modest and there was no hint of a famine.
6. The Chinese figure was nevertheless well below the 26.3m. tonne-km figure recorded in the Soviet Union in the 1980s (World Bank, 1990*b*: 218 n.).

Chapter 10. The Growth of Productivity

1. One of the problems with many accounts of technical progress under Mao is that they compare the level reached by China in the late 1970s with the level reached in other advanced countries. For example, Smil (1988: 88) notes that labour productivity in China's coal mines was only 0.9 tonnes per miner-shift in 1982 compared to 2.4 tonnes in the UK, 3.4 in West Germany, and 10 in the USA. This is an entirely reasonable comparison if one is simply showing that China lagged behind other countries at the time. But it can say nothing about the achievements of the Maoist regime because there is no consideration of China's relative standing at the beginning of the Maoist period. In other words, the hypotheses that (a) China was technologically backward in 1980, and (b) rapid technical progress occurred under Mao are entirely compatible.
2. Not surprisingly, the farmers knew nothing about its properties. Some of those in Hunan, having refined it into crude yellow cake, took it to the local market town where it sat on the shelves of a shop near the Zhuzhou railway station until collected by an appalled specialist (Lewis and Xue, 1988: 90).
3. A rare exception to the usual pessimistic appraisals is that of Simon (1989) who notes that China's record was relatively successful up to the mid-1960s. However, he argues, the Cultural Revolution did enormous damage and led to a widening of the technology gap between China and the West.
4. For a recent account of the Chinese steel industry, see Etienne (1992).
5. The five industries (*wuxiao*) selected for promotion in rural areas were chemical fertilizer, farm machinery, iron and steel, cement, and electricity.

6. Summary views on Maoist technical progress in industry are given in Baark (1991: 533), Fischer (1989: 121), and Conroy (1989).
7. Many other less formal studies also report improved total factor productivity. According to a study by Svejnar (1990: 249–50) based on data on enterprises located in very different parts of China for the early 1980s, collective enterprises 'have achieved a significant rate of technical progress over time, with the most rapid gains occurring in 1985. The estimates confirm that the rapid development of the TVP sector has not been brought about merely by extensive growth; intensive growth has contributed significantly to the observed success.'
8. A useful summary of these and other studies is given in Otsuka, *et al.* (1998: 36–42).
9. Chen, *et al.* (1988*b*) report rapid growth, but that may be because they include the period 1978–80—when productivity was arguably recovering from the trough of 1976.
10. Discussions of the role of science and technology after 1978 are to be found in Conroy (1989), Simon (1989), Simon and Goldman (1989), Baark (1991), Suttmeier (1991), and Simon (1991).
11. Including heavy Taiwanese investment in the Xiamen special economic zone between 1988 and 1995.
12. These data necessarily measure little more than the flow of various types of equipment and are certainly not comprehensive.
13. Huang and Duncan (1997), for instance, used only 60 firms drawn from Guangzhou, Shenzhen, Xiamen, and Shanghai.
14. The underlying theory is discussed by Vickers and Yarrow (1988), and Stiglitz (1994).
15. The official data in fact show a rather slight, but significant, decline.
16. The data on employment and GVIO for shareholding enterprises are given for 1993, 1994, and 1995 in ZGTJNJ (1994; 1995; 1996).
17. Tobacco provides a classic illustration of the trade-off between social and more narrowly economic goals. It is a high-productivity sector, and therefore its promotion will significantly increase overall productivity. However, the social costs are well known.
18. Labour productivity only regained its 1957 level in 1982, the year in which decollectivization reached its flood tide.
19. Another recent study is by Fan (1991) but his estimate—TFP rises at 2.1 per cent per annum—applies only to the period 1965–85. A Chinese study (Feng, 1990: 48) reports annual TFP growth rates of 3.4 per cent during 1953–7 and –0.7 per cent during 1967–78. However, the methodology used in this study is not specified.
20. Anthony Tang (1985: 203), whose growth-accounting approach is used heavily by Wen, puts the problem thus: 'The problem of complementarity or package, in general, tends to undermine the methodology of growth accounting according to factor contributions. What it all comes down to is a question of tastes basically. As Solow put it (1957), either the methodology appeals or it doesn't.'
21. It can only ever be arguable because there is no unambiguous way of estimating long-run social marginal costs. World prices cannot be used (because then one has to assume the world economy is perfectly competitive) and the problems with using the labour theory of value for this sort of exercise are well known.
22. The price paid to farmers for a tonne of processed rice was only 138 *yuan* in 1952, compared to a retail price for chemical fertilizer of 370 *yuan* per tonne (ZGTJNJ, 1983: 477–8). By comparison, the 1978 prices were 263 *yuan* for rice and 231 *yuan* for chemical fertilizer—a very marked change from 1952. It is obvious that the use of 1978 relative prices would produce a very different result in terms of trends in total factor productivity.

23. Although these yield increases reflected in part increased use of fertilizer and improvements in irrigation as well as the use of new seed varieties.
24. It is interesting that nobody claims here—in contrast to the debates on industrial TFP—that the absence of land *ownership* has prevented agricultural productivity from rising, yet the property rights of farm households are decidedly insecure.
25. As Stone (1988*a*: 792) points out, hybrid corn actually made its appearance in the early 1960s but its adoption was comparatively slow.
26. Some Chinese sources suggest the impact was rather greater; see Bramall (1995*a*). However, some of these claims probably reflect increased chemical fertilizer use as well as the impact of HYVs per se.

Chapter 11. Differences in Prefectural Growth Rates

1. The difference in the growth rates achieved in Liangshan compared to the other prefectures may partly reflect the use of an appropriate price deflator. However, Liangshan's counties were by no means self-sufficient in the 1980s. They marketed a significant volume of agricultural commodities, and purchased consumer goods, on the national market and were therefore affected by national price trends (see also the discussion in Chapter 13).
2. A rare exception is the entry under Wuxi city in JSSXGK (1989: 124), where it is explicitly stated that to be classified as a road, a route must be at least 3.5 metres wide.
3. This is especially true for the Wenjiang data. Although few two-lane carriageways were completed before 1985 in the Chengdu area—even on the key links between Chengdu and the airport, and between Chengdu and Guanxian (this latter was only under construction in late 1985)—that changed dramatically in the late 1980s and the early 1990s.
4. This was true for all Sichuan's western prefectures (Aba, Garze, Liangshan, and Ya'an) in the early 1980s. In 1982, these four 'exported' to the rest of the province some 15,000 tonnes of coal, 2,000 tonnes of non-ferrous metals, and a colossal 1.8 million cubic metres of timber (SCJJDL, 1985: 704). This latter amounted to 85 per cent of total production. Major producer good 'imports' were iron, steel, and cement.
5. Data on the capital stock in the prefectures is not readily available. There are data on the capital–labour ratio in state-owned enterprises in Liangshan and Wenjiang (SCZL, 1990), but these only cover a part of the total industrial capital stock. SOEs under the control of central government are not included in these figures, nor are COEs. The output data used here can only be a poor proxy for the capital stock. Nevertheless, all the more qualitative evidence suggests that Liangshan's per capita industrial capital stock was small compared to the other prefectures. To some extent, this is reflected in its low level of rural industrial output. The total gross output value of *xiangzhen* enterprises in Liangshan was 37.1m. *yuan* in 1976 compared to 255.1m. *yuan* in Wenjiang (*Sichuan xiangzhen qiye shinian*, 1988: 84).
6. The differential between Suzhou and Liangshan was much less in terms of per capita industrial value-added than gross output because of higher rates of value-added in Liangshan, where industrial activity typically focused on basic mining and logging. In Suzhou, low value-added textile production was a key type of industrial activity.
7. This is the official line (as reported in Drèze and Sen, 1995: 66) but it remains uncertain whether this was followed in practice in ethnic minority areas. We also know that, in Han areas, literacy was assessed by the number of years of education completed rather by any formal test of ability.
8. There is a large literature on pre-1949 industrialization in the Sunan area. In English, this includes Fei (1939; 1983; 1986; 1992), Wu and Xu (forthcoming), and Li (1986)

but perhaps the best sources of all are the *Industrial Handbooks* for Jiangsu and Zhejiang (JIH, 1933; ZIH, 1935). The Chinese language literature is of course even larger, but one very useful recent monograph is Shanghai shehui kexueyuan jingji yanjiusuo (1991). For industrialization in Suzhou in the Maoist period, see Leeming (1985), Lee (1991), and Huang (1990).

9. According to Leeming (1985: 115): 'Much of what is reported from Wuxi appears to be genuine manufacturing industry, as opposed to craftsmen's work or farm processing. In exceptional cases, very big industrial jobs have been done—the county organised a group of communes to build gates for the floating dry-dock at Shanghai.'
10. Although many of those employed in proto-industry were women and children, and therefore not subject to conscription.
11. According to Ogilvie (1993: 161): 'proto-industrialization [in Europe] did not invariably lead to factory industrialization—quite often it led to "de-industrialization" and a return to agriculture.'
12. Liangshan's principal industrial products were coal, timber, sugar, salt, and beverages in 1952 (SCZL, 1990: 376).
13. By contrast, Han Chinese accounted for 92 per cent of the population in Liangshan's Huidong county (LYZG, 1985: 347).
14. There is a substantial literature on Liangshan written from this perspective. For general English-language accounts, see Cheng (1984) and Zhong (1984). For Chinese-language economic surveys of Liangshan, see LSL (1985), LYZG (1985), *Muli Zangzu zizhixian gaikuang* (1985), Yin (1986), Wenshi ziliao weiyuanhui (1993), and Zhu (1992).
15. One anecdotal piece of evidence on this comes from a survey conducted in Liangshan in the mid-1980s: 'A cadre told us that per capita incomes in Zhaojue are the lowest in the province, but the volume of alcohol consumed per person was the highest' (Zhang, 1985: 10).
16. Farmers in Sichuan reached the same conclusion about double rice cropping in the 1980s (Bramall, 1993, 1995*a*). It was rapidly abandoned in all but a handful of regions (where the length of the growing season was much longer) during the late 1970s.
17. That in turn made little sense because the externality arguments were weaker by the early 1980s than they had been in the mid-1970s. Increases in agricultural production had effectively resolved the food problem (at least until the demand for dairy and meat products exploded) and there was less justification for an autarkic development strategy given China's growing (and willing) integration with the world economy; this made grain imports a much more palatable option.
18. And if the release of the labour that was available depressed industrial productivity (for the reasons discussed in Chapter 7), Suzhou may have been doubly disadvantaged.
19. The data discussed in this section are problematic because they exclude SOEs controlled by central government.
20. This is calculated from the current price mean rate of growth of NVIO deflated by the all-China industrial producer price index (from ZGTJNJ, 1995: 249).
21. This regression is for only eight counties because of the absence of employment data on Guanghan and Qionglai.
22. Data problems are of course another possibility, but it is unlikely that output growth was systematically under-reported in Liangshan as distinct from Wenjiang.

Chapter 12. The Master Discourse and the State

1. As Stiglitz (1994: 7) says in describing the orthodoxy: 'The market failures approach argues there is indeed a role for government, but it is a limited role. Government

simply needs to correct the well-defined market failures, which it can do with simple tools having minimal effects on the mode of operation of the market economy.'

2. The literature on the need to apply this orthodoxy to Eastern Europe is now enormous. Significant contributions are those of Blanchard, *et al.* (1991), Blanchard, *et al.* (1993), Lipton and Sachs (1992), Sachs (1993*b*), Aslund (1995), Gros and Steinherr (1995), WDR (1996), and Woo, *et al.* (1997). As Krugman (1996) points out, this consensus has unravelled somewhat since its high water mark in the aftermath of the collapse of the USSR. In Europe, the successful creation of a single currency is by no means assured in the aftermath of the EMS debacle in 1992. In the USA, the election of President Clinton in 1992 signalled a move away from some of the policies of the Reagan era, but most American economists still advise against industrial policy.
3. Hence Nozick's (1974: 26) vision of 'the night-watchman state of classical liberal theory, limited to the functions of protecting all its citizens against violence, theft, and fraud, and to the enforcement of contracts, and so on'.
4. Matters are more complex in real business-cycle models. Fiscal expansion financed by bond sales may raise output because higher interest rates cause intertemporal effects; agents supply more hours of work in order to save more and hence take advantage of higher interest rates (or, because of Ricardian equivalence, agents recognize that taxes will have to be higher in the future to repurchase the bonds).
5. There are a number of other assumptions here. First, Stiglitz ignores the whole question of whether equilibria exist; his emphasis is on the uniqueness proofs of a general competitive equilibrium. If positive feedback is unbounded, then an equilibrium will not even exist. Secondly, Stiglitz assumes that most of the externalities in an economy cannot be internalized; in his phrase, they are diffuse.
6. This view is more usually called the notion of the 'developmental state' first used by Johnson (1982). This name is misleading because those who take this stance are concerned primarily with growth promotion rather than development in the more general sense of improving capabilities and reducing income inequality. The term 'governed market' is therefore used here instead.
7. But note that the governed-market approach can be distinguished from the narrowly gradualist view—that state intervention may still be needed to effect transition from state socialism to capitalism but that this sort of intervention will 'wither away' in the long run. For the governors of the market, the pervasive nature of market failure in some areas of the economy is such that permanent intervention in those areas will be needed.
8. Another criticism from the left is that competition is an evil because it destroys community (Roemer, 1994: 117–18).
9. There is also (inevitable) disagreement amongst socialists over the precise degree of state control, especially of the industrial sector. This reflects the difficulties inherent in trying to determine whether ownership of a given industry generates sufficient externalities to make it worthwhile. The problem is particularly acute in the case of heavy industries (which often produce an output that is arguably of strategic importance).
10. This survey of the international evidence does not attempt to be comprehensive. This is because there is now a large and growing body of such evidence (especially on East Asia) which demonstrates that state intervention can lead to a faster pace of economic growth. The essentially short-run crisis that affected the region in 1996–7 in no sense undermines that body of evidence, largely because it was *caused* (especially in South Korea) by these countries accepting the dictates of the master discourse. This section therefore does no more than summarize the essentials of this increasingly well-known evidence.

11. This in large measure reflects the role of Japan, which was the second largest shareholder in the World Bank by the early 1990s and which funded much of the 1993 Report (Wade, 1996).
12. Ellman (1994); OECD (1995). Thatcherism had precisely the same effect in the UK; there was a clear regional correlation between levels of poverty/unemployment and mortality by 1990.
13. And the continued use of exchange controls on capital-account transactions means that the economy remains rather different from the neoclassical ideal.
14. One can hardly explain the *level* of per capita incomes in the US without some recognition of its abundant natural resources.
15. A point recognized by Fukuyama (1995). His earlier book (1992) blithely ignored these differences between OECD countries.
16. However, as Krugman (1996) notes, recent discussion of East Asia bears an eerie similarity to discussion of the USSR in the early 1960s. Then it was claimed that the USSR had 'succeeded', that its rise threatened Western hegemony and that authoritarianism could work. Now the same is claimed of East Asia. As Krugman (1996: 167–8) implies, the following is true of both the USSR in the early 1960s and East Asia in the early 1990s: 'The leaders of these nations did not share our faith in free markets or unlimited civil liberties. They asserted with increasing self-confidence that their system was superior: societies that accepted strong, even authoritarian governments and were willing to limit individual liberties in the interest of the common good, take charge of their economies, and sacrifice short-run consumer interests for the sake of long-run growth would eventually outperform the increasingly chaotic societies of the West. And a growing minority of Western intellectuals agreed.'
17. Yet even here, one has to be careful. As we have seen, work by orthodox economists like Young, Kim, and Lau has alleged that rapid growth in the NICs is due largely to the mobilization of factor inputs—and not to productivity growth. The same sort of argument has been applied to the rise and fall of the USSR (Krugman, 1996).
18. As might be expected, some gradualists are sceptical about market socialism. Putterman (1995: 1061–2), for example, argues that privatization in China has developed a momentum of its own and cannot easily be reversed. In arguing, however, that a market-socialist economy might not look very different to post-war France, he largely ignores the emphasis on poverty alleviation and the progressive taxation of wealth that are core values for many market socialists. In these areas, countries like Germany, France, and Japan fall woefully short.
19. Conventional monetarism was abandoned by the UK in the mid-1980s and its successor (international monetarism) was swept away by the recovery of the economy following the abandonment of its membership of ERM. The growth of the US in the 1980s and 1990s was of course very largely due to fiscal and monetary expansion.
20. There are substantial disagreements on this issue even amongst economists who do not share the Washington consensus. Krugman (1996: 148) thinks that the Washington view is largely correct in terms of its espousal of free markets (and especially free trade), but largely wrong in its affection for 'sound money' and fixed exchange rates. Rodrik (1996) accepts the need for sound money but argues that one of the East Asian lessons is the need for selective state intervention. British economists tend to agree that there is a problem of demand deficiency in the 1990s but disagree on the question of whether Thatcherism revitalized the supply side (Minford, 1994) or left industry bereft of adequate capital (Rowthorn, 1995; Michie and Grieve Smith, 1996).

21. Some of Rawski's writings place him close to the border between this group and the market socialists discussed below. For example, he notes with approval some of Stiglitz's criticisms of orthodox economic theory, the standard Vickers-Yarrow result that market conditions are probably more important than ownership per se in determining corporate performance and even notes—on the basis of the evidence from Korea and Taiwan—that full bank privatization may not be needed (Rawski, 1995: 1168, 1170–1). This criticism of neoclassical economic theory is very different from its espousal in Rawski's earlier book (Rawski, 1989; Huang, 1991).
22. As Rawski (1995: 1167) puts it: 'Reform means improvement, not perfection. . . . Attempting more may accomplish less.'
23. 'There is absolutely no reason to delay the beginning of a gradual privatization process. . . . It is hard to see what benefit the Chinese people gain from state ownership of, say, a textile firm in Wuhan' (Naughton, 1995*a*: 324).
24. Blecher (1991) draws a distinction between the more entrepreneurial role played by government in Sichuan's Guanghan county and the developmental state found in Shulu, and others have stressed the chronic weakness of local government in many of the poorer parts of China.

Chapter 13. Aggregate Demand and Relative Prices

1. The analysis here holds not just for Shulu, but generally across China.
2. Some *xiangzhen* enterprises are privately owned and shelter under the umbrella of local government status for tax and legal purposes. The majority, however, are owned or subordinated to local government. As Oi (1995: 1135) says: 'Township and village enterprises, which are the most economically significant portion of rural industry, are not privately owned, nor are they forms of hybrid privatization, but forms of local government. . . . to suggest that all rural industry is partially or secretly "private" misses the essential character of the process that has spurred China's rapid rural industrialization.' The World Bank (WDR, 1996) has persisted in calling these non-state enterprises but this makes little sense. They may not be part of the state plan, but the operation of all of them is heavily constrained by local government (Blecher and Shue, 1996) and they operate in a fashion far removed from the norm in OECD economies. However, for a view that many of the *xiangzhen* enterprises are in fact private, see Zhou (1996).
3. By 1988–9, significant bottlenecks existed because of shortages of energy and foreign exchange, and these bottlenecks contributed to the inflationary upsurge of that period (Lo, 1997). The situation was very different at the end of the 1970s.
4. A significant number of Chinese economists argued that the inflationary problems of 1985–6 could not be explained in terms of macroeconomic imbalance. They therefore rejected the view that inflation could be brought under control by fiscal and monetary contraction without adverse effects upon the growth rate. They viewed inflation as the result of microeconomic imbalance (or what Kornai calls 'shortage') which could be corrected by enterprise reform aimed at reallocating factors of production to more productive sectors of the economy. Not surprisingly, most of these economists were advocates of ownership, rather than price, reform (Naughton, 1995*a*: 188–96; Fewsmith, 1994: 180–4). By contrast, economists advocating price reform—notably Wu Jinglian—were adamant in their view that relative price changes could only be successfully achieved against a background of fiscal and monetary contraction (Fewsmith, 1994: 162–6).
5. Naughton (1995*b*: 1087 n.) argues that China is little different from other countries in this respect: 'Chinese policy-makers are in the same position as American policy-makers

or those of most other countries. Very few countries are currently able to use fiscal policy as a flexible element of overall macroeconomic policy.'

6. Fiscal policy is generally less effective (for the usual Mundell–Fleming reasons) under floating exchange rates. Even so, there is considerable evidence that output was affected by fiscal policy in the OECD countries in the 1980s, notably in the USA during the episode of 'military Keynesianism' under Reagan.
7. Philip Huang (1990: 244) makes a similar point about Songjiang county (near Shanghai), arguing that none of his interviewees mentioned relative prices. This, he argues, was for three reasons: the price structure was very difficult to understand, cropping decisions were controlled by the state and the bulk of grain was self-consumed. Liu Minquan, a former Wuxi production team leader, has also suggested to me that prices played only a limited role (pers. comm.). However, this perspective is probably more valid in parts of Sunan—where yields were very high by Chinese and international standards by 1980. There was therefore less supply-side slack than elsewhere in China.
8. One cannot attribute this changed behaviour to family farming because decollectivization did not begin on a significant scale in the province until 1981–2 (Bramall, 1995*a*).
9. In some of China's most advanced counties, the price rise was crucial in raising agricultural income because the limits to output expansion had been reached. This was particularly true of Suzhou prefecture, a point emphasized by Huang (1990). In some of Suzhou's richest counties, almost all of the increase in agricultural income that occurred in the early 1980s was down to price rises. According to He (1990: 114): 'The change in procurement prices transferred considerable amounts of industrial profits to the farmers, which gave them a financial foundation for entering non-agricultural business. In relatively developed Wuxi, price rises between 1980 and 1984 generated 81.9 per cent of the total increase in agricultural incomes. This ratio, of course, was not as high in underdeveloped counties because of their greater potential for increasing agricultural output.'
10. This is not to suggest that the price elasticity of supply was high in Sunan, especially for grain crops. The evidence suggests that Sunan farmers did not respond to higher grain prices by increasing either sales or production (Huang, 1990; Du, 1995).

Chapter 14. The Chinese State and Agriculture

1. The literature claiming that decollectivization played the key role in the acceleration of agricultural growth in the early 1980s is substantial. For general accounts of agricultural reform, see Ash (1988), Saith (1987), Domes (1982), Kelliher (1992), and Fewsmith (1994). For Chinese-language literature, useful studies include Su (1982), Zhu (1992), Chen, *et al.* (1993), and Zhang and Xu (1995). For the debate about whether decollectivization was 'bottom up' or 'top down', see Watson (1984), Unger (1985–6), Kelliher (1992), Zhou (1996), and Zweig (1997). For some of the econometric studies of decollectivization, see McMillan, *et al.* (1989), Lin (1992), and Putterman (1993). For some dissenting voices, see Bramall (1993, 1995*a*), Hinton (1990), Huang (1990), Potter and Potter (1990), and Liu (1991*a*, 1994).
2. Accounts of the decollectivization process at a village level can be found in Hinton (1992), Endicott (1988), Judd (1992), and Wang (1988). A detailed chronology is given in Zhonggong zhongyang xuanchuanbu xuanchuanju (1988).
3. The development of household farming was slow initially because it lacked the approval of central government. The Third Plenum explicitly banned household contracting on the grounds that it was a threat to collective farming. Even Central Committee

document 75 ('Several Questions on Strengthening and Perfecting the Production Responsibility System in Agriculture' issued on 27 Sept. 1980), which officially sanctioned *baochan dao hu* for the first time, permitted its use only in poor counties. Nevertheless, the direction of national policy was clear from the attack on Dazhai in December 1980; Dazhai's legendary success, it was claimed, reflected massive state investment rather than the 'spirit of self-reliance'. Full approval for *baochan* and *baogan dao hu* systems was finally granted in Central Committee document 1 ('Summary of the National Rural Work Conference') of 1 Jan. 1982. At that time, only about 45 per cent of rural households had adopted the production responsibility system (Lin, 1996: 19).

4. According to Garnaut, *et al.* (1996), land reform in the early 1950s was the first revolution, and decollectivization the second.
5. In many areas across China, *nongyezu* (agricultural groups) replaced teams after 1984. In addition, the 1980s saw the re-emergence of smaller lineage groups which farmed co-operatively during at least part of the year (Judd, 1992).
6. Similar arguments apply to the north China plain. Indeed, as Blecher and Shue note (1996: 193), group farming was the norm in some parts of Hebei's Shulu county even at the end of the 1980s.
7. This is a view now widely shared; see, for example, Zweig (1997: 14–15). Zhou's (1996) view that the process was driven from below is a rare exception.
8. For some of the literature on Dazhai, see Meisner (1978), Tsou, *et al.* (1979, 1982), Hinton (1983, 1990), and Qin (1995). For a critique of Dazhai's record, see Chen, *et al.* (1993).
9. The Gang criticized Dazhai because Chen Yonggui was closely associated with Hua Guofeng in the later stages of his career. The campaign against Dazhai developed after the publication of a newspaper article in 1980 entitled 'Dazhai's Departure From the Spirit of Dazhai' and has continued throughout the reform era; for example, the polemical tract *The Rise and Fall of the Red Flag of Dazhai* was published in 1990. One of the main criticisms against Dazhai in the late 1980s was its very low labour productivity by international standards; paradoxically, this reflected the low level of mechanization, itself a product of decollectivization. A lengthy summary of the charges against Dazhai is to be found in Chen, *et al.* (1993).
10. Putterman (1993: 119) and his team working on Dahe are aware of this problem. However, they nevertheless are of the view that Dahe was not very unusual: 'A general summary of our findings might be that while Dahe was certainly not average, due to its proximity to a provincial capital and the intensity of cultivation that it achieved during the collective era, it was also not entirely atypical of portions of the coastal region of rural China. . . . it is reasonable to proceed on the assumption that even if they are not precisely the norm, it is also unlikely that they [the findings] have no wider applicability.'
11. Some other writers have emphasized the importance of technological and climatic factors as the key determinant of crop yields. Hinton is one. So, too, Philip Huang (1990: 244), who characterizes the process of agricultural growth in Songjiang county (near Shanghai) thus: 'Finally, the form of organization of labor for crop production, whether collective or family, does not seem to have mattered much. . . . If we can trust the testimony of the peasants and technical cadres, as opposed to the political cadres, crop yields in Songjiang were shaped primarily by technological and climatic factors, and only secondarily by policy choices involving cropping patterns and procurement, and least of all by the reorganization of farm labor.'
12. The force of these objections is greatly reduced by the fact that the worst flooding since 1934 occurred in the Minjiang valley during 1980–1, despite the fabled Dujiangyan

irrigation system. Furthermore, the very fact that grain yields were already high by provincial standards on the Chengdu plain meant that it was more difficult for these counties to raise them further—which ought to have depressed their potential growth rate.

13. Not perhaps surprisingly, the four were Shanghai, Beijing, Zhejiang, and Guangdong; all these registered irrigation declines in the 1988–96 sub-period and over the transition period as a whole. Both Shanghai and Beijing experienced rapid urban expansion during this period, which took its toll on farmland. It should, however, be noted that the ratio of irrigated to total cultivated area declined from 80 per cent in 1978 to 77 per cent by 1994 in Beijing (LSTJ, 1990: 74, and ZGTJNJ, 1995: 331, 337). (A decline is also recorded for Shanghai, but then the figure of 100 per cent given for 1978 may have been an exaggeration). In other words, declining irrigated area was not due solely to the use of arable land for building and roads. In Guangdong and Zhejiang, the pace of industrial growth was so fast that the neglect of farming was almost to be expected. In Zhejiang, the irrigation ratio did at least rise from 82 per cent in 1978 to 87 per cent in 1994. In Guangdong, however, it declined sharply from its 1978 level of 71 per cent to only 63 per cent in 1994.

Chapter 15. The Open Door

1. On foreign trade reforms, see Jacobson and Oksenberg (1990), Lardy (1992), and World Bank (1994*c*; 1997*b*). On foreign direct investment, see Kamath (1990) and Kueh (1992). For special economic zones, see Jao and Leung (1986), Osborne (1986), Vogel (1989), Kleinberg (1990), and Wall, *et al.* (1996).
2. This omission was acknowledged in 1992 by Deng to have been a mistake: 'when I review my work in retrospect, I think one of the great mistakes I committed is that I did not make Shanghai one of the special economic zones at the time when the four existing special economic zones were founded' (in Yabuki, 1995: 292).
3. For the counties and municipalities covered, see Zhongguo tongjiju (1989*b*).
4. The concessions granted to these areas varied somewhat from the original SEZs, and few received the scale of infrastructural investment enjoyed by Shenzhen. However, the underlying principles involved were the same.
5. This document gave legitimacy to a process that had been going on for some time under the auspices of local government. Some of the zones certainly do date from 1992 and after; for example, the Suzhou industrial park, set up in collaboration with Singapore's government, formally came into being in May 1994. However, the Chengdu Economic and Technological Development Zone was established in July 1990, and the one in Kunshan dates from as early as 1985. For the history of these zones, see the official Special Economic Zone website (http://www.sezo.gov.cn).
6. For some early discussions of the Three Gorges project, see Fearnside (1988), Yabuki (1995), and Dai (1994).
7. Although Nurkse—and others such as W. A. Lewis (1980)—saw trade as the engine of growth, their policy conclusion was to advocate import substitution. This seemingly paradoxical conclusion reflected their view, unsurprising in view of world depression in the 1930s and after 1973, that growth in OECD countries had slowed down dramatically. The only solution, therefore, was for LDCs to generate the necessary demand themselves (Riedel, 1984).
8. This is discussed in more detail below. Once adjusted for the price differentials, it is unlikely that the share of exports in GDP reached 10 per cent.
9. For an introduction to the vast literature on Prebisch-Singer, see Spraos (1983).

10. Corden (1971) also stressed the supply-side role of trade, though his emphasis was more on capital accumulation rather than technical progress.
11. This creates difficulties for the master discourse, which attributes East Asian growth on the one hand to factor accumulation and on the other hand to the impact of international competition on technical progress. As Srinivasan (1995: 57) comments: 'This creates a problem for those who attribute the spectacular growth of NICs to the dynamic productivity gains arising from their outward orientation!'
12. A rare exception to this is the analysis of late Victorian British economic growth offered by Matthews, *et al.* (1982) which argues that the British growth slowdown in the late nineteenth century was due to slower export growth. Although there is probably something in this (the growth of textile exports did slow and, more generally, the growth of competition from other countries made it hard for Britain to maintain its share of world exports) most specialists have concluded that the main constraints on British growth were domestic—reflecting either 'failure' of one sort or other or simply binding supply-side constraints (Harley, 1994: 320). A more recent study by O'Brien (1999) has also argued that the growth of the Industrial Revolution itself owed much to the expansion of overseas trade.
13. The rationale is of course that, in the absence of foreign trade, substitution would have occurred via domestic production. That would have reduced real incomes via the higher cost of import substitutes, but not by a crippling amount. This type of conclusion parallels the calculation of the social savings engendered by railways; for most countries, it has typically been concluded that the impact of railways was quite small (McCloskey, 1987).
14. However, Japanese growth was probably export-led during two relatively short periods. First, during World War I when the European powers were no longer able to satisfy LDC demand. Second, during the recovery of the 1930s which 'was ignited by deficit spending and exchange rate depreciation, and sustained and accelerated by the expansion of exports to East Asia regions as well as by the high level of deficit spending' (Okura and Teranishi, 1994: 13).
15. For the distinction between trans-shipment and re-export in the context of China and Hong Kong, see Sung (1991: 15).
16. In ZGTJNJ, 1993; see Yabuki (1995: 161).
17. The theory is discussed in Fewsmith (1994) and Hsu (1991).
18. To be sure, processed oil is not really a primary product. Equally, however, it shares only some of the characteristics of a manufacture.
19. Conversely, it is not surprising that Tianjin, Shanghai, and Liaoning, the pre-war exporting centres of China, all experienced export growth rates of much less than 10 per cent per year.
20. The only way to 'rescue' the external trade hypothesis would be to show that, although the average degree of integration of the Chinese interior into the world economy was low, external trade and investment at the *margin* had a critical effect. But this is little more than clutching at straws because the incredibly powerful backward and forward linkage effects that this would presuppose between the handful of key sectors affected by the open door simply did not exist. Nor can one argue that provinces like Henan, Ningxia, and Sichuan began to grow quickly because of a sudden closing of Romer's 'ideas gap'. The key area of technical advance in the early 1980s was in agriculture, and much of this technical progress was indigenous in origin (Stone, 1988).
21. Although the American recession of 1990 and 1991 did not help those Chinese provinces that were relatively outward-orientated in the late 1980s by reducing the growth rate of their export markets.

22. These data are for actual or realized FDI. They are the sum of what the official Chinese sources report as foreign direct investment and other foreign investment (which is in fact commercial credit). The figures are inflated by round-tripping.
23. These data cover enterprises owned by entrepreneurs based in Hong Kong, Macao, and Taiwan as well other countries. They cover all *sanzi* enterprises, i.e. joint ventures, cooperative enterprises, and enterprises wholly owned by foreigners. In 1995, there were almost 50,000 *sanzi* industrial enterprises operating at the township level and above with independent accounting systems (Disanci, 1997: 484) and 234,000 *sanzi* enterprises of all sorts (ZGTJNJ, 1997: 609).
24. The other exports were generated by SOEs and foreign trade corporations.
25. Beijing, Tianjin, Liaoning, Shanghai, Jiangsu, Zhejiang, Fujian, Shandong, and Guangdong.
26. Though it would not significantly alter comparisons with other LDCs, where GDP is also underestimated by official exchange rate data.
27. The rate was of course faster still in some of Guangdong's regions such as Dongguan and Shenzhen.
28. I am grateful to a referee for this suggestion.
29. These figures are at 1970 and 1980 prices respectively. However, the difference between 1970 and 1980 industrial prices is virtually non-existent.
30. However, given that per capita real GDP was about four times higher in Shanghai than in Guangdong in 1978, there was manifestly some justice in a much higher rate of (implicit) taxation on the municipality.
31. For a discussion, see Yang (1994), Wong (1991*b*) and Wong, *et al.* (1995).
32. A rather different account is given in Vogel (1989: 89–90) but the picture remains in essence the same. Guangdong's contribution to the national exchequer was higher than its notional contribution suggests.
33. It is not entirely clear that this was unreasonable. It is true that Shanghai's total GDP, at 2.728bn. *yuan* in 1978, was not much higher than Guangdong's 18.473bn. *yuan* (LSTJ, 1990: 311, 619). However, in per capita terms, the gap between 2,498 *yuan* (Shanghai) and 369 *yuan* (Guangdong) was large enough to justify some sort of differential treatment.
34. A notable exception to this general trend was during 1986–9, when the real exchange rate appreciated (Lardy, 1992: 114–15).
35. Or—less satisfactorily—that prices are simply sticky.
36. Not surprisingly, a simple regression of the *yuan* value of exports on the dollar exchange rate yields both a very high R^2 and a highly significant t statistic.
37. The share of consumer goods was to some extent depressed by the deflationary macroeconomic policies pursued from late 1988 to early 1992. However, even in 1993—when recovery was in full swing—the consumer goods share of imports was only 8 per cent, well down on its 1981 level.
38. Indeed it is interesting that Hua Guofeng's attempt to hasten modernization in the late 1970s was ridiculed as the 'foreign leap forward' because of his intention to rely so heavily upon capital imports from abroad.

Chapter 16. The State, Industry, and Infrastructure

1. In 1985, state appropriations provided about 23 per cent of funds for investment by state-owned enterprises (industrial and non-industrial combined). 40 per cent was self-funded and 23 per cent came from borrowing. By 1994, however, state appropriations

provided only 5 per cent—compared to 26 per cent from loans and the 51 per cent that was self-funded (ZGTJNJ, 1995: 141).

2. These data are for *xiang*-level enterprises and above. They therefore cover a part of local government industry as well as industry controlled by central government.
3. As did the fall of Chen Yonggui, the former leader of the Dazhai production brigade, in February 1980.
4. The early 1980s also saw increased investment in the pesticide industry. None of this is to suggest that central government policy was entirely successful. Shortages of chemical fertilizers were viewed as a severe problem by many Chinese farmers in the late 1980s.
5. For price reforms, see Chan (1989) and World Bank (1993*b*). The reforms to agricultural prices in the early 1990s are discussed in Garnaut, *et al.* (1996).
6. This was initially a very slow process. However, a large proportion of state enterprises had been affected by 1988; the proportion of firms where manager responsibility was the norm increased from less than 10 per cent in 1984 to 40 per cent by 1986 and more than 90 per cent by 1988 (Naughton, 1995*a*: 205).
7. Though never entirely so because many prices remained out of line with marginal costs. It was, for example, almost impossible for the coal industry to make a significant profit because of its low state-imposed product price.
8. Many of the 'reformers' were advocates of prior enterprise reform because they were enriching themselves via the dual-track pricing system and therefore had an incentive to maintain it. Many of those close to Zhao, and many of the young 'reformers' (influential because of their family background and contacts rather than any intellectual distinction), were tainted by corruption.
9. The restructuring programme was nevertheless still its infancy in 1996. Small steel companies like Handan (Hebei province), which employed only 28,000 workers in 1996, continued to co-exist alongside giants like Shougang, Angang, and Baogang. Furthermore, the problems which afflicted Shougang in the mid-1990s show that the need for further re-structuring was much greater than initially realized.
10. In some parts of China, these sources of competitive pressure were highly significant. In Wenzhou, private enterprises posed a serious threat to state enterprises (Nolan and Dong, 1990). The same was true of Hong Kong-based enterprises in Guangdong.
11. It does, however, capture the extremes of the non-state sector distribution. Zhejiang and Fujian are typical of provinces where marketization has advanced rapidly; Zhejiang's non-state share in 1993 was actually higher than Guangdong's (79.5 per cent of current price GVIO compared to 72.5 per cent respectively—ZGTJNJ, 1994: 376–7). At the other end of the scale, Xinjiang had the lowest non-state share in 1993 (21.5 per cent), and Yunnan and Gansu were third and fourth lowest respectively. Data on Guangdong for 1978 to 1989 are not available in LSTJ (1990). The sample also covers a wide range of income levels (Gansu compared to Zhejiang) and both provinces with large (Liaoning) and small (Yunnan) industrial bases.
12. One of the reasons was Liaoning's high level of labour productivity in 1978. Given this high base—reflecting Liaoning's long history of industrialization—it is not surprising that the subsequent growth rate was lower than in provinces where industrialization was in its infancy.
13. This probably had much to do with their low level of industrial development in 1978—in sharp contrast to Liaoning.
14. Some recent work by Lo (1999) does suggest that competition was playing an important role in improving performance, but he is careful not to claim too much for his results.

15. For the growth of collective enterprises in rural China in the 1980s, see Wong (1988), Huang (1990), Byrd and Lin (1990), Findlay, *et al.* (1994), and Ho (1994). For the private sector, see Odgaard (1992*b*), Nolan and Dong (1990) and Zhou (1996). On the continuing links between local government and rural enterprises, see Oi (1990), Blecher (1991), Odgaard (1992*b*), and Blecher and Shue (1996).
16. Private enterprises hiring large numbers of workers posed a number of ideological problems for the Party in that it was difficult to reconcile such 'capitalist' enterprises with a development strategy that was avowedly 'socialist'. These residual ideological shackles were thrown off in 1988, when large, labour-hiring, households were granted legal status.
17. Moreover, this is the growth rate of *real* output; industrial prices rose by 24 per cent in 1993 and 20 per cent in 1994 (ZGTJNJ, 1995: 249).
18. Although the RCCs are under the supervision of the Agricultural Bank of China, the lending activities of the two are largely separate. Both lent funds to TVEs during the 1980s (Tam, 1988).
19. These growth rates overstate the rate of increase because of the change of definition of rural industry to incorporate all of the 'five wheels' (*wuge lunzi*)—*xiang*, *cun*, team, cooperative, and private—after 1984. Where relatively complete time series data are provided in the *xian zhi*, a distinct leap in the series is evident in 1984.
20. The rate of growth between 1978 and 1983 in Guanghan—which refers to *xiang*- and *cun*-level enterprises only—was 38 per cent.
21. At least until its Party Secretary (Yu Zuomin) received a 20-year prison sentence in 1993 for (*inter alia*) planning a murder and 'unlawful control of the people'.
22. The five small industries were chemical fertilizer, energy, iron and steel, farm machinery, and cement. Their development dates from 1958.
23. In sharp contrast to Wong's analysis, Blecher (1991: 286–9) argues that Shulu's relative success—and Guanghan's failure—reflects the way in which Shulu has grown out of, rather than abandoned, 'developmental Maoism'.
24. The routes taken in these two areas have been so distinctive that they have been labelled the Wenzhou and Sunan models. The Wenzhou model is discussed in Nolan and Dong (1990), Kok (1991), Dong (1992), and Liu (1992). For rural industrialization in Sunan, see Leeming (1985), Huang (1990), and Ho (1994).
25. One cannot really argue that poor areas in Zhejiang and Jiangsu lacked the necessary prerequisites for industrial growth. Although more deficient in human and physical capital than other parts of the provinces, the poor counties of Zhejiang and Jiangsu faced none of the crippling geographical or ethnic problems that were usual in western China. For example, the average illiteracy rate at the 1982 Census in Wenzhou—one of Zhejiang's poorest prefectures—was 38 per cent. By contrast, the figure was 58 per cent in Liangshan prefecture in Sichuan. Given also that local government was assiduous in its promotion of private industry in many parts of both provinces (Wenzhou is again the classic example), one cannot argue that the poor performance of the private sector reflects systematic discrimination against it by local government.
26. Weitzman and Xu explain the success of TVEs in terms of trust, which makes the introduction of formal property rights unnecessary; in Eastern Europe, where trust is lower, there is a much greater need for legally enforceable rights. Their argument is very different from that offered by Fukuyama (1995), who sees a pervasive lack of trust in Chinese cultures as a significant obstacle to the creation of large private corporations; family enterprises will thrive, but modern corporations will not. The Weitzman–Xu argument is not very convincing. If China were such a high trust society, the sort of precautions against

theft (luggage locked to racks in trains and iron bars on almost all ground floor windows) that are ubiquitous throughout the People's Republic would not be needed. Furthermore, it makes it difficult to explain the 'failure' of collective farming. That system has usually been criticized because of its flawed, workpoint-based, incentive system, But if there was a high level of trust within villages, there would have been little need for formal material incentive systems.

27. Investment by local government to some extent compensated for these lacunae. That is especially true of road building. However, the nature of large-scale infrastructural programmes is such that *central* government agency is imperative. It is in this respect that the record of the Dengist state on infrastructure is problematic.
28. However, it is unlikely that anyone who travelled long distance in one of China's hard-seat railway carriages during the 1980s would use 'adequate' to describe the conditions.
29. This policy was also designed to discourage the movement of peasants—usually seen as a potent force of unrest by the Chinese authorities, and especially so in the year of the Tiananmen massacre—into urban areas.
30. If Guanghan county in Sichuan is representative, most of the increased county-level spending between 1978 and 1985 was included within the budget; only about 10 per cent of county spending in 1984 on education was extra-budget (*Guanghan xian zhi*, 1992: 313).
31. This in part reflects the lengthening of lower middle school from two to three years in 1979.

Chapter 17. Origins of the Growth-Promoting State

1. Trotsky (1937: 254) was not wrong in suspecting that a 'backslide to capitalism is wholly possible' when he wrote of the Soviet Union; the same analysis seems equally prophetic about some aspects of the transition in China.
2. Accordingly, this book disagrees with Grabowski's view (1994) that the key issue is where the successful *developmental* state comes from.
3. To be sure, the common distinction made between gradualism in China and shock therapy in the USSR is exaggerated. In the latter, privatization of the assets of state industry was by no means instantaneous and, more generally, the pace of reform was sometimes slow. In Ukraine, the extent of liberalization that occurred between late 1991 (independence) and the summer of 1994 was very limited (Kaufmann, 1994). Moreover, when reform began under Gorbachev in the late 1980s, his intention was to gradually restructure the economy (*perestroika*), rather than to embark upon a programme of marketization. Furthermore, some writers have argued (wrongly) that reform was actually rapid in China, at least in the agricultural sector where 'privatization' is said to have occurred very quickly (Sachs and Woo, 1994; Balcerowicz, 1994: 37). Nevertheless, taken as a whole, the distinction between rapid transition towards a market economy in East Europe, and slow transition in China, is largely correct.
4. Private enterprises were allowed in the urban sector from 1981 onwards (Yabuki, 1995: 59).
5. The fourth reason is of course the ideological and political hegemony of the master discourse.
6. Although it is not unreasonable to deny the validity of a country's objective if that objective is military conquest. Arguably, too, there are human rights that are universal.
7. 'The East Asian success stories show that the same types of intervention that in Latin America have impeded growth (such as subsidized interest rates) have been used in countries like Taiwan and South Korea by these governments to accelerate growth (Streeten, 1996: 37).

8. There were of course earlier non-Chinese historical precedents. The most famous was Soviet New Economic Policy during the 1920s, which was similar in many respects to Chinese economic policy in the early 1950s (Bramall, 1995*b*). This may well have influenced Deng's thinking, not least because he studied in Moscow between January 1926 and January 1927 en route from Paris back to China.
9. Few of the ideas were Deng's. In fact, the three key working groups set up during 1961–2 assigned Chen Yun and Li Fuchun to economic issues, Peng Zhen to culture and education, whilst Deng was assigned to political and legal affairs. Nevertheless, as all these activities were coordinated via the Secretariat—that is, via Deng's office—he was closely involved in all three areas. See also Naughton (1993: 494–5).
10. Yongjia county in Zhejiang province's Wenzhou prefecture is a case in point. Its use there was championed in early 1957 by Li Yunhe—in charge of agriculture in the county. However, Li came under attack from the prefecture's newspaper in the summer, and from *Renmin Ribao* in October as the Hundred Flowers was abandoned. With these attacks came an attend to household farming; Li was styled a rightist in February 1958 (Fewsmith, 1994: 23–4). For an interesting, albeit rather euphoric, account of pre-1978 experiments with household responsibility, see Zhou (1996).
11. For Chinese accounts of this period, see Liu and Wu (1986, chs. 18 and 19), Zhongguo shehui zhuyi zhengtai jingjixue sishinian (1991, ch. 3), and Sun (1992, ch. 15).
12. In analysing the politics of the 1980s, it is the disagreements between Chen Yun and Deng Xiaoping that tended to be emphasized. In fact, there was much common ground. Both had strongly supported the *zerentian* system in the early 1960s, and both had enraged Mao in the process. Both were also in agreement about the way that disagreements within the CCP should be handled. For example, the falls of Hu Yaobang (January 1987) and Zhao Ziyang (June 1989) resulted merely in their loss of office rather than exile to the countryside or death—as would have happened during the Cultural Revolution.
13. Unprocessed (*yuanliang*) grain output per head was 268 kg in China in 1965. In Sichuan, the figure was 288 kg, and in Anhui and Guizhou grain available was 294 and 269 kg respectively (LSTJ, 1990).
14. The evidence that is available—albeit very anecdotal—suggests that those teams which adopted the *zerentian* system outperformed those that continued to use the production team as the basic unit of account. A survey conducted in 36 *xian* in Anhui in October 1961 found that grain output had increased by 36 per cent over the previous year in those teams using the household as the basic unit of account. The increase recorded in teams using team-level accounting was only 12 per cent (Lu, 1992: 173).
15. In retrospect, it is evident that most of the debates in the late 1970s were not so much about how to promote growth, but about whether other developmental objectives (class struggle and narrow income differentials) should give way to growth.
16. The answer to McCloskey's 'American question'—'If you're so smart, why aren't you rich?'—is thus very simple: not everyone wants to be rich.
17. Grabowski's (1994) internalist argument—that the size of the domestic market is the critical factor because that makes possible big gains (rents) for firms if they are willing to cooperate with the state—is not very convincing because of its very limited relevance in explaining both India's unsuccessful and Taiwan's successful experiment with dirigisme.
18. This is a point emphasized by Gramsci. Precisely because the scope for overt coercion is extremely limited, the capitalist state can only govern by eliciting consent. That does not preclude the possibility that the state and the capitalist class can manufacture consent via its control of the media (as suggested by Chomsky).

19. This is certainly not true of the best writers in the state-centred tradition. Myrdal (1968: i. 67) is very clear on this: 'the success of planning for development . . . would not in principle conflict with the ideal of political democracy, which only concerns the manner in which policies are decided upon.' See also Myrdal (1968: ii. 895).
20. According to Yabuki (1995: 227–8): 'In summary, if there is no underpinning of economic development, it is futile to attempt frontally to ameliorate human rights in China. Only by taking a slightly circuitous route to democracy via economic development can the problem of the human rights of the Chinese people truly be resolved . . . The difficulties of perestroika versus the success of the Deng Xiaoping line of separating politics and economics are indirect proof of the correctness of the strategy of proceeding from economic reform to political reform and the futility of attempting the reverse.'
21. One of the oddest features of Vanhanen's work is that his index of power resources, which he uses as an independent variable to explain the emergence of democracy, actually has many of the characteristics of a wider index of democracy itself. For example, literacy rates, the proportion of the population in higher education and the extent to which the control of non-agricultural means of production are dispersed—which feature in his index—are all indicators of the 'positive' freedom of the population.
22. For a summary of this argument, see Eggertsson (1990).
23. The conventional wisdom on authoritarianism is summarized by Rodrik (1996: 19) as: 'Authoritarianism may have had something to do with the East Asian government style, but there are too many mismanaged dictatorships around the world to take the hypothesis seriously. One need only look at sub-Saharan Africa.'
24. Though some have taken this route, e.g. Deepak Lal (1995).
25. Some economists have argued that an external threat may actually promote development by forcing states to pursue industrialization strategies. For example, Grabowski (1994) argues that the Chinese threat was important in promoting economic growth in South Korea and Taiwan. Yamamura (1977) has taken a similar view of pre-war Japanese industrialization: 'the "strong army" policy, combined with the wars, was the principal motivation behind creating and expanding the arsenals and other publicly-financed shipyards and modern factories which acted as highly effective centers for the absorption and dissemination of Western technologies and skills' (Yamamura, 1977: 113). While it is true that Germany and Japan outperformed other Western economies during the 1930s, it is clear that a policy of defence industrialization is second-best. The clearest demonstration of this is the acceleration in growth rates in both countries after 1945 when their large industrial companies shifted from defence to civilian production. Lockwood puts the point best: 'The drain of empire building went far to nullify the more constructive use of state power to mobilize savings for investment in productive enterprise . . . Significantly, the war which profited Japan most was World War I, when she remained neutral in all but name' (Lockwood, 1954: 577–8). Note also that slow British growth after World War II has been blamed by some on the fiscal consequences of a vain attempt to maintain Britain's position as a world power (Barnett, 1995).
26. An excellent summary of Sino-American relations during the Maoist era is given in Cohen (1990).
27. The guidance system was based on that used by Germany's V-2 rockets in the latter stages of World War II.
28. Part of the reason for this was that the PLA was itself disunited. Peng's status in the Army was by no means unassailable for two reasons. First, his abandonment of guerrilla tactics in August–December 1940 in the war against Japan (the 'Hundred

Regiments' campaign) involved very high casualties. Secondly, the PLA suffered extremely heavy casualties in the Korean War under Peng's command. As a result, a sizeable fraction of the army supported Lin Biao, whose reputation as tactician was second to none.

29. Paradoxically, Gorbachev was regarded much more favourably by the neo-authoritarian movement in China in the late 1980s; at that time, *perestroika* had not yet failed and Deng's physical frailty was becoming increasingly apparent. The neo-authoritarians advocated the separation of politics from economics, but also stressed the importance of having a 'Bonapartist' leader like Gorbachev. Zhao Ziyang, himself a sympathizer with neo-authoritarianism, increasingly cast himself in this role in the late 1980s.
30. Much remains unclear about Deng's early career, and will doubtless remain so until Party archives are made available. This brief sketch is based upon Yang (1998).
31. It is worth noting that the prestige enjoyed by Chen Yun and Yang Shangkun in the late 1980s also stemmed from their participation in the March, and their presence at the key Politburo meeting at Zunyi in January 1935 (Salisbury, 1985: 121).
32. As Lieberthal (1997: 99) says: 'The record makes clear that Liu Shaoqi, Deng Xiaoping, and most other leaders supported the GLF strategy wholeheartedly throughout 1958. Indeed, the only obvious civilian dissenters at the Politburo level that year were Premier Zhou Enlai and the top economic administrator, Chen Yun.'
33. Nevertheless, Deng's conversion to critic was rather late. As Dittmer (1993: 5) points out 'both Liu Shaoqi and Deng Xiaoping subsequently became enthusiastic supporters of the Great Leap Forward, which re-enacted the errors of overhasty collectivization in spades.'
34. The initial conference at Lushan at which Peng wrote his celebrated 'Letter of Opinion' to Mao was held in July. It was followed immediately after by the 8th Plenum of the 8th Central Committee, also at Lushan (August 1959). As for the reasons for Deng's absence, some accounts say that he broke his leg whilst playing billiards (Shambaugh, 1993; 470). Others attribute the break to a game of table tennis (MacFarquhar, 1983: 229). Goodman (1994: 62) has it that another person broke Deng's leg with a billiard cue and in Yang (1998: 145) he has an injured foot. All this is a fair measure of how much of Deng's career remains shrouded in mystery.
35. This paragraph is based primarily upon Yang (1998).
36. A very different argument is put forward by Campos and Root (1996), who argue that East Asian success was (in part) built upon shared growth. In other words, wealth redistribution meant that the bulk of the population had a share in the fruits of growth and therefore were willing to go along with the growth-promoting strategy. The problem with this is that it assigns too much importance to the great mass of the population in influencing the actions of the state. To be sure, revolutions can and do occur, but in general the collective-action problem is very hard to solve when those involved number millions. Accordingly, the main obstacle to the governed market should be seen as elite groups and not the mass of the population.
37. On the grounds that the tobacco industry is one of the main reasons for the high demand for health care.
38. The assumption here is of course that the marginal propensity to save (and therefore to invest) is higher out of profits than out of wages.
39. There are some exceptions, but these tend to support rather than refute the argument. For example, China has managed to achieve rapid—even accelerating—growth after 1985 despite rising inequality. But it is doubtful whether this is sustainable; the rising

inequality of the late 1980s was one factor precipitating the Tiananmen demonstrations in 1989. There has also been a tendency in the 1990s towards growing inflationary pressures (a product of inequality), which have been choked off only by draconian fiscal and monetary contraction.

40. It should be said that one would have more confidence in this kind of interpretation were the data on the East Asian income distributions reliable. As it stands, however, substantial doubts surround both the level and trend in income inequality in South Korea, Taiwan, and Japan (there is no doubt that the Hong Kong income distribution was highly unequal in 1960 as Rodrik's (1996: 20) own data show). In the case of Taiwan, the first proper national sample survey covering 3,000 households took place only in 1964. Although that is quite a large sample, there are doubts about its quality. First, the income estimates derived from the family surveys are typically between 17 and 27 per cent less than income estimates based on national accounts. Secondly, whereas wages and salaries are understated by between 22 and 33 per cent (as a per cent of national account estimates), interest and rent are understated by between 31 and 51 per cent (Kuznets, 1979: 103, 104, 106). This suggests strongly that rich households were either under-represented or that rich households systematically understated their real income. One cannot therefore disagree with Kuznets' (1979: 106) conclusion that 'we have to accept the major conclusions of the comparisons, which suggest significant shortages in the family survey income totals [and] . . . the possibility of wider inequalities in the conventional size distribution of income among households than are now indicated by the family survey reports.' As for South Korea, the 1960 gini coefficient was higher than for Taiwan but this was also probably an underestimate. This is because the South Korean data understate true inequality by excluding 'wealthy households [the urban rich], single-person households [the urban poor], non-farm households in rural areas [the rural rich] and small farmers [the rural poor]' (Hart-Landsberg, 1993: 199). In other words, the Korean data exclude the top and bottom ends of the income distribution. As for Japan, often regarded as a model amongst OECD economies for its low level of inequality, substantial doubts surround the data. Atkinson, *et al.* (1995: 69–70) deemed the official Japanese data so unreliable—they excluded top and bottom ends of the income distribution—that he did not include Japan in his comparison of OECD countries. Moreover, an alternative estimate by Ishizaki for the late 1960s put the gini coefficient at 0.41, substantially above the official figure of 0.34. Ishizaki's figures may themselves be on the high side because of his exclusion of farmer self-consumption (Minami, 1998) but it is nevertheless clear that the Japanese data are problematic. Whether any of this significantly undermines the view that inequality was comparatively low in East Asia is more debatable. After all, and as Little (1979: 498) says in commenting on the Taiwan data, 'understatement of property income is probably true of most surveys, especially in developing countries.' Nevertheless, one does need to tread with a degree of caution here.

41. The argument in this paragraph is the antithesis of Michael Lipton's (1977: 13) well-known view that 'The most important class conflict in the poor countries of the world today is not between labour and capital. Nor is it between foreign and national interests. It is between the rural classes and the urban classes.' The problem with Lipton's analysis is that one cannot talk of a single urban class, and that there is little evidence to suggest that revolutionary struggles have ever been primarily the result of urban–rural tensions.

42. As the events of 1988–9 proved, it was not easy to significantly reduce their living standards via price reform without provoking an explosive reaction.

43. In a democracy, the problem is as much about winning power as using it effectively. One possible solution is for a growth-promoting faction to make a credible, pre-regime change, commitment to the status quo. In many respects this is precisely the approach adopted by the Labour Party in Britain between 1992 and 1997. By committing itself to not raising income taxes or renationalizing utilities (and changing its constitution to make that pre-election commitment credible), it gained sufficient credibility to make itself electable. The problem for the post-1997 Labour government was that its pre-commitments (almost by definition) forced it to rule out the very type of policy changes —income tax rises to fund investment in infrastructure and other public goods—that are essential for growth promotion.
44. In inter-war Japan, the existence of the *zaibatsu* did not prevent growth. However, that growth was suboptimal because it was geared primarily towards the needs of the military sector.
45. Some of these issues are discussed in Rodrik (1996).
46. An alternative way of looking at Chiang's role is to give him the credit for the land reform but to note the massacre of up to 20,000 citizens at his behest in 1947. In other words, transition in Taiwan was made possible not by prior equality but by the use of force to liquidate one of the most vocal sections of the opposition.
47. According to Trotsky (1937: 255): 'The Soviet Union is a contradictory society halfway between capitalism and socialism, in which . . . on the road to socialism the workers would have to overthrow the bureaucracy.'
48. The composition of the Politburo and its standing committee are given in MacFarquhar (1993: 474–7). Deng Xiaoping, technically only Secretary to the Standing Committee, is also included in this list.
49. Most of the biographical information in this paragraph comes from Salisbury (1985).
50. In effect, the Chinese military were bought off with a side payment. In return for a reduction in their political influence, they were promised a substantial modernization of their equipment and—equally importantly—were granted the freedom to set up money-making enterprises themselves.

Chapter 18. Conclusion

1. 'Genuine' TFP growth excludes the static impact of labour reallocation from agriculture to industry, which contributed a further 1.1 per cent per year.
2. All the East Asian states began their phase of rapid growth with a low level of income and wealth inequality, but have not sustained it. Taiwan has managed to look good on paper, but much of that is due to the exclusion of the top and bottom ends of the income distribution in calculations of the gini coefficient.
3. Chile avoided the economic collapse which swept across Asia in the late 1990s by retaining capital controls. In that sense, it was much less market-orientated than usually thought. However, the sustainability of its growth remains uncertain given that it has been built around the primary sector.

References

Abramovitz, M. (1956): 'Resources and Output Trends in the United States since 1870', *American Economic Review*, 46, 5–23.

—— (1986): 'Catching Up, Forging Ahead, and Falling Behind', *Journal of Economic History*, 46 (2) (June), 385–406.

—— (1989): *Thinking About Growth*, Cambridge, Cambridge UP.

—— (1993): 'The Search for the Sources of Growth: Areas of Ignorance, Old and New', *Journal of Economic History*, 53 (2) (June), 217–43.

—— (1994): 'Catch-up and Convergence in the Postwar Growth Boom and After', in Baumol, W. J., Nelson, R. R., and Wolff, E. N. (eds.) (1994): *Convergence of Productivity*, New York, Oxford UP.

—— and David, P. (1973): 'Reinterpreting Economic Growth: Parables and Realities', *American Economic Review*, 63 (2), 428–39.

—— —— (1996): 'Convergence and Deferred Catch-up: Productivity Leadership and the Waning of American Exceptionalism', in Landau, R., Taylor, T., and Wright, G. (eds.) (1996): *The Mosaic of Economic Growth*, Stanford, Stanford UP.

Adelman, I. (1992): 'What is the Evidence on Income Inequality and Development?', in id. (1995): *Dynamics and Income Distribution*, Aldershot, Edward Elgar.

—— and Morris, C. T. (1971): *Economic Growth and Social Equity in Developing Countries*, Stanford, Stanford UP.

—— and Sunding, D. (1987): 'Economic Policy and Income Distribution in China', *Journal of Comparative Economics*, 11 (3) (Sept.), 444–61.

Administrative Divisions of the People's Republic of China, 1980 (1981), Beijing, Cartographic Publishing House.

Afanas'yeskiy, Ye. A (1960): 'Natural Conditions and Special Agricultural Features of the Province of Szechwan', in *The Geography of Agriculture in Communist China*, JPRS, Translation No. 3401; originally published in Russian by Publishing House of Oriental Literature, Moscow, 1959.

—— (1962): *Szechwan*, New York, JPRS Translation No. 15308; originally published in Russian by the Publishing House of Oriental Literature, Moscow.

Aghevli, B. (1996): 'Controlling Inflation', in Guitián, M. and Mundell, R. (eds.) (1996): *Inflation and Growth in China*, Washington, IMF.

Aghion, P. and Howitt, P. (1992): 'A Model of Growth through Creative Destruction', *Econometrica*, 60 (2) (March), 323–51.

—— —— (1998): *Endogenous Growth Theory*, Cambridge, Mass., MIT Press.

Aird, J. (1990): *Slaughter of the Innocents*, Washington, AEI Press.

Akerlof, G. A. and Yellen, J. L. (1986): *Efficiency Wage Models of the Labour Market*, Cambridge, Cambridge UP.

Alesina, A. and Perotti, D. (1992): 'Income Distribution, Political Instability and Investment', in Campos, J. E. and Root, H. L. (1996): *The Key to the Asian Miracle*, Washington, Brookings.

—— and Rodrik, D. (1992): 'Distribution, Political Conflict and Economic Growth', in Cuckierman, A., Hercowitz, Z., and Leiderman, L. (eds.) (1992): *Political Economy, Growth and Business Cycles*, Cambridge, Mass., MIT Press.

Alesina, A. and Rodrik, D. (1994): 'Distributive Politics and Economic Growth', *Quarterly Journal of Economics*, 109 (2) (May), 465–90.

Allen, R. (1988): 'The Growth of Labour Productivity in Early Modern English Agriculture', *Explorations in Economic History*, 25, 117–46.

—— (1992): *Enclosure and the Yeoman*, Oxford, Clarendon Press.

—— (1994): 'Agriculture during the Industrial Revolution', in Floud, R. and McCloskey, D. (eds.) (1994): *The Economic History of Britain Since 1700*, i, Cambridge, Cambridge UP.

Althusser, A. (1990 edn.): *For Marx*, London, Verso.

Amin, S. (1976): *Uneven Development*, New York, Monthly Review Press.

Amsden, A. H. (1989): *Asia's Next Giant*, Oxford, Oxford UP.

—— (1990): 'Third World Industrialization', *New Left Review*, 182 (July/August), 5–32.

—— Kochanowicz, J., and Taylor, L. (eds.) (1994): *The Market Meets Its Match*, Cambridge, Mass., Harvard UP.

Anand, S. and Kanbur, R. (1993): 'Inequality and Development: A Critique', *Journal of Development Economics* (Dec.).

Anderson, K. (1992): 'China's Industrialization and Fibre Self-Sufficiency', in Findlay, C. (ed.) (1992): *Challenges of Economic Reform and Industrial Growth: China's Wool War*, Sydney, Allen and Unwin.

Anderson, P. (1987): 'The Figures of Descent', *New Left Review*, 161 (Jan.–Feb.).

Anderson, R. S., Levy, E., and Morrison, B. (1991): *Rice Science and Development Politics*, Oxford, Clarendon Press.

Anhui nongye dili (1980), Hefei, trans. in JPRS (1980): *Anhui Agricultural Geography*, JPRS-CAG-85-017, Washington, Government Printing Office.

Anhui sheng renmin zhengfu banggongting (General Office of the Anhui People's Government) (ed.) (1987): *Anhui sheng qing* (Anhui Provincial Conditions), iii, Hefei, Anhui renmin chubanshe.

Anyue xian zhi (Anyue county record) (1993): Chengdu, Sichuan renmin chubanshe.

Arrow, K. (1962): 'The Economic Implications of Learning by Doing', *Review of Economic Studies*, 29 (June), 155–73.

—— and Hahn, F. H. (1971): *General Competitive Analysis*, London, Oliver and Boyd.

AS—Zhonggong zhongyang shujichu nongcun zhengce yanjiushi ziliaoshi (Rural Policy Research Office of the Central Committee Secretariat) (1988): *Zhongguo nongcun shehui jingji dianxing diaocha* (A Typical Example Survey of China's Rural Economy and Society), Beijing, Zhongguo shehui kexue chubanshe.

Ash, R. F. (1988): 'The Evolution of Agricultural Policy', *China Quarterly*, 116 (Dec.), 529–55.

—— (1991): 'The Peasant and the State', *China Quarterly*, 127 (Sept.), 493–526.

—— (1992): 'The Agricultural Sector in China', *China Quarterly*, 131 (Sept.), 545–76.

—— (1997): 'The Performance of China's Grain Sector', in OECD (1997): *Agricultural Policies in China*, Paris, OECD.

—— and Kueh, Y. Y. (1993): 'Economic Integration Within Greater China', *China Quarterly*, 136 (Dec.), 711–45.

Asimakopulos, A. (1977): 'Post-Keynesian Growth Theory', in Weintroub, S. (ed.) (1977): *Modern Economic Thought*, Oxford, Blackwell.

—— (1991): *Keynes's General Theory and Accumulation*, Cambridge, Cambridge UP.

Aslund, A. (1995): *How Russia Became a Market Economy*, Washington, Brookings.

Aston, T. H. and Philpin, C. E. (1985): *The Brenner Debate*, Cambridge, Cambridge UP.

Atkinson, A. B. and Micklewright, J. (1992): *Economic Transformation in Eastern Europe and the Distribution of Income*, Cambridge, Cambridge UP.

—— Rainwater, L., and Smeeding, T. M. (1995): *Income Distribution in OECD Countries*, Paris, OECD.

Aubert, C. (1990): 'The Agricultural Crisis in China at the End of the 1980s', in Delman J., Ostergaard, C. S., and Christiansen, F. (eds.) (1990): *Remaking Peasant China*, Aarhus, Aarhus UP.

—— (1992): 'Problems of Agricultural Diversification', in Vermeer, E. (ed.) (1992): *From Peasant to Entrepreneur*, Wageningen, Pudoc.

Baark, E. (1991): 'Fragmented Innovation', in Joint Economic Committee (1991): *China's Economic Dilemmas in the 1990s*, ii, Washington, US Congress.

Bachman, D. M. (1986): *Chen Yun and the Chinese Political System*, Berkeley, University of California Press.

Bacon, R. and Eltis, W. A. (1976): *Britain's Economic Problem*, London, Macmillan.

Ba dachengshi—Ba dachengshi zhengfu diaoyuan jigou lianhe ketizu (Joint Government Research Group for Eight Large Cities) (1990): *Zhongguo dachengshi renkou yu shehui fazhan* (Population and Social Development in China's Large Cities), Beijing, Zhongguo chengshi jingji shehui chubanshe.

Baer, W. (1995, 4th edn.): *The Brazilian Economy*, London, Praeger.

Bailey, F. G. (1966): 'The Peasant View of the Bad Life', in Shanin, T. (ed.) (1987): *Peasants and Peasant Societies*, Oxford, Blackwell.

Bain, I. (1993): *Agricultural Reform in Taiwan*, Hong Kong, Chinese UP.

Balassa, B. (1989*a*): *Comparative Advantage, Trade Policy and Economic Development*, Hemel Hempstead, Harvester Wheatsheaf.

—— (1989*b*): 'Outward Orientation', in Chenery, H. and Srinivasan, T. N. (eds.) (1989): *Handbook of Development Economics*, Amsterdam, North Holland.

Balcerowicz, L. (1994*a*): 'Common Fallacies in the Debate on the Transition to a Market Economy', *Economic Policy* (Supplement), 19, 16–50.

—— (1994*b*): 'Transition to the Market Economy: Poland, 1989–93', *Economic Policy* (Supplement), 19, 71–98.

Banister, J. (1987): *China's Changing Population*, Stanford, Stanford UP.

—— (1992): *Demographic Aspects of Poverty in China*, World Bank Working Paper for World Bank (1992): *China: Strategies for Reducing Poverty in the 1990s.*

—— and Preston, S. H. (1981): 'Mortality in China', *Population and Development Review*, 7 (1), 98–110.

Baran, P. A. (1957): *The Political Economy of Growth*, New York, Monthly Review Press.

Bardhan, P. K. and Roemer, J. E. (1992): 'Market Socialism', *Journal of Economic Perspectives*, 6 (Summer), 101–16.

—— —— (eds.) (1993): *Market Socialism*, Oxford, Oxford UP.

Barker, R. and Herdt, R. W., with Rose, B. (1985): *The Rice Economy of Asia*, Washington, Resources for the Future.

—— Sinha, R., and Rose, B. (eds.) (1985): *The Chinese Agricultural Economy*, London, Croom Helm.

Barnett, C. (1995): *The Lost Victory*, London, Macmillan.

Barro, R. (1996): 'Democracy: A Recipe for Growth?', in Quibria, M. G. and Dowling, J. M. (eds.) (1996): *Current Issues in Economic Development*, Hong Kong, Oxford UP.

—— and Lee, J. W. (1993): 'International Comparisons of Educational Attainment', *Journal of Monetary Economics*, 32 (3) (Dec.), 363–94.

—— and Sala-i-Martin, X. (1995): *Economic Growth*, New York, McGraw-Hill.

Bates, R. H. (1981): *Markets and States in Tropical Agriculture*, Berkeley, University of California Press.

Bates, R. H. (1983): *Essays on the Political Economy of Rural Africa*, Cambridge, Cambridge UP.
—— (1989): *Beyond the Miracle of the Market*, Cambridge, Cambridge UP.
—— and Krueger, A. O. (eds.) (1993): *Political and Economic Interactions in Economic Policy Reform*, Oxford, Blackwell.
Beasley, W. G. (1990): *The Rise of Modern Japan*, London, Weidenfeld and Nicolson.
Beckett, J. V. (1990): *The Agricultural Revolution*, Oxford, Blackwell.
Behrman, J. R. (1993): 'Macroeconomic Policies and Rural Poverty', in Quibria, M. G. (ed.) (1993): *Rural Poverty in Asia*, Hong Kong, Oxford UP.
Bergère, Marie-Claire (1989): *The Golden Age of the Chinese Bourgeoisie*, Cambridge, Cambridge UP.
Bernstein, T. P. (1977): *Up to the Mountains and Down to the Villages*, New Haven, Yale UP.
Bettleheim, C. (1988): 'Economic Reform in China', *Journal of Development Studies*, 24 (4) (July), 15–49.
Bhaduri, A. (1993): 'Alternative Development Strategies and the Rural Sector', in Singh, A. and Tabatabai, H. (eds.) (1993): *Economic Crisis and Third World Agriculture*, Cambridge, Cambridge UP.
Bhalla, A. S. (1992): *Uneven Development in the Third World*, London, Macmillan.
Bhalla, S. S. (1988): 'Is Sri Lanka an Exception?', in Srinivasan T. N. and Bardhan, P. K. (eds.) (1988): *Rural Poverty in South Asia*, New York, Columbia UP.
Bianco, L. (1971): *Origins of the Chinese Revolution, 1915–1949*, Stanford, Stanford UP.
Blanchard, O., Dornbusch, R., Krugman, P., Layard, R., and Summers, L. (eds.) (1991): *Reform in Eastern Europe*, Cambridge, Mass., MIT Press.
—— Boycko, M., Dabrowski, M., Dornbusch, R., Layard, R., and Shliefer, A. (eds.) (1993): *Post-Communist Reform*, Cambridge, Mass., MIT Press.
Blecher, M. (1990): 'The Contradictions of Grass-Roots Participation and Undemocratic Statism in Maoist China and their Fate', in Womack, B. (ed.) (1991): *Contemporary Chinese Politics in Historical Perspective*, Cambridge, Cambridge UP.
—— (1991): 'Development State, Entrepreneurial State', in White, G. (ed.) (1991): *The Chinese State in the Era of Economic Reform*, London, Macmillan.
—— and Shue, V. (1996): *Tethered Deer*, Stanford, Stanford UP.
—— and Wang, S. G. (1994): 'The Political Economy of Cropping in Maoist and Dengist China: Hebei Province and Shulu County, 1949–90', *China Quarterly*, 137 (March), 63–98.
Block, F. (1992): 'Capitalism without Class Power', *Politics and Society*, 20, 277–303.
—— (1996): 'Finance and Market Socialism', in Roemer, J. E. (1996): *Equal Shares*, London, Verso.
Blumenthal, T. (1972): 'Exports and Economic Growth: The Case of Postwar Japan', *Quarterly Journal of Economics*, 86 (4) (Nov.), 617–31.
Borensztein, E. and Ostry, J. D. (1996): 'Accounting for China's Growth Performance', *American Economic Review* (Papers and Proceedings), 86 (2) (May), 224–8.
Boserup, E. (1981): *Population and Technology*, Oxford, Blackwell.
Bosworth, B. P., Dornbusch, R., and Laban, R. (1994): *The Chilean Economy*, Washington, Brookings.
Bowles, P. and Dong, X. Y. (1994): 'Current Successes and Future Challenges in China's Economic Reforms', *New Left Review*, 208 (Nov./Dec.), 49–76.
Bowles, S. and Gintis, H. (1986): *Democracy and Capitalism*, New York, Basic Books.
Bowman, M. J. and Anderson, C. A. (1963): 'Concerning the Role of Education in Development', in Geertz, C. (ed.) (1963): *Old Societies and New States*, New York, Free Press.

Boyer, G. R. (1993): 'England's Two Agricultural Revolutions', *Journal of Economic History*, 53 (4) (Dec.), 915–23.

Brainard, W. C. and Perry, G. L. (eds.) (1992): *Brookings Papers on Economic Activity*, no. 2, Washington, Brookings.

Bramall, C. (1989): *Living Standards in Sichuan, 1931–1978*, Contemporary China Institute Research Notes and Studies No. 8, London.

—— (1990): 'The Wenzhou "Miracle": An Assessment', in Nolan, P. and Dong, F. R. (eds.) (1990*a*): *Market Forces in China*, London, Zed.

—— (1993): *In Praise of Maoist Economic Planning*, Oxford, Clarendon Press.

—— (1995*a*): 'Origins of the Agricultural "Miracle": Some Evidence from Sichuan', *China Quarterly*, 143 (Sept.), 731–55.

—— (1995*b*): 'The Lessons of History: New Economic Policy in China and the USSR', in Chang, H. J. and Nolan, P. H. (eds.) (1995): *The Transformation of the Communist Economies*, London, Macmillan.

—— and Jones, M. E. (1993): 'Rural Income Inequality in China Since 1978', *Journal of Peasant Studies*, 21 (1) (Oct.), 41–70.

Brandt, L. L. (1985): 'Chinese Agriculture and the International Economy, 1870–1930s', *Explorations in Economic History*, 22 (2) (April), 168–93.

—— (1989): *Commercialization and Agricultural Development*, Cambridge, Cambridge UP.

Bray, F. (1986): *The Rice Economies*, Oxford, Blackwell.

Brenner, R. (1977): 'The Origins of Capitalist Development', *New Left Review*, 104.

—— (1985*a*): 'Agrarian Class Structure and Economic Development in Pre-Industrial Europe', in Aston, T. H. and Philpin, C. E. (1985): *The Brenner Debate*, Cambridge, Cambridge UP.

—— (1985*b*): 'The Agrarian Roots of European Capitalism', in Aston and Philpin (1985).

—— (1986): 'The Social Basis of Economic Development', in Roemer, J. (ed.) (1986): *Analytical Marxism*, Cambridge, Cambridge UP.

—— (1994): *Merchants and Revolution*, Cambridge, Cambridge UP.

—— (1998): 'Uneven Development and the Long Downturn', *New Left Review*, 229 (May/June).

Broadman, H. G. (1995): *Policy Options for Reform of Chinese State-Owned Enterprises*, Washington, World Bank.

Brömmelhörster, J. and Frankenstein, J. (1997): *Mixed Motives, Uncertain Outcomes: Defence Industry Conversion in China*, London, Lynne Rienner.

Brown, L. (1995): *Who Will Feed China?*, London, Earthscan.

Buck, J. L. (1937): *Land Utilization in China*, Oxford, Oxford UP.

—— (1947): 'Some Basic Agricultural Problems of China', repr. in Buck, J. L. (1980): *Three Essays on Chinese Farm Economy*, London, Garland.

—— and Chen, D. T. (1944): 'The Most Capable Use of Land in Hwayang Hsien, Szechwan', *Economic Facts*, 38, repr. in Department of Agricultural Economics, University of Nanking (ed.) (1980): *Economic Facts*, iv. 575–86, London, Garland.

Byrd, W. A. (1990): 'Entrepreneurship, Capital, and Ownership', in Byrd and Lin (1990).

—— and Gelb, A. (1990): 'Why Industrialize? The Incentives for Rural Community Governments', in Byrd and Lin (eds.) (1990).

—— and Lin, Q. S. (eds.) (1990): *China's Rural Industry*, Oxford, Oxford UP.

Campbell, B. M. S. and Overton, M. (1991): *Land, Labour and Livestock*, Manchester, Manchester UP.

Campos, J. E. and Root, H. L. (1996): *The Key to the Asian Miracle*, Washington, Brookings.

Cao, M. G. (1988): *Zhongguo renkou—Jilin fence* (China's Population—Jilin), Beijing, Zhongguo caizheng jingji chubanshe.

Carr, E. H. (1980): *From Napoleon to Stalin and Other Essays*, London. Macmillan.

Catephores, G. (1994): 'The Imperious Austrian: Schumpeter as Bourgeois Marxist', *New Left Review*, 205 (May/June), 3–30.

CEF—Centre of Economic Forecasting, State Planning Commission (1987): *Input–Output Tables of China, 1981*, Honolulu, University of Hawaii Press.

Central Committee (1981): 'On Questions of Party History', in Liu, S. N. and Wu, Q. G. (1986): *China's Socialist Economy*, Beijing, Beijing Review Press.

—— (1991): *Major Documents of the People's Republic of China*, Beijing, Foreign Languages Press.

Chai, J. C. H. (1994): 'Transition to a Market Economy', *Communist Economies and Economic Transformation*, 6 (2) (June), 231–45.

Chan, A., Madsen, R., and Unger, J. (1984): *Chen Village*, Berkeley, University of California Press.

Chan, T. M. H. (1989): 'China's Price Reform in the 1980s', in Cheng, J. Y. S. (ed.) (1989): *China: Modernization in the 1980s*, Hong Kong, Chinese UP.

Chang, H. J. (1993*a*): *The Political Economy of Industrial Policy*, London. Macmillan.

—— (1993*b*): 'The Political Economy of Industrial Policy in Korea', *Cambridge Journal of Economics*, 17 (June), 131–57.

—— and Nolan, P. H. (eds.) (1995): *The Transformation of the Communist Economies*, London, Macmillan.

Chang, J. (1991): *Wild Swans*, London, HarperCollins.

Chattopadhyay, M. (1984): 'Transformation of Labour Use in Indian Agriculture', *Cambridge Journal of Economics*, 8 (3) (Sept.), 289–96.

Chen, E. K. Y. and Ho, A. (1994): 'Southern China Growth Triangle: An Overview', in Thant, M., Tang, M., Kakazu, H. (eds.) (1994): *Growth Triangles in Asia*, Hong Kong, Oxford UP.

Chen, J. Y., Chen, J. J., and Yang, X. (1993): *Zhongguo nongcun shehui jingji bianqian* (Changing Economic and Social Conditions in Rural China), Taiyuan, Shanxi jingji chubanshe.

Chen, K., Jefferson, G. H., and Singh, I. (1992): 'Lessons from China's Economic Reform', *Journal of Comparative Economics*, 16 (2) (June), 201–25.

—— —— Rawski, T., Wang, H. C., and Zheng, Y. X. (1988*a*): 'New Estimates of Fixed Investment and Capital Stock for Chinese State Industry', *China Quarterly*, 114 (June), 243–66.

—— Wang, H. C., Zheng, Y. X., Jefferson, G. H., and Rawski, T. G. (1988*b*): 'Productivity Change in Chinese Industry, 1953–85', *Journal of Comparative Economics*, 12 (4) (Dec.), 570–91.

Chen, L. Y. and Buckwell, A. (1991): *Chinese Grain Economy and Policy*, Oxford, CAB International.

Chen, P. C. (1994): 'Foreign Investment in the Southern China Growth Triangle', in Thant, M., Tang, M., Kakazu, H. (eds.) (1994): *Growth Triangles in Asia*, Hong Kong, Oxford UP.

Chen, R. M. (1990): 'A Preliminary Analysis of the "Big Labour-Hiring Households"' in Nolan, P. and Dong, F. R. (eds.) (1990*a*): *Market Forces in China*, London, Zed.

Cheng, J. Y. S. (ed.) (1989): *China: Modernization in the 1980s*, Hong Kong, Chinese UP.

Cheng, N. (1986): *Life and Death in Shanghai*, London, Collins.

Cheng, X. M. (1984): 'A Survey of the Demographic Problems of the Yi Nationality in the Greater and Lesser Liang Mountains', *Social Sciences in China*, 5 (3), 207–31.

Chengdu shi renmin zhengfu jingji yanjiu zhongxin (Economic Research Centre of the People's Government of Chengdu Municipality) (ed.) (1987): *Chengdu jingji* (The Economy of Chengdu), Chengdu, Xinan zhengjing daxue chubanshe.

Chevrier, Y. (1990): 'Micropolitics and the Factory Director Responsibility System, 1984–1987', in Davis, D. and Vogel, E. F. (eds.) (1990): *Chinese Society on the Eve of Tiananmen*, Cambridge, Mass., Harvard UP.

'China's Reform of the Taxation System', in *China in Brief* (1996), www.china.or.cn/.

Chinn, D. L. (1980): 'Cooperative Farming in North China', *Quarterly Journal of Economics*, 94 (2) (March), 279–99.

Chongqing shi jihua weiyuanhui (Planning Committee of Chongqing Municipality) (1991): *Chongqing shi jingji zonghe zhi* (Summary Gazetteer on the Economy of Chongqing City), Chongqing, Chongqing chubanshe.

Chongqing shi jingji dili (An Economic Geography of Chongqing) (1987), Chongqing, Chongqing chubanshe.

Chossudovsky, M. (1986): *Towards Capitalist Restoration? Chinese Socialism After Mao*, London, Macmillan.

Chow, I. H. S. (1989): 'Trends in the Application and Impact of Work Incentives in the Chinese Industrial Enterprises', in Cheng, J. Y. S. (ed.) (1989): *China—Modernization in the 1980s*, Hong Kong, Chinese UP.

Christiansen, F. (1990): 'The Ambiguities of Labor and Market in Periurban Communities in China During the Reform Decade' in Delman, J., Ostergaard, C. S., and Christiansen, F. (eds.) (1990): *Remaking Peasant China*, Aarhus, Aarhus UP.

Chuan, H. S. and Kraus, R. A. (1975): *Mid-Ch'ing Rice Markets and Trade*, Cambridge, Mass., Harvard UP.

Clark, G. (1993): 'Agriculture and the Industrial Revolution, 1700–1850', in Mokyr, J. (ed.) (1993): *The British Industrial Revolution*, Boulder, Westview.

Clark, J. C. D. (1986): *Revolutions and Rebellions*, Cambridge, Cambridge UP.

Coale, A. J. and Hoover, E. M. (1958): *Population Growth and Economic Development in Low Income Countries*, Princeton, Princeton UP.

Coen, R. M. and Hickman, B. J. (1987): 'Keynesian and Classical Unemployment in Four Countries', in Brainard, W. C. and Perry, G. L. (1987): *Brookings Papers on Economic Activity*, no. 1, Washington, Brookings.

Cohen, W. L. (1990): *America's Response to China*, New York, Columbia UP.

Conroy, R. (1989): 'China's Science and Technology Policy' in Cheng, J. Y. S. (ed.) (1989): *China—Modernization in the 1980s*, Hong Kong, Chinese UP.

Corden, W. M. (1971): 'The Effects of Trade on the Rate of Growth', in Bhagwati, J. N. (ed.) (1971): *Trade, Balance of Payments and Growth*, Amsterdam, North Holland.

Corry, D. and Glyn, A. (1994): 'The Macroeconomics of Equality, Stability and Growth', in Glyn, A. and Miliband, D. (eds.) (1994): *Paying for Inequality*, London, Rivers Oram Press.

Crafts, N. F. R. (1980): 'Income Elasticities of Demand and the Release of Labor by Agriculture during the British Industrial Revolution', repr. in Mokyr (1985).

—— (1985): *British Economic Growth During the Industrial Revolution*, Oxford, Clarendon Press.

—— (1989): 'The New Economic History and the Industrial Revolution', in Mathias, P. and Davis, J. A. (eds.) (1989): *The First Industrial Revolutions*, Oxford, Blackwell.

Crafts, N. F. R. (1994): 'The Industrial Revolution', in Floud, R. and McCloskey, D. (eds.) (1994, 2nd edn.): *The Economic History of Britain Since 1700*, i, Cambridge, Cambridge UP.

—— (1995): 'Exogenous or Endogenous Growth? The Industrial Revolution Reconsidered', *Journal of Economic History*, 55 (4) (Dec.), 745–72.

—— (1996): 'Deindustrialisation and Economic Growth', *Economic Journal*, 106 (1) (Jan.), 172–83.

—— (1997): 'Endogenous Growth', in Kreps, D. M. and Wallis, K. F. (eds.) (1997): *Advances in Economics and Econometrics*, ii, Cambridge, Cambridge UP.

—— and Harley, C. K. (1992): 'Output Growth and the British Industrial Revolution', *Economic History Review*, 45 (4) (Nov.), 703–30.

—— Toniolo, G. (1996): 'Postwar Growth: An Overview', in Crafts, N. F. R. and Toniolo, G. (eds.): *Economic Growth in Europe since 1945*, Cambridge, Cambridge UP.

Crawcour, E. S. (1988): 'Industrialization and Technological Change, 1885–1920', in Duus, P. (ed.) (1988): *The Cambridge History of Japan*, vi, Cambridge, Cambridge UP.

Crompton, R. (1993): *Class and Stratification*, Cambridge, Polity Press.

Crook, F. W. (1991): 'Primary Issues in China's Grain Economy in the 1990 Decade', in Joint Economic Committee (1991): *China's Economic Dilemmas in the 1900s*, ii, Washington, US Congress.

—— (1997): 'An Assessment of China's Agricultural Economy: 1980–2005', in Joint Economic Committee (1997): *China's Economic Future*, Washington, US Congress.

Cross, R. (ed.) (1995): *The Natural Rate of Unemployment*, Cambridge, Cambridge UP.

Cui, X. H., Shi, Z. K., Fan, G. Z., and Xiong, Z. Y. (1985): *Sichuan chengshi jingji* (Sichuan's Urban Economy), Chengdu, Sichuan kexue jishu chubanshe.

Cullenberg, S. (1994): *The Falling Rate of Profit*, London, Pluto Press.

Cumings, B. (1998): 'The Korean Crisis and the End of "Late" Development', *New Left Review*, 231 (Sept./Oct.), 43–72.

Dai, Q. (1994): *Yangtze! Yangtze!*, London, Earthscan.

Dangdai Sichuan congshu bianjibu (Editorial Committee for the 'Sichuan Today' Series) (1991): *Dangdai Sichuan dikuang shiye* (The Mineral Industry in Sichuan Today), Chengdu, Sichuan renmin chubanshe.

David, C. C. and Otsuka, K. (eds.) (1994): *Modern Rice Technology and Income Distribution in Asia*, London, Lynne Rienner.

Davis, D. and Vogel, E. (eds.) (1990): *Chinese Society on the Eve of Tiananmen*, Cambridge, Mass., Harvard UP.

Davies, R. W., Harrison, M., and Wheatcroft, S. G. (eds.) (1994): *The Economic Transformation of the Soviet Union, 1913–45*, Cambridge, Cambridge UP.

Davis, R. (1979): *The Industrial Revolution and British Overseas Trade*, Leicester, Leicester UP.

De Long, B. and Summers, L. H. (1992): 'Equipment Investment and Economic Growth', in Brainard, W. C. and Perry, G. L. (eds.) (1992): *Brookings Papers on Economic Activity*, no. 2, Washington, Brookings.

—— —— (1993): 'How Strongly do Developing Economies Benefit from Equipment Investment?', *Journal of Monetary Economics*, 32 (4) (Dec.), 395–415.

Delman, J. (1992): '"We Have to Adopt Innovation": Farmers' Perception of the Extension-Farmer Interface in Renshou County', in Vermeer, E. (ed.) (1992): *From Peasant to Entrepreneur*, Wageningen, Pudoc.

—— Ostergaard, C. S., and Christiansen, F. (eds.) (1990): *Remaking Peasant China*, Aarhus, Aarhus UP.

Denison, E. F. (1967): *Why Growth Rates Differ*, Washington, Brookings.
—— (1974): *Accounting for United States Economic Growth, 1929–1969*, Washington, Brookings.
Department of Agricultural Economics, University of Nanking (ed.) (1941): 'The Rice Problem', repr. id, (1980): *Economic Facts*, ii, London, Garland.
Diamond, L. (1992): 'Economic Development and Democracy Reconsidered', in Marks, G. and Diamond, L. (eds.) (1992): *Re-examining Democracy*, London, Sage.
Disanci (1997)—Disanci quanguo gongye pucha bangongshi (Office of the Third National Industrial Census) (ed.) (1997): *Zhonghua renmin gongheguo 1995 nian disanci quanguo gongye pucha ziliao huibian—diqu juan*) (Collected Materials from the 1995 3rd National Industrial Census of the People's Republic of China—Provincial Volume), Beijing, Zhongguo tongji chubanshe.
Dittmer, L. (1993): 'Chinese Reform Socialism under Deng Xiaoping', in Kau, M. Y-M. and Marsh, S. H. (eds.) (1993): *China in the Era of Deng Xiaoping*, New York, M. E. Sharpe.
Dollar, D. (1992): 'Outward-Oriented Developing Economies Really Do Grow More Rapidly: Evidence from 95 LDCs, 1976–85', *Economic Development and Cultural Change*, 40 (3), 523–44.
Domes, J. (1982): 'New Policies in the Communes', *Journal of Asian Studies*, 41 (2) (Feb.), 253–67.
Dong, F. R. (1988): 'Development Theory and Problems of Socialist Developing Economies', in Ranis, G. and Schultz, T. P. (eds.) (1988): *The State of Development Economics*, Oxford, Blackwell.
—— (1992): *Industrialization and China's Rural Modernization*, London, Macmillan.
—— Lin, C., and Naughton, B. (forthcoming): *Reform of China's State-Owned Enterprises*, London, Macmillan.
Dong, X. Y. and Putterman, L. (1997): 'Productivity and Organization in China's Rural Industries', *Journal of Comparative Economics*, 24 (2) (April), 181–201.
Dore, R. P. (1965): 'Land Reform and Japanese Economic Development—A Reactionary Thesis', repr. in Shanin, T. (ed.) (1987): *Peasants and Peasant Societies*, Oxford, Blackwell.
—— (1984): *Education in Tokugawa Japan*, London, Athlone.
Drèze, J. and Sen, A. K. (eds.) (1991): *The Political Economy of Hunger*, iii, Oxford, Clarendon Press.
—— —— (1995): *India: Economic Development and Social Opportunity*, Oxford, Clarendon Press.
Du, W. C. (1995): *Agricultural Marketed Surplus Response in China*, Aldershot, Avebury.
Du, W. Z. (1987): *Zhongguo renkou: Jiangsu fence* (China's Population: Jiangsu), Beijing, Zhongguo caizheng jingji chubanshe.
Dutt, A. K. (1984): 'Stagnation, Income Distribution and Monopoly Power', *Cambridge Journal of Economics*, 8 (1) (March), 25–40.
Dyker, D. A. (1992): *Restructuring the Soviet Economy*, London, Routledge.
Easterly, W. (1995): 'Explaining Miracles', in Ito, T. and Krueger, A. O. (eds.) (1995): *Growth Theories in Light of the East Asian Experience*, Chicago, University of Chicago Press.
—— Rodriguez, C. A., and Schmidt-Hebbel, K. (1994): *Public Sector Deficits and Macroeconomic Performance*, New York, Oxford UP.
Eatwell, J. (1982): *Whatever Happened to Britain*? London, Duckworth.
—— (1996): 'The International Origins of Unemployment', in Michie, J. and Grieve Smith, J. (eds.) (1996): *Creating Industrial Capacity*, Oxford, Oxford UP.

Eckstein, A. (1964): 'Sino-Soviet Economic Relations', in Cowan, C. D. (ed.) (1964): *The Economic Development of China and Japan*, London, Allen and Unwin.

Edmonds, R. L. (1994): *Patterns of China's Lost Harmony*, New York, Routledge.

Edwards, S. (1993): 'Openness, Trade Liberalization and Growth in Developing Countries', *Journal of Economic Literature*, 31 (3) (Sept.), 1358–93.

Eggertsson, T. (1990): *Economic Behaviour and Institutions*, Cambridge, Cambridge UP.

Ellman, M. (1979): *Socialist Planning*, Cambridge, Cambridge UP.

—— (1994): 'The Increase in Death and Disease Under Katastroika', *Cambridge Journal of Economics*, 18, 329–55.

Eltis, W. (1996): 'How Low Profitability and Weak Innovation Undermined UK Industrial Growth', *Economic Journal*, 106 (1) (Jan.), 184–95.

Elvin, M. (1973): *The Pattern of the Chinese Past*, Stanford, Stanford UP.

—— (1984): 'Why China Failed to Create an Endogenous Industrial Capitalism: A Critique of Max Weber's Explanation', *Theory and Society*, 13 (3) (May), 379–92.

Emmanuel, A. (1972): *Unequal Exchange*, New York, Monthly Review Press.

Endicott, S. (1988): *Red Earth*, London, I. B. Tauris.

Engels, F. (1972): *The Origins of the Family, Private Property and the State*, New York, Pathfinder.

Etienne, G. (1992): *Asian Crucible: The Steel Industry in China and India*, London, Sage.

Evans, P. B., Rueschemeyer, D., and Skocpol, T. (1985): *Bringing the State Back In*, Cambridge, Cambridge UP.

Fagerberg, J. (1994): 'Technology and International Differences in Growth Rates', *Journal of Economic Literature*, 32 (3) (Sept.), 1147–75.

Fan, G. (1994): 'Incremental Change and Dual-Track Transition', *Economic Policy*, 9 (Dec.), 99–122.

—— Hai, W., and Woo, W. T. (1996): 'Decentralized Socialism and Macroeconomic Stability', in Guitian, M. and Mundell, R. (eds.) (1996): *Inflation and Growth in China*, Washington, IMF.

Fan, S. G. (1991): 'Effects of Technological Change and Institutional Reform on Production Growth in Chinese Agriculture', *American Journal of Agricultural Economics* (May), 266–75.

Fearnside, P. M. (1988): 'China's Three Gorges Dam', *World Development*, 16 (5) (May), 615–30.

Fei, J. C. and Ranis, G. (1964): *Development of the Labor Surplus Economy*, Homewood, Ill., Irwin.

Fei, X. T. (1939): *Peasant Life in China*, London, Routledge and Kegan Paul.

—— (1983): *Chinese Village Close-Up*, Beijing, New World Press.

—— (1986): *Small Towns in China*, Beijing, New World Press.

—— (1992): *From The Soil*, Berkeley, University of California Press.

Feldman, G. A. (1928): 'On the Theory of Growth Rates of National Income', in Spulber, N. (ed.) (1964): *Foundations of Soviet Strategy for Economic Growth*, Bloomington, Ind., Indiana UP.

Feng, H. F. (1990): 'Zhongguo nongye zongyaosu shengchan shuai biandong qushi ji zengzhang mushi' (The Changing Trend and Pattern of Total Factor Productivity in Chinese Agriculture), *Jingji yanjiu* (Economic Research), 5 (May), 47–54.

Fewsmith, J. (1994): *Dilemmas of Reform in China*, Armonk, NY, M. E. Sharpe.

Field, R. M. (1988): 'Trends in the Value of Agricultural Output', *China Quarterly*, 116 (Dec.), 556–91.

—— (1992): 'China's Industrial Performance since 1978', *China Quarterly*, 131 (Sept.), 577–607.

Fields, G. S. (1980): *Poverty, Inequality and Development*, Cambridge, Cambridge UP.

—— (1991): 'Growth and Income Distribution', in Psacharopoulos, G. (ed.) (1991): *Essays on Poverty, Equity and Growth*, Oxford, Pergamon.

Findlay, C., Watson, A., and Wu, H. X. (eds.) (1994): *Rural Enterprises in China*, London, Macmillan.

Fischer, W. A. (1989): 'China's Industrial Innovation', in Simon, D. F. and Goldman, M. (eds.) (1989): *Science and Technology in Post-Mao China*, Cambridge, Mass., Harvard UP.

Fishlow, A. (1994): *Miracle or Design? Lessons from East Asia*, Washington, Overseas Development Council.

Floud, R. and McCloskey, D. (eds.) (1994, 2nd edn.): *The Economic History of Britain Since 1700*, i, Cambridge, Cambridge UP.

Folta, P. (1992): *From Swords to Plowshares? Defence Industry Reform in the PRC*, Boulder, Westview.

Fouquin, M. and Lemoine, F. (eds.) (1998): *The Chinese Economy*, Economica, London.

Francks, P. (1984): *Technology and Agricultural Development in Pre-War Japan*, New Haven, Yale UP.

—— (1992): *Japanese Economic Development*, London, Routledge.

Frank, A. G. (1967): *Capitalism and Underdevelopment in Latin America*, New York, Monthly Review Press.

Fridley, D. (1991): 'China's Energy Outlook', in Joint Economic Committee (1991): *China's Economic Dilemmas in the 1990s*, ii, Washington, US Congress.

Friedman, E., Pickowicz, P. G., and Selden, M. (1991): *Chinese Village, Socialist State*, New Haven, Yale UP.

Friedman, M. (1990): 'Using the Market for Social Development', in Dorn, J. A. and Wang, X. (eds.) (1990): *Economic Reform in China—Prospects and Problems*, Chicago, University of Chicago Press.

Fukuyama, F. (1992): *The End of History and the Last Man*, London, Hamish Hamilton.

—— (1995): *Trust*, London, Hamish Hamilton.

Gaiha, R. (1985): 'Poverty, Technology and Infrastructure in Rural India', *Cambridge Journal of Economics*, 9 (3) (Sept.), 221–43.

Galenson, W. (ed.) (1979): *Economic Growth and Structural Change*, Cornell, Cornell UP.

Gan, Y. P. and Yang, L. F. (1984): 'Wo sheng xiaofeipin gongye mianlin de jueze' (Identifying the Obstacles that Sichuan's Consumer Goods Industry Faces) in Sichuan jihua jingji xuehui (Sichuan Institute of Economic Planning) (ed.) (1984): *Jihua jingji de lilun yu shijian* (The Theory and Practice of Planned Economy), Chongqing, Chongqing chubanshe.

Gansu tongjiju (1988): *Gansu sheng shaominzu diqu jiben tongji ziliao* (Basic Statistical Materials on the Ethnic Minority Prefectures of Gansu Province), no publisher or place of publication.

Gao, B. H. and Zheng, Y. L. (eds.) (1987): *Zhongguo renkou: Anhui fence* (China's Population: Anhui), Beijing, Zhongguo caizheng jingji chubanshe.

Garnaut, R., Guo, S. T., and Ma, G. N. (eds.) (1996): *The Third Revolution in the Chinese Countryside*, Cambridge, Cambridge UP.

Gates, H. (1996): *China's Motor*, Ithaca, NY, Cornell UP.

Gelb, A., Jefferson, G., and Singh, I. (1993): 'Can Communist Economies Transform Incrementally?', in Blanchard, O. J. and Fischer, S. (eds.) (1993): *NBER Macroeconomics Annual 1993*, Cambridge, Mass., MIT Press.

Geography Department, Hunan Teachers' College (1981): *Hunan nongye dili* (Hunan Agricultural Geography), trans. in JPRS (1984): *China Report: Agriculture*, JPRS-CAG-84-022, 13 Aug., Washington, Government Printing Office.

Giddens, A. (1995): *Politics, Sociology and Social Theory*, Cambridge, Polity Press.

Glyn, A. (1992): 'The Productivity Miracle, Profits and Investment', in Michie, J. (ed.) (1992): *The Economic Legacy, 1979–92*, London, Academic Press.

Godley, W. (1996): 'America's Unaccountable Admiration for Mrs. Thatcher's Economics', in Eatwell, J. (ed.) (1996): *Global Unemployment*, London, M. E. Sharpe.

Gold, T. B. (1988): 'Still on the Collective Road: Limited Reform in a North China Village', in Reynolds, B. L. (ed.) (1988): *Chinese Economic Policy*, New York, Paragon.

Gomulka, S. (1986): *Growth, Innovation and Reform in Eastern Europe*, Madison, University of Wisconsin Press.

Goodman, D. (1986): *Centre–Province Relations in the PRC*, Cambridge, Cambridge UP.

—— (1994): *Deng Xiaoping and the Chinese Revolution*, London, Routledge.

—— and Feng, C. Y. (1994): 'Guangdong', in Goodman, D. and Segal, G. (eds.) (1994): *China Deconstructs*, London, Routledge.

Gordon, D. (1992): 'Discussion', *Economic Policy*, 15 (Oct.), 414–21.

Gowan, P. (1996): 'Eastern Europe, Western Power and Neo-Liberalism', *New Left Review*, 216 (March/April), 129–40.

Grabowski, R. (1994): 'The Successful Development State: Where Does It Come From?', *World Development*, 22 (3) (March), 413–22.

Griffin, K. and Zhao, R. W. (eds.) (1993): *The Distribution of Income in China*, Basingstoke, Macmillan.

Gros, D. and Steinherr, A. (1995): *Winds of Change*, London, Longman.

Grossman, G. M. and Helpman, E. (1991): *Innovation and Growth in the Global Economy*, Cambridge, Mass., MIT Press.

—— —— (1994): 'Endogenous Innovation in the Theory of Growth', *Journal of Economic Perspectives*, 8 (1) (Winter), 23–44.

Groves, T., Hong, Y. M., McMillan, J., and Naughton, B. (1994): 'Autonomy and Incentives in Chinese State Enterprises', *Quarterly Journal of Economics*, 109 (1) (Feb.), 183–209.

—— —— —— —— (1997): 'Productivity Growth in Chinese State-Run Industry', in Dong, F. R., Lin, C., and Naughton, B. (eds.) (1997): *Reform of China's State-Owned Enterprises*, London, Macmillan.

GSNJ—Gansu nianjian bianweihui (Gansu Yearbook Editorial Committee) (1997): *Gansu nianjian 1997* (Gansu Yearbook), Beijing, Zhongguo tongji chubanshe.

Gu, J., Shi, Y. L., Gao, E. S., and Gu, X. Y. (1991): 'Zhongguo ying'er siwangshuai jiqi yingxiang yinsu fenxian' (An Analysis of China's Infant Mortality Rate and Its Effects) in *Renkou yu jingji* (Population and Economics), 4 (Aug.), 26–33.

Gu, Z. C. (1985): 'Sichuan gongye jiegou de tedian yuji gaishan de tujing' (Peculiarities in Sichuan's Industrial Structure and Ways to Improve It) in Sichuan sheng shehui kexueyuan jingji yanjiusuo (Economic Research Institute of the Sichuan Academy of Social Sciences) (ed.) (1985): *Zhongguo shehuizhuyi jingji yanjiu* (Research on China's Socialist Economy), Chengdu, Sichuan sheng kexueyuan chubanshe.

Guangdong sheng difang shizhi bianzuan weiyuanhui (Compilation Committee for the Historical Record of Guangdong Province) (ed.) (1996): *Guangdong shengzhi: Liangshi zhi* (Guangdong Provincial Records: Grain Records), Guangzhou, Guangdong renmin chubanshe.

Guanghan xian zhi (Guanghan County Records) (1992): Chengdu, Sichuan renmin chubanshe.
Guitian, M. and Mundell, R. (eds.) (1996): *Inflation and Growth in China*, Washington, IMF.
Guizhou sheng qing bianji weiyuanhui (Guizhou sheng qing Editorial Committee) (1986): *Guizhou sheng qing* (Conditions in Guizhou Province), Guiyang, Guizhou renmin chubanshe.
Guizhou tongjiju (Guizhou Statistical Bureau) (ed.) (1984): *Guizhou jingji shouce* (Guizhou Economic Handbook), Guiyang, Guizhou renmin chubanshe.
Guojia kewei quanguo zhongda ziran zaihai zonghe yanjiuzu (Research Group for the National Scientific Committee on Major Chinese Natural disasters) (1993): *Zhongguo zhongda ziran zaihai ji jianzai duice* (Major Chinese Natural Disasters and Strategies to Prevent Them), Beijing, Kexue chubanshe.
Guowuyuan quanguo gongye pucha lingdao xiaozu bangongshi (Leading Group of the State Council for the National Industrial Census) (ed.) (1987): *Zhonghua renmin gongheguo 1985 nian gongye pucha ziliao* (Materials from the 1985 Industrial Census of the People's Republic of China), i, Beijing, Zhongguo tongji chubanshe.
GZTJNJ—Guizhou tongjiju (Guizhou Statistical Bureau) (1997): *Guizhou tongji nianjian 1997*, Beijing, Zhongguo tongji chubanshe.
Haggard, S. (1990): *Pathways from the Periphery*, Ithaca, NY, Cornell UP.
—— Cooper, R. N., and Moon, C. I. (1993): 'Policy Reform in Korea', in Bates, R. H. and Krueger, A. (eds.) (1993): *Political and Economic Interactions in Economic Policy Reform*, Oxford, Blackwell.
Hahn, F. H. (1986): 'Of Marx, Keynes and Many Things', in Sinclair, P. J. N. (ed.) (1987): *Prices, Quantities and Expectations*, Oxford, Oxford UP.
—— and Matthews, R. C. O. (1964): 'The Theory of Economic Growth: A Survey', *Economic Journal*, 74 (Dec.).
Hall, J. W. (1962): 'Feudalism in Japan', *Comparative Studies in Society and History*, 5, 15–51.
Hamberg, D. (1977): 'Early Growth Theory', in Weintraub, S. (ed.) (1977): *Modern Economic Thought*, Oxford, Blackwell.
Han, Z. R. and Feng, Y. F. (1992): *Xin Zhongguo nongchanpin jiage sishinian* (Agricultural Product Prices over the Forty Years of New China), Beijing, Shuili dianli chubanshe.
Hanley, S. and Wolf, A. P. (eds.) (1985): *Family and Population in East Asian History*, Stanford, Stanford UP.
Hanley, S. and Yamamura, K. (1977): *Economic and Demographic Change in Preindustrial Japan, 1600–1868*, Princeton, Princeton UP.
Harding, H. (1993): 'The Chinese State in Crisis, 1966–69', in MacFarquhar, R. (ed.) (1993): *The Politics of China, 1949–89*, Cambridge, Cambridge UP.
—— (1994): 'Comment', in Shirk, S. L. (1994): *How China Opened its Doors*, Washington, Brookings.
Hargreaves Heap, S. P. (1992): *The New Keynesian Macroeconomics*, Aldershot, Edward Elgar.
Harley, K. (1994): 'Foreign Trade', in Floud, R. and McCloskey, D. (eds.) (1994, 2nd edn.): *The Economic History of Britain Since 1700*, i, Cambridge, Cambridge UP.
Harral, C. G. (ed.) (1992): *Transport Development in Southern China*, Discussion Paper no. 151, Washington, World Bank.
Harrell, S. (ed.) (1995): *Cultural Encounters on China's Ethnic Frontiers*, Seattle, University of Washington.
Harrison, M. (1994): 'National Income', in Davies, R. W., Harrison, M., and Wheatcroft, S. G. (eds.) *The Economic Transformation of the Soviet Union, 1913–45*, Cambridge, Cambridge UP.

Harrod, R. (1939): 'An Essay in Dynamic Theory', *Economic Journal*, 49 (June), 14–33.
Hart Landsberg, M. (1993): *The Rush to Development*, New York, Monthly Review Press.
Hartford, K. (1985): 'Socialist Agriculture, Long Live Socialist Agriculture', in Perry, E. and Wong, C. (eds.) (1985): *The Political Economy of Reform in Post-Mao China*, Cambridge, Mass., Harvard UP.
Hawke, G. R. (1970): *Railways and Economic Growth in England and Wales, 1840–1870*, Oxford, Oxford UP.
Hay, D. A., Morris, D. J., Liu, G., and Yao. S. J. (1994): *Economic Reform and State-Owned Enterprises in China, 1979–1987*, Oxford, Clarendon Press.
Hayami, Y. and Yamada, S. (1991): *The Agricultural Development of Japan*, Tokyo, Tokyo UP.
He, J. C. (1990): 'Development Issues and Policy Choices', in Byrd, W. A. and Lin, Q. S. (eds.) (1990): *China's Rural Industry*, Oxford, Oxford UP.
Henan yanjiushi—Henan sheng renmin zhengfu diaocha yanjiushi (Research Unit of the People's Government of Henan Province) (1987): *Henan sheng qing* (Conditions in Henan Province), Henan renmin chubanshe, Zhengzhou.
Hènin, P. Y. (1986): *Macrodynamics*, London, Routledge.
Hinton, W. (1983): *Shenfan*, New York, Random House.
—— (1990): *The Privatization of China*, London, Earthscan.
—— (1995): 'Afterword', in Qin, H. L. (ed.) (1995): *Ninth Heaven, Ninth Hell*, New York, Barricade.
HNH—*Heilongjiang nongye hezuoshi* (History of Agricultural Collectivization in Heilongjiang) (1990), Beijing, Zhonggong dangshi ziliao chubanshe.
Ho, S. P. S. (1994): *Rural China in Transition*, Oxford, Clarendon Press.
Honig, E. (1990): 'Invisible Inequalities: The Status of Subei People in Contemporary Shanghai', *China Quarterly*, 122 (June), 273–92.
—— (1992): 'Native Place Hierarchy and Labor Market Segmentation', in Rawski, T. G. and Li, L. M. (eds.) (1992): *Chinese History in Economic Perspective*, Berkeley, University of California Press.
Horrell, S., Humphries, J., and Weale, M. (1994): 'An Input–Output Table for 1841', *Economic History Review*, 47 (3) (Aug.), 545–66.
Howe, C. (1971): *Employment and Economic Growth in Urban China 1949–57*, Cambridge, Cambridge UP.
—— (1996): *The Origins of Japanese Trade Supremacy*, London, Hurst and Company.
Hsiao, K. H. (1987): *The Government Budget and Fiscal Policy in Mainland China*, Taipei: Chung-hua Institution for Economic Research.
Hsu, J. C. (1989): *China's Foreign Trade Reforms*, Cambridge, Cambridge UP.
Hsu, R. C. (1991): *Economic Theories in China, 1979–1988*, Cambridge, Cambridge UP.
Hua, S., Zhang. X. J., and Luo, X. P. (1993): *China: From Revolution To Reform*, London, Macmillan.
Huang. P. C. C. (1985): *The Peasant Economy and Social Change in North China*, Stanford, Stanford UP.
—— (1990): *The Peasant Family and Rural Development in the Yangzi Delta, 1350–1988*, Stanford, Stanford UP.
—— (1991): 'A Reply to Ramon Myers', *Journal of Asian Studies*, 50 (3) (Aug.), 629–33.
Huang, X. L. (ed.) (1988): *Zhongguo renkou: Guangxi fence* (China's Population: Guangxi), Beijing, Zhongguo caizheng jingji chubanshe.
Huang, Y. P. and Duncan, R. (1997): 'How Successful Were China's State Sector Reforms?', *Journal of Comparative Economics*, 24 (1) (Feb.), 65–78.

Huang, Y. S. (1996): *Inflation and Investment Controls in China*, Cambridge, Cambridge UP.

Huber, E., Rueschemeyer, D., and Stephens, J. D. (1993): 'The Impact of Economic Development on Democracy', *Journal of Economic Perspectives*, 7 (3) (Summer), 71–85.

Huber, J. R. (1971): 'Effect on Prices of Japan's Entry into World Commerce after 1858', *Journal of Political Economy*, 71 (3), 614–28.

Huenemann, R. W. (1984): *The Dragon and the Iron Horse: The Economics of Railroads in China, 1876–1937*, Cambridge, Mass., Harvard UP.

Hughes, G. and Senik-Leygonie, C. (1992): 'Industrial Profitability and Trade Among the Former Soviet Republics', *Economic Policy*, 15 (Oct.), 353–86.

Hunan sheng nongye quhua weiyuanhui (Editorial Committee for Hunan Province Agricultural Districts) (ed.) (1989): *Hunan sheng nongye quhua* (Agricultural Districts of Hunan Province), v, Changsha, Hunan kexue jishu chubanshe.

Hunan tongjiju (Hunan Statistical Bureau) (1987): *Hunan tongji nianjian 1987* (Hunan Statistical Yearbook), Beijing, Zhongguo tongji chubanshe.

Huntington, S. P. (1968): *Political Order in Changing Societies*, New Haven, Yale UP.

Hussain, A. (1989): 'Science and Technology in the Chinese Countryside', in Simon, D. F. and Goldman, M. (eds.) (1989): *Science and Technology in Post-Mao China*, Cambridge, Mass., Harvard UP.

Hutson, J. (1915): *Mythical and Practical in Szechwan*, Shanghai, National Review Office.

Hutton, W. (1995): *The State We're In*, London, Jonathan Cape.

Hyde, C. K. (1977): *Technological Change and the British Iron Industry, 1700–1870*, Princeton, Princeton UP.

IMF (1998): *World Economic Outlook* (Sept.), Washington, IMF.

Inada, K. I., Seikiguchi, S., and Shoda, Y. (1992): *The Mechanism of Economic Development*, Oxford, Clarendon Press.

Ishikawa, S. (1967): 'Resource Flow Between Agriculture and Industry: The Chinese Experience', *The Developing Economies*, 5 (1) (March).

—— (1971): 'Changes in the Structure of Agricultural Production in Mainland China', in Jackson, W. A. D. (ed.) (1971): *Agrarian Policies and Problems in Communist and Non-Communist Countries*, Seattle, University of Washington Press.

—— (1987): 'Sino-Japanese Economic Co-operation', *China Quarterly*, 109 (March), 1–21.

—— (1988): 'Patterns and Processes of Intersectoral Resource Flows', in Ranis, G. and Schultz, T. P. (eds.) (1988): *The State of Development Economics*, Oxford, Blackwell.

Ito, T. and Krueger, A. O. (eds.) (1995): *Growth Theories in Light of the East Asian Experience*, Chicago, University of Chicago Press.

Jacobson, H. K. and Oksenberg, M. (1990): *China's Participation in the IMF, the World Bank and GATT*, Ann Arbor, University of Michigan Press.

James, W. E., Naya, S., and Meier, G. M. (1989): *Asian Development*, Madison, University of Wisconsin Press.

Jansen, M. B. and Rozman, G. (1986): *Japan in Transition*, Princeton, Princeton UP.

Jao, Y. C. and Leung, C. K. (1986): *China's Special Economic Zones*, Oxford, Oxford UP.

Jefferson, G. H. (1989): 'Potential Sources of Productivity Growth within Chinese Industry', *World Development*, 17 (1) (Jan.), 45–57.

—— (1990): 'China's Iron and Steel Industry', *Journal of Development Economics*, 33, 329–55.

—— and Rawski, T. G. (1994): 'Enterprise Reform in Chinese Industry', *Journal of Economic Perspectives*, 8 (2) (Spring), 47–70.

Jefferson, G. H. and Xu, W. Y. (1991): 'The Impact of Reform on Socialist Enterprises in Transition: Structure, Conduct and Performance in Chinese Industry', *Journal of Comparative Economics*, 15 (1) (March), 45–64.

—— —— (1994): 'Assessing Gains in Efficient Production Amongst China's Industrial Enterprises', *Economic Development and Cultural Change*, 42 (3) (April), 597–616.

—— Chen, K., and Singh, I. (1992*a*): 'Lessons from China's Economic Reform' in *Journal of Comparative Economics*, 16 (2) (June).

—— Rawski, T. G., and Zheng, Y. X. (1992*b*): 'Growth, Efficiency and Convergence in China's State and Collective Enterprises', *Economic Development and Cultural Change*, 40 (2) (Jan.), 239–66.

—— —— —— (1996): 'Chinese Industrial Productivity', *Journal of Comparative Economics*, 23 (2) (April), 146–80.

Jiangshan shi zhi (Jiangshan City Records) (1990), Hangzhou, Zhejiang renmin chubanshe.

Jiangsu tongjiju (Jiangsu Province Statistical Bureau) (ed.) (1989): *Jiangsu sishinian* (Forty Years of Jiangsu), Nanjing, Zhongguo tongji chubanshe.

Jiangsu tongjiju (Jiangsu Statistical Bureau) (ed.) (1992): *1992 nian Jiangsu shixian jingji* (The Economy of Jiangsu's Cities and Counties in 1992), Beijing, Zhongguo tongji chubanshe.

JIH—Bureau of Foreign Trade, Ministry of Industry (1933): *China Industrial Handbooks—Kiangsu*, Shanghai, repr. Ch'eng Wen Publishing Company, Taipei, 1973.

Johnson, C. A. (1962): *Peasant Nationalism and Communist Power*, Stanford, Stanford UP.

—— (1985): *MITI and the Japanese Miracle*, Stanford, Stanford UP.

Johnston, B. F. and Mellor, J. W. (1961): 'The Role of Agriculture in Economic Development', *American Economic Review*, 51 (4) (Sept.), 566–93.

Joint Economic Committee (1991): *China's Economic Dilemmas in the 1990s*, ii, Washington, US Congress.

—— (1997): *China's Economic Future*, Washington, US Congress.

Jones, M. E. (1994): 'Poverty, Inequality and Living Standards in Rural China, 1978–1990', unpub. Ph.D. diss., London, School of Oriental and African Studies.

Jorgenson, D. W. (1961): 'The Development of a Dual Economy', *Economic Journal*, 71, 309–34.

—— (1966): 'Testing Alternative Theories of the Development of a Dual Economy', in Adelman, I. and Thorbecke, E. (eds.) (1966): *The Theory and Design of Economic Development*, Baltimore, Johns Hopkins UP.

—— and Griliches, Z. (1967): 'The Explanation of Productivity Change', *Review of Economic Studies*, 34 (July), 249–80.

JSSXGK—Jiangsu sheng difangzhi bianzuan weiyuanhui bangongshi (Compilation Committee of the Office for the Local Records of Jiangsu Province) (1989): *Jiangsu shixian gaikuang* (Survey of Jiangsu's Cities and Counties), Nanjing, Jiangsu jiaoyu chubanshe.

JSTJNJ—Jiangsu tongjiju (Jiangsu Province Statistical Bureau) (ed.) (1994): *Jiangsu tongji nianjian 1994 and 1997* (Jiangsu Statistical Yearbook), Beijing, Zhongguo tongji chubanshe.

Ju, F. T. and Wu, D. S. (1986): 'The Formation and Development of the Silk Town Shengze', in Fei, X. T. (1986): *Small Towns in China*, Beijing, New World Press.

Judd, E. R. (1992): 'Land Divided, Land United', *China Quarterly*, 130 (June), 338–56.

—— (1994): *Gender and Power in Rural North China*, Stanford, Stanford UP.

Kaijiang xian zhi (Kaijiang County Records) (1989), Chengdu, Sichuan renmin chubanshe.

Kalain, R. (1984): 'Mao Tsetung's "Bukharinist" Phase', *Journal of Contemporary Asia*, 14 (1), 147–55.

Kaldor, N. (1957): 'A Model of Economic Growth', *Economic Journal*, 67 (3) (Sept.), 591–624.
—— (1961): 'Capital Accumulation and Economic Growth', in Targetti, F. and Thirlwall, A. P. (eds.) (1989): *The Essential Kaldor*, London, Duckworth.
—— (1966): 'Causes of the Slow Rate of Economic Growth in the United Kingdom', in Targetti and Thirlwall (1989).
—— (1972): 'The Irrelevance of Equilibrium Economics', in Targetti and Thirlwall (1989).
—— (1975): 'Economic Growth and the Verdoorn Law', *Economic Journal* (Dec.).
Kalecki, M. (1963): 'Introduction to the Theory of Growth in a Socialist Economy', in Osiatynski, J. (ed.) (1993): *Collected Works of Michal Kalecki*, Oxford, Clarendon Press.
Kamath, S. J. (1990): 'Foreign Direct Investment in a Centrally Planned Economy: The Chinese Case', *Economic Development and Cultural Change*, 39 (1) (Oct.).
Karshenas, M. (1995): *Industrialization and Agricultural Surplus*, Oxford, Oxford UP.
Käsler, D. (1988): *Max Weber*, Cambridge, Polity Press.
Katzman, M. T. (1977): *Cities and Frontiers in Brazil*, Cambridge, Mass., Harvard UP.
Kaufmann, D. (1994): 'Diminishing Returns to Administrative Controls and the Emergence of the Unofficial Economy', *Economic Policy* (Supplement), 19 (Dec.), 51–70.
Kelliher, D. (1992): *Peasant Power in China*, New Haven and London, Yale UP.
Kendrick. J. W. (1961): *Productivity Trends in the United States*, Princeton, Princeton UP.
Kenen, P. B. (1991): 'Transitional Arrangements for Trade and Payments among the CMEA Countries', *IMF Staff Papers*, 38 (June), 235–67.
Kerridge, E. (1967): *The Agricultural Revolution*, London, Allen and Unwin.
Khan, A. R. and Riskin, C. (1998): 'Income and Inequality in China', in *China Quarterly*, 154 (June).
—— Griffin, K., Riskin, C., and Zhao, R. W. (1993): 'Household Income and its Distribution in China', in Griffin, K. and Zhao, R. W. (eds.) (1993): *The Distribution of Income in China*, Basingstoke, Macmillan.
Khan, M. H. (1995): 'State Failure in Weak States', in Harriss, J., Hunter, J., and Lewis, C. M. (eds.) (1995): *The New Institutional Economics and Third World Development*, London, Routledge.
Kim, S. J. (1990): 'Productivity Effects of Economic Reforms in China's Agriculture', unpub. Ph.D. diss., Brown University, cited in Putterman (1993).
Kitson, M. and and Michie, J. (1996): 'Manufacturing Capacity, Investment, and Employment', in Michie, J. and Grieve Smith, J. (eds.) (1996): *Creating Industrial Capacity*, Oxford, Oxford UP.
Kiyokawa, Y. (1984): 'Entrepreneurship and innovation in Japan', *The Developing Economies*, 22 (3) (Sept.), 211–36.
—— (1987): 'Transplantation of the European Factory System and Adaptations in Japan: The Experience of the Tomioka Filature', *Hitotsubashi Journal of Economics*, 28 (1) (June), 27–39.
Kleinberg, R. (1990): *China's Opening to the Outside World*, Boulder, Westview.
Knight, J. and Song, L. (1993): 'The Spatial Contribution to Income Inequality in Rural China', *Cambridge Journal of Economics* (June).
Kohli, A. (1987): *The State and Poverty in India*, Cambridge, Cambridge UP.
—— (1994*a*): 'Where Do High Growth Political Economies Come From?', *World Development*, 22 (9) (Sept.), 1269–93.
—— (1994*b*): 'Centralization and Powerlessness: India's Democracy in a Comparative Perspective', in Migdal, J. S., Kohli, A., and Shue, V. (eds.) (1994): *State Power and Social Forces*, Cambridge, Cambridge UP.

Kok, C. T. (1991): 'Small Towns and Regional Development in Wenzhou', in Veeck, G. (1991): *The Uneven Landscape*, Baton Rouge, Louisiana State University.

Kornai, J. (1989): 'Some Lessons from the Hungarian Experience for Chinese Reformers', in Van Ness, P. (ed.) (1989): *Market Reforms in Socialist Societies*, London, Lynne Rienner.

—— (1992): *The Socialist System*, Oxford, Clarendon Press.

Kravis, I. (1970): 'Trade as a Handmaiden of Growth', *Economic Journal*, 80 (4) (Dec.), 850–72.

Kremer, M. (1993): 'Population Growth and Technological Change', *Quarterly Journal of Economics*, 108 (3) (Aug.).

Krueger, A. O. (1974): 'The Political Economy of the Rent-Seeking Society', *American Economic Review*, 64 (3) (June), 291–303.

—— (1985): 'Trade Policies in Developing Countries', in Jones, R. W. and Kenen, P. B. (eds.) (1985): *Handbook of International Economics*, Amsterdam, North Holland.

Krugman, P. (1990): *Rethinking International Trade*, Cambridge, Mass., MIT Press.

—— (1991): *Geography and Trade*, Cambridge, Mass., MIT Press.

—— (1993*a*): 'Protection in Developing Countries', in Dornbusch, R. (ed.) (1993): *Policy-making in the Open Economy*, Oxford, Oxford UP.

—— (1993*b*): 'The Current Case for Industrial Policy', in Salvatore, D. (ed.) (1993): *Protectionism and World Welfare*, Cambridge, Cambridge UP.

—— (1994*a*): *Peddling Prosperity*, New York, W. W. Norton.

—— (1994*b*): *The Age of Diminished Expectations*, Cambridge, Mass., MIT Press.

—— (1995): *Development, Geography, and Economic Theory*, Cambridge, Mass., MIT Press.

—— (1996): *Pop Internationalism*, Cambridge, Mass., MIT Press.

—— and Obstfeld, M. (1994): *International Economics*, New York, HarperCollins.

Kuchler, J. (1990): 'On the Establishment of a Poverty-Oriented Rural Development Policy in China', in Delman, J., Ostergaard, C. S., and Christiansen, F. (eds.) (1990): *Remaking Peasant China*, Aarhus, Aarhus UP.

Kueh, Y. Y. (1985): 'The Economics of the Second Land Reform in China', *China Quarterly*, 101, 122–31.

—— (1988): 'Food Consumption and Peasant Incomes in the Post-Mao Period', *China Quarterly*, 116 (Dec.), 634–70.

—— (1992): 'Foreign Investment and Economic Change in China', *China Quarterly*, 132 (Sept.).

—— (1995): *Agricultural Instability in China, 1931–1991*, Oxford, Clarendon Press.

—— and Ash, R. F. (1996): 'The Fifth Dragon', in Hook, B. (1996) (ed.) *Guangdong: China's Promised Land*, Hong Kong, Oxford UP.

Kumar, A. (1994): 'Economic Reform and the Internal Division of Labour in China', in Goodman, D. and Segal, G. (eds.) (1994): *China Deconstructs*, London, Routledge.

Kunshan xian zhi (Kunshan County Records) (1990), Shanghai, Shanghai renmin chubanshe.

Kuznets, S. (1979): 'Growth and Structural Shifts', in Galenson, W. (ed.) (1979): *Economic Growth and Structural Change*, Ithaca, NY, Cornell UP.

Kwon, J. (1994): 'The East Asia Challenge to Neoclassical Orthodoxy', *World Development*, 22 (4) (April), 635–44.

Lal, D. (1995): 'India and China: Contrasts in Liberalization?', *World Development*, 9 (23) (Sept.), 1475–94 .

Landes, D. S. (1969): *The Unbound Prometheus*, Cambridge, Cambridge UP.

—— (1993): 'The Fable of the Dead Horse', in Mokyr, J. (ed.) (1993): *The British Industrial Revolution*, Boulder, Westview.

Lardy, N. R. (1978): *Economic Growth and Distribution in China*, Cambridge, Cambridge UP.
—— (1984), 'Consumption and Living Standards in China, 1978–83', *China Quarterly*, 100 (Dec.), 849–65.
—— (1989): 'Dilemmas in the Pattern of Resource Allocation in China, 1978–1985', in Nee, V. and Stark, D. (eds.) (1989): *Remaking the Institutions of Socialism*, Stanford, Stanford UP.
—— (1992): *Foreign Trade and Economic Reform in China, 1978–1990*, Cambridge, Cambridge UP.
—— (1995): 'The Role of Foreign Trade and Investment in China's Economic Transformation', *China Quarterly*, 144 (Dec.), 1065–82.
—— and Lieberthal, K. (1983): *Chen Yun's Strategy for China's Development*, London, M. E. Sharpe.
Lau, L. J. (1996): 'The Sources of Long-Term Economic Growth', in Landau, R., Taylor, T., and Wright, G. (eds.) (1996): *The Mosaic of Economic Growth*, Stanford, Stanford UP.
Lavely, W., Xiao, Z. Y., Li, B. H., and Freedman, R. (1990): 'The Rise in Female Education in China: National and Regional Patterns', *China Quarterly*, 121 (March), 61–93.
Lawrence, R. Z. (1996): *Single World, Divided Nations?*, Paris, OECD.
Lee, Y. S. F. (1991): 'Rural Nonagricultural Development in an Extended Metropolitan Region: The Case of Southern Jiangsu', in Ginsburg, N., Koppel, B., and McGee, T. G. (eds.) (1991): *The Extended Metropolis*, Honolulu, University of Hawaii Press.
Leeming, F. (1985): *Rural China Today*, London, Longman.
Lenin, V. I. (1918; 1992 edn.): *The State and Revolution*, London, Penguin.
Lewis, J. W. and Xue L. T. (1988): *China Builds the Bomb*, Stanford, Stanford UP.
—— —— (1994): *China's Strategic Seapower*, Stanford, Stanford UP.
Lewis, W. A. (1954): 'Economic Development with Unlimited Supplies of Labour', *Manchester School of Economic and Social Studies*, 22, 139–91.
—— (1980): 'The Slowing Down of the Engine of Growth', *American Economic Review*, 70 (4) (Sept.), 555–64.
Leys, C. (1996): *The Rise and Fall of Development Theory*, London, James Currey.
Li, B. H. (1990): 'Woguo 28 gesheng zizhiqu zhixiashi shengyushaui de bianhua' (Changes in the Fertility Rate in Our 28 Provinces, Autonomous Regions and Cities), *Renkou yu jingji* (Population and Economics), 3 (June), 3–12.
Li, B. K. (1985): 'Guanyu jiandaocha dingliang fenxi de jige wenti' (Several Issues Concerning the Analysis of the Determination of the Price Scissors), in He, H. S. (ed.) (1985): *Nongye jingji luncong* (Collected Essays on the Agricultural Economy), Beijing, Nongye chubanshe.
Li, B. Z. (1986): *The Development of Agriculture and Industry in Jiangnan, 1644–1850*, Hangzhou, Zhejiang Academy of Social Sciences.
Li, C. R. (1992): *A Study of China's Population*, Beijing, Foreign Languages Press.
Li, L. C. L. (1997): 'Provincial discretion and national power: investment policy in Guangdong and Shanghai, 1978–1993', *China Quarterly*, 152, 778–804.
Li, R. S. (1996*a*): 'Dui dangqian woguo liudong renkou de renshi he sikao' (Reflections on China's Current Floating Population) in *Renkou Yanjiu* (Population Research), 20 (1) (Jan.), 10–15.
—— (1996*b*): 'Dui dangqian woguo nongcun renkou liudong de zai renshi' (A Reconsideration of China's Current Rural Floating Population) in *Renkou Yanjiu* (Population Research), 20 (6) (Nov.), 17–21.
Li, S. (1990): 'The Growth of Household Industry in Rural Wenzhou', in Nolan, P. and Dong, F. R. (eds.) (1990*a*): *Market Forces in China*, London, Zed.

Lieberthal, K. (1997): 'The Great Leap Forward and the Split in the Yenan Leadership', in MacFarquhar, R. (ed.) (1997; 2nd edn.): *The Politics of China*, Cambridge, Cambridge UP.

Lin, G. C. S. (1997): *Red Capitalism in South China*, Vancouver, UBC Press.

Lin, J. Y. F. (1988): 'Rural Factor Markets in China', in Reynolds, B. L. and Kim, I. J. (eds.) (1988): *Chinese Economic Policy*, New York, Paragon.

—— (1992): 'Rural Reforms and Agricultural Growth in China', *American Economic Review*, 82 (1).

—— (1994): 'The Nature and Impact of Hybrid Rice in China', in David, C. C. and Otsuka, K. (eds.) (1994): *Modern Rice Technology and Income Distribution in Asia*, London, Lynne Rienner.

—— (1996*a*): 'Inflation and Growth in China's Transition', in Guitian, M. and Mundell, R. (eds.) (1996): *Inflation and Growth in China*, Washington, IMF.

—— (1996*b*): 'Success in Early Reform: Setting the Stage', in Garnault, R., Guo, S. T., and Ma, G. N. (eds.) (1996) *The Third Revolution in the Chinese Countryside*, Cambridge, Cambridge UP.

—— Cai, F., and Li, Z. (1996): *The China Miracle*, Hong Kong, Chinese UP.

Lin, L. and Gu, Z. C. (1985): 'The Course of Reform in Sichuan's Economic Structure', *Social Sciences in China*, 6 (1), 179–205.

Lin, M. (1974): *Red Flag Canal*, Beijing, Foreign Languages Press.

Lin, Z. L. (1980): 'Initial Reform in China's Economic Structure', *Social Sciences in China*, 1 (3), 172–94.

Linhai xian zhi (Linhai county records) (1989), Hangzhou, Zhejiang renmin chubanshe.

Lipset, S. M. (1959): 'Some Social Requisites of Democracy', *American Political Science Review*, 53 (1), 69–105.

—— (1993): 'The Social Requisites of Democracy Revisited', *American Sociological Review*, 59 (Feb.), 1–22.

Lipton, D. and Sachs, J. (1992): 'Prospects for Russia's Economic Reforms', in Brainard, W. C. and Perry, G. L. (eds.) (1992): *Brookings Papers on Economic Activity*, no. 2, Washington, Brookings.

Lipton, M. (1977): *Why Poor People Stay Poor*, London, Temple Smith.

Little, I. M. D. (1979): 'An Economic Renaissance', in Galenson, W. (ed.) (1979): *Economic Growth and Structural Change*, Cornell, Cornell UP.

—— (1982): *Economic Development*, New York, Basic Books.

Liu, H. K. (1988): *Zhongguo renkou—Sichuan fence* (China's Population—Sichuan), Beijing, Zhongguo caizheng jingji chubanshe.

Liu, M. Q. (1991*a*): 'Work Incentives and Labour Allocation on China's Communes', unpub. D. Phil. diss., Oxford University.

—— (1991*b*): 'Intersectoral Labor Allocation on China's Communes', *Journal of Comparative Economics*, 15 (4), 602–26.

—— (1994): 'Commune, Responsibility System and China's Agriculture', in Fan, Q. M. and Nolan, P. (eds.) (1994): *China's Economic Reforms*, London, Macmillan.

Liu, S. N. and Wu, Q. G. (1986): *China's Socialist Economy*, Beijing, Beijing Review Press.

Liu, T. C. and Yeh, K. C. (1965): *The Economy of the Chinese Mainland*, Princeton, Princeton UP.

Liu, Y. L. (1992): 'Reform From Below: The Private Economy and Local Politics in the Rural Industrialization of Wenzhou', *China Quarterly*, 130 (June), 293–316.

Liu, Z. (1990): *Dangdai Zhongguo de Hunan* (China Today: Hunan), 2 vols., Beijing, Zhongguo shehui kexue chubanshe.

Lo, D. (1997): *Market and Institutional Regulation in Chinese Industrialization, 1978–94*, London, Macmillan.

Lo, D. (1999): 'Reappraising the Performance of China's State-Owned Industrial Enterprises', *Cambridge Journal of Economics*, 13 (4) (Dec.).

Lo, L. N. K. (1989): 'Chinese Education in the 1980s', in Cheng, J. Y. S. (ed.) (1989): *China: Modernization in the 1980s*, Hong Kong, Chinese UP.

Lockwood, W. (1954): *The Economic Development of Japan*, Princeton, Princeton UP.

LSL (1985): *Sichuan sheng Liangshan zhou Yizu shehui lishi diaocha* (An Investigation into the Social History of the Yi Minority Living in Sichuan's Liangshan Prefecture), Chengdu, Sichuan sheng shehui kexueyuan chubanshe.

LSTJ—Zhongguo guojia tongjiju (Chinese State Statistical Bureau) (ed.) (1990): *Quanguo gesheng zizhiqu zhixiashi lishi tongji ziliao huibian* (Collection of Historical Statistical Materials on China's Provinces, Autonomous Regions and Centrally Administered Cities), Beijing, Zhongguo tongji chubanshe.

Lu, R. J. (1992): *Dangdai Zhongguo de Anhui* (China Today: Anhui), Beijing, Dangdai Zhongguo chubanshe.

Lu, X. Y. and Zhang, H. Y. (1990): 'Nongmin de fenhua wenti yu duice' (The Differentiation of the Peasantry: Problems and Remedies), *Nongye jingji wenti* (Problems of Agricultural Economics), 1, 16–21, trans. in JPRS, CAR-90-040, 29 May 1990, 59–67, Washington, Government Printing Office.

Lucas, R. E. (1988): 'On The Mechanics of Economic Development', *Journal of Monetary Economics*, 22 (July), 3–42.

—— (1993): 'The Making of a Miracle', *Econometrica*, 61 (2) (March), 251–72.

Luk, S. H. and Whitney, J. B. R. (eds.) (1993): *Megaproject: A Case Study of China's Three Gorges Project*, Armonk, NY, M. E. Sharpe.

LYZG—*Liangshan Yizu zizhizhou gaikuang* (A Survey of the Liangshan Yi Minority Autonomous Region) (1985), Chengdu, Sichuan minzu chubanshe.

Ma, B. (1991): *Nanyang diqu liangshi zhi* (Nanyang Prefecture Grain Records), Zhengzhou, Zhongzhou guji chubanshe.

Ma, H. (ed.) (1990): *Modern China's Economy and Management*, Beijing, Foreign Languages Press.

—— and Sun, S. Q. (1995): *Zhongguo jingji xingshi yu zhanwang* (China's Economic Situation and Prospects), Beijing, Zhongguo fazhan chubanshe.

McCloskey, D. N. (1981): *Enterprise and Trade in Victorian Britain*, London, Allen and Unwin.

—— (1987): *Econometric History*, London, Macmillan.

—— (1990): *If You're So Smart*, Chicago, University of Chicago Press.

McCombie, J. S. L. and Thirlwall, A. P. (1994): *Economic Growth and the Balance of Payments Constraint*, London, Macmillan.

MacFarquhar, R. (1983): *The Origins of the Cultural Revolution*, ii: *The Great Leap Forward*, Oxford, Oxford UP.

—— (ed.) (1993; 1st edn.): *The Politics of China, 1949–89*, Cambridge, Cambridge UP.

—— and Fairbank, J. K. (eds.) (1987): *The Cambridge History of China*, xiv, Cambridge, Cambridge UP.

—— Cheek, T., and Wu, E. (eds.) (1989): *The Secret Speeches of Chairman Mao*, Cambridge, Mass., Harvard UP.

McGuckin, R. H., Sang V. Nguyen, Taylor, J. R., and Waite, C. A. (1992): 'Post-Reform Productivity Performance and Sources of Growth in Chinese Industry, 1980–85', *Review of Income and Wealth*, 38 (3) (Sept.), 249–66.

McGuire, M. C. and Olson, M. (1996): 'The Economics of Autocracy and Majority Rule', *Journal of Economic Literature*, 34 (1) (March), 72–96.

McKhann, C. F. (1995): 'The Naxi and the Nationalities Question' in Harrell, S. (ed.) (1995): *Cultural Encounters on China's Ethnic Frontiers*, Seattle, University of Washington.

McMillan, J. and Naughton, B. (1992): 'How to Reform a Planned Economy', *Oxford Review of Economic Policy*, 8 (1) (Spring).

—— Whalley, J., and Zhu, L. J. (1989): 'The Impact of China's Economic Reforms on Agricultural Productivity Growth', *Journal of Political Economy*, 97 (4), 781–807.

Maddison, A. (1991): *Dynamic Forces in Capitalist World Development*, Oxford, Oxford UP.

—— (1994): 'Explaining the Economic Performance of Nations, 1820–1989', in Baumol, W. J., Nelson, R. R., and Wolff, E. N. (eds.) (1994): *Convergence of Productivity*, New York, Oxford UP.

—— (1998*a*): 'Chinese Economic Performance in Historical and Comparative Perspective', in Fouquin, M. and Lemoine, F. (eds.) (1998): *The Chinese Economy*, Economica, London.

—— (1998*b*): *Chinese Economic Performance in the Long Run*, Paris, OECD.

Mallick, R. (1992): 'Agrarian reform in West Bengal', *World Development*, 20 (5) (May), 735–50.

Mankiw, N. G. (1995): 'The Growth of Nations', in Brainard, W. C. and Perry, G. L. (eds.) (1995): *Brookings Papers on Economic Activity*, no. 1, Washington, Brookings.

—— Romer, D., and Weil, D. N. (1992): 'A Contribution to the Empirics of Economic Growth', *Quarterly Journal of Economics*, 107 (2) (May), 407–37.

Mann, M. (1993): *The Sources of Social Power*, ii, Cambridge, Cambridge UP.

Marglin, S. (1984): *Growth, Distribution, and Prices*, Cambridge, Mass., Harvard UP.

Marx, K. (1867; 1954 edn.): *Capital*, i, London, Lawrence and Wishart.

—— (1875): 'Critique of the Gotha Programme', in McLellan, D. (ed.) (1977): *Karl Marx: Selected Writings*, Oxford, Oxford UP.

—— (1885; 1956 edn.): *Capital*, ii, London, Lawrence and Wishart.

—— (1894; 1959 edn.): *Capital*, iii, London, Lawrence and Wishart.

—— *Critique of Hegel's Philosophy of the State*, in Marx, K. and Engels, F. (1975): *Collected Works*, i, London, Lawrence and Wishart.

Matthews, R. C. O., Feinstein, C. H., and Odling-Smee, J. C. (1982): *British Economic Growth, 1856–1973*, Oxford, Oxford UP.

Mauro, P. (1995): 'Corruption and Growth', *Quarterly Journal of Economics* (Aug.).

Meisner, M. (1978): 'Dazhai', *Modern China*, 4 (1) (Jan.), 27–62.

Mellor, J. W. (1973): 'Accelerated Growth in Agricultural Production and the Intersectoral Transfer of Resources', *Economic Development and Cultural Change*, 22 (1) (Oct.), 1–17.

—— and Ahmed, R. (eds.) (1988): *Agricultural Price Policy for Developing Countries*, Baltimore, Johns Hopkins UP.

Mianzhu xian zhi (Mianzhu county records) (1992), Chengdu, Sichuan kexue jishu chubanshe.

Michie, J. and Grieve Smith, J. (eds.) (1994): *Unemployment in Europe*, London, Academic Press.

—— —— (eds.) (1995): *Managing the Global Economy*, Oxford, Oxford UP.

—— —— (eds.) (1996): *Creating Industrial Capacity*, Oxford, Oxford UP.

Microresearch Department (1988): 'Market Structure and the Enterprise System in Microeconomic Reform', *Social Sciences in China*, 9 (4) (Dec.).

Migdal, J. S., Kohli, A., and Shue, V. (eds.) (1994): *State Power and Social Forces*, Cambridge, Cambridge UP.
Miliband, R. (1968): *The State in Capitalist Society*, London, Weidenfeld and Nicolson.
Minami, R. (1986): *The Economic Development of Japan*, London, Macmillan.
—— (1994*a*; 2nd edn.): *The Economic Development of Japan*, London, Macmillan.
—— (1994*b*): *The Economic Development of China*, London, Macmillan.
—— (1998): 'Economic Development and Income Distribution in Japan', *Cambridge Journal of Economics*, 22 (1) (Jan.), 39–58.
—— Kim, K. S., Makino, F., and Seo, J.-H. (eds.) (1995): *Acquiring, Adapting and Developing Technologies*, London, Macmillan.
Minford, P. and Riley, J. (1994): 'The UK Labour Market', in Barrell, R. (ed.) (1994): *The UK Labour Market*, Cambridge, Cambridge UP.
Misra, K. (1998): *From Post-Maoism to Post-Marxism*, London, Routledge.
Mitch, D. (1993): 'The Role of Human Capital in the First Industrial Revolution', in Mokyr, J. (ed.) (1993): *The British Industrial Revolution*, Boulder, Westview.
Mo, X. Y. (1989): 'Hunan Lacks Agricultural Inputs', *Hunan Ribao*, 22 Feb. 1989 and 6 March 1989, trans. in JPRS (1989): *China Report: Agriculture*, JPRS-CAR-89-041, 9 May 1989, Washington, Government Printing Office.
Mokyr, J. (ed.) (1985): *The Economics of the Industrial Revolution*, London, Allen and Unwin.
—— (ed.) (1993): *The British Industrial Revolution*, Boulder, Westview.
Morishima, M. (1982): *Why Has Japan 'Succeeded'?*, Cambridge, Cambridge UP.
Morris-Suzuki, T. (1994): *The Technological Transformation of Japan*, Cambridge, Cambridge UP.
Mosher, S. (1994): *A Mother's Ordeal*, London, Little Brown.
Mosk, C. (1996): *Making Health Work*, Berkeley, University of California Press.
Muli Zangzu zizhixian gaikuang (A Survey of Muli Autonomous County's Tibetan People) (1985), Chengdu, Sichuan minzu chubanshe.
Murphy, R., Shleifer, A., and Vishny, R. (1989): 'Industrialization and the Big Push', *Journal of Political Economy*, 97, 1003–26.
Murrell, P. and Olson, M. (1991): 'The Devolution of Centrally Planned Economies', *Journal of Comparative Economics*, 15, 239–65.
Myers, R. H. and Peattie, M. R. (1984): *The Japanese Colonial Empire, 1895–1945*, Princeton, Princeton UP.
Myrdal, G. (1957): *Economic Theory and Under-Developed Regions*, London, Duckworth.
—— (1968): *Asian Drama*, London, Allen Lane.
Nairn, T. (1988): *The Enchanted Glass*, London, Radius.
Nakagane, K. (1989): 'Intersectoral Resource Flows in China Revisited', *The Developing Economies*, 27 (2).
Nakamura, J. (1965): 'Growth of Japanese Agriculture, 1875–1920', in Lockwood, W. W. (ed.) (1965): *The State and Economic Enterprise in Japan*, Princeton, Princeton UP.
—— (1966): *Agricultural Production and the Economic Development of Japan*, Princeton, Princeton UP.
Nanchong xian zhi (Nanchong County Records) (1993), Chengdu, Sichuan renmin chubanshe.
National Population Census Office (1991): *Major Figures of the Fourth National Population Census of China*, Beijing, Zhongguo tongji chubanshe.
Naughton, B. (1987): 'Macroeconomic Policy and Response in the Chinese Economy', *Journal of Comparative Economics*, 11 (3) (Sept.), 334–53.

Naughton, B. (1988): 'The Third Front', *China Quarterly*, 115 (Sept.), 351–86.

—— (1990): 'China's Experience with Guidance Planning', *Journal of Comparative Economics*, 14.

—— (1991*a*): 'Industrial Policy during the Cultural Revolution', in Joseph, W. A., Wong, C. P. W., and Zweig, D. (eds.) (1991): *New Perspectives on the Cultural Revolution*, Harvard, Harvard UP.

—— (1991*b*): 'Macroeconomic Management and System Reform in China', in White, G. (ed.) (1991): *The Chinese State in the Era of Economic Reform*, London, Macmillan.

—— (1991*c*): 'Inflation', in Joint Economic Committee (1991) *China's Economic Dilemmas in the 1990s*, ii, Washington, US Congress.

—— (1992): 'Implications of the State Monopoly Over Industry and Its Relaxation', *Modern China*, 18 (1) (Jan.), 14–41.

—— (1993): 'Deng Xiaoping: The Economist', *China Quarterly*, 135 (Sept.), 491–514.

—— (1994): 'Chinese Institutional Innovation and Privatization from Below', *American Economic Review* (Papers and Proceeding), 84 (2) (May), 266–70.

—— (1995*a*): *Growing Out of the Plan*, Cambridge, Cambridge UP.

—— (1995*b*): 'China's Macroeconomy in Transition', *China Quarterly*, 144 (Dec.), 1083–1104.

—— (1997): 'China's Emergence and Prospects as a Trading Nation', in Brainard, W. C. and Perry, G. L. (eds.) (1997): *Brookings Papers on Economic Activity 1996*, no. 2, Washington, Brookings.

Nee, V. and Su, S. J. (1990): 'Institutional Change and Economic Growth in China', *Journal of Asian Studies*, 49 (1) (Feb.).

Needham, J. (1970): *Clerks and Craftsmen in China and the West*, Cambridge, Cambridge UP.

Neijiang shi zhi (Neijiang City Records) (1987), Chengdu, Bashu shushe.

Nelson, R. R. (1973): 'Recent Exercises in Growth Accounting', *American Economic Review*, 63, 462–8.

—— and Winter, S. G. (1982): *An Evolutionary Theory of Economic Change*, Cambridge, Mass., Harvard UP.

Nicholas, S. and Nicholas, J. (1992): 'Male Illiteracy and Workforce Deskilling During the Industrial Revolution', *Journal of Interdisciplinary History*, 22, 1–18.

—— and Oxley, D. (1993): 'The Living Standards of Women during the Industrial Revolution, 1795–1820', *Economic History Review*, 46 (4) (Nov.), 723–49.

Nickum, J. E. (1990): 'Volatile Waters: Is China's Irrigation in Decline?', in Tso, T. C. (ed.) (1990): *Agricultural Reform and Development in China*, Washington, Ideals.

Ningxian zhi (Records of Ning County) (1988), Lanzhou, Gansu renmin chubanshe.

Nolan, P. (1988): *The Political Economy of Collective Farms*, Cambridge, Polity Press.

—— (1993): *State and Market in the Chinese Economy*, London, Macmillan.

—— (1995*a*): *China's Rise, Russia's Fall*, London, Macmillan.

—— (1995*b*): 'Political Economy and the Reform of Stalinism', in Chang, H. J. and Nolan, P. (eds.) (1995): *The Transformation of the Communist Economies*, London, Macmillan.

—— (1996): 'Large Firms and Industrial Reform in Former Planned Economies', *Cambridge Journal of Economics*, 20 (1) (Jan.), 1–29.

—— and Ash, R. F. (1995): 'China's Economy on the Eve of Reform', *China Quarterly*, 144 (Dec.), 980–98.

—— and Dong, F. R. (eds.) (1990*a*): *Market Forces in China*, London, Zed.

—— —— (eds.) (1990*b*): *The Chinese Economy and Its Future*, Cambridge, Polity Press.

—— and Sender, J. (1992): 'Death Rates, Life Expectancy and China's Economic Reforms', *World Development*, 20 (9) (Sept.), 1279–1303.

Nongcun yanjiuzu—Zhonggong Sichuan sheng wei nongcun jingji shehui fazhan zhanlue yanjiuzu (Research Group for the CCP's Sichuan's Committee on the Development Strategy for Rural Economy and Society) (ed.) (1986): *Sichuan nongcun jintian he mingtian* (Rural Sichuan Today and Tomorrow), Chengdu, Sichuan kexue jishu chubanshe.

Nongcun zijin ketizu (Study Group on Rural Investment Funds) (1990): 'Yindao nongcun zijin zengjia nongye touru' (Direct Rural Funds in Order to Increase Agricultural Investment', *Nongye jingji wenti* (Problems of Agricultural Economics), 4 (April), 20–5.

Nongye bu (Ministry of Agriculture) (1985): *Zhongguo nongye jingji gaiyao 1983* (An Outline of the Chinese Agricultural Economy), Beijing, Nongye chubanshe.

—— (1989): *Zhongguo nongcun jingji tongji daquan 1949–86* (Complete Statistics on China's Rural Economy), Beijing, Nongye chubanshe.

—— (1990): *Zhongguo liangshi fazhan zhanlue duice* (A Grain Development Strategy for China), Beijing, Nongye chubanshe.

—— (1997): *Zhongguo nongye nianjian 1997* (Chinese Agricultural Yearbook), Beijing, Nongye chubanshe.

Norman, E. H. (1940): *Japan's Emergence as a Modern State*, New York, Institute of Pacific Relations.

North, D. C. (1981): *Structure and Change in Economic History*, New York, Norton.

—— (1990): *Institutions, Institutional Change and Economic Performance*, Cambridge, Cambridge UP.

—— (1994): 'Institutional Change in American Economic History', in Weiss, T. and Schaefer, D. (eds.) (1994): *American Economic Development in Historical Perspective*, Stanford, Stanford UP.

—— and Thomas, R. P. (1973): *The Rise of the Western World*, Cambridge, Cambridge UP.

—— and Weingast, B. W. (1987): 'The Evolution of Institutions Governing Public Choice in 17th-Century England', *Journal of Economic History*, 49, 803–32.

Nove, A. (1983): *The Economics of Feasible Socialism*, London, Allen and Unwin.

Nozick, R. (1974): *Anarchy, State and Utopia*, New York, Basic Books.

Nurkse, R. (1961): *Patterns of Trade and Development*, Oxford, Blackwell.

O'Brien, P. K. (1977): 'Agriculture and the Industrial Revolution', *Economic History Review*, 30, 166–81.

—— (1999): 'Imperialism and the Rise and Decline of the British Economy, 1688–1989', *New Left Review*, 238 (Nov./Dec.).

Odgaard, O. (1992*a*): 'Entrepreneurs and Elite Formation in Rural China', *Australian Journal of Chinese Affairs*, 28 (July), 89–107.

—— (1992*b*): *Private Enterprise in Rural China*, Aldershot, Avebury.

OECD (1995): *OECD Economic Surveys: The Russian Federation 1995*, Paris, OECD.

—— (1997): *Agricultural Policies in China*, Paris, OECD.

Offe, C. (1974): 'Structural Problems of the Capitalist State', in von Beyme, K. (ed.) (1974): *German Political Studies*, London, Sage.

Ogilvie, S. C. (ed.) (1993): 'Proto-Industrialization in Europe', *Continuity and Change*, 8 (2) (Aug.).

Ohkawa, K., Takamatsu, N., and Yamamoto, Y. (1974): *Estimates of Long-Term Economic Statistics of Japan since 1868*, i: *National Income*, Tokyo, Toyo Keizai Shinposha.

Oi, J. C. (1989): *State and Peasant in Contemporary China*, Berkeley, University of California Press.

—— (1990): 'The Fate of The Collective After the Commune', in Davis, D. and Vogel, E. (eds.) (1990): *Chinese Society on the Eve of Tiananmen*, Harvard, Harvard UP.

Oi, J. C. (1993): 'Reform and Urban Bias in China', in Varshney, A. (ed.) (1993): *Beyond Urban Bias*, London, Frank Cass.

—— (1994): 'Rational Choices and Attainment of Wealth and Power in the Countryside', in Goodman, D. and Hooper, B. (eds.) (1994): *China's Quiet Revolution*, Melbourne, Longman Cheshire (and New York, St. Martin's Press).

—— (1995): 'The Role of the Local State in China's Transitional Economy', *China Quarterly*, 144 (Dec.), 1132–49.

Okimoto, D. I. (1989): *Between MITI and the Market*, Stanford, Stanford UP.

Okura, M. and Teranishi, J. (1994): 'Exchange Rate and Economic Recovery of Japan in the 1930s', *Hitotsubashi Journal of Economics*, 35 (1) (June), 1–22.

Olson, M. (1965): *The Logic of Collective Action*, Cambridge, Mass., Harvard UP.

—— (1982): *The Rise and Decline of Nations*, New Haven, Yale UP.

—— (1983): 'The Political Economy of Comparative Growth Rates', in Mueller, D. C. (ed.) (1983): *The Political Economy of Growth*, New Haven, Yale UP.

—— (1996): 'The Varieties of Eurosclerosis', in Crafts, N. F. R. and Toniolo, G. (eds.) (1996): *Economic Growth in Europe since 1945*, Cambridge, Cambridge UP.

Osborne, M. (1986): *China's Special Economic Zones*, Paris, OECD.

Otsuka, K., Liu, D. Q., and Murakami, N. (1998): *Industrial Reform in China*, Oxford, Clarendon Press.

Oulton, N. and Young, G. (1996): 'How High is the Social Rate of Return to Investment?', *Oxford Review of Economic Policy*, 12 (2) (Summer), 48–69.

Overton, M. (1996): *Agricultural Revolution in England*, Cambridge, Cambridge UP.

Owen, W. E. (1966): 'The Double Development Squeeze on Agriculture', *American Economic Review*, 56 (March), 43–70.

Page, J. (1994): 'The East Asian Economic Miracle', in Fischer, S. and Rotemberg, J. J. (eds.) (1994): *NBER Macroeconomics Annual 1994*, Cambridge, Mass., MIT Press.

Paine, L. W. (1994): 'Progress and Problems in China's Educational Reform', in Joseph, W. A. (ed.) (1994): *China Briefing 1994*, Boulder, Westview.

Pan, Z. F. (ed.) (1988): *Zhongguo renkou: Guizhou fence* (China's Population: Guizhou), Beijing, Zhongguo caizheng jingji chubanshe.

Pasinetti, L. L. (1974): *Growth and Income Distribution*, Cambridge, Cambridge UP.

—— (1977): *Lectures on the Theory of Production*, London, Macmillan.

Peng, H. K. and Zou, H. F. (1988): 'Sichuan sheng Xichang shi Yizu juju diqu jingji fazhan tansuo' (An Exploration into the Economic Development of Yi Areas around Xichang Prefecture, Sichuan', *Minzu Yanjiu* (Minority Research), 2, 24–9.

Penn World Tables (1995) at http://bizednet.bris.ac.uk.

Pepper, S. (1987*a*): 'Education for the New Order', in MacFarquhar, R. and Fairbank, J. K. (eds.) (1987): *The Cambridge History of China*, xiv, Cambridge, Cambridge UP.

—— (1987*b*): 'New Directions in Education', in MacFarquhar and Fairbank.

—— (1990): *China's Education in the 1980s*, China Research Monograph, no. 36, Berkeley, University of California Press.

—— (1996): *Radicalism and Education Reform in Twentieth Century China*, Cambridge, Cambridge UP.

Perdue, P. C. (1987): *Exhausting the Earth: State and Peasant in Hunan, 1500–1850*, Cambridge, Mass., Harvard UP.

Perkins, D. H. (1967): 'Government as an Obstacle to Industrialisation: The Case of Nineteenth-Century China', *Journal of Economic History*, 27 (4) (Dec.).

—— (1969): *Agricultural Development in China, 1368–1968*, Edinburgh, Edinburgh UP.

—— (1994): 'Completing China's Move to the Market', *Journal of Economic Perspectives*, 8 (2) (Spring), 23–46.
—— and Yusuf, S. (1984): *Rural Development in China*, London, Johns Hopkins UP.
Persson, T. and Tabellini, G. (1994): 'Is Inequality Harmful for Growth?', *American Economic Review*, 84 (3) (June), 600–21.
Piazza, A. (1983): *Trends in Food and Nutrient Availability in China, 1958–1981*, Washington, World Bank Staff Working Paper no. 607.
—— (1986): *Food Consumption and Nutritional Status in the PRC*, Boulder, Westview.
Pollin, R. (1995): 'Financial Structures and Egalitarian Economic Policy', *New Left Review*, 214 (Nov./Dec.), 26–61.
Population Census Office (1987): *The Population Atlas of China*, Oxford, Oxford UP.
Potter, S. H. and Potter, J. M. (1990), *China's Peasants*, Cambridge, Cambridge UP.
Poulantzas, N. (1968): *Political Power and Social Classes*, London, New Left Books.
Powell, S. G. (1992): *Agricultural Reform in China*, Manchester, Manchester UP.
Prebisch, R. (1949): 'The Economic Development of Latin America and Its Principal Problems', repr. in *Economic Bulletin for Latin America* (1962), 7, 1–22.
Prybyla, J. (1991): 'The Road from Socialism', *Problems of Communism*, 40 (Jan.–April).
Przeworski, A. and Limongi, F. (1993): 'Political Regimes and Economic Growth', *Journal of Economic Perspectives*, 7 (3) (Summer), 51–69.
Psacharopoulos, G. and Woodhall, M. (1985): *Education for Development*, New York, Oxford UP.
Pujiang xian zhi (Pujiang County Records) (1992), Chengdu, Sichuan renmin chubanshe.
Putterman, L. (1988): 'Group Farming and Work Incentives in Collective-Era China', *Modern China*, 14 (4) (Oct.).
—— (1993): *Continuity and Change in China's Rural Development*, Oxford, Oxford UP.
—— (1995): 'The Role of Ownership and Property Rights in China's Economic Transition', *China Quarterly*, 144 (Dec.), 1047–64.
Qianwei xian zhi (Qianwei County Records) (1991), Chengdu, Sichuan renmin chubanshe.
Qin, H. L. (ed.) (1995): *Ninth Heaven, Ninth Hell*, New York, Barricade.
Quibria, M. G. and Dowling, J. M. (eds.) (1996): *Current Issues in Economic Development*, Hong Kong, Oxford UP.
Raiser, M. (1995): 'Lessons for Whom, From Whom?', *Communist Economies and Economic Transformation*, 7 (2) (June), 133–58.
Ramseyer, J. M. and Rosenbluth, F. M. (1995): *The Politics of Oligarchy*, Cambridge, Cambridge UP.
Rawski, E. S. (1979): *Education and Popular Literacy in Ch'ing China*, Ann Arbor, University of Michigan Press.
Rawski, T. G. (1989): *Economic Growth in Prewar China*, Berkeley, University of California Press.
—— (1994): 'Progress without Privatization', in Milor, V. (ed.) (1994): *Changing Political Economies*, Boulder, Lynne Rienner.
—— (1995): 'Implications of China's Reform Experience', *China Quarterly*, 144 (Dec.), 1150–73.
Ren, R. E. (1997): *China's Economic Performance in An International Perspective*, Paris, OECD.
Ren, T., Sun, H. Y., and Liu, J. L. (1980): 'Enterprises in Sichuan Acquire Greater Independence', *Social Sciences in China*, 1 (1), 201–15.
Renkou yu jiuye tongjisi (1997)—Guojia tongjiju renkou yu jiuye tongjisi (Department of Population and Employment Statistics, State Statistical Bureau) (ed.) (1997): *Zhongguo*

laodong tongji nianjian (Yearbook of Chinese Labour Statistics), Beijing, Zhongguo tongji chubanshe.

Richman, B. M. (1969): *Industrial Society in Communist China*, New York, Random House.

Riedel, J. (1984): 'Trade as the Engine of Growth in Developing Countries Revisited', *Economic Journal*, 94 (1) (March), 56–73.

Riskin, C. (1987): *China's Political Economy*, Oxford, Oxford UP.

—— (1991): 'Feeding China', in Drèze, J. and Sen, A. K. (eds.) (1991): *The Political Economy of Hunger*, Oxford, Clarendon Press.

Riskin, C. (1993): 'Income Distribution and Poverty in Rural China', in Griffin, K. and Zhao, R. W. (eds.) (1993): *The Distribution of Income in China*, Basingstoke, Macmillan.

Robinson, J. V. (1956): *The Accumulation of Capital*, London, Macmillan.

—— (1962): *Essays in the Theory of Economic Growth*, London, Macmillan.

Rodrik, D. (1995): 'Getting Interventions Right', *Economic Policy*, 20 (April), 53–107.

—— (1996): 'Understanding Economic Policy Reform', *Journal of Economic Literature*, 34 (1) (March), 9–41.

Roemer, J. E. (1994): *A Future for Socialism*, London, Verso.

—— (1996): *Equal Shares*, London, Verso.

Romer, D. (1996): *Advanced Macroeconomics*, New York, McGraw Hill.

Romer, P. M. (1986): 'Increasing Returns and Long-Run Growth', *Journal of Political Economy*, 94 (5) (Oct.), 1002–37.

—— (1990): 'Endogenous Technological Change', *Journal of Political Economy*, 98 (5), pt. 2 (Oct.), S71–S102.

—— (1991): 'Increasing Returns and New Developments in the Theory of Growth', in Barnett, W. A., Cornet, B., D'Aspremont, C., Gabszewicz, J., and Mas-Colell, A. (eds.) (1991): *Equilibrium Theory and Applications*, Cambridge, Cambridge UP.

—— (1993): 'Idea Gaps and Object Gaps in Economic Development', *Journal of Monetary Economics*, 32 (Dec.), 543–73.

—— (1994): 'The Origins of Endogenous Growth', *Journal of Economic Perspectives*, 8 (1) (Winter), 3–22.

—— (1995): 'Comment', in Brainard, W. C. and Perry, G. L. (eds.) (1995): *Brookings Papers on Economic Activity*, no. 1, Washington, Brookings.

Rosen, S. (1990): 'The Impact of Reform Policies on Youth Attitude', in Davis, D. and Vogel, E. F. (eds.) (1990): *Chinese Society on the Eve of Tiananmen*, Cambridge, Mass., Harvard UP.

Rosenberg, N. (1992): *Inside the Black Box*, Cambridge, Cambridge UP.

—— (1994): *Exploring the Black Box*, Cambridge, Cambridge UP.

Rosenstein-Rodan, P. N. (1943): 'Problems of Industrialization of Eastern and South-Eastern Europe', *Economic Journal*, 25, 202–11.

Rowe, W. T. (1984): *Hankow: Commerce and Society in a Chinese City, 1796–1889*, Stanford, Stanford UP.

—— (1989): *Hankow: Conflict and Community in a Chinese City, 1796–1895*, Stanford, Stanford UP.

Rowthorn, R. E. (1975): 'What Remains of Kaldor's Law?', *Economic Journal* (March).

—— (1995): 'Capital Formation and Unemployment', *Oxford Review of Economic Policy*, 11 (1) (Spring), 26–39.

—— and Wells, J. R. (1987): *De-Industrialization and Foreign Trade*, Cambridge, Cambridge UP.

Rozelle, S. (1994): 'Decision-Making in China's Rural Economy', *China Quarterly*, 137 (March).

Sabin, L. (1994): 'New Bosses in the Workers' State', *China Quarterly*, 140 (Dec.), 944–70.

Sachs, J. (1993*a*): 'Comment on Gelb, Jefferson, and Singh', in Blanchard, O. J. and Fischer, S. (eds.) (1993): *NBER Macroeconomics Annual 1993*, Cambridge, Mass., MIT Press.

—— (1993*b*): *Poland's Jump to the Market Economy*, Cambridge, Mass., MIT Press.

—— (1995): 'Reform in Eastern Europe and the Former Soviet Union in Light of the East Asian Experience', *Journal of the Japanese and International Economies*, 9 (4) (Dec.), 454–85.

—— and Warner, A. (1995): 'Economic Reform and the Process of Global Integration', in Brainard, W. C. and Perry, G. L. (eds.) (1995): *Brookings Papers on Economic Activity* no. 1, Washington, Brookings.

—— and Woo, W. T. (1994): 'Structural Factors in the Economic Reforms of China, Eastern Europe, and The Former Soviet Union, *Economic Policy*, 18 (April), 101–46.

—— —— (1997): 'Chinese economic growth', in Joint Economic Committee (1997): *China's Economic Future*, Washington, US Congress.

SAG (1986)—*Sichuan Agricultural Geography*, trans. from ZKCDY (1980), in JPRS Translation no. CAG-86-026, 25 June.

Saith, A. (1987): *The Re-emergence of the Chinese Peasantry*, London, Croom Helm.

Salisbury, H. (1985): *The Long March*, London, Pan Books.

Samuelson, P. A. (1939): 'Interaction between the Multiplier Analysis and the Principle of Acceleration', *Review of Economic Statistics*, 21 (May), 75–8.

Sanderson, M. (1991, 2nd edn.): *Education, Economic Change and Society in England 1780–1870*, London, Macmillan.

Sato, K. (1966): 'On the Adjustment Time in Neo-Classical Growth Models', *Review of Economic Studies*, 33 (July), 263–8.

Saxonhouse, G. (1985): 'Technology Choice in Cotton Textile Manufacturing', in Ohkawa, K. and Ranis, G. (eds.) (1985): *Japan and the Developing Countries*, Oxford, Blackwell.

Scheper-Hughes, N. (1992): *Death Without Weeping*, Berkeley, University of California Press.

Schneider, L. (1989): 'Learning From Russia', in Simon, D. F. and Goldman, M. (eds.) (1989): *Science and Technology in Post-Mao China*, Cambridge, Mass., Harvard UP.

Schofield, R. S. (1973): 'Dimensions of Illiteracy, 1750–1850', *Explorations in Economic History*, 10 (4) (Summer).

Schram, S. R. (1989): *The Thought of Mao Tse-Tung*, Cambridge, Cambridge UP.

Schultz, T. W. (1960): 'Capital Formation by Education', *Journal of Political Economy* (Dec.), 571–83.

—— (1961): 'Investment in Human Capital', *American Economic Review*, 51 (1) (March), 1–17.

—— (1990): 'Investing in People', in Eicher, C. K. and Staatz, J. M. (eds.) (1990): *Agricultural Development in the Third World*, Baltimore, Johns Hopkins UP.

Schumpeter, J. (1943; 1987 edn.): *Capitalism, Socialism and Democracy*, London, Unwin.

Schurmann, F. (1974): *The Logic of World Power*, New York, Pantheon Books.

SCJJDL—*Sichuan jingji dili* (1985), Chengdu, Sichuan kexue jishu chubanshe.

SCJJNJ—*Sichuan jingji nianjian 1986* (Sichuan Economic Yearbook), Chengdu, Sichuan kexue jishu chubanshe.

Scott, J. C. (1976): *The Moral Economy of The Peasant*, New Haven, Yale UP.

Scott, M. F. (1989): *A New View of Economic Growth*, Oxford, Clarendon Press.

SCTJNJ—Sichuan tongjiju (Sichuan Statistical Bureau): *Sichuan tongji nianjian, 1987, 1989, 1990, 1992, 1993, 1994, 1995 and 1997* (Sichuan Statistical Yearbook), Beijing, Zhongguo tongji chubanshe.

SCZL—*Sichuan gongye qiye zonglan* (A Summary Account of Sichuan's Industrial Enterprises) (1990), Beijing, Zhongguo renmin chubanshe.

Selden, M. (1988): *The Political Economy of Chinese Socialism*, London, M. E. Sharpe.
—— (ed.) (1979): *The People's Republic of China: A Documentary History*, New York, Monthly Review Press.
Sen, A. K. (1981): *Poverty and Famines*, Oxford, Oxford UP.
—— (1987): *The Standard of Living*, Cambridge, Cambridge UP.
—— (1988): 'Sri Lanka's Achievements', in Srinivasan, T. N. and Bardhan, P. K. (eds.) (1988): *Rural Poverty in South Asia*, New York, Columbia UP.
—— (1989): 'Food and Freedom', *World Development*, 17 (6) (June), 769–81.
—— (1992): 'Life and Death in China: A Reply', *World Development*, 20 (9) (Sept.), 1305–12.
Shambaugh, D. (ed.) (1982): 'Zhao Ziyang's "Sichuan Experiment"', *Chinese Law and Government*, 15 (1) (Spring).
—— (1993): 'Deng Xiaoping: The Politician', *China Quarterly*, 135 (Sept.).
Shang, J. C. (1989): *Dangdai Zhongguo de Zhejiang* (China Today: Zhejiang), 2 vols., Beijing, Zhongguo shehui kexue chubanshe.
Shanghai shehui kexueyuan jingji yanjiusuo (Economic Research Institute of the Shanghai Academy of Social Sciences) (1991): *Jindai Jiangnan sizhi gongye shi*, Shanghai, Shanghai renmin chubanshe.
Shangye Bu (Ministry of Commerce) (ed.) (1984): *Xin Zhongguo shangye shigao* (A Draft History of Commerce in New China), Beijing, Zhongguo caizheng jingji chubanshe.
Shanin, T. (ed.) (1987): *Peasants and Peasant Societies*, Oxford, Blackwell.
Shapiro, S. (1981): *Experiment in Sichuan*, Beijing, New World Press.
Shen, Y. M. and Tong, C. Z. (1992): *Zhongguo renkou qianyi* (Population Migration in China), Beijing, Zhongguo tongji chubanshe.
Sheng, Y. M. (1993): *Intersectoral Resource Flows and China's Economic Development*, London, Macmillan.
Shinohara, M. (1962): *Growth and Cycles in the Japanese Economy*, Tokyo, Kinokuniya.
Shirk, S. L. (1993): *The Political Logic of Economic Reform in China*, Berkeley, University of California Press.
—— (1994): *How China Opened Its Doors*, Washington, Brookings.
Shmelev, N. and Popov, V. (1990): *The Turning Point*, London, I. B. Tauris.
Shue, V. (1980): *Peasant China in Transition*, Berkeley, University of California Press.
—— (1988): *The Reach of the State*, Stanford, Stanford UP.
—— (1990): 'Emerging State–Society Relations in Rural China', in Delman, J., Oostergaard, C. S., and Christiansen, F. (eds.) (1990): *Remaking Peasant China*, Aarhus, Aarhus UP.
Sichuan Ribao (1982): 'Cadre with Responsibility for Flood and Drought-Fighting Answers Questions', trans. as 'Eastern Sichuan Flood-Fighting Effort Described', in JPRS (1982): *China Report: Agriculture*, CR-AGR-231, 7 Oct. 1982, Washington, Government Printing Office.
Sichuan shehui kexueyuan (Sichuan Academy of Social Science) (ed.) (1988): *Sichuan shehui jingji qingshi zonghe kaocha ji fazhan duice yanjiu* (A Summary Study of Sichuan's Economy and Society, and Research on How to Develop Them), Chengdu, Sichuan sheng shehui kexueyuan.
Sichuan sheng renkou pucha bangongshi (Sichuan Province Population Census Office) (1988): *Zhongguo 1987 nian one per cent renkou chouyang diaocha ziliao: Sichuan fence* (Materials from the China 1987 One Per Cent Population Sample survey: Sichuan Volume), Beijing, Zhongguo tongji chubanshe.

Sichuan tongjiju (Sichuan Statistical Bureau) (ed.) (1986): *Sichuan tongji nianjian 1985* (Sichuan Statistical Yearbook), Chengdu, Sichuan tongjiju.

Sichuan xiangzhen qiye shinian (Sichuan's Township and Village Enterprises Over the Decade, 1977–1986) (1988), Chengdu, Sichuan renmin chubanshe.

Sicular, T. (ed.) (1989): *Food Price Policy in Asia*, Ithaca, NY, Cornell UP.

—— (1991): 'China's Agricultural Policy during the Reform Era', in Joint Economic Committee (1991): *China's Economic Dilemmas in the 1990s*, ii, Washington, US Congress.

—— (1995): 'Redefining State, Plan and Market', *China Quarterly*, 144 (Dec.), 1020–46.

Simon, D. (1989): 'China's Drive to Close the Technological Gap', *China Quarterly*, 119 (Sept.), 598–630.

—— (1991): 'China's Acquisition and Assimilation of Foreign Technology', in Joint Economic Committee (1991): *China's Economic Dilemmas in the 1990s*, ii, Washington, US Congress.

—— and Goldman, M. (eds.) (1989): *Science and Technology in Post-Mao China*, Cambridge, Mass., Harvard UP.

Simon, J. J. (1977): *The Economics of Population Growth*, Princeton, Princeton UP.

—— (1981): *The Ultimate Resource*, Princeton, Princeton UP.

Singer, H. (1950): 'The Distribution of Gains between Investing and Borrowing Countries', *American Economic Review*, 40 (2) (May), 473–85.

—— (1992): 'Lessons of Post-War Development Experience, 1945–1988', in Adriaansen, W. L. M. and Waardenburg, J. G. (eds.) (1992): *A Dual World Economy*, Bombay, Oxford UP.

Singh, A. (1977): 'UK Industry and the World Economy', *Cambridge Journal of Economics*, 1, 113–36.

Siu, H. F. (1989): *Agents and Victims in South China*, New Haven, Yale UP.

—— (1990): 'The Politics of Migration in a Market Town', in Davis, D. and Vogel, E. (eds.) (1990): *Chinese Society on the Eve of Tiananmen*, Cambridge, Mass., Harvard UP.

Skinner, G. W. (1965–6): 'Marketing and Social Structure in Rural China', *Journal of Asian Studies*, 24 (1, 2, 3) (Nov., Feb., May).

Skocpol, T. (1979): *States and Social Revolutions*, Cambridge, Cambridge UP.

—— (1994): *Social Revolutions in the Modern World*, Cambridge, Cambridge UP.

Smil, V. (1988): *Energy in China's Modernization*, London, M. E. Sharpe.

—— (1993): *China's Environmental Crisis*, New York, M. E. Sharpe.

Smith, T. C. (1959): *The Agrarian Origins of Modern Japan*, Stanford, Stanford UP.

—— (1977): *Nakahara*, Stanford, Stanford UP.

—— (1988): *Native Sources of Japanese Industrialization, 1750–1920*, Berkeley, University of California Press.

Sobhan, R. (1993): *Agrarian Reform and Social Transformation*, London, Zed.

Solow, R. M. (1956): 'A Contribution to the Theory of Economic Growth', *Quarterly Journal of Economics*, 70 (Feb.), 65–94.

—— (1957): 'Technical Change and the Aggregate Production Function', *Review of Economics and Statistics*, 39 (Aug.), 312–20.

—— (1970, repr. 1988): *Growth Theory*, Oxford, Oxford UP.

—— (1996): 'Growth Theory' in Greenaway, D., Bleaney, M., and Stewart, I. (eds.) (1996): *A Guide to Modern Economics*, London, Routledge.

Song, N. G. (ed.) (1987): *Zhongguo renkou: Nei Menggu fence* (China's Population: Inner Mongolia), Beijing, Zhongguo caizheng jingji chubanshe.

Spence, J. (1996): *God's Chinese Son*, London, HarperCollins.

Spraos, J. (1983): *Inequalizing Trade?*, Oxford, Clarendon Press.
Srinivasan, T. N. (1995): 'Long-Run Growth Theories and Empirics', in Ito, T. and Krueger, A. O. (eds.) (1995): *Growth Theories in Light of the East Asian Experience*, Chicago, University of Chicago Press.
—— and Bardhan, P. K. (eds.) (1988): *Rural Poverty in South Asia*, New York, Columbia UP.
State Statistical Bureau (ed.) (1994): *China Foreign Economic Statistical Yearbook*, Beijing, Zhongguo tongji chubanshe (English and Chinese edn.).
—— (1996): 'Statistical Communiqué of the State Statistical Bureau of the PRC on 1995 National Economic and Social Development', *Beijing Review*, 39 (14) (April).
—— (1997): 'Statistical Communiqué on Socio-Economic Development in 1996', *Beijing Review*, 40 (17) (April–May).
Stiglitz, J. E. (1994): *Whither Socialism?* Cambridge, Mass., MIT Press.
—— (1995): 'Social Absorption Capability and Innovation', in Koo, B. H. and Perkins, D. H. (eds.) (1995): *Social Capability and Long-Term Economic Growth*, London, Macmillan.
—— (1997): 'Reflections on the Natural Rate Hypothesis', *Journal of Economic Perspectives*, 11 (1) (Winter), 3–10.
Stone, B. (1988*a*): 'Developments in Agricultural Technology', *China Quarterly*, 118 (Dec.).
—— (1988*b*): 'Relative Prices in the People's Republic of China', in Mellor, J. W. and Ahmed, R. (eds.) (1988): *Agricultural Price Policy for Developing Countries*, Baltimore, Johns Hopkins UP.
Streeten, P. (1996): 'Governance', in Quibria, M. G. and Dowling, J. M. (eds.) (1996): *Current Issues in Economic Development*, Hong Kong, Oxford UP.
Stross, R. E. (1986): *The Stubborn Earth*, Berkeley, University of California Press.
Su, S. Z. and Zhang, X. Y. (1989): *Sanzhong quanhui yilai Makesizhuyi zai Zhongguo de fazhan* (The Development of Marxism in China since the Third Plenum), Beijing, Zhongguo renmin chubanshe.
Su, X. (1982): 'Zerenzhi yu nongcun jitisuozhi jingji de fazhan' (The Responsibility System and the Development of Collectivized Agriculture in Rural Areas), *Jingji yanjiu*, 11 (Nov.), 3–9.
Sun, C. C. (1959): *Economic Geography of North-East China*, trans. JPRS, New York, Government Printing Office.
—— (1960): *Economic Geography of South-West China*, trans. JPRS, New York, Government Printing Office.
Sun, J. (1992): *Zhonghua renmin gongeheguo jingjishi 1949–90* (An Economic History of the People's Republic of China), Beijing, Zhongguo renmin daxue chubanshe.
Sun, Y. (1995): *The Chinese Reassessment of Socialism, 1976–92*, Princeton, Princeton UP.
Sung, Y. W. (1991): *The China–Hong Kong Connection*, Cambridge, Cambridge UP.
—— (1995): 'Comment', in Ito, T. and Krueger, A. O. (eds.) (1995): *Growth Theories in Light of the East Asian Experience*, Chicago, University of Chicago Press.
Sutton, A. C. (1973): *Western Technology and Soviet Economic Development, 1917–1965*, Stanford, Hoover Institute.
Suzhou tongjiju (1996): *Suzhou tongji nianjian 1996* (Suzhou Statistical Yearbook), Beijing, Zhongguo tongji chubanshe.
Svejnar, J. (1990): 'Productive Efficiency and Employment', in Byrd, W. A. and Lin, Q. S. (eds.) (1990): *China's Rural Industry*, Oxford, Oxford UP.
SWB (1980*a*): 'Sichuan', FE/W1092/A/5, 23 July 1980, London, BBC.
—— (1980*b*): 'Sichuan', FE/W109/A/4–5, 27 Aug. 1980, London, BBC.

—— (1980*c*): 'Sichuan', FE/W1097/A/7, 27 Aug. 1980, London, BBC.
—— (1981*a*): 'Floods: Sichuan', FE/W1148/A/5, 26 Aug. 1981, London, BBC.
—— (1981*b*): 'Floods: Sichuan', FE/W1157/A/3, 28 Oct. 1981, London, BBC.
Taira, K. (1978): 'Factory Labour and the Industrial Revolution in Japan', in Mathias, P. and Postan, M. (eds.) (1978): *The Cambridge Economic History of Europe*, vii (pt. 2), Cambridge, Cambridge UP.
Taiwan Statistical Databook, 1990 (1990), Taipei, Council for Economic Planning and Development.
Tam, O.-K. (1988): 'Rural Finance in China', *China Quarterly*, 113 (March), 60–76.
Tang, A. M. (1985): *An Analytical and Empirical Investigation of Agriculture in Mainland China*, Seattle, University of Washington Press.
Tang, R. J. (1996): 'Grain Marketing', in Garnault, R., Guo, S. T., and Ma, G. N. (eds.) (1996): *The Third Revolution in the Chinese Countryside*, Cambridge, Cambridge, UP.
Tang, Z. J. (1986): *Da Xinan ziran jingji shehui ziyuan pingjia* (An Evaluation of the Natural Economy and Social Resources of the South-West), Chengdu, Sichuan sheng shehui kexue chubanshe.
Targetti, F. and Thirlwall, A. P. (eds) (1989): *The Essential Kaldor*, London, Duckworth.
Tawney, R. H. (1937, repr. 1990): *Religion and the Rise of Capitalism*, London, Penguin.
Taylor, J. R. (1988): 'Rural Employment Trends and the Legacy of Surplus Labour, 1978–1986', *China Quarterly*, 116 (Dec.).
Teiwes, F. C. (1971): 'Provincial Politics in China', in Lindbeck, J. M. H. (ed.) (1971): *China: Management of a Revolutionary Society*, Seattle, University of Washington Press.
—— (1988): 'Mao and His Lieutenants', *Australian Journal of Chinese Affairs*, 19/20, 1–80.
—— (1993, 2nd edn.): *Politics and Purges in China*, New York, M. E. Sharpe.
—— and Sun, W. (eds.) (1993): *The Politics of Agricultural Cooperativization in China*, Armonk, NY, M. E. Sharpe.
Thant, M., Tang, M., and Kakazu, H. (eds.) (1994): *Growth Triangles in Asia*, Hong Kong, Oxford UP.
Thomas, B. (1985): 'Food Supply in the United Kingdom During the Industrial Revolution', in Mokyr, J. (ed.) (1985): *The Economics of the Industrial Revolution*, London, Allen and Unwin.
Thompson, E. P. (1968): *The Making of the English Working Class*, New York, Vintage.
Thorbecke, E. (1992): 'The Process of Agricultural Development in Taiwan', in Ranis, G. (ed.) (1992): *Taiwan*, Boulder, Westview.
Tobin, J. (1980): *Asset Accumulation and Economic Activity*, Oxford, Blackwell.
Todaro, M. P. (1969): 'A Model of Labor Migration and Urban Unemployment in Less Developed Countries', *American Economic Review*, 59 (1) (March), 138–48.
Tonglu xian zhi (Tonglu County Records) (1991), Hangzhou, Zhejiang renmin chubanshe.
Trevithick, J. A. (1992): *Involuntary Unemployment*, Hemel Hempstead, Harvester Wheatsheaf.
Trotsky, L. (1937, 1972 edn.): *The Revolution Betrayed*, New York, Pathfinder.
Tseng, C. W. and Mao, W. L. (1994): 'Fiscal Policy and Economic Development in Taiwan', in Aberbach, J. D., Dollar, D., and Sokoloff, K. L. (eds.) (1994): *The Role of the State in Taiwan's Development*, New York, M. E. Sharpe.
Tsou, T., Blecher, M., and Meisner, M. (1979): 'Organization, Growth and Equity in Xiyang county', *Modern China*, 5 (1) (Jan.), 3–40; and 5 (2) (April), 139–85.
—— —— —— (1982): 'The Responsibility System in Agriculture: Its Implementation in Xiyang and Dazhai', *Modern China*, 8 (1) (Jan.).

Tsurumi, E. P. (1990): *Factory Girls*, Princeton, Princeton UP.

Tuchman, B. W. (1970): *Sand Against the Wind*, London, Macmillan.

UNCTAD (1997): *Trade and Development Report 1997*, New York, United Nations.

UNDP—United Nations Development Programme (various years): *Human Development Report 1992 and 1994*, Oxford, Oxford UP.

UNESCO (1995): *Statistics on Education, 1995*, Geneva, UNESCO.

Unger, J. (1986): 'The Decollectivization of the Chinese Countryside', *Pacific Affairs*, 58 (4) (Winter), 585–606.

—— (1993): 'Urban Families in the Eighties', in Davis, D. and Harrell, S. (eds.) (1993): *Chinese Families in the Post-Mao Era*, Berkeley, University of California Press.

van Elkan, R. (1995): 'Singapore's Development Strategy', in Bercuson, K. (ed.): *Singapore*, Washington, IMF.

Vander Elst, P. (1981): *Capitalist Technology for Soviet Survival*, London, IEA.

Vanhanen, T. (1997): *Prospects of Democracy*, London, Routledge.

Varshney, A. (ed.) (1993): *Beyond Urban Bias*, London, Frank Cass.

Veeser, H. A. (ed.) (1989): *The New Historicism*, London, Routledge.

Vermeer, E. B. (1977): *Water Conservancy and Irrigation in China*, The Hague, Leiden UP.

—— (1988): *Economic Development in Provincial China*, Cambridge, Cambridge UP.

—— (ed.) (1992): *From Peasant to Entrepreneur*, Wageningen, Pudoc.

Vickers, J. and Yarrow, G. (1988): *Privatization*, Cambridge, Mass., MIT Press.

Vogel, E. F. (1989): *One Step Ahead in China*, Cambridge, Mass., Harvard UP.

Volkogonov, D. (1991): *Stalin*, London, Weidenfeld and Nicolson.

von Neumann, J. (1937): 'A Model of General Equilibrium', *Review of Economic Studies*, 13, 1–9.

von Tunzelmann, G. N. (1978): *Steam Power and British Industrialization to 1860*, Oxford, Oxford UP.

Wade, R. (1990): *Governing the Market*, Princeton, Princeton UP.

—— (1996): 'Japan, The World Bank, and The Art of Paradigm Maintenance', *New Left Review*, 217 (May/June), 3–37.

—— and Veneroso, F. (1998): 'The Asian Crisis: The High Debt Model Versus the Wall Street–Treasury–IMF Complex', *New Left Review*, 228 (March/April), 3–23.

Wakashiro, N. (1990): 'Rural Reform and Agricultural Production in China', *The Developing Economies*, 28 (4) (Dec.), 482–502.

Walder, A. G. (1987): 'Wage Reform and The Web of Factory Interests', *China Quarterly*, 109 (March).

—— (1990): 'Economic Reform and Income Distribution in Tianjin, 1976–1986', in Davis, D. and Vogel, E. (eds.) (1990): *Chinese Society on the Eve of Tiananmen*, Cambridge, Mass., Harvard UP.

—— (1991): 'Workers, Managers and The State', *China Quarterly*, 127 (Sept.).

Walker, K. R. (1984): *Food Grain Procurement and Consumption in China*, Cambridge, Cambridge UP.

Wallerstein, I. (1974): *The Modern World System*, New York, Academic Press.

—— (1979): *The Capitalist World Economy*, Cambridge, Cambridge UP.

Wang, F. L. (1998): *From Family to Market*, Oxford, Rowman and Littlefield.

Wang, G. C. and Zhou, Q. R. (1985): *Smashing the Communal Pot*, Beijing, New World Press.

Wang, L. X. (1988): 'Mao's Legacy in Anhui', *Kunlun*, 6 (Dec.), trans. in JPRS (1989): *China Report: Agriculture*, CAR-89-079, July, 1–65, Washington, Government Printing Office.

Wang, M. K. and Lu, Z. Y. (1997): *Chengzhen jumin shouru chaju yanjiu* (Research on Income Differentials between Urban Residents), Beijing, Zhongguo yanshi chubanshe.
Wang, S. J. (1988): *Zhongguo renkou: Zhejiang fence* (China's Population: Zhejiang), Beijing, Zhongguo caizheng jingji chubanshe.
Wang, X. L. (1990): 'Capital Formation and Utilization', in Byrd, W. A. and Lin, Q. S. (eds.) (1990): *China's Rural Industry*, Oxford, Oxford UP.
Wang, X. Q. and Bai, N. (1991): *The Poverty of Plenty*, London, Macmillan.
Wang, Y. (1987): *Zhongguo shixian shouce* (Handbook of China's Counties and Cities), Hangzhou, Zhejiang renmin chubanshe.
Warren, B. (1980): *Imperialism: Pioneer of Capitalism*, London, Verso.
Watson, A. (1984): 'Agriculture Looks for 'Shoes that Fit': The Production Responsibility System and Its Implications', in Maxwell, N. and McFarlane, B. (eds.) (1984): *China's Changed Road to Development*, Oxford, Pergamon.
—— (1989*a*): 'The Family Farm, Land Use and Accumulation in Agriculture', in Cheng, J. Y. S. (ed.) (1989): *China: Modernization in the 1980s*, Hong Kong, Chinese UP.
—— (1989*b*): 'Investment Issues in the Chinese Countryside', *Australian Journal of Chinese Affairs*, 22 (July), 85–128.
—— (ed.) (1992): *Economic Reform and Social Change in China*, London, Routledge.
—— and Findlay, C. (1992): 'The Wool War in China', in Findlay, C. (ed.) (1992): *Challenges of Economic Reform*, Sydney, Allen and Unwin.
—— —— and Du, Y. T. (1989): 'Who Won the "Wool War"? A Case Study of Rural Product Marketing in China', *China Quarterly*, 118 (June), 213–41.
WDR—World Bank (various years): *World Development Report 1982, 1990, 1991, 1992, 1993, 1994, 1995, 1996, and 1997*, Oxford, Oxford UP.
Weber, M. (1956; 1978 edn.): *Economy and Society*, Berkeley, University of California Press.
Wedeman, A. (1997): 'Stealing From the Farmers: Institutional Corruption and the 1992 IOU Crisis,' *China Quarterly*, 152 (Dec.), 805–31.
Wei, S. J. (1995): 'The Open Door Policy and China's Rapid Growth', in Ito, T. and Krueger, A. O. (eds.) (1995): *Growth Theories in Light of the East Asian Experience*, London, University of Chicago Press.
Weil, R. (1996): *Red Cat, White Cat*, New York, Monthly Review Press.
Weitzman, M. L. and Xu, C. G. (1994): 'Vaguely Defined Cooperatives and Cooperative Culture', in Nove, A. and Thatcher, I. D. (eds.) (1994): *Markets and Socialism*, Aldershot, Edward Elgar.
Wen, J. G. Z. (1993): 'Total Factor Productivity Change in China's Farming Sector, 1952–89', *Economic Development and Cultural Change*, 42 (1) (Oct.), 1–42.
Wenshi ziliao weiyuanhui (Historical and Cultural Materials Committee) (1993): *Liangshan wenshi ziliao xuanji* (Selected Materials on the History and Culture of Liangshan), xi, Xichang, no publisher.
Wenzhou cidian (A Dictionary of Wenzhou) (1995): Shanghai, Fudan daxue chubanshe.
Wenzhou tongjiju (Wenzhou Statistical Bureau) (ed.) (various years): *Wenzhou tongji nianjian 1985 and 1989* (Wenzhou Statistical Yearbook), Wenzhou, no publisher.
Westphal, L. E. (1990): 'Industrial Policy in an Export-Propelled Economy', *Journal of Economic Perspectives*, 4 (3) (Summer), 41–59.
White, G. (ed.) (1988): *Developmental States in East Asia*, London, Macmillan.
—— (1991): *The Chinese State in the Era of Economic Reform*, London, Macmillan.
Whyte, M. K. and Parish, W. L. (1984): *Urban Life in Contemporary China*, Chicago, Chicago UP.

Wiener, M. J. (1981): *English Culture and the Decline of the Industrial Spirit, 1850–1980*, Cambridge, Cambridge UP.
Wilkinson, R. (1994): 'Health, Redistribution and Growth', in Glyn, A. and Miliband, D. (eds.) (1994): *Paying for Inequality*, London, Rivers Oram Press.
Williamson, J. G. (1965): 'Regional Inequality and the Process of National Development', *Economic Development and Cultural Change*, 13 (4) (July), 3–84.
—— (1985): *Did British Capitalism Breed Inequality?*, London, Allen and Unwin.
—— (1990): *Coping with City Growth during the British Industrial Revolution*, Cambridge, Cambridge UP.
—— (1991): 'Did English Factor Markets Fail During the Industrial Revolution?', in Crafts, N. F. R., Dimsdale, N. H., and Engerman, S. (eds.) (1991): *Quantitative Economic History*, Oxford, Clarendon Press.
Wirtschaffer, R. M. and Shih, M. (1990): 'Decentralization of China's Electricity Sector', *World Development*, 18 (4) (April).
Wong, C. P. W. (1982): 'Rural Industrialization in China', in Barker, R., Sinha, R., and Rose, B. (eds.) (1982): *The Chinese Agricultural Economy*, London, Croom Helm.
—— (1988): 'Interpreting Rural Industrial Growth in the Post-Mao Period', *Modern China*, 14 (1) (Jan.).
—— (1989): 'Between Plan and Market', in Gomulka, S., Ha, Y. C., and Kim, C. O. (eds.) (1989): *Economic Reforms in the Socialist World*, London, Macmillan.
—— (1991*a*): 'Central Planning and Local Participation under Mao', in White, G. (ed.) (1991): *The Chinese State in the Era of Economic Reform*, London, Macmillan.
—— (1991*b*): 'Central–Local Relations in an Era of Fiscal Decline', *China Quarterly*, 128 (Dec.).
—— (1991*c*): 'The Maoist "Model" Reconsidered', in Joseph, W. A., Wong, C. P. W., and Zweig, D. (eds.) (1991): *New Perspectives on the Cultural Revolution*, Cambridge, Mass., Harvard UP.
—— (1994): 'China's Economy', in Joseph, W. A. (ed.) (1994): *China Briefing 1994*, Boulder, Westview.
—— Heady, C., and Woo, W. T. (1995): *Fiscal Management and Economic Reform in the People's Republic of China*, Hong Kong, Oxford UP.
Woo, W. T. (1998): 'Chinese Economic Growth', in Fouquin, M. and Lemoine, F. (eds.) (1998): *The Chinese Economy*, Economica, London.
—— Parker, S., and Sachs, J. D. (eds.) (1997): *Economies in Transition*, Cambridge, Mass., MIT Press.
—— Hai, W., Jin, Y. B., and Fan, G. (1994): 'How Successful Has Chinese Enterprise Reform Been?', *Journal of Comparative Economics*, 18 (June), 10–37.
Wood, E. M. (1991): *The Pristine Culture of Capitalism*, London, Verso.
World Bank (1988): *China: Growth and Development in Gansu Province*, Washington, World Bank.
—— (1990*a*): *China: Between Plan and Market*, Washington, World Bank.
—— (1990*b*): *China: Macroeconomic Stability and Industrial Growth Under Decentralized Socialism*, Washington, World Bank.
—— (1992): *China: Strategies for Reducing Poverty in the 1990s*, Washington, World Bank.
—— (1993*a*): *The East Asian Miracle*, Oxford, Oxford UP.
—— (1993*b*): *China: The Achievement and Challenge of Price Reform*, Washington, World Bank.
—— (1993*c*): *World Debt Tables*, Washington, World Bank.
—— (1994*a*): *China: GNP Per Capita*, Washington, World Bank.

—— (1994*b*): *Adjustment in Africa*, Oxford, Oxford UP.
—— (1994*c*): *China: Foreign Trade Reform*, Washington, World Bank.
—— (1995): *Bureaucrats in Business*, Oxford, Oxford UP.
—— (1996): *The Chinese Economy*, Washington, World Bank.
—— (1997*a*): *China 2020*, Washington, World Bank.
—— (1997*b*): *China Engaged*, Washington, World Bank.
—— (1997*c*): *Sharing Rising Incomes*, Washington, World Bank.
Wright, M. C. (1957): *The Last Stand of Chinese Conservatism*, Stanford, Stanford UP.
Wrigley, E. A. and Schofield, R. S. (1981): *The Population History of England, 1541–1871*, Cambridge, Cambridge UP.
WT—World Bank (various years): *World Tables 1992 and 1994*, Baltimore, Johns Hopkins UP.
Wu, H. X. and Wu, Y. R. (1994): 'Rural Enterprise Growth and Efficiency', in Findlay, C., Watson, A., and Wu, H. X. (eds.) (1994): *Rural Enterprises in China*, London, Macmillan.
Wu, N. K. (1993): *A Single Tear*, London, Hodder and Stoughton.
Wushan xian zhi (Wushan County Records) (1991), Chengdu, Sichuan renmin chubanshe.
Wuxi tongjiju (Wuxi Statistical Bureau) (ed.) (1997): *Wuxi tongji nianjian* (Wuxi Statistical Yearbook), Beijing, Zhongguo tongji chubanshe.
WXGY—Wuxi xian jingji weiyuanhui (Wuxi County Economic Committee) (1990): *Wuxi xian gongye zhi* (Wuxi County Industrial Records), Shanghai, Shanghai renmin chubanshe.
Xin, M. (1990): 'The Rural Labor Market', in Byrd, W. A. and Lin, Q. S. (eds.) (1990): *China's Rural Industry*, Oxford, Oxford UP.
Xiong, Q. Q. (1990): *Dangdai Zhongguo de Hunan sheng* (China Today: Hunan Province), Beijing, Zhongguo shehui kexue chubanshe.
Xizang zizhiqu renkou pucha bangongshi (Tibet Population Census Office) (1992): *Jindai Zhongguo Xizang renkou* (The Tibetan Population in China Today), Beijing, Zhongguo zangxue chubanshe.
Xu, D. X. (ed.) (1982): *China's Search for Economic Growth*, Beijing, New World Press.
—— and Wu, C. M. (forthcoming): *Chinese Capitalism, 1552–1840*, London, Macmillan.
Xu, W. S. (ed.) (1988): *Zhejiang nongcun gaige de zuji* (The Path of Zhejiang's Rural Reform), Hangzhou, Nongcun duwu chubanshe.
Xue, M. Q. (1981): *China's Socialist Economy*, Beijing, Foreign Language Press.
Yabuki, S. (1995): *China's New Political Economy*, Boulder, Westview.
Yager, J. A. (1988): *Transforming Agriculture in Taiwan*, Ithaca, NY, Cornell UP.
Yamamura, K. (1977): 'Success Illgotten? The Role of Meiji Militarism in Japan's Technological Progress', *Journal of Economic History*, 36 (1) (March).
—— (1986): 'Caveat Emptor: The Industrial Policy of Japan', in Krugman, P. (ed.) (1986): *Strategic Trade Policy and the New International Economics*, Cambridge, Mass., MIT Press.
Yamazawa, I. (1990): *Economic Development and International Trade*, Honolulu, Resource Systems Institute.
Yan, R. Z., Gong, D. G., Zhou, Z. X., and Bi, B. D. (1990): 'Zhongguo gongnongye chanpin jiagc jiandaocha de xianzhuang fazhan qushi yu duice (The Current Situation, Development Trends and Solutions to the Scissors Differential Between Agriculture and Industry in China), *Jingji yanjiu*, 2 (Feb.), 64–70.
Yan, Y. X. (1996): *The Flow of Gifts*, Stanford, Stanford UP.
Yang, B. (1993): 'The Making of a Pragmatic Communist', *China Quarterly*, 135 (Sept.), 444–56.
—— (1998): *Deng: A Political Biography*, New York, M. E. Sharpe.

Yang, C. (1990): *Dangdai Zhongguo de Sichuan* (China Today: Sichuan), 2 vols., Beijing, Zhongguo shehui kexue chubanshe.

Yang, D. L. (1994): 'Reform and the Restructuring of Central–Local Relations', in Goodman, D. and Segal, G. (eds.) (1994): *China Deconstructs*, London, Routledge.

Yang, X. and Liu, J. R. (1986): *Zhongguo nongcun gaige de daolu* (Rural China's Reform Path), Beijing, Beijing daxue chubanshe.

Yang, Z. W. (1988): 'Woguo tinghuo pengzhang de zhenduan' (A Diagnosis of Inflation in Our Country), *Jingji yanjiu* (Economic Research), 4 (April), 3–11.

Yeh, K. C. (1979): 'China's National Income, 1931–36', in Hou, C. M. and Yu, T. S. (eds.) (1979): *Modern Chinese Economic History*, Seattle, University of Washington Press.

—— (1992): 'Macroeconomic Issues in China in the 1990s', *China Quarterly*, 131 (Sept.), 501–44.

Yeung, G. (1998): *Foreign Investment and Socio-economic Development in Dongguan*, unpubl. Ph.D. diss., University of Cambridge (forthcoming, Macmillan).

Yeung, Y. M. (1994): 'Infrastructural Development in the Southern China Growth Triangle', in Thant, M., Tang, M., and Kakazu, H. (eds.) (1994): *Growth Triangles in Asia*, Hong Kong, Oxford UP.

Yin, C. Y. (1986): 'Dui Liangshan shehui jingji fazhan wenti de zai renshi' (Some Further Insights into the Problems of Economic and Social Development in Liangshan) in Zhongjue minzu xueyuan shaoshu minzu jingji yanjiusuo (The Ethnic Minority Economic Research Institute of the Central Nationalities School) (ed.): *Xibu minzu diqu jingji kaifa tansuo* (An Exploration into the Economic Development of Ethnic Minority Regions in Western China), 126–74, Beijing, Zhongjue minzu xueyuan chubanshe.

You, J. (1991): 'Zhao Ziyang and the Politics of Inflation', *Australian Journal of Chinese Affairs*, 25 (Jan.), 69–91.

Young, A. A. (1928): 'Increasing Returns and Economic Progress', *Economic Journal* (Dec.).

Young, A. (1992): 'A Tale of Two Cities', in Blanchard, O. J. and Fischer, S. (eds.) (1992): *NBER Macroeconomics Annual 1992*, Cambridge, Mass., MIT Press.

—— (1993): 'Invention and Bounded Learning By Doing', *Journal of Political Economy*, 101, 443–72.

—— (1995): 'The Tyranny of Numbers', *Quarterly Journal of Economics* (Aug.).

Young, S. and Yang, G. (1994): 'Private Enterprises and Local Government in Rural China', in Findlay, C., Watson, A., and Wu, H. X. (eds.) (1994): *Rural Enterprises in China*, London, Macmillan.

Yu, C. L. and Buckwell, A. (1991): *Chinese Grain Economy and Policy*, Wallingford, CAB International.

Yu, D. C. (1989): *Quanguo baicun laodongli qingkuang diaocha ziliaoji* (Collected Materials from a National Multi-Village Survey of the Situation of the Labour Force Across China), Beijing, Zhongguo tongji chubanshe.

Yu, G. Y. (ed.) (1984): *China's Socialist Modernization*, Beijing, Foreign Languages Press.

Yuan, P. (1994): 'Capital Formation in Rural Enterprises', in Findlay, C., Watson, A., and Wu, H. X. (eds.) (1994): *Rural Enterprises in China*, London, Macmillan.

Yue, W. (1990): *Dangdai Zhongguo de tongji shiye* (China Today: Statistics), Beijing, Zhongguo shehui kexue chubanshe.

ZGFX—Zhongguo tongjiju (Chinese State Statistical Bureau) (ed.) (various years): *Zhongguo fenxian nongcun jingji tongji gaiyao 1980–1987, 1989, 1990, and 1992* (An Outline of Rural Economic Statistics by County in China), Beijing, Zhongguo tongji chubanshe.

ZGGYJJTJNJ—Zhongguo tongjiju (Chinese State Statistical Bureau) (various years): *Zhongguo gongye jingji tongji nianjian 1990, 1991, 1992, 1993, 1994, and 1995* (Yearbook of Economic Statistics on Chinese Industry), Beijing, Zhongguo tongji chubanshe.

ZGJYNJ—*Zhongguo jiaoyu nianjian 1949–1981, and 1995* (Chinese Educational Yearbook), Beijing, Zhongguo renmin chubanshe.

ZGNCTJNJ—Zhongguo tongjiju (Chinese State Statistical Bureau) (various years): *Zhongguo nongcun tongji nianjian 1985, 1990, 1993, 1994, and 1995* (Yearbook of Statistics on Rural China), Beijing, Zhongguo tongji chubanshe.

ZGNMYYTJZL—Nongye bu (various years): *Zhongguo nongmuyuye tongji ziliao 1984 and 1986* (Statistical Materials on Chinese Farming, Animal Husbandry, and Fisheries), Beijing, Nongye chubanshe.

ZGNYNJ—Nongye bu (various years): *Zhongguo nongye nianjian 1983, 1985, 1990, 1996, and 1997* (Chinese Agricultural Yearbook), Beijing, Nongye chubanshe.

ZGNYTJZL—Nongye bu (various years): *Zhongguo nongye tongji ziliao 1987, 1988, 1989, 1990, 1991, 1992, 1994* (Statistical Materials on Chinese Agriculture), Beijing, Nongye chubanshe.

ZGRKNJ—Zhongguo shehui kexueyuan renkou yanjiusuo (Population Institute of the Chinese Academy of Social Sciences) (ed.) (various years): *Zhongguo renkou nianjian 1985, 1991 and 1992* (Chinese Population Yearbook), Beijing, Jingji guanli chubanshe.

ZGRKTJNJ—Zhongguo tongjiju (Chinese State Statistical Bureau) (various years): *Zhongguo renkou tongji nianjian 1988, 1991, 1992, and 1993* (Chinese Population Statistics Yearbook), Beijing, Zhongguo tongji chubanshe.

ZGSWY—Zhonggong Gansu sheng wei yanjiushi (Research Unit of the Gansu Committee of the CCP) (ed.) (1988): *Gansu sheng qing* (Conditions in Gansu Province), i, Lanzhou, Gansu renmin chubanshe.

ZGTJNJ - Zhongguo tongjiju (Chinese State Statistical Bureau) (various years): *Zhongguo tongji nianjian 1981, 1983, 1984, 1985, 1987, 1988, 1989, 1990, 1991, 1992, 1993, 1994, 1995, 1996, and 1997* (Chinese Statistical Yearbook), Beijing, Zhongguo tongji chubanshe.

Zhan, J. (1993): 'The Role of Foreign Direct Investment in Market-Oriented Reforms and Economic Development: The Case of China', *Transnational Corporations* (Dec.).

Zhang, H. A. and Xu, Y. (eds.) (1995): *Zhongguo nongcun zhengzhi wending yu fazhan* (Political Stability and Development in Rural China), Wuhan, Wuhan chubanshe.

Zhang, J. (1985): 'Gaige jingji xinli shi fazhan shaozu minzu diqu jingji de zhongyao huanjie' (The Reform of Economic Psychology is an Important Element in the Economic Development of Ethnic Minority Regions), *Minzu yanjiu* (Minority Research), 4, 7–11.

Zhang, S. D. and Hou, Z. Y. (ed.) (1990): *Dangdai Zhongguo de Henan* (China Today: Henan), 2 vols., Beijing, Zhongguo shehui kexue chubanshe.

Zhang, T. Z. (1993): *Jiangsu sheng jingji dili* (An Economic Geography of Jiangsu Province), Beijing, Xinhua chubanshe.

Zhang, X. H. (1992): *Enterprise Reforms in a Centrally Planned Economy: The Case of the Chinese Bicycle Industry*, London, Macmillan.

Zhang, X. L. (1991): *Getting Used to Dying*, London, Flamingo.

Zhao, Y. J. and Zhang, S. J. (1988): 'Restraining the Payments Capability of China's Grass-Roots Banks', *Chinese Economic Studies*, 21 (3) (Spring).

Zhejiang sheng jingji yanjiu zhongxin (Zhejiang Economic Research Centre) (1986): *Zhejiang sheng qing gaiyao* (An Outline of Conditions in Zhejiang Province), Hangzhou, Zhejiang renmin chubanshe.

Zhejiang tongjiju (Zhejiang Statistical Bureau) (1984): *Zhejiang jingji gaikuang* (A Summary of Zhejiang's Economy), Hangzhou, Zhejiang tongji chubanshe.

Zheng, P. L. (1985): *Zhongguo jiamu pinzhong jiqi shengtai tezheng* (Chinese Domestic Animals and the Characteristics of Their Environment), Beijing, Nongye chubanshe.

Zhong, X. (1984): *Emerging from Primitivity*, Beijing, New World Press.

Zhonggong zhongyang wenxian yanjiushi (Document Office of the Central Committee) (ed.) (1982): *Sanzhong quanhui yilai* (After the Third Plenum), Beijing, Renmin chubanshe.

Zhonggong zhongyang xuanchuanbu xuanchuanju (Propaganda Office of the Central Committee's Department of Propaganda) (1988): *Jidang Zhongguo nongcun de biange* (The Transformation Surging Across Rural China), Beijing, Guangming ribao chubanshe.

Zhongguo nongmin bao (China Peasant News) (1983): 'Rapid Spread of Contracting Linked to Output in Northeast China', trans. in JPRS (1983): *China Report: Agriculture*, 261, 15 June 1983, Washington, Government Printing Office.

Zhongguo tongjiju (Chinese State Statistical Bureau) (1985*a*): *Zhongguo gongye jingji tongji ziliao* (Economic Statistics on Chinese Industry), Beijing, Zhongguo tongji chubanshe.

—— (1985*b*): *Zhongguo shehui tongji ziliao* (Statistical Materials on Chinese Society), Beijing, Zhongguo tongji chubanshe.

—— (1989*a*): *Zhongguo laodong gongzi tongji ziliao 1978–1987* (Statistical Materials on the Chinese Labour Force and Wages), Beijing, Zhongguo tongji chubanshe.

—— (1989*b*) (ed.): *Yanhai jingji kaifangqu jingji yanjiu he tongji ziliao* (Economic Research and Statistical Materials on the Open Coastal Economic Region), Beijing, Zhongguo tongji chubanshe.

—— (1990): *Zhongguo laodong gongzi tongji nianjian 1990* (Statistical Yearbook on the Chinese Labour Force and Wages), Beijing, Zhongguo tongji chubanshe.

—— (1998): *Zhongguo tongji gaiyao* (A Statistical Survey of China), Beijing, Zhongguo tongji chubanshe.

Zhongguo tongjiju renkou tongjisi (Population Office of Chinese State Statistical Bureau) (1993): *Zhongguo 1990 nian renkou pucha ziliao*, ii (Materials on the 1990 Population Census of China), Beijing, Zhongguo tongji chubanshe.

Zhongguo Xinan minzu yanjiu xuehui (South-West China Ethnic Research Institute) (ed.) (1986): *Xinan minzu diqu jingji gaikuang* (An Economic Survey of Ethnic Minority Areas in South West China), Chengdu, Sichuan sheng minzu yanjiusuo.

Zhonghua quanguo funu lianhehui funu yanjiusuo (Research Institute of the All China Women's Federation) (1991): *Zhongguo funu tongji ziliao* (Statistics on Chinese Women), Beijing, Zhongguo tongji chubanshe.

Zhongyang minzu xueyuan shaoshu minzu jingji yanjiusuo (Ethnic Minority Economic Research Institute of the Central Nationalities School) (1986): *Xibu minzu diqu jingji kaifa tansuo* (An Exploration of Economic Development in the Ethnic Minorities Regions of Western China), Beijing, Zhongyang minzu xueyuan chubanshe.

Zhou, K. X. (1996): *How The Farmers Changed China*, Boulder, Westview.

Zhu, H. M. (1992): *Dangdai Liangshan* (Liangshan Today), Chengdu, Bashu shushe chubanshe.

Zhu, L. (1991*a*): *Rural Reform and Peasant Income in China*, London, Macmillan.

—— (1991*b*): 'The Changing Role of the State in Chinese Agriculture' in White, G. (ed.) (1991): *The Chinese State in the Era of Economic Reform*, London, Macmillan.

—— and Jiang, Z. (1993): 'From Brigade to Village Community', *Cambridge Journal of Economics*, 17/4 (Dec.), 441–62.

Zhu, R. (1992): *Dangdai Zhongguo de nongye* (China Today: Agriculture), Beijing, Dangdai Zhongguo chubanshe.

ZIH—Bureau of Foreign Trade, Ministry of Industry (1935): *China Industrial Handbooks: Chekiang (Zhejiang)*, Ministry of Industry, Shanghai (repr. 1973 by Ch'eng Wen Publishing Company, Taipei).

Zita, K. (1991): 'China's Telecommunications and American Strategic Interests', in Joint Economic Committee (1991): *China's Economic Dilemmas in the 1990s*, ii, Washington, US Congress.

ZJTJNJ—Zhejiang tongjiju (Zhejiang Statistical Bureau) (various years): *Zhejiang tongji nianjian 1988, 1989, 1990, 1991, 1992, 1993, 1994, 1995, and 1996* (Zhejiang Statistical Yearbook), Beijing, Zhongguo tongji chubanshe.

ZKCDY—Zhongguo kexueyuan Chengdu dili yanjiusuo (Chengdu Geographical Research Institute, Chinese Academy of Science) (ed.) (1980): *Sichuan nongye dili* (An Agricultural Geography of Sichuan), Chengdu, Sichuan renmin chubanshe.

Zong, H. W. (1989): *Years of Trial, Turmoil and Triumph*, Beijing, Foreign Languages Press.

Zou, Q. Y. and Miao, W. J. (eds.) (1989): *Zhongguo renkou: Yunnan fence* (China's Population: Yunnan), Beijing, Zhongguo caizheng jingji chubanshe.

ZSDSWY—Zhonggong Shandong sheng wei yanjiushi (Research Office of the Shandong Committee of the Chinese Communist Party) (1989): *Shandong sishinian* (Forty Years of Shandong), Jinan, Shandong renmin chubanshe.

ZSSWY—Zhonggong Sichuan sheng wei yanjiushi (Research Unit of the Sichuan Committee of the CCP) (ed.) (1984): *Sichuan sheng qing* (Conditions in Sichuan), Chengdu, Sichuan renmin chubanshe.

Zu, L. Y. (1985): 'Jiangsu sheng nongchanpin chengben fazhan qushi qianxi' (An Outline of Trends in Agricultural Production Costs in Jiangsu Province), in He, H. S. (ed.) (1985): *Nongye jingji luncong* (Collected Essays on the Agricultural Economy), 6, 240–50, Beijing, Nongye chubanshe.

Zweig, D. (1989): *Agrarian Radicalism in China, 1968–1981*, Cambridge, Cambridge UP.

—— (1991): 'Rural Industry', in Joint Economic Committee (1991): *China's Economic Dilemmas in the 1990s*, ii, Washington, US Congress.

—— (1997): *Freeing China's Farmers*, Armonk, NY, M. E. Sharpe.

Zysman, J. (1983): *Governments, Markets and Growth*, London, Martin Robertson.

ZYSWZY—Zhonggong Yunnan sheng wei zhengce yanjiushi (Policy Research Office of the Yunnan Province Party Committee) (1986): *Yunnan sheng qing* (Conditions in Yunnan Province), Kunming, Yunnan renmin chubanshe.

Index